WINDOWS
NT
Professional
Library

WINDOWS NT

Windows NT Performance Tuning & Optimization

Kenton **Gardinier**

Osborne/**McGraw-Hill**

Berkeley   New York   St. Louis   San Francisco
Auckland   Bogotá   Hamburg   London   Madrid
Mexico City   Milan   Montreal   New Delhi   Panama City
Paris   São Paulo   Singapore   Sydney
Tokyo   Toronto

Osborne/**McGraw-Hill**
2600 Tenth Street
Berkeley, California 94710
U.S.A.

For information on translations or book distributors outside the U.S.A., or to arrange bulk purchase discounts for sales promotions, premiums, or fund-raisers, please contact Osborne/**McGraw-Hill** at the above address.

Windows NT Performance Tuning & Optimization

1234567890 AGM AGM 901987654321098

ISBN 0-07-882496-6

Publisher
   Brandon A. Nordin
Editor-in-Chief
   Scott Rogers
Acquisitions Editor
   Wendy Rinaldi
Project Editor
   Nancy McLaughlin
Contributing Authors
   Brian Moran, MCSE, MCSD
   Rand Morimoto, MCSE
   Toby J. Velte, Ph.D.
   Glen Hodgins
Technical Editor
   John McMains
Copy Editors
   Judy Ziajka
   Lysa Lewallen

Editorial Assistants
   Marlene Vasilieff
   Betsy Manini
Proofreaders
   Stefany Otis
   Karen Meade
Indexer
   Valerie Perry
Computer Designers
   Ann Sellers
   Jani Beckwith
Illustrator
   Brian Wells
Cover Design
   Regan Honda
Series Design
   Peter F. Hancik

This book is dedicated to
my mom and my sister Kim,
and to my dad, who is no longer with us,
for their support, their unconditional love,
and for believing in me.

ABOUT THE AUTHOR...

Kenton Gardinier is an MCSE and Senior Systems Engineer specializing in performance analysis and optimization of Windows NT networks. Gardinier also lectures on various NT-related issues, such as capacity planning, performance optimization, fault tolerance management, and enterprise management, and frequently contributes to **Windows NT Magazine** and **Windows NT Systems.** He serves on the board of the Triangle NT User Group.

WINDOWS NT
Professional Library

CONTENTS

ACKNOWLEDGMENTS

I would first like to thank Wendy Rinaldi at Osborne for her insight and motivation throughout this project. Wendy has always been extremely supportive, and I appreciate her giving me the opportunity to write for this series. I would also like to extend my appreciation to the rest of the Osborne staff, including Nancy McLaughlin, Judy Ziajka, and Marlene Vasilieff, for their patience, diligence, and professionalism.

I would like to personally thank John McMains for his support, advice, and generosity. John has been a huge influence on my life and has been a true friend from the very beginning. I have the utmost respect and admiration for him.

This book would not have been able to cover the range of topics that it does if it were not for the help of my contributing authors. Glen Hodgins at ITS, Brian Moran at Spectrum Technology Group, Rand Morimoto at Inacom Information Systems, and Toby Velte at Velte Systems have provided a wealth of experience and expertise, for which I am thankful.

There are many others that deserve to be mentioned by name, but I would specifically like to thank the following people for their support: Nick Baran at *Windows NT Systems* magazine, Scott Blanchard at Cadre Systems, Maggie Collarini at Information Systems Manager, Matt Drake at Persimmon IT, Charles Kelly at WANTUG, John Klekner, Dean Rogers at Cisco Systems, Amy Sigrist at Syntel, and Graham Zoller at the Federal Reserve Bank of Minneapolis.

INTRODUCTION

Over the last few years, Windows NT has proven itself to be a robust, reliable, enterprise-level network operating system. NT is now running more large networks and mission critical applications than ever before. As a result, the importance of Windows NT performance is paramount. This book is designed to be an all-inclusive, definitive guide to identifying potential performance bottlenecks and minimizing their effects on overall system performance. It is the direct result of careful analysis and the gathering of techniques proven to maximize Windows NT's effectiveness and efficiency.

There is more to performance tuning and optimization than simply throwing more financial and hardware resources at the system or buying the latest and greatest equipment. Optimum system performance is the consummation of careful planning, empirical analysis, and proactive monitoring. These processes are certainly more challenging than they sound. Today's typical NT systems are made up of numerous different parameters and components, all of which can potentially influence overall system performance. Such complexity makes it all the more challenging—and all the more important—to tune your system for optimal performance. This book analyzes the most important and influential components that can impact performance, and provides recommendations that will help you extract every drop of performance from your system.

Challenges of Performance Management

Reality in today's business world is harsh, competitive, and demanding. Streamlining resources and working more efficiently have become focal points in strategic business planning. Many companies, large and small, are faced with the fact that they must strive for more, with fewer resources, in order to survive. Some companies find themselves restructuring their business strategies not necessarily to stay ahead of the game, but instead, simply to keep up with their competition.

The "more for less" approach to conducting business stems from rapid advancements in technology and the possibility that, in such a dynamic environment, anyone can come out on top. Fierce competition, combined with the availability of a vast amount of information, forces everyone to aim for a business strategy in which work quality, efficiency, and productivity can increase simultaneously. Those companies that can achieve such status are bound to succeed and satisfy the customers' needs.

The same principle of efficient, cost-effective productivity applies to system performance. If a system is not optimized for efficiency, then work cannot be accomplished effectively. The system will not perform at maximum capacity. The system may be running "just fine," but is it performing at its optimal level, or can performance be improved? When and how is it appropriate to optimize computer resources?

What Is Performance Optimization?

Performance optimization, defined in its most elementary form, is simply the completion of an objective or task in the shortest amount of time with minimal wasted effort or resources. It means harmonizing hardware and software resources to perform duties in a timely and efficient manner. The ultimate goal of performance optimization is to use your server's limited resources in such a way that it provides the best level of service to your internal and/or external customers.

On the surface, performance optimization may appear to be simply a matter of tweaking a few settings and expecting a performance boost. Unfortunately, it is often difficult to tell whether or not the system is experiencing delay due to wasted or overworked components. What guidelines do you follow to measure your server's performance? How do you establish baseline values to represent server efficiency? How do you configure your system's settings to increase capacity? When should you perform configuration changes? Will the changes uncover—or even cause—other problems within the system? All of these questions and more are answered within the context of this book. It delves into the art of performance tuning and offers concise recommendations that are guaranteed to boost performance, increase efficiency, and streamline server resources.

The following outline briefly explains the topics covered here. If you feel unfamiliar with the theory and techniques of performance optimization, then by all means begin with Chapter 1 and proceed to the end of the book. If you are looking to solve one or more specific system problems, this outline will point you to the chapter you need.

Chapter 1: Understanding Your Windows NT Server Environment

This chapter gives you a general overview of the art of performance optimization. It examines hardware and Windows NT operating system architectures to give you a fundamental understanding of Windows NT, which is essential if you wish to begin optimizing your system.

Chapter 2: Capacity Planning

Capacity planning has traditionally been practiced only on mainframe and UNIX platforms, but has recently begun to emerge from its infancy in the PC world. It is now becoming a crucial element to managing and maintaining the Windows NT environment. This chapter examines both the formal and informal approaches to capacity planning. Moreover, it analyzes available capacity planning tools for Windows NT, whether those tools are built-in or produced by third party vendors. Here you will also find a thorough discussion of the principles and methodologies used to adequately examine and predict system utilization.

Chapter 3: Domain Planning

Proper NT domain planning and implementation is crucial to optimizing your Windows NT environment. This chapter discusses the four NT domain models, as well as possible alternatives, to help you structure the domain that will best suit your needs. It also explains how to configure domain controllers for optimum performance and maximum stability.

Chapter 4: Boosting Memory Performance

Memory contention is one of the most common causes of performance degradation. Typically, NT professionals would just add memory, but this chapter shows that there is more to memory optimization than simply adding more resources. This chapter presents other optimization techniques, such as hardware configuration and paging, that can be used to increase overall system performance.

Chapter 5: Boosting Network Performance

Tuning the network may appear to be an overwhelming, if not impossible, task. However, this chapter simplifies the process and uncovers important ways that you can achieve maximum network throughput and capacity. It illustrates proper planning procedures, as well as analyzing commonly used protocols and network-related services, to help you maximize network efficiency.

Chapter 6: Optimizing the Disk Subsystem

The disk subsystem is one of the slowest system components, and its configuration plays a critical role in optimum server performance. This chapter examines the various components of the disk subsystem, such as different types of drives, file systems, and disk configurations, and provides concrete recommendations as to what should be used and how. It also describes performance indicators and other tools used to measure and analyze performance.

Chapter 7: Tweaking Graphics Subsystem Performance

The graphics subsystem is often the most neglected of Windows NT subsystems. This is surprising, considering that Windows NT relies on a graphical user interface for most of the duties that it performs. Chapter 7 analyzes how the graphical subsystem affects performance, both on the server and your workstations; it then provides recommendations for the different configurations.

Chapter 8: A New Look at the Powerful Performance Monitor

The Performance Monitor is one of the most widely used utilities for monitoring and analyzing system activity. This chapter examines many different aspects and uses of the Performance Monitor, spells out those resources that must be monitored, and explains how to overcome the utility's limitations by running it as a service. Moreover, this chapter shows you how to go beyond simple monitoring capabilities and use the Performance Monitor proactively to support the Windows NT environment.

Chapter 9: Printing

Printing is rarely regarded as a means of boosting performance, but this chapter sets out to prove otherwise. Here you will learn which specifications have the greatest effect on printing performance, and discover how you can optimize your own printing performance.

Chapter 10: Tuning with the Registry

The Windows NT Registry is a critical component of the operating system because it contains the hardware and software configuration parameters. Many of the configuration recommendations throughout this book require modifications that can only be done through the Registry. This chapter describes the Registry's organizational structure, the tools used to modify the Registry, and how to keep the Registry operating efficiently for optimal performance.

Chapter 11: Internet Information Server and the Proxy Server

Internet Information Server (IIS) can greatly affect the ways in which companies conduct business on the Internet, as well as how they provide information through internal Intranets. This chapter analyzes the factors influencing IIS performance, and provides proven recommendations aimed at boosting the performance of both IIS and the Proxy Server.

Chapter 12: SQL Server

This chapter focuses on the most important factors affecting SQL Server performance. It examines planning considerations, hardware configurations, SQL Server configuration options, database application design, and much more. The recommendations in this chapter are intended to minimize any negative effects that SQL Server sometimes has on overall system performance.

Chapter 13: Optimizing Exchange Server

This chapter takes an extensive look at Exchange Server, focusing on the intricacies that affect performance—such as planning considerations, groupware functionality, hardware configurations, and future resource demands. It furnishes insightful recommendations and configuration parameters that you can use to increase performance for internal and external messaging and groupware functions. Here you will find an analysis of currently available utilities aimed at proactively monitoring and boosting performance.

Chapter 14: Getting the Most Out of Systems Management Server

This chapter analyzes the most influential factors affecting performance, including various planning considerations, and provides concrete recommendations for boosting performance and gaining control over this extremely powerful, complex, and resource-intensive enterprise management tool.

Appendix A: Windows NT Performance Monitor Objects & Counters

The appendix at the end of this book provides a complete listing of objects and counters available to Windows NT. Many of these objects and counters have been referenced and examined throughout the book, but they are gathered here to provide you a handy reference.

Top Ten Performance Tips

Although many of your performance problems cannot be solved overnight, here are the ten best tune-ups that you can make if you wish to delve immediately into the art of performance tuning. These concise recommendations are by no means "cure-alls" or guarantees for huge performance differences, but they do help alleviate burdens that may be taxing your system. The procedures listed here are examined much more thoroughly in the chapters of this book.

▼ Add more memory! Windows NT is a resource-intensive operating system that requires a considerable amount of physical memory. No matter how much memory you currently have on your system, give it more. This is the most effective and the least expensive way to upgrade your system's performance.

■ Turn on write-back cache and zero wait states for memory within your system's BIOS.

■ Create a paging file for each physical disk. Spreading the I/O load among multiple disk drives and controllers greatly enhances performance because it allows information to be written simultaneously.

■ Set the minimum paging file size to the highest anticipated system and user-level application requirements. Eliminating the need to increase the paging file size for initial values speeds up application startup times and reduces disk fragmentation.

■ Turn off animated or 3-D screen savers. They typically boost processor utilization to 100 percent.

■ If your budget permits, use SCSI hard disk drives and hardware RAID controllers.

■ If you have any 8- or 16-bit adapters (network, disk, etc.), you can significantly increase performance by replacing them with high-performance 32-bit cards.

■ Balance the workloads of your servers.

■ Remove unnecessary software components, such as services, device drivers, and protocols. For example, if you are not using a system for remote access services, but you have the Remote Access Server service running, stop it—and then either set it to "disabled" through the Services applet in the Control Panel, or simply remove it altogether.

▲ Minimize the number of protocols used. If you are running more than one protocol, use the Network applet in the Control Panel to set the binding order. You can decide which protocol binds to the network interface card first either by frequency of use or by examining the speed of each protocol.

CHAPTER 1

Understanding Your Windows NT Server Environment

One of the most important yet often overlooked aspects of performance tuning and optimization is understanding your Windows NT Server environment. It may seem difficult enough keeping up with daily administrative and maintenance tasks without also taking the time to understand the roles of individual server components. Nevertheless, however daunting a task this may seem, it is imperative that you have at least a basic understanding of each component and how they interact. For example, knowing that the secondary cache plays a vital role in how the CPU anticipates the next instruction to be executed can greatly influence your ability to gain peak performance from your server. Understanding the environment will also help you predict future resource requirements and proactively solve problems.

This chapter provides a general overview of server hardware and the Windows NT operating system architecture. It first examines hardware architectures and describes how devices interact with one another. Then it explores the Windows NT operating system architecture, including the self-tuning mechanisms that promote efficiency. The internal components of the operating system play an integral role in every aspect of your system. This chapter describes each component's characteristics and their interactions with your system's hardware.

A SELF-SUFFICIENT OPERATING SYSTEM

Windows NT is by far one of the most self-sufficient operating systems. It takes over some performance responsibilities often fulfilled by users and administrators, dynamically changing parameters as resources require them. For example, Windows NT dynamically increases the size of pagefile.sys as the need to swap data to disk increases. Similarly, work demands placed on Windows NT are constantly changing as work habits and application requirements change. It would be extremely burdensome on administrators and users if they constantly had to manually change settings in the Registry to reflect changes in requirements. To prevent such inconvenience, Microsoft has built self-tuning mechanisms into the operating system that dynamically adjust to current demands on the system.

Windows NT automatically controls certain resources. It focuses on controlling parameters pertaining to memory and disk resources. For the most part, Windows NT dynamically handles memory configurations, such as how much RAM is allocated to services and applications, disk cache usage, and the sizing of the virtual memory's pagefile.sys. Windows NT does not, however, change all configurations dynamically. For example, it will not try to increase read/write transfers to disk by moving an application to a faster drive or deplete the memory resources of one application for the benefit of another. If Windows NT had this much control, many changes could have disastrous consequences.

The Server Service

The Server service offers another example of how Windows NT is self-sufficient. The Server service is a file-system driver responsible for interacting with other file-system drivers to perform I/O requests. It establishes the connections requested by other redirectors but does not request connections from other redirectors. Each time the server is booted, the Server service parameters are auto-configured. This self-tuning mechanism is particularly useful when you add memory to your existing configuration, because Windows NT's Server service automatically adjusts its parameters to reflect the additional random access memory (RAM).

CAUTION: Running the command NET CONFIG SERVER with the /AUTODISCONNECT, /SRVCOMMENT, or /HIDDEN parameter will overwrite the Server service's Registry parameters and permanently disable its self-tuning capabilities. Moreover, you will no longer be able to configure the Server service through the Network applet in the Control Panel.

Registry entries pertaining to the Server service are located in the HKEY_LOCAL_ MACHINE hive within the following subkey:

```
\SYSTEM
    \CurrentControlSet
     \Services
         \LanmanServer
          \Parameters
```

If the self-tuning capabilities have been accidentally disabled, you can use the Registry Editor (REGEDT32.EXE) to restore the auto-configuration parameters.

CAUTION: When editing or modifying the Registry directly, use extreme caution. An incorrectly set parameter can cause serious, irrecoverable damage or system failure. Always have an updated Emergency Repair Disk (ERD) or a recent backup ready for such emergencies.

To restore the Server service's self-tuning properties, remove every entry except the following:

```
EnableSharedNetDrives
Lmannounce
NullSessionPipes
NullSessionShares
Size
```

Once the modifications are complete, restart Windows NT. Windows NT can once again automatically adjust Server service settings.

CHOOSING THE RIGHT HARDWARE CONFIGURATION

You will quickly find that Windows NT can cause migraines, sleepless nights, and countless other stress-related problems if it is not set up on compatible hardware. To avoid needless hassles and wasted time, make sure you have the hardware that Windows NT requires. Selecting supported hardware is your first step in performance tuning and optimization.

Compatible hardware means that a Windows NT device driver exists for a device, such as an internal adapter, modem, or external storage device, and has successfully passed Microsoft's hardware compatibility test (HCT). The HCT is a suite of rigorous testing procedures that stress the hardware and driver beyond normal operating ranges. Original equipment manufacturers (OEMs) usually test their products in-house first and then ship the hardware to Microsoft for the HCT. All device-driver testing is performed at Microsoft to verify the interoperability of Windows NT, the device driver, and the system or device.

Microsoft makes available many documents that discuss compatibility with Windows NT. For example, the documents "General Compatibility Information," "Compatibility and Usability," and "Hardware Compatibility List (HCL)" are all packaged with the shipping version of Windows NT. In addition, the HCL is updated and published quarterly. You can obtain the latest version of the HCL at **ftp://ftp.microsoft.com/ bussys/ winnt/winnt-docs/hcl/** or **http://www. microsoft.com/hwtest.**

The HCL contains a complete list of all supported hardware devices. The HCL is grouped into the following categories:

▼ Systems (Intel *x*86, DEC Alpha, and MIPS)

■ PowerPC-based systems and devices

■ SCSI devices

■ Non-SCSI tape backup and CD-ROM devices

■ Communication devices (such as network adapters and modems)

■ PCMCIA systems and devices

■ Video display adapters

- Drive systems
- Printers
- ▲ Accessories (such as keyboards, pointing devices, multimedia adapters, tablets, and uninterruptable power supplies [UPS])

If a system or device is not specifically listed on the HCL, then it most likely is not supported. Even if various models of a product are listed but the one you are using is not, you should assume that your particular model will not work. For example, if models 540, 540e, and 540ex are in the HCL, but your model, 540xl, is not, you must assume that it is not supported unless the vendor guarantees compatibility.

Checking the HCL for every system or device for compatibility with Windows NT sounds like a hassle. However, it is well worth the effort because you will spend much more time troubleshooting an unsupported system or device than you would have verifying that it is supported.

WINDOWS NT AND HARDWARE ARCHITECTURES

This section provides a broad overview of the Windows NT architecture and sheds light on how operating system components interact with hardware and with one another. It is important to have an understanding of the architecture because it will strengthen your understanding of your environment and enhance your ability to successfully tune Windows NT. The Intel-based PC architecture is the focus of this section, but the concepts presented here can be applied to other platforms, such as DEC Alpha, MIPS, and PowerPC, that Windows NT supports. At this time, it appears that only the Intel and DEC Alpha platforms will be supported under future versions of NT. This may cause further questioning of the RISC architecture for NT.

The architecture used for the processor chip defines the way Microsoft designs and builds versions of Windows NT. The operating system is the interface between your system's software (such as MS Office and MS BackOffice) and hardware. If it is not optimized to take full advantage of your system, it may not adequately support your technological needs, such as the need to handle a specified number of transactions per day.

Processor Architecture

The Intel-based PC architecture is one of many platforms that Windows NT currently supports. The other platforms are different than Intel's architecture because they are based on the *reduced instruction set computer* (RISC), while Intel uses a *complex instruction set computer* (CISC). The major difference between the two architectures is that a computer using CISC performs more tasks to process instructions than its RISC counterpart. The distinction between CISC and RISC architectures in Intel's processors is gradually diminishing. Since the introduction of the Pentium processor, the architecture has incorporated both CISC and RISC characteristics. This is not saying that Intel will eventually produce chips based on RISC, but it appears that the company is definitely working on a compromise between the two architectures.

Generally speaking, RISC processors are faster and more efficient than CISC processors with the same speed rating. This should not completely convince you to move to a RISC platform, however. You must also look at the number of applications that are supported. Application support for Intel's CISC platform is tremendous. Thousands of applications have been written that can run on Windows NT with the Intel or Intel-compatible processor chip. However, other platforms—especially the OEC Alpha—are playing catch-up in the applications-support area.

Another aspect of architecture that you should consider is the different generations of Intel's family of processors. Intel traditionally named successive processors *x*86. Now it uses names such as the Pentium, Pentium Pro, and Pentium II. Each processor is rated in terms of MHz, which basically translates into the number of instructions per second that the processor can handle. The Pentium family operates with a 32-bit architecture. You can expect to see later generations use 64-bit or higher architectures.

NOTE: A 200-MHz Pentium Pro operates faster than a 200-MHz Pentium despite the same speed rating. The difference lies within each processor's architecture and the family to which each processor belongs. The Pentium Pro architecture's read-ahead algorithms use the second-level cache more efficiently than the Pentium. Moreover, the Pentium Pro communicates with the second-level cache via a private internal bus, whereas the Pentium communicates with the cache externally.

Processors and Memory

The heart or foundation of the computer is the central processing unit (CPU). The CPU, whether it is CISC or RISC based, is connected to two very important resources— second-level cache memory and main random access memory (RAM)—by a 32-bit system bus.

NOTE: A feature of the Pentium, Pentium Pro, and Pentium II families that is often misinterpreted is the incorporation of an external 64-bit data bus used to communicate with system memory. This does not mean that these processor families use 64-bit architectures, but the bus does greatly increase the amount of data that can be passed to and from the CPU and system memory.

You can think of this bus as a major interstate with 32 lanes of traffic, with each lane handling one bit of information at a time. RAM serves as your system's main memory storage area. It holds instructions from the operating system as well as applications that you execute. Cache memory is similar to RAM but is much faster. Information is stored in both memory areas; the difference lies in when and how the information is used. Generally, the instructions from the operating system and applications are loaded into RAM for storage. As the operating system and applications are used, the instructions are temporarily copied to the faster cache medium. When the processor needs to retrieve particular instructions, it first checks the cache. If the instructions are in the cache, the retrieval time is greatly reduced compared to the time required to retrieve instructions directly from RAM. Typical speeds for cache retrieval are between 10 and 20 nanoseconds, while RAM retrieval speeds range from 60 to 80 nanoseconds. The difference between cache and RAM speeds may seem minute (only 50 to 60 nanoseconds), but to your system this represents an enormous latency period. To understand what this time difference means, consider the millions of instructions your system executes multiplied by the latency period. You can then begin to imagine how quickly the latency time adds up, leading to a noticeable performance difference between cache and RAM. This is why computers with more cache memory generally outperform those with less.

Bus Architectures

Communication from the CPU, RAM, and cache to other system components is off-loaded from the system bus to other data transfer buses. This releases the system bus from this responsibility and keeps it clear of slower traffic that may impede performance. There are several types of data transfer buses that communicate with other system components. Common varieties are *Industry-Standard Architecture* (ISA), *Enhanced Industry-Standard Architecture* (EISA), *VESA Local* (VL), and *Peripheral Component Interconnect* (PCI) bus architectures. Figure 1-1 shows CPU, RAM, and cache communication with other data transfer buses.

The buses are interfaces between the system bus and the devices on your system. Their sizes are 8, 16, or 32 bits, depending on the bus used. To ensure optimum performance, you should use 32-bit buses whenever possible. However, some components, such as floppy disk drives, may not be able to use 32-bit buses. In such cases, use a 16-bit bus. Table 1-1 summarizes the differences between the expansion buses.

The PCI expansion bus is becoming the industry standard. Its design overcomes the limitations of other expansion buses. PCI also offers a 32-bit bus and full support of plug-and-play technology. Plug-and-play is similar to self-tuning technology in that it

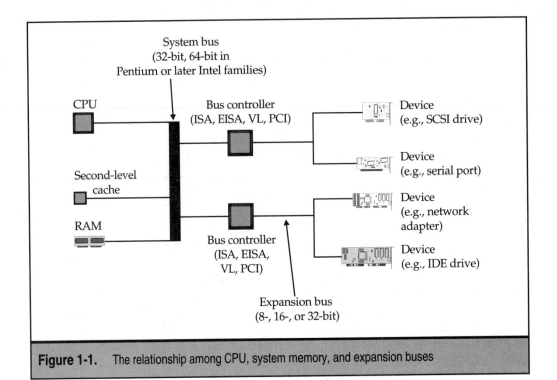

Figure 1-1.　The relationship among CPU, system memory, and expansion buses

recognizes hardware changes and configures devices without any human intervention. Although Windows NT 4.0 does not fully support plug-and-play, you can expect to see it implemented in later versions.

Expansion Bus Architecture	Bus Width (in Bits)	Notes
ISA	8 or 16	Older bus architecture that should be avoided
EISA	16 or 32	Backward compatible with ISA
VL	32	Simplistic in design
PCI	32	Supports plug-and-play

Table 1-1.　Expansion Bus Architectures

NOTE: It may not be fair to say outright that NT does not support plug-and-play. Windows NT 4.0 can automatically detect some plug-and-play devices such as a mouse, while a few others need special plug-and-play drivers located in the \drvlib\pnpisa\x86 directory on the Windows NT 4.0 CD-ROM. The first beta release of Windows NT 5.0 is incorporating major changes to fully support plug-and-play.

When configuring a new system, make sure to incorporate a PCI/EISA or PCI/VL combination. Either combination offers you the optimal configuration with both architectures supporting 32-bit data paths. The PCI/EISA combination also increases the compatibility of your system components through EISA's support for adapters that must use a 16-bit expansion bus. EISA expansion slots can also use ISA adapters for backward compatibility. For your existing systems using PCI, install PCI disk controllers and network adapters. Installing any other type of card (ISA, EISA, or VL) does not provide the maximum performance levels you need with such components.

Intelligent I/O (I_2O)

An emerging standard for Intel-based bus architectures, called *Intelligent I/O*, or I_2O, is expected to quickly saturate the PC market. The goal of this industry initiative is to advance I/O systems by reducing the workload on the primary PCI bus, standardizing I/O messaging between the operating system and devices, and establishing a higher level of interoperability among different operating systems—thus increasing a system's overall efficiency and performance.

In current system designs, the processor handles most I/O interrupts. This design bottlenecks the processor's performance because the attention paid to the interrupts disrupts data processing. The I_2O standard, however, releases the processor from having to manage I/O interrupts originating from peripheral devices (such as NICs and hard drive controllers). This frees the processor to do more useful work, allowing the system to handle greater workloads and support more users.

In addition to providing performance benefits, the I$_2$O standard creates opportunities for developers who write device drivers. Developers can now design drivers that are independent of the operating system platform and device. This independence is achieved through a split-driver model in which the OS services module and hardware device module are separated. Neither of the components needs to be aware of the specific implementation details of the other, such as its system structure or type of bus architecture, because communication occurs through a standard messaging interface.

Controller Specifications

Devices (network adapters, hard disk controllers, serial expansion devices, and so on) connect to your system via an expansion bus interface. It is important to know which type of interface you have so you can match the devices according to the bus architecture. Like expansion buses, hard disk controllers come in many industry-standard flavors such as *Integrated Drive Electronics* (IDE), *Enhanced Integrated Drive Electronics* (EIDE), *Small-Computer Standard Interface* (SCSI), and *Fast-Wide SCSI,* to name a few. SCSI variations and EIDE are among the top competing standards because of their high transfer rates and reliability.

EIDE

The EIDE specification, introduced in 1994, was designed to overcome the limitations of the older IDE drives. The two main disadvantages of the IDE drive are slow transfer rates and the dependency on INT13 BIOS calls that limit the maximum drive size to 528MB. EIDE drives boast faster transfer rates than IDE, and they break the 528MB barrier. EIDE uses logical block access (LBA) instead of INT13 BIOS calls to extend beyond this drive-size limitation. EIDE drives require either special drivers that simulate LBA mode, or a BIOS dating from 1994 or later.

EIDE controllers are the preferable choice for many because the transfer rates are comparable to some SCSI variations and because they are much less expensive. Moreover, obtaining the proper drivers to support a variety of platforms is as easy as hopping on the Internet and going to any number of sites to download them. On the other hand, EIDE does not scale as well as SCSI. One EIDE controller supports only two drives per channel interface (for a total of four devices), while some SCSI variations support up to 15 drives on one controller. In addition to hard disk drives, a SCSI controller can support SCSI tape backup, CD-ROMs, and many more types of devices. SCSI is the preferred choice when considering secondary storage for file servers or systems with large storage requirements. Device driver support is a little harder to come by, but scalability often outweighs the inconvenience it causes.

SCSI

As already mentioned, SCSI controllers come in many different flavors. There are SCSI, SCSI-2, SCSI-3, Fast SCSI, Fast-Wide SCSI, Ultra SCSI, Wide Ultra SCSI, Ultra2 SCSI, and Wide Ultra2 SCSI controllers. Table 1-2 provides some important statistics about each type of SCSI controller. Each flavor is designed to a standard SCSI specification. The specifications exist to ensure that certain criteria are met and that drives from different vendors can coexist. The

Specification	Transfer Speed (in MB/Second)	Bus Width	Maximum Device Support (Including the Controller)
SCSI-1	5	8	8
Fast SCSI	10	8	8
Fast-Wide SCSI	20	16	16
Ultra SCSI	20	8	8
Wide Ultra SCSI	40	16	16
Ultra2 SCSI	40	8	8
Wide Ultra2 SCSI	80	16	16

Table 1-2.   SCSI Specifications

Fast-Wide SCSI controller specification has become a popular choice over its predecessors because of its higher transfer rates and increased peripheral support. It uses a data transfer bus that is twice the size of those used in earlier specifications, and boasts a performance of roughly twice the speed.

NOTE: To take advantage of the performance ratings for particular specifications, the controller type and device type must match. Linking a Fast-Wide SCSI device (20 MB/sec) to a Fast SCSI controller (10 MB/sec) will limit the device to the transfer rate of the controller.

Two emerging SCSI specifications soon will be saturating the market. The first specification, based on the SCSI-3 specification, is called Fibre Channel (FC). The FC specification is designed for implementations in which a fiber optic cable connects the SCSI adapter and its chain of devices. The actual specification has been around since 1988, but there are few, if any, implementations with fiber optics. Instead, a modified FC has been used that supports copper cabling. As drives become faster and more efficient, the use of this technology is likely to explode. Transfer speeds are approximately 100MB per second and above. Don't be surprised in the near future to see FC with fiber optic implementations exceeding 400 MB/sec.

The second emerging technology is SCSI plug-and-play. With this technology, the controller checks each device on the chain and makes any changes necessary to resolve conflicts. The controller then configures each SCSI device without human intervention, thus eliminating some of the problems occasionally associated with SCSI technology.

WINDOWS NT OPERATING SYSTEM ARCHITECTURE

Now you have a general understanding of the hardware architecture. This section delves into the operating system internals and describes the interaction between the operating system and the hardware.

The goal of any operating system design is to provide an interface between the system's hardware and the applications the user executes. Windows NT goes one step further by supplying an intuitive interface that enables users to perform tasks with minimal technical training. Unlike UNIX, it shelters most users by providing an easy-to-use interface to perform daily administrative tasks, general performance tuning, and other common operations. However, it is important to understand the basic Windows NT internals if you expect to successfully optimize your system. For example, you would not try to fix an electrical problem in your house without first gaining a thorough understanding of electricity, wiring, and so on. The same principle applies to tuning Windows NT. Knowing your system and the interactions among the system components helps you optimize and troubleshoot so that you can provide the best level of service.

NT Internals

The Windows NT operating system design is both modular and layered. The core of the system is divided into discrete objects according to functionality. Each of these objects has its own characteristics and responsibilities within the operating system and interacts with the other objects to perform tasks or instructions. These components can run in either the microprocessor's *kernel mode* (privileged mode) or *user mode* (application mode).

The Windows NT Executive represents the subsystems and components that run in kernel mode, including the *microkernel, hardware abstraction layer* (HAL), and *management services.* The number of components privileged enough to run in kernel mode is limited because a component must have direct access to both hardware and software resources. This restriction provides a more secure and stable environment, almost completely eliminating the possibility of an erratic program or subsystem disturbing or crashing the entire system.

All other subsystems and components, such as server subsystems and applications, execute in user mode. User mode components operate in their own address spaces and can communicate with other user mode components, as well as with the Windows NT Executive, through well-defined software interfaces. Figure 1-2 shows the internal components of Windows NT and the interactions among them.

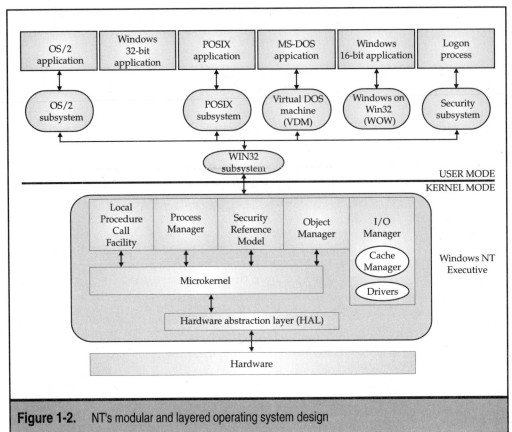

Figure 1-2. NT's modular and layered operating system design

Kernel Mode

The Windows NT Executive represents the components that run in kernel (privileged) mode. It is the underlying structure for the operating system, and it provides the basic functionality for the rest of the system. For example, when a user mode application or process requests information, it communicates directly with the OS/2, Portable Operating System Interface (POSIX), or Win32 subsystem. The subsystem then communicates with the Windows NT Executive.

The Windows NT Executive consists of four main components:

▼ HAL

■ Microkernel

- ■ Management services
- ▲ Client-server subsystem

HAL   The hardware abstraction layer, or HAL, provides a direct link from the operating system to the hardware. It operates underneath the rest of the operating system so that applications and subsystems do not need to be aware of hardware-specific information. Each hardware platform (Intel, DEC Alpha, and so on) requires its own unique HAL. Since Windows NT is a modular and layered operating system, and the HAL is a modular component, porting to a different system requires that only the HAL be replaced.

The HAL is also responsible for symmetrical multiprocessing (SMP) functionality (discussed in more detail later in this chapter). Microsoft packages two versions of the HAL for each supported processor type: one supports a single processor, and the other can handle up to eight processors, with Windows NT Server, Enterprise Edition. Previous versions of NT could support only four processors out of the box. At this time, you must contact an OEM or a hardware vendor for scalability beyond eight processors.

MICROKERNEL   The microkernel is the heart of the operating system. You may wonder why this component is not called the kernel as it is in many other operating systems. The difference is that kernels in other operating systems are responsible for almost all actions and functions within the system, whereas in microkernel architecture, some of those responsibilities are passed on to other components. Windows NT's microkernel delegates some of these services, such as I/O management, to other components within the Windows NT Executive.

Since NT's microkernel is responsible for system-wide functionality, it is always resident in physical memory. Its duties include the following:

- ▼ **Thread scheduling**   *Threads* are pieces of code from a particular process that are assigned a scheduling priority (a number from 0 to 31). The microkernel allows a thread to execute for a specified time period before preempting it to allow other process threads to execute. This is the foundation of Windows NT's ability to multitask preemptively. The microkernel itself cannot be preempted; it always has the highest priority.

■ **SMP synchronization** A copy of the microkernel runs on every processor present on the system. This ensures efficient use of all processors and system resources.

▲ **Interrupts and exceptions** *Interrupts* (hardware generated delays) and exceptions (software generated delays) are managed by the microkernel. When an interrupt occurs, the microkernel preempts any thread currently executing so it can service the interrupt.

MANAGEMENT SERVICES Management services interact directly with user mode subsystems (OS/2, POSIX, and Win32). These services include the I/O Manager, Object Manager, Security Reference Monitor (SRM), Process Manager, Local Procedure Call (LPC) Facility, and Virtual Memory Manager. Each service is very important to the stability, reliability, and manageability of the operating system and, ultimately, to user-level applications.

▼ **I/O Manager** As the name implies, the I/O Manager oversees the system's input and output tasks. This responsibility includes managing device, cache, network, and installable file system (FAT, HPFS, NTFS, CDFS, and so on) drivers. In order to preserve communication and compatibility, the I/O Manager provides a uniform interface for all driver types. For example, the uniform interface allows multiple installable file systems to reside on the same system.

■ **Object Manager** The Object Manager has the greatest responsibility among the management services, supporting all other NT Executive subsystems. Windows NT treats its physical and logical resources as objects. This includes, but is not limited to, files, disk drives, memory, and processes. The Object Manager creates, defines, modifies, and deletes these objects and makes an object's resources available for other resources to use. In addition, the Object Manager supplies each object with a handle containing access control information that is required when a process requests access to the object.

- **Security Reference Monitor**   The SRM operates in conjunction with the logon process, security subsystem, and Object Manager to enforce system security policies. When a user logs onto the system, he or she is assigned a security access token. Every time a user requests a resource, the SRM consults the object's handle and security access token to decide if the user has sufficient privileges to use the requested resource.

- **Process Manager**   The Process Manager supervises processes and threads. This includes creating, modifying, and deleting processes and threads. Each time an application, subsystem task, or microkernel function is executed, the Process Manager is called to create a process. The Process Manager is called at least once more to create a thread, depending on how many threads are associated with the process. A process must contain at least one thread to execute. As you might expect, the Process Manager works closely with the Object Manager and the microkernel to create objects and perform scheduling, respectively. It also communicates with the SRM to ensure security between processes and process resource requests.

- **Local Procedure Call Facility**   The LPC Facility enables two different processes to communicate. It is a messaging mechanism based upon the Remote Procedure Call (RPC) facility and conforms to the client-server model. The clients are Windows NT-supported applications (MS-DOS, Win16, Win32, POSIX, and OS/2), and the servers are the environment subsystems (Win32, POSIX, and OS/2). The difference between RPC and LPC is that LPC supports and is optimized for communication only on the local machine, whereas RPC messaging can span other machines.

- ▲ **Virtual Memory Manager**   Many of today's applications require large amounts of memory that sometimes may not be accommodated by the limited amount of physical memory on your system. To ensure that applications have enough memory to execute, Windows NT uses virtual memory to compensate for limited memory resources. Virtual memory management is a combination of memory and disk management. Upon execution, each process is allocated its own address space. The address space is subdivided into pages that are used to store data. As RAM resources deplete, pages are swapped to disk. The data that is swapped to disk can later be retrieved. The Virtual Memory Manager keeps track of which memory address space belongs to which process. It also manages the retrieval of pages from disk.

CLIENT-SERVER SUBSYSTEM   New to the kernel mode in Windows NT 4.0 are the *graphics device interface* (GDI) and *Window Manager* (USER). Collectively, these are called the *client-server subsystem*. Traditionally, graphical user interface (GUI) functions were performed through the Win32 application programming interface (API). In Windows NT 4.0, these functions have been moved to the kernel, both to improve operating system performance for graphics operations and to reduce memory requirements. This move also simplifies the design and reduces the responsibilities of the Win32 environment subsystem. Chapter 7 provides a more detailed explanation of this change.

Figure 1-3 shows the change in NT 4.0's operating system architecture.

User Mode

All subsystems and applications that do not run in kernel mode run in user mode. This includes the environment subsystems (OS/2, POSIX, and Win32), logon process, security subsystem, and user-level applications.

The environment subsystems handle process requests for service or information. These subsystems then initiate communication with the Windows NT Executive to provide the service or information that the process has requested. Only the environment subsystems can

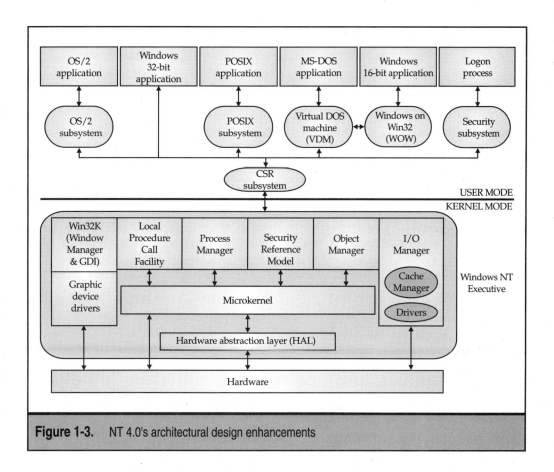

Figure 1-3.   NT 4.0's architectural design enhancements

issue requests to kernel-mode operations; they are the software interfaces for user mode applications.

The environment subsystems are also the key to compatibility with other platforms such as DOS, 16-bit Windows 3.*x*, OS/2, and POSIX-compliant applications. Each subsystem emulates a particular operating system in a protected address space. Their functionality, except I/O management (keyboard, mouse, and display management) and messaging (object linking and embedding, or OLE, and dynamic data exchange, or DDE), is segregated into 16- and 32-bit operations. This ensures that a misbehaving user-level application does not disrupt the operations of the other subsystems or the operating system itself. For example, an erratic DOS application will not have any affect on the stability of a running POSIX application.

WIN32 SUBSYSTEM   The Win32 subsystem is Windows NT's primary environment subsystem. This was not always the case, however. Microsoft tried to give equal responsibility to the other environment subsystems but soon realized that this caused too much duplication of operations and ultimately degraded performance. As a result, Microsoft has placed most of these redundant responsibilities on the Win32 subsystem and strengthened the Win32 set of APIs.

An additional change has been implemented in the Windows NT 4.0 operating system architecture. As mentioned earlier, the USER and GDI facilities have been removed from the Win32 subsystem and placed in the kernel mode to enhance graphics performance and decrease memory requirements. In making this modification, Microsoft also changed the Win32 environment subsystem's name to the CSR subsystem. To avoid any confusion, however, this book continues to use the Win32 name. Other than the loss of the functionality of the two components that were removed, the functionality of the subsystem remains the same.

The Win32 subsystem provides extensive resources and functionality to other subsystems and user-level applications through a set of APIs. This structure models the client-server architecture in that Win32 acts as the server, and all other user mode processes are clients. There are two reasons for this type of structure: First, Win32 controls all user mode I/O, including interactions with the keyboard, mouse, and display. Second, other systems may need to communicate with each other through OLE or DDE. Both of these types of operations are accomplished through the set of APIs. When the OS/2 or POSIX subsystem needs either one of these services, it translates its API calls to a corresponding Win32 API call to request service.

OTHER USER MODE SUBSYSTEMS   In addition to the Win32 subsystem, Windows NT has two other protected environment subsystems: OS/2 and POSIX. Both subsystems extend NT's application support and conform to open systems standards. Each subsystem can communicate with the rest of the system by translating its API calls to the respective Win32 API calls to be serviced by the Win32 subsystem.

The Institute of Electrical and Electronics Engineers (IEEE) developed POSIX to provide portability on UNIX systems. A set of standards has evolved ranging from POSIX.1 to POSIX.12. Windows NT uses the POSIX.1-compliant subsystem, meaning that it complies with the basic POSIX standards. These standards include case sensitivity and support for multiple filenames. Applications conforming to this standard can execute within the POSIX subsystem in their own protected memory space.

The OS/2 subsystem supports OS/2 1.*x* character-based applications on Intel-based architectures, but does not provide any support for OS/2 2.*x* GUI applications (Presentation Manager applications).

NOTE: The OS/2 subsystem is not supported on RISC machines, but OS/2 real-mode applications can execute on RISC machines within an MS-DOS session.

OS/2 operates in much the same manner as the POSIX subsystem in that it can communicate with the rest of the system through API translation, and that applications run in their own protected memory spaces. However, it has one additional capability that the POSIX subsystem does not: networking support. OS/2 provides networking support through LAN Manager APIs, NetBIOS, named pipes, and mail slots.

Symmetrical Multiprocessing

Symmetrical multiprocessing (SMP) support allows a system to efficiently use multiple processors for increased performance. Microsoft has concentrated on scaling Windows NT Server linearly up to four processors without any alterations in the operating system. Four-processor SMP scalability has become an industry standard because there has not been a strong demand for anything higher, and because the use of more than four processors has not proven to be any more cost-effective than the use of load balancing on multiple servers. Also, very few applications have been written to take advantage of more than four processors. However, the trend in high-end enterprise environments is moving gradually toward SMP architectures that support six, eight, or even more processors.

 NOTE: Windows NT Server supports four processors out of the box, while Windows NT Workstation supports only two.

Windows NT 4.0 incorporates enhancements that allow it to efficiently scale beyond four processors. Some OEMs have even successfully modified Windows NT to scale up to 32 processors.

When upgrading or buying an entirely new system, you may want to consider taking advantage of NT's SMP support. Four-way servers currently dominate the SMP market, but you should plan ahead by making sure that your hardware can easily be upgraded to include six or more processors.

If your system currently has only one processor and you would like to upgrade to more than one, the Windows NT 4.0 Resource Kit contains a utility to help you. The UPTOMP.EXE utility makes upgrading a Windows NT computer from a single- to multiple-processor system an easy process. It first verifies that the system currently runs only one processor, and then prompts you to specify the location of the multiprocessor HAL (located either on the Windows NT 4.0 CD-ROM or a disk provided by the vendor). Once the setup is complete, you need to restart your system to make the changes take effect.

CONCLUSION

This chapter helps you develop a fundamental understanding of your environment by examining hardware and Windows NT operating system architectures and how the various components interact. This knowledge is essential to understanding how and when you can successfully optimize and tune your Windows NT system. Now that you know the basics of the internal hardware and software architectures, you can delve right into the art of performance tuning.

WINDOWS
NT
Professional
Library

CHAPTER 2

Capacity Planning

Almost everyone at some point has experienced server resource shortages or even resource surpluses where resources were not being utilized as anticipated. Everyone can relate to such problems as hard disk drives that have reached their maximum capacity, or network saturation due to increased network activity. When problems such as these arise, you usually find yourself in fire-fighting mode, trying to solve the problem as quickly as possible so that users either do not notice the problem or feel that it was handled in a timely, efficient manner. If you are successful (or lucky), you may be looked upon as a highly skilled engineer by those who do not know the real cause of the problem. However, more often than not, these small catastrophes damage not only your professional relationship with users but your Windows NT environment.

Like it or not, the user's perception is reality. Consider, for example, a situation in which the response time for an application residing on a server is abnormal during only a 30-minute period after lunch. A person using this application notices the lag time. The user may now feel that there is something wrong with the application or with the network. Either way, the user's perception is that something is amiss. If situations become commonplace in which users feel that there is a problem with computing resources, you may soon be looking for a job with another company.

How can you change users' perceptions? How can you create or maintain a reliable, efficient Windows NT environment and minimize or eliminate fire fighting? These questions and many more are addressed in this chapter. By no means will this chapter be your savior for all computing problems, but it will give you a solid understanding of why you need adhere to *capacity planning procedures,* and will show you the benefits you can reap from doing so. It also describes the methodologies and tools you can use to examine and proactively monitor your environment to ensure reliability, availability, and serviceability.

WHAT IS CAPACITY PLANNING?

Capacity planning originated and matured in the mainframe and minicomputer environments as a way to ensure reliability, availability, and serviceability of computer resources. The capacity planning concept was also carried over quite successfully to UNIX environments. These systems often grew to support a large number of users. Engineers and administrators responsible for the systems quickly recognized the need for proactive monitoring to provide adequate support, immediately and in the future, to end-users and the business structure.

History is definitely repeating itself, except that now large numbers of users and businesses are using PCs instead of mainframes or UNIX workstations to perform tasks and transactions. More and more businesses are converting their legacy systems and UNIX environments to PC-based systems because of their cost efficiency, application support, and processing power, among many other reasons. However, when compared to the mainframe and UNIX environments, the PC world still has a long way to go to bring capacity planning to fruition. Even so, the PC industry is finally beginning to emphasize capacity planning, especially with the increasing popularity of Windows NT systems in the business world. The responsibilities now placed on Windows NT make the capacity planning process crucial to the successful management of your environment.

Capacity planning is one of the most important and most difficult responsibilities you face with both small- and large-scale Windows NT environments. It requires a combination of disciplines and can always be improved upon because work habits and environments continually change. Capacity planning encompasses many aspects of systems management, performance management, deductive reasoning, and forecasting. However, there is more to capacity planning than just using formulas or statistical information. You must use your subjective, creative, and intuitive insight in addition to relying on purely analytical solutions.

Capacity planning can mean many different things to, and be applied to, many aspects of business. Its central concept, however, revolves around several key questions:

▼ How quickly can a task be accomplished?

■ How much work can be performed?

▲ What costs are associated with different business strategies?

Capacity planning enables you to stay one step ahead of your system and anticipate future resource requirements by evaluating existing system behavior.

Benefits of Capacity Planning

The benefits of capacity planning are astounding. It helps define the overall system by establishing baseline performance values and then, through trend and pattern analysis, provides valuable insight into where the system is heading. It is an invaluable aid for uncovering both current and potential bottlenecks. Properly implemented capacity planning procedures can reveal how specific system management activities (software and hardware upgrades, changes in network topologies, and so on) may affect performance, future resource requirements, and budgeting strategies. Capacity planning allows you to attend to performance issues proactively instead of retroactively.

DEFINING SERVICE LEVELS AND GOALS

Capacity planning seeks a balance between resources and workloads. It is extremely difficult to provide just the right amount of computing power for the tasks to be performed. If a system is powerful but underutilized, then a lot of resources are of little value and a waste of money. On the other hand, if a system cannot handle the workload, then tasks or transactions are delayed, opportunities are lost, costs increase, and the user (or customer) perceives a problem. Thus, a primary goal of capacity planning is *balance*.

Capacity planning involves working with unknown or immeasurable aspects of a system, such as the number of gigabytes or terabytes of storage the system will need in the next few years. Other issues may relate to the user workload capacity, such as the number of system administrators that will be needed to maintain the operability of the company's Internet server. All of these questions are related to capacity planning methodologies, and their answers cannot be predicted with complete accuracy. Estimating future resource requirements is not an easy task. However, capacity planning provides a process in which you can establish benchmarks and analyze characteristics of present system resource utilization and use these to make predictions about future needs. Your level of understanding and control of your system needs is limited; to achieve a balance between capacity and workload, you must gain as much understanding and control of the environment as possible. Controlling the aspects that are within your reach greatly increases your chances of successfully maintaining the reliability, serviceability, and availability of your system.

How can you begin to proactively manage your system? First, you should establish *system-wide policies and procedures*. Policies and procedures help define service levels and shape users' expectations. Once these are defined, you can easily begin characterizing workloads, which will, in turn, help you define the *baseline performance values* needed to gauge the health of your system.

POLICIES AND PROCEDURES

You should first of all realize that whatever policies and procedures you decide to implement depend entirely on your environment. The process of defining levels of service and objectives for your system gives you a certain level of control over the system's resources. For example, you will gain a thorough understanding of how different components interact with one another and how you can expect the system to function. Without this level of control, it is difficult to manage and optimize system performance. Policies and procedures also help you winnow out empirical data and transform it into information that you can use to determine current as well as future capacity requirements. In essence, policies and procedures define how the system is supposed to be used, establishing guidelines to help users understand that they can't always have total freedom to use system resources any way they see fit. In a system where policies and procedures are working successfully, and where network throughput suddenly slows to a crawl, you can assume that the reason is not, for instance, that some people were playing a multi-user network game or that a few individuals were sending enormous e-mail attachments to everyone throughout the company.

Two sets of policies and procedures can be established: a set that you communicate to users, and a set used internally by the information systems (IS) department and systems support staff. For example, policies and procedures for users might include a limitation on the size of e-mail attachments and discouragement of the use of beta products (other than ones internally developed) on your network. Internal policies or procedures might include rules that all backups should be completed by 5:00 A.M. each work day and that routine system maintenance (server refreshes, driver updates, and so on) should be performed on Saturday mornings between 6:00 and 9:00 A.M. The following list provides additional examples of policies and procedures that might be applied to your environment:

▼ You can specify that computing resources are intended for business use only—i.e., that no gaming or personal use of computers is allowed.

■ You can specify that only certain applications are supported and allowed on the network.

■ You can establish space quotas on private home directories.

■ You can establish replication intervals for certain databases.

▲ You can specify that users must follow a set of steps to receive technical support.

DEFINING BASELINE VALUES

By now you may be asking, "What do I do to begin performance monitoring?" or "How do I perform capacity planning for a new Windows NT network or stand-alone machine?" In fact, you already have begun the process by defining policies and procedures, which cut down the amount of empirical data that you face. The next preparatory step for capacity planning is establishing baseline values so you can monitor performance. You need a starting point against which you can compare results. In determining baseline values, you deal with a lot of hard facts (statistical representations of system performance), but there are also a few variables that require your judgment and intuition. These variables are workload characterization, benchmarks, vendor-supplied information, and of course, your data collection results.

Workload Characterization

Identifying the *workloads* of a system can be an extremely challenging task, in part because resources often intertwine among different workloads and vary in processing time as well as in the amount of data being processed. Workloads are grouped, or characterized, according to the type of work being performed and the resources used. The following list shows how workloads can be characterized:

▼ Department function (research and development, manufacturing, and so on)

■ Volume of work performed

■ Batch processing

■ Real-time processing

■ Service requests needing attention within a specified time

▲ On-line transactions

Once you have identified your system's workloads, you can determine the resource requirements for each and plan accordingly. This process will also help you understand the performance levels the workloads expect and demand from the system.

Benchmarks

Benchmarks are values that are used to measure the performance of products such as processors, video cards, hard disk drives, applications, and entire systems. They are one of the most sought-after performance indicators in the computer industry. Almost every company in the computer industry uses these values to compare themselves against the competition. As you might suspect, benchmarks are used heavily in sales and marketing, but their real purpose is to indicate the levels of performance you can expect when using the product.

Most benchmarks are provided by the vendors themselves, but they can originate from a variety of other sources as well, such as magazines, benchmark organizations, and in-house testing labs. Table 2-1 lists companies and organizations that provide benchmark statistics and tools for evaluating product performance. Benchmarks can be of great value in your decision-making process, but they should not be your only source for evaluating and measuring performance. When consulting benchmark results during capacity

Company/Organization Name	Web Address
Transaction Processing Performance Council	http://www.tpc.org
AIM Technology	http://www.aim.com
Ziff-Davis Benchmarking Operation	http://www.zdnet.com/zdbop/
Windows Magazine	http://www.winmag.com/software/wt.htm
BYTE Magazine	http://www.byte.com/bmark/bmark.htm

Table 2-1.   Organizations That Provide Benchmarks

planning, use them as guidelines only and use care in their interpretation.

The Windows NT Resource Kit also provides a utility called Response Probe (PROBE.EXE) that can be used to benchmark resources. Response Probe can be used to establish performance measurements for particular resources by exposing them to predefined workloads. The workloads are produced using scripts that simulate real work being performed. Since this utility produces certain levels of stress on the system, it should be used only in a test or lab environment and not in production.

CAPACITY PLANNING MODELS

Because of the diversity of components that play pivotal roles in capacity planning, the process can be approached in many different ways. Capacity planning models can be tailored and applied to virtually any planning need. Some use less formal techniques and general problem-solving strategies, while others involve systematic procedures and distinct capacity planning methodologies. The example in this chapter reflects a more formal approach to capacity planning. However, this model also has characteristics of the less formal approach because capacity planning does not rely on standardization or discrete steps to resolve planning issues.

The general problem-solving process described here stems from the many times my dad drilled into me the problem-solving skills he acquired as a Dale Carnegie instructor. Figure 2-1 shows the general problem-solving process.

As you can see in Figure 2-1, problem solving begins with the recognition that a problem exists. In capacity planning, this might be a file server's slow performance, the anticipation or effects of company growth, or the need to increase workload capacity, for example.

The next step is identifying the source of the problem. One way this is accomplished is by collecting data. Once you have identified the problem's source, you can present and then try possible solutions. Try one solution at a time and then analyze the results. Finally, ask yourself whether the problem is solved. If the problem still exists or

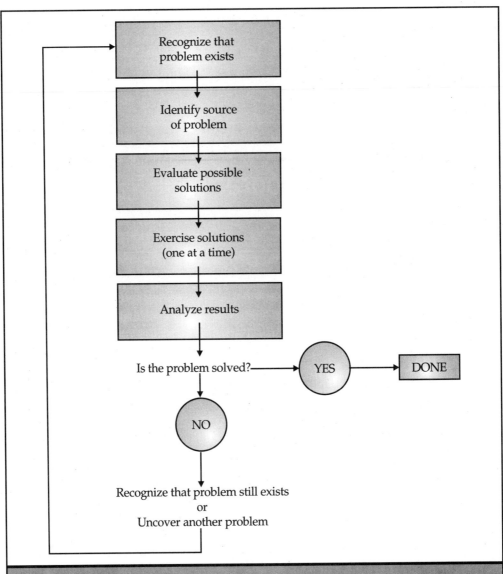

Figure 2-1. The general problem-solving process

the solution presents another problem, you return to the beginning of the problem-solving process. Otherwise, the problem is solved, and you can move on to other issues. Like capacity planning, problem solving is an ongoing process.

The more formal approach to capacity planning uses discrete stages. Each of these stages builds and relies on the other. Throughout these stages, you apply the general problem-solving principles just described. Two important preparatory stages— defining service levels and determining baseline values—integrated into the capacity planning model have already been discussed. The following list shows the stages of capacity planning. Each one, with the exception of the two previously mentioned, is thoroughly examined later in this chapter.

▼ Define service levels and goals.

■ Determine baseline values.

■ Monitor system resources.

■ Create a measurement database.

■ Interpret the data.

▲ Report the results.

It is not essential that you follow these stages in the order they are listed here. However, each stage progressed logically from the other. For example, you cannot create a measurement database without first collecting the necessary data. The capacity planning model presented here is extremely flexible and can be tailored to any type of environment.

CAPACITY PLANNING TOOLS

A growing number of tools are available for collecting and analyzing system data and forecasting system capacity on the Windows NT platform. Microsoft offers some useful utilities that are either built into Windows NT or sold as separate products that can be used to collect and analyze data. These include Task Manager, Network Monitor, and Performance Monitor, which are built into the operating system, and Systems Management Server (SMS), which is a stand-alone product. Data collected from these applications can be exported to other applications, such as Microsoft Excel or Access, for storage and analysis.

Built-in Utilities

The Task Manager, Network Monitor, and Performance Monitor come with the Windows NT operating system.

Task Manager

The Windows NT Task Manager provides multifaceted functionality. It allows you to monitor system activity in real time and to view processor, memory, application, and process status information. You can switch to other running applications or processes, and you can easily end a task or process.

To start using Task Manager, you can use any of the following four methods:

▼ Right-click the Taskbar and select Task Manager.

■ Press CTRL-SHIFT-ESC.

■ Press CTRL-ALT-DELETE and then click Task Manager.

▲ Type **taskman.exe** at the command prompt.

When you execute the Task Manager, the screen that you see in Figure 2-2 will appear.

This window contains three tabs—Applications, Processes, and Performance—that you can toggle between. In addition, a status bar at the bottom of the window displays the number of running processes and the percentage of CPU and memory used, as shown in Figure 2-3.

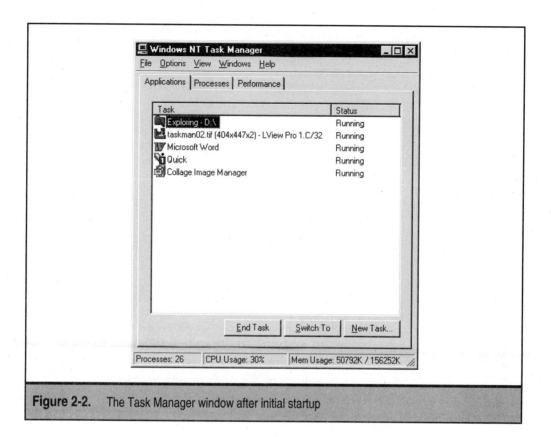

Figure 2-2.   The Task Manager window after initial startup

The Task Manager presents valuable real-time performance information that can help you determine what processes or applications are problematic and give you an overall picture of the health of your system. Unfortunately, its limitations, such as its inability to store collected performance information and the breadth of its monitoring capabilities, do not make it a prime candidate for capacity planning purposes. Moreover, it can give you information pertaining only to the local machine. You must be physically at the machine to gauge performance with the Task Manager.

Network Monitor (NT Server and SMS)

There are two flavors of Network Monitor that can be used to check network performance. One is packaged within Windows NT, and the

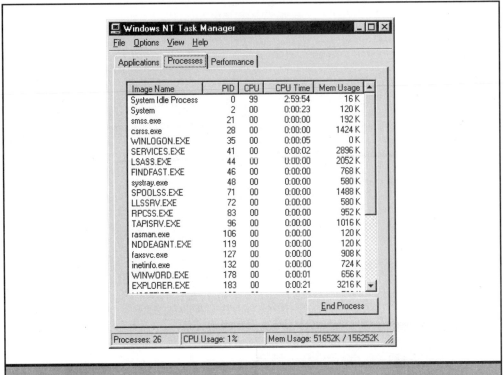

Figure 2-3.   The Task Manager displaying all processes running on the system

other is a component of SMS. Both versions have the same interface, as shown in Figure 2-4, and many functional components, but there are few differences in what they can monitor.

The Network Monitor, built into Windows NT, is intended to monitor only the network activity on the local machine. For security reasons, you cannot capture traffic on remote machines. The Network Monitor can, however, capture all frame types traveling into or away from the local machine.

To use the Network Monitor, you must have the Network Monitor Tools and Agent service installed. To install this service, follow these steps:

1. Double-click the Network applet in the Control Panel.

2. Select the Services tab and then choose Add.

3. Scroll down the list of services until you find the Network Monitor Tools and Agent service.

4. Select the service and choose OK.

5. Specify the path to the Windows NT source files.

6. After the source files are installed, click Close in the Network dialog box. When you are prompted to reboot your machine, click Yes.

7. After the machine has restarted, locate and execute the Network Monitor from the Start | Programs | Administration Tools (Common) menu.

The SMS version of the Network Monitor is essentially an enhanced version of the one integrated into Windows NT Server.

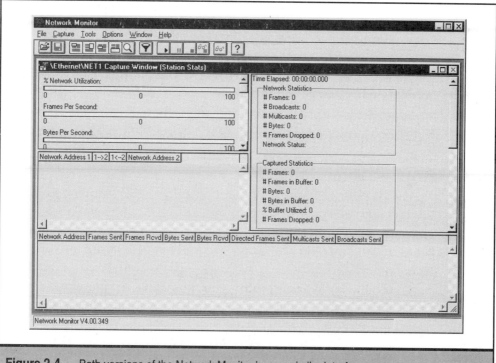

Figure 2-4. Both versions of the Network Monitor have a similar interface.

The primary difference between them is that the SMS version can run promiscuously throughout the network and monitor remote machines. In addition to monitoring remote machines, it can find routers present on the network and monitor the traffic circulating through it as well as resolve addresses from names.

CAUTION: The SMS version of the Network Monitor presents possible security risks due to the nature of its monitoring techniques and privileges. It can monitor network traffic traveling into and away from remote machines. Any sensitive data that the Network Monitor captures could possibly be revealed. Consequently, it is imperative that you limit the number of administrators or IS staff members that can use this version of the Network Monitor.

The SMS version of Network Monitor coincides more with capacity planning objectives because it can monitor several machines at once from a centralized location. Using the Windows NT Server version limits the scope of your monitoring and data collection. It also forces you to install the Network Monitor Tools and Agent service on every machine that needs to be monitored. This results in additional memory requirements and processing power for each machine. For capacity planning purposes, the SMS version of the Network Monitor is an excellent tool for providing real-time network analysis and establishing historical network performance statistics that can be used to examine the health of your network.

Performance Monitor

The Performance Monitor is the most commonly used performance monitoring tool both because it is bundled with the operating system and it allows you to monitor every system object that has measurable counters associated with it. Figure 2-5 shows the Performance Monitor startup screen.

The Performance Monitor is also an excellent tool because it allows you to analyze data through charts, reports, and logs that you can save for future scrutiny. This chapter assumes that you will use the Performance Monitor as your capacity planning tool since it is

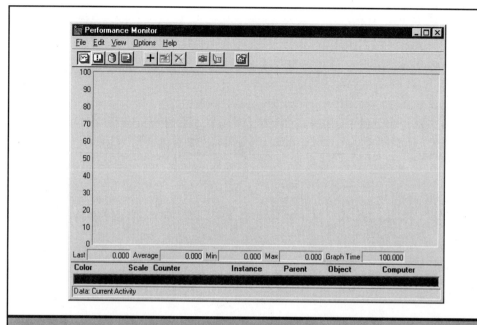

Figure 2-5.   The Performance Monitor startup screen (default)

available to everyone running Windows NT and its principles can be applied to other utilities. Refer to Chapter 8 for a more complete explanation of the Performance Monitor and its uses.

There are many Windows NT Resource Kit utilities that complement the Performance Monitor. One that is particularly useful for capacity planning is the Data Logging Service: MONITOR.EXE and DATALOG.EXE. MONITOR.EXE is the tool used to configure and manage the service, DATALOG.EXE. The Data Logging Service is similar to the Performance Monitor's Alert and Logging function except it is easier to use when managing log files on many remote machines. You can also use the AT Scheduler to start and stop the Data Logging Service so you can monitor specific counters at set times. The Performance Monitor and other applications such as Microsoft Excel or Microsoft Access can then analyze the log files that are generated.

To install the Data Logging Service, follow these steps:

1. Use the Performance Monitor to create a log file (*.LOG).

2. Add appropriate objects to the log file, but do not start logging data.

3. From the File menu, select Save Workspace to save the settings (*.PMW).

4. Copy DATALOG.EXE and the settings file to the %SYSTEMROOT%\SYSTEM32 folder for every machine for which you want to use the Data Logging Service.

5. Register the Data Logging Service on every machine to which you copied DATALOG.EXE and the settings file by typing **monitor setup** at the command prompt.

After the Data Logging Service stops, you can use the Performance Monitor to view and analyze the log files that the service produces.

THIRD-PARTY UTILITIES

In addition to the Microsoft tool set, a number of third-party capacity planning utilities are available for Windows NT. Some of these tools are listed in Table 2-2.

Many companies are porting their UNIX capacity planning applications over to the NT platform. These products commonly provide a means for collecting, analyzing, storing, and reporting statistical system information much as NT's Performance Monitor does. Most, if not all, of the products also incorporate enhancements such as scheduling or graphical reporting capabilities. Some even integrate innovative functionality that promises to automate many aspects of capacity planning. For example, some of the more advanced programs, such as PerformanceWorks, perform historical trend analysis and incorporate decision-support models to help you predict future system use.

Whether third-party products add enhanced storage features or GUI enhancements, most are superior in overall functionality to NT's Performance Monitor. However, there are advantages and disadvantages to using these utilities instead of NT's free utility. A few of these products are briefly described in the following sections

Utility Name	Company
PerformanceWorks	Landmark Systems Phone: 800-333-8666 Web site: http://www.landmark.com E-mail: info@landmark.com
HP Openview	Hewlett Packard Phone: 800-637-7740 Web site: http://www.hp.com/openview/
Dynameasure	Bluecurve, Inc. Phone: 510-267-1500 Web site: http://www.bluecurve.com/ E-mail: sales@bluecurve.com
Unicenter TNG	Computer Associates Phone: 888-864-2368 Web site: http://www.cai.com/
PerfMan	Information Systems Phone: 610-865-0300 Web site: http://www.infosysman.com E-mail: services@infosysman.com
RoboMon NT	Heroix Phone: 800-229-6500 Web site: http://www.robomon.com/ E-mail: info@heroix.com

Table 2-2.   Third-Party Capacity Planning Tools

to give you a comparative overview that will help you decide whether to try them. As mentioned earlier, the capacity planning model used in this chapter is based on the Performance Monitor, but the concepts presented can be applied to the following capacity planning tools as well.

PerfMan

PerfMan, shown in Figure 2-6, is by far one of the easiest-to-use capacity planning utilities available for Windows NT. I have used this product and find that it adequately meets requirements for capacity planning in large or small environments. Setup and configuration take minimal effort, and its intuitive interface makes the management aspects of system monitoring a breeze.

PerfMan is essentially the Performance Monitor on steroids. It provides enhanced versions of such Performance Monitor functions as data storage, monitoring, and alerting. PerfMan consists of two main components: the server and analyst modules. The server component is the 32-bit module that handles all data collection and summarization. Collection and summarization intervals can be set in seconds, minutes, hours, days, and so on to suit your capacity planning goals. The analyst component is a 16-bit module that analyzes the summarized performance data from the server module.

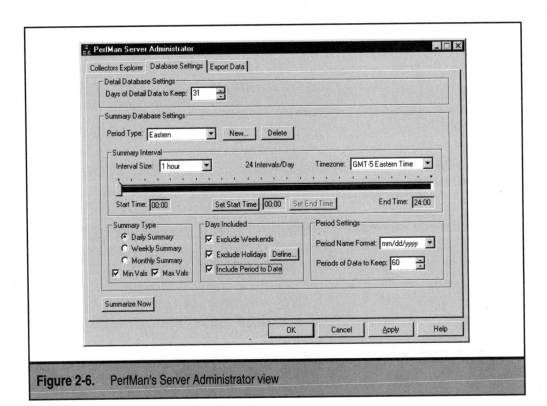

Figure 2-6. PerfMan's Server Administrator view

It can be installed separately from the server module and can be used on any client machine.

You may wonder why the analyst module is a 16-bit application and the server module is a 32-bit application. The reason is actually quite simple. Writing the analyst as a 16-bit application allows you to view performance data from other platforms such as Windows 3.*x* and OS/2. You may think that very few companies, if any, still support those operating systems. However, I have found that an unbelievable number of companies do, in fact, still run those operating systems.

PerfMan offers three distinct advantages: it automatically manages historical information, it offers extremely flexible monitoring configuration options, and its reporting functionality is highly intuitive. We will examine each of these benefits.

The first advantage is PerfMan's management of historical information. It creates a measurement database for you and manages administrative operations such as the organization associated with the storage of historical information. The amount of data that is collected can grow exponentially, leaving you with bewildering amounts of data to sift through to find relevant information. With PerfMan creating and managing your management database, you can easily retrieve any relevant data on the fly. Moreover, PerfMan saves you lots of time and removes the hassle of manually searching through heaps of data.

The second advantage of using PerfMan is the flexibility with which you can configure counter monitoring. When logging data statistics, you are not forced to monitor entire objects as you are with the Performance Monitor. Instead, you can selectively choose which counters to monitor from each object. You simply select the server that you wish to monitor and apply the appropriate counters. PerfMan also permits you to configure default collectors, shown in Figure 2-7. A default collector is essentially a template of performance counters that you can apply to individual servers. For example, if a network has five Microsoft Exchange servers supporting the company's messaging infrastructure, you can create a default collector for a Microsoft Exchange server that has all the counters you want to monitor. You can then simply apply the default

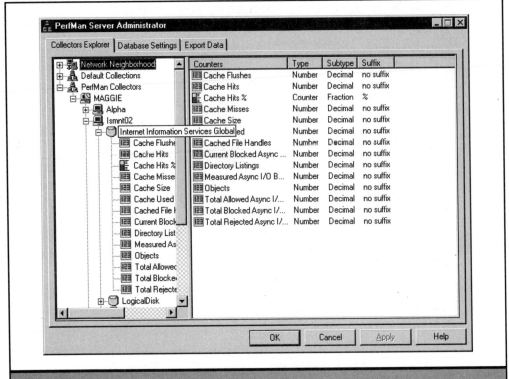

Figure 2-7.   Default collectors can be applied to individual servers in your network environment.

collector to the other four servers, and each one will inherit the properties of that default collector. If PerfMan did not have this functionality, you would be forced to manually configure each of the servers. This saves valuable amounts of time.

The third advantage of using PerfMan is its reporting functionality. As mentioned earlier, the analyst module is responsible for interpreting the summarized performance data. It also controls reporting. Reports can be generated in a variety of formats such as pie, 2-D, and 3-D charts, as shown in Figure 2-8, for three types of intervals: none, peak interval, and peak planned interval. Interval designs can be configured through the server module on the Database Settings tab. Depending on the setting you select, you can view averages and peak performances for every period that you

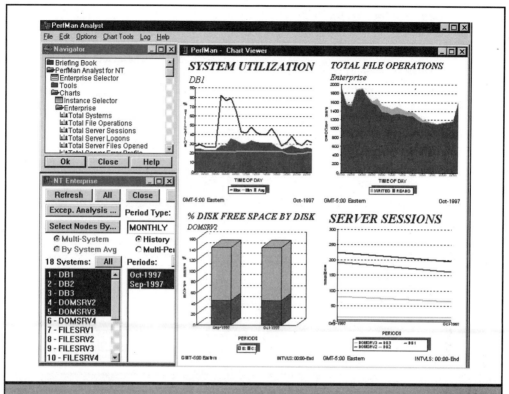

Figure 2-8. PerfMan provides a variety of useful charting formats to analyze summarized data.

specify. The peak planned interval charts are the best to use when you already know what times of the day that are the busiest.

Selecting PerfMan as your third-party utility gives you the ability to automate many capacity planning procedures pertaining to data collection and storage. It is an effective yet not overly complex tool that monitors system resources, stores historical data, and can even alert you to potential problems before they arise.

PerformanceWorks

PerformanceWorks is one of the more advanced utilities available for capacity planning purposes. It provides centralized administration of the monitoring, alerting, storing, and reporting of performance statistics. Moreover, it incorporates decision-support models that can help you accurately analyze real-time and historical data. Figure 2-9 shows the PerformanceWorks screen.

PerformanceWorks reflects the client/server model in that the Domain Station component acts as a server and SmartAgents are the clients. Domain Station is the control center for all of Performance-Works' functionality, such as configuration and monitoring. It monitors any server on your network that has the SmartAgent installed, including servers that reside in other domains. A SmartAgent is a service that runs on the machine. It communicates with the Domain Station to provide performance information regarding that particular server. The service uses very few resources to run on the server, so its effect on performance is minimal.

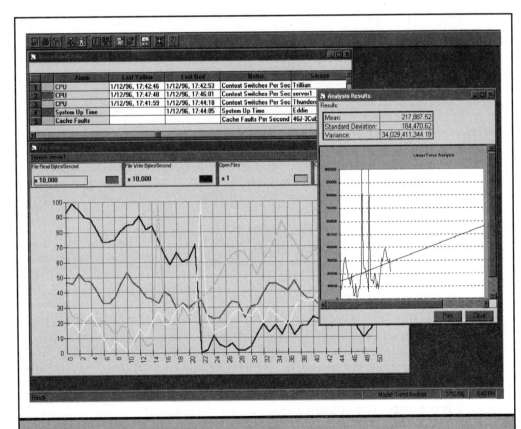

Figure 2-9.   PerformanceWorks displaying performance statistics

Performance Works can be used with Microsoft's SMS to install the SmartAgent on multiple servers. This saves you the time and trouble of going to each machine to install the agent.

One of the more advanced features of PerformanceWorks is its ability to help you analyze the data you collect. It includes decision-support models to analyze data and predict what system resources requirements may be needed in the future. These models rely on Microsoft Excel to examine the data for trends or patterns.

PerformanceWorks is an effective capacity planning utility for monitoring and analyzing performance. The next release, expected soon, is expected to incorporate functionality that will record user response times directly from the user's desktop. This capability has existed in UNIX capacity planning products but not for the Windows NT platform.

Dynameasure Enterprise

Dynameasure Enterprise takes a slightly different approach to capacity management from the rest of the third-party capacity planning utilities. Most other products are focused around some form of monitoring technique, whereas Dynameasure relies on actual system testing to get accurate representations of system use. This allows you to create real-world scenarios for your environment. These scenarios can be tailored to best represent system use characteristics.

This section presents a general overview of Dynameasure; to determine whether it will work for you, you will need to evaluate it yourself. This section will, however, provide you with enough information to give you a solid understanding of Dynameasure's capabilities.

Dynameasure Enterprise has many features that can be used in your capacity planning process. It can be used to perform benchmarking, perform stress testing, and evaluate the effects of implementing new technologies. Even though Dynameasure's measurements result from stress testing, it is not simply a load tester. It is flexible enough to be used to create what-if scenarios, and stress testing is not limited to one particular application or system component.

Dynameasure includes two services: Dynameasure for SQL and Dynameasure for File Services. Both simulate real-world scenarios by stressing the system with customizable or predefined workloads. Dynameasure for SQL uses on-line transaction processing to simulate workloads for Oracle 7 Server and Microsoft SQL Server. Dynameasure for File Services can simulate workloads for every imaginable aspect of network file operations. It can simulate file transfers, loads placed on the network by the execution of server-based applications, installations over the network, and more. You can tailor the amount of stress on the system to create what-if scenarios for your system. Figure 2-10 shows some examples of Dynameasure reports.

Dynameasure Enterprise is an excellent tool that measures the capabilities of the hardware and software components of your system. It also helps you gain insight on how certain systems

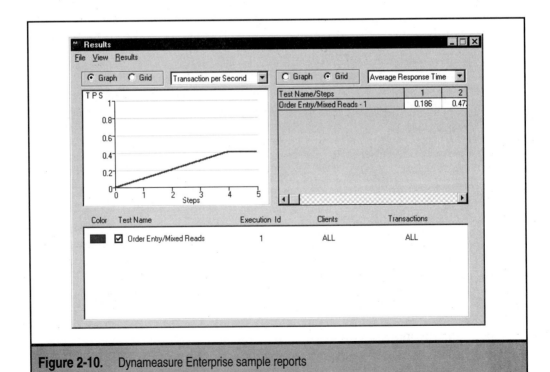

Figure 2-10. Dynameasure Enterprise sample reports

management decisions, such as the addition of new technologies, will affect your system's performance.

MONITORING SYSTEM RESOURCES

You can monitor numerous system resources for the purpose of capacity planning. In fact, there are so many objects and counters that you can monitor that you can quickly become overwhelmed with the amount of data that you collect. If you do not carefully choose what to monitor, you may collect so much information that the data will be of little use. Large amounts of data can be unwieldy and can cause you to spend most of your time organizing instead of analyzing. Keep in mind that one of the key concepts behind capacity planning is *efficiency.* Tailor your monitoring to the server's configuration as accurately as possible.

There are a few important resources that you should always monitor for every server: the memory, processor, disk subsystem, and network subsystem. These resources are the four most common contributors to system bottlenecks. A *bottleneck* is the slowest component of your system and can be either hardware or software. Bottlenecks limit a system's performance because your system runs only as fast as its slowest resource. For example, a file server may be equipped with a 100MB Fast Ethernet network interface card (NIC), but if the disk subsystem is relatively antiquated, the system cannot take full advantage of the network throughput provided by the NIC. There are also residual effects of bottlenecks, such as the under-consumption of hardware resources. Resources may not be utilized because the system is trying to compensate for the bottleneck.

In addition, the way a Windows NT Server is functionally configured influences what other resources or services you should consider monitoring. The most common Windows NT Server configurations enable file and print sharing, application sharing, domain controller functions—or some combination of these. For example, you may want to monitor the effects of replication and synchronization on domain controllers but not for an application or for file and print servers. It is important to monitor the most common contributors to system bottlenecks as well as those that pertain to the particular server configuration.

This section discusses specific counters you should monitor for each common contributor to bottlenecks. Note, however, that there are many other counters that you should consider monitoring in addition to the ones described here. This section is intended to give you a baseline or an absolute minimum number of counters to start your monitoring process. You will find more information on counters and the values you should look for in subsequent chapters.

Monitoring Memory

Of the four common contributors to bottlenecks, memory is usually the first resource to cause performance degradation. This is simply because Windows NT tends to devour as much memory as possible. Fortunately, adding more memory is also the easiest and most economical way to upgrade performance. Figure 2-11 shows the Performance Monitor's screen for monitoring memory counters in real time. Refer to Chapter 4 for more information on memory and for techniques to optimize server memory configurations.

Memory has many significant counters associated with it. However, the two counters that should always be monitored are Page Faults/sec and Pages/sec. These indicate whether the system is configured with the proper amount of RAM. For more information on memory performance, refer to Chapter 4.

A page fault occurs when a process requires code or data that is not in its working set. This counter includes both hard faults (those that require disk access) and soft faults (where the faulted page is found elsewhere in memory). Most systems can handle a large number of soft faults without sacrificing performance. However, hard faults can cause significant delays because of hard disk access times. Even the seek and transfer rates of the fastest drive available on the market are slow compared to memory speeds. The enormous latency associated with hard page faults should immediately convince you to configure the system with as much RAM as possible.

The Pages/sec counter reflects the number of pages read from or written to disk to resolve hard page faults. Hard page faults occur

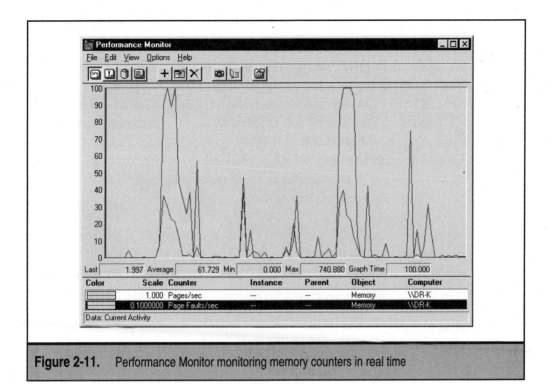

Figure 2-11.   Performance Monitor monitoring memory counters in real time

when a process requires code or data that is not in its working set or elsewhere in memory. The code or data must be found and retrieved from disk. This counter is the primary indicator of thrashing (relying too much on the hard disk drive for virtual memory) and excessive paging. Pages/sec values that are consistently above 20 indicate insufficient memory.

Monitoring the Processor

The processor is often the first resource analyzed when there is a noticeable decrease in system performance. For capacity planning purposes, there are two significant counters to monitor in the processor object: % Processor Time and Interrupts/sec. The % Processor Time counter indicates the percentage of overall processor utilization. If more than one processor exists on the system, an instance for each one is included along with a total (combined) value counter. If the % Processor Time counter sustains a processor use rate of 50 percent or greater for long periods of time, you should consider upgrading. When the average processor time consistently exceeds 80 percent utilization, users may notice a degradation in performance that will not be tolerable.

The Interrupts/sec counter is also a good indicator of processor utilization. It indicates the number of device interrupts the processor is handling per second. The device interrupt can be hardware or software driven. The number of interrupts handled by the processor should not exceed 3,500 in Pentium or higher-level machines. Some ways to improve performance include off-loading some services to another less-used server, adding another processor, upgrading the existing processor, and distributing the load to an entirely new machine.

Monitoring the Disk Subsystem

The disk subsystem consists of two main types of resources: hard disk drives and hard disk controllers. The Performance Monitor does not have an object directly associated with the hard disk controller because the values given in the Physical and Logical Disk objects accurately represent disk subsystem performance. Refer to Chapter 6 for more information on configuring and optimizing the disk subsystem. Disk performance counters are disabled by default because they cause a slight performance degradation in systems dating before the Pentium architecture. In Pentium or higher-level machines, the effects of the counters are negligible. Even though the performance degradation is minimal, however, you should disable disk performance counters when you are not actively monitoring the disk subsystem. To begin viewing statistics for your disk subsystem, you must first activate the disk performance counters with the command **diskperf -y** for the local machine, **diskperf -y \\mycomputer** for remote machines, or **diskperf -ye** for machines with software stripe sets. After you have finished monitoring, you can disable the disk performance counters with the command **diskperf -n**.

The best disk performance counters to monitor for capacity planning are % Disk Time and Avg. Disk Queue Length. The % Disk

Time counter monitors the amount of elapsed time that the selected physical or logical drive is busy servicing read and write requests. Avg. Disk Queue Length indicates the number of outstanding requests (requests not yet serviced) on the physical or logical drive. This value is an instantaneous measurement rather than an average over a specified interval, but it still accurately represents the number of delays the drive is experiencing. The request delays experienced by the drive can be calculated by subtracting the number of spindles on the disk from the Disk Queue Length measurement. If the delay is frequently greater than 2, then the disks are degrading performance.

Monitoring Network Performance

Because of its many components, the network subsystem is one of the most complicated subsystems to monitor for bottlenecks. Protocols, NICs, network applications, and physical topologies all play important roles in your network. To further complicate matters, your environment may implement multiple protocol stacks. Therefore, the network performance counters you should monitor vary depending upon your system's configuration.

The important information to gain from monitoring network subsystem components is the amount of network activity and throughput. When monitoring network subsystem components, you should use other network monitoring tools in addition to the Performance Monitor. For example, consider using Network Monitor (either the built-in or SMS version). Using these tools together broadens the scope of monitoring and more accurately represents what is occurring within your network infrastructure. The Network Monitor displays network utilization percentages, collision rates, and other information that complements the statistics you gather with the Performance Monitor. Figure 2-12 shows the Network Monitor at work.

This discussion of capacity planning for the network subsystem focuses on two protocols, NetBEUI and TCP/IP, that are commonly installed on Windows NT systems. Consider a Windows NT Server configured to use the NetBEUI protocol. NetBEUI has both connection and connectionless delivery properties. The Datagrams/sec counter

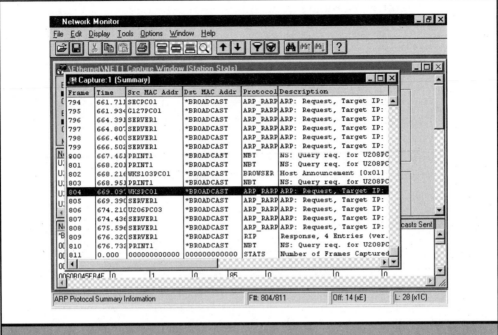

Figure 2-12.   Network Monitor analyzing captured TCP/IP and other network traffic information

is a significant indicator of network activity because datagrams are associated with unreliable, connectionless delivery methods. Datagrams are packets that may or may not reach the intended recipient.

This data transfer method is analogous to mass-mailing a letter because datagrams typically are broadcast to every node, and no acknowledgments are generated to indicate that the packet was successfully delivered. A key indicator of network throughput for the NetBEUI protocol is the Bytes Total/sec counter. This counter tracks both frame-based and datagram activity but counts the bytes only in the frames that carry data.

Another common protocol in use today is TCP/IP. In fact, with all the craze surrounding the Internet, TCP/IP is probably the most widely used protocol. If you are implementing this protocol, it is imperative that you closely monitor it so that it does not negatively affect network performance. TCP/IP is not necessarily any more likely to affect performance than other protocols, but it is less efficient compared to some protocols such as NetBEUI.

The counters for TCP/IP are added to the system after you install the protocol and the Simple Network Management (SNMP) service. If you do not install the SNMP service, you will not see the TCP/IP counters because the associated objects and counters are contained within the service.

The objects available for monitoring TCP/IP are FTP Server, ICMP, IP, NIC, NetBT, TCP, UDP, and WINS Server, and there are many significant counters that you should consider monitoring. This section discusses just two for capacity planning purposes; refer to Chapter 5 for more information on what else you may want to monitor for your network configuration.

Two important counters to use for TCP/IP monitoring pertain to the NIC object. They are the Bytes Total/sec and the Output Queue Length counters. The Bytes Total/sec counter indicates the amount of inbound and outbound TCP/IP traffic experienced by your server. The Output Queue Length indicates whether there are congestion or contention problems on your NIC. If the Output Queue Length value is consistently above 2, check the Bytes Total/sec counter for abnormally high values. High values for both counters suggests that there is a bottleneck in your network subsystem, and it may be time to upgrade your server network components.

There are many other counters that need to be monitored and consulted before you can accurately pinpoint the cause of abnormal counter values or network performance degradation. For example, were the abnormal Bytes Total/sec and Output Queue Length values the result of a temporary burst in network activity or unusually high collision rates? If you know that the collision rate is greater than 10 percent, then the problem may be the performance of the overall network and not just the Windows NT Server in question.

CREATING A MEASUREMENT DATABASE

Now you should have a pretty good idea of what you need to measure for capacity planning purposes: four contributors to bottlenecks as well as the counters pertaining to the server's functionality. You are now ready to start gathering system information and creating a measurement database. Before you begin, note that there are two monitoring phases in capacity planning. The first stage lasts for about a week or two. This is the stage where you will be collecting snapshots of system performance at frequent intervals. The second stage is a process that you will continue throughout your capacity planning implementation.

Initial data gathering intervals are more frequent than routine capacity planning intervals because you are trying to obtain a solid understanding of system statistics. During the first week, use the Performance Monitor to monitor the system counters you have chosen at up to one-minute intervals. Increasing the frequency of collection increases the amount of data that you gather. Create separate log files for each day to help organize the abundance of data you will collect. It is also very important that you have plenty of disk space for the log files. In fact, my latest capacity planning setup at a client site required approximately 90MB for the first week of gathering performance data!

Once you've begun to record your data, you can immediately start building your measurement database. The measurement database is not used only to store historical data; it serves as an organizational structure so that the data does not become unwieldy and ultimately worthless to your capacity planning efforts. Most third-party utilities provide excellent measurement databases without any intervention on your part. You just specify what to monitor, and they automatically handle measurement database creation and management. The Performance Monitor simply stores historical data in log files. To work around Performance Monitor's limited ability to create a measurement database, you can export the

Performance Monitor log files to another application such as
Microsoft Access or Microsoft Excel, as shown here:

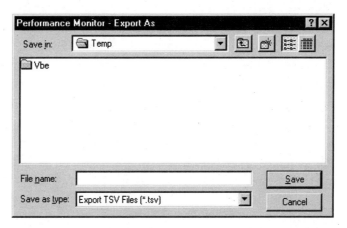

Exporting the data to these types of applications will allow you to
more efficiently organize, analyze, and report on the collected data
than if you use only the Performance Monitor. To export a file that
can later be analyzed by another application, use the following
procedure:

1. From the File menu, select Export Log.

2. In the Performance Monitor's Export As dialog box, type a
   name for the log file.

3. Choose either the CSV or TSV file type.

NOTE: The TSV file type has its columns separated by tabs, while the
CSV file type has its columns separated by commas. TSV files are typically
used in spreadsheet applications, and CSV files are typically suitable for
databases.

4. Click Save.

With the data exported for use in another application, you can easily perform queries and create graphs to help you interpret your data or even present system information in a non-technical format. Creating and maintaining a measurement database helps you gain a fundamental understanding of the performance data by organizing your records.

Scaling Down the Data Collection

After a week of initial data collection, you should have a pretty good idea of typical system performance levels. You can now scale down the amount of data collection to a more suitable level. This will save a considerable amount of disk space plus the hassle of organizing and interpreting large amounts of data. Typically, capacity planning measurements are taken at 10-minute (600-second) and 15-minute (900-second) intervals. To scale down the amount of data collected even more, monitor the system only during peak activity. By increasing the time interval and narrowing the range of monitoring times, you can greatly reduce the size of the log files.

Another way to reduce the amount of data collected is to reduce the number of counters in the objects being monitored. It may not be necessary to monitor all counters for each object. However, you may always want to monitor the following:

▼ **Memory**   Page Faults/sec, Pages/sec

■ **Processor**   % Processor Time, Interrupts/sec

■ **Logical disk and physical disk**   % Disk Time, Avg. Disk Queue Length

▲ **Network subsystem**   Dependent on the protocols used

The counters you monitor for the network subsystem depend on the server's function and the protocols it uses. For instance, with Gateway Service for NetWare, you would monitor the Bytes Total/sec and Packets/sec counters. An important counter to always monitor for all Windows NT Servers is Server: Total Bytes/sec.

Even after you reduce the amount of data you collect, you must keep an organized approach to data collection because your data still can quickly grow to an enormous size. Without organization, the data will become unwieldy, overwhelming, and ultimately useless for capacity planning purposes.

Table 2-3 shows sample performance data from the four common contributors to system bottlenecks. These values are simply examples and should not be consulted for target values.

Category	Object	Counter	Minimum	Average	Maximum
Memory	Memory	Pages/sec	0	2.611	22.193
		Page Faults/sec	6.977	29.963	388.202
Processor	Processor	% Processor Time	0.496	2.693	16.854
		% Processor Time 1	0	2.67	9.184
Disk Subsystem	Logical Disk	% Disk Time	3.221	27.952	100.000
		Avg. Disk Queue Length	0	0.884	3.591
	Paging File	% Usage	5.069	5.075	5.079
		% Usage Peak	27.542	27.542	27.542
Network Subsystem	Gateway Service for the NetWare	Bytes Total/sec	0	519.924	6323.248
		Packets/sec	0	8.039	9686

Table 2-3.   Sample Counter Statistics from the Performance Monitor

INTERPRETING THE DATA

You must not only understand how and when to collect data but also how to interpret the results. Interpretation requires insight to fully understand the overall health of your system. You can use the collected data to profile current resource demands, characterize workloads on each system, and uncover over- and underutilized resources. Data can also be analyzed for trends or patterns to provide historical snapshots of the system.

For example, suppose that the recent popularity of a server-based application has brought the application server's processor utilization rate to an astounding average of 85 percent. This increase may signal a need for a multiprocessor machine or simply for a processor upgrade. A capacity planning procedure can allow system management staff to predict and prepare for this event proactively. The information obtained through the capacity planning stage can yield an understanding of the general health of the system and help forecast future requirements.

REPORTING

The reporting stage is often overlooked in the capacity planning process. However, reporting directly benefits both IS staff and management.

The IS staff benefits from reports because they provide a wealth of system configuration information such as resource utilization levels, historical capacities, and forecasts in easy-to-comprehend, graphical formats. Reports can also uncover unexplored or unanticipated trends in performance or relationships among resources. The reporting stage essentially takes the technical information that you have been gathering and presents it in a format that is easier to understand. By making the available information as clear and concise as possible, reports enable the IS staff to make support decisions that benefit the system. Without a reporting process, it would be difficult, if not impossible, for staff to assess system requirements before problems arise.

Reports also provide many benefits to various management levels. System performance reports presented graphically, as shown in Figure 2-13, can be understood by almost everyone, including people without a technical background. Using charts, for example, a report can visually present a system's current performance levels and possible performance scenarios. Many business decision makers cannot afford to be bombarded with raw data and tedious details. Graphical presentations remove the unnecessary details and present clear, concise summaries of information so rational decisions can be made.

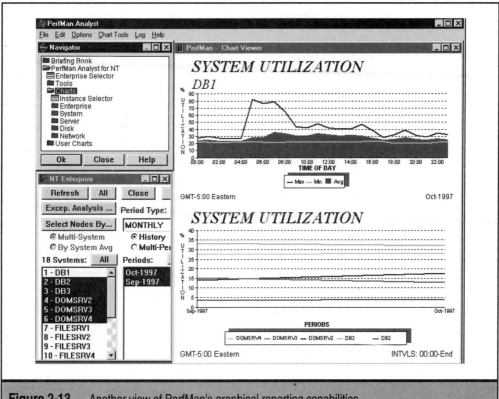

Figure 2-13. Another view of PerfMan's graphical reporting capabilities

CONCLUSION

Capacity planning is of growing importance in the Windows NT environment, especially with its increasing responsibility for mission-critical applications. The ultimate goal of capacity planning is to stay one step ahead of your system so you can make educated forecasts of resource requirements and minimize performance problems, such as bottlenecks, before they occur. Proactively attending to system performance reduces the amount of time you spend reacting to performance degradation issues because you will discover problems before they negatively affect the system.

This chapter defined capacity planning and provided a set of procedures for attaining your capacity planning goals. It also described some of the built-in and third-party tools that you can use to successfully manage your system.

CHAPTER 3

Domain Planning

This chapter expands your understanding of Windows NT's domain hierarchy and examines performance considerations for domains and domain strategies. Before focusing on technical issues relating to performance optimization and other concepts relating to efficiency, we will examine the logic behind domain architecture as well as other issues relating to domain strategies, such as trust relationships and the logon process. These and other aspects of domains can profoundly affect the performance of Windows NT Server and the network.

Domains are logical groupings of users and computer resources. They are analogous to departments or entire organizations in that they consist of one or several components that operate as a single entity. Domains can be designed based on location or function; that is, they can encompass departments, users, resources, spatial requirements, or entire organizations.

Domains provide a level of organization to the network environment. A network can have one or more domains depending on your company's organization. There are many configurations that you can choose from, and Microsoft publishes four domain models, which will be discussed shortly. The model you choose for your environment will depend on a number of factors, including the number of users your environment supports, the need to centralize or decentralize administration, company politics, and location.

One reason Microsoft decided to implement this type of grouping is security. However, this discussion focuses primarily on the performance aspects of domains.

A Windows NT network can consist of workgroups or domains. However, because the workgroup model is suitable only for small networked environments, this chapter discusses only domain performance issues. It starts with an overview of the four domain models, trust relationships, and the authentication process and then delves into the performance optimization aspects of domains.

CREATING A DOMAIN

When you install Windows NT Server, the system asks you whether the machine should be configured as a *primary domain controller* (PDC), a *backup domain controller* (BDC), or a stand-alone server. To create a domain, you must configure the server as a PDC. It will then prompt you for a name for the domain you wish to create. Only one PDC can exist for each domain. If you configure the server as a PDC and then decide that it should either join an existing domain or be a stand-alone server, your only choice will be to completely reinstall the operating system. Therefore, it is extremely important to plan the server's role in your environment.

The PDC provides the foundation for the domain and holds the master copy of the *Security Accounts Manager* (SAM) database, which contains user, group, and machine account information. The PDC also handles user authentication and manages the synchronization and replication of information to any existing BDCs. As its name implies, the BDC is designed to help the PDC with domain controller functions. It takes on some of the PDC's responsibilities by authenticating users who want to log onto the domain and provides fault tolerance for the domain by keeping a copy of the SAM database. The domain can include other machines, including Windows NT stand-alone servers and workstations, LAN Manager servers, Windows for Workgroups 3.*x* clients, Windows 95 clients, and MS-DOS clients. However, only Windows NT Server, Windows NT Workstation, and LAN Manager servers participate as members of the domain.

FOUR DOMAIN MODELS

Microsoft has defined four domain models that you can choose from to match your business needs and organization. The models represent different ways NT can logically organize groups of computers into a single functional unit and provide a secure system.

The four domain models—*single, single master, multiple master,* and *complete trust*—are defined by the number of domains present in the organization, the domain type (user, resource, or master), and the trust configuration among the domains.

From a performance standpoint, the way in which you define your domain infrastructure can affect costs (additional hardware, time involved managing the domain, and so on), user logon times, and network activity and throughput. The following descriptions of the domain models will help you decide which model best fits your organization's needs.

The Single Domain Model

The single domain model is the simplest of all the models. It represents a centralized management scheme where all users and resources are contained in one domain. The single domain contains one PDC and possibly one or more BDCs. Figure 3-1 shows the single domain model.

This model is the building block for all other domain models. Depending on its size and the proximity of servers, the single domain can be an advantageous model from a performance and administrative point of view because of its centralization of management. This domain model is suitable for companies that need to support 5,000 or fewer users.

The Single Master Domain Model

An extension of the single domain model is the single master domain model. This model consists of a master domain and one or more resource domains. The master domain contains all account types (user, group, and machine) to provide centralized management of these accounts; the resource domains contain only computer resources such as servers and printers. All accounts, including machine accounts, are created and managed from the master domain. User accounts log onto only the master domain and with proper access privileges can use the resources in the resource domains through established trust relationships. Each resource

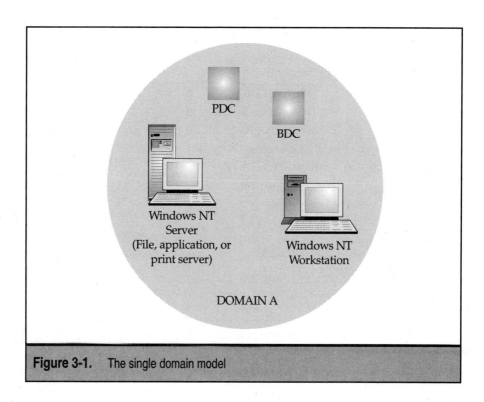

Figure 3-1.   The single domain model

domain establishes a one-way trust relationship with the master domain. Figure 3-2 shows the single master domain model with one-way trust relationships established. This model segments the accounts from the resources to provide easier, centralized management and control over the domain.

The Multiple Master Domain Model

The multiple master domain model consists of at least two master domains and one or more resource domains. There is complete trust bonding between the master domains. This means that the master domains all have two one-way trust relationships established between them. The resource domains, containing servers, printers, and other services, trust each master domain with an established one-way trust. Since master domains completely trust each other, users can log onto any master domain even if they have an account

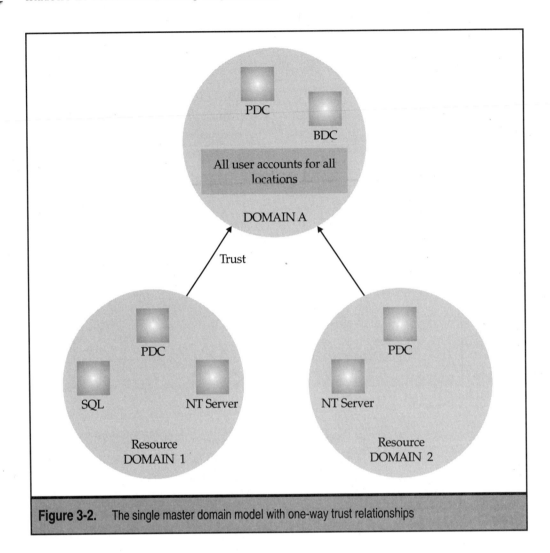

Figure 3-2. The single master domain model with one-way trust relationships

only in one of the other master domains. The user's account is stored in only one master domain, but because of the trust relationship between master domains, the account can be verified for logon. Moreover, a user from any master domain can use any resources or services in any other master or resource domain unless the user's account specifically restricts the user from doing so. Figure 3-3 shows the multiple master domain model.

The master domain model provides flexibility in account and resource management. Domain administrators can not only manage their own domain but also other master domains. This model is best

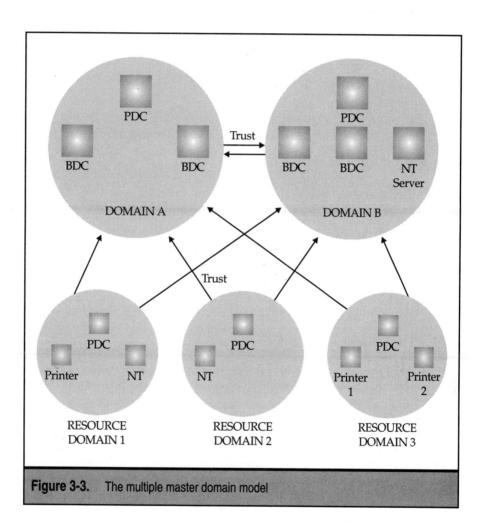

Figure 3-3.   The multiple master domain model

suited to companies that have two or more organizational units that have separate needs and functions. It is also suitable for companies with more than 10,000 users. Accounts can be managed separately in each master domain, and users need only one NT account to access resources and services from any resource domain.

The Complete Trust Domain Model

The last model that Microsoft proposes is one in which every domain is a master domain—that is, in which every domain completely trusts every other domain. In other words, each domain is a separate entity that can use resources in other domains. No resource domains exist in this model, because all domains have their own resources that they manage. What distinguishes this domain model from the others is that every domain trusts all other domains completely. Between every domain there are two established one-way trust relationships. Users with domain administrator privileges can manage accounts as well as resources in all domains. This model should be used only when account management is minimal and security is not a major concern. This model can quickly become overwhelming because managing the trust relationships alone can be an administrative nightmare. Figure 3-4 shows the complete trust domain model.

DO YOU TRUST ME?

We have discussed that domains have a certain degree of trust between them, but we have not completely defined what a *trust relationship* means to domains. The concept of trust relationships can be confusing, but without a thorough understanding of its impact on the structure of the Windows NT environment, it can be difficult to enhance the manageability and performance of your system.

Trust relationships between domains establish a bond between these domains. Depending on the configuration, a trust gives one domain the authority to use the other's Security Accounts Management database (SAM). This segments the organization

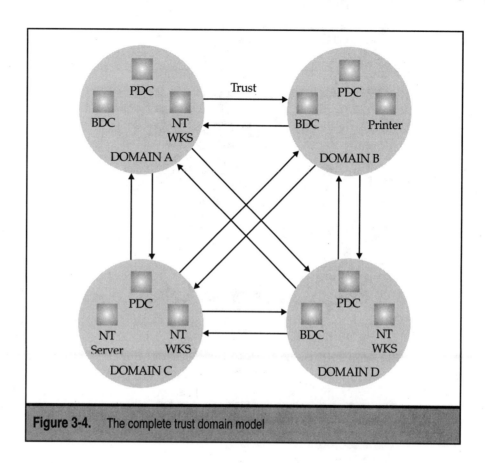

Figure 3-4.   The complete trust domain model

into more manageable groups than what domains themselves can provide. For example, without trust relationships, the single master model would not be possible; there would be either just a single domain or two separate domains.

Trust relationships go only in one direction. For example, when domain A trusts domain B, domain B users can use resources in domain A but not vice-versa. To bridge the domains so that each side can use the other's resources, two one-way trusts must be established. In the single master domain model, one-way trust relationships are established so that resource domains trust users to come over and use printing services, file services, and more. However, there is no need for the master domain to trust the resource domains, because a resource domain does not contain user accounts.

Calculating the Number of Trusts

You can perform two different calculations to determine the number of trust relationships needed for a particular domain model. You can determine the number of trusts between master domains, and you can determine the number of trusts between master and resource domains. It is important to perform these calculations during the planning stages so you know exactly how many trust relationships your design requires. Trusts affect network performance especially when WAN links are brought into the equation. How trust relationships affect network performance will be discussed shortly.

To calculate the number of trusts between master domains (T_m), use the formula

$$T_m = N_m(N_m - 1)$$

where N_m is the number of master domains.

To calculate the number of trusts between master and resource domains (T_r), use the formula

$$T_r = N_m N_r$$

where N_m is the number of master domains and N_r is the number of resource domains.

Table 3-1 shows the results of these formulas applied to different domain model scenarios.

The total number of trusts involved in a multiple master domain implementation is computed by adding the total number of trusts between the master domains to the total number of trusts between master and resource domains: $T = T_m + T_r$, or $T = N_m(N_m - 1) + N_m N_r$. As Table 3-1 shows, with the multiple master model, the number of trusts escalates with each domain addition. The more domains in your Windows NT environment, the more impact trust relationships have on performance, especially on the network subsystem. This is another reason why the complete trust domain model is not recommended.

Model	Number of Master Domains	Number of Resource Domains	Total Number of Trusts
Single	1	0	0
Single master	1	2	2
Multiple master	2	2	6
	2	3	8
	7	20	182
Complete trust	8	0	56

Table 3-1.   Sample Calculations of the Number of Trust Relationships Needed for Different Scenarios

SIZE DOES MATTER

The size of the domain is limited by the size of the SAM database and nonpaged pool memory. The maximum recommended size of the SAM database is 40MB. This file size determines the number of users that can be supported. The maximum number of users that can be supported in a single domain is 40,000. This number is based on a single SAM database. If the multiple master domain model or complete trust domain model is implemented, then there are multiple instances of the SAM database. To calculate the maximum number of users that can be supported with these domain models, multiply the number of users supported in a single domain (40,000) by the number of master domains. Thus, your organization is not limited to 40,000 user accounts if the domain structure follows the multiple master or complete trust domain model.

User, Group, and Machine Accounts

User, group, and machine account information makes up the bulk of the information stored in the SAM database. Each type has a certain size associated with it that can be used to calculate the number of users a domain can support.

The user account contains information that identifies the user. This includes the user name, account password, group associations, and account restrictions. Each user account requires 1K in the SAM database.

Group accounts vary in size. The size of each group account depends on the number of user accounts belonging to the group. For this reason, you should assume that each group account requires approximately 4K of space in the SAM database.

When machines, such as an NT Workstation, NT Server, or BDC, join the domain, a machine account is created. Each account that is created requires approximately 0.5K in the SAM database.

Table 3-2 outlines the space requirements in the SAM database for each type of account.

Using this information on account space requirements, you can compute the SAM database size for your environment. This will give you a close approximation to what the actual size of the SAM database will be. For example, assume that a domain will have 26,000 users, 250 group accounts, and 26,000 machine accounts. Now multiply these numbers by the respective space requirements for each account and then add the products:

$$(26,000 \times 1K) + (250 \times 4K) + (26,000 \times 0.5K)$$

Account	Space Required (in Kilobytes)
User	1.0
Group	4.0
Machine	0.5

Table 3-2.   Account Space Requirements in the SAM Database

Your result will be the approximate size of the SAM database. After a quick calculation, you find that the resulting size of the SAM will be around 40MB, which pushes the recommended limit of the SAM database size. From a performance point of view, you should consider dividing the accounts in this example among other domains to minimize the administrative demands and the system load needed to maintain such a large database, and to allow for future growth.

In addition to the size limitations of the SAM database, the nonpaged pool memory also affects the number of users that a domain can support. *Nonpaged pool memory* is a reserved portion of RAM that cannot be paged to a paging file. This means that it is constantly resident in main memory. Algorithms based on the amount of physical memory determine the maximum amount of nonpaged pool memory in a Windows NT system. Each account in the PDC's SAM resides in nonpaged pool memory. Consequently, the size of the domain also depends on the amount of physical memory of the PDC and other domain controllers. The following formulas can be used to approximate the nonpaged pool memory of a domain controller:

$$NonpagedPoolSize = MinimumNonpagedPoolSize \\ + ([PhysicalMB - 4] \times MinimumAddition \\ NonpagedPoolPerMB)$$

$$MaximumNonpagedPoolSize = DefaultMaximumNonpagedPool \\ + ([PhysicalMB - 4]) \times Maximum \\ AdditionNonpagedPoolPerMB)$$

where

MinimumNonpagedPoolSize = 256K
MinimumAdditionNonpagedPoolPerMB = 32K
DefaultMaximumNonpagedPool = 1024K (1MB)
MaximumAdditionNonpagedPoolPerMB = 400K

For example, a machine with 64MB of RAM will have:

$$NonpagedPoolSize = 256K + ([64 - 4] \times 32K) \\ = 2176K \approx 2.2MB$$

$$MaximumNonpagedPoolSize = 1024K + ([64 - 4] \times 400K)$$
$$= 25,024K \approx 25MB$$

Although you should know these values to calculate the maximum number of users that a domain can support, your master (account) domains should not approach these limits. There is noticeable performance degradation in server response time as well as administrative management processes when a domain supports more than 15,000 users.

THE LOGON PROCESS

The logon process is mandatory in Windows NT environments whether a user is accessing resources on the local machine or in a domain. The user must provide security credentials to gain access to resources. A user logging onto the local machine supplies a user name and password that is then validated by the machine's local SAM database. Logging onto a domain is much like logging onto the local machine except that the domain controller validates the account instead of the local machine.

The user's request to log onto the domain is handled by either a PDC or one of the BDCs in the domain. It is essentially a race between the controllers to determine which processes the request. Typically, the BDC wins the race simply because it usually is not as busy as the PDC and can consequently respond to the request more quickly. The client machine accepts the first response, and the winner (PDC or BDC) begins processing the request. This process may involve loading user profiles, logon scripts, and drive mappings. Once a user is logged onto the domain, the user can access resources (with proper access permissions) within the domain. This entire process is called *authentication* and is performed by the NetLogon Service.

NetLogon Service

One of the primary responsibilities of the NetLogon Service is processing logon requests on either the local machine or domain. There are two types of logons that occur within a Windows NT domain environment to start the authentication process: *interactive logons* and *remote logons*. Interactive logons take place when a user supplies a user name and password in the logon dialog box. Users also specify whether they want to log onto the local machine or domain. A remote logon takes place when a user who is already logged on attempts to connect to resources located on another computer. For example, remote logon occurs when a user attempts to connect to a remote printer or map a network drive.

The NetLogon Service has three responsibilities with regards to user authentication: discovery, secure channel setup, and pass-through authentication.

▼ **Discovery**   This process occurs during machine initialization. As the machine starts up, the NetLogon Service tries to locate a domain controller for the specified domain. More specifically, it looks for a machine that responds to the name *DOMAINNAME<1C>*. Domain controllers go through this process as well, except that they search for domain controllers in all trusted domains.

■ **Secure channel setup**   A secure communications channel is established between an NT machine and the domain controller by a series of challenges that they issue to and from each other. This verifies the validity of machine accounts and ensures a secure channel between the two machines. This channel is then used to pass user identification information.

▲ **Pass-through authentication**   Pass-through authentication takes place when a user requests a service or attempts to connect to a resource where the user cannot be authenticated by a domain controller in the domain in which the user is logged on. The computer that is asked to provide a resource sends the user's request to the destination's domain controller for authentication. The same logon process occurs when a user with proper accesses privileges logs onto a domain controller except that the user can log onto only the domain. Users cannot log onto a domain controller locally, because domain controllers do not store a local SAM database in addition to the domain SAM database.

NOTE: A user must be a member of the Administrators, Server Operators, Print Operators, Account Operators, or Backup Operators group, or have been granted the Log On Locally right, to log onto a domain from a domain controller.

Now that you have an understanding of general domain planning concepts—domain models, trust relationships, and the logon process—you can look at what aspects of domains can be optimized to increase Windows NT Server and network proficiency.

DOMAIN DESIGN AND PERFORMANCE

Domain design is vital to the performance of your Windows NT environment. Implementation of an incorrectly designed domain structure can have profound effects on your systems and network. Performance issues related to domains also affect system administration. For example, an incorrect design can cause additional administrative demands that consume time, money, and resources. Managing a domain's security policies, trust relationships, and accounts can become a constant source of administrative work. When designing or reengineering a domain environment, it is important to pay close attention to the enterprise's organizational structure to ensure that the most suitable domain model is applied to the Windows NT environment.

Choosing a Suitable Domain Model

Choosing the best domain model for your own environment can be difficult. However, the good news is that every model offers some degree of flexibility so you can link domains as your network grows. When choosing a domain model, you need to take into account such factors as the level of control and flexibility the model provides, geographic location of domain controllers, network topology, security needs, and the number of users the system supports.

Even though Microsoft states that a master domain can support up to 40,000 users (with no group or machine accounts) or 26,000 users (with group and machine accounts), actually reaching these maximums is not recommended. A general rule to follow when considering the number of users per domain is that a master domain should support no more than 10,000 users, and an additional BDC should be available for every 1,000 users.

Single domains are best for small to mid-size companies (less than 5,000 employees) even if the human resources department anticipates an explosion in the growth of the workforce, because master or resource domains can be added when the growth actually occurs. Single domains also offer good security and centralized administration. Companies with more than 5,000 employees should consider using the master domain model, because it segments user accounts and resources. However, a company needing to support 10,000 or more users in one geographic location should strongly consider using the multiple master domain model to split the accounts in half, thus increasing performance and facilitating management.

Location

The location or placement of domain controllers is just as important as which domain model you choose. The most important location consideration is the placement of the BDC to perform authentication and minimize network traffic generated by synchronization of the SAM database.

The proximity of the BDC to the location where users log on can affect logon times for users. The BDC holds a copy of the SAM database from the master domain and uses it to authenticate accounts. If the BDC is placed close to the users, it can handle logon requests locally, thus ensuring that requests are handled in a timely manner. For this reason, it is imperative that all BDCs receive regular updates to the SAM database from the PDC. If the BDC handling a logon request does not have recent updates, the domain may not be able to correctly validate the user. The NetLogon Service is responsible for database synchronization.

In addition to faster logon times for users, a BDC placed close to where the users log onto the domain can significantly reduce the amount of network traffic, especially over WANs or other slow links (anything less than 10 MB/sec), as shown in Figure 3-5. These links are also often less reliable than LAN connections. If a link goes down, users can still log onto the domain through the local BDC.

Domain-Related Network Traffic

Depending on the domain model in use, the location of domain controllers, and the network's makeup, the amount of network activity generated by domains can significantly affect network performance. Much of this traffic is generated without client or user interaction. Trust relationships and synchronization are examples of nonclient-related network activity that can generate network traffic. Other factors, such as user requests to log onto the domain, also affect network performance. The following sections discuss domain-related network traffic in a TCP/IP environment.

LOGON VALIDATION You can increase performance by configuring domain controllers to perform more logon validations simultaneously. One of the easiest ways to do this is to choose Maximize Throughput for Network Applications in the Server service. By default, the Server service uses the option Maximize Throughput for File Sharing to configure the domain controllers. With this simple configuration change, you can possibly triple the number of simultaneous logons domain controllers perform.

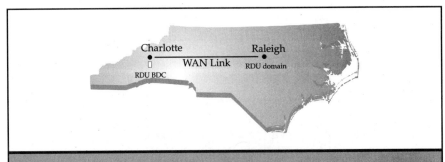

Figure 3-5. A BDC validating users locally so that logon requests do not have to travel across the WAN link

Typically, domain controllers handle six or seven requests per second, but the changed configuration boosts this number to 20 or more per second.

Here are the steps to follow if you wish to change the default setting:

1. In the Control Panel, double-click the Network applet.

2. Select the Services tab.

3. Select the Server service and choose Properties. The following dialog box appears:

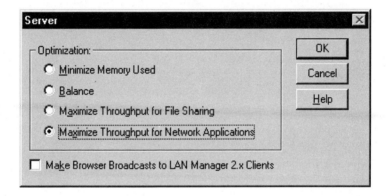

4. Check the radio button beside Maximize Throughput for Network Applications and click OK.

5. Close the Network applet.

6. When the NT prompts you to restart your machine, select Yes.

LOGON REQUEST TRAFFIC   The logon process must be completed before the user can access and use resources on the domain. For simplicity, this process is divided here into three parts: discovery, account validation, and post-validation.

DISCOVERY   During the discovery phase, the client machine uses either the Windows Internet Naming System (WINS) or broadcasts to find a domain controller to handle the logon request. Using WINS to find a domain controller is more efficient because it uses H-node queries rather than B-node broadcasts. *H-node* and *B-node* are two examples of *NetBIOS over TCP/IP* (NBT) modes. The other NBT modes include:

▼ **P-node**   Uses a point-to-point communication with WINS to resolve a machine name

▲ **M-node**   Uses B-node first, then P-node if the first resolution fails

If a WINS server is present on the domain and it is specified in either the Dynamic Host Configuration Protocol or TCP/IP configuration, the client defaults to using H-node for resolution. H-node tries communicating directly with WINS (P-node) to resolve a machine name before it broadcasts throughout the entire domain (B-node). Only when the P-node fails will the client resort to broadcasting. The reason H-node is more efficient than B-node is that H-node generates significantly less traffic. In most cases, the machine name will be resolved using WINS. Each method (H-node and B-node) generates two frames of information, but the broadcast method generates approximately 300 more bytes of information.

ACCOUNT VALIDATION   The next phase of the logon process is the validation of the account information that the user specified. It begins when the client machine accepts the first response it receives from a domain controller. The client then resolves the NetBIOS name of the domain controller, establishes a TCP and NetBIOS session with the domain controller, and after SMB negotiation, connects to \\domaincontroller\IPC$. When this process is complete, the client machine uses two API calls to finish logon validation and synchronize timing for time stamping. The overall process generates 15 frames and approximately 2KB of network traffic.

POST-VALIDATION   After the account is validated, the user account continues logging onto the domain and executes any logon scripts or user profiles. The amount of traffic that this process generates depends entirely on what is being processed. Once the logon scripts and user profiles finish executing, all connections (TCP, NetBIOS, and SMB) are dropped. Disconnecting these sessions generates five frames and about 400 bytes of traffic.

LOGON TIME   The amount of time required for a user to log on is of major importance. In fact, authentication is one of the primary responsibilities of domain controllers. Part of this process may involve logon scripts. Logon scripts are batch files that run automatically when a user logs onto a domain. They can be used to provide services to configure a user's environment. For example, logon scripts can be used to synchronize the time between the client machine and server, connect network drives, and run network applications at startup. Usually, logon scripts take only a few seconds to complete, but sometimes they may take longer. This can be the result of the script itself or because of network performance issues.

With the help of the Event Logging Utility (LOGEVENT.EXE) in the Windows NT Resource Kit, you can calculate the amount of time required to process the logon script. This utility writes events to the Windows NT event log on local or remote machines. Its primary purpose is to provide and store historical information from application or batch file execution. For example, you can call LOGEVENT from within batch files, from an AT command, or from a logon script. Since it can be executed from the command prompt or a batch file, it is a great utility for calculating the time it takes for logon scripts or logon script components to finish executing. Moreover, you can associate comments and category numbers to identify unique events each time you call LOGEVENT.

You need to specify parameters to log an event in the Event Viewer. Simply type **LOGEVENT** to see the syntax for the utility. The following is the syntax for LOGEVENT and the parameters that can be used to specify what is logged in the Event Viewer:

```
logevent [–m \\MACHINENAME] [–s SIWEF]
         [–c CategoryNumber] "Message"
```

where S (Success), I (Information), W (Warning), E (Error), or F (Failure) denotes the severity of the event. For example, LOGEVENT–S F –C 911 "Connection Failed" records a failed event on the local machine, stating that a connection failed.

NOTE: When an event is logged using LOGEVENT, it is stored in the Event Viewer's application log.

The next example illustrates how LOGEVENT can be used in a logon script. The information can later be used to calculate processing time. The logon script in this example is called LOGON.BAT, and it contains various LOGEVENT entries that signify that certain events have occurred.

```
LOGON.BAT
-----------------------------------------------------------------
@ECHO OFF
REM The LOGEVENT entry directly below signals the start of
the REM logon script and logs the event into a remote server's
REM application log.
LOGEVENT -M \\PERFSERV -S I -C 100 "LOGON SCRIPT STARTED"
ECHO.
ECHO.
ECHO COMPANY NAME, Inc.
ECHO.
ECHO.

REM **** RUN SMS UTILITY ****
REM LOGEVENT can be used to time an application within a batch
REM file as well. Shown here is LOGEVENT logging the time it
takes for the SMS utility to execute.
LOGEVENT -M \\PERSERV -S I -C 300 "START SMS PROCEDURE"
NET USE Y: /DEL /Y
NET USE Y: \\SMS-SERVER\SMS_SHR
CALL Y:\RUNSMS.BAT
NET USE Y: /DEL /Y
LOGEVENT -M \\PERSERV -S I -C 301 "STOP SMS PROCEDURE"

REM **** MAP NETWORK DRIVES    ****
NET USE H: \\SERVERNAME\HOME /Y
NET USE P:  \\SERVERNAME\APPS /Y
NET USE Q: \\SERVERNAME\NET /Y
```

```
NET USE S: \\SERVERNAME\SHARED /Y
:END

REM LOGEVENT signals the end of the logon script.
LOGEVENT -M \\PERSERV -S S -C 100 "LOGON SCRIPT FINISHED"
EXIT
```

This batch file provides several examples of how to use the Event Logging Utility in a logon script. For instance, the script here is segmented, and the events, except the logon script's start and stop points, have unique category numbers to help distinguish them. The logon script uses the same category number for its start and end points to identify the execution of the entire logon script.

How can these events be used to calculate logon times? Each time LOGEVENT records an event in the Event Viewer, the Event Viewer automatically time stamps it. Figure 3-6 shows how the LOGEVENT entries appear in the Event Viewer's application log. You then calculate the difference in time between two events to determine the total time needed to execute that segment in the logon script. For example, to find out the total processing time for the entire logon script, find the start and end of the logon script using the category number (100). Then subtract the start time from the end time to get the total time. You can apply the same procedure to calculate the execution time of any area that you sectioned off with LOGEVENT.

NOTE: You should check the event message as well as the category number to be sure there is no confusion as to the start and end points for a logon script execution sequence. This is particularly useful when there are many logon script execution sequences.

Trust Traffic

As mentioned previously, trust relationships link domains and allow users to access resources in other domains. In this sense, trusts contribute to a domain's scalability and flexibility. There is also a

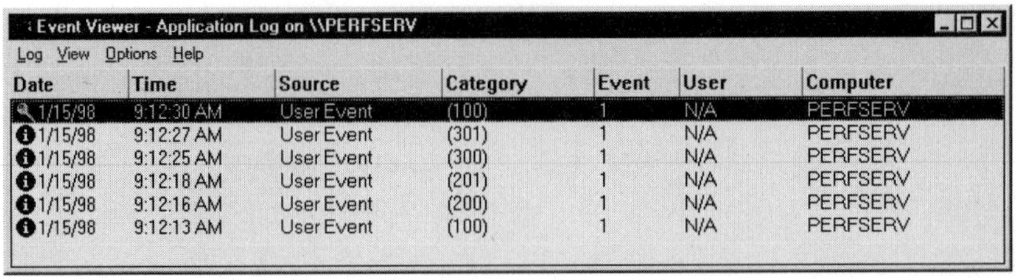

Figure 3-6. LOGEVENT entries in the Event Viewer

downside to trust relationships, however. The number of trusts can quickly increase as you add more domains to your Windows NT environment. For example, a complete trust domain model with five domains requires 20 trust relationships. Adding only three more domains would boost the requirement to 56 trust relationships! This is why it is extremely important to choose a suitable domain model for your environment to keep the number of domains to a minimum. Trust relationships can become a burden to administer and can also negatively affect network performance.

Traffic generated from trust relationships can be separated into three categories: traffic from establishing a trust, from importing trusted user or group accounts, or from pass-through authentication. Table 3-3 summarizes the approximate amount of traffic generated by each category.

Category	Number of Frames	Data Size (in Kilobytes)
Establishing a trust	100	15
Importing trusted accounts	110	24
Pass-through authentication	20	4

Table 3-3. Network Traffic Generated by Trust Relationships

Once a trust is established, little traffic is generated to maintain the trust; however, traffic is generated by pass-through authentication every time a user attempts to connect to a resource in another domain. Moreover, traffic is generated every time a trusted user or group account is imported into another domain. The amount of traffic may seem small for the three categories alone, but if you multiply this amount by the hundreds or thousands of imported accounts and users that may use pass-through authentication, the amount quickly adds up.

Domain Controller Hardware Requirements

Domain controllers are responsible for maintaining the overall health of the domain by, for example, maintaining the SAM database, authenticating users, replicating the directory, and synchronizing the database. For this reason, it is important to design a domain controller to perform adequately under the anticipated workloads of the domain. Microsoft recommends using the size of the SAM as a guideline for selecting the hardware. You can get the actual size of the SAM database by locating it in the %SystemRoot%\System32\ Config directory. For example, if the anticipated size of the SAM database is 5MB or less, then the minimum recommended CPU is a 486DX/33 with 32MB of RAM. Also, the amount of RAM for a domain controller should be approximately 2.5 times the size of the SAM database. There are other important aspects that you should consider, too, such as disk space and the transfer rate of the NIC. More often than not, the network subsystem and memory pose the greatest risk of bottlenecks to domain controllers. Windows NT 4.0 requires a great deal of memory, and can easily devour 32MB by itself.

Your hardware configuration will depend on your budget constraints, the number of users you need to support, the network configuration, any other functionality the domain controller will provide, and the size of the SAM database. However, the absolute minimum hardware configuration that I recommend for a domain controller performing only domain-related functions is as follows:

Pentium 133 MHz
2 = 1GB HD (with mirroring)

48MB RAM
High-performance NIC (100 Mbps)

The most important components for machines performing only domain controller functions are memory and the network subsystem. Therefore, the more memory and network bandwidth that can be provided, the better performance will be. Domain controllers with 64MB RAM and 100-Mbps connection do wonders for authentication throughput.

Synchronization

Synchronization is the process in which the NetLogon Service on all BDCs synchronizes the SAM database with the master copy on the PDC. This synchronization is performed automatically at specified intervals. The default configuration settings for this process can sometimes negatively affect the network by generating a lot of traffic. The amount of traffic generated by the synchronization process is a major concern over slow links. However, you can modify parameters within the Registry to control the network traffic generated by the synchronization process. The NetLogon Registry parameters are located in

HKEY_LOCAL_MACHINE\
   SYSTEM\
      CurrentControlSet\
         Services\
            Netlogon\
               Parameters

ReplicationGovernor

The ReplicationGovernor NetLogon parameter controls the percentage of network bandwidth that the service can use for synchronization purposes. The default value (100 percent) allows NetLogon service to use the entire bandwidth if necessary. Having the potential to use 100 percent of the network bandwidth may or may not affect synchronization in LAN environments, but it does significantly affect performance on WANs or other slow links.

To improve performance, you should change the percentage of network bandwidth to a value between 25 and 50 percent in both LAN and WAN environments. This ensures that synchronization still occurs in a timely manner but without controlling the entire bandwidth. If you set the ReplicationGovernor value below 25 percent, you run the risk of never completing the synchronization process. In order to change the percentage of network bandwidth used by the ReplicationGovernor, you must add an entry within the Registry. To add this entry, do the following:

1. Start the Registry editor by typing REGEDT32 at either the command prompt or from the Start | Run option.

NOTE: It is recommended to use only the REGEDT32 registry editor to make these changes.

2. Go to this key:

   HKEY_LOCAL_MACHINE\
      SYSTEM\
         CurrentControlSet\
            Services\
               Netlogon\
                  Parameters

3. Select Add Value from the Edit menu to display the Add Value dialog box.

4. In the Value Name box, type in ReplicationGovernor and then select REG_DWORD for the Data Type, as shown here:

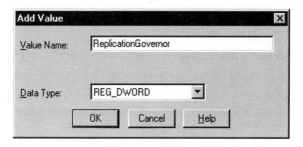

5. Click OK. This will cause the DWORD Editor dialog box to pop up.

6. In the Radix grouping, select Decimal and then type in the maximum percentage of network bandwidth that you want the ReplicationGovernor to take. Here you see a case where the maximum network bandwidth allowed is 50 percent:

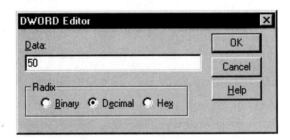

7. Click OK to add the new value.

Pulse

Pulse is another NetLogon configuration parameter that can be used to optimize the synchronization process. Pulse controls the rate at which the PDC checks for SAM changes and sends a message to all BDCs announcing that it is time to update. By default, the PDC checks every five minutes. However, this parameter can be set to check as seldom as every two days.

When changing the Pulse value, you need to balance the amount of network traffic that could potentially be generated and the frequency with which the SAM database needs to be updated. Do not set this value too high because a user logging onto the domain may not be correctly validated if the BDC has not been updated for a long time. It is recommend that you change the Pulse parameter to a value between 15 and 30 minutes, which decreases the amount of generated traffic but also keeps the SAM database synchronization updated.

As was the case with the ReplicationGovernor, in order to change the default setting for the Pulse rate, you must manually add the value in the Registry. To change the default setting for Pulse rate, do the following:

1. Start the Registry editor by typing REGEDT32 at either the command prompt or from the Start | Run option.

2. Go to the Registry key specified above in step 2 within the ReplicationGovernor section.

3. Select Add Value from the Edit menu to display the Add Value dialog box.

4. In the Value Name box, type in Pulse and then select REG_DWORD for the Data Type, as shown here:

5. Click OK. This will cause the DWORD Editor dialog box to pop up.

6. In the Radix grouping, select Decimal and then type in the number of seconds between a synchronization. For example, if you want a synchronization to take place every 15 minutes you would specify 900 seconds ($15 \times 60 = 900$):

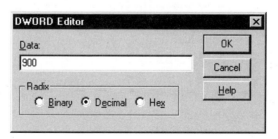

7. Click OK to add the new value.

The alternative to automatic synchronization is manual, or on-demand, synchronization. This type of synchronization is accomplished through the Server Manager. To manually synchronize the domain, do the following:

1. Choose Start | Programs | Administrative Tools (Common) and then run Server Manager.
2. In the main display window, select the PDC.
3. From the Computer menu, select Synchronize Entire Domain. A dialog box will pop up and ask you if you are sure that you want to resynchronize the domain.
4. Choose Yes.

It is recommended that you perform synchronization automatically. Use manual synchronization only under extreme conditions, when you need to ensure that unnecessary network traffic is not generated by this process.

CONCLUSION

Domain planning is essential to optimizing your Windows NT environment. It provides a flexible and scalable foundation that can be tailored to fit a company's needs. This chapter described the domain structures that can be used as models for your own environment and how your decisions regarding the domain structure can affect performance. This chapter also recommended optimal configurations to make your domain infrastructure as efficient as possible.

CHAPTER 4

Boosting Memory Performance

R unning out of memory is one of the most common problems with Windows NT Server systems. Basically, when a system runs out of memory, the combined memory requirements of all processes exceed the amount of physical memory on the system. NT must then resort to its virtual memory to keep the system and processes running. Running out of memory creates serious problems in response times and in the running of mission-critical applications. It is especially disastrous if the system is also low on disk space. NT's virtual memory mechanism is a vital component to the operating system, but it is not nearly as fast as physical memory. A depletion of physical memory resources should be avoided at all costs, because it will cause extreme performance degradation.

NT is a hungry beast; once you give it more memory, it can—and more than likely will—immediately devour it. A viable solution to the problem of insufficient memory is simply to add more memory. In fact, doing nothing else but adding more memory will usually take care of most of your memory performance problems. Unfortunately, adding more memory is not always possible because of budget constraints or the physical limitations of the hardware. However, there are ways to optimize memory with the server's existing configuration. In fact, as mentioned earlier, covering up a problem by just adding resources may lead to greater problems down the road.

There are many ways to gauge and maintain NT Server memory performance. The key is to know what to look at and when. This chapter provides real steps for successfully boosting memory performance. You will first develop your understanding of the hardware and software aspects of memory, such as the types of memory and how NT manages its memory resources, so you can effectively use the available resources to fine-tune the server's memory configuration. This will also benefit you in your purchasing decisions by helping you understand which types of memory provide the best level of performance. You will then learn what should and can be tuned.

MEMORY FUNDAMENTALS

Many of the operating systems and applications available today are resource intensive, especially when it comes to memory requirements. They require large amounts of memory to run effectively and efficiently. Windows NT is no exception. It requires a lot of memory, but it is designed to accommodate its own memory requirements as well as those of even the most resource-intensive applications.

NT uses two different memory schemes, physical and virtual, to satisfy potentially large memory requirements. Physical memory is the amount of RAM that is installed on the system. On the other hand, virtual memory is a logical extension of physical memory that frees up physical memory on the system and allows more processes to execute. In other words, if Windows NT did not use virtual memory, the system could only afford to execute processes within the capacity of the amount of physical memory available. Since virtual memory is logical and not physical, it can either be related to unused address space or, more importantly, to the space on the hard disk that it treats as physical memory. When Windows NT resorts to the hard disk for virtual memory, the process is called *paging*. Paging is described in more detail later in this chapter. Virtual memory is completely different from physical memory, but applications are not aware of this. Applications view physical and virtual memory as a single entity, and do not even know that NT uses two memory schemes. NT fools applications into thinking that there is more memory on the system than there actually is. Only the operating system knows how much physical memory is actually on the system; applications cannot differentiate between physical and virtual memory.

Applications use a linear 32-bit offset to specify the memory addresses they want to reference. NT's use of a 32-bit logical binary addressing scheme lets applications think they can reference up to

4GB of virtual memory (2^{32} = 4,294,967,296 = 4GB). The amount of memory on the system may be as little as 16MB, but each application will still think that it has 4GB available for its own use. Applications think they have so much memory available because they view memory as linear; an application just specifies a memory location and does not care or need to know if the code or data is actually in virtual or physical memory.

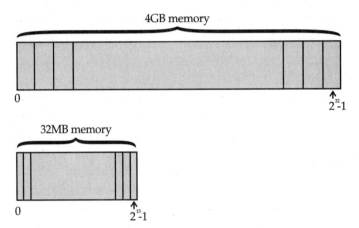

When an application requests code or data from a memory address, the address is a virtual address, not a physical one. It is then NT's responsibility to translate the virtual address into a physical memory address to retrieve the requested code or data. Would it not be simpler to just let the application keep up with its own memory use and locations? Surprisingly, the overhead from making virtual references to information stored in memory is minimal. More important, the virtual addressing scheme gives the operating system control over memory management operations and extends the perceivable amount of available memory. The component responsible for loading data into main memory and assigning it a virtual address is the Virtual Memory (VM) Manager, located within the NT Executive, as shown in Figure 4-1. The VM Manager is also responsible for behind-the-scenes translation from virtual to physical addresses. The VM Manager provides a level of control over memory resources and shields the applications from having to know where code or data actually resides. For more information on the VM Manager, refer to Chapter 1.

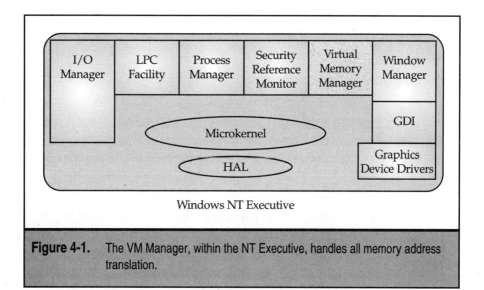

Figure 4-1. The VM Manager, within the NT Executive, handles all memory address translation.

The Paging Process

As mentioned earlier, applications do not have to worry about memory management. For all they know, every time they refer to a particular memory address, it resides in main memory—but this is not always the case. If the information is not contained in main memory, where is it? Code or data that has not been used for a while is swapped out to the hard disk to free main memory. This allows more efficient use of main memory.

Paging, the process of moving information from main memory to a hard disk for temporary storage, is illustrated in Figure 4-2. The information is moved to a paging repository called pagefile.sys. If the information is referenced later, it can be returned to main memory. The next time the applications need code or data, the VM Manager translates the address and checks to see if it is in main or virtual (pagefile.sys) memory. Information located in virtual memory must then be swapped back into main memory so the processor can use it. Only the information in main memory is of any use to the processor. The VM Manager automatically locates or, in some cases, creates a block of main memory that this information can be loaded into. It

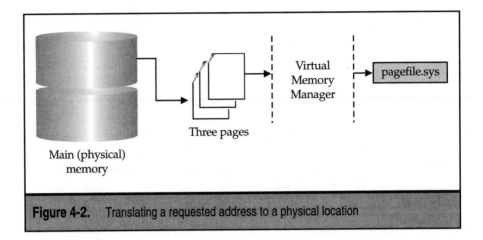

Figure 4-2.   Translating a requested address to a physical location

then updates the addressing tables and informs the processor of the physical address where the code or data reside.

Memory Sharing

Often applications need to communicate with each other and share information. To provide this capability, NT must allow access to certain memory space without jeopardizing its security and integrity or that of other applications. Therefore, the VM Manager divides the 4GB virtual memory equally and assigns privilege levels to control access. The upper 2GB of address space is dedicated to kernel mode (privileged) operations to protect the operating system and ensure stability. The lower 2GB of address space allows both privileged and unprivileged code, such as user applications, to access it.

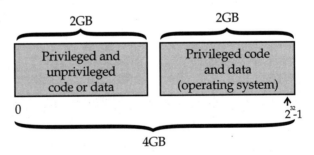

The VM Manager keeps track of each process' memory space with separate translation tables. However, it can dynamically adjust the translation tables so that certain addresses translate to the same pages of main memory for more than one process. This controls the level of access that processes have to another process' memory space. This does not mean, however, that a process can access any memory address defined within the upper 2GB of virtual memory.

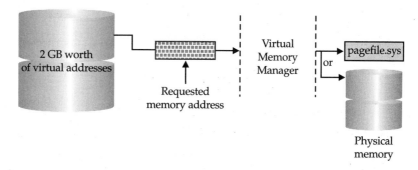

From a performance standpoint, the ability to share memory greatly reduces the amount of memory used by an application. When more than one copy of an application is running, each instance can use the same code and data. This means that it is not necessary to maintain separate copies of the application's code loaded and using memory resources. No matter how many instances of the application are running, the amount of memory needed to adequately support the application's code remains relatively the same. There may be a slight increase in memory requirements, but this is due mainly to new data having to be maintained by the application. For example, if an instance of an application requires 4MB of memory, the next instance will not require that the system provide an additional 4MB to support it. A quick way to verify this is to check the Task Manager's Process tab. To see the memory requirements of an application with more than one instance, do the following:

1. Start the application you wish to monitor (for example, Netscape).

2. Start the Task Manager by right-clicking on the Taskbar.

3. In the Windows NT Task Manager dialog box, select the Process tab.

4. Scroll down the list of processes running on the system and find the application you wish to monitor.

5. Note the amount of memory the application is using with one instance. This is located under the Mem Usage column.

6. Next, start another instance of the application and watch its memory requirements. You will notice that the second instance uses much less memory than the first.

Paging Is Inevitable

At first thought, you might think that buying a ton of additional memory would prevent NT from using its paging scheme, thus increasing performance. Paging is the process of temporarily transferring some of the contents of a system's physical memory to the hard disk until the system needs the contents of that memory again. However, this is not the case; NT is designed to use paging no matter how much physical memory is available. Simply put, paging is inevitable. Even if you have 100MB of available memory, NT will still use its paging scheme. The more memory you have, however, the less the system will have to rely on paging—although added memory will not altogether eliminate the need to page. The good news, however, is that there are more ways to increase paging performance than just adding more memory.

NOTE: Since memory is ridiculously inexpensive these days, adding memory to the system configuration is *always* a good idea because it will increase performance.

Windows NT is extremely stingy with its memory resources. When you give it more memory, it keeps as much as possible for itself. In fact, NT tries to minimize the amount of available memory on reserve. Most of the additional memory is used for caching. This is one of the reasons why paging exists on Windows NT systems. There is no way to remove the Windows NT paging scheme (for example, you can't delete it through the Registry), but there are ways you can minimize paging. Techniques for boosting paging performance will be discussed shortly.

NONPAGED POOLED VERSUS PAGED POOLED MEMORY

NT determines which system memory components can and cannot be paged out to disk. Obviously, some code, such as the kernel, should not be swapped out of main memory. Therefore, NT further differentiates memory used by the system as either nonpaged pooled or paged pooled. These sections of main memory play active roles in determining how the VM Manager handles the paging process.

Nonpaged pooled memory contains occupied code or data that must stay resident in memory. This structure is similar to that used by old MS-DOS programs, where relatively small terminate and stay resident (TSR) programs were loaded into memory at startup. These programs stayed in a certain portion of memory until the system either restarted or shut down. For example, an anti-virus program would be loaded as a TSR program to protect against possible virus attacks.

Paged pooled memory is the portion of memory that holds pageable code or data that may be needed sooner rather than later. Any system process that is in paged pooled memory can be paged out to disk, but it is held temporarily in this section of main memory in case the system needs it immediately. Windows NT pages other processes before paging system processes out to disk.

Nonpaged Pooled Memory

Processes contained within nonpaged pooled memory stay in main memory and cannot be paged out to disk. This portion of physical memory is used for kernel mode operations, the SAM database, NIC drivers, and other processes that must stay in main memory to operate efficiently. Without this section of main memory, kernel components would be pageable, and the system itself would become unstable.

The amount of main memory allocated to the nonpaged memory pool depends on the amount of physical memory the server has and the demands that processes place on the system for memory pool space. However, Windows NT does limit nonpaged pooled memory to 32MB. Complex algorithms dynamically determine the maximum amount of nonpaged pool memory on a Windows NT system at startup, based on the amount of physical memory in the system. This self-tuning mechanism within NT automatically adjusts the size according to the current memory configuration. For example, if you increase or decrease the amount of RAM in the system, NT automatically adjusts the size of nonpaged pooled memory to reflect that change.

CAUTION: If the NonPagedPoolSize key entry in the Registry, located in HKEY_LOCAL_MACHINE
  \System
    \CurrentControlSet
      \Control
        \Session Manager
          \Memory Management,
is set to anything other than zero, NT may not correctly allocate the amount of nonpaged pooled memory needed by the system.

You can approximate the size of the nonpaged pooled memory by using the following formulas:

NonPagedPoolSize = MinimumNonPagedPoolSize + ([Physical MB – 4]
$$\times \text{MinAdditionNonPagedPoolPerMB})$$

MaximumNonPagedPoolSize = DefaultMaximumNonPagedPoolSize
+ ([Physical MB – 4]
$$\times \text{MaxAdditionNonPagedPoolPerMB})$$

where

MinimumNonPagedPoolSize = 256K
MinAdditionNonPagedPoolPerMB = 32K
DefaultMaximumNonPagedPoolSize = 1,024K (1MB)
MaxAdditionNonPagedPoolPerMB = 400K

For example, if a system has 64MB of RAM, it will have approximately NonPagedPoolSize = 256K + ((64-4) × 32K) = 2,176 K (or roughly 2.2MB) allocated to the nonpaged memory pool. NonPagedPoolSize can reach a maximum size of 32MB.

There are also easier ways to approximate the size of nonpaged pooled memory. For starters, there are counters that can be monitored using the Performance Monitor (for information on using the Performance Monitor, see Chapter 8). You can monitor the following:

▼ Memory: Pool Nonpaged Bytes

■ Memory: Pool Nonpaged Allocations

▲ Process: Pool Nonpaged Bytes

The Memory object counters are nonpaged pooled memory approximations for the entire system; the Process counter reflects the size allocated to each process.

The easiest way to approximate the size of nonpaged pooled memory, however, is to use the Task Manager. The estimated size of the nonpaged pooled memory is shown in the Kernel Memory section of the Task Manager's Performance tab. You can also use the Task Manager to view how much nonpaged pooled and paged pooled memory an individual process is using. Simply follow these steps:

1. Start the Task Manager by right-clicking on the Taskbar or pressing CTRL-ALT-DEL and selecting Task Manager.

2. Select the Processes tab, and then from the View menu, choose Select Columns to display the available viewing options for the Processes tab.

3. In the Select Columns dialog box, check the boxes beside the Paged Pool and Non-paged Pool options and click OK.

When you return to the Windows NT Task Manager Processes window, you will see how much space in the paged pooled and nonpaged pooled memory that is occupied by individual processes.

From a performance standpoint, the larger the size of nonpaged pooled memory, the more data can be fit into this space. Since this is physical memory space, information can be written and read much faster than it can on a hard disk. The recommendation for nonpaged pooled memory is simple: give the system enough physical memory so that the nonpaged pooled memory is at least 2MB in size. The more physical memory you have, the larger the nonpaged pooled memory can be. So, in order to increase the amount of nonpaged pooled memory, you must increase the amount of physical memory on the system. However, remember that NonPagedPool memory is limited to 32MB, so adding memory beyond this point has no effect on the nonpaged pooled memory.

Page Pooled Memory

Any code or data in privileged mode processes that does not always need to be in main memory is considered pageable, and can reside in paged pooled memory. This pool typically contains pages of memory that are frequently referenced by the system for processing by the CPU. If the frequency with which pages are referenced decreases or the paged pool approaches capacity, pages can be swapped out to the paging file (pagefile.sys) on the hard disk.

Like nonpaged pooled memory, the paged pooled memory configuration parameters are located in the Registry in

HKEY_LOCAL_MACHINE
　\System
　　\CurrentControlSet
　　\Control
　　　\Session Manager
　　　　\Memory Management

When the PagedPoolSize parameter is set to zero, the system calculates the amount of physical memory allocated to this pool. This approximation is based on the system's memory configuration. Generally, the size ranges from a few megabytes to a maximum of 192MB of RAM. Obviously, your system is going to need a large amount of RAM before the paged pooled memory size reaches its maximum capacity of 192MB.

You can also determine the size of the paged pooled memory by hand. The following formulas require you to know the value of the variable MaximumNonPagedPoolSize. Thus, before you begin calculating the size of paged pooled memory, use the formulas presented earlier to calculate the maximum size of nonpaged pooled memory. Then use the following formulas to find out how much physical memory can be used for paged pooled memory.

$$\text{Temp\_Size} = (2 \times \text{MaximumNonPagedPoolSize [in MB]}) \div \text{PAGE\_SIZE}$$

$$\textbf{Size} = (\text{Temp\_Size} + [\text{PTE\_PER\_PAGE} - 1]) \div \text{PTE\_PER\_PAGE}$$

$$\textbf{PagedPoolSize} = \text{Size} \times \text{PAGE\_SIZE} \times \text{PTE\_PER\_PAGE}$$

where

PTE_PER_PAGE = 1,024 bytes
PAGE_SIZE = 4,096 bytes

NOTE: if your calculations result in a number greater than 192MB for the size of paged pooled memory, the system will allocate only 192MB.

If this area of physical memory begins to reach capacity or becomes completely full, the system tries to compensate for the lack of paged pooled address space by swapping out those pages of memory that have been least requested to the paging file on the hard disk. As a result, it is very important that the system's memory configuration be sufficient for the tasks that it performs. The more the system has to rely on paging to and from the hard disk, the greater the likelihood that performance will degrade.

TYPES OF MEMORY

Deciding what kind of memory to purchase for a server is as important, if not more important, than tweaking what you already have to increase performance. There are many different flavors and configurations of memory to choose from, which can be confusing. The following list shows you some of the choices you will need to make when purchasing memory for Windows NT Server:

▼ Parity or nonparity

■ Fast page mode (commonly referred to as dynamic random-access memory, or DRAM) or EDO SIMMs (enhanced data out single inline memory modules)

■ SIMMs or DIMMs (dual inline memory modules)

■ 30-pin or 72-pin SIMMs

■ RAM speed (typically 50, 60, or 70 nanoseconds)

■ Cache memory size

▲ Cache memory type

You should be concerned with all of these choices regardless of whether you are purchasing a new system or upgrading an existing configuration. The decisions you make may also depend on your system. For instance, some motherboards and BIOS types support only certain RAM access times, or the motherboard may have slots that match only the 72-pin SIMMs. Whatever you decide should be the result of well-thought-out planning, because the various memory options can significantly affect the system and system performance. Adding more memory of the wrong type or speed, for example, can severely degrade the system instead of boosting performance.

You can use the following sections as guidelines for your memory purchasing decisions. Each section highlights individual issues that you must be aware of and provides recommendations regarding the best possible configuration for your Windows NT system.

Parity versus Nonparity

As a machine boots up, the system's BIOS performs a rudimentary memory test. Contrary to what you may believe, the test does not detect whether there are any impending memory failures. The BIOS test will probably reveal SIMMs or DIMMs that are no longer useful (damaged by static or other means), but in general, memory failures are detected only when the affected areas are accessed. Some memory failures are of little concern, but you may not know which are important until some of your data is corrupted.

What can be done to protect against performance problems due to damaged or corrupted memory? Some memory chips have error checking built directly into their design. *Parity memory* is capable of parity checking, which determines whether the memory has any errors or failures by adding an extra bit to every byte (8 bits). *Nonparity memory*, on the other hand, does not use an extra bit, and consequently does not detect memory errors. This means that parity memory can detect a problem area before data is written to it, whereas nonparity memory would let the data be written.

CAUTION: You can mix parity and nonparity memory, but it is better to use just one or the other.

If you are deciding between parity and nonparity memory, remember that it is always safer to go with parity checking. That way, you will always know when there is a physical problem with memory. Otherwise, you may never know that a problem exists until it is too late. Moreover, the extra checking routines performed with parity SIMMs do not impact memory performance.

Many vendors, including Intel, are now applying a type of parity checking called *error-correcting codes* (ECC) within the machine hardware. ECC helps intercept and correct parity errors before they cause an application, or the entire system, to halt. More specifically, it corrects all single-bit errors and detects all double-bit errors. It employs the same number of bits as traditional parity memory, but all bits serving as parity checks are grouped together instead of spread across the 64-bit span. This requires a more organized approach to the physical structure of memory, which enables expanded error-checking capabilities.

DRAM, EDO, BEDO RAM, and SDRAM SIMMs

DRAM, EDO, BEDO RAM, and SDRAM are common types of SIMMs that make up the system's main memory. They are not the fastest types of memory available, but because of their price and performance, they are the most suitable for configuring a system with large amounts of memory.

DRAM

DRAM SIMMs have been the most widely used type of main memory storage because of their relatively low cost. They can be purchased with or without parity. From a performance standpoint, however, DRAM SIMMs have a drawback: the access time is the slowest of the SIMM types. Windows NT Server performance will suffer if this type of SIMM is used; therefore, it is not the recommended choice, especially considering the cheap price of faster memory. DRAM is not the recommended SIMM type to use on Windows NT Server systems, because it simply cannot read or write fast enough to transfer information as fast as the processor wants it. When this occurs, the processor patiently waits until it receives the code or data that it needs. This idle time is called the *wait state*. The more time the processor spends in the wait state, the slower the computations will be.

DRAM should be your absolute last choice, but if for some reason (such as cost) you decide to use DRAM, make sure you have an ample amount of Level 2 (L2) cache space (this will be discussed shortly). Systems using DRAM and a large amount of L2 cache space can achieve performance somewhat comparable to that of systems using EDO or SDRAM with smaller caches.

EDO

EDO memory is an improvement over the traditional DRAM chip set because it offers better read-ahead algorithms, thus increasing the amount of information that can be transferred to and computed by the processor. This SIMM type is becoming more prevalent in server systems as its price matches DRAM prices. EDO memory may be as much as 15 percent faster than conventional DRAM. It comes in three speeds: 70, 60, and 50 ns. However, if the system is a Pentium 100 or higher, you should completely avoid 70-ns SIMMs, because this speed does not adequately support the processor or bus transfer rates. These components will actually be slowed down by 70-ns SIMMs.

In general, it is more advantageous to use EDO memory instead of DRAM. Most 486-class and higher motherboards support EDO memory. Also, EDO memory is highly recommended if the system lacks L2 cache.

NOTE: Parity is not an available option with EDO memory.

BEDO RAM

Burst extended data output RAM, or BEDO RAM, is a step higher in performance than EDO memory. As the name implies, BEDO RAM reads data in bursts. This means that once one memory address is requested, three additional addresses are provided. Each additional address is read in one CPU clock cycle, compared to approximately five clock cycles for the first address (5-1-1-1).

Why read additional addresses when only one is requested? If the next instruction is located in one of the three sequential addresses read, the CPU will not have to wait for another five clock cycles to receive the data in the requested address space. This method of anticipating the next instruction is very similar to caching, discussed later in this chapter.

The only potential problem with BEDO RAM is its inability to adequately support bus speeds of 66 MHz or greater. This may not be a problem with your current hardware, but it will pose a problem when bus speeds exceed 66 MHz.

SDRAM

Synchronous DRAM, or SDRAM, is the next generation of SIMM. This memory type offers faster access times than DRAM and EDO memory, but it is not as widely accepted. There are several reasons why SDRAM is faster than its counterparts. SDRAM is based on DRAM, but it incorporates three features that reduce the time needed to coordinate the operations between memory and the processor: synchronous operation, cell banks, and burst mode.

▼ **Synchronous operation**   This feature reduces the amount of time the processor spends in the wait state by using clock input that tightly integrates timing between the processor and itself.

■ **Cell banks**   SDRAM uses two separate cell banks to allow the flow of data between the processor and memory to remain continuous. When one cell fills up or is busy, the other cell continues operation.

▲ **Burst mode**   At times the processor may request code or data from only a single address space. Instead of supplying just one address space, SDRAM apportions an array of consecutive address spaces in the expectation that the next instruction will be located within the block already sent out. The principle behind burst mode is similar to that behind the caching mechanisms.

SDRAM has approximately the same access time as BEDO RAM, but the differentiating factor is that it can be used with bus speeds of up to 100 MHz. Most architectures do not incorporate such high bus speeds yet, but with bus speeds becoming faster every day, it won't be long before such speeds are commonplace. Because of its ability to adapt to the rapidly changing bus and processor architectures, SDRAM is the preferred type of SIMM for your Windows NT Server.

SIMMs versus DIMMs

SIMMs and DIMMs determine how memory is packaged rather than what type of RAM it is. The most notable difference between SIMMs and DIMMs is that the metal connectors on either side of a SIMM are grouped together, whereas the metal connectors on a DIMM are independent of one another. Independent connectors mean more possible signals, which increases the number of address lines and widens the bus interface. In other words, with DIMMs, more data can travel simultaneously between main memory and the processor, which significantly boosts memory performance.

Not every motherboard supports DIMMs, due to architectural differences between DIMMs and SIMMs. Instead of using 72-pin connectors, DIMMs use 168 pins to connect to the rest of the system. As a result, only one DIMM is required in Pentium architectures, whereas two SIMMs are required for Pentium or higher class machines. Since you can install DIMMs one at a time, you can easily mix different sizes of DIMMs together without any repercussions. At the current time, DIMMs use only SDRAM memory. DIMMs are gradually becoming the preferred type of main memory, but they are less common than DRAM or EDO SIMMs, not only because of architectural constraints, but also because DIMMs are more expensive than SIMMs.

Mixing Memory

Is it possible to mix different types and speeds of memory? Mixing different types or speeds of memory is analogous to buying hardware that is not on the HCL for a Windows NT Server: It may not necessarily cause a problem, but it is not the recommended route to take. Moreover, mixing different types and speeds is not the best way to optimize system performance.

Memory speed is a key component in your decision-making process. First you must find out what speeds the motherboard and BIOS can support. Installing 60-ns memory on a system that can support only 70-ns access times will not increase performance; in fact, the system will access the memory only at the slower rate, providing no performance gain or other benefits from using faster memory. Mixing different memory speeds may present another obstacle, too. Unless the mixed speeds meet the requirements of the processor and motherboard, you will have to manually set the memory speed in the BIOS to reflect the slower speed. Also, mixed memory speeds may confuse the CPU if speeds are mixed within the same memory bank. For instance, a memory bank consisting of two memory modules of different speeds will assume the speed of the slower module. For this reason, it is best to keep speed consistency throughout the system.

Mixing memory types is another story altogether. Mixed types should be avoided wherever possible, especially on Windows NT Server systems, because the results are highly variable from system to system. The only memory types you should even consider mixing memory are parity and nonparity memory. Even though mixing parity types is not recommended, it can be done if you turn off parity detection.

NOTE: Even mixing memory from different manufactures may be problematic. Therefore, stick to using one type of memory from a single manufacturer.

Caching

If you compare main memory speeds to processor speeds, you'll notice that the processor is overwhelmingly faster. In addition, hardware architectures that support parallel processing and enhanced hard-coded read-ahead algorithms only widen the gap in speed. The rate at which data travels from memory to the processor is critical to system performance. Unfortunately, RAM speeds are many times slower than processor speeds, so a mechanism must be in place to enable the processor to spend more time doing useful work rather than waiting on memory. One way that the system copes with the significant difference between memory and processor speeds is caching.

A *cache* is a smaller, faster type of memory that temporarily stores the most recently accessed data. It takes advantage of the likelihood that the system or application will access the same information again in the near future. If the needed data is in the cache, it can be retrieved directly from the cache without relying on the bus to push the data to the processor. This reduces the amount of time that the processor sits idle doing nothing.

The type of memory used for caching purposes is called static RAM (SRAM). Some SRAM chip sets have been clocked as fast as 4.5 ns—there is still a performance difference between processor speed and SRAM access times, but the difference is smaller. SRAM can achieve such a quick access time because it has approximately six times more transistors than a SIMM.

Why not use SRAM instead of DRAM, EDO, BEDO RAM, or SDRAM? Although this would be a dream come true for everyone, it is not likely to happen in the near future. For starters, most hardware designs don't accommodate such an implementation. Also, in most cases, the increased speed does not justify the difference in price between SIMMs (or DIMMs) and SRAM chips. When SRAM prices do fall to more suitable levels, however, do not be surprised to see engineers scrambling to design systems to accommodate large amounts of SRAM.

There are three types of cache: internal (Level 1) cache, external (Level 2) cache, and file system cache.

Level 1 Cache

Internal, or Level 1 (L1), cache is internal to the processor itself. L1 cache is finite and usually ranges from 8 to 16K in size. A cache controller located on the processor controls the cache. The cache controller enhances the cache's performance by attempting to predict the address space that the processor will need next and then reads the addresses into the cache before the address space is requested. The fact that the cache is integrated with the processor itself makes the travel time from memory to the processor almost negligible. The chances that the processor will experience a wait state when code or data is found in the L1 cache are minimal.

Since the size of L1 cache is extremely small and NT handles memory pages in 4K segments, the L1 cache can store a maximum of four pages (with 16K of L1 cache) at a time. Unfortunately, the only way to optimize the performance of the L1 cache is to configure the system with as much L1 cache memory as possible.

Level 2 Cache

The external, or Level 2 (L2), cache is typically larger than the L1 cache, but it is not directly integrated with the processor. Instead, it is located on the motherboard and is controlled by a separate cache controller. In other words, if the system has both an L1 and an L2 cache, the system will also have two separate cache controllers.

The L2 cache is much larger than the L1 cache because it is responsible for mapping large amounts of system RAM. The size ranges from 64K to 2,048K (2MB), but systems are typically configured with either 256K (for systems with up to 32MB of RAM) or 512K (for systems with more than 32MB of RAM) of L2 cache memory. Using more than the typical amount greatly increases server performance, because it helps reduce the amount of wait time experienced by the processor. The L2 cache can also serve as a buffer between the processor and memory to improve access times associated with writing to memory. If main memory is busy, the L2 cache records what the processor wants to write to memory, freeing up the processor.

Contrary to popular belief, adding more main memory to the system does not always provide the performance boost that you may need. The reason for this is directly related to the amount of L2 cache in the system. Any time you add more main memory to the system, the L2 cache must map the additional address space created by the increase in main memory. As a result, the efficiency of the L2 cache slightly decreases. This is yet another reason why you should configure servers with as much L2 cache memory as possible. Windows NT Servers with up to 32MB of RAM should have an L2 cache of at least 512K, and systems with more than 32MB of RAM should be configured with at least 1,024K.

Are there different varieties of SRAM? Which one provides the best overall performance? SRAM, used for L2 cache, comes in three distinct flavors: asynchronous SRAM (async SRAM), synchronous burst SRAM (sync SRAM), and pipelined burst SRAM (PB SRAM).

ASYNC SRAM   Async SRAM has been commonly used in systems dating back to the 386. Access times for this cache are typically 12 to 15 ns, which is faster than SIMM types but not fast enough to keep up with modern processors such as the Pentium or higher-class machines. This type of cache actually can hinder performance because it causes the processor to experience wait states. It operates much the same way as main memory in that it retrieves code or data after the processor asks for it. For this reason, it is recommended that you not use async SRAM for your Windows NT Servers.

SYNC SRAM   Sync SRAM uses the burst method described earlier, reading in three more memory addresses than the number originally requested. In addition, its synchronous operation provides an extremely fast rate, so the processor does not experience wait states to receive code or data. The catch, however, is that sync SRAM provides exceptional performance only when bus speeds are 66 MHz or less. Performance actually begins to decline when sync SRAM is used with higher bus speeds. However, if you are using a system with a 66 MHz or slower bus speed and it supports sync SRAM, then this type of cache will out-perform all other cache types.

PB SRAM   PB SRAM, another high-speed synchronous burst cache, employs an innovative technology called pipelining. Pipelining uses registers to load code or data that can be used by the processor. The first cache cycle, initiated by the processor, takes three clock cycles to complete, but the speed advantage comes from the additional three sequential read operations: The next three cache cycles are each completed in one clock cycle (3-1-1-1). No matter what bus speed the system runs at, PB SRAM always operates at 3-1-1-1. It is the fastest of the three cache types for systems with bus speeds above 66 MHz.

File System Cache and the Windows NT Cache Manager

The third type of cache used by Windows NT is the file system cache. It is different from the other caches because it uses a portion of main memory instead of any of the different varieties of SRAM. As you may suspect, the file system cache is not nearly as fast as the other types, but it does help boost performance.

The Windows NT Cache Manager is responsible for adjusting the size of the file system cache. It determines the size of the file system cache based on whether the system is a workstation or server, the amount of physical memory the system has, and the functional configuration of the system. For instance, a Windows NT file server with ample physical memory will typically have a larger file system cache than a machine being used as a print server, firewall, etc. Windows NT Server systems use a large system cache model, in which any available memory not used by applications or the system is allocated to the file system cache. The Windows NT Cache Manager dynamically controls the actual size of the file system cache since memory requirements continually fluctuate.

Does your system have enough memory to support an effective file system cache? The most effective way to find out is to use the Performance Monitor to watch the cache counters. Your primary concern when monitoring cache counters is the percentage of *hits* and *misses*. A hit occurs when the requested data is found in the file system cache, and a miss occurs when the system has to search elsewhere to find the data. A high percentage of hits and a low percentage of misses means that the system is configured with enough memory to support a large enough file system cache.

When browsing the list of counters within the Cache object, you will notice four different counters relating to the cache hit ratio:

▼ Copy Read Hits %

■ Data Map Hits %

■ MDL Read Hits %

▲ Pin Read Hits %

Here are some other Performance Monitor counters that are useful for gauging cache performance:

Cache   Copy Reads/sec
             Data Flushes/sec
             Lazy Write Flushes/sec
             Lazy Write Pages/sec
             Read Aheads/sec

Memory   Cache Bytes
             Cache Faults/sec
             Pages Input/sec

Why are there four Performance Monitor counters gauging the cache hit ratio? Because Windows NT, and applications running under Windows NT, can read data from the cache in four different ways:

▼ **Copy read**   When a process requests to read a file, the file system copies the data from the cache into the application's buffer (within main memory).

■ **Fast read**   Fast reads are similar to copy reads, with one major exception: Instead of communicating with the file system to retrieve the data from the cache, the process retrieves the data directly from the cache. Fast reads typically occur after the initial read request.

■ **Pin read**   A pin read occurs when data is mapped into the cache so that it can be modified and then written back to the disk. The unusual name stems from the idea that the data is *pinned* in the cache, meaning that it stays in the same memory location and cannot be paged out to disk. This method reduces the number of page faults that may occur when data is requested.

▲ **Read Ahead**   Cache read aheads occur when the VM Manager identifies a process reading a file sequentially. The VM Manager then expects that future read requests will be sequential as well, so it begins mapping larger blocks of data than what the process is asking for. Generally speaking, read aheads offer better performance than the other cache read methods, but performance is also dependent on the process' read patterns.

One of the most common types of read operations used by Windows NT, especially on a server running Internet Information Server (IIS), to retrieve pages containing data from the file system cache is measured by the Memory Descriptor List (MDL) counter. Therefore, on Windows NT Servers running IIS, the MDL Read Hits % counter is the primary counter to watch to find out if Windows NT has enough memory to supply a large enough file system cache. As stated earlier, a high cache hit ratio shows that there is plenty of memory for the file system cache, and this ratio also indicates how effectively Windows NT uses this cache. A realistic goal for this counter, as well as the other cache hit ratio counters, is a ratio of 70 percent or higher; ratios higher than 80 percent indicate exceptional performance. A system experiencing a cache hit percentage below 70 percent may be experiencing a memory shortage. It is advised to increase the amount of physical memory on such a system.

To figure out the percentage of cache misses, simply subtract the percentage of cache hits from 100 percent. For example, if MDL Read Hits % equals 85 percent, then the cache miss rate is 15 percent.

No matter what the functionality of the server is, the Copy Reads Hits % counter gives a good overall picture of a server's cache hit ratio for file read operations. When a process requests data from a file that it has not previously accessed, it is usually a copy read. Moreover, this type of read is more prevalent with small transfers. For this reason, you should always monitor this counter when analyzing the file system cache performance.

BOOSTING PAGING PERFORMANCE

As stated earlier, NT is designed to use paging no matter how much physical memory is available on the system. There are many benefits stemming from NT's use of a paging scheme, but they come with a price. Paging frees up physical memory on the system and allows more processes to execute. When a process needs code or data that has been swapped to the hard disk, the system puts the data back into physical memory and transfers other information to the hard disk if necessary. The difference in performance between a hard disk and physical memory is astounding. For example, a hard disk typically has an access time of approximately 10 ns, whereas physical memory has an access time of around 60 ns. Memory is several orders of magnitude faster than disk speed. In fact, it is roughly 160,000 times faster than even the most technologically advanced disk drive! This fact alone should make you rush out and buy more memory.

How can you minimize the effects of paging on the system? Adding more memory is the first choice for many to reduce paging activity, because the additional memory reduces the likelihood that the system has to constantly rely on the hard disk. However, there is more to increasing paging performance than simply adding more memory. You can also maximize performance for those times when the system must resort to paging by proactively monitoring the changing memory requirements and properly configuring the paging file (pagefile.sys).

Paging File Location Considerations

During Windows NT's installation process, the paging file (pagefile.sys) is automatically created using contiguous disk space. The file is always placed in the root directory of the system partition, but this is not always the optimal placement for the file. To get the best performance from paging, you should first look at the system's disk subsystem configuration to find out whether your system has more than one physical hard disk drive. You can use the Disk Administrator by choosing Start | Programs | Administrative Tools | Disk Administrator to view the system's disk configuration, as shown in Figure 4-3. (Refer to Chapter 6 for more information on the Disk Administrator.) If your system has only one hard disk, it is highly recommended that you configure the system with an extra drive if at all possible. The reason for this recommendation is simple: Windows NT supports up to 16 separate paging files that can be distributed across multiple drives. Configuring the system with

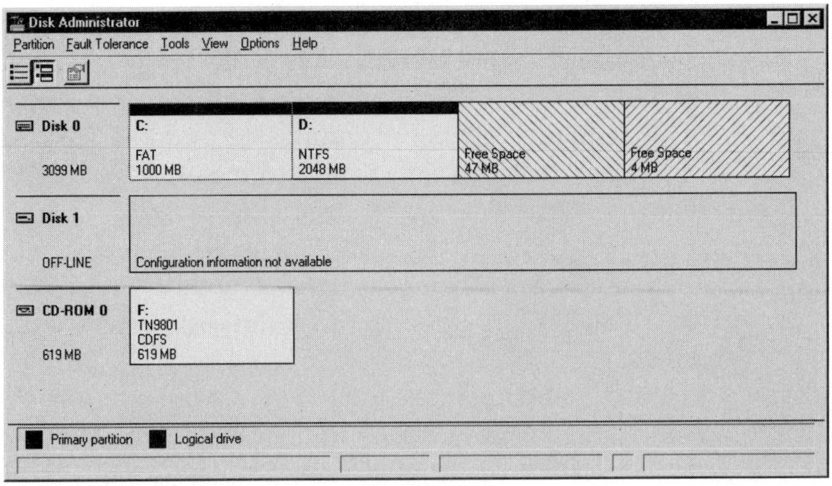

Figure 4-3.   Viewing the number of physical drives on the system

multiple paging files allows simultaneous I/O requests to the various disks, greatly boosting page file performance for I/O requests.

A system with only one physical hard drive limits your ability to optimize paging performance. The drive must take care of system and application requests as well as accessing the paging file. The physical drive may have multiple partitions, but you would be ill advised to disperse the paging file among the partitions. Paging files spread across multiple partitions do not increase the hard drive's ability to read or write any faster to pagefile.sys. In fact, this may even hamper system performance, because the drive must handle paging requests for more than one paging file. Only when a partition does not have enough space to contain the entire paging file should you place paging files on multiple partitions on the same disk.

Servers with multiple physical drives can use multiple paging files to increase paging performance. The key is to spread the load from paging requests to more than one physical disk. Essentially, the system can handle more than one paging request at a time with paging files on separate physical drives. Each physical drive can access or write information to its paging file simultaneously, which increases the amount of information that can be transferred. The optimal configuration for multiple paging files is to place each paging file on a separate drive that has its own drive controller. However, this may not be a viable solution for most server-based configurations because of the additional expense and the limited number of interrupts available on a system.

Calculating the Size of the Paging File

The most important configuration parameter for paging files is size. No matter how many paging files your system has, if they are not properly sized, the system may have performance problems. If the initial size is too small, the system may have to enlarge the paging file to compensate for the additional paging activity. When the system has to increase the size of the paging file on the fly, it has to create new space for it along with handling paging requests. The system will experience a large number of page faults, and may even start thrashing. A *page fault* occurs when the system must find information outside the process' working set, either elsewhere in physical memory or in the pagefile. *Thrashing* occurs when the system lacks the memory resources (both physical and virtual) to satisfy usage requirements, and thus experiences excessive paging. The system will spend more time paging than executing applications. When the system is thrashing, the Memory: Pages/sec counter is consistently above 100 pages per second. Thrashing severely decreases system performance. In addition, dynamically expanding the paging file causes fragmentation. The paging file could be scattered throughout the disk rather than created in contiguous space at boot time, adding overhead to the system and causing severe performance degradation. You should, at all costs, avoid having the system increase the size of the paging file.

NOTE: In order for the system to be able to write memory dumps to disk after a system crash, the system partition must have a pagefile with a size equal to or greater than the amount of physical memory plus one.

NOTE: On NTFS drives, always keep at least 25 percent of the drive's capacity free to ensure that the paging file can be created in contiguous space.

What should the minimum and maximum paging file size be? Microsoft recommends using the sum of the amount of physical RAM plus 11 as the minimum size for a paging file. However, you should first approximate the paging requirements under normal or typical use. Compare your approximation with Microsoft's recommendation and use the higher value as the minimum.

NOTE: For systems configured with multiple paging files, the minimum recommended size should be spread across each of the paging files. In other words, it is not necessary to set the minimum requirement as the minimum size for each paging file.

For example, suppose your system's typical paging activity requires 40MB from a paging file, and your system has 64MB of RAM. Following Microsoft's recommendation for the minimum paging file size gives you 75MB (64MB RAM + 11). Under normal operation, you have approximately 35MB of swap space that is not being used. If your system can spare the space, you should use the minimum size Microsoft recommends, because even if your system jumps to 60MB in paging activity, the paging file will not have to grow to handle the increased load. The important thing to remember here is that you should avoid having the system expand the paging file, because this will have negative effects on performance.

To change the paging file location or size configuration parameters, do the following:

1. Double-click the System applet icon in the Control Panel or right-click the My Computer icon on the desktop and select Properties.

2. On the Performance tab (shown in Figure 4-4), click the Change button.

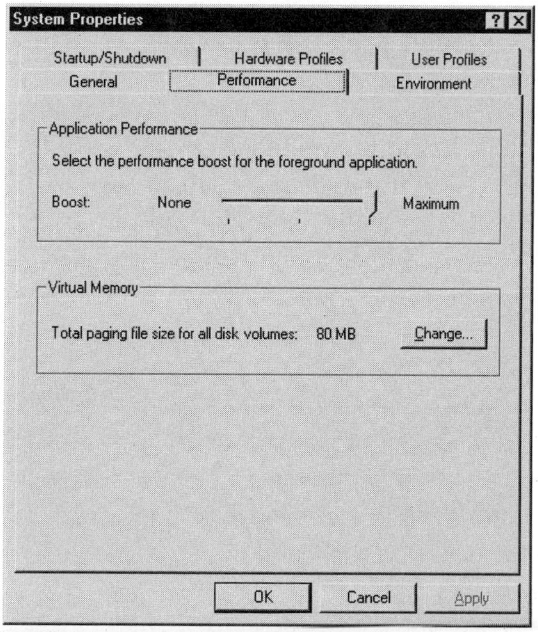

System Properties

| Startup/Shutdown | Hardware Profiles | User Profiles |
| General | Performance | Environment |

Application Performance

Select the performance boost for the foreground application.

Boost: None   ————————   Maximum

Virtual Memory

Total paging file size for all disk volumes: 80 MB   Change...

OK   Cancel   Apply

Figure 4-4. Changing paging file configuration parameters

3. To add another paging file to the existing configuration, select a drive that does not already have a paging file. Then specify the initial size and maximum size of the paging file (in megabytes), click Set, and click OK.

NOTE: Make sure that you reconfigure the other paging files so that the sum of their minimum sizes reflects the minimum required size for the entire system.

4. To change the minimum and maximum size of an existing paging file, select the drive where the paging file resides. Then specify the initial size and maximum size of the paging file (in megabytes), click Set, and click OK.

5. Click Close in the System Properties dialog box.

6. When the system prompts you to restart the computer, select Yes.

There are several methods you can use to determine the system's paging requirements so you can set the right minimum paging file size. You can use the Task Manager, Windows NT Diagnostics (WINMSD), or the Performance Monitor to find the proper size so the paging file does not have to expand during normal operation.

NOTE: Believe it or not, the absolute minimum size of the paging file is only 2MB. Obviously, however, performance will suffer if you set the size this low, because the system will be forced to expand the paging file until paging requests can be handled adequately.

Task Manager

An easy way to check whether you have configured the correct size for the paging file is to use the Task Manager. This gives you an accurate representation of how the system is using the paging file along with other vital system information.

NOTE: A system's *Commit Peak* is the highest amount of physical and virtual memory the system has allocated to processes thus far.

After starting the Task Manager (by right-clicking the Taskbar), click the Performance tab to see real-time system statistics, as shown in Figure 4-5. The information that is most pertinent for paging file size is located in the Commit Charge section. This section shows whether the Commit Peak approaches or exceeds the Commit Limit, and whether it exceeds the amount of physical memory on the system.

As the system experiences increases in paging activity, the amount of committed memory (Commit Total) increases. Once it approaches the Commit Limit value, the system needs to expand the paging file. The Commit Limit indicates the amount of virtual

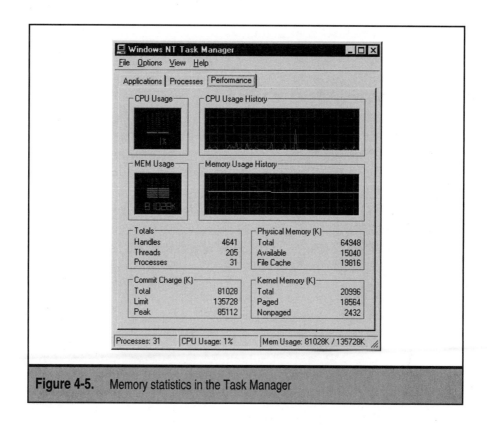

Figure 4-5.   Memory statistics in the Task Manager

memory that can be committed to memory without having to expand the paging file. Since the goal is to keep the paging file from expanding, it is imperative that you keep Commit Total and Commit Limit far apart. If these values meet, the system must dynamically increase the size of the pagefile. The worst case scenario, however, is when the Commit Total meets the sum of RAM plus the maximum pagefile size because the paging file can no longer grow to meet expectations. (This may cause system instability, prevent applications from starting, and other anomalies.)

The information presented by the Task Manager's Commit Charge section also shows you whether the system's main memory is sufficient to accommodate the tasks the system performs. If the Commit Total value regularly exceeds the amount of RAM in the system, the system may not have enough physical memory. For example, if a system with 64MB (64,948K) of RAM has a Commit

Total value of approximately the same amount (64,948K), it is time to increase the amount of physical memory on the system.

Windows NT Diagnostics

The WINMSD utility is similar to the Task Manager in that it displays system statistics such as the state of services and memory, but it does not present information in real time. You must manually refresh the display to get current information. For this reason, it is recommended that you do not rely heavily on this tool to calculate the minimum size of the paging file. However, this utility does provide you with a way to quickly approximate the minimum paging file size by looking at the information on the Memory tab, shown in Figure 4-6.

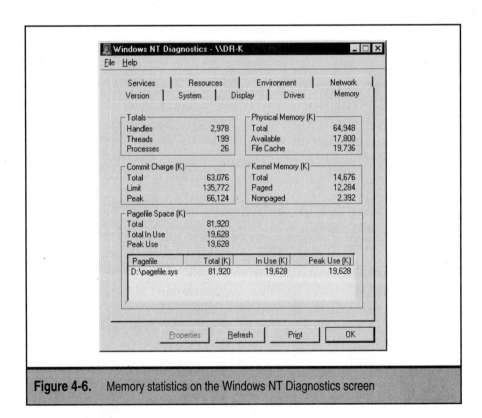

Figure 4-6.   Memory statistics on the Windows NT Diagnostics screen

Performance Monitor

The best and most reliable method for determining the minimum paging file size is to use the Performance Monitor to monitor counters that pertain to virtual memory. Before you start monitoring the counters, follow Microsoft's recommendation to set the minimum paging file size (amount of physical RAM + 11). Now you are ready to monitor the memory use for typical operations.

You should start by using four counters to monitor virtual memory: Memory: Committed Bytes and Commit Limit, and Paging File: % Usage and % Usage Peak. Other memory counters are useful to monitor, but you should hold off measuring them until later in the monitoring process, because the ones you immediately use are the best for discovering the minimum paging file requirements. The four counters you should monitor first are described here:

▼ **Memory: Committed Bytes** This counter indicates the amount of virtual memory currently used by all processes. It is the amount of virtual memory actually committed, not merely reserved.

■ **Memory: Commit Limit** The Commit Limit is the maximum amount of virtual memory that can be committed without running the risk of expanding the paging file. This value is just below the sum of the physical memory and the current paging file size. This value does not quite equal the sum of the physical memory and the paging file size, because it subtracts the amount of memory reserved for the operating system.

■ **Paging File: % Usage** This is the percentage of the paging file that is currently in use by all processes.

▲ **Paging File: % Usage Peak** This counter indicates the highest percentage of space used in the paging file.

The Commit Limit and Committed Bytes counters work together; if you monitor the counters separately, you will not get the information you need to properly set the paging file's minimum size. Only by monitoring both counters can you correctly determine whether the paging file is approaching or has already reached full capacity. When the size of the Committed Bytes counter approaches the Commit Limit, the system is running out of virtual memory. In fact, the system will warn you if these two values are equal or if the Committed Bytes counter exceeds the limit. It displays a warning advising that you manually increase the paging file and restart the system:

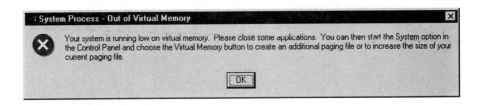

You must then close some applications, manually increase the paging file, and restart the system.

During normal system use, the Committed Bytes counter should never exceed the amount of physical RAM on the system, especially with a properly configured minimum paging file size. You can provide yourself with some extra reassurance that this situation will not occur during normal operation by adding an alerting mechanism. As an additional precaution, you can use the Performance Monitor to alert you when the Committed Bytes value comes within 20 percent of the Commit Limit value.

If the Committed Bytes counter does equal or exceed the Commit Limit value, it is very important to check the number of hard page faults the system is experiencing. Hard page faults introduce significant performance delays because they indicate pages that have had to be retrieved from disk instead of main memory. The counter that shows the number of hard page faults is Memory: Pages/sec. Check this counter for consistently abnormal activity (above 20 pages per second) to further verify that the system is running out of virtual memory and must expand the paging file to compensate.

The two other counters that you should immediately monitor to help determine the minimum paging file size are the Paging File: % Usage and % Usage Peak counters. You can use these two counters together or monitor them separately to get an accurate picture of the percentage of the paging file that is being used. You should keep the % Usage counter equal to or below 40 percent, and the % Usage Peak should stay below 75 percent. Keeping paging activity within these acceptable ranges protects against having to increase the paging file. You can also use these counters to get a rough estimate of how much more physical memory the system needs to keep reliance on the paging file to a minimum. For example, suppose the minimum paging file size is set to 80MB, and the % Usage counter averages around 20 percent. In this case, the 20 percent use rate for the paging file is essentially telling you that if you add memory equal to 20 percent of the paging file, you will accommodate the majority of server functions with main memory instead of the paging file. You can reduce the usage percent to a bare minimum by configuring the system with an additional 16MB of RAM.

A little less important than the minimum paging file size but still important to boosting paging performance is the maximum size of the paging file. The maximum value is the largest size to which you ever expect the paging file to grow in the worst-case scenario. Of course, you must have enough free disk space to accommodate this limit. A general rule of thumb is that you should set the maximum value to the minimum value plus 50 percent. In most cases, if you have properly configured the minimum paging file and have set the maximum paging file size to the recommended amount, this value should never be approached.

NT's reliance on paging provides many benefits to the system as well as to user applications. However, paging can also negatively affect performance. Adding more memory to the system is not always feasible, and it does not always correct the performance problems associated with paging activity. Fortunately, there is more than one way to increase the system's paging performance. Proactive monitoring and proper paging file configuration and location all play key roles in boosting paging performance. Keep in mind that if you properly configure the minimum and maximum paging file sizes, you drastically reduce the risk of compromising performance even during periods of peak memory use.

MEMORY AND APPLICATION PERFORMANCE

Memory and application performance are interrelated. Applications depend on memory and Windows NT's memory management to perform duties and tasks effectively and efficiently. Windows NT's Virtual Memory Manager is responsible not only for the efficiency of the operating system's memory use, but also for maintaining the optimal memory configuration for applications.

Memory requirements are dynamic because system components and user applications do not always use the same code or data every time they run. Consequently, it is to your advantage to develop a mechanism to monitor memory requirements so you can act and not react to increases in memory use. Increases in memory use can often lead to memory shortages. There are several counters that help you monitor the overall effects of memory as well as the relationship between the Virtual Memory Manager and applications on the system. There are also other steps you can take to ensure optimal performance.

Monitoring Counters

The wealth of information you get from the available memory counters enables you to make informed decisions regarding how to maximize memory performance. In addition to the counters that have already been mentioned in previous sections (Paging File: % Usage and % Usage Peak, and Memory: Commit Limit and Committed Bytes), you can use the following counters to help you determine whether the system is configured for maximum memory efficiency:

Memory	Available Bytes
	Page Faults/sec
	Pages/sec
Process	Page Faults/sec
	Working Set

Page Faults/sec and Pages/sec

The most important memory counters for you to monitor are Page Faults/sec and Pages/sec. These two counters accurately indicate the amount of paging activity that the system is experiencing.

Paging activity can result from two types of faults: hard and soft. Paging activity occurs when a process, needing code or data, references a virtual address where it thinks the code or data resides. However, only NT knows the actual location. If the information being sought does not reside in the process' working set, it is looked for elsewhere in memory or in the paging file. Soft faults occur when the needed information is found outside of the process's working set but still in main memory. The code or data could be in a number of places within main memory. It may be in the file system cache, in the transition to disk, or in the working set of another process. Soft faults can occur frequently without reducing system performance, because usually the processor is only briefly interrupted.

Hard faults have much more of an effect on system performance. A hard fault occurs when the code or data that the process requested is located within the paging file. The Virtual Memory Manager then must search the paging file for the requested information and pull it back into main memory so the process can use it. The Virtual Memory Manager must contend with slow disk speed as well as possibly the need to swap enough code or data from main memory to the disk to make room for the process's request. Hard faults can drastically reduce overall system performance and should therefore be kept to a minimum.

To maximize memory efficiency, it is imperative to keep paging to a minimum. NT is designed to page code and data no matter how much memory is available. However, if it has to constantly swap data to disk, performance and memory efficiency will begin to decline, because the disk is several orders of magnitude slower than RAM. Using the Page Faults/sec and Pages/sec counters to check the amount of paging will also tell you whether the system needs more physical memory, since NT's dependency on the disk subsystem for paging rapidly increases only when the amount of physical memory is low.

The Page Faults/sec counter reflects both hard and soft faults, and the Pages/sec counter indicates the number of pages read from or written to disk to resolve hard page faults. The Pages/sec counter is essentially tucked away in the Page Faults/sec counter. You can expect the Page Faults/sec counter to be much higher than Pages/sec, because a Windows NT system can tolerate large numbers of soft faults without significantly compromising performance. For most Pentium class or higher machines, acceptable values for the Page Faults/sec counter can be as high as 250 page faults per second, depending on the number of hard page faults the system experiences at this rate.

A key to minimizing paging is keeping the Pages/sec counter consistently lower than 20 pages per second. The counter may occasionally reach 60 pages per second or more, but this value should be reached only for a brief time. For instance, when an application is first executed, you can expect to see the counter sharply peak for a moment while the application is being loaded into memory. The Pages/sec counter also tells you whether the system is excessively paging, or thrashing. The system is thrashing when the Pages/sec value consistently exceeds 100 pages per second. Thrashing should be avoided at all costs because it drags down server performance to intolerable levels. It puts so much stress on the system that you will hear the disk drive constantly churning.

Available Bytes and Working Set

The Virtual Memory Manager is responsible for keeping track of the system's memory resources. One critical responsibility is maintaining a minimum amount of available memory for the operating system and for active processes. On the Windows NT Server, the Virtual Memory Manager tries to keep at least 4MB available so the system can handle any sudden increases in memory requirements resulting from applications being loaded into memory, the allocation of more memory to a process, and so on. The Virtual Memory Manager maintains this minimum level of available bytes by dynamically adjusting the space used in physical memory and the paging file.

The Memory: Available Bytes counter measures the amount of free memory dynamically controlled by the Virtual Memory Manager. The goal of monitoring this counter is to make sure that it does not dip below 4MB. In fact, you should strive to keep this counter value well above 4MB to minimize paging activity. The number of available bytes fluctuates by default because of its close relationship to paging activity and the size of a process' working set.

The working set for a process contains code and data that has been recently used by the process, and its size is the amount of physical memory allocated to that process. It does not include process code or data that exists in the paging file. The Virtual Memory Manager manages the working set dynamically according to the amount of available memory. The maximum size of the working set is determined by the amount of physical memory installed on the machine. There are three categories of working set size:

▼ **Small**   16MB of RAM or less

■ **Medium**   16 to 20MB of RAM

▲ **Large**   More than 20MB of RAM

The size of the working set is finite, and its minimum and maximum values are hard-coded within the operating system. As a result, the minimum and maximum sizes cannot be changed or tuned. You can, however, force NT to let applications use as large a working set as possible by setting the Maximize Throughput for Network Applications option for the Server service. Use the Network applet Services tab located in the Control Panel to configure the Server service.

When a process requests a piece of code or data, it assumes that it will be located in its working set. The process continues uninterrupted if the code or data is found within the working set. Otherwise, either a hard or soft fault occurs. You can use the Process: Page Faults/sec counter to examine the page faults for a specific process. This counter is similar to the one in the Memory object except that it shows the paging activity only for the process, not for the entire system. An increase in a process' paging activity indicates that the working set is not large enough to handle the process and signals the Virtual Memory Manager to increase the size of the working set for the process. If the amount of available bytes is above the minimum required by the system (4MB), the size of the working set is increased. Otherwise, the Virtual Memory Manager will temporarily increase the working set so that the page faults caused by the process decrease.

In general, when the amount of available bytes approaches the system's minimum toleration level, the Virtual Memory Manager attempts to recover lost bytes by trimming the working sets of active processes. Of course, this only continues the cycle. The chance that requested code or data can be found in the working set of a process is reduced as the working sets are trimmed. The page fault rate increases because more code and data has to be retrieved from disk instead of the working set of the process. The system finds itself once again trying to compensate for the increase in page faults.

There is no recommended size for working sets because their size varies with each process and system configuration. Keep in mind that performance is at its best when page faults are kept to a minimum and the number of available bytes is well above the minimum required by the system. At present, there is no way to monitor the hard page faults caused by a specific process, so you have to rely on the Process: Page Faults/sec and Memory: Available Bytes counters to keep the system running efficiently. Since there are limited tuning parameters for working sets, the most viable way to optimize the working set of a process is to simply configure the system with enough physical memory so that working sets can be increased to their maximum capacity.

Plugging Memory Leaks

There may come a time when you notice that system responsiveness is gradually decreasing to a crawl, when even a simple mouse movement takes what seems like hours to complete. Gradual degradation in performance usually means that a process is leaking memory. Memory leaks are a result of poorly written code. A memory leak occurs when a process robs the system of its memory resources. All processes at one point or another ask the system to allocate more memory for their use. Then when the process is done with that particular memory segment it releases the memory. A leaky process keeps the memory allocation instead of releasing it to the system for other processes to use. This process repeats itself until memory resources are depleted. At this point, the only way to stop the drain is to either stop the process or reboot the system.

Identifying Memory Leaks

If you experience a gradual decline in performance or abnormal unresponsiveness, you should immediately assume that there is a possible memory leak. You have won half the battle once you identify a memory leak as a possible cause of the system's performance degradation. Memory leaks are difficult to detect before they degrade performance, because to locate them, you would need to constantly watch every process and possibly every thread for abnormal trends. Moreover, you may have to watch for as much as a few weeks before you begin to notice that a process is not releasing memory back to the system.

To correctly conclude that a memory leak is causing sluggish system behavior, you should verify that the system is allocating memory and that the memory resource is continuously being depleted before you begin searching for the source of the problem. Use the Performance Monitor to watch every counter in the Memory object. Pay close attention particularly to the Pool Nonpaged Allocs, Pool Nonpaged Bytes, Pool Paged Allocs, Pool Paged Bytes, System Code Total Bytes, and System Driver Total Bytes counters, since they provide the best indications of whether a certain memory resource is being depleted. Under normal circumstances these counters may fluctuate between high and low values. However, if a memory leak exists, one or more of these counters will only rise in value because the memory is not being returned. You can also monitor the Objects: Threads and Objects: Sections counters to see if memory leaks exist. The Threads counter indicates the number of active threads in the system at that given instant, and the Sections counter reports the number of sections created by processes. A section is an area of virtual memory that a process creates to store data for itself or other processes. Both of these counters will continually increase during a memory leak. You should use the Chart view to monitor activity in real time so you can come to a conclusion about the problem as soon as possible.

NOTE: Your chances of discovering memory leaks before they have disastrous effects are greatly increased if proper capacity planning methodologies are used as outlined in Chapter 2. You may notice, through trends or patterns, that memory is gradually being depleted and never properly returned to the system.

When you are charting the memory activity, you will see only increases in memory allocation, though you may also periodically see plateaus, where the process has temporarily stopped requesting more memory. It is important to understand that during this period of inactivity, the process has only reached a level where it is not requesting more memory. After a short time, it will once again request more memory resources and continue to hold onto what it already has.

At this point, you have verified that a memory leak exists in the system. Next you need to find out which process is responsible for slowly devouring memory resources and reducing server performance. A good way to simplify your search is to run a second instance of the Performance Monitor, and then place both Performance Monitor windows side by side. Then you can have one window displaying the counters relating to total system memory (Memory: Available Bytes, Memory: Committed Bytes, and so on), and another displaying the memory used by each process. Now you can more easily track the times at which memory allocations increase against the memory usage of individual processes. As you can see in Figure 4-7, reducing the number of counters that are displayed in a single window makes this tracking process easier on the eyes.

Start by monitoring the counters within the Process object. Before you get overwhelmed by the sheer number of counters available for

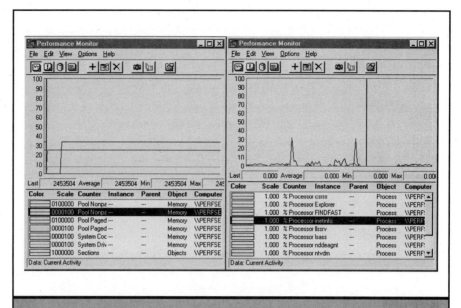

Figure 4-7. Running two instances of the Performance Monitor

the object, be assured that you do not need to monitor every single one. You should single out those counters that will supply you with enough information to accurately pinpoint the source of the memory leak. Each counter has a separate instance for each process (or program) currently running on the system as well as a Total instance for the combined processes. Figure 4-8 shows the Thread Count counter with all possible instances. The following is a list of recommended Process counters to include when monitoring to find the cause of a memory leak:

▼ **Page File Bytes**   This counter indicates the number of bytes that a process has used in the paging file.

■ **Private Bytes**   Private bytes are the number of bytes that a process has allocated to itself that it cannot share with other processes. This counter was used to detect a memory leak caused by SERVICES.EXE in Windows NT versions 3.51 and 4.0.

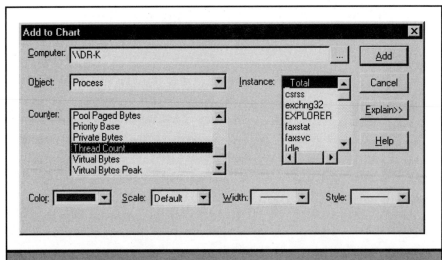

Figure 4-8.   Assessing the number of instances that can be monitored for each Process counter

- **Pool Nonpaged Bytes**   This counter includes the number of bytes in nonpaged pooled memory. Nonpaged pooled memory is a limited amount of memory dedicated solely to privileged mode components within the operating system. If a memory leak affects this pool, the amount of memory can be quickly depleted and cause vital system services to fail. If the nonpaged pooled area is affected by a memory leak, the leak could be related to a service running.

- **Pool Paged Bytes**   This counter is similar to the Pool Nonpaged Bytes counter in that the resource it monitors has limited capacity and is dedicated to system components. Also, as the resource is depleted and not replenished, system services are likely to fail. The difference between this area of memory and nonpaged pooled memory is that pages contained within the pool paged memory can be swapped out to disk.

- **Thread Count**   The thread count is the number of active threads for each process. By definition, there is at least one thread executing instructions for a process. A process can be multithreaded, meaning that more than one thread can simultaneously execute instructions. The process leaking memory may spawn many threads, which will increase the counter value.

■ **Virtual Bytes** This counter indicates the amount of virtual address space an active process is using. This value does not necessarily mean that disk or main memory pages are being used or committed by the process.

▲ **Working Set** This counter indicates the size of a process' working set in bytes. The working set consists of the amount of physical memory that the process is using. It includes pages of memory that have been used by the process's threads. When the process needs more memory resources, it attempts to pull pages from main memory to satisfy the request. If memory resources are low or if the page resides in virtual memory (pagefile.sys), the VM Manager will not allow the process to add to its working set. Under normal circumstances, NT can trim the working set of a process when memory resources are low. However, if the process is leaking memory, the system will not be able to reduce the size of the process's working set.

Since the goal of using these counters is to discover which process is causing problems, you should observe every instance of each counter, with the possible exception of the Total instance, since it does not reflect a specific process running on the system. Once you have added all of the recommended counters and their respective instances, you can begin to watch for places where an increase in memory allocation coincides with a process' use of memory resources. For example, if you notice that Memory: Pool Paged Bytes and the RASMON process always simultaneously increase in value, this process may be the cause of the memory leak.

Once the guilty process has been discovered, you should either replace or correct the process so it no longer leaks or uses memory inefficiently. Usually you can apply patches or upgrades to alleviate the problems caused by a process. Check with Microsoft or with the company that developed the application to obtain a fix. Remove the process altogether if a remedy does not exist and it causes intolerable system behavior.

Preventing Memory Leaks

Memory leaks can cause severe performance degradation if they are not caught in time. In most cases, they also cause unnecessary downtime that affects every aspect of the business that relies on the server. Fortunately, there are preventative measures that you can take to help avoid performance reductions caused by memory leaks.

First, it is imperative to keep Windows NT current with the latest service packs and hot fixes from Microsoft. Service packs and hot fixes contain operating system enhancements as well as bug fixes. If you do not keep up with these small upgrades, you increase your chances of running into memory leak problems.

Even with the latest service packs and hot fixes, you still run the risk of a greedy process that continually takes memory without returning it to the system. To reduce this risk, establish a burn-in period where you test any new software, including service packs and hot fixes, on a server before you apply the software to Windows NT Servers in a production environment. The burn-in period should last at least a few days to ensure that the new software does not leak memory or have other negative side-effects. This may not always be feasible because of the cost of having another machine available solely for testing, and it may be difficult to mimic a server in the production environment. Allotting the time and equipment will be to your advantage in the long run, however, because you will greatly reduce the chance of downtime associated with memory leaks as well as other problems that might arise from a new installation.

Using RAM Disks

Disk access is clearly the bottleneck in NT's virtual memory mechanism. Physical memory access times are several orders of magnitude faster than those of the best drives on the market. Despite this overwhelming difference in speed, NT still relies heavily on disk drives for many tasks such as storage and paging.

Are there any ways, other than disk caching, to lessen NT's reliance on the disk subsystem? One possible solution is to create a RAM disk. A RAM disk device driver segments a portion of the system's physical memory during startup to emulate a disk drive. NT recognizes this part of memory as another disk drive on the system. You can specify the size of the RAM disk, but the size is ultimately determined by the amount of physical memory on your system. The RAM disk serves the same purpose as other drives on your system: as a storage medium for code and data. It is essentially a hard disk that operates at RAM speeds.

Windows NT Server does not natively support RAM disks. However, there are shareware RAM disk device drivers as well as commercial software packages that allow you to create and manage this type of storage medium.

The advantage of using a RAM disk is the speed at which you can launch processes. Depending on the amount of code and data the RAM disk can hold, load times for processes are greatly reduced. The information primarily resides in main memory, which consequently reduces the number of times it must be retrieved from a disk drive.

The disadvantages of RAM disks are not so obvious, but you should consider them. First, a procedure must be in place to copy code and data from a storage medium to the RAM disk before a process can take advantage of the RAM disk's speed. The time spent copying information to the RAM disk will more than likely be greater than the time needed to load the information from disk. You can automate the copy procedure through batch or logon script processing, but by the time you are through copying, the process could have already been loaded and running.

The other disadvantage of using a RAM disk is more of a fault tolerance rather than a performance issue. Since RAM disks are volatile, anything contained within the RAM disk is lost when the system loses power or is shut down. Some commercial applications offer a degree of fault tolerance by mirroring the RAM disk to a partition on a disk drive, but usually you have to configure both the RAM disk and the partition so they are of equal size. For example, if your RAM disk is 20MB, you would need to create a 20MB partition for the application to automatically mirror the RAM disk to the partition. For this reason, you should not use a RAM disk for mission-critical processes or data that is dynamic. Although some may argue that the advantages outweigh the disadvantages, one indisputable fact remains: RAM disks expose the system to additional risks.

Trimming Server Fat

An easy way to create more available memory for Windows NT and applications is to remove anything that the server is not using. This could mean removing or disabling services and processes that are not being used as well as minimizing the number of protocol stacks that the server is using. What you decide to trim depends on the server's configuration, which obviously will vary from system to system. Be careful not to remove anything that the server requires to function. For instance, if the system is configured as a proxy server, you shouldn't disable the WWW service, but you may want to turn off the Socks, FTP, and Gopher services.

The amount of memory you conserve or gain also depends on how much memory the process uses. The more memory you can free, the more memory becomes available to the resources and system components that need it. Table 4-1 lists a few common services that you may or may not want to disable, or set to manual, in order to save memory resources.

Service	Description	Recommendation
Alerter	Lets you send administrative alert messages to other users on the Windows NT network. This service requires that the Messenger service be running.	Keep this service active unless your machine is a stand-alone server, not participating in a Windows NT network.
Clipbook Server	Allows your machine to share data with other machines through the clipboard.	Disable this service unless you plan to share clipboard data.

Table 4-1. Services That Might Be Disabled to Conserve Memory

Service	Description	Recommendation
Directory Replicator	Allows entire directory trees to be replicated to other machines on the Windows NT network, as long as those machines also have this service enabled.	Disable this service if the NT machine is not participating in replication.
Event Log	Allows a machine to record application, security, and system events that can be viewed with the Event Viewer.	Keep this service active so that you'll receive information pertaining to the system. The information generated is key to troubleshooting the server.
Messenger	Lets you send and receive pop-up messages, such as administrative alerts.	Keep this service active in order to receive pop-up messages. These messages may prove very useful in remote communications, and may also alert you to important system information.
NetLogon	Required in order to participate in a Windows NT domain. This service is used for authentication purposes.	Keep this service active unless your machine is a stand-alone server, not participating in a Windows NT network.
Schedule	Lets you schedule the execution of certain events using the AT command or other scheduling tools.	Disable this service unless you use or plan to use the AT command or other scheduling tools.

Table 4-1. Services That Might Be Disabled to Conserve Memory (*continued*)

Service	Description	Recommendation
Server	Allows your machine to share resources with other computers.	Keep this service active unless the machine is a non-networked, stand-alone machine.
TCP/IP NetBIOS Helper	Runs the NetBIOS API on top of the TCP/IP protocol.	Keep this service active unless the machine is a non-networked, stand-alone machine.

Table 4-1.   Services That Might Be Disabled to Conserve Memory (*continued*)

The following sections discuss several other features that you may wish to disable in order to free additional memory for the system.

Disabling the Spooler Service

If you do not have a printer connected to the machine either locally or over a network, then there is no reason to keep the spooler service running. Removing this service will reduce the amount of committed memory by approximately 600K and the amount of nonpaged pool memory by approximately 10K. To disable the Windows NT Spooler service, do the following

1. In the Control Panel, double-click the Services applet icon to display the Services dialog box:

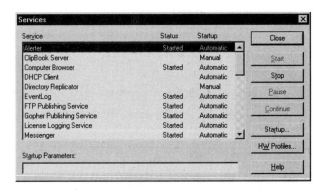

2. Scroll down the alphabetical list until you find the Spooler service and then select it.

3. Click the Startup button to display the Spooler service properties.

4. Click the radio button beside Disabled to disable the Spooler service, as shown here:

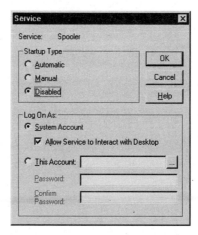

This prevents the service from starting when the machine boots up.

5. Click OK.

6. To begin saving memory resources, click the Stop button to immediately stop the service. Then click Close.

Removing or Unbinding Protocols

Remove or unbind any protocols that the network is not using to communicate. This not only frees memory resources, but it also optimizes your server's network I/O performance. For instance, you may not need (or want) the WINS Client (TCP/IP) bound to every adapter or service. The gain in memory resources may be minute, but every little bit improves performance.

Disabling Atdisk

Disable the Atdisk device if the system has only SCSI devices. The Atdisk device supports the IDE interface and therefore is not necessary if the system does not have any IDE devices. You disable a device similar to the way you disable a service. Do the following:

1. In the Control Panel, double-click the Devices applet.

2. Scroll down the list of devices until you find the Atdisk device and then select it.

3. If the device is active and you only have SCSI devices, stop the device by clicking the Stop button, as shown here:

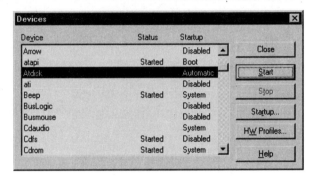

4. To prevent the device from starting when the system starts, click the Startup button and select the radio button next to Disabled:

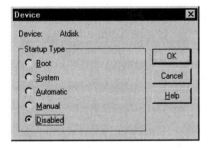

5. Click OK. Then click Close.

CONCLUSION

Memory contention is one of the most common causes of performance degradation. The key to successfully managing the system's dependency on memory is to supply the system with enough physical memory to adequately support the operating system and all other processes running on the system. There is more to memory optimization, however, than simply adding more memory. Throughout this chapter, other optimization techniques, such as hardware configuration, paging, and trimming resources, were examined to show you what you can do to increase overall system performance.

CHAPTER 5

Boosting Network Performance

Mﾠore and more users are sharing resources and applications, and accessing information stored either on local servers or on servers located great distances across electronic networks. Sometimes remote resources are so transparent that a user does not realize how great a distance their requested information has traveled, nor that a reply has likely been returned in a fraction of a second.

Users do become acutely aware of network use when the delay becomes longer than a fraction of a second. Here the fastest, most optimized system can appear to crawl because of insufferable delays introduced by a slow network.

Tweaking and optimizing the network may seem like an insurmountable task. There are numerous pieces of hardware from a myriad of different vendors—all commanding their own configuration language—servers of all types, a variety of network topologies, and countless applications that comprise your network. How can you optimize this amalgamation of technology? The key is to divide and conquer. This chapter examines how to break down the network into more easily manageable components and then optimize each part. Finally, this chapter will put them all back together so that you can see the big picture again to optimize for future network demands.

NETWORK ARCHITECTURE

A network can be divided into two systems. First, hardware forms the network topology including the wires, routers, servers, the usage protocols, and the configuration of all these components. The second system is the amount and timing of the network traffic over each link. Together they make a unique and always changing environment. However, you must first acquaint yourself with the terminology and characteristics of the network components before you can jump in and start tweaking these two seemingly disparate systems. This section outlines some basic principles of networking, but if you are well versed in this area, you may skip ahead to the next section, "Finding and Removing Network Bottlenecks."

The OSI Reference Model

The International Standards Organization (ISO), founded in 1946, published the Open Systems Interconnect (OSI) reference model in 1978 to define standards allowing vendors of different devices and systems the ability to communicate with each other on a network. This seven-layer model has become the standard for designing communication methods among network devices. It is not important to memorize all the responsibilities of each layer, but it is helpful to know the basic function of each, because many hardware devices and configurations reference them.

Each layer of the OSI reference model illustrated in Figure 5-1 defines a function or a set of functions performed when data is transferred between applications across the network. Any number of protocols, rules that control how a process or function works, may control this function.

Each protocol communicates with other protocols above and below it on the same computer, and with a peer at the same layer on a remote system. Information is passed down through the layers until it is transmitted across the network, where it is passed back up the stack to the application at the remote end. Although each layer only

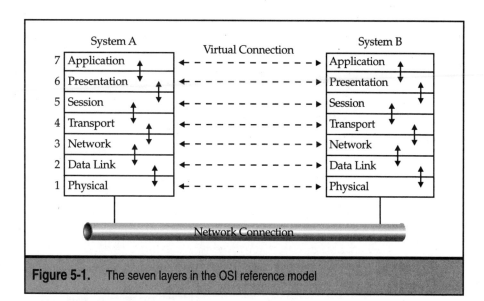

Figure 5-1.   The seven layers in the OSI reference model

needs to know how to pass information up or down from one layer to the next, they rely on the fact that each layer will perform its respective function. This is tremendously useful because you can use a high-level protocol, such as TCP, layer 4, with a variety of layer one and two protocols, such as, Ethernet over coax cable or Token Ring over twisted-pair cable.

Each protocol layer is concerned only with communication to a peer at the other end of a link, and thus creates a *virtual link* to the other system at the equivalent level. For example, File Transfer Protocol (FTP) is an application layer protocol that communicates with peer FTP applications on remote systems. FTP applications are only concerned with FTP functions, and do not care whether the physical layer is a serial modem line or a twisted-pair Ethernet connection.

Starting from the bottom, the layers are numbered one to seven, and have the following basic functions in the network operations:

▼ **Layer one**   This *physical layer* deals with the actual transport medium being used, and is sometimes referred to as "the wire." It defines the electrical and mechanical characteristics of the medium carrying the data signal, such as coaxial cable, fiber optics, twisted-pair cabling, and serial lines.

■ **Layer two**   The *data link layer* controls access onto the network, and is one of many layers to ensure the reliable transfer of packets across the network. Token passing (Token Ring and FDDI) and Carrier Sense Multiple Access with Collision Detection (Ethernet) are techniques included in layer two of the OSI model.

■ **Layer three**   The *network layer* is concerned with moving data between different networks. Protocols at this layer, such as IP and IPX, are responsible for finding the data's destination device.

■ **Layer four**   Primary responsibility of the *transport layer* is to ensure that data reaches its destination intact and in the proper order. The Transmission Control Protocol (TCP) and User Datagram Protocol (UDP) operate at this level.

- **Layer five** The *session layer* establishes and terminates connections and arranges sessions between two computers. The Lightweight Directory Access Protocol (LDAP) and Remote Procedure Call (RPC) provide some functions at this level.

- **Layer six** The *presentation layer* formats data for display or for printing. Examples of presentation layer protocols are NetBIOS and the Lightweight Presentation Protocol (LPP).

▲ **Layer seven** The *application layer* defines the protocols to be used between the application and the lower layers. Examples of protocols at this level include electronic mail (Simple Mail Transfer Protocol), file transfers (File Transfer Protocol), and remote login.

Physical Protocols

The physical protocols fall into two main categories: the token passing and the collision-based protocols. These differ primarily in how they gain access to the physical medium (the wire or fiber).

Collision-Based Protocols

Ethernet, Fast Ethernet, and Gigabit Ethernet all use a collision-based method to access the wire. Before attempting to transmit a message, a computer listens to the wire to determine if another computer is already transmitting a message. If it does not hear a carrier for the standard Ethernet span of 9.6 microseconds, the computer will attempt to transmit the message. It must continue to listen while transmitting, because if two computers transmit at the same time, a collision occurs resulting in incomplete frames, called *runt frames*. Both computers must back off from their transmissions, and then retry after a random period of time.

Token-Passing Protocols

Fiber Distributed Data Interface (FDDI) and Token Ring are two types of token-passing protocols that use completely different methods for accessing the media. Instead of generating a message for the media whenever the computer has one queued, it must wait to receive the token that is quickly and continuously passed around the ring of computers. The computer can only place a message on the media when it has the token, and it only has the token for a limited time before it must be relinquished to its neighbor, giving all participants an equal opportunity to send messages.

Optimizing Ethernet

LAN protocols operate at speeds in excess of 100 Mbps. However, the achievable data rate or *throughput,* which is measure in bits per second, is never as high as the protocol's specification. In the case of the collision-based protocols, it is easy to see that collisions cause a decrease in throughput because each computer must stop transmitting and restart after a short break, resulting in lost time and productivity.

Collisions are such a big problem with collision-based protocols that you rarely expect to get better than 40 percent of the promised throughput. A 10-Mbps Ethernet segment usually provides a transfer rate of 4 Mbps. Divide this number by eight to get bytes, subtract another five percent for protocol overhead and you will be lucky to see a 400 KB/sec transfer rate.

Not to worry, there are several things you can do to increase your throughput on Ethernet.

▼ **Reduce users per segment**   For starters, reduce the number of computers sharing the same Ethernet segment. This will reduce the potential for collisions and increase the success rate at which completed frames are transmitted onto the media.

■ **Decrease the length of your segment**   Shortening the physical media will decrease the detection and recovery time from a collision and will increase your throughput. When a computer at one end of the media wants to send a message, it places bits onto the wire one at a time until the entire frame is on the wire. If the media is long, it will take longer for the bits to travel the length of the wire, and longer for the collision to be detected than if the wire is very short.

▲ **Use duplexing and switches**   Traditionally Ethernet used what is called *half-duplexing,* meaning that a computer could not receive and send data at the same time. Now some network devices use full-duplex Ethernet, allowing for simultaneous sending and receiving of data, thus providing for faster throughput. Also, Ethernet switching helps to limit the chances for a collision by reducing the number of stations on a particular Ethernet segment. Many computers are connected to the same switch, and communicate with each other. Instead of everybody receiving everybody else's messages, and causing collisions, the switch keeps the messages separate from the other members of the switch unless the message is intended for one of them.

Optimizing Token-Passing Protocols

Both token-passing protocols and collision-based protocols benefit from having a small physical length. Surprisingly, increasing the number of active stations in token-ring networks has a different result than that of Ethernet.

▼ **Reduce the physical length of the ring**   Token-passing protocols, like collision based protocols, can be improved by reducing the physical size of the network (a ring in this case). The time a token spends traveling through the empty spaces between stations is time lost for transmitting useful data. By reducing the physical length between stations, you can cut down on the travel time between stations and, subsequently, improve utilization of the ring. In addition to improving utilization, the ring will appear to be faster as data is travelling around the ring in less time.

▲ **Increase the number of active stations**   As odd as it sounds (since the same is not true with Ethernet), you can increase your throughput utilization by increasing the number of active stations. Here is how it works: The time a token takes to travel to the next station is downtime for the ring, so it decreases throughput. Valuable time is further lost when the token travels to a station that has nothing to say. Even though the station doesn't add data to the ring, it still takes some of the token's time before it sends the token on its way around the ring. Therefore to get the most utilization (i.e., the time during which useful data is being transmitted) from your available bandwidth, every station should transmit data when it has the token. This way you can begin to approach the advertised throughput for your ring (usually 4 or16 Mbps.

Network Protocols

In the enterprise, Windows NT has to be able to communicate effectively with all sorts of computer systems, including legacy systems, the Internet, and even competitors' products that use proprietary protocols. Much of NT's acceptance into the enterprise will depend on how easily it can be integrated with existing hardware and network protocols.

As we saw in the previous section, physical layer protocols define how to communicate with the physical media. In turn, a network protocol helps one computer deliver a message to its intended recipient. This section gives an overview of the primary network layer protocols used in the NT networking environment, paying particular attention to TCP/IP, which is quickly becoming the protocol of choice for all networking.

TCP/IP

The Internet Protocol (IP) is the workhorse of what is now commonly called the TCP/IP Protocol Suite. All of the upper layer protocols in the upcoming list work through this IP layer of the stack. IP works at the network layer (layer 3) allowing lower layer protocols (the physical network layers) to communicate with higher layer protocols. IP provides the method to control the transmission of packets from one computer to another. However, it does not provide for guaranteed delivery, flow control, or error recovery usually handled by the higher layers.

Because IP works at the network layer and up, it can work with Ethernet, Token Ring, FDDI, WANs, or all of these. TCP/IP is rapidly becoming the protocol of choice because of its efficiency and widespread acceptance among the PC and UNIX community. A few of the many protocols included in the TCP/IP protocol suite are listed here:

▼ **ARP**   Address Resolution Protocol

■ **FTP**   File Transfer Protocol

■ **HTTP**   Hypertext Transfer Protocol

■ **ICMP**   Internet Control Message Protocol

■ **IP**   Internet Protocol

■ **NFS**   Network File System

■ **RPC**   Remote Procedure Call

■ **SMTP**   Simple Mail Transfer Protocol

■ **SNMP**   Simple Network Management Protocol

■ **TCP**   Transmission Control Protocol

■ **Telnet**   Character oriented terminal emulation

■ **TFTP**   Trivial File Transfer Protocol

▲ **UDP**   User Datagram Protocol

Typically there is little to change about the IP protocol that will increase network performance. Most variables, such as frame size, are set by default to very reasonable values and do not need to be changed. Most TCP/IP optimization occurs at the level of the application (see the section "Optimizing Network Applications" later in this chapter) or with NT services using IP over the network (see "Optimizing Network-Related Services").

NetBEUI

NetBEUI is the Extended User Interface for NetBIOS, which is an older LAN protocol developed by IBM in the mid-1980s. NetBEUI provides a standard frame format for locating and communicating with other devices on the LAN by using NetBIOS machine names. Each device on the LAN is given a NetBIOS name consisting of no more than 15 characters that NT uses to identify your computer. When a computer has data it needs to send to another device on the LAN, it broadcasts the specific NetBIOS name onto the LAN. Every computer on the LAN reads the broadcast packet, but only the device with the matching name responds. In this process, called *NetBIOS name resolution*, the receiving device sends its hardware name to the source device so the two computers can communicate directly.

Although the protocol lends itself to being very quick on a small network, as the size of the network grows and more devices attempt NetBIOS name resolution, this broadcast methodology can quickly consume the available bandwidth. This is especially harmful when networks are connected over slower wide area network (WAN) links.

Since NetBEUI uses broadcasts to resolve names, networks with more than a few users can easily clog the system with broadcasts. Called a *broadcast storm*, this type of clog is common in large networks that use protocols to broadcast messages to all their users. Although NetBEUI is easy to set up with Windows, it is so chatty that only the smallest of networks should use it.

Fortunately, NetBEUI is not routable so the broadcasts stop when they encounter a router producing the undesirable condition of isolating all the computers on that segment from the rest of the network. To enable routing of NetBIOS, TCP/IP or IPX can be used to wrap around the NetBEUI packets before placing them on the network. As you will see in the next section, Windows NT uses NetBIOS over TCP/IP (NBT) to run on a routed TCP/IP network.

NetBIOS over TCP/IP

Since NetBIOS uses common names for addressing, and IP uses numbers, there needs to be a way to map the two so they are compatible. The NetBIOS over TCP/IP service is used to resolve NetBIOS names to IP addresses, and vice versa.

NAME MAPPING   Windows Internet Naming System (WINS) is one of several ways to associate an IP address with a NetBIOS name. When you configure TCP/IP on NT systems, you can enter the IP addresses of WINS servers so your system knows how to reach them even if they are on different subnets. The WINS database is then populated by the clients.

Another way to associate an IP address with a NetBIOS name is through the LMHOSTS or HOSTS files (located in the %SYSTEMROOT%\System32\drivers\etc directory). These files must be updated manually as the IP address mappings change, and the chore can become quite tedious as more computers are added to the system even if you use automatic scripting routines.

THE NBTSTAT COMMAND   There are times when it becomes essential to have static mapping in a computer. To help troubleshoot NetBIOS name resolution problems, NT has a useful command-line tool called NBTStat that has the following arguments:

▼ **nbtstat –n**   Displays NetBIOS names that were registered locally by the system using the server or redirector services

■ **nbtstat –c**   Lists the IP address mapping name that is cached in the system

■ **nbtstat –R**   Causes the system to purge the cache and reload it from the LMHOSTS file (only entries with the #pre designator in the LMHOSTS file are reloaded automatically)

■ **nbtstat –a <name>**   Returns the NetBIOS name table for the computer <name> as well as the MAC address of its NIC

▲ **nbtstat –S**   Lists the current NetBIOS sessions, their status, and some basic statistics

You can find more information about NBTStat by typing **nbtstat /?** at the command prompt.

IPX/SPX

Novell's IPX/SPX is another popularly used protocol. The Internetwork Packet Exchange/Sequenced Packet Exchange (IPX/SPX) is used within NetWare for file and print sharing.

SPX operates on the transport layer (layer 4) of the OSI model, and ensures the reliability of the end-to-end communication link. Although SPX guarantees packet delivery and sequencing, it does not play a direct role in packet routing. IPX operates at the network layer (layer 3) of the OSI model and handles the addressing of network devices, keeps track of the routes within the IPX network, and identifies and locates all the services available on the IPX network.

Unlike NetBEUI, IPX is a routable network protocol. Routing protocols help to keep track of other IPX network locations and provide the best route for data to travel between two network devices.

The Service Advertising Protocol (SAP at layer 5) enables networked devices, such as network servers and routers, to exchange information about available services in an IPX network. Like NetBEUI, SAP messages (SAPs) are used to advertise their services and network addresses to workstations that need access to particular addresses and services.

Since SAPs are broadcast onto the network every 60 seconds, they can become a problem as the network grows. In larger networks, it is advantageous to filter SAPs at the routers so their broadcasts do not bog down the network.

SNMP and MIBs

The Simple Network Management Protocol (SNMP) runs at the application layer (layer 6) of the OSI model, and is used to manage TCP/IP-based networks and gather statistics on how the network is being used. Usually, an application queries SNMP agents for information from other SNMP-enabled network devices. The most common SNMP queries are listed in Table 5-1.

SNMP Query	Description
Get Request	Retrieves the values of specific MIB variables from an SNMP agent
Get-Next Request	Retrieves the next instance of information for a particular variable or device
Set Request	Alters the value of objects that can be written to the MIB
Get Response	Contains the values of the requested variables
Trap	Contains information about an event that caused an unsolicited message from an SNMP agent

Table 5-1. Common SNMP Queries

A Management Information Base (MIB) is used to keep statistics on how SNMP agents are being used. The MIB provides a standard representation on the information available to the SNMP agent and where it is stored. For easy analysis and reporting, the SNMP application keeps a database of all its managed SNMP agents and the information extracted from the MIBs.

POLLING INTERVALS   SNMP agents help you manage your network, but they can become part of the problem if their numbers grow too large. As the number of SNMP agents being managed in a network increases, the amount of overhead for network management may become excessive. To reduce the amount of information transferred from the SNMP agents to the centralized database, increase the *polling interval* between each SNMP request. You can further reduce network traffic generated by SNMP agents by directing them to only report when an unusual event has occurred. You might, for example, use frequent reporting at first to generate your baseline, then set traps on the SNMP agents to report only when a specific threshold, such as percent utilization, has been exceeded.

SNMP WITH NT   Windows NT has built-in support to act as an SNMP agent. In this case, the SNMP service accesses the Registry on the local machine and converts this information into a MIB that can be queried by standard SNMP managers.

Here are some examples of the MIBs you can use as they may contain extensive amounts of information:

▼ **Internet MIB-II**   Defines objects used for fault analysis as defined in RFC 1213

■ **LAN Manager MIB-II**   Defines objects used for user and logon information

■ **Microsoft DHCP Server MIB**   Contains information about the use of the DHCP server

■ **Microsoft Internet Information Server MIB**   Defines statistics describing the use of the HTTP, Gopher, and FTP servers

▲ **Microsoft WINS Server MIB**   Defines statistics and database information about the use of the WINS Server

The Windows NT Server Resource Kit CD contains the definition files for these MIBs and two applications that you can use to enable an NT system to act as an SNMP manager: SNMPutil.exe and SNMPmon.exe.

You can export Performance Monitor counters to a MIB using a utility called Perf2MIB.exe. This utility, found in the NT Resource Kit, allows you to create MIBs based only on the counters you specify.

NOTE: More information about SNMP can be found in the Internet Engineering Task Force (IETF) Request for Comments (RFCs) 1155, 1157, and 1213.

Network Hardware

It is often the case that there is not a lot to configure when it comes to networking hardware. Basically you buy a machine that has certain specifications, plug it in, and let it run. This applies more to "dumb" devices such as simple bridges and repeaters. However, more intelligent devices such as routers can be configured, and some configurations lend themselves to faster throughput than others. But perhaps the biggest optimization you can make with networking hardware is using the appropriate hardware in a solid network design. This section describes the basic technologies that comprise the network infrastructure necessary for proper deployment in your network.

Bridges and Repeaters

The physical size of any network is limited, because the quality of electrical signals tend to weaken as the length of the wire increases. A simple device called a *repeater* is used to amplify the electrical signals and to extend the size of a segment. Repeaters take packets from one Ethernet segment and regenerate them onto an adjoining Ethernet segment. They operate only at the physical layer (layer one) of the

OSI model, and they make no decisions based on the content of the packet. They simply repeat all packets on the segment.

They also allow you to add more stations to an Ethernet segment. However, be aware of the problems associated with overloading the segment with too many stations as discussed previously.

BRIDGES BLOCK BROADCASTS   Bridges operate at layer two of the OSI model, the data link layer. They make intelligent decisions about packet forwarding based on information in the data link header of the packet. Therefore, they do not automatically re-transmit broadcasts from one segment to another. Instead they only forward frames that are destined for workstations on other segments. Bridges can join segments of a similar topology, such as Token Ring or Ethernet, or can be used for *translational bridging* by bridging two LAN segments of different topologies, such as connecting a Token Ring segment to an Ethernet segment.

Switches

Switches operate on the same basic principles as bridges, although switches typically are faster than traditional bridges and offer a higher number of ports that can be made up of different topologies. We now see switches with combinations of Token Ring, Ethernet (10, 100, 1,000 Mbps), FDDI, and Asynchronous Transfer Mode (ATM), although very few switches incorporate all these topologies in the same switch.

SWITCHES ARE FAST   Switches contain ports where you can connect either a dedicated device or a shared media LAN. Dedicated devices can often run in full-duplex mode, because there is no other traffic on the link to contend with, effectively doubling the throughput of the topology. For example, a 10-Mbps Ethernet port can theoretically run at 20 Mbps if it is running in full-duplex mode, allowing you to connect other switches, routers, or heavily used servers as dedicated devices. Routers, however, use software to determine the port that the traffic will be sent out on and, thus, are inherently slower than switches that perform these sorts of decisions in hardware.

Switches allow you to logically group different switch ports to form virtual LANs (VLANs), giving network administrators some flexibility in creating workgroups or managing broadcast domains. A manager can control which LANs are directly connected to other LANs.

Switches can vary tremendously on the speed of their ports and the speed of the switching fabric. Therefore, evaluate the amount of traffic on each port in both incoming and outgoing directions before implementing a switch. The switching fabric is the internal speed of the switch that must keep up with the incoming information and send it out of the switch without delay. For example, switches often have several 100-Mbps ports and several 10-Mbps ports. You obviously would not want to place a 100-Mbps device onto a 10-Mbps port, or vice versa.

Routers

Routers are "intelligent" networking components that work at the network layer, or layer three, of the OSI model. They implement routing techniques to determine the best path between a source and destination, and to forward packets between them. To do this, a router has memory to store the routing table and a processor to run the software that examines each packet as it is coming through. The router opens each packet and examines its destination address. Looking the address up on the routing table tells the router which port the packet should be sent out on. The ports are always different segments, and may use different physical protocols such as FDDI or Ethernet.

ROUTERS ADD FUNCTIONALITY   In addition to keeping broadcasts contained to a single segment, routers also incorporate many other features to enhance the stability and security of the network. They often come with redundant power supplies, have complete MIBs containing information about traffic patterns and errors, and can include access lists to control data that is put onto or taken off of the network.

Routers, unlike some of the other hardware products mentioned, have sophisticated configurations that are vendor-specific, and somewhat complicated. Apply these configurations with a good dose of common sense when optimizing your networking infrastructure.

Here are a few recommendations you should apply to your router configurations:

▼ **Activate only the ports that you are using.**   Unused ports sap CPU cycles and pose a security risk.

■ **Activate only the protocols that you are using.**   Tighten up security by not burdening the router's CPU with unused routing or network protocols.

▲ **Use access lists only if necessary.**   Although access lists provide a useful security filter for your traffic, they are CPU- and memory-intensive. You might implement access lists only on the routers at the border of your network.

Starting with a good network design and using high-quality, reliable components will help you ensure optimal throughput from your network infrastructure. If possible, it is an especially good idea to use equipment from the same manufacturer for maximum compatibility.

Some networking hardware vendors and their contacts are listed in Table 5-2.

Device	Company	Type	Contact Information
Network Interface Cards (NICs)	3Com	Ethernet	http://www.3com.com
	Adaptec	ATM, Ethernet	http://www.adaptec.com
	IBM	ATM, Ethernet, Token Ring	http://www.networking.ibm.com
	Madge	Token Ring	http://www.madge.com
	Olicom	ATM, Ethernet, Token Ring	http://www.olicom.com
Hubs	3Com	Ethernet	http://www.3com.com

Table 5-2.   Network Hardware Vendors

Device	Company	Type	Contact Information
	Accton Technology	Ethernet	http://www.accton.com
	Bay Networks	Ethernet, Token Ring	http://www.baynetworks.com
	Cabletron	Ethernet, Token Ring	http://www.cabletron.com
	Cisco	Ethernet, FDDI	http://www.cisco.com
	Hewlett-Packard	FDDI, Ethernet	http://www.hp.com
	IBM	Ethernet, Token Ring	http://www.networking.ibm.com
	Intel	Ethernet	http://www.intel.com
Switches	3Com	Fast Ethernet, Gigabit Ethernet, Token Ring, ATM, FDDI	http://www.3com.com
	Bay Networks	Fast Ethernet, Token Ring, ATM, FDDI	http://www.baynetworks.com
	Cabletron	Fast Ethernet, Gigabit Ethernet, Token Ring, ATM, FDDI	http://www.cabletron.com
	Cisco	Fast Ethernet, Gigabit Ethernet, Token Ring, FDDI, ATM	http://www.cisco.com
	Extreme Networks	Fast Ethernet, Gigabit Ethernet	http://www.extremenetworks.com
	Hewlett-Packard	Fast Ethernet, ATM, FDDI	http://www.hp.com

Table 5-2. Network Hardware Vendors (*continued*)

Device	Company	Type	Contact Information
	IBM	Fast Ethernet, Token Ring, ATM, FDDI	http://www.networking.ibm.com
	Newbridge Networks	Fast Ethernet, Gigabit Ethernet, FDDI, ATM, Token Ring	http://www.newbridge.com
Routers	3Com	Fast Ethernet, Token Ring, FDDI	http://www.3com.com
	Ascend	Fast Ethernet, FDDI	http://www.ascend.com
	Bay Networks	Fast Ethernet, Token Ring, FDDI	www.baynetworks.com
	Cabletron	Ethernet, Token Ring	http://www.cabletron.com
	Cisco	Fast Ethernet, FDDI, Token Ring	http://www.cisco.com
	Extreme Networks	Fast Ethernet, Gigabit Ethernet	http://extremenetworks.com

Table 5-2.   Network Hardware Vendors (*continued*)

FINDING AND REMOVING NETWORK BOTTLENECKS

Every network connection has a bottleneck—a piece of hardware or software that limits the flow of information being sent from one computer to another. It is the goal of the network administrator to find and eliminate the most pervasive bottlenecks. Sometimes time and money limit the network engineer from eliminating bottlenecks, but usually the problem is a lack of knowledge and of the ability to locate bottlenecks. This section outlines some basic steps you can follow to prevent creating bottlenecks in your network, and explains how to properly identify and eliminate them.

Network Design Considerations

The network design should be reviewed for any possible bottlenecks even before the first packet travels across a network. More often than not, a basic understanding of the hardware components—and a dose of common sense—will guide you in proper network design. Nonetheless, here are a few points to remember when evaluating a network design.

▼ **Put similar pipes together.** Do not force a 100-Mbps Ethernet segment into a 10-Mbps port on a router. This example illustrates the importance of being familiar with your hardware's capabilities, and can save you time and money by helping you to eliminate mismatched pieces.

■ **LANs are rarely the bottleneck.** Even though 80 percent of network traffic is usually local and 20 percent is destined for remote sites, most often the bottleneck in your network will be your Wide Area Network (WAN) links. Focus your attention on optimizing the WAN, because WAN speeds are often much lower than typical LAN speeds, and purchasing a WAN link with LAN speeds is prohibitive.

■ **Familiarize yourself with your network's traffic patterns.** Knowing how much information is being moved around your network, and knowing the source and destination of the traffic, will be of tremendous help in finding future bottlenecks. For example, a server farm located on a 10-Mbps segment might normally be a flag for an upgrade—unless *you* know that those servers are rarely used and that 10 Mbps easily fulfills their demands.

▲ **Monitor, monitor, monitor.** To successfully optimize any network, you must be constantly watching the traffic patterns, hardware usage, and application response times. The next section provides a description on how to use tools to monitor some of the more crucial statistics.

Performance Monitor Counters

In NT network environments, network bottlenecks usually reside in the network hardware or at the servers. You can use the Performance Monitor to help locate the bottleneck and take corrective measures. Refer to Chapter 8 for more information about using the Performance Monitor.

Network Performance

Client-server programs operate in a request/answer paradigm. The client computer sends a request to a server, and the server provides an answer to the client. Most NT functions operate in this regard although any NT system can act as the server or the client. Workstation and Server are the two services providing this functionality to NT systems, and monitoring these services can be quite useful.

▼ **Workstation service (Redirector)**   The Redirector (RDR.SYS) transmits requests destined for servers onto the physical network.

▲ **Server service**   The Server service (SRV.SYS) receives the incoming requests and passes them up into the NT system.

NOTE: NT has built in an efficient auto tuning mechanism for these services so it is not recommended that you edit the Registry manually to change their settings.

THE REDIRECTOR SERVICE   Typically, a bottleneck will not be at the client, although this is not always the case. The Redirector service helps connect clients to servers, and has several counters that you can monitor to gauge its use. One of the more useful counters is the Redirector: Bytes Total/sec, which represents the total bytes for the client. To get a more global picture of network utilization, you can use the Network Monitor tool included with NT Server and SMS, as covered in more detail in the next section. The Network Monitor will tell you the current utilization percentage and the type of packet.

Remember that on collision-based networks, you should not let this value exceed 40 percent.

Another counter to watch is the Redirector: Current Commands counter. This counter describes the length of the queue for frames waiting to get on the network segment. The value increases when there is a delay in placing frames onto the network, which may indicate a bottleneck inside the computer. This value should not get much larger than the number of NICs installed in the computer.

THE SERVER SERVICE   The Server service receives requests for work, and its ability to keep up with the request can be monitored via the Server: Work Item Shortages counter. This counter advances when the Server service denies work requests because it is too busy. Naturally, if this counter continues to increase above a value of one, you have a serious resource shortage at that computer. Review the use of disk resources as well as CPU utilization to further pinpoint the bottleneck.

The number of failed memory allocations, from either the physical memory or the paged memory, is recorded in the Server: Pool Nonpaged Failures and Server: Pool Paged Failures counters. Normally these values should hover around zero. If you have excessive errors, it is a result of running low on resources, especially memory. To resolve this bottleneck, you can add more physical RAM.

Capacity Planning with the Performance Monitor

To get ahead of your network problems, it is useful to monitor network resources for potential shortages or future bottlenecks, and the Performance Monitor can help with this task. The key counters listed in Table 5-3 cover the essential bases, including the network segments, memory, hard drive space, and processor utilization on servers. You might find it useful to watch only a few counters at a time, as the amount of data to observe and store can become quite large when so many counters are active.

The Performance Monitor counters can be set to alert you if an event occurs, thereby reducing the amount of unnecessary information

Object	Counter
LogicalDisk	% Free Space
Memory	Pages/sec
Network Segment	% Network Utilization, Total bytes received/sec
Paging File	% Usage Peak
PhysicalDisk	% Disk Time, Avg. Disk Queue Length
Processor	% Processor Time

Table 5-3.   Performance Counters for Capacity Planning

that you may receive. For example, you could have the Performance Monitor send you an alert if the Network Segment: % Network Utilization exceeded 30 or 40 percent on a crucial Ethernet segment. For more information on sending Performance Monitor alerts, refer to Chapter 8.

Network Monitoring Utilities

Collecting network traffic is not as mysterious as most people believe. You do not need special hardware other than a computer and a Network Interface Card (NIC) that operates in *promiscuous mode,* meaning that the card does not discard traffic messages destined for other computers. To receive data from SNMP agents, you will need special software to coordinate the communication process for you.

Tools

For the sake of simplicity we are going to break network monitoring devices into two overlapping groups: network analyzers and network probes. For basic network utilization measurements you will only need to use network , but both will be covered here.

NETWORK ANALYZERS   Network analyzers are primarily used for troubleshooting because they work at the lower two layers of the OSI model, the physical and data link layers, and they sometimes contain SNMP support for remote management. Analyzers allow you to capture detailed statistics about the number and types of frames that are currently coursing through the network. When used in troubleshooting, network engineers look for collisions, beaconing Token Ring stations (indicating a problem with a neighbor), and percent utilization. They can also peer into each frame on the network and read its contents, which occasionally hold nuggets of useful information about a user or an application to help you resolve a problem. Obviously this ability poses a security risk, because protocols that send information in clear text format such as FTP are considered unsecured. You can easily use an analyzer to capture an FTP session and read the username and password from inside the frame.

Analyzers have uses other than just snooping around frames, such as recording network traffic and playing it back to the network at a later time. This can be quite useful when you want to test how other systems react to a specific request and you want control over the request. Additionally, you can play back a high-volume traffic capture to stress test your systems and determine the exact level when traffic breaks down.

Because you can filter traffic based on host or destination addresses, analyzers can be used to capture a single traffic conversation between two machines. We will use this feature later to test an application's performance on the network.

NETWORK PROBES   Network probes provide added functionality by gathering information about higher layers in the OSI model, and are usually more permanent fixtures. Probes are very often PCs with probe software installed on them, or they can be separate hardware devices that are smaller than PCs and have no monitor or keyboard attached to them. Either way, they sit quietly attached to the network gathering network statistics. Administration is done remotely, via a serial port connected to the back of the probe or on the probe console if there is one available. Although they are not used to read the contents of packets, they can give you information about network layer protocols such as how much of your traffic is IP vs. IPX. Table 5-4 lists some vendors for both network analyzers and probes.

Company/Product	Solution Format	Type	Contact
Ascend/ NetClarity	Software	Probe	http://www.ascend.com
Bay Networks/ StackProbe	Software and hardware	Probe	http://www.baynetworks.com
Compuware/ EcoScope	Software	Probe	http://www.compuware.com
HP/Network Node Manager for NT	Software	Probe	http://www.hp.com/openview
NetScout Systems	Software and hardware	Probe	http://www.netscout.com
Cinco Networks/ NetXRay	Software	Analyzer	http://www.cinco.com
Digitech Industries/ WAN900	Software and hardware	Analyzer	http://www.digitechinc.com
LANQuest/ Frame Thrower	Software and hardware	Analyzer	http://www.lanquest.com
Network General/ Distributed Sniffer System	Software and hardware	Analyzer	http://www.ngc.com

Table 5-4. Third-Party Network Probes and Analyzers

Company/Product	Solution Format	Type	Contact
RadCom/ RC-155-c ATM Traffic Generator/ Analyzer	Software and hardware	Analyzer	http://www.radcom-inc.com
Xyratex/ Gigabit Ethernet Protocol Analyzer	Software and hardware	Analyzer	http://www.xyratex.com

Table 5-4. Third-Party Network Probes and Analyzers (*continued*)

The Microsoft Network Monitor

As mentioned earlier, you do not need a special system to monitor network traffic, and you may already have what it takes right on your computer. Windows NT Server comes with a network monitoring tool, called the Network Monitor. The version of Network Monitor bundled with NT Server allows you to capture traffic coming from or destined to the machine you are running it on. However, the version that ships with SMS can monitor all stations using that segment. See Chapter 14 for more information about SMS.

The first component to be installed is called the Network Monitor Agent; it is available with NT Workstation and Server. Once installed, it allows a Microsoft Network Monitor Tool (running on NT Server) to monitor the traffic that the Agent sees. This is one way to circumvent the limitation of only being able to install the Network Monitor Tool on an NT Server. When both components are installed on an NT Server, it is called the Network Monitor Tools and Agent.

The Microsoft Network Monitor is a powerful tool you can use to help optimize your network. It can track packets up to the network layer, perform filters on stations or protocols, and conduct packet analysis. To start the Network Monitor, click Network Monitor from the Administrative Tools menu. You will be prompted to select an agent if your local agent is not running. To connect to an agent running on another system, click Capture, Networks and then select the computer running the Monitoring Agent. Note that you will need to have administrative rights on both machines to do this.

Once the Network Monitor has connected to an active agent, you will see the main Capture window. Click the Capture button and statistics will start to accumulate, as shown in Figure 5-2, for two computers, "Net Server" and "Net Client."

This window contains information on the utilization of the network. Network Monitor continuously captures traffic until the user-defined buffer is filled up. Subsequently, newly arrived packets overwrite older packets. You can watch the statistics change over time, or stop the capture to view individual packets.

From the Capture menu, click the Stop and View item. This will end the capture and bring up the packet analysis window, as shown in Figure 5-3. Double-clicking a particular frame will open it and display the contents for you.

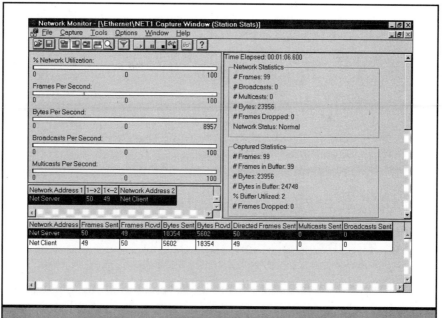

Figure 5-2.   Capturing frames between two machines

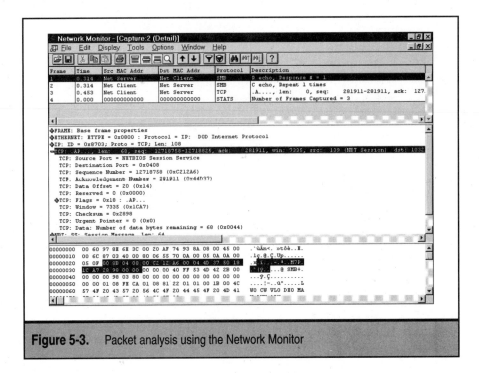

Figure 5-3. Packet analysis using the Network Monitor

A tremendous amount of detail can be gleaned from the analysis of the Network Monitor at the general statistics level and at the individual packet level. Monitoring general use of the network segment is most useful for overall network optimization. Some statistics reported by Network Monitor to keep an eye on include:

▼ % Network Utilization

■ Broadcast per Second

■ Multicasts per Second

▲ Number of Dropped Frames

TCP/IP Optimization

To tune your TCP/IP network you will need to familiarize yourself with some of NT's built-in TCP/IP commands. The more useful commands are listed in Table 5-5.

Command-line Tool	Description
arp	Allows you to view and modify the Address Resolution Protocol table. This table shows the TCP/IP numerical address to hardware address comparison.
ipconfig	Displays the current TCP/IP configuration and allows you to update or release DHCP configuration values. This is a quick way to view the IP address and the gateway address for a computer.
nbtstat	Displays the NetBIOS over TCP/IP connections, reloads the LMHOSTS cache, and determines the registered name and scope ID. As described earlier, this command can save you time troubleshooting LMHOST file entries.
netstat	Displays IP information including active ports, routing tables, and other statistics.
net statistics	Lists basic statistics about general network traffic. Lists statistics for the Server or Workstation services on that computer.
nslookup	Queries DNS servers for host aliases, services, and record information. Checks the DNS and name resolution processes.
ping	Sends echo requests to target workstations. The ubiquitous utility is used to gauge the most basic connectivity between two computers.
route	Used to add, change, or view the current route table. A powerful command to enter static routes if your NT system has at least two NICs and is acting as a router.
tracert	Determines and lists the hops to the target workstation. You can view which computers and routers your traffic has taken to the destination machine.

Table 5-5. TCP/IP Command-line Tools

More information can be found for each of these commands by typing the command followed by **/?** at the command prompt. For example, to learn more about the NBTStat command, you would type

```
nbtstat /?
```

You would then see the following description of how to use nbtstat:

```
Displays protocol statistics and current TCP/IP connections
using NBT(NetBIOS over TCP/IP).

NBTSTAT [-a RemoteName] [-A IP address] [-c] [-n]
        [-r] [-R] [-s] [-S] [interval] ]
  -a   (adapter status) Lists the remote machine's name
                        table given its name
  -A   (Adapter status) Lists the remote machine's name
                        table given its IP address.
  -c   (cache)          Lists the remote name cache
                        including the IP addresses
  -n   (names)          Lists local NetBIOS names.
  -r   (resolved)       Lists names resolved by broadcast
                        and via WINS
  -R   (Reload)         Purges and reloads the remote
                        cache name table
  -S   (Sessions)       Lists sessions table with the
                        destination IP addresses
  -s   (sessions)       Lists sessions table converting
                        destination IP addresses to host
                        names via the hosts file.

  RemoteName            Remote host machine name.
  IP address            Dotted decimal representation of
                        the IP address.
  interval              Redisplays selected statistics,
                        pausing interval seconds
                        between each display. Press Ctrl+C
                        to stop redisplaying
                        statistics.
```

OPTIMIZING NETWORK APPLICATIONS

To get the most out of your network, it is only natural to optimize application traffic, which will usually make up the majority of network traffic. Whether you are testing a prepackaged application (such as Microsoft Word) before deploying it on your network, or evaluating an in-house application, the basic question you want to answer is the same: How will the application behave in a networked environment? To answer this question, it would be wise to build a laboratory network away from the production network to analyze applications that may one day flow through your network. If you do not have the budget to build a laboratory network, you will have to test applications on the production network. Unfortunately, the production network environment is not as controlled as a lab, and testing could disrupt your production services.

Setting Up a Test Network

A simple design for a test network is illustrated in Figure 5-4. The cloud shape represents a WAN link, a router connection, or perhaps other devices that emulate the production network. If you are testing on your production network, just replace the cloud with all devices in your network between the client and server computers. At one end of the test network is a server computer, and at the other end is a

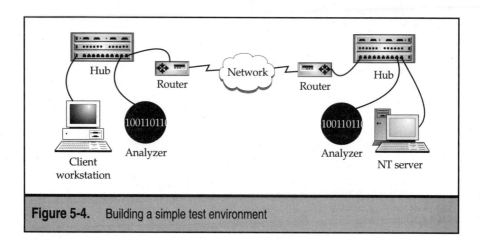

Figure 5-4.   Building a simple test environment

client computer. Network analyzers are placed at each end of the network, one on each network segment, and will be used to monitor the conversation and record precisely when packets leave and arrive at the two computers.

Running a Test

The object of testing an application for the network is to record a conversation and track the number and timing of packets that are sent between two computers, usually a server and a client, during a typical application function. For example, if you are going to test a database application, you might run several tests, one for each of the main types of application function, such as a database query, a record save, or edit a previous record.

Follow these steps when running a test:

1. Configure the analyzers to only capture packets from the client and server computers by filtering out all other stations.

2. Coordinate the analyzers to start capturing packets at the same time.

3. Use the client to perform an application function, thereby requesting information from the server.

4. Stop capturing when the function is complete.

5. Repeat these steps for each different type of function.

When you are finished, you will have a collection of analyzer trace files holding the packets used for each function in each direction. Using a simple spreadsheet, you can organize the data to highlight the number of packets travelling in each direction, as well as the number of delays at each computer and on the network. Obviously, it is essential to keep track of each analyzer and its respective files and transactions. Currently, there are no commercial programs available to run analysis automatically, so you will have to do most of this organization by hand. Therefore, it make sense to keep the analysis as simple as possible.

Analyzing the Results

To keep track of the different types of results, use the following variables:

- ▼ *Pkt*   The size of the packet (bits, b)
- ■ *BW*   The bandwidth of the network connection (bps)
- ■ *RT*   The round trip network delay (seconds, sec)
- ■ P_c The processing time of the client (sec)
- ▲ P_s The processing time of the server (sec)

Figure 5-5 schematically illustrates the traffic flow from the server to the client and back again during a simple conversation. In this

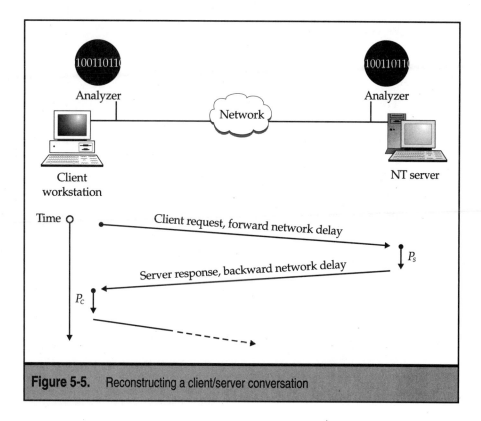

Figure 5-5.   Reconstructing a client/server conversation

figure, the client initiates the conversation by sending a request packet to the server, which will arrive after a short network delay. The server does some internal processing for a length of time (P_s) and returns a reply to arrive at the client after a second network delay, producing a total round trip (RT) delay. The client then performs a processing task for a given length of time (P_c) and the process begins again. This set of simple numbers can be used to describe the application properties.

All these numbers are available to you because you recorded the conversation between the two computers with two analyzers. Unless the analyzers are time-synchronized, however, you can only use this method to determine the one-way network delay. The analyzer clocks are offset by some unknown period of time, and only tell you when packets arrive using an absolute internal time. Because the internal clocks are probably off by some unknown value, you cannot be certain that the delay between one packet leaving at three seconds and arriving at five seconds is actually two seconds.

Recording the *total* round trip delay from the client analyzer is the first step towards determining the round trip delay of the network. This is the amount of time it took from when the packet was sent out to when the reply was sent back. Next, subtract the processing time of the server from the total round trip delay to determine the round trip *network* delay. The server processing time is the time elapsed from when the analyzer saw the request enter the server to when the analyzer saw the reply leave the server.

How can you use these numbers to optimize applications? First of all, to be a little more precise, you should better define the processing times of the client and server, P_c and P_s. The processing time is measured by analyzers that are already on the wire or network, and includes the time it takes for the computer to place and read the packet on the wire. The time it takes to place a packet on the wire and pull it off the wire is $2 \times Pkt/BW$. Therefore, to get the correct client and server processing times, you must subtract the delays as follows:

$$P_c = P_{c\,(measured)} - (2 \times Pkt/BW_c)$$

$$P_s = P_{s\,(measured)} - (2 \times Pkt/BW_s)$$

Now for the really useful part. You can put all these variables together in a single variable that describes the rate at which the application is running on the network. This variable is called the *application rate (AppRate)*, and it is measured in bits per second:

$$AppRate = \frac{Pkt}{RT + P_c + \dfrac{2Pkt}{BW_c} + P_s + \dfrac{2Pkt}{BW_s}}$$

Although this equation is illustrated for use on a single transaction, it is easy to imagine how the equation could be extrapolated or generalized for a whole application. The basic goal is to maximize the AppRate value for every network application so that it has low latency and appears faster to your users. The following are some general rules to help increase the AppRate.

For the Application Designer:

▼ Decrease the client and server processing time, P_c, P_s.

■ Reduce the number of packets used.

▲ Make the packet larger (*Pkt*) instead of having several small packets.

For the Network Designer:

▼ Increase the bandwidth (*BW*) to reduce the time it takes to place and read data from the wire.

▲ Reduce the network delays (*RT*) as much as possible.

Using the AppRate equation will help you pinpoint the bottleneck, usually found in the network delay (*RT*), that prevents your applications from running faster. This variable is very complicated because it involves every piece of hardware that transports the conversation and all the other traffic that was present at the time of the conversation. Nonetheless, narrowing your bottleneck down to the physical network has eliminated the application, the client computer, the server computer, and their immediate network connections as the source of delays. To further delve into the delays found on the network it is very useful to run the simulations described in the upcoming section, "Proactive Planning."

OPTIMIZING NETWORK-RELATED SERVICES

As mentioned before, many of Windows NT's network components are made more efficient through initial network design rather than by haphazardly attempting to tweak performance through the Registry. This section examines how to properly integrate DNS and WINS name services to increase name resolution.

DNS

With the advent of larger networks and booming use of the Internet, naming services are becoming more and more important. A faulty naming service can prevent workstations from seeing computers found locally on their segment either through broadcasts or cached names. Workstations are also unable to see computers that have an IP to other name mapping sites defined in their HOSTS of LMHOSTS files. Updating these files can become administratively unfeasible as the number of workstations grows.

Designing DNS for Speed

Implementing and optimizing DNS on a network starts with careful planning. Part of the process should include a detailed review and documentation of the existing network infrastructure. At a minimum, you should assess the following items:

▼ The total number of nodes on the network

■ The capacity and reliability of WAN circuits

■ The topology of network backbones

■ The type of Internet connectivity

- The type of firewall(s) used to secure the network

- The geographical and business layout of the organization

- The NT domain architecture

- The existing WINS architecture

- The type of client workstations on the network

- The availability of DHCP and the number of nodes using it

- The TCP/IP addressing scheme currently in place

▲ The availability of DNS servers at your ISP

Having this information on hand before you begin to design your DNS service strategy will greatly help you create an optimized naming solution. The following points should receive specific attention.

DOMAINS   DNS can be divided into domains and subdomains to serve naming requests. Plan now for the correct number of domains and subdomains, because this aspect of the design is more difficult to change later. If you have too many domains, you will have too many machines to administer. If there are too few, then requests from the users will overwhelm the DNS servers and cause considerable delays.

There are many factors to consider when deciding on the domain architecture.

▼ The number of nodes

- The number of remote sites with servers

- The available bandwidth between larger sites

▲ The company's geographical organization

REDUNDANT DNS   At a minimum you must have two DNS servers for each DNS domain or zone, thus eliminating a DNS server as a single point of failure for your network. These servers should always be placed in a secure environment with reliable power and network connectivity. For fault tolerance, you might consider locating the primary server and two or more secondary servers in different physical locations.

LOAD BALANCING DNS SERVERS   You will certainly want to balance the load of DNS traffic across several DNS servers, if they are available. This can be accomplished by alternately configuring NT systems to use one or the other DNS server, provided that you use static addressing instead of DHCP. If you use DHCP, alternate which DNS server is listed as the default DNS host in the DHCP scope definition to balance DNS server usage. Regularly monitor the DNS servers to ensure equal usage.

USING CACHING NAME SERVERS   Caching name servers can speed up name resolution especially when users must traverse a WAN link to reach the DNS server. To the client, a caching server looks like a DNS server, but it actually does nothing more than remember recent DNS queries and provide them to the client. If the client requests a name resolution that has not been queried recently, then the caching name server asks the primary DNS server for this information and then stores it in its memory. Caching servers are best deployed at sites that do not have a DNS server but have many clients using TCP/IP with only a slow WAN connection to the primary DNS server.

Figure 5-6 illustrates a typical DNS architecture using both primary and multiple secondary servers. In addition, a caching server is deployed at the large site containing local TCP/IP-based servers. You could configure the clients to use the two secondary servers, but not the primary when resolving names. This is done to reduce the load on the primary so additional secondary servers can be added to the environment as required. To increase capacity, additional secondary and/or caching servers can be deployed without having to redesign the DNS architecture.

Integrating DNS with WINS

To allow DNS to resolve NetBIOS names, Microsoft's DNS can be integrated with WINS. The performance of this exchange can be tuned using a couple of variables found in Microsoft's DNS Manager utility. Open the DNS Manager, right-click the zone you want to set,

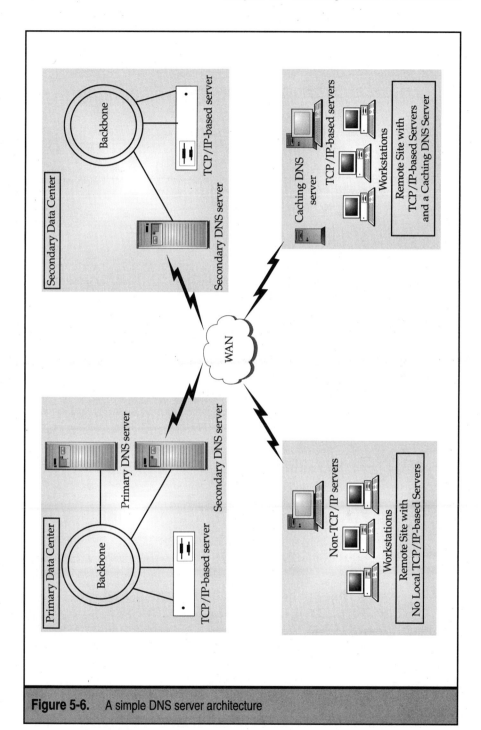

Figure 5-6.   A simple DNS server architecture

select Properties | WINS Lookup | Advanced. The window is shown here:

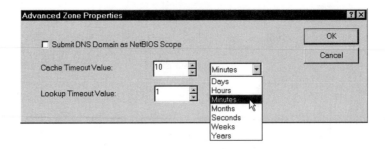

The first variable, the cache timeout value, sets the amount of time a particular query can be cached in the DNS server for reuse. The default value is ten minutes but can be increased if the WINS information changes infrequently. If you have an extremely high number of updates to WINS, the value should be set from 1 to 5 minutes.

The second variable is the lookup timeout value; it sets the amount of time the DNS server will wait for a response from the WINS server. Although the default is one second, if your closest WINS server resides over a slow, highly utilized WAN link, or if your WINS server is running at high utilization, you may need to set this value higher. This will prevent the DNS server from timing out while waiting for the WINS server.

The Future of DNS

Future releases of Microsoft's implementation of DNS will include the ability for dynamic updates (Dynamic DNS). Client machines will be able to register its host name with DNS just as they do with WINS today. This will greatly reduce the administration of IP addresses because it allows DNS to populate its host tables not only with static host entries, but also with host entries or workstations that have their IP addresses dynamically assigned using DHCP.

PROACTIVE PLANNING

The best way to optimize your network is not to tweak existing, ill-conceived network designs, but rather to design a network topology that will perform to its fullest from the start before deployment.

Planning for Success

A successful network design must start with a goal, such as providing server access to 5,000 users or dial-up access for 300 remote users. You will probably have budgetary constraints to work with, but even if you had unlimited funds, you should follow the following points when planning to upgrade a site:

▼   **Baseline your network usage.**   A baseline gives you a snapshot of network usage for certain links or components over a given period of time. A good baseline will watch most links at many different times in the day and throughout the week. Depending on how your organization functions, usage may be affected by the time of the month or even the time of the year. The baseline defines the absolute minimum of throughput requirements needed, and provides a starting point to help guide design and optimization of the network.

■   **Trend your usage.**   If a baseline is a snapshot, think of a trend as a movie. It will illustrate how your network is being utilized over time, usually up to the present. Values for trending can be obtained from the Performance Monitor or from a third-party network monitoring utility. These products generally store values for every day or week, and provide a graph showing usage of a link or computer resource during a specified time. Trending is especially important because it allows you to make a prediction about the future needs of your network resources. If, for example, you have had a 5 percent increase in network traffic over a specific WAN link during the one year, you can be reasonably certain this increase will continue. You can incorporate this data into your network design and plan for future increases.

▲ **Simulate your network.**   Although you can predict the need for network resources using trends, you cannot predict what will happen if you add more user segments, change the type of routers, or add a new application to the network. These sorts of questions can be answered in two ways: make the change on the production network and watch what happens, or make the change on a model of your network and watch what happens. The latter solution is cheaper, faster, and can help you keep your job.

Using Simulations to Optimize the Network

Simulators are software tools that allow you to test a model of your network under different designs or traffic loads. It becomes impossible to predict with any accuracy how network changes will affect the overall performance once the network grows too large. There are simply too many devices, too many routes, and too many traffic conversations going on simultaneously.

A good model of your network will incorporate many of its details such as router characteristics, frame relay properties, and traffic patterns. Because all models operate under the axiom "garbage in, garbage out," you must ensure that as much detail as possible has been included into the network model.

Simulators usually use an *analytical* or a *discrete* approach to modeling network traffic. Discrete-event simulation analyzes each packet to determine its behavior, and is usually slower than the analytical approach, which makes more assumptions about the traffic. However, some have argued that the analytical method is just as accurate as the discrete event method. Because of the long simulation time involved in using the discrete-event method, it is recommended that you use the analytical method of simulation for larger networks of more than 50 routers or switches.

Obviously, a model must include simplifications, but how do you know which aspects can be simplified without compromising the integrity of the model? This section outlines the simulation process and helps you understand where to make simplifications to your model.

Preparing to Simulate

Earlier in this chapter, you saw how to conduct a simple application analysis to determine how much traffic a given application generates on the network. This analysis was conducted in a test environment without all the nuances of a real production network. You need to run a simulation before you deploy your application, both to see how it will behave on your production network and to determine what changes must be made to the network in order to insure optimum application performance.

Network Topology

Before you can run a single simulation, you must create a representation of the production network, including the topology and the network traffic.

The *network topology* is the framework of the network, and refers to both the physical devices that comprise the network and their logical settings. Later you are going to add network traffic on top of this framework to emulate your production network.

Some physical devices that should be included in the representation of the network are:

- ▼ Routers
- ■ Computers
- ■ Switches
- ■ WAN links
- ■ LANs
- ▲ Point-to-point connections

Some logical parameters that must be considered are as follows:

▼ Interface settings on routers

■ LAN speeds

■ WAN speeds

■ Router capabilities (such as backplane speed)

■ Routing protocols

▲ Naming conventions

Fortunately, you do not need to enter all this information in manually. There are programs that use SNMP to query the devices and that can access information stored in the MIB to discover the physical and logical settings on your network.

Network Traffic

It is essential to model the network traffic in as much detail as is computationally possible, because the current applications will greatly impact the performance of any new applications. Capturing network traffic can be challenging, but can be accomplished by strategically placing network probes at locations where traffic either originates or terminates. Placing and managing many probes can be time-consuming and expensive, but there is currently no other method available for obtaining a snapshot of packets for your entire network.

The better probes obtain information about the traffic all the way up to the application layer, generating usage statistics based upon applications. Some things you should expect from your probes include:

▼ Network protocol

■ Application name

■ Source computer

■ Destination computer

■ Number of packets in each direction

■ Number of bytes in each direction

■ Latency for application

▲ Duration of conversation

Although you are going to use the traffic information to complete your model of the network, this information can also be used in other respects. For example, you can check the latency for applications to see if they are meeting a minimum quality of service, check how much throughput is being used by each application, investigate web usage, and more.

Increasing Simulation Speed

Running simulations of medium-sized networks, less than 50 routers or switches, is very computationally intensive, and can take hours even using the fastest processors due to the number of different conversations the probes will record during the sampling period. To increase simulation performance, you can remove or consolidate traffic conversations.

REDUCING CONVERSATIONS   Removing conversations will artificially reduce the amount of traffic represented in the model, and will ultimately prove to be undesirable. However, when you have multiple probes capturing simultaneously, some conversations will be picked up by more than one probe. The conversations are duplicates, and they must be removed. The management console that controls the probes usually removes the probes, but if not, then you should remove them yourself.

Conversations with small byte counts have a very small impact on the network, and can be removed without affecting the integrity of the model. You can probably remove 40 percent of the conversations and only lose about three percent of the network traffic, because many conversations are very small.

CONSOLIDATING CONVERSATIONS   Another method you can use to lower the number of total conversations, and make the simulator run faster, is to consolidate conversations that have the same source, destination, and are of the same application type. All packets and bytes are added to this consolidation so no traffic load is lost. You may want to define a specific timeframe that both conversations must reside in before consolidation. A simple utility can be created to perform this function. You will enjoy a 40-70 percent decrease in the number of conversations by eliminating small conversations and consolidating those that remain.

Running Simulations

At this point, you have a detailed description of the network traffic and the topological layout of your network incorporated into your model. Plus, you have taken measures to optimize the performance of the simulation by reducing the number of conversations that will run during the simulation. The next step is to run simulations. To start, you should have a specific question in mind, though most questions will relate to network optimization. Essentially you want to know how the performance, as measured by application response time for example, is effected when you make a change to the network. Some things you might change about the network include:

▼ Change or add WAN links or LANs

■ Change or add routers

■ Change routing protocols

■ Move servers or add servers

■ Move users or add users

▲ Add or remove an application

CONCLUSION

The network is an extremely important component for any environment, including Windows NT, because it serves as the backbone for communication. The concepts and considerations of the network appear to be overwhelming, and optimizing the network may even seem impossible. This chapter showed how you could demystify the complexity of the network by segmenting it into manageable sections. Then, the chapter examined how to design and tune these sections and finally piece them together to optimize the network as a whole.

CHAPTER 6

Optimizing the Disk Subsystem

Storage devices are vital components of Windows NT Server systems. They must not only house operating system and application code but also valuable data that your company depends on. How reliable the information is and how fast it can be retrieved are also key factors in Windows NT systems. The importance of the disk subsystem should be reflected in the configuration; by no means should you try to cut costs by purchasing lower-quality products.

Equally important to system reliability, availability, and operability is how well the disk subsystem performs under every imaginable condition the server may face. You should—and can—expect high-quality performance from the components that comprise the disk subsystem, even when server use is at its highest. To realistically obtain the best performance, you must look at the many factors that effect it. You must look at who manufactures the component, the type of drive, the type of controller, transfer rates, seek times, configurations, and much more. Get the best equipment that you can afford, and you have won half the battle.

While this chapter focuses on optimizing performance, it also sheds some light on the issues of fault tolerance. It also discusses the importance of striking a balance between fault tolerance and performance optimization. Unfortunately, it is extremely difficult to optimize performance and still maintain the most reliable configuration to protect against disaster. In reading this chapter, however, you will learn many ways to compromise without losing sight of either need.

DISK SUBSYSTEM DEVICES

One of the most important decisions you face when configuring a Windows NT Server is choosing the type of hardware components you will use for the disk subsystem. Your decision includes the drive type, disk controller type, and bus interface. As with many other components that make up a Windows NT system, there are plenty of choices. Thankfully, though, when it comes to performance and reliability, the choices for the disk subsystem hardware boil down to just a few.

This section focuses on the choices that you have for the type of disk drive your system will use. The other hardware components are discussed later in this chapter.

In the past several years, hard drives have undergone numerous changes that affect not only how much data you can store but, more importantly, the speed at which you can retrieve and use stored data. There are two types of drives that are currently still in the race for high performance: drives that use IDE/EIDE and SCSI interfaces. However, new standards, such as the Fibre Channel and FireWire technologies, which promise even greater performance enhancements, are just around the corner. This section examines the IDE/EIDE and SCSI interfaces and compares the two technologies. It also discusses some of the new technologies on the horizon.

Primary and Secondary Storage

Hard disk drives are the primary storage devices you will be most concerned with when it comes to performance. However, you should keep in mind that many forms of secondary storage devices offer storage alternatives as well as fault tolerance. These include tape drives, solid state drives (SSDs), removable drives, DVDs, and optical drives.

If you are considering SSDs, you should note that although this technology is rapidly improving and SSDs could potentially improve Windows NT disk subsystem performance, SSD technology is still relatively new, and some time will pass before they will be recommended for use with Windows NT Server systems. It is certainly too early to count SSDs out of the performance race because they are already boasting very fast access times and transfer rates. An SSD is essentially a RAM disk housed in its own casing, but instead of using the system's physical memory, SSDs commonly use Flash RAM or other high-speed chipsets. SSDs do not contain movable parts, so performance is not hindered by mechanical latencies. However, solid-state drives are not recommended at this time because Flash RAM, despite its high speed, has a finite life. It also can be written to only a finite number of times, which also limits its use.

Hard Drive Mechanics and Terminology

Before you begin considering hard disk specifications, controller cards, and so on, it is important to have an understanding of the physical makeup of the hard disk drive and to be familiar with the terminology associated with the disk subsystem. Arming yourself with this knowledge will help you shop wisely when purchasing disk subsystem components and achieve optimum performance for your system.

The hard disk drive consists of many moving parts that work together to read, store, and transfer data. The primary components are the platters, read/write heads, and actuator.

▼ **Platters** The platters are the actual magnetic media that store the data. The number of platters in the disk drive depends on the capacity of the drive. Each platter is attached to a central spindle and motor that spins the platters.

■ **Read/write heads** The heads that read and write data onto the platters are attached to a head stack assembly. The number of heads on the disk drive depends on the drive's capacity and performance characteristics. Typically, the higher the performance rating of the drive, the more heads it has. Most modern drives have heads located on either side of the disk to decrease the time it takes to read and write data. These heads (and the rest of the drive's assembly) are extremely sensitive. In fact, if dust particles were to contaminate the inside drive mechanics, the drive could be severely damaged. This is why it is so important not to open the drive chassis.

▲ **Actuator** This is the motor that rapidly moves the entire head stack assembly so the heads can read and write data.

When information is read from or written to the disk, the process proceeds in an orderly fashion. Formatting the hard drive gives the platters organization. The platter is divided into tracks, sectors, and cylinders. Figure 6-1 shows the organizational structure of each platter.

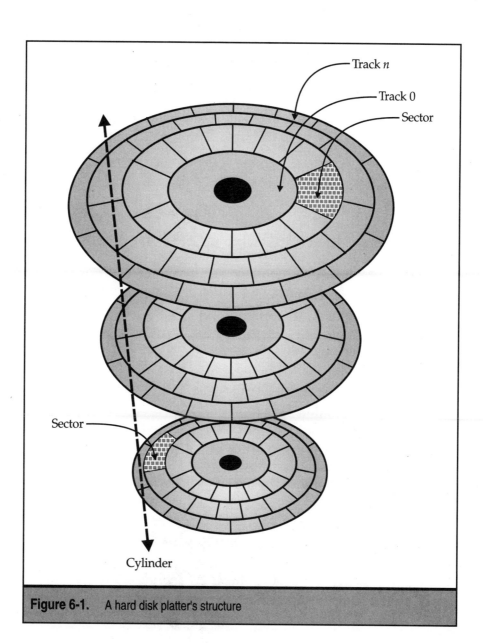

Figure 6-1. A hard disk platter's structure

▼ **Track**   Tracks are analogous to the lanes of a running track. They are narrow lanes circulating the platter. Track 0 is the innermost track, and track *n* (where *n* is the number of tracks on the platter) is the outermost track.

■ **Sector**   Platters are further segmented by sectors, which are essentially containers for storing data. Typically, each sector is 512 bytes.

▲ **Cylinders**   Cylinders are similar to tracks, but a cylinder is a pair of tracks on opposite sides of the platter. For example, on a disk drive with five platters, each cylinder has ten tracks.

Now that you have an understanding of a hard disk drive's mechanics, you can begin thinking about performance. What factors determine a drive's performance? The most important are the data transfer rate, rotation speed, rotational latency, seek time, head switch time, cylinder switch time, and access time.

▼ **Data transfer rate**   The data transfer rate is the overall transfer rate of data from the hard disk to the CPU for processing and is typically measured in megabytes per second (MB/sec). It combines the disk transfer rate (the speed at which data is transferred to or from the platter to the drive controller) and the host transfer rate (the speed at which data travels from the drive controller to the CPU).

■ **Rotation speed**   The rotation speed of the drive is sometimes referred to as spindle speed. It is measured in revolutions per minute (rpm). Hard disk drives spin at a constant rate, with speeds ranging from 3,000 to 10,000 rpm. Typical speeds, however, are 5,400 and 7,200 rpm. The rotation speed and data transfer rate are directly proportional, meaning that the faster the rotation, the higher the data transfer rate. It is important to note that as the rotation speed increases, so does the amount of heat that the drive produces. Thus, to keep the drive operating efficiently and to maintain the drive's life expectancy (mean time between failures), it is very important to keep the drives cool. It is always a good idea to configure the system with additional fans to keep the drives from overheating.

> **NOTE:** *The mean time between failures*, or *MTBF*, is the average time that a disk drive will run before it fails. Manufacturers commonly boast that the MTBF is between 500,000 and a million hours—57 to 114 years!—assuming the drive runs 24 hours a day. In truth, the drive might fail tomorrow—especially if you let it overheat—or it may last beyond your lifetime.)

- **Rotational latency**   Rotational latency, measured in milliseconds (ms), is the amount of time it takes for the drive head to locate the requested sector after being positioned over the appropriate track. The rotational latency is inversely proportional to the rotational speed: the faster the rotation speed, the lower the rotational latency. For example, at 5,400 rpm, the latency is approximately 6 ms; at 7,200 it is approximately 4 ms; and at 10,000 rpm it is slightly under 3 ms. Notice that the rotational latency decreases at a slightly reduced rate as the rotation speed increases.

- **Seek time**   This is a measurement (in ms) of the amount of time it takes the actuator arm to move from one track to the next. Obviously, the fastest seek times occur when the head reads or writes data sequentially, and the worst times occur when the actuator arm must move from the outermost to the innermost track (known as a *full-stroke seek*). The most relevant seek time is the average seek time because it better represents a drive's ability to find the requested data than does any single seek time. The average seek time is defined as the time it takes to locate a track during a random read. Typical average seek times for most modern drives range from 6 to 13 ms.

- **Head switch time**   Head switch time is the average amount of time (in ms) required to switch to another head to read or write data. Since all heads are connected to a single actuator arm and only one head can read or write data at a time, this measurement helps define the drive's actual performance capabilities.

- **Cylinder switch time**   The cylinder switch time is the average amount of time (in ms) required to move the head from one track to another located on a different cylinder.

▲ **Access time**   The access time is a convenient combination of seek time, head switch time, and cylinder switch time.

IDE/EIDE

The IDE interface has been around since 1985 and was originally called the AT-Attachment (ATA) because of its interoperability with the IBM PC/AT computer. Its original design offered simplicity and cost efficiency—benefits it still offers today, with prices continually dropping.

However, the IDE interface provides its benefits at the cost of performance. Promises that the drives could sustain approximately 8 MB/sec were replaced with the reality of speeds of about 3 MB/sec, because the IDE architecture relies on Programmed I/O (PIO), where the CPU handles all data transfers in a nonsynchronized fashion. Thus, only one transfer can take place at a time. During PIO transfers, the disk controller sends the data (ranging from 512 bytes to 64K) to memory. The CPU then moves the data to its destination. This process impedes performance and creates overhead for the CPU. In addition, because of DOS and BIOS limitations, the capacity of IDE drives is limited to 528MB. These performance inefficiencies crippled the system.

To deal with IDE's problems, Western Digital offered the Enhanced IDE (EIDE) specification. Since EIDE's introduction, higher transfer rates have improved considerably. EIDE still relies on PIO but achieves higher transfer rates through PIO and Direct Memory Access (DMA) mode changes. DMA, also known as bus mastering, reduces a drive's reliance on the CPU to handle data transfers. To gain the advantages of DMA, make sure your system is running the latest version of the BIOS and the IDE/EIDE device drivers.

In addition, extensions to the EIDE specification, such as ATA-2 and ATA-3, have introduced new PIO and DMA modes with even better transfer rates. Table 6-1 lists the various mode types and their respective transfer rates for the IDE/EIDE drive type. The ATA-3 specification, for example, uses PIO mode 5, which has a maximum transfer rate of 22.2 MB/sec, and DMA mode 5, which claims an astounding 33.3 MB/sec.

NOTE: At the time of this writing, NT supports only DMA modes 0 and 2.

EIDE has also incorporated changes to remove the drive capacity limitation and the number of devices that can be supported on a system. It alleviates the drive capacity limitation by supporting Logical Block Access (LBA) mode. LBA is a BIOS function that translates track, head, and sector information into logical block numbers to allow the entire disk to be recognized and used. EIDE also provides an additional channel so an extra two drives can be attached to the system (for a total of four IDE/EIDE devices) as well

Specification	Mode	Transfer Rate (in MB/sec)
ATA	PIO mode 0	3.3
	PIO mode 1	5.2
	PIO mode 2	8.3
	DMA mode 0	4.2
ATA-2	PIO mode 3	11.1
	PIO mode 4	16.6
	DMA mode 1	13.3
	DMA mode 2	16.6
ATA-3/Ultra ATA	PIO mode 5	22.2
	DMA mode 3	33.3

Table 6-1. IDE/EIDE Modes and Transfer Rates

as AT Application Programming Interface (ATAPI) support for nondisk peripherals such as CD-ROMs and tape drives.

Note that to gain the best performance possible when configuring the system with more than just hard drives, the hard drives should be placed on the primary channel, and the nondisk drives should be on the secondary channel, as shown in Figure 6-2. There are two reasons for this. First, the more advanced PIO and DMA modes are generally not supported on the second channel, which would severely hamper performance if the hard drives were put on the secondary channel. Second, devices on the same channel cannot operate independently; only the channels can operate independently. Therefore, if the hard drive and nondisk drive are mixed on both channels, the hard drive will have to wait for the slower device before it can begin its next task.

The physical design of EIDE drives is similar to that of the original IDE drives, where the controller functions are located on the drive rather than on the disk controller itself. This keeps the price of EIDE drives comparable as well. The relatively low cost of EIDE drives and the performance enhancements achieved make the EIDE specification a viable choice for your Windows NT Server disk subsystem.

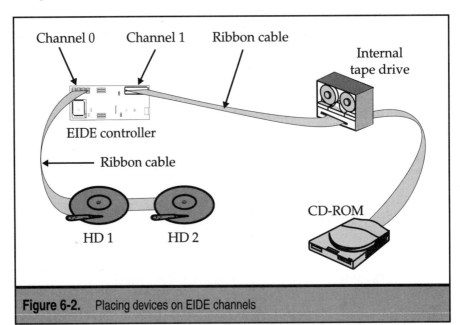

Figure 6-2.   Placing devices on EIDE channels

SCSI

SCSI is a communication standard that hosts specifications SCSI-1, SCSI-2, and SCSI-3. Each succeeding specification improves on the one before, providing better performance and compatibility.

Microsoft has always touted the use of SCSI in Windows NT Server systems for maximum disk subsystem performance. Why has Microsoft recommended SCSI over IDE/EIDE? For starters, SCSI is device independent, which means that the machine does not need to know about the SCSI controller or the devices attached to it. Its design also facilitates scalability. For example, devices (including nondisk drives) can be daisy-chained on a single controller, enabling many devices to be supported simultaneously. Some SCSI controllers allow as many as 15 additional devices to be connected! More important, however, is the performance SCSI allows. As the specifications are defined, you will clearly see why SCSI maximizes performance. The section "EIDE versus SCSI" later in this chapter describes more reasons why Microsoft urges you to use SCSI for optimal performance.

SCSI-1

SCSI-1 was introduced in the early 1980s as the first interface specification that let a single controller manage up to seven devices in a daisy chain. It uses an 8 bit-wide data path to synchronously transfer data at rates up to 5 MB/sec. Although the transfer rates were clearly faster than IDE rates (approximately 3 MB/sec) at the time, there were also other advantages to using the new specification. It is scaleable (it supports up to seven SCSI devices), it uses bus-mastering techniques instead of PIO to reduce CPU processing overhead, and it multitasks I/O operations. The use of bus mastering or DMA removes much of the responsibility placed on the CPU for data transfers.

Clearly, the SCSI-1 specification started off on the right foot, and it consequently rapidly gained acceptance from the industry. However, with today's demands for large disk capacity and fast transfer rates, SCSI-1 should not be considered, not even for low-end servers or workstations much less for your Windows NT Server.

SCSI-2

As you might expect, SCSI-2 defines faster transfer rates and wider data paths than SCSI-1. In addition, SCSI-2 eliminated many incompatibility problems by including more device models such as CD-ROMs, tape drives, and scanners.

SCSI-2 is blazingly fast in comparison to its predecessor. The specification offers synchronous data rates of up to 10 MB/sec (called Fast SCSI-2) on an 8 bit-wide data path. It also incorporates a 16 bit-wide data path (Fast/Wide SCSI-2) with double the transfer rate of Fast SCSI-2 (20 MB/sec).

SCSI-2 also supports more devices on a single controller (from 7 to 15) and offers improved cache management and parity checking compared to SCSI-1.

SCSI-3

While SCSI-2 is treated as a single specification, the SCSI-3 standard can be broken into subsets, each with its own SCSI specification. SCSI-3 is divided into subsets because the standard is still evolving. As with the other versions of the SCSI communication standard, SCSI-3 improves upon performance and maintains backward compatibility. Even though the specification is still evolving, many notable features have emerged from SCSI-3, including FAST-20, FAST-40, Fibre Channel, and FireWire. The FAST-20 specification can achieve data transfer rates of up to 20 MB/sec, and FAST-40 essentially can achieve data rates twice as fast (40 MB/sec). The Fibre Channel and FireWire specifications are discussed in detail later in this chapter.

NOTE: Refer to Table 1-2 in Chapter 1 for a summary of some of the different SCSI flavors and their related transfer rates.

EIDE versus SCSI

The debate over which interface technology—EIDE or SCSI—is the best has been going on for ages, with each side claiming to offer the best solution for storage requirements. This section examines the differences between the two interfaces and the implications for Windows NT Server performance. More specifically, this section looks at the cost, ease of use, speed, and scalability aspects of these two interface technologies. The best choice for your Windows NT disk subsystem will become more apparent as you read this section.

Cost

As we know all too well, money is not an infinite resource. Most IT budgets are limited, and as a result, care must be taken when purchasing new equipment. From a price perspective, EIDE is definitely a sound choice. It offers excellent quality and relatively high performance at unbelievably low cost. A SCSI drive offers high-end drive performance and scalability—but you bear the cost; don't be surprised to pay 15 to 40 percent more for SCSI drives. Moreover, SCSI controllers are considerably more expensive than EIDE controllers.

Ease of Use

EIDE technology aims for simplicity and ease of use. When designing a system to use the EIDE interface, you have to configure at most four drives on two separate channels. Furthermore, you can set up multiple drives in a master-slave relationship without worrying about terminating electrical signals.

Ease of use is definitely one of SCSI's shortcomings. The terminology alone makes SCSI difficult to use. Design plans require you to match drive controllers types to the particular SCSI specification being used, determine the number of channels the drive controller should have, choose between single-ended or differential SCSI and active or passive electrical termination, configure SCSI IDs, and so on.

In fact, most, if not all, of the hardware problems associated with SCSI result from cabling or termination issues. It is imperative that you purchase the highest quality cabling and terminators to avoid these unnecessary hassles. For more information on cabling and terminators, refer to "Avoiding Cabling and Termination Problems" later in this chapter.

There is one area where SCSI does surpass EIDE in terms of ease of use. SCSI allows you to attach external devices with little additional configuration. EIDE does not let you attach external devices at all; there is no such thing as an external EIDE device that can attach to the EIDE controller. The ability to attach additional devices externally is very useful when, for instance, you need to expand hard disk drive capacity or install a device such as a scanner.

Speed

The ability to transfer large amounts of data in a small amount of time is one of the most important aspects of the disk subsystem that you should be concerned with. Both EIDE and SCSI have come a long way since their debuts, and each provide exceptional performance. The methods that these two standards use to obtain their high transfer rates have always been different. It is this difference that separates the two.

From the start, SCSI has used bus-mastering techniques for data transfers to system memory; only a few of the older SCSI drives relied on PIO for data transfers. This approach not only increases transfer rates, but it also reduces CPU use relating to data transfers. This technique uses the SCSI drive controller DMA logic rather than the system DMA controller; no CPU intervention is required to transfer data to memory. Most SCSI drive controllers are equipped with a RISC-based processor (typically from the 68000 series) that assists in processing data transfers.

In addition, SCSI easily handles the multiple simultaneous I/O operations common in NT and other multitasking environments. NT uses an asynchronous I/O model that allows it to communicate with multiple devices simultaneously, and SCSI is designed to take advantage of this model. When a request for a file is issued, NT informs the controller, and the controller passes the request over the SCSI bus. A device on the SCSI bus, called the responder, responds to the request. At this point, the device disconnects (goes offline) to find the file. Shortly thereafter, it reports to the controller that the file has been found. During the disconnection phase, another request can be initiated and sent over the SCSI bus.

The advantages of SCSI's ability to handle overlapping I/O requests can be truly appreciated only in a preemptive multitasking operating system environment such as Windows NT. The benefits of multitasking I/O are especially salient when the system has more than one SCSI drive. This makes sense because where else would the next request go to if there were only one drive and it were temporarily disconnected? When the system is configured with more than one SCSI disk drive, you can expect significant performance advantages. Multitasking and bus mastering are the two primary reasons why SCSI transfer rates can reach 20 or 40 MB/sec, and in some cases, more than 100 MB/sec.

NOTE: The SCSI-3 standard includes Fibre Channel technology, which currently claims maximum transfer rates in excess of 100 MB/sec.

In comparison to the SCSI standard, EIDE transfer rates are much slower. Even the new ATA-3 interface supports a maximum transfer rate of only 33.3 MB/sec. This may be sufficient for workstations or low-end Windows NT Server systems but not for high-end servers that need to support heavy transfer loads. For example, you would not want to use EIDE on SQL servers, Exchange Servers, and so on.

EIDE also has some other performance drawbacks. The ATA-2 and ATA-3 implementations do indeed enhance EIDE by providing bus mastering techniques. However, the CPU still is responsible for significantly more data transfers than is the case in systems employing SCSI. In addition, many EIDE devices still support only PIO modes of operation. You may recall that this requires the CPU to handle all data transfers, which entails CPU overhead. Performance is also hampered by the fact that EIDE can handle only one I/O operation at a time per channel, and you are limited to two channels.

Scalability

The ability to easily scale systems to meet the continually changing and challenging demands placed on the system is of utmost importance. It is critical to be able to add devices without having to go through a major system overhaul. Disk subsystems employing the

EIDE standard are limited from the very beginning. As previously mentioned, EIDE can support up to 4 disk drives. What happens when maximum disk capacity has been reached? Your only choice is to replace one or more drives. With SCSI, this is not the case even if the existing SCSI channels contain their maximum limit of 7 or 15 devices. To extend capacity, you simply install an additional SCSI controller adapter or add external devices. Neither of these options are available with EIDE.

SCSI also supports a wider variety of device types than EIDE. It supports both internal and external devices such as hard disk drives, CD-ROM drives, tape drives, and scanners. Although the ATAPI specification enables EIDE to support more than just hard disk drives, support is generally limited to CD-ROM drives and tape drives. External devices are presently not supported by the EIDE interface.

The Best Device for Windows NT Performance

SCSI defends its title as the preferred choice in a Windows NT Server environment. It provides exceptional performance and offers the most advanced solution available for configuring Windows NT Servers with large amounts of drive capacity.

The SCSI specification continues to evolve at a more rapid pace than the IDE/EIDE specification. For instance, SCSI drives are constantly breaking speed records and now have speeds equaling 10,000 rpm.

The following list summarizes the reasons why you should choose SCSI over EIDE for a Windows NT Server:

▼ True multitasking support

■ High data transfer rates in excess of 100 MB/sec

■ Compatibility; SCSI supports more devices (internally and externally)

■ Bus mastering efficiency

▲ Scalability; some SCSI specifications can support up to 15 additional devices on a single channel, depending on the type of controller used

All these performance benefits make SCSI the best choice for Windows NT Server systems, especially on systems such as file servers that handle primarily I/O-related functions. Here is a general rule of thumb: always use SCSI, but if your budget forces you to choose less expensive EIDE, you should limit its use to low-end servers or servers primarily running memory-resident applications such as a firewall.

Fibre Channel Arbitrated Loop (FC-AL)

Based on the SCSI-3 standard and a subset of the Fibre Channel Specification Initiative, Fibre Channel Arbitrated Loop (FC-AL) is an up-and-coming architecture that promises incredibly amazing transfer speeds and device support. It uses a serial loop rather than a bus architecture, which allows data to be transferred from device to device, as shown in Figure 6-3. In a single-channel configuration, FC-AL boasts speeds of approximately 100 MB/sec, and in a dual-channel configuration, speeds can easily exceed 200 MB/sec. As you can see, FC-AL easily overcomes the bandwidth limitations of standard SCSI.

FC-AL is actually one of three Fibre Channel topologies. The others are Fabric and Point-to-Point. FC-AL devices can be connected using either fiber optics or copper serial cables (which are commonly used in SCSI implementations). Copper cables are cheaper and work for devices in close proximity, but devices separated by a distance

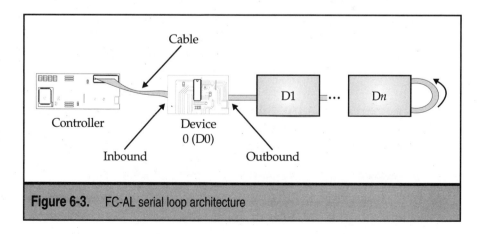

Figure 6-3. FC-AL serial loop architecture

greater than 30 meters need fiber optics for reliable connections. The Arbitrated Loop topology attaches devices to each other in a daisy chain, which makes connecting devices a piece of cake. The last device in the chain completes the loop by connecting to a loopback connector or its own outbound connector. FC-AL currently supports up to 126 devices.

Despite the physical differences between FC-AL and standard parallel SCSI, FC-AL can incorporate parallel SCSI devices into its topology. This makes the transition from parallel SCSI to FC-AL an easier process. It is anticipated that FC-AL will eventually replace SCSI all together.

FireWire

FireWire is another technology originating from the SCSI-3 specification. Texas Instruments and Apple developed it, and when the IEEE approved it, it also became known as the 1394 initiative. Cable versions of FireWire currently support data transfer rates of 100 (S100), 200 (S200), and 400 MB/sec (S400). FireWire was intended to replace standard parallel SCSI, but it will more likely replace EIDE in workstations and low-end servers.

FireWire topology is analogous to an upside-down tree, with the leaves of the tree being nodes or devices. It maps the devices through a 64 bit-wide addressing model, with 10 bits for the network IDs, 6 bits for node IDs, and 48 bits for the memory address. One of the advantages of using this addressing model is that it can support an amazing number of devices (theoretically, more 65 thousand!).

FireWire supports both asynchronous and isochronous (time-synchronized delivery) types of data transfers. Isochronous data transfers broadcast data based on channel numbers rather than a specific address and provide high bandwidth consistently. The advantage of supporting both asynchronous and isochronous formats is that both nonreal-time and real-time applications are supported. In other words, processes such as printing (nonreal time) and streaming multimedia video (real time) can coexist on the same bus.

Windows NT does not currently natively support FireWire, but future versions of Windows NT are expected to support it. Then you can expect to reap the benefits from its ability to support high data transfer rates (S1600, or 1.6 GB/sec, is soon expected), large numbers of devices, both nonreal-time and real-time applications, and hot plugging (device connection and removal without powering down the machine).

SCSI CONTROLLERS AND BUSES

At this point, it should be clear that SCSI devices have significant performance advantages over EIDE for Windows NT. Now you need to decide what type of SCSI host adapter, system bus, and SCSI bus to choose. You have an abundance of choices, each with different specifications that yield different levels of performance. Because even a SCSI system will run only as fast as its slowest component, when it comes to disk subsystem components, faster is almost always better. More important, whatever choice you make, it is critical that you match device performance with bus performance. For example, you will reap little or no performance advantage by using slow, less expensive disk drives with a high-end 40 MB/sec SCSI controller unless you employ multiple disk drives that together can fully utilize the bandwidth of the controller.

From a performance standpoint, it makes no sense to discuss any system bus architecture except PCI. PCI outperforms ISA, EISA, and VLB architectures in a variety of ways and is the best choice for SCSI because of its speed. PCI has a throughput of roughly 32 MB/sec and can reach speeds as high as 132 MB/sec in burst mode. Table 6-2 defines the various system buses and their bandwidths. Moreover, the I_2O initiative is expected to further enhance the throughput

Bus Type	Bandwidth (in MB/sec)
ISA	0.5 to 3
EISA	5 to 12
VLB	32
PCI	32 to 132

Table 6-2. Bus Architectures and Their Associated Bandwidths

capabilities of PCI by reducing the workloads placed on the bus. Refer to Chapter 1 for more information regarding I_2O and system bus architectures.

When determining which SCSI specification to use, it is recommended that you purchase the highest performance standard that you can afford. Clearly, this will achieve the best level of performance within your reach, and it will also mean you do not need to upgrade system components as soon.

As mentioned earlier, one of the key factors in optimizing performance is matching device performance with SCSI bus performance. In other words, if you decide to go with the Ultra Wide SCSI disk drives, make sure that you use a SCSI controller that will not hamper their high-end, 40-MB/sec transfer rates.

Tables 6-3 and 6-4 present examples of simplified SCSI disk subsystems to show the importance of matching the throughput capabilities of disk subsystem components to achieve optimal performance.

As you can see in Table 6-3, the two SCSI disk drives on the system can have a combined bandwidth of approximately 10.2 MB/sec, and the SCSI bus itself can handle 20 MB/sec. This is slightly more than half of the SCSI bus's utilization capability. Is this a waste of resources? From a performance standpoint, yes. However, it does leave room to expand the capacity of the disk subsystem without having to add an additional SCSI host adapter or upgrade to a specification with a higher transfer rate.

Figure 6-4 shows this configuration.

Device	Average Transfer Rate (in MB/sec)	Specification
Host adapter	32	PCI
SCSI bus	20	Fast/Wide SCSI
SCSI disk drive 1	5.1	7,200 rpm
SCSI disk drive 2	5.1	7,200 rpm

Table 6-3.   Matching Disk Subsystem Component Bandwidths: Wasting Resources

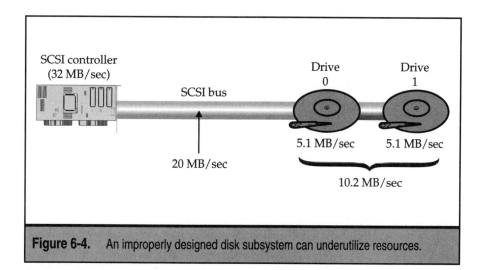

Figure 6-4.   An improperly designed disk subsystem can underutilize resources.

The three SCSI disk drives in Table 6-4 have a combined bandwidth of approximately 15.3 MB/sec. This is a result of SCSI's ability to multitask I/O operations even on a single channel. The system in this example has been improperly configured because the bandwidth of the SCSI bus has been exceeded. The system will never reach beyond the 10 MB/sec limit. To rectify the problem, use a Fast/Wide SCSI or another SCSI specification that allows 20 MB/sec or greater transfer rates. It is always better to have a slightly greater bandwidth capability on the SCSI host adapter rather than to have the adapter's capacity limit the total bandwidth of all the devices on the SCSI chain.

Device	Average Transfer Rate (in MB/sec)	Specification
Host adapter	32	PCI
SCSI bus	10	Fast SCSI
SCSI disk drive 1	5.1	7,200 rpm
SCSI disk drive 2	5.1	7,200 rpm
SCSI disk drive 3	5.1	7,200 rpm

Table 6-4.   Matching Disk Subsystem Component Bandwidth: Overloading the Bus

CHOOSING A FILE SYSTEM

Windows NT presently supports the following file systems:

- ▼ MS-DOS FAT
- ■ OS/2 HPFS
- ■ NTFS
- ▲ CDFS (CD-ROM)

Each supported file system is made up of three components: the file system driver, the file system utility DLL, and the file system recognizer used during startup to determine the file systems present on the system. Information regarding the file system components, such as the file system driver, can be found in the Registry. Specifically, file system driver information can be found in

HKEY_LOCAL_MACHINE\SYSTEM\CurrentControlSet\
Services\DriverName

where DriverName is the file system driver name without the extension (for example, NTFS). The default settings for the file system driver are listed in Table 6-5.

Information on the file system recognizer, which determines whether the file system needs to be loaded, is located in the HKEY_LOCAL_MACHINE\SYSTEM\CurrentControlSet\Services\

Parameter	Default Value
ErrorControl	0×1 (normal)
Group	Boot file system
Start	0×4 (disabled)
Type	0×2 (file system driver)

Table 6-5. File System Driver Default Registry settings

RecognizerName subkey. As is the case with the name for the file system driver, *RecognizerName* is the name of the file system recognizer driver without the extension. The default settings for this driver are listed in Table 6-6.

In this discussion of performance issues, only the FAT file system and NTFS will be examined. These two file systems affect the performance of the disk subsystem the most and are fully supported by Windows NT. Both file systems are examined to highlight their strengths and weaknesses before recommendations are made as to which one you should use on your Windows NT Server system.

NOTE: The HPFS file system in Windows NT 4.0 has only read-only support. It is anticipated that future versions of Windows NT will completely remove HPFS support because of application support, file system inefficiency, and security issues.

FAT

Since the early MS-DOS era, the File Allocation Table (FAT) has served as a useful file system for storing code and data. It is one of the simplest file systems that Windows NT supports. Of course, FAT was designed without concern for true preemptive multitasking environments like Windows NT—but can it nevertheless be useful within a Windows NT Server environment?

Parameter	Default Value
ErrorControl	0 (startup halts)
Group	Boot file system
Start	0×1 (system)
Type	0×8 (file system recognizer)

Table 6-6.   File System Recognizer Default Registry Entries

Windows NT supports FAT primarily to provide backward compatibility. This allows older applications that were created for MS-DOS to run under Windows NT. Of course, some DOS-based applications are not capable of running under Windows NT due to incompatibilities, such as DOS-based applications trying to write directly to the hardware.

FAT uses a table stored at the root of a volume; the size of the volume dictates the size of the table. When files are created or deleted, FAT is updated to reflect the change. The FAT file system is most efficient for use with volumes of less than 200MB. Volumes greater than 200MB present challenges to the FAT file system because of the size of the table, and performance begins to suffer with volumes greater than 200MB.

Figure 6-5 shows the organization of the FAT file system. Each partition contains a section for BIOS parameters and two copies of the File Allocation Table in addition to any files and directories.

FAT has many more disadvantages than advantages in a Windows NT environment. The disadvantages include the following:

▼ It provides no means to ensure security.

■ It cannot ensure file integrity. FAT does not keep track of file system transactions like NTFS does, which guards against single-sector failures. Also, NTFS keeps multiple copies of the Master File Table. The actual number of copies it keeps depends on the size of the volume.

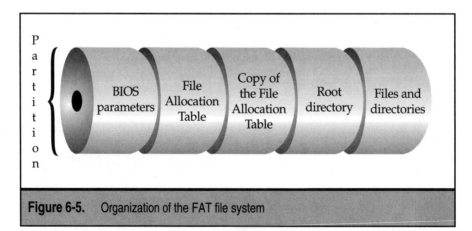

Figure 6-5. Organization of the FAT file system

■ It does not support long filenames. However, NT does provide a workaround. You can use the bits for the file attributes to support up to 256 characters in the name without affecting MS-DOS or OS/2 access. In addition, if a file created on a FAT partition exceeds the 8.3 format, NT creates a conventional directory entry to support the 8.3 format and also creates one or more secondary directory entries, depending on the number of characters in the filename. A secondary directory entry is created for every 13 characters in the filename.

■ File size is limited. Although it could be argued that the maximum FAT file size of 4GB is large enough to support most system needs, NTFS clearly exceeds this boundary, with the current maximum file size being an amazing 16 exabytes (or 18,446,744,073,709,551,616 bytes). The more important consideration is how efficiently FAT can work with such a large file size, which is unwieldy at best.

▲ Its unorganized structure hinders volume management. The size of the volume is inversely proportional to the efficiency of the FAT file system; as the volume size increases, the efficiency of the file system drops dramatically. Table 6-7 shows how the cluster size increases as the volume size increases. Because the cluster size increases rapidly, there is potential for a lot of wasted space. For example, on a 2GB partition, the cluster size is 32K. If a file is only 10K in size, then there will be 22K of space that is not utilized. If the partition were larger than 2GB, then there would be 54K worth of wasted space. To see the repercussions of using FAT, multiply this wasted amount by the hundreds or even thousands of files that are smaller than the cluster size. The amount of underutilized space quickly adds up.

With all these limitations, it is strongly recommended that you not use the FAT file system on your disk subsystem.

Volume Size (in MB)	Cluster Size (in K)
0 to 32	<1
33 to 64	1
65 to 128	2
129 to 255	4
256 to 511	8
512 to 1,023	16
1,024 to 2,047	32
2,048 to 4,095	64

Table 6-7.   The Relationship Between Volume (Partition) Size and Cluster Size

NOTE: Volumes larger than 4GB are supported only under Windows NT 4.0 and later. Cluster sizes continue to double for each successive volume increase. For instance, volumes between 4 and 8GB use 128Kb clusters, while volumes between 8 and 16GB use 256Kb clusters.

NTFS

Microsoft designed the NT File System (NTFS) to overcome the limitations of FAT and HPFS. It was also designed to accommodate future demands for efficiency in large-scale (multigigabyte and multiterabyte) disk subsystems. In fact, NT can handle sizes that probably will not be implemented until a few years from now. For example, NT currently supports up to a 64Kb sector size, which could potentially support a partition up to 256 terabytes!

Note that NTFS is efficient only with partitions greater than 400MB because NT requires some overhead to maintain security (NTFS uses NT's security model, which includes discretionary and system access control lists), transactional logging (which adds fault tolerance), and other disk management information. This is why some people use FAT instead of NTFS; FAT is more efficient than

NTFS on small partitions because it does not require as much overhead. However, there is little, if any, reason why Windows NT should have a partition of that size or smaller, especially on a server.

NOTE: The overhead NTFS requires is why you cannot format a floppy with NTFS: there is simply not enough room for the NTFS file system and data.

Table 6-8 compares some of the advantages and disadvantages of the NTFS file system.

NTFS is clearly the file system of choice for Windows NT. It succeeds in overcoming the limitations of the other file systems that NT supports. Moreover, its design promotes efficiency when used

Advantages	Disadvantages
Supports partition sizes up to 256 terabytes	Reduces capacity and causes slight performance degradation on partitions of less than 400MB
Models NT security	Can be accessed only with Windows NT, unless a third-party driver or the Network File System (NFS), commonly used on UNIX machines, is used
Adds fault tolerance at the file level	Cannot use standard DOS utilities such as Undelete
Supports file sizes of up to 2^{64} bytes (16 exabytes)	
Supports both 8.3 and long filename formats	
Supports 255-character filenames (UNICODE)	

Table 6-8. Advantages and Disadvantages of NTFS

with partitions of greater than 400MB. You can also expect future versions of Windows NT to continue to build upon NTFS with enhancements such as encryption support, increased efficiency, improved fault tolerance capabilities, and support for larger file sizes.

RAID

RAID—or Redundant Array of Independent Disks—technology has been incorporated into Windows NT since the birth of NT. RAID offers many advantages, including a safe means of storing data, easy addition of disk capacity, and enhanced disk drive performance. Simply put, RAID brings improved performance and reliability to a system's disk subsystem.

Five different levels of RAID can be implemented. Generally, only one is used at a time on a given system, but as you shall see later in this section, some of these levels can be combined.

NOTE: Windows NT offers software support for RAID levels 0, 1, and 5 only.

Although it is important to know what the RAID levels are, it is critical to know how to integrate RAID with your system's functionality. In other words, depending on the server's role in your Windows NT environment, you may be better off using a level of RAID that promotes speed and throughput more than reliability, or vice versa.

If speed were the only goal when configuring RAID on the disk subsystem, the recommended choice would be RAID level 0. There would be little need to examine the other levels. However, disk subsystem performance entails much more than just speed. You must consider data integrity and fault tolerance issues as well, because an unreliable or failed system does not yield high performance. Although this book focuses on tuning and optimizing Windows NT performance, this section provides an overview of the various types of RAID and how you can effectively use them to gain both performance and reliability.

Hardware versus Software RAID

There are two types of RAID (not to be confused with the levels of RAID): hardware based and software based. Hardware RAID uses on-board processors on the drive controller to perform all the RAID functions instead of using the CPU and operating system. Most hardware RAID solutions support all levels of RAID and typically allow you to combine levels as well. This type also offers an enhanced level of fault tolerance and controller diagnostic utilities that are not included with software RAID solutions.

Software RAID relies on the operating system, and consequently the CPU, to perform RAID-related I/O operations such as calculating parity information. Software RAID thus places more strain on Windows NT and can potentially degrade server performance. However, there is one irrefutable advantage to software RAID and that is cost. RAID levels 0, 1, and 5 can be implemented through Disk Administrator, Windows NT's built-in disk management utility.

As a general rule, hardware solutions perform substantially faster than software solutions. Consequently, hardware-based RAID is strongly advised. It not only is the faster option, it is also more reliable than software-based solutions. Note, too, that some hardware-based RAID arrays offer hot-swappable drives and expansion capabilities. Hot-swappable drives provide an added layer of reliability because if a drive fails, it can easily be swapped out and replaced without powering down the system. The expansion capabilities allow you to add drives without having to reconfigure your existing setup.

Hardware-based RAID arrays do not come with a small price tag, but there is an abundance of vendor support. Vendors such as Compaq, Dell, Hewlett Packard, and IBM provide complete hardware-based RAID solutions (drive controller, array chassis, and monitoring software) for Windows NT. Even though hardware-based RAID is more expensive than software-based RAID, you should consider using it if your budget permits because it offers the best overall performance.

If finances are tight but you need relatively high performance and reliability (most configurations do), then software-based RAID will suffice. You cannot argue the price because it is built into Windows

NT without any extra charge. By definition, software-based RAID can cause sluggish server performance because the operating system is used for all RAID functions. If you must use software-based RAID, implement only RAID level 1 (disk mirroring) and possibly RAID level 0 (disk striping without parity) but never RAID level 5 (disk striping with parity). The overhead involved in calculating parity is simply way too much for any operating system to adequately handle along with other system responsibilities. You also face serious fault tolerance issues with software RAID level 5. For instance, software RAID level 5 does not allow a damaged or nonfunctional drive to be hot-swapped.

The following sections describe the RAID levels. You will notice that some offer excellent performance while others are better for increasing fault tolerance, for example, by eliminating downtime or reducing the risk of data loss. The level most appropriate for you will depend on your server's individual characteristics. RAID offers you the ability to strike a balance between performance and reliability.

RAID Level 0: Disk Striping

RAID 0 requires two or more disks so that data can be striped (or split) across multiple disks simultaneously. The group of disks actively striping data is called the stripe set. The more disks that you have in the stripe set, the faster the performance of the disk subsystem. Figure 6-6 shows a RAID 0 stripe set.

Performance increases as the number of disks in the stripe set increases because there are more drives working in parallel, allowing each disk to take a smaller portion of the workload. Because all the drives can perform I/O simultaneously, the work is completed more quickly. With each additional disk, throughput increases at a rate slightly less than twice the previous throughput rate. However, as the number of drives increases, so does the amount of traffic on the bus, and the rated throughput of the controller may be exceeded.

Before deciding to implement RAID 0, consider a few points. First, hardware-based RAID 0 is preferred over software-based RAID 0 because striping does cause some overhead. If software-based RAID 0 is used, NT must calculate the striping instead of just letting the controller handle it. The slower the processor, the greater the impact of striping on overall system performance.

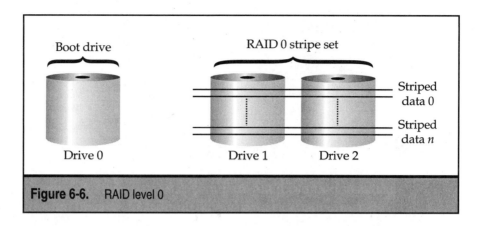

Figure 6-6.   RAID level 0

Second, to gain the full benefit of RAID 0's performance capabilities, the disks should be of equal capacity because only one I/O operation occurs at a time since the system perceives the stripe set as one disk.

Third, RAID 0 does not offer any redundancy or parity control and so offers no fault tolerance. If speed is all you are after or you need high performance and maximum disk capacity, then RAID 0 is an excellent choice. However, if your data is extremely important, you should consider other RAID levels or implement a well-planned backup strategy.

The disk subsystem is by definition slower than the CPU and memory. When compared to these two components, it will always be the bottleneck. However, RAID 0 provides the highest level of performance for systems that require extremely fast read and write operations. Moreover, it provides maximum capacity for the disk subsystem.

NOTE: You will see large performance gains if the system's paging file is placed on a RAID 0 stripe set.

Creating a Striped (RAID 0) Array

Using Disk Administrator, Windows NT's built-in disk management tool, you can configure and manage the hard disk drives within

the system. To build a software-based RAID 0 stripe set, do
the following:

1. Click the first partition to be included in the stripe set to select
   it. This partition should be considered free space.

NOTE: The system partition (the partition containing %SYSTEMROOT%,
typically the \WINNT directory) cannot be a part of the RAID 0 stripe set.

2. While pressing the CTRL key, click at least one more drive to
   be included in the stripe set. Each drive that you select will be
   highlighted as shown in Figure 6-7. Each partition to be
   included in the stripe set should be free space and on a
   separate physical disk.

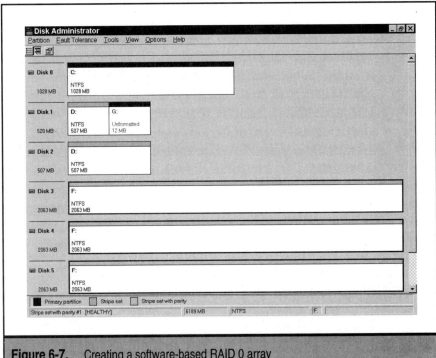

Figure 6-7.   Creating a software-based RAID 0 array

3. Once you have selected all of the drives to be used in the stripe set (you can select up to 32 partitions, but each must be on a separate physical drive), choose Create Stripe Set from the Partition menu. Then select Commit Changes Now.

4. Format the drives by choosing Format from the Tools menu.

5. From the Partition | Configuration menu, select Save. This last step saves the RAID 0 configuration information.

RAID Level 1: Disk Mirroring

RAID 1, also known as disk duplexing, mirrors disks. Each disk mirrors, or clones, itself onto another drive of equal size. When data is written to one drive, it is simultaneously written to the other, as illustrated in Figure 6-8. Performance is slightly better than that of a system using no RAID at all. In fact, read performance is almost always better, but write performance is not because a write must occur on two disks instead of one. However, you can slightly increase this performance by placing the drives on their own separate controller.

RAID 1 offers moderate performance with exceptional fault tolerance. If the drive being mirrored develops a problem or even fails, the second drive can immediately take over, though usually only if you are using hardware-based RAID 1. The controller takes the mirrored disk offline and, depending on the controller, may even attempt to alleviate the problem by reformatting the drive and copying the data back to the original disk. Another advantage of hardware-based RAID 1 is that the boot drive can be mirrored.

The drawback of RAID 1 is that you immediately lose 50 percent of disk capacity. For example, if you have two 1GB hard disks, the maximum capacity is 1GB, not 2GB, because the second disk is mirroring the other and cannot be used for anything else. Figure 6-9 shows the drop in capacity when using RAID 1 with the Disk Administrator.

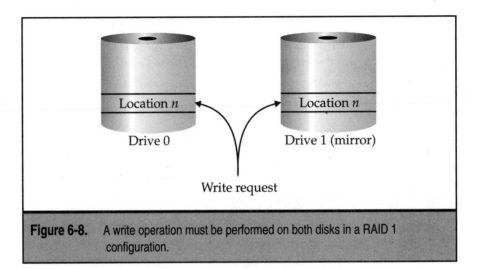

Figure 6-8. A write operation must be performed on both disks in a RAID 1 configuration.

Creating a Mirrored (RAID 1) Array

Hardware-based RAID 1 is highly recommended over software-based RAID with NT's Disk Administrator, though the performance drop does not affect the system as much as with other forms of software-based RAID.

NOTE: Software-based RAID 1 does not limit your ability to include the system partition.

To establish a software-based RAID 1 configuration (mirroring between two drives), do the following:

1. Click the first drive to be included in the RAID array to select it.

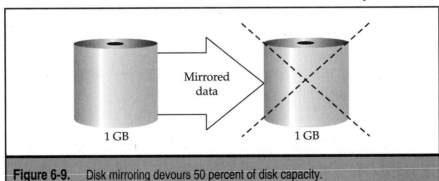

Figure 6-9. Disk mirroring devours 50 percent of disk capacity.

2. While pressing the CTRL key, click the second drive to be included. This selects the second drive. As Figure 6-10 shows, both drives are now highlighted.

3. Select Establish Mirror from the Partition menu to create the mirror. Then select Commit Changes Now.

4. From the Tools menu, select Format to format the second drive.

5. From the Partition | Configuration menu, select Save. This last step saves the RAID 1 configuration information.

At this point, the system begins writing the information from the first disk to the second disk to establish the mirror.

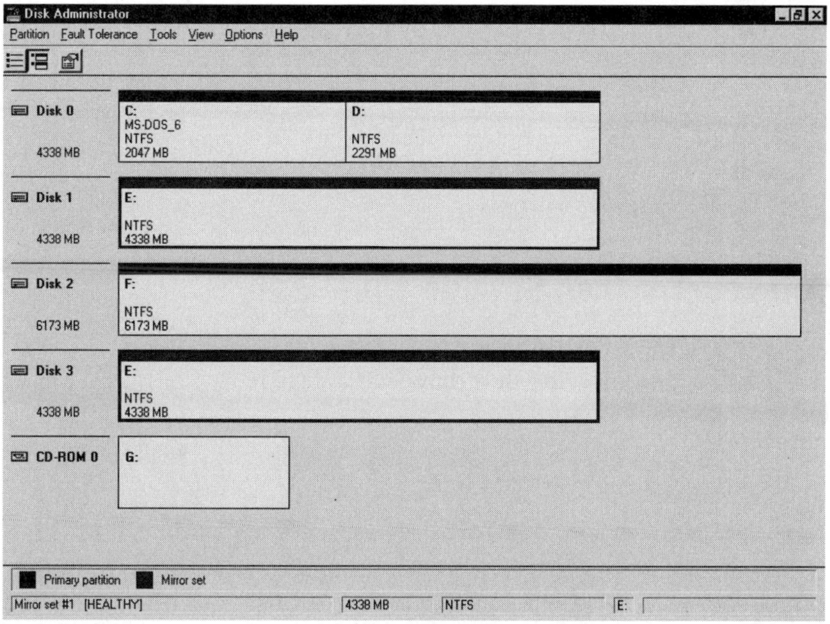

Figure 6-10.   Creating a mirrored array

RAID Level 2: Disk Striping with Parity

Windows NT does not inherently support RAID 2, and its implementation is almost never practical. RAID 2 uses a form of striping that requires a parity bit for every byte of code or data. This puts a substantial amount of overhead strain even on high-end controllers, but read and write operations can be performed slightly faster than with RAID 1 implementations. However, to achieve this slightly faster throughput, many drives need to be included in the array. Because the return on investment is minimal, RAID 2 is not recommended.

RAID Level 3: Disk Striping with Parity

RAID 3 should be used with caution, if it is used at all. Windows NT does not inherently support it. It does stripe data, like RAID 0, and it contains parity information, like RAID 5, but instead of striping the parity information, it places it all on a single drive. For example, if a RAID 3 configuration contains four disks, three disks will stripe data and the fourth will contain all of the parity information. Moreover, for this level of RAID to operate efficiently, all drive spindles must be synchronized. For these reasons, RAID 3 is not a popular RAID implementation and is not recommended for your Windows NT Server environment.

RAID Level 4: Disk Striping with Parity

RAID 4 overcomes some of the limitations of RAID 2 and RAID 3 by sequentially striping data in blocks instead of bit by bit. The way in which this level reads data also differs from RAID 2 and RAID 3 because the read operation is multithreaded. Multiple I/O requests can be handled simultaneously because not every drive is used for the operation. For instance, consider a system with four disk drives using RAID 4. If a chunk of data occupies two data words (a data word is 16 bits long), then one word is read (or written) to the first disk, and the second data word is read (or written) to the second disk. The request is completed without involving the third disk at all. The last disk is used only for parity information as with RAID 3.

Despite its improvements over levels 2 and 3, RAID 4 is typically not a practical solution for performance or reliability. It can be implemented with hardware-based RAID solutions, but Windows NT does not support a software-based solution. RAID 4 should not be considered for enhancing performance or for ensuring reliability.

RAID Level 5: Disk Striping with Parity

Hardware-based RAID 5 implementations are by far the most popular RAID implementations, largely because it achieves a balance among performance, reliability, and cost. Software-based RAID 5 can also be implemented through NT's Disk Administrator, but this approach is strongly discouraged because of the overhead involved in calculating parity information. If software-based RAID 5 is used, the CPU must calculate the parity information and then send it to the SCSI bus.

As shown in Figure 6-11, RAID 5 does not use a single dedicated drive for parity information. Instead, it spreads the parity information across all disks in the array. In this regard, RAID 5 offers true disk striping with parity, with each drive containing both parity information and data. The advantage to this implementation is that if any single drive in the array fails, the parity information can be used to regenerate the lost data. In addition, some hardware-based RAID 5 solutions provide hot-swap capability as mentioned earlier. In this case, however, simply replacing the drive will initiate the regeneration process without bringing the system down. You can even use a hot spare drive so that if a drive does fail, the controller can automatically detect the failure and begin regeneration without any human intervention.

NOTE: The regeneration process will increase the server's workload and slow performance until the process is complete.

The amount of parity information needed with RAID 5 decreases as the number of drives in the array increases. The overhead accrued with parity information is equal to $1/n$, where n equals the number of drives in the array. For example, a RAID 5 drive array consisting

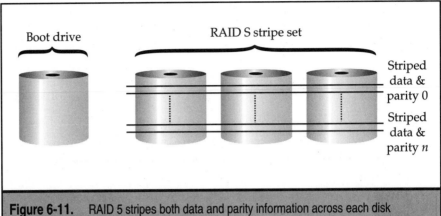

Figure 6-11. RAID 5 stripes both data and parity information across each disk in the array.

of four 1GB disks will have approximately 25 percent of disk capacity dedicated to parity information. That leaves roughly 3GB for code and data. Table 6-9 shows some sample calculations regarding parity and total storage capacities for RAID 5.

As you can see, if the disks all have the same capacity, calculating the amount of space needed for parity information is easy. The total essentially equals the space of one of the drives.

NOTE: Using the same disk capacity for every drive in the array is highly recommended. In addition, every drive in the array should come from the same vendor.

Number of 1GB Drives in the Array (n)	Parity Overhead (1/n)	Total Capacity for Code and Data (in GB)
6	1/6	5
7	1/7	6
8	1/8	7

Table 6-9. Calculating the Parity Overhead and Total Disk Space in RAID 5

One of the primary reasons why RAID 5 offers better read and write performance than other RAID levels with parity checking is that these operations are multithreaded. Multiple requests can be handled on multiple drives simultaneously. Read performance is only slightly less than that for striping without parity (RAID 0), but write performance is no more than 60 percent that of RAID 1. However, the cost of implementing RAID 5 is much less than the cost of implementing RAID 1.

RAID 5 is clearly the best choice for overall disk subsystem performance, reliability, scalability, and cost. Remember, though, that hardware-based, not software-based, RAID 5 should be used on a Windows NT Server.

RAID Level 6: Disk Striping with Parity

RAID 6 is RAID 5 on steroids. It incorporates an enhanced level of fault tolerance by backing up the striped parity information with additional parity information. In short, there are two sets of parity information: one for data (as in RAID 5) and one for the parity information calculated from the data. RAID 6 can be thought of as a form of redundant redundancy because it adds additional fault tolerance to the parity information used in RAID 5. The result is that if two drives were to fail at approximately the same time, both drives could be regenerated to recover the lost data.

RAID 6 is a new addition to the various levels of RAID and is currently not supported by Windows NT. It is clearly geared toward guarding against disk failures and other related disk catastrophes, but it places an additional performance burden on the system, particularly when writes are made to the stripe set. From a performance standpoint, the additional parity information does not justify the degradation in performance that occurs even in high-end hardware-based solutions.

This new implementation may prove to be a viable solution, for both performance and reliability, as hardware-based solutions become faster. However, it is unlikely that Windows NT will incorporate software-based RAID 6 because of the drastic reduction in performance caused by the parity information overhead.

Combining Levels of RAID

Another benefit of using RAID is that you can combine two levels and reap the benefits of what they offer together. This way, you can increase both performance and fault tolerance. You can choose from many combinations of RAID levels, but there are only two viable ways to configure your system for any of these combinations. Both require a hardware RAID controller.

Some RAID controllers support two levels of RAID. When you are evaluating controllers and the likelihood is great that you will incorporate a combination of RAID levels, make sure that the controller supports RAID combinations. The recommended route is to let the controller take responsibility for performing I/O functions for the RAID combination. This approach is recommended for the same reason that a hardware controller is recommended for a single level of RAID: it increases performance.

As you might expect, hardware RAID controllers that support RAID combinations are more expensive than those that do not. If this is discouraging news, you have another option: you can combine hardware RAID with NT's software RAID. In this case, the hardware controller will be dedicated to providing one level of RAID, and Windows NT will handle the other level. This option does not yield the same performance gains as a completely hardware-based solution, but it still provides noticeably increased performance and enhanced fault tolerance.

Many variations of combined RAID levels exist, including RAID 0+1 (RAID 01), RAID 1+0 (RAID 10), RAID 3+0 (RAID 30), and so on. The most popular and, not surprisingly, the best performers are RAID 01 and RAID 10. Both combine mirroring (RAID 1) and striping without parity (RAID 0) to gain the advantages of each level. RAID 01, which mirrors the stripe set, offers impressive read and write performance whether the I/O transactions are random or sequential. When compared with all of the other RAID levels and combinations, RAID 01 delivers the best overall performance and fault tolerance. The primary disadvantage of RAID 01 is that your drive capacity drops by 50 percent as it does with RAID 1. Therefore you will lose the capacity equal to half of the number of drives that are striped. Figure 6-12 illustrates a RAID 01 configuration in which six striped 1GB disk drives are mirrored, thus reducing drive capacity by 50 percent, or 3GB—but still leaving a 3GB capacity.

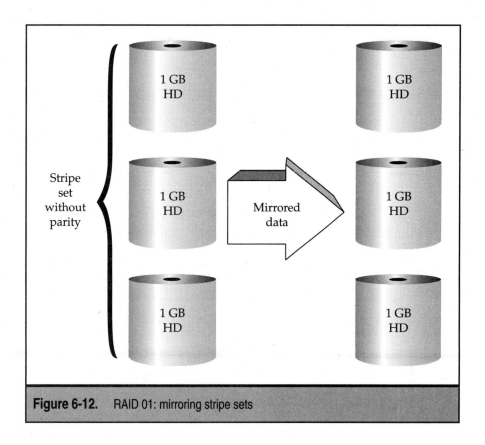

Figure 6-12.   RAID 01: mirroring stripe sets

RAID 01's sidekick, RAID 10, is essentially the inverse of RAID 01. In this case, mirrored drives are striped. The performance and fault tolerance of RAID 10 configurations, such as the one in Figure 6-13, are comparable to those of RAID 01.

RAID Vendors

Table 6-10 lists vendors that manufacture RAID supplies. Some vendors, such as Compaq, Dell, Hewlett Packard, and IBM, supply complete RAID systems preconfigured, while others focus their attention primarily on RAID controllers or array chassis.

MAINTAINING A HEALTHY DISK SUBSYSTEM

Common sense tells us that a healthy disk subsystem performs much better than one with problems such as corrupted files, damaged

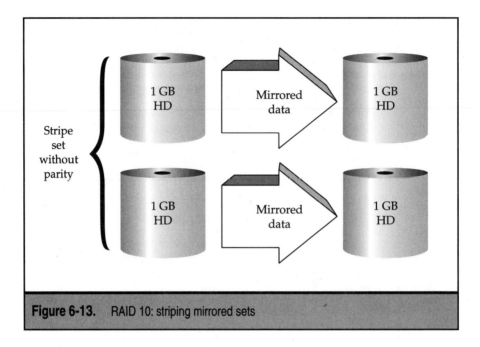

Figure 6-13. RAID 10: striping mirrored sets

sectors, corrupt boot records, poor device driver performance, and fragmentation.

What can be done when a problem does occur? What preventative measures can be taken to reduce the likelihood that the disk subsystem will experience these problems? This section discusses ways to remedy problems if they occur, and offers some preventative medicine to head off problems before they affect your disk subsystem. This section is not intended as an all-inclusive guide to disaster recovery.

NOTE: For a good book dedicated to disaster recovery and fault tolerance issues, check out *Windows NT Backup & Recovery* by John McMains and Bob Chronister (Osborne/McGraw-Hill, 1998). It offers plenty of advice to help you ensure that your disk subsystem maintains its expected level of performance.

Company Name	Contact Information
Adaptec	1-800-442-7274
	http://www.adaptec.com
Adjile Systems	1-800-347-7621
	http://www.adjile.com
Amdahl Corporation	1-800-223-2215
	http://www.amdahl.com
Antrone Research	1-714-237-1527
	http://www.antrone.com
Box Hill Systems	1-800-727-3863
	http://www.boxhill.com
CLARION	1-800-672-7729
	http://www.clarion.com
CMD Technology	1-800-426-3832
	http://www.cmd.com
Cybernetics	1-757-833-9000
	http://www.cybernetics.com
Infotrend	1-707-541-3400
	http://www.infotrend.com
nStor	1-800-724-3511
	http://www.nstor.com
Raidtec	1-770-664-6066
	http://www.raidtec.com
Artecon Storage Dimensions	1-800-765-7895
	http://www.storagedimensions.com
Winchester Systems	1-800-325-3700
	http://www.winsys.com

Table 6-10.   RAID Vendors

In Case of an Emergency

In a perfect world, all of the preventative measures that you take to ensure reliability and performance would keep the system operational. Unfortunately, mechanical parts have limited lifetimes and are prone to failure. This is why it is critical to take as many precautions as possible to ensure that you are prepared for the worst.

Creating an Emergency Repair Disk (ERD)

The ERD contains a backup of the system's Registry files so you can restore damaged NT system files. Although you cannot reboot the system with the ERD alone, the ERD can help get NT to boot on its own by correcting damaged system files. Creating an ERD takes only a few minutes, yet the potential returns are tremendous. It can drastically reduce the amount of downtime if a boot failure occurs.

To create an ERD, do the following:

1. Choose Start | Run and then type **RDISK** in the Open box to execute the application, or type **RDISK** at the command prompt.

2. The Repair Disk Utility dialog box appears:

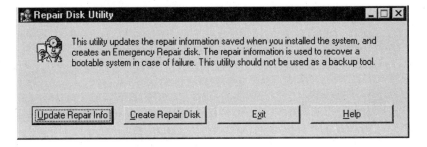

3. Click Update Repair Info to update the repair information.

4. Once the update process is complete, you are asked whether you want to create a floppy disk (ERD) with the new information. Select Yes to create the ERD.

NOTE: The Update Repair Info option automatically updates the repair information only on the hard disk drive. The information is stored in the %SYSTEMROOT%\repair directory.

The second option on the Repair Disk Utility screen, Create Repair Disk, formats the disk you plan to use as the ERD and then copies the information from the %SYSTEMROOT%\repair directory to the freshly formatted floppy disk. Note that RDISK does not check to see if the repair information is up-to-date. For this reason, it is crucial for you to execute the Update Repair Info option first.

You may notice that running the RDISK utility does not supply or update security and user account information on the ERD automatically. To update the repair information and copy these files to the ERD, you must run RDISK with the /S parameter. The process is slightly different from that described to run RDISK without any parameters. After you enter and execute RDISK /S, the update process immediately begins (no dialog box appears). When the update is complete, the Setup dialog box appears, asking whether you want to update the ERD. Select Yes to update the ERD:

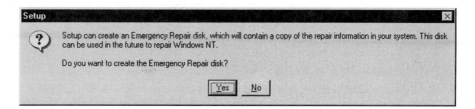

CAUTION: In most cases, you will not be able to store the SAM database on the ERD despite NT's use of compression algorithms in the update repair information process to compact the SAM. Only information from relatively small domains can be stored on the ERD. Because of this limitation, make sure your backup routine includes the Registry.

Boot Floppies

The idea of using a boot floppy to gain access to the system is not new, but the usefulness of this approach with Windows NT is limited, especially if you are using only NTFS. Nevertheless, boot floppies have their benefits. You may need to create two types of boot floppy: a DOS boot disk and an NT boot disk. This section examines the use of these boot floppies to access and possibly repair the system.

USING A DOS BOOT DISK   A DOS boot disk can be used only on systems using FAT, because DOS cannot recognize NTFS partitions. Some system configurations use both FAT and NTFS, with FAT being used on the boot partition. If that is the case in your system, then it is highly recommended that you create a DOS boot disk. Here's how:

1. At a DOS based machine or a machine running Windows 95, open a DOS session and type **FORMAT A: /S** at the command prompt to create the boot floppy.

2. Copy the FDISK utility (FDISK.EXE) to the boot disk. (The FKISK utility is useful for repairing damaged boot sectors.)

Now if you ever experience a problem with booting into the system and the boot partition uses FAT, you can use the DOS boot disk to gain access to the system. Once you have gained access, use the FDISK utility to attempt to rectify the problem. More specifically, run FDISK with the undocumented /MBR parameter. This replaces the boot sector. If the problem was caused by a damaged boot sector, the problem will usually be resolved, and you will be able to access the system with NT.

NOTE: If your system uses FAT for the boot partition but NTFS for all other partitions, it may be to your advantage to include a shareware utility, NTFSDOS, which allows you to access NTFS volumes from DOS. Otherwise, you will not be able to access NTFS after booting to DOS with the DOS boot disk.

USING AN NT BOOT DISK   Do you need to create an NT boot disk? The question can be argued both ways. You should already have a boot disk from the three installation floppies provided by Microsoft, and these can be used to access and repair system files. In one particular case, however, an NT boot disk can save you a lot of time and worry. If your system mirrors the boot partition, you should create an NT boot disk so that if the system fails to start, you can boot to the mirrored (working) drive.

In any case, an NT boot disk will allow you to gain access to the system, and it is easy to create:

1. Format a floppy disk.

2. Copy the NT startup files (BOOT.INI, NTDETECT.COM, and NTLDR) located on the root of the boot partition to the newly formatted floppy disk.

3. If you are mirroring the boot partition, remove the Read-Only attribute from BOOT.INI on the NT book disk. Then add the mirrored boot partition to the list of choices. For example, add the following line:

    ```
    multi(0)disk(0)rdisk(1)partition(1)\WINNT="Boot From NT
    Mirrored Partition"
    ```

NOTE: The general procedure for creating an NT boot disk stops after step 2. Use step 3 only if you are mirroring the boot partition.

Maintaining File Integrity with CHKDSK

You are probably already familiar with the CHKDSK utility used in DOS-based systems. NT's CHKDSK, however, is more advanced because it scans for file system integrity on FAT, HPFS, and NTFS partitions. It checks for lost clusters, cross-linked files, and more, and it attempts to correct any errors it finds. It also gives you lots of other file system information, as shown in Figure 6-14.

NT automatically runs CHKDSK at startup if it senses file system corruption. You can also manually start the utility. CHKDSK runs in five modes. The first doesn't have any parameters. This is a read-only mode used just to check for any errors in the file system. CHKDSK

```
Command Prompt                                              _ □ ✕

D:\>chkdsk
The type of the file system is NTFS.
Warning! F parameter not specified
Running CHKDSK in read-only mode.

CHKDSK is verifying files...
File verification completed.
CHKDSK is verifying indexes...
Index verification completed.
CHKDSK is verifying security descriptors...
Security descriptor verification completed.

 2096608 kilobytes total disk space.
 1589962 kilobytes in 17794 user files.
    5352 kilobytes in 1163 indexes.
   31785 kilobytes in use by the system.
    4096 kilobytes occupied by the logfile.
  469508 kilobytes available on disk.

     512 bytes in each allocation unit.
 4193216 total allocation units on disk.
  939017 allocation units available on disk.

D:\>
```

Figure 6-14.   File system information reported by CHKDSK

reports but does not attempt to repair any errors in this mode, so the process is completed quickly. The four other options use the following parameters:

▼ **/FILENAME**   Checks for fragmentation on the specified file

■ **/F**   Attempts to fix any errors in the file system

■ **/V**   Provides the name and full path of every file located on the partition

▲ **/R**   Locates bad sectors on the partition and attempts to recover readable information

To run CHKDSK, do the following:

1. From the command prompt, go to the partition in question. For example, type **C:**.

2. Type **CHKDSK** without any parameters simply to check for file system errors. If any errors are found, proceed to step 3.

3. Run the CHKDSK utility with the /F parameter to attempt to fix errors found in the file system.

Avoiding Cabling and Termination Problems

Many of the problems you are likely to encounter with SCSI-based disk subsystems stem from faulty cabling or improper termination. For example, cables may come loose, lightly shielded cables may not filter electrical noise, or shoddy terminators may not cancel signals. These are simple problems, but they can have serious consequences and can have a large impact on disk subsystem performance. To minimize problems and maintain optimal performance, it is extremely important that you buy high-quality cabling and terminators. Here are some guidelines that you should follow:

▼ Cables should have an impedance rating of at least 90 ohms.

■ SCSI devices must be terminated at both ends.

■ Match termination ends (use active termination whenever possible).

▲ Avoid using external SCSI devices whenever possible.

Using the highest quality cabling and terminators does not guarantee that you will never encounter problems caused by faulty equipment, but it does shift the odds in your favor. Also, these components are the least expensive in your disk subsystem, so it is easier to squeeze top quality into tight budgets. One source of high-quality SCSI cables and terminators is Granite Digital (**http://www.scsipro.com/**). Generally, higher-quality products cost more than less reliable products, but in this case, the price is well justified.

Keeping Your Disk Defragmented

Whether disk defragmentation needs to be performed at all on the Windows NT platform has become a topic of hot debate in the last few years, even though defragmentation utilities have been around for ages on DOS- and Windows-based platforms. Microsoft claims that using an efficient file system such as NTFS alleviates the need for defragmentation, but this is only partially true. The FAT file system is more susceptible to fragmentation problems than NTFS, but the NTFS file system is not immune to fragmentation either. Up until

Windows NT version 4.0, Microsoft did not provide any internal coding that would support third-party disk defragmentation tools. Needless to say, Microsoft now has undocumented built-in support for disk defragmentation so that third-party developers can write disk defragmentation tools for Windows NT that work with both FAT and NTFS.

What is disk fragmentation and how does it occur? Both the FAT and NTFS file systems allocate disk sectors into logical units called clusters. Whenever you create or modify a file, NT assigns a group of clusters to the file based on the file size. Most files are dynamic, meaning that their sizes can increase or decrease over time, changing the size requirements for the file. Also, when files are deleted, they release free clusters. Over time, the disk becomes fragmented with free clusters and bits of files scattered across the disk, as shown here.

For example, suppose you create a text file, and NT allocates four clusters. You then create many more files on the disk. Sometime later, you add text to the first file you created, and an additional four clusters are needed to accommodate this additional text. Where do these additional clusters go? They do not fit contiguously with the original clusters and must be placed elsewhere on the disk. Now the file is fragmented.

Here is an example showing how data might be organized on a fragmented disk:

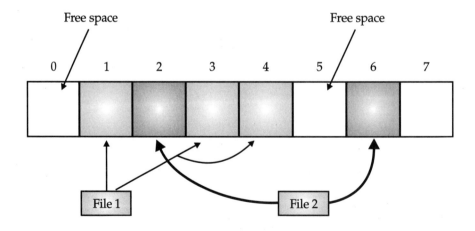

This is how the disk would be organized after defragmentation:

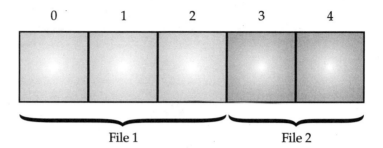

How can you defragment disks when Windows NT does not
provide such a utility? There are a growing number of third-party
utilities that offer exceptional performance. Two products that offer
excellent disk defragmentation capabilities are Executive Software's
Diskeeper (**http://www.execsoft.com**), shown in Figure 6-15, and
Symantec's Speed Disk in the Norton Utilities for Windows NT

NOTE: Fragmentation can also occur when the paging file is forced to
increase beyond its minimum size. This is yet another reason why it is critical
to properly size the paging file. Refer to Chapter 4 for more information on
configuring the paging file.

Fragmentation negatively affects system performance by
significantly reducing the rate at which data can be read from the
disk. To read a fragmented file, the disk drive head has to move to
various locations to read each fragment. The more a single file is
fragmented and the more fragmented files there are on the disk, the
more the head has to move from fragment to fragment. This increases
the amount of work that must be done to read a file and can
drastically reduce the disk's throughput speed. To keep the disk
subsystem running at optimal capacity, you should always keep disk
fragmentation to less than 10 percent.

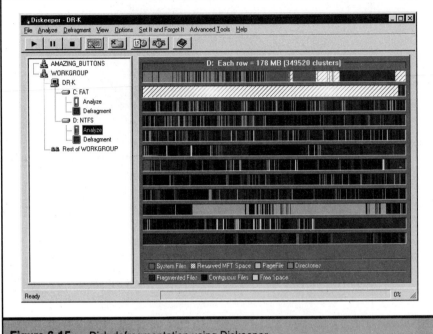

Figure 6-15.   Disk defragmentation using Diskeeper

(**http://www.symantec.com**), shown in Figure 6-16. Both products let you do the following:

▼ Schedule disk defragmentation at a specific time

■ Defragment files, free space, or both

■ Record defragmentation events

■ Minimize defragmentation effects on overall system performance

▲ Maintain NTFS file system properties such as security

In addition, the server version of Diskeeper adds remote capabilities. For example, you can remotely schedule and control disk defragmentation levels. It also lets you install a client piece on a

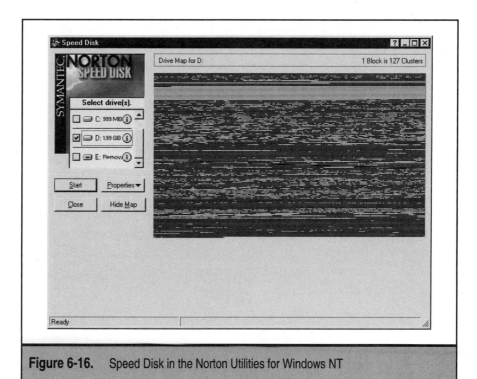

Figure 6-16. Speed Disk in the Norton Utilities for Windows NT

Windows NT Workstation and monitor the fragmentation levels of remote servers.

Despite the fact that these products strive to minimize their effects on system performance, you should schedule disk defragmentation for off-peak hours. For example, schedule disk defragmentation between midnight and 2:00 A.M. nightly, and schedule your backup routine to begin after 2:00 A.M.

MEASURING DISK PERFORMANCE WITH PERFORMANCE MONITOR

Many factors play important roles in disk subsystem performance. If you have chosen to configure your system with SCSI, NTFS, and

RAID, you are well on your way to optimizing server I/O performance.

Once you have a configuration in place, you need to monitor the disk subsystem to ensure that it can handle your resource requirements now and in the future as they change.

How do you begin monitoring disk subsystem performance? If you try to use the disk counters to monitor performance, chances are good they will all report zeros, because the drivers necessary to gather data from the disk subsystem are not enabled by default. These drivers can cause a slight performance degradation for I/O operations, though their actual effects depend on the system. For instance, performance degradation is greater on 486-class machines and low-end Pentiums than on more powerful machines.

To enable the disk performance counters for the local machine, do the following:

1. Display the command prompt by choosing Start | Programs | Command Prompt.

2. For a system without RAID, type **DISKPERF–Y**. For a system with software-based RAID, type **DISKPERF –YE** as shown in Figure 6-17.

3. Restart the machine to activate the drivers.

You can also enable the disk performance counters on a remote machine by specifying the UNC name of the machine as an additional parameter. Simply type **DISKPERF–Y** *SERVERNAME* for a system without RAID, or **DISKPERF–YE** *SERVERNAME* for a system with RAID.

Once the machine has restarted, you can begin monitoring disk subsystem performance.

Disk Subsystem Performance Characteristics

Performance characteristics for the disk subsystem vary from system to system. In addition to the disk components themselves, many variables, such as memory, workloads placed on the system, and the machine's processing power, also affect disk subsystem performance.

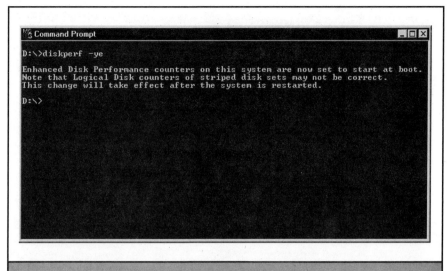

Figure 6-17.   Enabling disk performance counters on a system configured with RAID

The capacity planning procedures described in detail in Chapter 2 provide an excellent means for gauging the performance of other system components and how they affect the disk subsystem. Capacity planning also helps you to calculate the minimum and maximum values your system needs for optimal performance so you can compare the results you obtain from monitoring your disk subsystem.

Keep in mind that the monitoring results may not necessarily represent the performance of the disk subsystem. The results may be a symptom of another problem rather than a cause. For example, the disk subsystem may be doing an unusual amount of work because the system is trying to compensate for a lack of memory. (The system relies on the hard disk drives for virtual memory.) If you know that the system is not paging excessively, then you can assume that a component in the disk subsystem is causing the bottleneck. Otherwise, you may just keep blaming the disk subsystem and never truly uncover the real problem. This is one of the many reasons why it is important to understand and monitor the other factors that affect disk subsystem performance as well.

Important Disk Counters to Monitor

All of the available counters for the disk subsystem are contained in the LogicalDisk and PhysicalDisk objects. The LogicalDisk object contains counters pertaining to logical drives or partitions. For example, if a single physical drive has three partitions—C:, D:, and E:—each counter would have these three instances. The PhysicalDisk object holds the counters that measure the characteristics of each physical disk in the system.

What counters within these two objects provide the most useful performance measurements for the disk subsystem? While it could be argued that every counter provides a wealth of knowledge that could prove useful in analyzing performance and capacity, there are a few that are strongly recommended. The disk counters described here can be found in both objects, and it is important to monitor these counters in both of the objects because they analyze components differently. For instance, the % Disk Time counter in the LogicalDisk object analyzes the time spent servicing requests for a partition, while the PhysicalDisk: % Disk Time looks at the disk as a whole.

% Disk Time

The % Disk Time counter is helpful in determining the amount of activity the disk is experiencing. Its value is the percentage of time that the disk spends servicing read and write requests. Figure 6-18 shows Performance Monitor capturing data from this counter.

Depending on the server's functions, this counter may reach levels as high as 100 percent consistently. The goal, however, is to keep its value below 55 percent. As % Disk Time exceeds 55 percent, the reduction in performance will become more and more noticeable. If this counter is consistently averaging above the recommended level, you should seriously consider either upgrading the disk subsystem or offloading some of the server's responsibilities to another server.

Current Disk Queue Length

Current Disk Queue Length indicates whether the disk subsystem can service requests in a timely manner. When a read or write request is sent to the disk subsystem, the request is either serviced

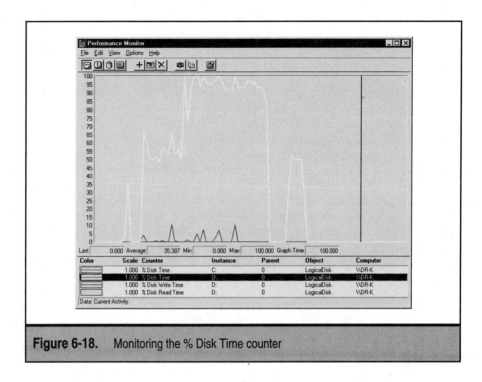

Figure 6-18.   Monitoring the % Disk Time counter

immediately or put into a queue. It is put into a queue if the disk subsystem is busy and cannot handle the request right away.

Since the disk subsystem is slower than the CPU and memory, you can expect to see requests frequently placed into the queue. This is not abnormal and does not mean that the disk subsystem is improperly configured. However, if Current Disk Queue Length is always greater than 2, the disk cannot keep up with the rest of the system, creating a traffic jam in which a request cannot be serviced until another has been completed. Using SCSI disk drives in a hardware-based RAID configuration will greatly reduce the likelihood that this type of congestion will occur.

Avg. Disk Bytes/Transfer

The Avg. Disk Bytes/Transfer counter displays the average number of bytes that are transferred to or from the disk. It includes both read and write requests.

There is not a magic number for this counter that tells you that disk subsystem performance is optimal. The appropriate counter value depends on the server's functions and the types of workloads placed on the disk. Generally, though, the larger the value, the better. If a large number of bytes are being transferred, this simply means that the system can handle a large capacity.

Even though your goal is as large a value as possible for this counter, there will come a point when the disk reaches its maximum transfer capability. Checking the Current Disk Queue Length in conjunction with this counter can help you determine the point at which requests start piling up in the queue. This will help you better understand the disk subsystem's saturation point so you can consider balancing loads between disks or even between servers.

MEMORY USE AND CACHING

Memory tuning and the file system cache (explained in detail in Chapter 4) are keys to ensuring that the disk subsystem performs at optimal capacity. Improper memory and file system cache configurations can have disastrous effects on disk subsystem performance. For example, a system configured with an insufficient amount of memory to support applications and services relies heavily on the disk subsystem for virtual memory, placing an added (and unnecessary) strain on the disk drives. The disks will constantly be accessed and used as a backup for memory, which limits the disk subsystem's ability to service its normal responsibilities.

Onboard Disk Cache

Several caching techniques are designed specifically to improve disk subsystem performance. More advanced drives, such as Seagate's Barracuda family of drives (**http://www.seagate.com**), incorporate caches on the drives themselves. Some drives are equipped with a full megabyte (1,024K) worth of cache space. The goal of caching is to anticipate requests for code or data and retrieve the requested object before the system asks for it. When the disk drive has a caching mechanism of its own, the amount of processing that the system itself must perform can be reduced significantly.

Is a bigger cache size better? The answer depends on how the cache is managed. Some advanced drives segment large caches and include enhanced caching algorithms to increase the cache hit rate and thus improve the effectiveness of the cache. Suppose, for example, a drive with 1MB of its own cache space does not use any of these enhancements. It fills the entire cache with anticipated code or data. Then another request comes in, and it tries to anticipate future requests by reading in this data (because the anticipated requests are not currently allocated in the cache). However, it must find room in the cache to handle the additional requests. The only choice now is to purge the entire cache memory to service the new request. All of the work performed earlier is essentially wasted because it can no longer be used.

If this large amount of cache space is segmented, however, the drive will essentially have two or more caches at its disposal. Some drives, such as the ones from Seagate, can have as many as four cache segments to divide the cache load. When a cache segment becomes saturated, only that segment is purged. The other segments can still keep their contents and maintain a potentially high cache hit/miss ratio.

What happens when all the cache segments are full? This is where the advanced caching algorithms make their mark. The drive must decide which cache to purge. It does not want to purge a segment that is about to be used; the drive purges the segment with the least amount of data likely to be used next.

It should be clear that disk read performance can be more efficient with an onboard disk cache. You should be sure to include this feature in your purchase if at all possible.

WINDOWS NT RESOURCE KIT UTILITIES

Several utilities packaged in the Windows NT Resource Kit allow you to manage disk resources and monitor the health of the disk subsystem to maintain optimal performance. One of the most useful is Response Probe. This utility helps you determine resource utilization levels, without using real or live data, so you can optimize the disk subsystem configuration.

Response Probe

Response Probe, in the Windows NT Resource Kit, uses scripts to create predefined workloads on the system. Response Probe tries to simulate as real an environment as possible by simulating the way in which a user actually works. For example, Response Probe may simulate time spent processing data as well as a user's idle time.

This utility is especially useful for evaluating disk subsystem performance characteristics because of its ability to closely model the behavior of users and because of the control it gives you over the workloads being performed. It also can help you establish disk subsystem benchmarks, such as minimum and maximum throughput, average disk usage, and response time with various amounts of stress upon the system.

Working with Response Probe will help you tailor the workloads you define and analyze the results. To help you get off to a quick start, Response Probe includes many scripts you can use to test the system. You can also create your own test scripts.

Test Scripts

Response Probe includes predefined workloads so you can quickly begin examining the disk subsystem. These include Diskmax, Minread, and Sizeread and are located in the \Perftool\Probe \Examples subdirectory. For each of the test scripts, an associated text file describes the test. The test scripts described here come with Response Probe and can be used to simulate workloads on the disk subsystem.

DISKMAX   The Diskmax test script is designed to stress the disk subsystem to evaluate a disk's maximum throughput. You can specify the type of read operation it uses. By default, it performs a sequential read operation, but it can read data randomly as well. Also by default, Diskmax reads from a file called WORKLOAD.DAT. This file is approximately 20MB and consequently is not installed in the installation process. You must manually copy the file to the \Perftool\Probe\Examples subdirectory or to another location. Since this file is used for testing purposes only, it is filled with zeros used as placeholders.

Optionally, you can create your own workload file with the CreateFile utility supplied with Response Probe. This tool must be run from the command prompt. The syntax for CreateFile is CREATFIL *FILENAME* [*FILESIZE*], where *FILENAME* is the file to be created and *FILESIZE* represents the size of the file. You can create files in 1MB increments.

The DISKMAX.SCT script file contents are shown here:

```
# Diskmax Thread Description File
#
# Description: This script file is part of a test of maximum
#              disk throughput.It creates a single threaded
#              process that does sequential, unbuffered reads
#              of 64K records from a 20Mb file.
#
# Format:
#              THINKTIME       Mean  SDev    (milliseconds)
#              CYCLEREADS      Mean  SDev    (number)
#              FILESEEK        Mean  SDev    (records)
#              CPUTIME         Mean  SDev    (milliseconds)
#              DATAPAGE        Mean  SDev    (page number)
#              FUNCTION        Mean  SDev    (function
#                                            number 1-1000)
#              FILEACCESS      fileaccess    (file name)
#              FILEATTRIBUTE   RANDOM | SEQUENTIAL
#              FILEACCESSMODE  BUFFER | UNBUFFER | MAPPED
#              RECORDSIZE      number_of_bytes (default - 4096
#                                            bytes)
#              FILEACTION      R | W
#
#              Mean  Sdev
#
THINKTIME     0     0           No think time.
```

CPUTIME	0	0	No other processing time.
CYCLEREADS	100	30	Reads 100 times/cycle on average, with a sdev of 30.
FILESEEK	0	0	Fileseek is ignored for sequential access.
DATAPAGE	0	0	No datapage activity.
FUNCTION	500	0	Reads the middle function repeatedly to simulate codepage access.
FILEACCESS	WORKFILE.DAT		Reads the 64K records from this file.
FILEATTRIBUTE	SEQUENTIAL		Reads the records sequentially.
FILEACCESSMODE	UNBUFFER		Reads directly from disk without the file system cache.
RECORDSIZE	65536		Reads 64K records.
FILEACTION	R		Reads only (no writes).

MINREAD   The format of the MINREAD.SCT test script is similar to that of the DISKMAX.SCT test script, but it reads smaller amounts of sequential or random data. Minread reads only 512 bytes at a time from WORKLOAD.DAT or from the file that you created with the CreateFile utility.

This test script is useful for determining a minimum, baseline performance value that you can compare against other test scripts or real data. It determines how disk performance may vary by reading information a sector at a time. This data is the smallest unit that is unbuffered by the file system cache. In other words, Minread determines the raw performance of the disk without any help from the file system cache.

Before you run this test script, it is imperative to make sure that the drive you are going to run it on uses 512 bytes for each sector. To find out how many bytes are used in each disk sector, follow these steps:

1. Start the Windows NT Diagnostics from the Administrative Tools (Common) group.

2. Select the Drives tab.

3. Select the Drives by Letter option to display all local and networked drives on the system.

4. Double-click the drive that you are planning to run the script on to display the number of bytes used for each sector on the partition, as shown here:

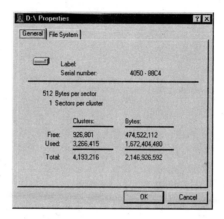

If the number of bytes is anything other than 512 bytes, you must change the size in MINREAD.SCT to reflect the size the partition is using. MINREAD.SCT is a text file, so you can use any text editor, such as Notepad, to change the test script.

```
# Minread Thread Definition File
#
# Description:  This file is part of a test of reading
#               the smallest possible records (512-bytes
#               = 1 sector, unbuffered) from a 20Mb
#               file,Workfile.dat. It is designed to
#               test how disk performance varies when
#               reading many small records.

# 512 bytes is a common sector size.  If your disk has a
# different sector size, change the value in the
# RECORDSIZE parameter, below.  You can also change from
# SEQUENTIAL to RANDOM.  If you do, change the  values
```

```
# for the FILESEEK parameter to mean = 20000, sdev
# = 6667.
#
#
# Format:
#              THINKTIME    Mean  SDev   (milliseconds)
#              CYCLEREADS   Mean  SDev   (number)
#              FILESEEK     Mean  SDev   (records)
#              CPUTIME      Mean  SDev   (milliseconds)
#              DATAPAGE     Mean  SDev   (page number)
#              FUNCTION     Mean  SDev   (function
                                         number 1-1000)
#              FILEACCESS   fileaccess   (file name)
#              FILEATTRIBUTE  RANDOM | SEQUENTIAL
#              FILEACCESSMODE  BUFFER | UNBUFFER | MAPPED
#              RECORDSIZE   number_of_bytes (default -
                                         4096 bytes)
#              FILEACTION   R | W
#
#         Mean    Sdev
#
THINKTIME     0      0        No think time.
CYCLEREADS  100     30        Reads 100 times/cycle
                              on average, with a
                              sdev of 30.
FILESEEK      0      0        Fileseek is ignored
                              for sequential access.
CPUTIME       0      0        No other processing
                              time.
DATAPAGE      0      0        No datapage activity.
FUNCTION    500      0        Reads the middle
                              function repeatedly to
                              simulate minimum
                              codepage access.
FILEACCESS  workfile.dat      Reads the 512-byte
                              records from this
                              file.
```

```
FILEATTRIBUTE        SEQUENTIAL      Reads the records
                                     sequentially.
FILEACCESSMODE       UNBUFFER        Reads directly from
                                     disk without the file
                                     system cache.
RECORDSIZE    512                    Reads 512K records.
FILEACTION    R                      Reads only (no
                                     writes).
```

Measuring and Testing
Disk Throughput with Response Probe

Are disk drives as fast or faster than what the manufacturer claims? Measuring and testing the speed of your disk drives not only gives you a good idea of actual transfer rate capabilities; it also will be an enormous help to you when you are matching the performance of the various disk subsystem components.

You can measure and test disk throughput in several ways. For example, you can use any of numerous third-party benchmarking utilities, Windows NT Resource Kit utilities (such as Response Probe), and Performance Monitor. This section describes how to use Performance Monitor in conjunction with Response Probe to determine a disk's transfer rate. The counters used here should also be consulted when running the Response Probe scripts described in the previous section.

The reason for discovering the maximum throughput of disk drives is to establish baseline estimations of drive performance so you can adequately match each drive's transfer capacity with the rest of the disk subsystem to achieve optimal performance. Your results will include such specifications as revolutions per minute and seek time, showing you what the drives can really do. The need for such measurements should be obvious; without them, you may inadvertently configure a disk subsystem that is a bottleneck.

To begin measuring and testing drive throughput, select the PhysicalDisk object for logging with Performance Monitor. Refer to Chapter 8 for more information on how to configure logging with Performance Monitor. It is also a good idea to include the Processor and Memory objects, even though you will be focusing your attention on the PhysicalDisk object. Including these additional objects will help you understand how the rest of the system copes when the disk subsystem is under extreme pressure to transfer large amounts of data. You should notice the correlation between processor utilization, hard page faults, and disk throughput.

Once you have begun to monitor the recommended objects, run the Response Probe Diskmax test script. After the test script has completed, you can begin viewing the data that Performance Monitor collected. Table 6-11 outlines the specific Performance Monitor counters that should be monitored when measuring and testing disk throughput.

Before you become overwhelmed with the data, particularly the large numbers for the disk bytes counters, you should convert the numbers from bytes to megabytes so you can more easily understand them. For example, in Figure 6-19, the Disk Bytes/sec counter shows 1363913.375 bytes, which roughly translates to 1.4MB.

The results from the Disk Bytes/sec counter show a mediocre transfer rate of 1.4MB, but notice that the Avg. Disk Queue Length averaged slightly less 2. Could a higher transfer rate be achieved?

Object	Counter
Memory	Pages/sec
PhysicalDisk	% Disk Time
	Avg. Disk Bytes/Read
	Avg. Disk Bytes/Transfer
	Avg. Disk Queue Length
	Disk Bytes/sec
Processor	% Processor Time
	Interrupts/sec

Table 6-11. Performance Monitor Counters for Evaluating Disk Throughput

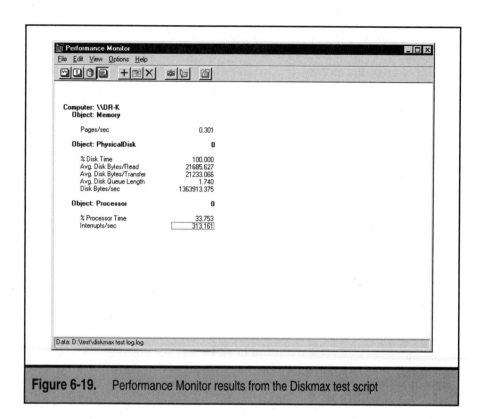

Figure 6-19.   Performance Monitor results from the Diskmax test script

Before trying to answer this question, look at the % Disk Time counter. Surprisingly, the percentage of time spent servicing read requests was high. This is like someone looking frantically busy all the time but rarely getting much work done. With this in mind, you can conclude that the drive itself is the bottleneck. In this case, the SCSI bus is being underutilized. (Return to the discussion of component matching in "SCSI Controllers and Buses" earlier in this chapter for more information.)

By examining the other counters, such as Processor: % Processor Time and Memory: Pages/sec, you can also determine whether the other system components contributed to the low transfer rate. In this example, you can see that these components did not contribute to the latency experienced by the drive because their counter measurements were well within their boundaries.

CONCLUSION

The disk subsystem is always a slower component than the CPU or memory subsystem and therefore is always likely to be a bottleneck. For this reason, it is critical to optimize the disk subsystem to perform at the highest level possible. This chapter examined the various components of the disk subsystem, such as the different types of drives, bus standards, file systems, and disk configurations, and provided concrete recommendations as to what should be used and how. It also described performance indicators and the tools used to measure and analyze performance and to predict subsystem resource requirements.

CHAPTER 7

Tweaking Graphics Subsystem Performance

W indows NT's graphics subsystem components are rarely the topic of discussions about Windows NT server performance. Most of the time, IT professionals talk about improving a server system's performance by increasing the amount of physical memory, upgrading processors or processor speed, upgrading to faster disks, and so on. However, the graphics subsystem on Windows NT servers is important as well. In fact, it should not be overlooked, because most of the information you get from the computer comes through this subsystem. Without a good graphics adapter and monitor, you may not be able to retrieve information at all.

Of course, the graphics subsystem is not nearly as important on a server as it can be on a workstation, because traditional server functionality requires simply that the information is properly displayed. Graphics subsystem performance is a different story altogether on client machines, especially on workstations using computer-aided design (CAD), computer animation tools, and other high-end rendering or graphics applications. These differences mean that some of the concepts and recommendations presented in this chapter are more applicable to a workstation than to a server system. Nevertheless, this chapter will give you the tools to improve the performance of both Windows NT Server and Windows NT Workstation systems.

Because most Windows NT functionality is built on a graphical user interface (GUI), it is logical to conclude that graphics and video performance can significantly affect other system components, such as memory and the disk subsystem, especially if the graphics subsystem causes conflicts among other system components. Unfortunately, the only time IT professionals look at the graphics and video components is after conflicts arise.

How you plan to use a server or workstation has a tremendous effect on how you configure the graphics subsystem and the importance of graphics subsystem performance. For instance, graphics subsystem performance in a typical server (domain controller, file and print server, application server, and so on) in an NT server environment is not as critical as it is for a workstation that has been set up to handle streaming video or graphic rendering.

To configure every server as if it were a graphics rendering workstation, however, would simply be overkill. Most workstations, on the other hand, must be able to handle high-end graphics applications, and they consequently should be configured for optimal graphics subsystem performance.

In addition to showing you how graphics and video performance affects overall system performance, this chapter also shows you how to tweak the graphics subsystem so your system runs as smoothly and efficiently as possible.

UNDERSTANDING THE NEW KERNEL ARCHITECTURE

As mentioned in Chapter 1, Windows NT received a new kernel design that reduces a lot of redundant operating system coding and consequently promotes more efficient use of resources. One of the major design enhancements involved moving portions of the Win32 subsystem (in user mode) to make them integral parts of Windows NT's Executive Services.

This subsystem move reduces Windows NT's memory requirements, offloads some of the Win32 environment subsystem responsibilities, and streamlines graphic operations. The change is generally transparent to users and applications on a Windows NT system, but the overall result is a leaner and meaner operating system, especially in the way that it now handles graphic operations.

Previous Architecture

Prior versions of NT incorporated the following five components in the Win32 subsystem:

▼ **Console**   Provides applications and the operating system with text window support.

- ■ **Graphics device drivers**   Graphics drivers specific to particular hardware implementations. Some of this functionality was repeated in the Windows NT Executive.

- ■ **Graphics device interface (GDI)**   A library of calls for the graphics devices.

- ■ **Operating system functions**   A group of DLLs that support the rest of the components in the Win32 subsystem.

- ▲ **Window Manager**   Handles all screen I/O as well as input from devices such as the mouse and keyboard.

Figure 7-1 shows these components in the Win32 subsystem and how they interact with the Windows NT Executive.

In this early design, it is evident that the Win32 subsystem was responsible for the majority of graphics operations for the entire system. Every time a graphics request was made, the Win32 subsystem components—namely, the Window Manager and GDI—had to temporarily hold the data being transferred between the client (requester) and server as well as manage the process threads needed to handle the request. As you might expect, with potentially several hundred graphics process threads, there was just too much information being processed in the Win32 subsystem. In addition,

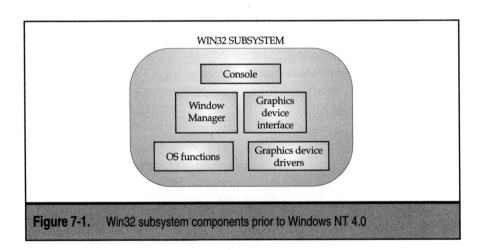

Figure 7-1.   Win32 subsystem components prior to Windows NT 4.0

some of these operations were duplicated in the NT Executive. The bottom line was that this design risked creating a bottleneck for the rest of the system because of the CPU and memory overhead involved in graphics calls to the system.

This should not imply, however, that the former design structure was inefficient and inherently minimized performance. In fact, several properties of this design promoted efficient operations. For example, the Win32 subsystem uses shared memory buffers that increase the throughput between Win32 and the client application by minimizing the number of process threads between these two components. Also, when a Win32 application (client) makes several graphics calls to the Win32 GDI, the calls are not immediately transferred through the Win32 subsystem to the output device. Only when the GDI queue is filled do the calls move to the output device for processing. This method is employed because the GDI uses batching and caching to handle incoming information. Batching allows more information to be handled at once by having the queue fill up before the entire batch is sent off for additional processing. Trying to service one call at a time would severely restrict the graphics subsystem performance.

The New, More Efficient Design

What design enhancements have been made in Windows NT? Three components—the Window Manager, GDI, and graphics device drivers—have been completely removed from the Win32 subsystem (or CSR subsystem) and placed in the Win32K Executive Service, otherwise known as the NT Executive. All other Win32 subsystem functionality (console and operating system services) is still intact. For example, both shutdown services and console management remain in the Win32 subsystem in user mode.

The benefits of this architectural change extend to areas such as application protection, security, and driver reliability, and some benefits are more apparent than others. This design enhancement also has implications for graphics performance as well as overall system performance, as the following sections explain.

Less Unnecessary Communication

The latest versions of Windows NT essentially strip away the communication middleman. They significantly reduce the amount of communication between user and kernel mode operations, which saves considerable time and resources. Graphics operation requests no longer have to communicate through paired threads (one in the Win32 subsystem and one in kernel mode) and memory buffers. For instance, when an application calls for a screen write operation, the graphics device drivers can interact directly with the hardware to produce results faster.

The performance gains from cutting out the middleman are significant enough. You can expect as much as a 90 percent decrease in the amount of time needed to switch between the user and kernel mode environments in comparison to the previous design! The jump in performance is noticeable to the naked eye.

Reduced Code

Since the code for the Window Manager and GDI are now in the NT Executive, the amount of code necessary to provide the same level of functionality is significantly reduced. Moreover, the number of processes and threads is reduced as well because the transition from the Win32 subsystem and kernel mode operations is more efficient.

How does this increase performance? Reducing the amount of code reduces Windows NT's burden in tracking and managing the potentially hundreds of calls per second it may receive, resulting in more calls supported with fewer processes and threads.

Transitions within the kernel mode generally take more resources and time to complete compared with direct access to the same privilege level, so the GDI still uses techniques such as batching and caching but to a lesser degree than in the previous architectural design. However, once a call has been made to the Window Manager or GDI, the subsystems can now access other resources (that is, other Windows NT Executive services) without having to go through a transition.

Improved Graphics Device Driver Reliability

Everyone knows that performance depends on whether the driver is stable. The enhancements made in the new Windows NT architecture have forced the rewriting of many, if not all, graphics-related drivers to conform to the kernel mode conditions, making them more stable and more efficient. For example, all video drivers need to be rewritten to comply with the new mode of operation. Previous versions of graphics drivers were typically written to run partially in user mode within CSR and also in kernel mode. Now the graphics drivers run entirely in kernel mode, which again bypasses the middleman and improves efficiency.

NOTE: The new architecture is the reason why video drivers written for Windows NT version 3.51 and earlier will not function properly in current Windows NT environments.

Better Memory Management

In the Windows NT 3.51 operating system architecture, a memory buffer was needed for transitions between user and kernel modes. However, the new design completely removes the need for the buffer because components, such as the Window Manager and GDI, that operate within kernel mode have the privilege of accessing an application's memory address space. Communication from the Window Manager and GDI to the application is established through a direct link. In other words, the transition between user and kernel modes no longer needs a memory buffer for communication.

Memory is also conserved because the amount of code is reduced. The code is less complex, so less memory is needed to get the same end results.

Are there visible results that would indicate that less memory is being used? The new design saves approximately between 256K to 1MB of a process' working set memory. This savings may then be used for other functionality, such as the Explorer interface shell. Consequently, the memory savings resulting from the new design will most likely not be obvious. In fact, you will note that the memory requirements of the current version of Windows NT are approximately the same as for earlier versions.

Improved Multitasking

The new kernel design raises two related questions: does it improve multitasking, and are threads originating in kernel mode subject to preemption? In fact, the present design does improve multitasking, even though many kernel mode threads cannot be preempted.

The new architectural design allows threads in both user and kernel modes, with the exception of those in the microkernel, to be preempted so they can execute alongside each other. Threads in the Windows Manager and GDI are no exception. The real performance gain from the improved multitasking occurs when a graphics application is multithreaded or the machine has more than one processor (an SMP-based machine). For instance, on an SMP machine, the two threads associated with an application will each run on a separate processor, which makes more efficient use of the machine's processing power. Also, each thread will tend to run on the same processor, resulting in a higher hit ratio in memory caches. (Refer to Chapter 4 for more information on caching.)

GRAPHICS TERMINOLOGY

To gain a clearer understanding of the graphics subsystem, you should become familiar with the following terms:

- ▼ **2-D graphics**　Two-dimensional graphics that present flat images, including text and windows, on the screen. These images do not have any depth, and they constitute the majority of the images on the screen.

- ■ **3-D graphics**　Three-dimensional graphics mimic real-world environments because they give the perception of depth through shading and various other means. 3-D graphics are becoming more commonplace in computer technology.

- **Audio-video interleave (AVI)**   A file format that contains both audio and video data. The two types of data are interleaved.

- **Color depth**   The number of colors displayed at a given resolution. For example, a 24-bit graphics adapter has a color depth of 2 to the twenty-fourth power (2^{24}), which is equivalent to 16.7 million colors. Color depth is also known as pixel or bit depth.

- **Dot pitch**   A measurement that indicates how fine a detail the monitor can display. The lower the dot pitch, the better the quality of the picture.

- **Frame**   A single complete pass from the top of the screen to the bottom by the monitor's electron beam.

- **Frame rate**   A measurement used for video. It is the number of video frames (at a given resolution) that can be displayed per second. The frame rate indicates the quality of the video. The higher the number of frames per second (FPS), the better the quality.

- **Graphics accelerator**   Graphics adapters that have onboard processors to reduce the processing that needs to be performed on the CPU. Most modern graphics adapters are configured with onboard processors and are thus considered graphics accelerators.

- **High color**   Screen display with 15- or 16-bit color depth, which displays up to 65,536 colors simultaneously.

- **Interleaving**   Memory interleaving is a technique used to address more than one memory segment at a time. Graphics adapters supporting memory interleaving will dramatically increase performance.

- **Pixels**   Tiny elements or dots that make up the picture that you see on the screen.

- **RAMDAC**   RAM digital-to-analog converter. It is used to convert the digital data (coming from video memory) into an analog signal that the monitor can understand. RAMDAC consists of four components: SRAM (used to store the color map) and three digital-to-analog converters (DACs). A single DAC is used for each of the colors (red, green, and blue) of the electron gun that is used to display the images on the screen.

- **Refresh rate** The rate at which the screen is redrawn per second. It is expressed in terms of MHz. Higher refresh rates, typically 60 Hz and above, reduce the amount of screen flicker.

- **Resolution** The number of active pixels on the screen. The higher the number of pixels, the better quality of the picture. Resolution is expressed by its horizontal and vertical values (for example, 800 × 600 pixels).

- **True color** Screen display considered to show picture-quality graphics because true color displays up to 16.7 million colors at once. Some argue that this is the limit for the number of colors that the human eye can perceive.

- ▲ **Video bandwidth** The maximum amount of data that can be transferred to and from video memory, measured in MB/sec.

VIDEO DISPLAY

Many look at the process of presenting data on the screen in a readable format as black-box technology. Although it is far from a simple process, it is certainly not too difficult to understand.

Why worry about how information travels to the monitor? It is important to understand this process because it not only gives you a better understanding of the system, but it also helps you pinpoint bottlenecks in the graphics subsystem. Remember that any system or subsystem is only as fast as its slowest component. When you understand the video display process, you will know which features of the adapter provide the best performance boost.

Figure 7-2 illustrates the movement of data from the CPU to the monitor for display.

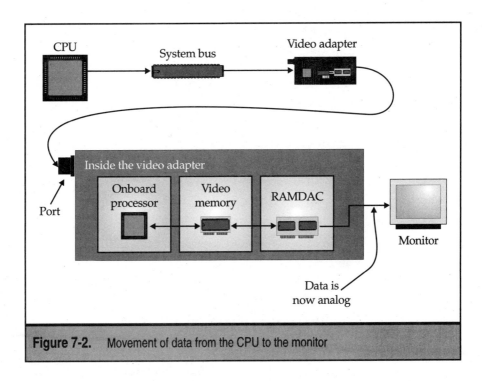

Figure 7-2.   Movement of data from the CPU to the monitor

The Video Display Process

Memory, the CPU, and the video adapter all work together to manipulate the data to produce images and text that the user can understand. The video display process begins at the CPU and ends at the monitor. Regardless of whether the graphics are 2-D or 3-D, the video display process follows these basic steps:

1. The CPU transfers digital data to the system bus, where it soon reaches the video adapter.

2. The video adapter processes the digital data and stores it in the adapter's video memory.

3. The RAM digital-to-analog converter (RAMDAC) reads the data from video adapter memory and converts the digital data to a signal (analog data) that can be read by the monitor.

4. The RAMDAC sends the analog data to the monitor for output to the screen.

The following sections examine each step to determine where potential bottlenecks may exist.

Step 1: CPU to Video Adapter

The transfer of data from the CPU to the graphics adapter involves many factors that can affect how fast the information travels to its destination. These factors include the CPU, the bus speed on the motherboard, and the bus speed on the graphics adapter. Since bus speeds are relatively slow compared to the CPU, the busses are usually the cause of a bottleneck.

To ensure that data transfer occurs at the fastest speed possible, you should use PCI, rather than ISA, EISA, or VLB, for the bus connecting the graphics adapter to the motherboard. Of course, this requires a system with a spare PCI slot for the graphics adapter. Another possibility is the new AGP specification, described in the section "Choosing a Graphics Adapter" later in this chapter.

NOTE: For performance reasons, some PCI devices take precedence over the graphics adapter. For example, if the system has only two PCI slots, you should use these slots for the NIC and hard disk controller instead of the graphics adapter. You are more likely to face this situation with servers than workstations.

Depending on the type of system you have, however, the PCI bus may not operate at the maximum 33 MHz (133 MB/sec) speed. For example, the earlier Pentium models (P75, P90, P120, and so on) usually operate at only 25 MHz, which further impedes performance.

The important point in this step is that you should use the best performing bus possible to achieve the highest possible data transfer rate.

Step 2: Video Adapter to Video Memory

There are two potential bottlenecks in the second stage of the video display process. The first involves the graphics adapter's onboard processor because it is the component that is responsible for processing the data that comes in from the CPU. To keep performance from slowing down, make sure that the graphics processor operates at a speed of at least 200 MHz. Some of the more advanced onboard processors that support 64-bit or even 128-bit processing have speeds in excess of 220 MHz.

The other potential bottleneck is the video memory. The key is to configure the graphics adapter with dual-port video memory as with VRAM, WRAM, and so on to ensure that performance is at its highest. You must use dual-port memory because the video memory must perform more than one operation at a time to successfully keep pace with the rest of the graphics subsystem. Dual-port video memory can be read from and written to at the same time.

The different types of video memory and their characteristics are examined in the section "Choosing a Graphics Adapter" later in this chapter. The video memory is situated in between the onboard processor and the RAMDAC, and it must communicate with both of these simultaneously to be effective. This is why it is important to use dual-port video memory whenever possible. The two devices that the video memory sits between are busy constantly, and the video memory must be fast enough to keep up with them both.

Step 3: Video Memory to RAMDAC

As data comes in from the onboard processor, it is temporarily stored in video memory until the RAMDAC is ready to use the data. The data is stored in video memory's frame buffer as a bitmap image. Then the data is transferred to the RAMDAC for more processing. Actually, the RAMDAC continuously reads data from video memory to maintain the display. Every time a new window is displayed, the mouse is moved, or the cursor changes, the display must be updated. Every update puts more pressure on the RAMDAC to read in more data.

Once the RAMDAC receives data, it transforms the data to analog signals that the monitor can recognize. As you may have already guessed, this transformation occurs continuously; the RAMDAC is always reading in data from memory and manipulating it for display on the monitor. If you increase the resolution or refresh rate, the amount of data that the RAMDAC must read and transform also increases.

Step 4: RAMDAC to the Monitor

This final step in the video display process, in which the RAMDAC passes the analog signal to the monitor, is the least likely place for a bottleneck in the graphics subsystem. Your concern here is with the monitor itself rather than the transfer of data. The monitor must be able to handle the workload given to it by the graphics adapter. Check the monitor's characteristics to be sure that the monitor supports the resolution, refresh rate, and color depth that the graphics adapter supports. Matching the two components' characteristics reduces the possibility of a performance bottleneck and decreases the likelihood that any incompatibility may be encountered. Consult the next section, "Graphics Hardware Considerations," for more information regarding performance issues with monitors.

GRAPHICS HARDWARE CONSIDERATIONS

Because most Windows NT operations are based on a graphical user interface (GUI), careful planning and consideration is needed in choosing your graphics hardware components. As with many other components of a Windows NT server, you have many choices when deciding how to achieve the best overall performance. The two primary components you should focus on are the video adapter and the monitor; these are important in any system.

Before you can determine what kind of video adapter and monitor to configure in your NT system, you need to look at what the video adapter will need to support. You should first consider the type of server it will be used for. For instance, will the server be used as a domain controller, file and print server, application server, or a server housing high-end graphics applications and data? Just as important, you must consider the types of applications that will be used on this server. Most business applications use 2-D graphics, but applications such as CAD and computer animation tools likely use 3-D graphics or OpenGL. OpenGL is an API standard for efficiently developing advanced 3-D graphics. It is an operating system independent API designed from the IRIS GL specifications by Silicon Graphics (SGI).

Choosing a Graphics Adapter

Once you have a general idea of what functions the server will be used for, you can begin to match these functions with the functions different video adapters support. The attributes that you need to consider when choosing a video adapter include the type of onboard processor or chipset the adapter uses, the amount and type of video memory, the bus type and width, whether the adapter supports 2-D or 3-D graphics (or both), the resolution and refresh rate, and Windows NT driver support.

Onboard Processor

Speeds in information technology are constantly increasing, and onboard processor technology for graphics adapters is no exception. Of course, the faster the onboard processor, the faster the graphics adapter and the less likely that the graphics subsystem will be a bottleneck. The onboard processor takes over much of the responsibility for processing video data from the CPU, which lets the CPU tend to other tasks. Typical onboard processors can process data 32, 64, or even 128 bits at a time. To realize the full potential of the onboard processor, it is imperative that you configure the card with the proper amount of video RAM. For example, a 64-bit card with only 1MB (1×8) of video RAM will not achieve its full processing power because only 32 bits of data will be addressed at a time. If the graphics adapter had 2MB (1×8) of video memory, then video memory could potentially be read or written to 64 bits (2×32) at a time.

Video Memory

Video adapters use several types of memory, most of which are specifically designed for use with video. These include EDO, VRAM, WRAM, and SDRAM, described in Table 7-1. As you can see, the various types of video memory can differ significantly in the amount of data traffic they can handle. Is it really necessary to configure the graphics adapter to use video memory with the highest possible bandwidth? Although this question may appear to have a relatively easy answer, it really depends on the type of graphics adapter you are using, how much money you are willing to spend, and what type of functionality the graphics adapter will support (2-D or 3-D graphics or both). From a performance standpoint, faster is usually better, but there is a point where the fastest available video memory may be overkill. The goal is to supply enough bandwidth so that performance is not hindered and you will not have to upgrade relatively soon. Because of the heavy demands placed on the graphics subsystem, video memory must be considerably faster than normal system RAM.

Memory Type	Description	Video Bandwidth
EDO	Extended data-out RAM	105 MB/sec
VRAM	Video RAM	80 MB/sec
WRAM	Window RAM	80 MB/sec
SDRAM	Synchronous DRAM	253 MB/sec or 100 MHz
SGRAM	Synchronous graphics RAM	490 MB/sec
RDRAM	Rambus DRAM	600 MHz
nDRAM	RDRAM offspring	1,600 MHz

Table 7-1. Memory Types and Throughput Capacity

The standard dynamic RAM (DRAM) that can be used on the main system was once considered the memory type of choice for graphics adapters. (For more information on DRAM and other types of system memory, refer to Chapter 4.) Now, usually only low-end graphics adapters use this type of video memory because of its many limitations, such as its reliance on the system clock to reset it before each screen refresh operation. Other memory types, by contrast, have undergone significant changes to meet the needs of today's graphics adapters. Also, the increasing popularity of graphics-based operating systems, such as Windows NT, and the increasing demands for higher resolution, more frequent screen refresh operations, and greater color depth necessitate the use of high-performance video memory. Video memory enhancements not found in standard DRAM include dual-port memory, masked writes to memory, clock speed synchronization—and much more.

The following paragraphs describe the types of video memory that should be considered for the system's graphics adapter.

VRAM   VRAM, otherwise known as video RAM, uses a totally different approach than that of conventional RAM. It can be accessed through two ports instead of just one, which means that it can be accessed by two different devices simultaneously, as illustrated in Figure 7-3. As discussed earlier in this chapter, video memory communicates with both the onboard processor and the RAMDAC simultaneously, which makes this dual-port feature extremely useful for providing high performance. VRAM allows the onboard processor and RAMDAC to access it simultaneously; while new information is rushing in, it is also being pumped out to the RAMDAC. As a result, VRAM yields substantially better performance than conventional RAM. The downside, however, is that VRAM is extremely expensive compared to other forms of video memory.

WRAM   Window RAM (WRAM) is another type of memory that supports two ports, like VRAM. Although WRAM uses the same dual-port technique as VRAM, it provides a performance increase of

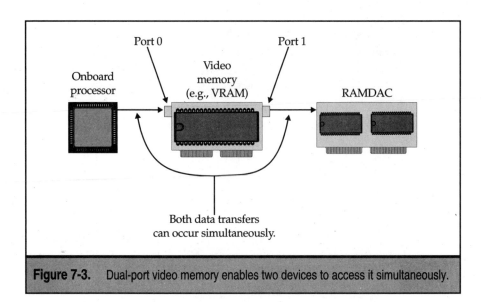

Figure 7-3.   Dual-port video memory enables two devices to access it simultaneously.

up to 50 percent over VRAM. In addition, WRAM is cheaper (by as much as 20 percent). Clearly, WRAM is a better memory choice than VRAM.

RDRAM   In Table 7-1 you can see that RDRAM offers blazingly fast performance. It offers data transfer rates as high as 600 MHz! This technology is gradually seeping into the market and is already in use on some graphics adapters. You can expect to see its effects in the system memory market as well. You should strongly consider this type of video memory, especially if your system will be used for CAD, rendering, computer animation, or other high-end graphics applications.

Intel has formed an alliance with Rambus, Inc., the company that designed this type of video memory. It is anticipated that Intel will use this technology in its future motherboard designs.

A new version of RDRAM, called nDRAM, is currently under development. It is expected to enable data transfer rates as high as 1,600 MHz!

SGRAM   Synchronous graphic RAM (SGRAM) is a single-port version of video memory. While it is true that two ports are more efficient than one, SGRAM relies on other techniques to achieve high data transfer rates. SGRAM can synchronize operations with the CPU bus clock at speeds reaching 100 MHz, and it also uses various write techniques to increase total bandwidth. Moreover, SGRAM can open two memory pages instead of just one, simulating the dual-port technology of VRAM and WRAM.

CALCULATING THE AMOUNT OF VIDEO MEMORY NEEDED   How much video memory does the graphics adapter need? There are two factors that determine how much video memory is needed: the number of colors to be displayed and the screen resolution. Table 7-2 summarizes the minimum amount of video memory required to display various resolutions and color depths in 2-D. It is important to note that these are the minimum amounts required and that some of the video memory is also used to store font metrics and other graphical information. Calculating the minimum amount, however, will help you understand how to configure the right amount of video memory on the graphics adapter. It is always a good idea to configure the graphics adapter with a little more video memory than the minimum required to account for the other graphical information that may be stored. For example, for a screen display with a resolution of 640 × 480 pixels and 256 colors, the minimum amount of video memory required is 1MB, but you would be wise to purchase a card with at least 2MB of video memory.

To calculate the minimum video memory requirements for the resolution and color depth that you plan to display, use the following formula:

resolution × (color depth ÷ 8) =
minimum video memory required (in bytes)

For example, suppose you want a resolution of 800 × 600 and 256 colors. You know that 256 colors is equivalent to 8-bit color ($2^8 = 256$),

Resolution (Horizontal × Vertical)	Approximate Number of Colors Supported	Color Depth (in Bits)	Minimum Memory Required (in MB)
640 × 480	256	8	1
	65,000	16	1
	16.7 million	24	2
800 × 600	256	8	1
	65,000	16	1
	16.7 million	24	2
1,024 × 768	256	8	1
	65,000	16	2
	16.7 million	24	3
1,280 × 1,024	256	8	2
	65,000	16	3
	16.7 million	24	4
1,600 × 1,200	256	8	2
	65,000	16	4
	16.7 million	24	6

Table 7-2.   Video Memory Requirements at Various 2-D Resolutions and Color Depths

so your calculation is as follows: 800 × 600 (8 ÷ 8) = 480,000 bytes, or approximately half a megabyte. Always round the result up to the nearest megabyte. It is unusual today to find a graphics adapter configured with less than 1MB of video memory. Therefore, in this example, the graphics adapter would need to have a minimum of 1MB of memory installed.

You are also strongly urged to take into account future requirements. You should purchase enough video memory so that if you do decide to run at a higher resolution, the amount of memory on the graphics adapter is sufficient. The alternative is adding video memory to the graphics adapter (if it supports additional memory). In the preceding example, for instance, 2MB would be needed to run at the next higher resolution. This may seem like overkill, but the extra memory can save you time and money in the future.

2-D AND 3-D MEMORY REQUIREMENTS   Generally, 3-D graphics require much more memory than 2-D graphics running at the same resolution. 3-D graphics adapters need more video memory because an extra buffer is needed to store the third-dimension depth value. That is, 3-D graphics adapters need a total of three buffers—front, back, and Z buffers—to display the images and text on the screen. A 2-D environment does not need a Z buffer; the front and back buffers are sufficient to support just two dimensions.

How much more memory do 3-D graphics require? To calculate the video memory requirements for 3-D graphics displays, you can use the following formula:

resolution $\times$ (color depth $\div$ 8) $\times$ 3 buffers =
minimum video memory required

For example, suppose you want a resolution of 800×600 and approximately 65,000 colors. You know that 65,000 colors is equivalent to 16-bit color ($2^{16} = 65,536$), so the calculation is (800×600 (2×3) = 2,880,000, or approximately 3MB.

Table 7-3 shows other minimum video memory requirements at different resolutions and color depths.

Bus Architecture

The subject of bus architectures for graphics adapters can be confusing because there are two bus architectures that are related to the graphics adapter. First, there is one bus that coincides with the system's bus architecture, such as ISA, VLB, EISA, or PCI, that is the actual connection point where the graphics adapter meets the rest of the system. The second bus is internal to the graphics adapter. The two buses are separate, but they are not completely independent of one another.

Resolution (Horizontal × Vertical)	Approximate Number of Colors Supported	Minimum Memory Required (in MB)
640 × 480	256	1
	65,000	2
	16.7 million	3
800 × 600	256	2
	65,000	3
	16.7 million	5
1,024 × 768	256	3
	65,000	5
	16.7 million	8
1,280 × 1,024	256	4
	65,000	8
	16.7 million	12
1,600 × 1,200	256	6
	65,000	12
	16.7 million	18

Table 7-3.   Video Memory Requirements at Various 3-D Resolutions and Color Depths

EXTERNAL BUS ARCHITECTURES   There is some debate over whether the graphics adapter on servers should be a low-end model (such as ISA) or a high-capacity model (such as EISA or PCI). The argument for the former is that typical servers do not need blazingly fast graphics adapters since many of them spend most of their time locked behind closed doors. Moreover, the graphics adapter takes up a precious, high-throughput EISA or PCI slot. The other side of the argument is that most graphics adapters now support only PCI configurations, and if an extra PCI slot exists, then configuring the server with a PCI graphics adapter can only improve server graphics performance.

PCI is definitely becoming commonplace, and its performance level is outstanding. If the server can give up a PCI slot, then it is highly recommended that you choose PCI over ISA or some other low-end bus architecture. Otherwise, you are limiting the amount of bandwidth from the graphics adapter to the rest of the system.

CAUTION: On systems that need to run at resolutions higher than 640 × 480 or that use high-end graphics applications such as CAD or rendering packages, ISA should not even be considered.

AGP: A NEW STANDARD IN ARCHITECTURE   The accelerated graphics port (AGP) acts like a bus, but it is, in fact, a port. For this reason, only one device (the graphics adapter) can use AGP. This newcomer is designed specifically to increase the bandwidth of graphics adapters. Although this new technology has not saturated the mainstream market and most applications, especially business applications, cannot take advantage of this new technology, its benefits are gradually becoming noticeable, especially in high-end graphics workstations. At this time, Windows NT does not support AGP, but you can expect to see it supported in later releases. Some motherboards, such as the Intel 440LX, have built-in AGP support so you can include an AGP graphics adapter in the system's configuration.

AGP is logical extension to the PCI 2.1 specification. For this reason, AGP graphics adapters can utilize the PCI slot and sometimes even the same PCI driver, though this practice is not supported or recommended. Unlike PCI, AGP is not shared with other devices, such as SCSI and network devices. It is dedicated solely to the graphics adapter. Figure 7-4 illustrates this distinction. AGP also boasts double the performance of PCI. It operates at a minimum of 66 MHz (a bandwidth of approximately 266 MB/sec), while PCI operates at 33 MHz (a bandwidth of 133 MB/sec), though significant improvements from AGP are generally noticeable only when moving large amounts of graphics data at high resolution. AGP also incorporates features, such as pipelined read and write operations, demultiplexed graphics data and addresses on the bus, and Direct Memory Execute (DIME), designed to minimize latencies and

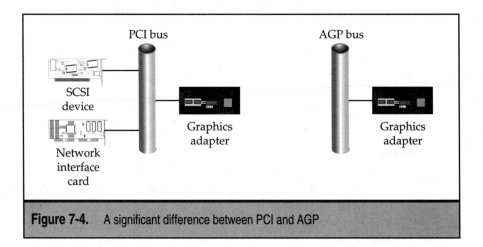

Figure 7-4.   A significant difference between PCI and AGP

increase bandwidth. DIME exploits system memory for *texture mapping* (applying surface characteristics, such as color, brightness, reflection, and more to 3-D objects) operations used in 3-D graphics, which can significantly reduce the movement of texture mapped data and reduce the overhead associated with 3-D graphics.

In conclusion, the performance advantages that you expect from AGP compared to PCI are not yet overwhelming. Don't be surprised, though, to see the AGP specification continually improving until it becomes the bus of choice. Future AGP specifications are expected to achieve transfer rates as high as 800 MB/sec. Moreover, AGP is likely to become the most popular bus for graphics adapters because of its benefits for the system's existing PCI devices. For example, the AGP adapter isolates all graphics data, which offloads an enormous amount of data from the PCI bus. This leaves more room for other devices (SCSI disk drives, network adapters, and so on) and boosts the ability of these devices to transfer data.

INTERNAL BUS ARCHITECTURES   The graphics adapter's internal bus fosters communication among the onboard processor, video memory, and RAMDAC. The width of the bus is typically 32, 64, or 128 bits. This means that 4 to 16 bytes of data can be transferred from one component to another at once. Generally, the wider the bus, the better the overall performance of the card.

To take advantage of a wider bus, such as the 64-bit bus, however, there must be sufficient memory. For instance, a card with a 64-bit data bus that is configured with 1MB of video memory would not be able to take advantage of the larger bus because the memory chip itself is only 32 bits wide, as illustrated in Figure 7-5. In this case, 2MB (1 × 8) of video memory is needed to use the 64-bit bus. Recall from Table 7-2 that a resolution of 1,024 × 768 with a color depth of 256 colors requires only 1MB of video memory. However, to provide the most efficient use of the internal bus architecture (64 bits and

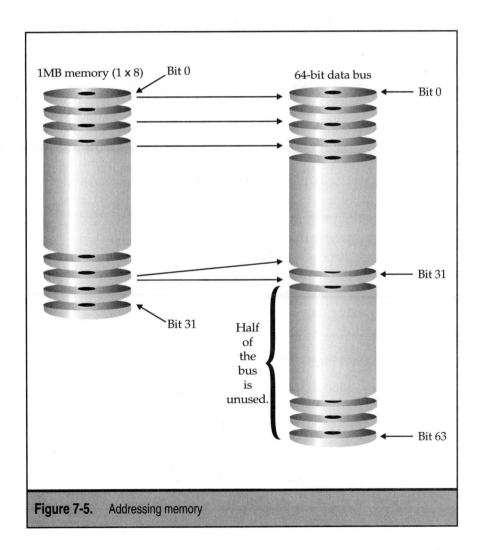

Figure 7-5.   Addressing memory

higher), the amount of addressable memory must match the internal bus width. Therefore, without taking into account the resolution and color depth, the minimum amount of memory needed to sustain performance in a 64-bit graphics adapter is 2MB, and a 128-bit card requires 4MB.

2-D and 3-D Video Adapters

Most of the work you do on a Windows NT server will use 2-D graphics. Most business applications support only 2-D graphics, as do most administrative tools, such as WINS Manager, Server Manager, and Internet Information Server Manager. When you consider 2-D performance, you are concerned mainly with such factors as the speed of screen refresh operations and how smoothly you can scroll through text and graphics; you are not concerned with such factors as texture mapping and rendering.

Much of what can be done to improve 2-D graphics has already been accomplished. Consequently, the 2-D graphics adapters available for the Windows NT platform do not have extreme variations in performance. Nevertheless, you still need to choose a good-quality 2-D graphics adapter that can adequately handle large graphical workloads, especially since Windows NT relies on a graphical user interface.

Graphics adapters today are moving away from purely 2-D technology to technology that supports 3-D graphics. This trend is reflected in Windows NT's support for OpenGL, DirectX, and so on. Depending on your server's function and the applications that run on the server, you may need support for 3-D graphics. 3-D performance is now becoming the distinguishing factor among graphics adapters.

What is the best choice for your Windows NT environment? The answer depends largely on what you will be using the server for. If the server handles CAD, rendering, or other graphics-intensive applications, then a 3-D graphics adapter is your optimal choice. For NT machines that rely heavily on 2-D graphics but that may require 3-D graphics in the future, you have the option of incorporating both 2-D and 3-D graphics capabilities in one graphics adapter. The best overall performance will come from a graphics adapter that provides exceptional quality with both 2-D and 3-D graphics capabilities.

Resolution and Refresh Rate

The screen resolution and refresh rate are closely related in terms of a graphics adapter's performance and should be the first things you consider when choosing a graphics adapter. These features define the quality and detail of images that are presented on the display. As the resolution increases, so does the number of pixels that make up the images on the screen. The more pixels on the screen, the finer the detail can be. However, to maintain the fine detail from the resolution, the graphics adapter must also provide an adequate refresh rate so there's no distortion or flicker.

Typical resolutions are 640 × 480, 800 × 600, 1,024 × 768, and 1,600 × 1,200, but Windows NT also supports resolutions of 1,152 × 882, 1,280 × 1,024, among others, as shown in Table 7-4. The first number in the resolution specification represents the horizontal resolution, and the second number represents the vertical resolution. Combining these values gives you the total resolution for the entire display.

Some graphics adapters support all resolutions, while others can handle only a few. In addition, the quality at which graphics adapters support different resolutions varies significantly, because graphics adapters support certain refresh rates at higher resolutions than others. It is more difficult to maintain high refresh rates as you increase the resolution because the amount of data passing through the graphics adapter increases greatly at each higher resolution. In

Common Resolutions	Uncommon Resolutions
640 × 480	1,152 × 864
800 × 600	1,152 × 882
1,024 × 768	1,280 × 1,024
1,600 × 1,200	

Table 7-4.   Resolutions Supported by Windows NT

addition, increases in the number of colors (the color depth) are also harder to support at higher resolutions, and this too can affect graphics performance.

When the resolution is increased, more resources, namely video memory and onboard processing power, are needed to achieve a particular color depth and refresh rate. The more memory and processing power the graphics adapter has to support higher resolutions, the better, because otherwise you will encounter severe performance degradation if you try to run your system in these modes. Higher resolution means that more data must be handled by the graphics adapter, and increases in the refresh rate and color depth add even more resource requirements.

In conclusion, if you plan to use the higher resolution modes, be sure that the graphics adapter can adequately support the refresh rate needed for those resolutions. The minimum refresh rate for any resolution should be 60 Hz. Also be sure to follow the recommendations outlined in Table 7-2 for the minimum video memory requirements. If the refresh rate and memory requirements are not met while running at higher resolutions, the graphics subsystem performance will suffer, and this will affect overall system performance.

Driver Support

The availability, stability, and reliability of graphics device drivers is extremely important on the Windows NT platform. Make sure that the drivers you use are certified by Microsoft to ensure that adequate testing has been done. In other words, check the NT HCL at **http://www.microsoft.com/hwtest/**, or verify with the manufacturer that the device drivers are optimized for NT. Using an uncertified or beta driver can wreak havoc on a Windows NT machine.

RECOVERING FROM A FAULTY DRIVER INSTALLATION   Sometimes incompatibility problems occur between even certified graphics device drivers and other system drivers. As a result, for instance, the screen may go blank or become severely distorted. If this happens, you can use the following steps to recover:

1. Restart the machine.

2. Press the spacebar when you are prompted to do so.

3. Select the Last Known Good configuration.

4. Press ENTER to revert back to the Last Known Good configuration.

   When you choose this option, Windows NT undoes any changes in the Registry that may have caused the problem to occur.

If you are absolutely certain that the graphics device driver caused the problem (that is, if this was the only configuration change made on the system), you have yet another option. By default on Intel-based machines, two paths to the Windows NT system folder are created, like these:

```
multi(0)disk(0)rdisk(0)partition(2)\WINNT="Windows NT Server
Version 4.00"
```

```
multi(0)disk(0)rdisk(0)partition(2)\WTNNT="Windows NT Server
Version 4.00 [VGA mode]" /basevideo /sos
```

You can choose the VGA mode option to start Windows NT with the standard VGA driver. Once you get into the system, be sure to reconfigure the graphics device driver so the problem does not recur.

Table 7-5 lists several graphics adapter manufacturers and provides web site information for each.

Monitors

Working in conjunction with the graphics adapter is the monitor, which, as you well know, is the component that you use to view the information passed from the graphics adapter. It is far too common for machines to be configured with just any type of monitor. Most people just make sure it is big enough and the manufacturer has a good reputation. However, you should be sure to choose not only a good-quality monitor, but also one that matches your graphics adapter's abilities. Otherwise, you will be wasting the capabilities of the monitor or the graphics adapter or both.

Company Name	Web Site
ATI Technologies	http://www.atitech.ca/
Canopus Corporation	http://www.canopuscorp.com/
Creative Labs	http://www.creaf.com/
Diamond Multimedia Systems	http://www.diamondmm.com/
Hercules	http://www.hercules.com/
Media Vision	http://www.svtus.com/
Number Nine Visual Technology	http://www.nine.com/
Oak Technology	http://www.oaktech.com/
S3 On Board	http://www.s3.com/
Trident Microsystems	http://www.trid.com/
Tseng Labs	http://www.tseng.com/
VideoLogic	http://www.videologic.com

Table 7-5.   Web Addresses for Graphics Adapter Manufacturers

As with graphics adapters, there are numerous factors to consider when choosing a monitor, including bandwidth, refresh rate, interlacing, dot pitch, resolution, size, and brand reputation. Although there is no one best choice for some of these attributes, it is important that you consider all of them to make sure your graphics adapter and monitor capabilities match. All of these attributes are discussed in the following paragraphs.

Table 7-6 provides contact information for several prominent monitor manufacturers.

Bandwidth

Bandwidth is a measure, in megahertz, that indicates the total amount of data that the monitor can handle per second. The manufacturer provides this specification. To take full advantage of

Company Name	Contact Information
Acer	1-800-733-2237
	http://www.acer.com/aac/index.htm
Compaq	1-800-888-0220
	http://www.compaq.com/
Dell	1-800-289-3355
	http://www.dell.com/
Hewlett Packard	1-800-553-2901
	http://www.hp.com/
Hitachi	1-800-448-2244
	http://www.hitachi.com/
Mitsubishi	1-714-220-2500
	http://www.mitsubishi.com/
NEC	1-650-528-6000
	http://www.nec.com/
Nokia	1-800-483-7952
	http://www.nokia.com/
Samsung	1-800-800-726-7864
	http://www.sosimple.com/
Sony	1-800-352-7669
	http://www.sony.com/
ViewSonic	1-800-888-8583
	http://www.viewsonic.com/

Table 7-6. Contact Information for Monitor Manufacturers

the graphics adapter, match this value with the graphics adapter's clock frequency, also provided by the manufacturer (and sometimes referred to as the pixel rate). The clock frequency indicates the total amount of data that the graphics adapter can handle per second.

Refresh Rate

As noted earlier, the refresh rate refers to the maximum number of frames that can be displayed at a given resolution. The refresh rate depends primarily on the horizontal scan rate (the number of lines of pixels that can be displayed per second) and the resolution. For example, the monitor may have a 85 Hz refresh rate at 640 × 480 resolution, but at a higher resolution such as 800 × 600, it may be capable of a refresh rate of only 72 Hz. Be sure to match the refresh rate with the video adapter's capabilities.

What is an acceptable refresh rate? Personal preference plays a role in this choice, but you should know that the higher the refresh rate, the higher the quality of the picture; at lower rates, the picture becomes grainy and flickers. For some people, 60 Hz is acceptable, but the higher the resolution and the larger the monitor, the higher the refresh rate needed to produce clear pictures.

Interlaced versus Non-interlaced Monitor

Interlaced monitors scan the display in two passes. On the first pass, they scan every other line, and then they return on a second pass and scan all the lines they previously skipped. The human eye can barely (or not at all) detect this subtle scanning technique, and it has been widely used to increase resolution and reduce flicker. Non-interlaced monitors, on the other hand, scan every line in a single pass to produce higher quality output at a given resolution.

Non-interlaced monitors are best even for servers that do not make heavy use of graphics because of the image quality they offer. Note, though, that some non-interlaced monitors revert to interlaced mode at high resolutions (usually 1,024 × 768 or higher). For this reason, you should carefully read the monitor's specifications.

Dot Pitch

The dot pitch is the diagonal distance between the center of any two dot triads. A dot triad is a triangular arrangement of three phosphor dots on the screen. Each of these dots is a different color: red, green, or blue. Together they comprise the images that are displayed on the monitor.

As the dot pitch increases, the dots on the screen become more noticeable. Therefore, a low dot pitch rating gives you a better quality picture. Aim for monitors that have a dot pitch of .28 or less to ensure that picture quality is not distorted in higher resolutions. Again, your decision here relates more to personal preference than to performance.

Resolution

Resolution is one of the most important attributes to consider when purchasing a monitor. This measurement indicates how fine a detail the monitor can display. The resolution is the maximum number of pixels that can be displayed at once and it coordinates with the monitor's dot pitch. For instance, a 800×600 resolution means that the screen can display 800 pixels horizontally and 600 pixels vertically. Generally speaking, the higher the resolution, the better the quality of the picture.

Your monitor must be capable of supporting the resolutions you want to use. You need to look at not only the resolution modes a monitor supports but also the screen size. For instance, a resolution of $1,024 \times 768$ viewed on a 14-inch monitor will yield difficult-to-read images even for someone with excellent vision. Table 7-7 shows the recommended matches between resolution and monitor size.

Resolution	Minimum Monitor Size (in Inches)
640×480	14
800×600	15
$1,024 \times 768$	17
$1,280 \times 1,024$	17
$1,600 \times 1,200$	21

Table 7-7. Matching Resolution and Monitor Size

GIVING VIDEO SERVERS A BOOST

Multimedia applications have exploded into Windows environments, and Windows NT is no exception. Computer video, especially, is hot because it can be used both for entertainment and as a business tool. The application possibilities for video over the Internet, intranets, and extranets are enormous. It can be used as a powerful training device, as a video-conferencing tool, and much more. Streaming video is a technique used for delivering video more rapidly over a network, and its use is expanding because of the increasing bandwidth capabilities of even remote connections.

Streaming Video

Many companies are catching on to the advantages of combining video technology with Windows NT and, in particular, are now employing Windows NT servers to provide streaming video for their Internet, intranet, and extranet connections. New techniques for configuring Windows NT video servers enable enhanced inter-operability between client and server as well as higher-quality video.

Prior to streaming video, the delivery of video from the server to the client was limited. Pushing video to a client meant that the client first had to download the entire video file before playing it. This approach works for some applications, but it does not allow video to be fully exploited. It limits the ability to use video for training purposes, presentations, and so on, for example, and it is unworkable for applications such as video conferencing, where the video data must be live or on demand.

Server-based streaming video overcomes many of these limitations. For instance, server-based streaming video is integrated into Internet Information Server. A client connects to the web server via the HTTP protocol and begins retrieving the video data, as with earlier video retrieval methods. However, instead of having to wait for the entire video to download, after a few seconds of buffering on the client machine, the client can start playing the video. In addition, the Windows NT video server constantly monitors the connection for any condition changes that may affect video quality such as drops in bandwidth. If such conditions occur, the Windows NT video server adjusts accordingly to minimize the changes in video quality for the client.

Configuring Server-based Streaming Video for Optimal Performance

Although server-based streaming video can provide powerful enhancements to your Windows NT environment, this technology can also profoundly affect system and network performance. The three primary factors that influence streaming video performance are video compression, the disk subsystem, and the network subsystem.

COMPRESSION To keep the amount of server disk space consumed by video files to a minimum and to prevent the network from being saturated by video data, the video data must be compressed. Otherwise, you will need enormous amounts of disk space (possibly hundreds of gigabytes or even terabytes) as well as enough network bandwidth to support all the video data traversing the network.

There are several different ways that you can compress video data, including decreasing the frame rate, reducing the color depth, and lowering the resolution. Generally, the more you compress the video data, the lower the picture quality. For example, reducing the resolution from 640×480 to 320×240 compresses the video data by about four times, but the quality will be lower, and the picture may even be hazy. If you are planning to compress video data by reducing the frame rate, it is important to keep in mind that 30 frames per second yields what is considered good quality, but that 10 frames per second yields picture quality generally considered unacceptable. The object to compressing data is to reduce the video data to a more manageable size while maintaining reasonable picture quality. The amount of compression applied to video should also match the resources that will store and process the video data.

The utilities used to compress streaming video are called *coders/decoders,* or *codecs.* Codecs available on the Windows NT platform vary widely in capability. Most of them, except Microsoft NetShow, use proprietary techniques that require special types of players to view the streaming video.

OPTIMIZING THE DISK SUBSYSTEM FOR VIDEO PERFORMANCE   The best performing drives for video application are those that provide fast, steady performance as opposed to drives that perform well but execute small transfers requiring bursts. This is because the vast majority of video transfers from the disk are read and written sequentially.

Another important device to consider for a video server's disk subsystem is a drive that incorporates thermal recalibration delay. Thermal recalibration delay is a process that recalibrates the drive heads during idle times to ensure read and write operability. Essentially, this is a self-tuning mechanism that promotes smoother flow of video data by preventing dropped video frames.

EFFECTS ON THE NETWORK   Although server-based streaming video does offer exceptional performance over a network compared to earlier video technologies, it still affects network performance more than it does any other subsystem. Reduced network performance has been one of the strongest arguments against the transmission of video over network connections. Because of its impact on the network, it is imperative that you optimize server-based streaming video.

Server-based streaming video does, however, tame the tremendous bandwidth requirements of video, thanks largely to the technologies used by streaming video, such as buffering and IP multicasting. IP multicasting is a type of broadcasting without the limitations or disadvantages of IP broadcasting. It can transmit data to a lot of users simultaneously without causing as big a performance hit as IP broadcasting. It also has the ability to cross router boundaries. The other video delivery option is unicasting, which is another type of IP data transmission. The difference between IP multicasting and unicasting is that unicasting attempts to provide a set bandwidth for each client, whereas multicasting segments a set amount of bandwidth for all clients. For example, if bandwidth has been set at 56 Kbps, unicasting will try to deliver 56 Kbps to each client, whereas multicasting will spread the 56-Kbps bandwidth across all the clients, as illustrated in Figure 7-6. For more information on network performance issues, refer to Chapter 5.

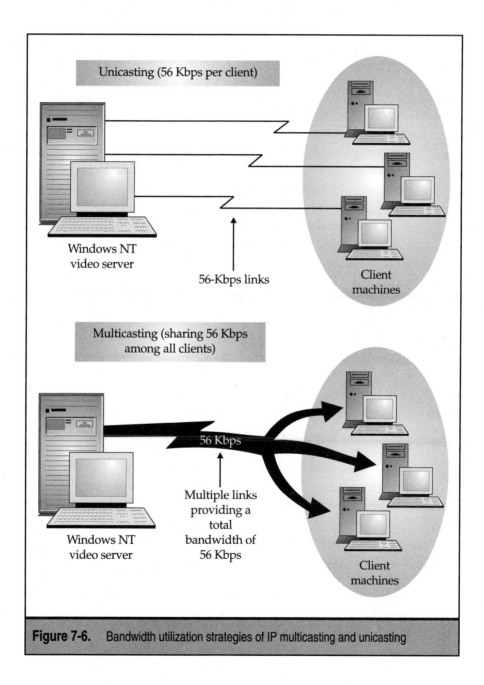

Figure 7-6.   Bandwidth utilization strategies of IP multicasting and unicasting

What can be done to further enhance a Windows NT video server using streaming video? In addition to the recommendations given in Chapter 5 for improving network performance, you can reduce the workload streaming video applications place on the network by using IP multicasting instead of unicasting whenever possible. Even when using IP multicasting, however it is a good idea to limit the number of users that can connect to the server simultaneously.

Video Server Products Available for Windows NT

As the popularity of multimedia applications such as server-based streaming video continues to grow, more and more sophisticated multimedia products are becoming available for Windows NT. Some of the more popular server-based streaming video products are listed in Table 7-8.

Product Name	Company	Contact Information
Microsoft NetShow	Microsoft	1-800-335-3100 http://www.microsoft.com/netshow/
RealNetworks RealVideo	RealNetworks	1-206-674-2700 http://www.real.com/
VDOnet VDOLive	VDOnet	1-617-528-6000 http://www.vdo.net/
Vxtreme Web Theater	Vxtreme	1-800-501-4689 http://www.vxtreme.com/
Xing Streamworks	Xing Technology	1-800-294-6448 http://www.xingtech.com/

Table 7-8.   Contact Information for Server-based Streaming Video Servers

MONITORING GRAPHICS SUBSYSTEM PERFORMANCE

Measuring the performance of the graphics subsystem is not an easy task, primarily because the methods you have used to measure other system components have to be modified for use here. The Performance Monitor does not include an object specifically for monitoring the graphics subsystem. Moreover, few vendors supply counters or even their own utilities to measure a graphics adapter's performance.

How, then, do you measure graphics subsystem performance? One of the best ways still involves using the Performance Monitor. You have to be resourceful when you are using it because there are not any objects that are dedicated to the graphics subsystem. Instead, you must monitor the Process object to find out if the graphics subsystem is a bottleneck in system performance.

Using the Process object, monitor the Client Server Runtime Subsystem (CSRSS) instance to obtain an indirect indication of the system's graphics activity. Recall from "Understanding the New Kernel Architecture" earlier in this chapter that the CSRSS is the subsystem responsible for graphics activities. There are many counters that you can use to watch the CSRSS instance. However, the most important counters to watch from the Process object are % Processor Time, % Privilege Time, and % User Time. Table 7-9 summarizes these counters.

How do the values obtained from these counters translate into actual graphics performance? Your primary concern with these counters is ensuring that their values are consistently low. For exceptional graphics performance, you want values ranging from 0 to 10 percent, while for good to acceptable performance, the counters should range between 11 and 40 percent. If your system is consistently experiencing values higher than 40 percent, the graphics subsystem most likely is a bottleneck.

In your daily monitoring routine, you may or may not include the CSRSS instance. If you do not and you are experiencing unusually high Processor: % Processor Time values, it is possible that the culprit is the CSRSS. Therefore, it is important that you watch the CSRSS

Counter	Exceptional Performance (%)	Good to Acceptable Performance (%)	Description
% Processor Time	0 to 10	11 to 40	This counter reflects the percentage of processing time used by all threads in a process (CSRSS) to execute instructions.
% Privilege Time	0 to 10	11 to 40	This counter takes into account the percentage of elapsed time needed to execute code in privileged mode. Instructions operating in privileged mode have access to system-private data that is protected from access by a process' threads executing in user mode.
% User Time	0 to 10	11 to 40	This counter indicates the percentage of elapsed time needed to execute code in user mode.

Table 7-9. Counters for Monitoring the CSRSS

instance when the processor is experiencing high percentages of processing time. This way you can trace the cause and determine whether the graphics subsystem is the reason the processor is being taxed. A faster video adapter or one with more onboard RAM would provide noticeable improvement in graphics subsystem performance.

The following two examples demonstrate how to monitor the CSRSS to determine graphics subsystem performance.

Example 1: Examining Graphics Activity While Playing a Game

One way to see how monitoring the CSRSS subsystem can help you determine graphics subsystem performance is to experiment with a game called Free Cell. In this example, Free Cell is set to play against itself until the game is completed. During the game, you will notice that the duties of the CSRSS increase, and you can see whether the additional load placed on the graphics subsystem can be handled without degradation in overall system performance. To perform this experiment, do the following:

1. Start the Performance Monitor from the Start | Programs | Administrative Tools menu.

2. Begin monitoring the Process counters % Processor Time, % Privileged Time, and % User Time with the CSRSS instance, as shown in Figure 7-7.

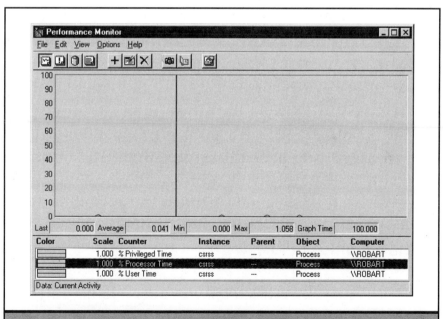

Figure 7-7.   Monitoring the CSRSS subsystem

3. Start the game Free Cell from the Start | Programs | Accessories | Games menu. If no games were installed on the server, you can add them through the Add/Remove Programs applet in the Control Panel.

4. From the Game menu, choose New Game to start a new game.

5. While holding down the SHIFT and CTRL keys, press F10 until the User-Friendly User Interface dialog box appears:

6. Select Abort so the computer will begin to play through to completion once you make a move.

7. Make any move you wish to allow the game to play itself.

8. After the game is complete, check the Performance Monitor to see the effects of the game on the CSRSS and the graphics subsystem.

The game's effects on the graphics subsystem will vary depending on your system's configuration. However, you should not encounter values above 10 percent if your graphics subsystem is configured with the proper hardware. In the example shown in Figure 7-8 (a Pentium Pro 200 with a Matrox Millenium 4MB video adapter), the game caused only a slight rise in activity in all three counters monitoring the CSRSS instance.

Example 2: OpenGL Screen Saver Effects on the Graphics Subsystem

In this next example, you will see how the dazzling 3-D graphics effects of the OpenGL screen savers can affect the graphics subsystem. In fact, this example illustrates why it is so important not to use these screen savers on servers because of their effects on the graphics

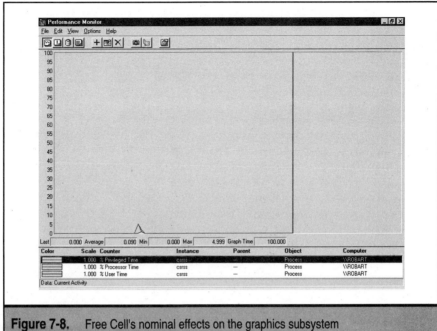

Figure 7-8.   Free Cell's nominal effects on the graphics subsystem

subsystem as well as on other system components. It is recommended that you run this experiment on a test machine rather than on a server in production.

To perform this experiment, do the following:

1. Start the Performance Monitor from the Start | Programs | Administrative Tools (Common) menu.

2. Begin monitoring the Process counters % Processor Time, % Privileged Time, and % User Time with the CSRSS instance.

3. In the Control Panel, double-click the Display applet to display the Display Properties dialog box.

4. On the Screen Saver tab, select an OpenGL screen saver of your choice from the Screen Saver drop-down menu, as shown in Figure 7-9.

5. Click the Preview button to run the screen saver for a short time.

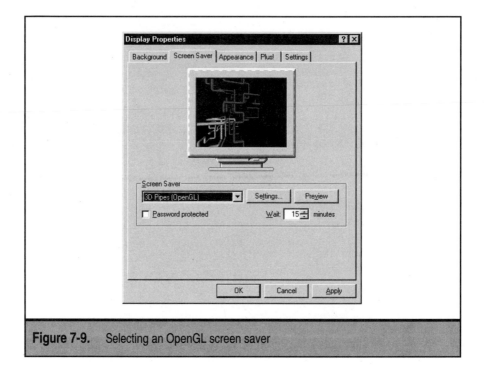

Figure 7-9.   Selecting an OpenGL screen saver

6. Once the screen saver demonstration is done, check the Performance Monitor to see its effects on the CSRSS and the graphics subsystem.

CONCLUSION

The graphics subsystem is often the most neglected Windows NT subsystems, especially when it comes to optimizing performance. This is surprising considering that Windows NT relies on a graphical user interface for most of the duties that it performs and the types of applications that it supports. This chapter showed the importance of optimizing graphical subsystem performance and provided recommendations regarding how to configure an optimal system. It also discussed the increasing popularity of multimedia, high resolutions, high color depths, and high refresh rates and the necessity of a high-performance graphics subsystem to support these features; otherwise, not only would the performance of the graphics subsystem suffer, but the entire system could be brought to its knees.

CHAPTER 8

A New Look at the Powerful Performance Monitor

You can use the Performance Monitor to measure individual system components or the overall performance of local and remote NT computers. This Win32 utility is bundled with Microsoft's operating system, and is one of the most commonly used monitoring and troubleshooting tools from Microsoft. It allows you to monitor and analyze system performance data in real time and to collect log data for future scrutiny. The Performance Monitor can also alert administrators when system values exceed or fall below specified values, and it can report on the data that it has collected.

This chapter begins by introducing the Performance Monitor provided with Windows NT, providing you with a basic understanding of this tool's capabilities. This chapter then explores the ways you can use the Performance Monitor to monitor your system, describing the various monitoring options available to you so you can more effectively use this utility. You will also learn about other applications that you can use in conjunction with the Performance Monitor to enhance your monitoring capabilities.

OVERVIEW OF THE PERFORMANCE MONITOR

The Performance Monitor is tailored for performance tuning for your Windows NT systems environment. It provides information that can be used to detect problems and optimize the system. It captures, or takes snapshots of, system performance characteristics at periodic intervals that can be used to see the behavior of the system, measure the load on system components, predict future resource requirements, and alert you to potential failures of system components.

Like any application, the Performance Monitor will use some of your system's resources. However, the amount of resources it uses depends on the frequency of data collection, the number of objects or counters being measured, and the location of log files. Typically, the Performance Monitor uses 2 to 4MB of memory and minimal processor time (1 to 5 percent). Adding the disk and network subsystem components to your monitoring scheme also adds to the resource load. Although the Performance Monitor's effects on system resources are minimal, you still should be aware of them.

What Is Monitored

Each Windows NT computer has components that the Performance Monitor can monitor. These components can be hardware or software components that perform tasks or support workloads. Many of these components have indicators that reflect certain aspects of their functionality that can be accurately measured in terms of the rate at which tasks are accomplished. For example, measuring the Network Segment: Total bytes received/second counter shows you the number of bytes placed on it by the network subsystem. In particular, all collected data comes from the counters that the Performance Monitor monitors.

Objects

In Windows NT systems, many of the components that comprise an entire system are grouped into *objects* based on their characteristics. For example, anything pertaining to the processor is located in the Processor object, and anything relating to memory is located in the Memory object. Objects are grouped according to functionality or association within the system. They can represent logical mechanisms, such as processes, or physical entities, such as hard disk drives.

The number of objects is not limited to what Windows NT provides. All Microsoft BackOffice products have objects that can be evaluated and tracked by the Performance Monitor. Objects can also be created by third-party vendors so that IT professionals like yourself can use the Performance Monitor to monitor your own components. Microsoft has purposely chosen to let outside vendors create objects and counters, specific to their own applications or devices, that the Performance Monitor can read.

The number of objects present on a system depends on the system configuration. For instance, Internet Information Server counters will not be present if the system is not running that application. However, the following common objects can be found in every system:

▼ Cache

■ Logical disk

- Memory
- Paging file
- Physical disk
- Process
- Processor
- Server
- System
- Thread
- ▲ Network-related objects (Browser, NetBEUI, Server, and so on)

In addition, many other objects are available to the Performance Monitor from third-party vendors or Microsoft BackOffice applications. Here are a few examples:

- ▼ SQL Server
- SQL Server Users
- SNA Logical Unit Sessions
- FTP Server
- Gopher Service
- HTTP Service
- Internet Information Services Global
- Microsoft Fax Server
- ▲ Telephony

Counters

Each object contains *counters*. Counters typically provide information about use, throughput, queue length, and so on for a particular object. For example, all counters pertaining to the paging file are contained in the Paging File object. The Performance Monitor uses the counters within an object to collect data. The information

gathered from these counters is then displayed in the Performance
Monitor window or dumped into a data file.

Instances

If your system has more than one similar component (two hard
drives, four processors, and so on), each one is considered an
instance of that component. Each instance in the system has an
associated counter that measures its individual performance.
Counters with multiple instances also have an instance for the
combined instances. Shown here is an example of the PhysicalDisk
counter with multiple instances:

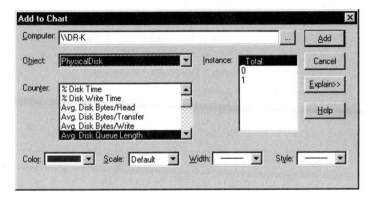

Uses of the Performance Monitor

So far we have seen that the Performance Monitor monitors and
collects system performance statistics and can be used to notify
support staff of impending bottlenecks and failures. Here is a
summary of some of the possible uses for the Performance Monitor:

▼ Monitoring performance in real time or historically

■ Monitoring the effects of system configuration changes

■ Identifying bottlenecks

■ Troubleshooting performance problems

■ Identifying trends and patterns in system performance

- Creating performance reports
- Determining resource capacity
- Monitoring local or remote machines
- Notifying administrators when specified resources approach thresholds
- ▲ Exporting data from counters to other products for further analysis

Charts

Counter statistics can be monitored in real time with the Chart view. The Chart view lets you actively watch the values of selected counters. The results of the collected data appear in a histogram (bar chart) or graph. As you can see in Figure 8-1, the graph format produces a chart that looks something like an electrocardiogram used for monitoring a heartbeat. The charting format you choose is determined mainly by personal preference. You may find one format more suitable than others for viewing your system.

To begin viewing counters in real time, follow these steps:

1. Select Chart from the View menu.

2. Select Add to Chart from the Edit menu. You'll see the following dialog box:

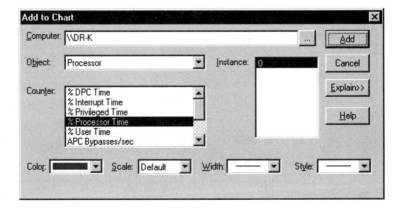

3. If you want to monitor a remote machine, enter the UNC name of the computer in the Computer box, or browse for the computer by clicking the button to the right of the Computer text box.

4. Choose the object you want to monitor.

5. Select the desired counters within the object.

NOTE: If you're not sure whether to add a certain counter, click Explain in the Add to Chart dialog box to gain a better understanding of the desired counter. This option is also available for alerts and reports.

6. Choose the Color, Scale, Width, and Style for the counter. The Scale factor is usually set to 1.00, but you can change this value to increase or decrease the counter's height within the graph.

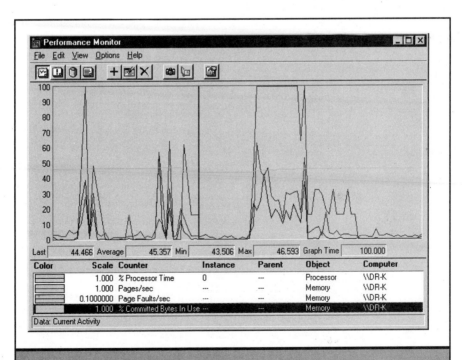

Figure 8-1.   A Performance Monitor graph

7. Click Add to add the counter to your monitoring scheme.

8. Add more counters if desired.

9. Click Done when you are finished.

 NOTE: You can highlight an individual counter by selecting the counter and pressing CTRL-H. This helps you differentiate that counter from the rest.

Exporting Charts

To export a chart for use with another application, such as Microsoft Excel or Access, do the following:

1. Select Export Chart from the File menu.

2. Choose the location for the chart and type the filename in the Performance Monitor – Export As dialog box.

3. Select one of the following file types.

   ■ TSV: Tab-delimited file

   ■ CSV: Comma-delimited file

4. Click Save.

Chart Options

There are a few chart options, shown in Figure 8-2, that can change the look and feel of the Performance Monitor and that can be of great service to you by helping to decipher the displayed values. These options can be set within the Options | Chart menu.

▼ **Legend**   Displays the chart legends at the bottom of the window. Removing this feature also removes the Value Bar option.

■ **Value Bar**   Displays the value bar at the bottom of the window. The value bar displays the last, average, minimum, and maximum values of the highlighted counter.

■ **Gallery**   Defines the graphical representation of the counters. The choices are Graph and Histogram.

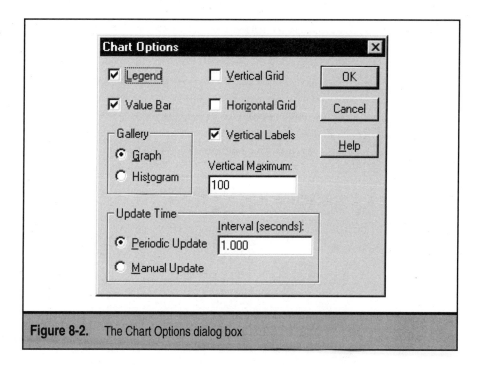

Figure 8-2.   The Chart Options dialog box

- **Update Time**   Indicates the frequency with which the Performance Monitor captures data from the selected counters. Selecting Periodic Update automatically captures data at the frequency you specify. Manual Update captures data only at your command.

- **Vertical Grid** and **Horizontal Grid**   Display vertical or horizontal grid lines to help you pinpoint values in the display window.

- **Vertical Labels**   Displays the Y-axis labels. By default, labels 0 to 100 are displayed (for 0 to 100 percent).

▲ **Vertical Maximum**   Indicates the maximum value displayed on the Y-axis. By default, the maximum value is 100 to reflect percentages, but you may want to change this value when monitoring counters that are not percentages, such as the number of frames sent and received from the TCP/IP protocol.

Logs

The Performance Monitor can store the data it collects in a data file, or log. Logged data is not viewed in real time, so logging provides a historical perspective on system performance. As mentioned in Chapter 2, logging is the preferred approach in capacity planning because it makes it easier to interpret trends or patterns in system performance. It also provides a mechanism for storing data in a convenient format for future scrutiny. You can use the Performance Monitor to replay the cataloged performance data, or you can easily export it to other applications.

To configure the Performance Monitor to log activity, follow these steps:

1. Select Log from the View menu.

2. Select Add to Log from the Edit menu to display the Add To Log dialog box:

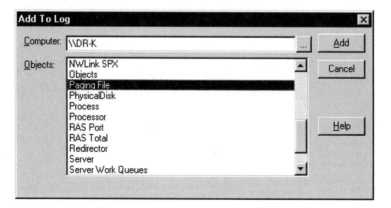

3. In the Computer text box, type the UNC name of the computer you want to monitor (the local machine is the default) or click the button to the right of the text box to browse for the computer you want to select.

4. In the Objects list, select the objects to be monitored and click Add.

5. When you're finished, click Done.

6. Select Log from the Options menu to display the Log Options dialog box:

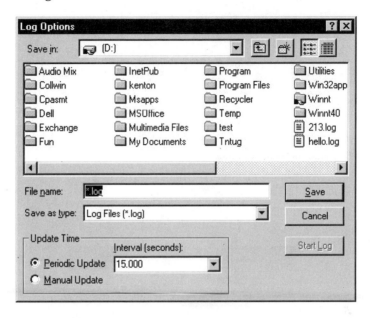

7. In the File Name text box, type a name for the log file in the format *logname*.log.

8. Specify the Update Time option by choosing Periodic Update, or select Manual Update.

9. Click Start Log to initiate logging. Note that when logging starts, the Start Log button changes to the Stop Log button.

It is very important to plan the update time for logging activity, because the size of the log file can quickly become overwhelming. Controlling the monitoring interval enables you to control the growth of log files as well as to analyze system statistics in specified time frames.

NOTE: There are no mechanisms within the Performance Monitor to cap the size of the log file. If hard disk space is limited, watch the growth of the log file closely to ensure that the file does not try to exceed disk capacity. You may also want to configure the Performance Monitor to alert you when drive space (LogicalDisk: % Free Space) drops below 25 percent.

Instant Replay

Once you have a log file containing raw system performance data, you can retrieve and analyze the data that has been collected. For now, we will just explore how to use the Performance Monitor to open the log file for analysis; later in the chapter we will explore how to use Microsoft Office applications to reduce and analyze log files.

Before attempting to open and analyze a log file, make sure the log file is not currently in use. Once data collection in the log file is stopped, you can open and display data from the file. Follow these steps:

1. Select Log from the Options menu.

2. In the Log Options dialog box, shown here, click Stop Log.

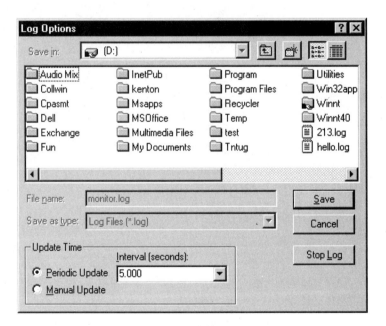

3. From the View menu, select Chart or Report, depending on how you want to display the data from the saved log file.

4. From the Options menu, choose Data From. You'll see this small box:

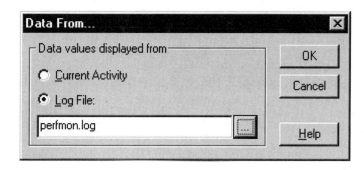

5. Select Log File, and either type the path and filename or click the button to the right of the text box to browse the directory structure for the log file you want to use.

6. Click OK.

   At this point you can either add counters to be displayed by selecting Add to Chart from the Edit menu, or you can specify a time frame that you want to examine. Specifying a time frame reduces the amount of data displayed at one time; that's what you'll do next.

7. Select Time Window from the Edit menu.

8. In the Input Log File Timeframe dialog box, shown here, use either the time line scroll bar or select the appropriate bookmarks to specify the start and stop times for the data you want to view.

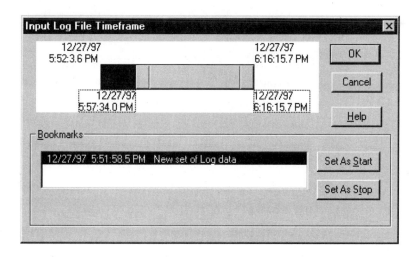

NOTE: If you use Bookmarks to specify the time frame, the time line scroll bar will reflect the times you specify.

9. Click OK.

    Now you're ready to display the log file data.

10. From the Edit menu, select Add to Chart or Add to Report.

11. Choose the object you want to view. Note that only the objects that you added to the log file are displayed.

12. Select the desired counters for the object.

13. Specify the Color, Scale, Width, and Style options for the counter. The Scale factor is usually set to 1.00, but you can change this value to increase or decrease the counter's height within the graph.

14. Click Add.

15. Add more counters if desired.

16. When you're finished, click Done.

Exporting Logs

To export a log file for use with another application, do the following:

1. Select Export Log from the File menu.

2. Choose the location for the file and specify the filename in the Performance Monitor – Export As dialog box.

3. Select one of the following file types.

    ■ TSV: Tab-delimited file

    ■ CSV: Comma-delimited file

4. Click Save.

Reports

You can also use the Performance Monitor's reporting mechanism to view data gathered from counters. The major difference between the Report view and the other views is that the Report view displays the data in a tabular format. Because this format is relatively easy to understand, Report view can be particularly useful in trouble-shooting problems or detecting bottlenecks.

The same technique you used before to display counters is applied to the Report view. You choose individual counters that you want to display from the objects that you select. To add counters to the Report view, do the following:

1. Select Report from the View menu.

2. To clear a report or create a new report, choose New Report Settings from the File menu.

3. Select Add to Report from the Edit menu.

4. If you want to monitor a remote machine, type the UNC name of the computer in the Computer text box or browse for the computer name by clicking the button to the right of the text box.

5. Select the object you want to monitor.

6. Select the desired counters for the object.

7. Click Add.

8. Add more counters if desired.

When you're finished, click Done.

Exporting Reports

If you want, you can export reports for use in another application. To export reports, do the following:

1. Select Export Report from the File menu.

2. Choose the location for the file and specify the filename in the Performance Monitor – Export As dialog box.

3. Select one of the following file types:

■ TSV: Tab-delimited file

■ CSV: Comma-delimited file

4. Click Save.

Alerts

Alerts can be set on any available counter to notify the administrator when a specified condition occurs, such as when processor use exceeds 90 percent. If a counter exceeds or falls below the value that you specify, the Performance Monitor triggers an alert that logs the event and notifies the administrator.

To add and configure alerts, do the following:

1. From the View menu, choose Alert.

2. Add counters by selecting Add to Alert from the Edit menu. The following dialog box will appear:

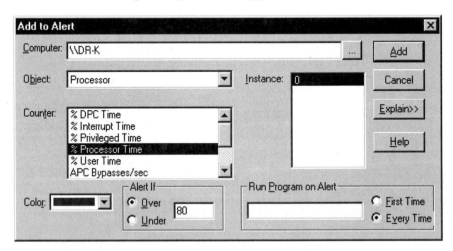

3. If you want to monitor a remote machine, type the UNC name of the computer in the Computer text box or browse for the computer by clicking the button to the right of the text box.

4. Choose the object you want to monitor.

5. Highlight the desired counter for the object.

6. Select the desired color of the alert. If don't specify a color, the Performance Monitor chooses different colors for each alert.

   For the Alert If option, specify a value for the counter and select Over if you want an alert triggered if the counter exceeds this value or Under if you want an alert triggered if the counter falls below this value.

7. If you want to run an application, such as paging software, when an alert occurs, type the path and filename for the application in the Run Program on Alert box. If you use this option, also specify whether this program will run the first time or every time the alert is triggered.

Alert Options

Other available options for alerts enhance the recording of events and provide other forms of notification to administrators. You can switch to the Alert view when a triggered event occurs, log events to the Event Viewer's Application log, send a message through the network to a specific user name, and specify the frequency with which the Alert log is updated. To display the Alert Options dialog box, shown here, choose Alert from the Options menu.

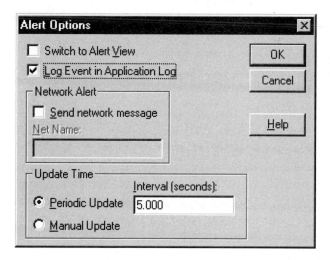

Monitoring a Remote Machine

The Performance Monitor is not limited to monitoring just the local Windows NT machine. It is configured to measure the performance of the local machine by default, but you can extend its monitoring scope to other Windows NT machines on the network. You can monitor a remote NT machine separately or at the same time that you monitor the local machine.

To monitor a remote NT machine or add one to the existing monitoring scheme, follow these steps:

1. Select one of the four views (Chart, Log, Report, or Alert) from the View menu.

2. Choose Add to View from the Edit menu.

3. In the Add to View dialog box, type the UNC name of the computer in the Computer text box and click Add. Alternatively, click the button to the right of the text box to see a list of available computers to monitor. Select the computer you want to monitor and then click OK.

4. Choose the object you want to monitor.

5. Select the desired counters for the object.

6. Click Add.

7. Add more counters if desired.

8. When you're finished, click Done.

CRITICAL RESOURCES TO MONITOR

The Performance Monitor can monitor several different counters available on NT systems, including counters provided by NT, Microsoft BackOffice, and third parties. It is imperative that you carefully select the counters to monitor, because the amount of information collected can quickly become unwieldy and, ultimately, useless. A general rule of thumb is that you should monitor the four common contributors to bottlenecks:

▼   Memory

■   Processor

■   Disk subsystem

▲   Network subsystem

As mentioned in Chapter 2, these critical resources are often the first components to degrade system performance. For example, it is more common for an application server to have slow response times due to slow disk access or lack of memory than it is for the server's performance to be degraded due to its remote access service.

In addition to monitoring the four common contributors to bottlenecks, it is also imperative that you closely watch the resources that affect the way the server functions within the NT environment. A Windows NT Server may be configured to handle file and print sharing, application sharing, domain controller functions, or any combination of these. The functions that you use determine which resources you should closely monitor. For example, monitoring disk subsystem counters for file and print servers will be more important than for domain controllers. Devising a monitoring scheme where you include the four common contributors as well as the resources pertaining to the server's functions will greatly increase your ability to boost your system's performance.

Memory

Two memory counters that should always be monitored are Page Faults/sec and Pages/sec. Together they can accurately tell you whether or not the system is configured with the proper amount of RAM. More specifically, they reflect the amount of paging activity within the system. You can refer to Chapter 4 for more information on memory and paging. Because the Page Faults/sec counter includes both hard and soft faults, an acceptable level is going to be much higher than that for the Pages/sec counter. Most systems can tolerate Page Faults/sec levels of only about 250 before performance is compromised. Pages/sec values consistently above 20 indicate that the system is not configured with enough physical RAM. In fact, if

Pages/sec values are always above 10, you need to start thinking about adding more memory.

Two other counters that are worth mentioning again are the Commit Limit and Committed Bytes counters. These two counters work together. This means that you need to look at both of the counters to gauge whether or not the system is using virtual memory efficiently. The Commit Limit counter indicates the total available virtual memory in the system. This is the sum of the amount of physical RAM and the maximum paging file size. As mentioned in Chapter 4, the paging file size is configured on the Performance tab within the Control Panel system applet.

The Committed Bytes counter shows the total amount of virtual memory that the system has already committed from its resources (Commit Limit). When the size of the Committed Bytes counter approaches the Commit Limit value, the system is running out of virtual memory. In fact, the system will warn you if these two values meet. You will also be warned to increase the paging file size and restart the system:

At this point, you will need to increase the amount of physical RAM or expand the paging file. As mentioned earlier, consult Chapter 4 for more information on memory, including how to increase the paging file size.

What should the minimum and maximum paging file size be? Microsoft recommends that the minimum paging file size should be the amount of physical RAM plus 11. However, a better strategy is to figure out the typical usage requirements of the paging file for a particular system, and then specify that value as the minimum—except, of course, if the value falls below the formula suggested by Microsoft. For example, if the paging file typically requires 83MB of space but the formula totals to 75MB (64MB RAM + 11), then you should set the minimum size of the paging file to at least 83MB. You do not want the system to have to worry about increasing the paging file size on its own. Placing the responsibility for increasing the paging file size on the system induces performance degradation. You can head off this problem by properly configuring the minimum paging file size.

The maximum value should be the highest value you ever expect the paging file to grow to. Of course, you must have enough free disk space to accommodate the maximum size of the paging file. One rule of thumb is to set the maximum value to the minimum value plus 50 percent.

Other than trial and error, what other methods can be used to calculate the paging file values? Actually, the required minimum size for the paging file is only 2MB. It is quite obvious, though, that performance will be severely degraded if the paging file is set to 2MB, because thrashing (excessive paging) will be inevitable. The best method that I have found to calculate an appropriate paging file size is to set the minimum paging file size to a relatively low value and then monitor the memory use for typical operations. The Memory: Committed Bytes and Paging File: % Usage counters will indicate the required amount of virtual memory. The Committed Bytes counter will show you the size of virtual memory currently in use by all applications, and the % Usage will show you what percentage of the paging file is currently being used.

During typical system use, the Committed Bytes counter should never exceed the amount of physical RAM in the system. If this counter approaches the physical RAM value, be sure to also check the number of hard page faults with the Memory: Pages/sec counter. A general rule of thumb is to keep the Memory: Pages/sec counter less than 20. Values higher than 20 force the system to expand the paging file, thus verifying that the system is paging excessively.

For the Paging File: % Usage counter, an acceptable value is below 40 percent. Keep in mind that if you properly configure the minimum and maximum paging file size, you drastically reduce the risk of compromising performance even during periods of peak memory use.

Processor

Recall that % Processor Time is the amount of time that the processor is doing useful work. This essentially means the amount of time that the processor is not executing non-idle threads or servicing interrupts. Each instance of % Processor Time should not exceed 50 percent use. If this counter consistently approaches or exceeds 50 percent, the first step in troubleshooting should be to check whether the Interrupts/sec counter is 3,500 or more. If the system is experiencing 3,500 or more interrupts per second, a device or device driver may be to blame for the high processor use.

Disk Subsystem

By default, the drivers necessary to collect information on the disk subsystem are disabled to avoid the overhead for this process. This overhead is negligible, however, and should not affect your results. To gather hard disk drive statistics, load the disk monitoring drivers by typing **DISKPERF -Y OR DISKPERF -Y \\REMOTEMACHINE** at the command prompt. This enables the disk performance monitoring drivers the next time the system is restarted. If you do not enable the disk performance monitoring drivers and you try to gather disk statistics, the Performance Monitor results will be only zeros.

NOTE: If the system is configured to use software-based RAID, type **DISKPERF -YE** instead of DISKPERF -Y at the command prompt. This enables more counters that are specific to RAID configurations.

When you are not monitoring the disk subsystem, you should disable the disk performance monitoring drivers. This will conserve the number of resources they take up. Entering the command **DISKPERF -N** at the command prompt disables the drivers. It is important to note here that the drivers are disabled only after the system is restarted.

Once you enable the disk performance monitoring drivers, you can monitor any counter within the disk subsystem. As mentioned in earlier chapters, the first counters to watch in the disk subsystem are % Disk Time and Disk Queue Length from either the LogicalDisk or the PhysicalDisk object. The acceptable values for these counters are less than 55 percent and less than 2, respectively.

One important circumstance that you should be aware of involves the disk subsystem and memory. A system that is not configured with the proper amount of memory can cause a tremendous amount of disk activity, because the system is trying to compensate for the lack of memory by paging. Thus, if you notice excess disk activity and it is supported by unacceptable % Disk Time and Disk Queue Length values, check to see if the paging file is properly configured and the system has enough RAM. If the paging file is properly configured, adding more RAM can solve the problem if it is memory related.

Network Subsystem

The network subsystem is the most difficult system to optimize and troubleshoot due to the complexity of the interactions among components. The operating system, network-based applications, network interface cards, protocols, and topologies all play pivotal roles in determining how well your network performs. Consequently, you cannot simply monitor a few particular counters as though they were the most important ones to watch.

However, there are two counters worth mentioning as good starting points for monitoring the network subsystem performance. These counters are Server: Bytes Total/sec and Network Segment: % Network utilization. By default, the Network Segment: % Network utilization counter is not enabled. You must load the Network Monitor Agent or the Network Monitor Tools and Agent service before the counter will appear in Performance Monitor. To install either service, do the following:

1. In the Control Panel, double-click on the Network applet to display the server's network properties.

2. On the Services tab, click Add to add the service.

3. In the Select Network Service dialog box, scroll down the list of services until you find either the Network Monitor Agent

or the Network Monitor Tools and Agent service. Select the service you wish to install and then click OK.

4. At this point, Windows NT prompts you to supply the location of the source files. Provide the appropriate path (for example, **d:\i386**) and click Continue.

5. Close the Network Properties dialog box by clicking Close.

6. When the system prompts you to restart the system, click Yes.

The Server: Bytes Total/sec counter indicates the amount of network activity experienced by the server. An acceptable value for the Server: Bytes Total/sec counter is approximately 0.8 Mbps for Ethernet-based networks and 0.5 Mbps on 16-Mbps Token Ring networks. Values exceeding these thresholds will increase the chances that the network will become saturated. For the % Network utilization counter, there are really two acceptable values: theoretical and actual. Theoretically, an Ethernet network should be able to use as much bandwidth as possible and sustain levels of 70 percent and higher. However, as the saturation level reaches 30 percent, the rate of collisions begins to rapidly increase. As collisions increase, Ethernet begins to use the network bandwidth less efficiently. For this reason, % Network utilization should always be kept under 30 percent. If your network is struggling to keep close to this level, you should consider performance enhancements for your network. These might include segmenting the network, increasing the speed (for example, from 10Mb to 100Mb), or using switches instead of hubs.

ANALYZING DATA WITH MICROSOFT EXCEL

Using the Performance Monitor by itself to analyze data collections is somewhat limiting. You should not complain, though, because the Performance Monitor is a free utility. It also has data export features so you can use other applications, such as Microsoft Excel or Access, to enhance the analysis process. The fact that the Performance

Monitor is a free utility that can easily share its information with other applications makes it a strong competitor against the more powerful third-party performance monitoring utilities.

Most third-party utilities have their own mechanisms for analyzing the data that they collect. However, there are costs associated with using any third-party performance monitoring utility. These include, but are not limited to, the price of application licensing, the learning required to use the utility, and the need to convince management that the benefits of investing in the third-party product far outweigh the costs. Even so, the capabilities of third-party products make them worthy of investigation.

Before you go out and buy one of these products, you should be aware of the analysis that can be performed with the Microsoft Office suite. Most Microsoft-based networks using Windows NT have at least a few of the products packaged in this suite. If your environment is one of the many out there that uses Microsoft Office products, you are in luck. The Performance Monitor integrates extremely well with Microsoft Excel and Access so that you can use these tools to help analyze system performance data. If you do not have these products, you can still use another spreadsheet or database application to overcome the Performance Monitor's limited ability to make sense of collected data.

The following example steps you through the process of exporting data to Excel to chart system performance. This example is relatively simple, but you can apply the concepts to larger data collections. The results you create from Excel can be used to more easily interpret the data as well as provide reports to management.

Reducing the Data Collection

The first step in using Excel is to open the log file with the Performance Monitor. You can then choose which object counters you want Excel to use. Selecting which counters to use can greatly reduce the data set, because the selection process enables you to use only the data relevant to your purposes instead of the entire object that you collected in the log file.

CAUTION: You should not delete log files less than a few months old, even if you think you have exported all the data that you need to Excel or some other application for analysis. You may find that you need to analyze another counter in addition to the ones currently being analyzed.

1. Start the Performance Monitor and choose either Chart or Report from the View menu.

2. From the Options menu, choose Data From.

3. When the Data From dialog box appears, click Log File. In the text box, either type the location and filename of the log file or click the button to the right of the text box to browse for the log file.

4. Click OK.

5. Add any counters you want for each object that you monitored. For detailed instructions for adding counters, see "Overview of the Performance Monitor" earlier in this chapter.

6. Depending on how long you logged data, you may want to narrow the time interval, further reducing the amount of data that you want to analyze. To narrow the time interval, choose Time Window from the Edit menu.

Obtaining a Good Sampling

The time interval value is also useful for getting a good sampling from the data. Without a good data sampling, it is hard to deduce what is really going on in the system. Moreover, some intervals are more important than others. For example, the hour right before lunch time might contain a lot of system activity, but during the time shortly thereafter, you find that activity dramatically decreased. Measuring system performance during the lull period does not mean as much to you as the hour before lunch time. The next time you log data, you may want to monitor only the hour before lunch time and not the period during lunch time.

Charting Performance with Excel

You are now ready to export your chart or report to a format that can be easily read by Excel. Excel can read both the .TSV and .CSV formats that the Performance Monitor uses for export, but the .CSV format is designed specifically for spreadsheets. For this reason, it is better to export the data to the .CSV format.

1. Choose Export Chart or Export Report from the Performance Monitor's File menu.

2. In the Performance Monitor – Export As dialog box, specify the path and filename of the file you want to export, using the .CSV extension.

3. Click Save.

4. Start Microsoft Excel.

5. From the File menu, choose Open.

6. In the Open dialog box, shown in Figure 8-3, select Text Files from the Files of Type drop-down list.

7. Specify the location and filename for the exported data by browsing the directory structure in the Open dialog box.

8. Click Open.

The exported data file is now opened in Excel. Notice the information in the top-left corner of the worksheet. It indicates the name of the machine from which the measurements were extracted, the date and time the collection took place, and the start and stop times for this particular selection of counters. The information may not appear to serve much purpose right now, but when you start looking at many different data sets and machines, it will help you keep organized.

You will also see a data set that looks similar to the one in Figure 8-4. The data set can be used in many different ways. For example,

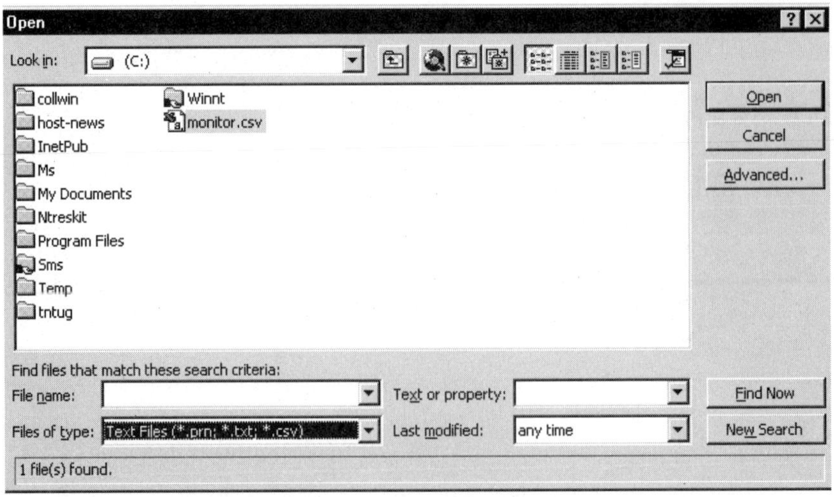

Figure 8-3. The dialog box for opening files in Excel

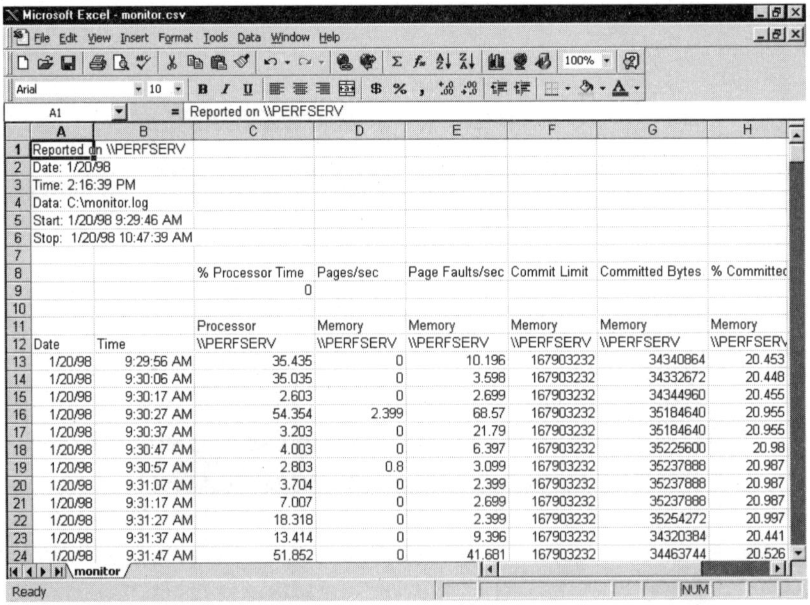

Figure 8-4. A sample data set exported to Excel from a Performance Monitor log file

you can use Excel's conditional formatting, PivotTables, to analyze the collected data. You can also chart the data to make it easier to interpret and search for trends or patterns. The rest of this example focuses on how to chart a given set of data.

Charting the Data with Excel

Now that the CSV file is opened within Excel, you can begin charting the data you select. To create a chart within Excel, do the following:

1. Highlight the cells containing data that you want to chart as shown in Figure 8-5.

2. Start the Chart Wizard by selecting Chart from the Insert menu.

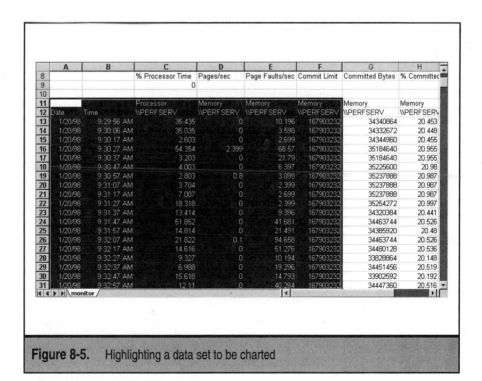

Figure 8-5.   Highlighting a data set to be charted

3. The Chart Wizard steps you through the chart creation process. On the first screen, select the type of chart you want to use, such as the Area Chart type.

NOTE: To view a sample chart for your selection, click and hold the "Press and hold to view" sample button.

4. Click Next.

5. Specify the data ranges to be charted, as shown in Figure 8-6. If you highlighted data before starting the Chart Wizard, the Data Range field is automatically filled in for you. You can change this value if it is not correct.

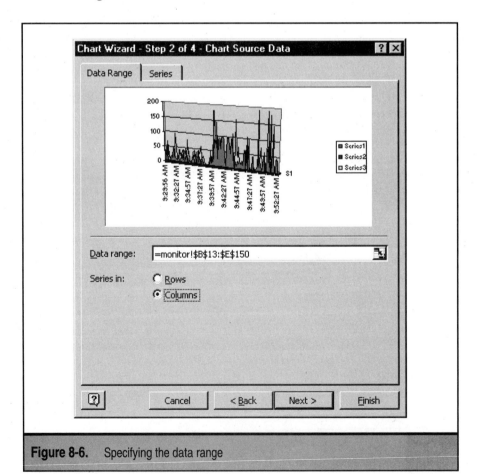

Figure 8-6.   Specifying the data range

6. Select the Series Tab, shown in Figure 8-7. A series represents an individual counter that will be displayed in the chart. The series legend is displayed beside the actual chart.

7. Select a series and type a name for the series in the Name box.

8. In the Values box, the values to use should be automatically specified. However, you can change these values if necessary. For example, the Pages/sec counter values are located in the C column from cells C$13 to C$40.

9. Repeat steps 7 and 8 for each series-to-counter relationship. If you need to add or remove a series, you can do so by clicking Add or Remove directly under the Series box.

10. Click Next.

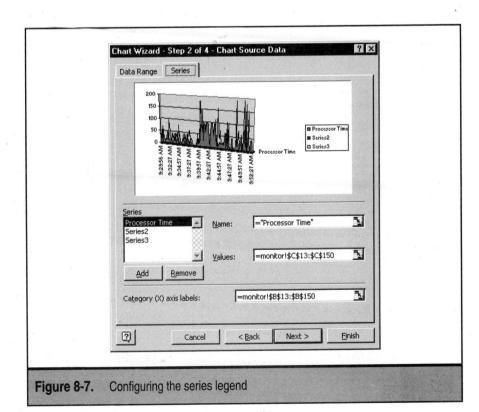

Figure 8-7. Configuring the series legend

11. In the next Chart Wizard dialog box, shown in Figure 8-8, give the chart a title and optionally provide names for the X-axis and Y-axis. This dialog box also lets you further customize the chart. For this example, you use the default custom configurations.

12. Click Next.

13. Specify whether you want to create a new worksheet for the chart or export it to an existing worksheet. (It is wise to keep the data and charts on separate sheets. To do this, click the button next to As New Sheet.)

14. Type a name of your choice for the new worksheet that will contain the chart.

15. Click Finish.

CREATING PERFORMANCE MONITOR TEMPLATES (*.PMW)

Saving your workspace can drastically reduce the amount of time you spend configuring the Performance Monitor to keep an eye on

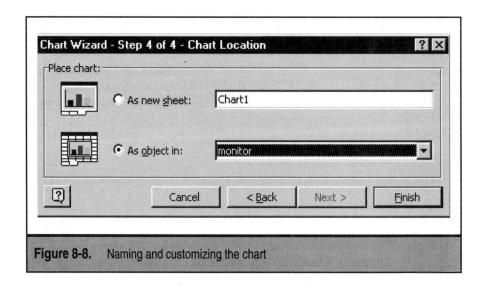

Figure 8-8. Naming and customizing the chart

your systems. The process involves simply selecting the view (Chart, Log, Report, or Alert) you want to use, adding the counters you want to monitor, and saving the workspace to a workspace file (*.PMW). The next time you want to monitor this group of counters, all you need to do is open the workspace file, and the configuration will be complete. The following procedure assumes that you have already selected a view to use and have added the counters you want to monitor.

To save the workspace to a file for later use, do the following:

1. From the File menu, choose Save Workspace.

2. In the Performance Monitor – Save Workspace As dialog box, specify the path and filename of the workspace file you want to save.

3. Click Save.

You can use the Open command on the File menu to open an existing workspace file the next time you want to use those particular settings.

The biggest advantages of using workspace templates are the time you save configuring the Performance Monitor to monitor resources and the consistency of what is being monitored. By starting the Performance Monitor using the saved workspace file, you can save yourself a lot of trouble, especially when you are monitoring several machines throughout the network.

There are actually two ways in which you can configure the Performance Monitor to start using a workspace template. You can either place the Performance Monitor icon on the desktop and modify the shortcut's target, or you can start the Performance Monitor from the command prompt with the workspace file as the parameter. To use the command prompt to start the Performance Monitor with a workspace file, type **PERFMON WORKSPACE.PMW**.

AUTOMATING THE PERFORMANCE MONITOR

The Performance Monitor has two major limitations. The first is that it cannot cap the size of the log files it creates. When you log performance data, the log file grows until you either manually stop data collection or the hard disk where the file resides fills up completely. (Obviously, this second way of stopping the log file from growing any further should not even be considered.)

The second—and probably the most significant—limitation of the Performance Monitor is that a user must be logged onto a machine to run it. This means that if a user logs off or if the server is restarted for any reason, the Performance Monitor stops and will not be restarted until a user executes it. In addition, the Performance Monitor cannot stop collecting data without user intervention.

To overcome these limitations, you can automate the Performance Monitor so that you do not have to constantly baby-sit its monitoring and data collection. There are two utilities within the Windows NT Resource Kit that complement the Performance Monitor: SRVANY and the Data Logging Service. SRVANY is an application that runs the Performance Monitor as a service. Running the Performance Monitor as a service allows you to start and stop monitoring and collection at times that you specify. By controlling the time interval, you can control the size of the log files. The Data Logging Service is a separate application, but it serves the same purpose as the logging and alerting capabilities within the Performance Monitor. It, too, regulates the size of the log file by controlling the collection times.

Performance Monitor as a Service

SRVANY.EXE is an NT Resource Kit utility used to run Windows NT applications as services. Any Windows NT application can be configured to execute as an NT service. This includes, but is not limited to, Win16 and Win32 applications. There are some limitations in running Win16 applications as services because of how they are written. Consequently, this utility works best with Win32 applications. The Performance Monitor's Win32 architecture makes it a great application to be run as a service.

SRVANY must be installed and configured properly to execute a Win16 or Win32 application as a service. This is done by supplying

SRVANY a parameter within the Registry key and renaming the service to reflect the application that is being launched as a service.

Installation

If you have used SRVANY.EXE before, make sure that you temporarily disable any services that it has created before you begin transforming the Performance Monitor to run as a service. You should also temporarily disable any SRVANY services when installing or upgrading the NT operating system or applications. There are two ways that you can easily stop the service. The first way is through the Services applet within the Control Panel, and the second is by typing **NET STOP SERVICENAME** at the command prompt.

The installation procedure is essentially a four-step process. It includes creating an account that the service will use, installing SRVANY as a service, configuring startup parameters for the service, and modifying the service's Registry parameters to reflect the new Performance Monitor service. I also recommend that you add a testing step to the process to ensure that the service has been installed correctly. Even though the focus here is on setting up Performance Monitor to run as a service, this process can be applied to any Win16 or Win32 application that you want to run as a service.

CREATING THE SERVICE ACCOUNT   The Performance Monitor service should run under its own account. This is not a requirement but, rather, a convenience. Having a separate account for the Performance Monitor service allows you to configure it with the proper access rights without affecting another account. For example, if you created the service using the LocalSystem account, it would not have the network access rights that are required to send alerts notifying administrators of potential problems nor the ability to monitor remote machines.

To create an account for the Performance Monitor service, do the following:

1. Using User Manager for Domains, create a new user account for the service. In this example, the account name is PerfServ, as you can see in Figure 8-9.

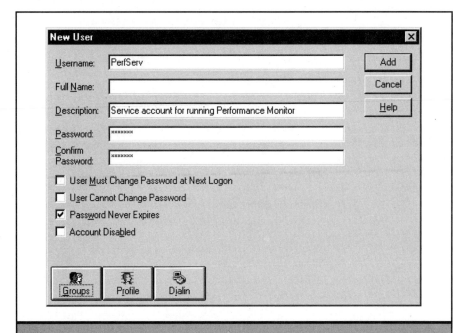

Figure 8-9. Creating the PerfServ account within User Manager for Domains

 NOTE: If this service is going to be used to monitor remote machines, it must have Domain Admin rights. Use the Groups button to add this account to the Domain Admin group.

2. Uncheck User Must Change Password at Next Logon.

3. Check Password Never Expires.

4. Click Add and then Close.

5. Choose User Rights from the Policies menu.

6. Check the Show Advanced User Rights box.

7. From the drop-down box on the right, select "Log on as a service."

8. Click Add and then click Show Users in the Add Users and Groups dialog box.

9. Use the scroll bar to scan for the PerfServ account. Select the service account name (PerfServ) and click Add. The PerfServ account should be listed in the Add Names box.

10. Click OK.

11. Click OK in the User Rights Policy dialog box.

INSTALLING THE SRVANY SERVICE   Another Windows NT Resource Kit utility, INSTSRV.EXE, is used to install SRVANY as a service. At the command prompt, type **INSTSRV PERFSERVICE C:\NTSERVICE\SRVANY.EXE**. This installs SRVANY as a service and creates the proper Registry entries.

> **NOTE:**   The command-line entry shown here is only an example. You can replace PERFSERVICE with whatever name you choose for the Performance Monitor service, and the path should reflect the location of the SRVANY executable.

CONFIGURING THE STARTUP PARAMETERS   The next step in installing the service is to assign it an account and to configure the startup type. Use the Services applet in the Control Panel to do the following:

1. Select the PERFSERVICE service and click the Startup button.

2. In the Startup Type section, select Automatic.

3. In the Log On As section, select This Account and enter the name of the service account (**PerfServ**), as shown in Figure 8-10.

4. Type the service account password and click OK.

5. Close the Control Panel.

MODIFYING THE PERFORMANCE MONITOR SERVICE REGISTRY PARAMETERS   SRVANY.EXE is now an installed service, but you must configure its parameters to permit it to launch the Performance Monitor as a service. Creating a pointer to the Performance Monitor

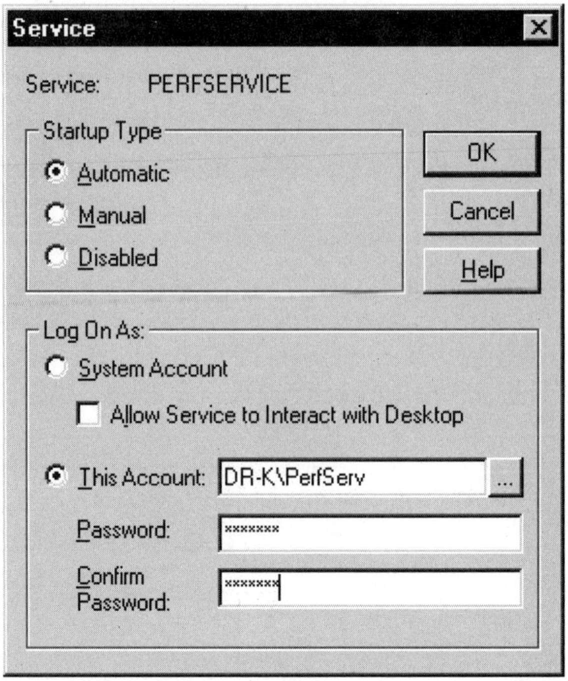

Figure 8-10.   Configuring the service parameters

executable within the utility's Registry key does this. To modify the Registry parameters, do the following:

1. Start the Registry Editor by typing **REGEDT32.EXE** at the command prompt or using the Start | Run command.

2. Select the following Registry key:

    HKEY_LOCAL_MACHINE\
      SYSTEM\
       CurrentControlSet\
        Services\
         PERFSERVICE

3. Choose Add Key from the Edit menu and type **Parameters** in the Key Name field, as shown here:

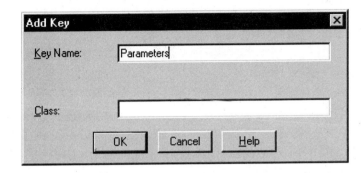

4. Click OK.

5. Select the Parameters key created in step 3.

6. Choose Add Value from the Edit menu and enter **Application** (use the default data type).

7. Click OK.

8. In the String Editor dialog box that appears, enter the path pointing to the Performance Monitor executable; for example, **c:\winnt\system32\perfmon.exe**, as shown here:

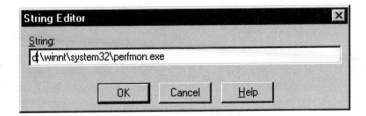

9. Click OK to add this string to the Application value.

10. Select the Parameters key again and choose Add Value from the Edit menu.

11. Type **AppParameters** for the value name.

12. Select REG_XZ as the data type.

13. Click OK.

14. In the String Editor dialog box that appears, enter the path pointing to the Performance Monitor workspace file; for example, **c:\winnt\system32\myworkspace.pmw**.

15. Click OK to add this string to the AppParameters value.

STARTING THE PERFORMANCE MONITOR SERVICE   The final installation procedure is to start the Performance Monitor service (PERFSERVICE). To start the service now (rather than waiting until the machine is rebooted), do the following:

1. Open the Services Applet in the Control Panel.

2. Highlight PERFSERVICE and click the Start button to start the service.

3. Once the service is started, close the Control Panel.

Disabling or Removing the Service

There may be times when you need to disable or remove services created with the SRVANY utility. For example, when you install or upgrade Windows NT or an NT application, it is recommended that you temporarily disable SRVANY services. You can temporarily disable the utility by using the Services applet in the Control Panel. Simply highlighting the service name and clicking Stop stops the service. It will not restart until you reboot or manually start it again.

Removing the service is no more complicated than disabling it. The easiest way (not using a Registry Editor to manually remove Registry entries) is to type **INSTSRV PERFSERVICE REMOVE** at the command prompt.

Data Logging Service

The second (and easier) way to automate performance monitoring is through the Data Logging Service. It offers logging and alerting functionality similar to that of the Performance Monitor. The Data

Logging Service is a separate utility, but it integrates well with the Performance Monitor. In fact, the Data Logging Service must use a workspace file created by the Performance Monitor to determine which components to measure.

The utility is comprised of two executables: MONITOR.EXE and DATALOG.EXE. MONITOR installs the service—DATALOG.EXE—and also manages service operation. The Data Logging Service is very easy to use, especially for managing log files on many remote machines.

To install and use the Data Logging Service, follow these steps:

1. Use the Performance Monitor to create a log file (*.LOG).

2. Add appropriate objects to the log file, but do not start logging data.

3. From the File menu, choose Save Workspace to save the settings (*.PMW). Type the filename with the .PMW extension.

4. Copy DATALOG.EXE and the settings file to the %SYSTEMROOT%\SYSTEM32 folder for every machine for which you want to use the Data Logging Service.

5. Register the Data Logging Service on every machine to which you copied DATALOG.EXE and the settings file by typing **monitor setup** at the command prompt. The service is now installed.

6. Direct the service to use the workspace file you created with the Performance Monitor by specifying the filename.

7. To tell the Data Logging Service what to monitor, type **MONITOR *WORKSPACE.PMW*** at the command prompt, where *WORKSPACE.PMW* is the file you created with the Performance Monitor.

Now you are ready to begin monitoring the system with the Data Logging Service. It is a registered service (one that you can control through the Control Panel), but you can also schedule it to start and stop at specific times. To control the times when it collects data or alerts you to problems, you must use the AT Scheduler. To schedule the service to start and stop at certain times, type the following at the command prompt:

> AT *SERVERNAME* 7:00 "MONITOR START"
> AT *SERVERNAME* 9:00 "MONITOR STOP"

NOTE: The Schedule service must be running for you to use the AT command.

You can also configure the Data Logging Service to start automatically at startup by typing the following at the command prompt:

MONITOR *SERVERNAME* AUTOMATIC

Before you can begin using the log files generated by the Data Logging Service, you must stop the Service. After it is stopped, you can open it just as you would a log file created by the Performance Monitor itself. Since the log file format is similar to the one the Performance Monitor uses, you can easily analyze the collected data with the Performance Monitor or another application, such as Microsoft Excel or Access.

REDUCING DATA COLLECTION'S IMPACT ON THE NETWORK

Monitoring a remote machine can negatively affect network performance. In fact, it affects the network more than it does the machine that it is monitoring, because each snapshot of performance data that is taken from the remote machine must traverse the network to reach the machine you are monitoring from. The more counters that you watch on the remote machine, the more impact monitoring has on the network. For this reason, it is extremely important to discriminate when selecting which counters to use.

One solution to this problem is to run the Performance Monitor on each of the machines you want to keep an eye on and then transfer the log files to a centralized location for review. However, if you plan to measure performance on many different machines, the traditional method of using the Performance Monitor by itself (without automation) can be an administrative burden simply because of the time involved in configuring and managing each remote machine. If you do not closely monitor a machine, you run the risk of filling up the disk space with the collected data.

By automating the entire process, you can save time and resources. First, automate the Performance Monitor by making it a service, or optionally you can use the Data Logging Service. This automation allows you to control the size of the log file by specifying the times when you want to monitor the remote machines. Then you can write a simple batch file that either copies or moves the log files that are created to a centralized location for reduction and analysis. Using the AT command to kick off the batch file allows you to schedule the transfer during off-peak hours.

To better understand this solution, I will use the Data Logging Service as an illustration. Keep in mind that this is a simple example intended to show you how easy it is to lessen the impact of remote data collection on the network.

```
MONITOR WORKSPACE.PMW
AT \\SERVER1 8:00 /EVERY:M,T,W,TH,F "MONITOR START"
AT \\SERVER1 12:00 /EVERY:M,T,W,TH,F "MONITOR STOP"
```

Batch file (TRANSFER.BAT) contents:

```
echo Moving log file to performance monitoring server...
REM if an existing log is present, but no old log, make an
REM old log
IF NOT EXIST \\perfserv\logs\server1_old.log
   IF EXIST \\perfserv\logs\server1.log
      COPY \\perfserv\logs\server1.log
           \\perfserv\logs\server1_old.log
REM if an old log is present, append the existing log to the
REM old log
IF EXIST \\perfserv\logs\server1_old.log
   COPY
\\perfserv\logs\server1_old.log+\\perfserv\logs\server1.log
```

```
\\perfserv\logs\server1_old.log
REM in all cases, write a new log (or replace the existing
REM log)
COPY d:\logs\server1.log \\perfserv\logs
End of batch file (TRANSFER.BAT)
AT 22:00 /EVERY:M,T,W,TH,F TRANSFER.BAT
```

NOTE: This batch file is only an example of how to transfer log files to a centralized location. You should consider developing a mechanism that renames a file if it exists on the remote machine. In this example, the new log file is simply appended to the remote machine's existing log file.

When you need to monitor a remote machine in real time, you must resort to the charting or reporting method. There is no way to postpone the workloads placed on the network as there is for logging. You cannot, for example, wait until 5:00 P.M. when everyone begins leaving to measure performance. Therefore, you must monitor the least amount of counters possible to minimize the strain placed on the network. It is also good practice to control the frequency of data collection. For example, if you know that you may be monitoring for an extended period (more than 20 or 30 minutes), consider reducing the frequency by adding 5 or 10 seconds to the interval. Use real-time monitoring on remote machines only when it is absolutely necessary and try to keep the time you spend on measuring performance to a minimum.

CONCLUSION

The Performance Monitor is a powerful built-in utility for monitoring and analyzing system activity in real time as well as historically through log files. This chapter examined many different aspects of the Performance Monitor, including what the utility monitors, the utility's various uses, the critical resources to monitor, and how to overcome the utility's limitations by running it as a service. This chapter also discussed how the Performance Monitor can be used to notify administrators when specified counters reach specified thresholds. As you can see, the Performance Monitor is more than a simple monitoring utility built into the operating system. It is a utility that can be used to proactively support the Windows NT environment.

CHAPTER 9

Printing

If there is one service that many take for granted on Windows NT systems, it is printing. Users assume quick and easy printing of their documents, letterhead, forms, graphics, and so on, and many IT professionals simply install printers on Windows NT and forget about them.

There is nothing wrong with sticking with the simple printing capabilities of your system, especially considering the ease with which Windows NT furnishes print services. However, there are many configurable options that help boost printing capabilities and streamline print server resources, though printing is usually the last place people look to improve performance.

Printing can be a major performance factor on Windows NT Server systems, though it is usually not much of a concern on workstations or client machines, even when a printer is installed locally. Even so, in either case the principles and recommendations presented in this chapter will help create a more efficient printing environment for both Windows NT Server and Windows NT Workstation.

TERMINOLOGY

To understand the printing process, hardware configuration considerations, and optimization techniques discussed in this chapter, you need to become familiar with a few terms:

▼ **Printer** Also known as the logical printer. The printer is the interface between Windows NT and the hardware (the printing device). This term is often incorrectly used interchangeably with the printing device.

■ **Printing device** The actual hardware that produces the output (that is, the physical printer). It is not uncommon for the printing device to be called the printer.

■ **Print device driver** The software driver that is loaded to communicate with the printing device.

- **Printer pool**   A logical grouping of two or more identical devices. Client machines perceive a printer pool as a single entity. In other words, from the user's standpoint, they appear to be printing to a single printing device.

- **Printer port**   The port to which the print device connects to communicate with the system. The printer port can either be a physical port (such as LPT1, LPT2, COM1, or COM2) or a logical port that uses the Universal Naming Convention (UNC) name (for example, *SERVERNAME*\ *PRINTERNAME*).

- **Spooler**   The component composed of dynamic link libraries (DLLs) responsible for receiving, processing, scheduling, and distributing print jobs.

- **Spooling**   One of several processes performed by the spooler. This process writes the contents of the print job to the spool file for temporary storage.

- **Despooling**   The exact opposite of spooling. This process reads the contents of the spool file and sends the contents to the print device.

- **Print job**   The source code, usually in a native print-control language, that results from a printing request.

- **Line printer daemon (LPD)**   A TCP/IP print service that receives print jobs from line printer remote (LPR) clients, such as UNIX machines.

- ▲ **Queue**   The sequence in which documents wait to be printed.

PRINTING BASICS

Before you can fine-tune any Windows NT subsystem or component, you must understand how it operates. Think of NT as a sports car. You may be able to drive it, but would you even think about trying to work on the car's engine if you did not know the first thing about mechanics? You would not know where to look for problems much less how to give it a tune-up. Printing under Windows NT is no different. This section explores the basic printing process and management concerns to give you a better understanding of what can and should be done to improve printing efficiency and speed.

The Printing Process Under Windows NT

Contrary to what you may believe, when a user prints a job, it does not go directly to the printer. Only after it has gone through a series of logical procedures does it finally reach the printer for output. This section describes the process when a Windows NT client issues a print request to a Windows NT print server. The printing process varies depending on the operating system that the client machine is running. These differences are outlined in Table 9-1.

Client Operating System	Client Redirector	Communication Protocol
Windows 95	LAN Manager MS Network Client 3.0 for Windows	NetBEUI NWLink (IPX/SPX) TCP/IP
Windows 98	LAN Manager MS Network Client 3.0 for Windows	NetBEUI NWLink (IPX/SPX) TCP/IP
Windows 3.x (16-bit)	LAN Manager MS Network Client 3.0 for Windows Windows for Workgroups Built-in Redirector	NetBEUI NWLink (IPX/SPX) TCP/IP
MS-DOS (assuming applications are network aware)	MS Network Client 3.0 for Windows Windows for Workgroups Built-in Redirector	NetBEUI TCP/IP

Table 9-1. Communication Structures for Print Clients

Client Operating System	Client Redirector	Communication Protocol
UNIX (with RFC 1179 LPR support)	RFC 1179 compliant LPR support to print to NT's TCP/IP print server (LPD service)	TCP/IP
Macintosh	Default Macintosh printing support	Appletalk TCP/IP
Windows NT	Default NetBIOS support and Workstation service	Any Windows NT supported protocol (for example, NetBEUI, NWLink, or TCP/IP)

Table 9-1. Communication Structures for Print Clients (*continued*)

Initially, when a user creates a printing job, the application that is being printed from issues a request to the graphics device interface (GDI) component. The GDI then communicates with the appropriate printer driver before generating the request in a print control language, such as PostScript. If the wrong printer driver has been installed, the print control language may not be compatible with the printing device. The new kernel architecture, described in Chapter 4, promotes faster printing because this initial step reduces the number of calls that need to be made to the Win32 subsystem, and the GDI runs in kernel mode instead of user mode.

NOTE: All Windows-based clients printing from a Windows application make application calls to the GDI.

After the print job request has been generated in a language the printer can understand, the client sends a remote procedure call (RPC) to the spooler server service (SPOOLSS.EXE) on the client machine. Then the spooler server service tells the spooler's router (SPOOLSS.DLL) to find and establish communication with a print server. The connection to the print server is established through an RPC call, and the print job is sent to the print server.

The spooler's router on the print server receives the print job. The data type of the print job received by the print server varies depending on the type of client that sent the request. The default data type for Windows NT clients is enhanced metafile format (EMF). Windows NT clients can use other data types as well, such as the commonly used RAW format. (See "Print Job Data Types" later in this chapter for more information.)

NOTE: If the data type is not specified, the print job defaults to the data type set for the print processor on the print server.

Next, the router hands the print job to the spooler's local print provider on the print server, which spools the print job to disk. Then the spooler's local print provider polls the print processors until a suitable data type is found, and that print processor then takes the print job. Depending on the data type, the print processor may need to alter the print job so that it prints correctly.

At this point, the separator page processor gains control over the print job and checks to see whether a separator page has been specified. If no separator page is specified, the print job is despooled to the print monitor. There are two paths the print job can take from here; the decision depends on whether the print device is bidirectional. If the device is bidirectional, the job goes to the language monitor before heading off to the port monitor. Otherwise, it goes directly to the port monitor, which transmits the print job data to the actual print device.

Finally, the print device receives the print job. As it receives the print job, it converts each page into a bitmap image before printing it on paper.

Figure 9-1 presents a simplified illustration of this process.

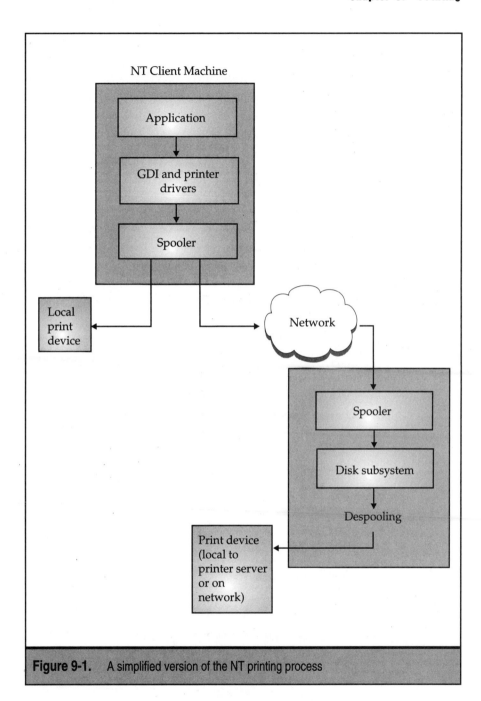

Figure 9-1.   A simplified version of the NT printing process

Creating a Printer

Installing and configuring printing services under Windows NT could not be easier. The Explorer interface shell makes this process simpler and more efficient than it is for most other operating systems, including earlier versions of Windows NT. Although the focus of this chapter is not the set up and management of printers, the administrative tasks for printing services must be well understood before you proceed to more advanced, technical topics.

When you create a printer, you are not configuring the printer hardware but, rather, providing a definition of the hardware that you are connecting to. The printer will appear to be connected directly to the server, regardless of whether the print device is local to the server or connected to the network via its own network interface. (The various types of interfaces are discussed later in the section "Printer Connection".)

To create a printer definition, you must be a member of one of the following groups:

▼ Administrators

■ Domain Administrators

■ Print Operators

▲ Server Operators

If you have the permissions associated with one of these groups, follow these steps to create a printer:

1. Double-click the Printers folder from the Control Panel, or open the Printers folder by choosing Start | Settings | Printers. You'll see this box:

2. Double-click the Add Printer icon to start the Add Printer Wizard, shown in Figure 9-2.

3. The Add Printer Wizard presents two choices: My Computer or Network Printer Server. Select My Computer because it is the only viable option here to create a printer on a print server; the Network Printer Server option is for client machines wishing to connect to a printer already created on a print server. Then click Next to continue.

4. The next window, shown in Figure 9-3, asks you to specify how the printer is connected to the print server. If it is physically connected to the server, select either a parallel (for example, LPT1) or serial (for example, COM1) port and then click Next. Otherwise, you can add either a DLC or TCP/IP port connection, as described in the next step.

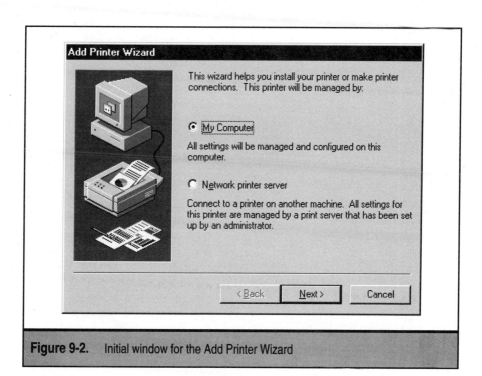

Figure 9-2.   Initial window for the Add Printer Wizard

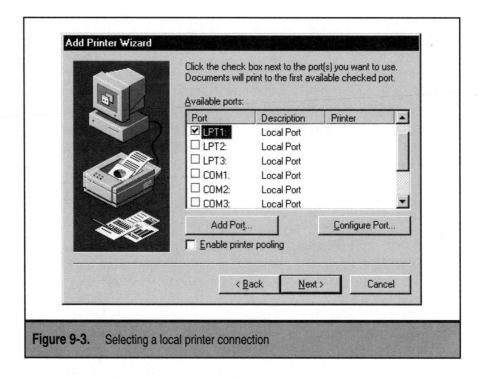

Figure 9-3. Selecting a local printer connection

5. If the printer has its own network connection, such as a DLC or TCP/IP connection, choose Add Port to select the port type, as shown here. Then click Next.

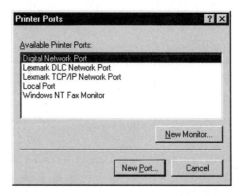

6. Select a printer driver. Windows NT supplies drivers for a variety of printers for you to choose from, as you can see in Figure 9-4. You can also install a driver from a diskette or other media by choosing Have Disk. To check whether NT natively supports the printer, scroll down the Manufacturers list to select the vendor and then choose your printer from the Printers list. When you are done, click Next.

7. Specify a name for the printer. This name identifies the printer on the network browse list.

8. If you are sharing the printer, you need to set it up so others can print to it through the print server, as shown in Figure 9-5. To do this, select the operating systems (on the client machines) that will need access to this printer. This will copy the appropriate drivers so they are available to users connecting

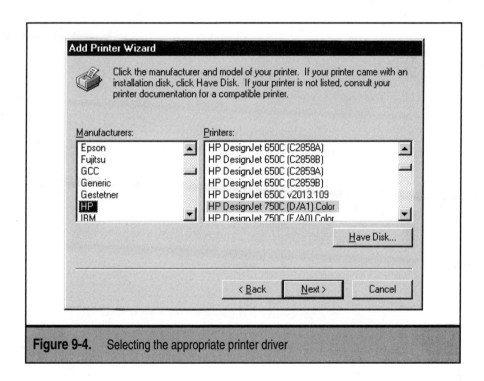

Figure 9-4.   Selecting the appropriate printer driver

to the printer. When you are finished with this screen, click Next.

9. Specify whether you want to print a test page.

10. Click Finish to complete the installation. When prompted, choose the path for the installation files.

Print Job Data Types

Windows NT maximizes interoperability with other operating system environments by defining different print job data types. This is a necessary piece in the printing process because not all environments handle printing in the same way, and different environments may use entirely different formatting and print commands.

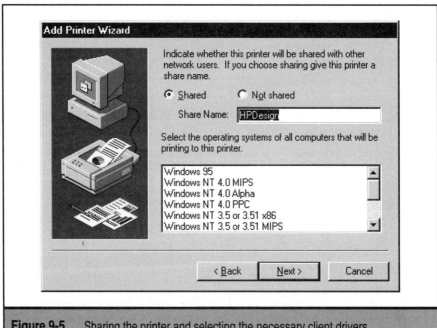

Figure 9-5. Sharing the printer and selecting the necessary client drivers

The data type tells the print server's spooler what kind of print job this is. The spooler can then determine whether the print job needs to be modified to print correctly. The print server service on the client machine is responsible for assigning the print job a data type. If no data type is assigned, then the default data type of the print server is used. For most Windows-based environments, the default data type typically is RAW. However, Windows NT's default data type is EMF.

EMF

Enhanced metafile format (EMF) is the default data type for Windows NT 4.0 or higher clients printing to a Windows NT 4.0 or higher print server. This data type has many advantages over many of the data types previously used.

NOTE: EMF is not the default data type for PostScript printers. In addition, when adding a printer to a Windows NT client, you must choose the Network Printer Server option rather than the My Computer option during installation to establish EMF as the default data type.

The EMF data type boosts printing performance in a variety of ways. First, EMF emulates client-server capabilities with its rendering functions. Only a small portion of the print job's rendering is done on the client machine, freeing the client machine to perform other duties in a more timely fashion. After the EMF information is generated by the GDI, the client regains control, and the information becomes a background process for spooling. The print job is then sent to the print server for completion of the rendering process. The greatest performance gains occur with the largest print jobs.

Another advantage of EMF is its *device independence*, which means that it can be used with any printing device and so is more flexible than other data types. Typically, print jobs with the EMF data type also are easier for devices to manage because they generally are smaller than the same print jobs with the RAW data type. In addition, this reduced size enables EMF print jobs to complete slightly faster than print jobs using the RAW data type.

The EMF data type also preserves print quality. EMF ensures that the fonts used on the client machine are the exact ones that the print server will use, which keeps font substitution to an absolute minimum and results in print jobs that retain the same quality as the original document on the screen.

The only time EMF is not the preferred data type is when using a PostScript printer. For PostScript printers, the RAW data type provides better performance, in part because of the different formatting associated with this type of printing, and is the default data type.

RAW

The RAW data type is formatted in the printing device's *native print control language.* This means that no additional alterations are needed, and that the print job is ready to print as is. Because the format uses the printer's native print control language, the RAW data type is device dependent. At first glance, RAW may seem to provide faster printing than EMF because the data type provides a ready-to-print format, and no additional encoding or decoding is necessary for the printer to recognize it. However, this is true only when printing to a PostScript printer, primarily because for other types of printers, the GDI and printer device drivers on the client machine perform all rendering operations.

RAW [FF Appended]

The RAW [FF Appended] data type is used on those rare occasions where the application being printed from is incapable of properly finishing the print request. In this situation, the application does not append a form-feed character to the end of the job, which prevents the last page from being printed when it is sent to a PCL print device. This data type tells the print server's spooler to add the form-feed character to the end of the print job. No other changes are made to the print job. Windows NT never automatically uses this data type by default. If you want to set it as the default data type, you must manually set it as the default. For instructions on how to override the default data type, see "Checking or Overriding the Default Data Type" later in this chapter.

RAW [FF Auto]

The RAW [FF Auto] data type is similar to the RAW [FF Appended] data type in that it also can tell the spooler to append a form-feed character to the end of a print job. The difference, however, is that this data type actually checks to see whether a form-feed character already exists. This adds to the time needed for a print job to complete, and for performance reasons it should be used only rarely. As with the RAW [FF Appended] data type, Windows NT never defaults to this data type; you must set it manually.

Text

The Text data type is used for print jobs that contain ANSI text. The print processor (WinPrint) and the printer device driver use this data type to create a new print job to print the text of the original print job. This ensures that ANSI text is printed correctly and conforms to the print device's default font, form, orientation, and resolution.

Generally, this data type is used only when the printing device cannot properly interpret a print job containing simple text. For example, the character set may be printed if a simple text file does not specify its character-mapping scheme.

PSCRIPT1 (PostScript)

The PSCRIPT1 data type is used only for print jobs from a Macintosh client that contain PostScript code when the printer shared by Windows NT is not PostScript compatible. This data type tells the spooler to interpret the PostScript code to create a bitmap image of the page. The GDI and print device driver convert the image into the printer's native print control language.

Checking or Overriding the Default Data Type

To check or modify the default data type for a particular printer on the Windows NT print server, do the following:

1. Choose Start | Settings | Printers or double-click the Printers folder in the Control Panel and then select the print device for which you want to check or modify the default data type.

2. Choose Properties from the File menu or right-click the printer icon.

3. On the General tab, shown in Figure 9-6, select Print Processor.

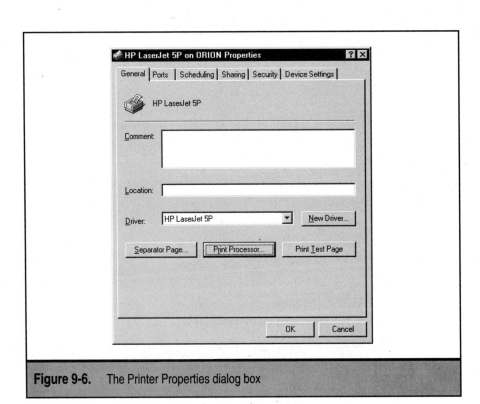

Figure 9-6.   The Printer Properties dialog box

4. The Print Processor dialog box that appears lists the type of print processor used and highlights the default data type. To change the default data type, simply select the data type you want, as shown here, and click OK.

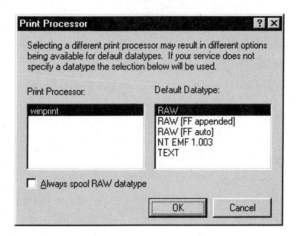

5. On the printer's Properties page, click OK.

PRINTER HARDWARE CONFIGURATIONS AND CONSIDERATIONS

Optimizing the printing process begins with choosing the most efficient hardware that also meets the functional needs of the environment. There are a large number of printing devices to choose from, such as dot-matrix, ink jet, laser, or thermal printers or plotters, as well as many other print devices, depending on your printing needs. It is important to choose the appropriate print device for the functions it will perform in the environment.

Despite the different functionality associated with these various print device types, you can judge their performance by measuring certain common characteristics, including the quality and type of output, speed of printing (typically measured in pages per minute, or PPM), and connection type. Each of these factors can greatly influence the printing process.

Quality and Type of Output

Your first consideration when purchasing a print device should be the quality and type of output the device produces. Some environments need dot-matrix print devices for impact printing, while others need non-impact print devices such as plotters, for instance, to produce architectural designs from CAD applications. Other environments, where space and money are factors, may opt for all-in-one print devices that include printing, faxing, and copying capabilities. Once you know what type of printing is needed, you can determine the type of output you require.

Resolution

The type of output you need also determines the output quality you require. No matter whether you are printing text or graphics, or both, the resolution determines the quality of the printed results. Resolution is typically measured in dots per inch (dpi). The higher the dpi value, the better the output quality. Print resolution is based on the same principles as for resolution in the graphics subsystem, discussed in Chapter 7.

It is not uncommon for print devices to support 1,200 dpi or higher resolution. However, a word of caution is needed here, because higher resolutions usually take longer to print. For example, a print job set at 600 dpi will print faster than the same print job set at 1,200 dpi on the same print device.

Printing Speed

Printing speed is measured either in characters per second (cps) or pages per minute (ppm). The cps rating is typically used only with dot-matrix print devices. The pages per minute attribute of a print device is the maximum number of pages that the print device can output in one minute. This characteristic also depends on resolution: the higher the resolution, the more time it takes to complete a print job. The rating also depends heavily on whether you are printing graphics or plain text. Get the highest ppm rating possible to ensure that print jobs complete as quickly as possible.

Printer Connection

How the print device is connected to Windows NT is as important as any of the characteristics discussed so far. Whether the print device is local or remote, it attaches to Windows NT through an interface specification. This interface can either expand or limit the amount of data that can be transmitted to the print device for output.

The primary types of interface connections can be divided into two categories: parallel and network. The two categories can be further broken down to individual print connection specifications. Each specification is defined by its special features and transfer rates.

It is important to note that there are two print connection interfaces that do not fit into any of these categories: the serial (RS-232) and infrared connections. These types of interfaces provide extremely slow transfer rates that are unacceptable for environments concerned with performance. Parallel interfaces generally provide transfer rates at least twice as fast as either of these specifications. There is not much growth potential for the serial specification, but it is anticipated that infrared technology will eventually overcome its limitations to provide acceptable transfer rates not only for print devices but for network connectivity as well.

Parallel Interfaces

Parallel interfaces are for print devices connected locally to the Windows NT print server or workstation. They also define how the print device is physically attached to the machine.

The first commonly used parallel interface relied on a unidirectional Centronics type of connection, pictured here:

There have since been many improvements on this specification to allow greater printing speeds and higher-quality output.

ECP   The Extended Capabilities Port (ECP) specification is a parallel-port standard that supports bidirectional communication between the print device and the rest of the system. ECP is roughly 10 times faster than the older Centronics standard. It is an intelligent parallel interface specification built from the IEEE 1284 specification.

With ECP, the printer port can operate at speeds from 500,000 to 1 million characters per second. This is a tremendous improvement over the Centronics standard, which has a maximum transfer rate of 125,000 characters per second.

EPP   The Enhanced Parallel Port (EPP) is another intelligent parallel port standard that supports bidirectional communication. Its features and performance are similar to those of the ECP specification. For example, its transfer speed is between 500,000 and 1 million characters per second.

Network Interface

Many print devices are becoming *network aware*, meaning that the device itself can be attached to the network instead of being physically connected to the Windows NT print server or workstation. This allows greater flexibility, especially in heterogeneous environments where more than one type of operating system platform uses a single print device.

Connecting the print device directly to the network also increases the transfer rate between the client requesting the print job and the actual print device. In fact, the printing device is more likely to cause a bottleneck than the network interface connection because there is more data coming into the print device than it can use efficiently.

There are many different network interfaces for the print device. Table 9-2 lists the most common network interfaces and their respective transfer rates.

OPTIMIZING THE PRINTING PROCESS

Windows NT offers excellent printing process optimization. This eliminates the need to tune the system to increase printing performance in environments where only limited printing is performed or on workstations. However, in environments with medium to heavy printing workloads or on a Windows NT Server dedicated as a print server, printing optimization is necessary to improve and maintain performance. This process includes choosing the appropriate hardware, as outlined earlier, as well as fine-tuning the operating system. This section highlights the most important areas that should be considered to increase printing performance.

Network Interface (Speed in Mbps)	Maximum Transfer Rate (in cps)
Ethernet (10)	1,250,000
Fast Ethernet (100)	12,500,000
Token ring (4)	500,000
Token ring (16)	2,000,000

Table 9-2. Network Printing Interfaces and Transfer Rates

Font Management

Font management can affect printing performance. The way you perform font management affects disk capacity, server memory requirements, and printing speed. You should pay particular attention to this aspect of printing performance if you are using an international version of Windows NT (supporting a large character set) or if Windows NT is used in a print shop environment. Print shops tend to use a large number of fonts and character sets, increasing resource requirements for the system.

In performing font management, you need to consider font drivers, the types and number of fonts on the system, and the font cache. Each of these aspects is described here.

Font Drivers

Windows NT natively supports many different types of fonts, including bitmap, vector, and TrueType fonts. However, sometimes additional font types are needed that require third-party (external) font drivers. Usually, though, this occurs only in print shops that have specialized printing needs. Although many font vendors do supply relatively reliable font drivers, it is recommended that you use as few additional drivers as possible.

Third-party font driver information is located in the following Registry subkey: HKEY_LOCAL_MACHINE\SOFTWARE\ Microsoft\Windows NT\CurrentVersion\Font Drivers. You should use the software provided by the font vendor to manipulate any entries in this subkey. The font drivers native to Windows NT do not have entries in the Registry.

Font Types and the Number of Installed Fonts

The type and number of fonts used on the system are closely related and can have a large impact on system performance if they are not properly managed. It is best to use the fonts natively supported by

Windows NT, but there are times when this will not suffice. Some systems have relatively few fonts installed, while others may have literally thousands. Keep the number of installed fonts to a minimum because they can quickly chew up memory and disk resources. Fonts typically vary in size from just a few kilobytes to several hundred kilobytes. Removing a few will not free up very much disk space, but when you remove a large number of them, you can potentially save vast amounts of disk space.

One way to keep the number of installed fonts to a minimum is to use only TrueType fonts in Windows-based applications. However, you must make sure that none of the Windows-based applications require other font types such as bitmap, vector, or third-party fonts. If this is a viable option, you can disable the use of non-TrueType fonts in Windows-based applications by manipulating the following Registry subkey: HKEY_USERS\SOFTWARE\Microsoft\Windows NT\CurrentVersion\TrueType.

There are two parameters in this Registry subkey: TTEnable and TTonly. To have only TrueType fonts available for Windows-based applications, do the following:

1. Start the Registry Editor by typing **REGEDT32** at the command prompt or in the Start | Run box.

NOTE: It is recommended that you use only the REGEDT32 Registry Editor to make these changes.

2. Open the TrueType Registry key listed earlier, as shown in Figure 9-7.

3. If the TTonly parameter exists, double-click it to display its properties and then change the value to 1.

4. If the TTonly parameter does not exist, then select Add Value from the Edit menu to add the TTonly parameter. This displays the Add Value dialog box.

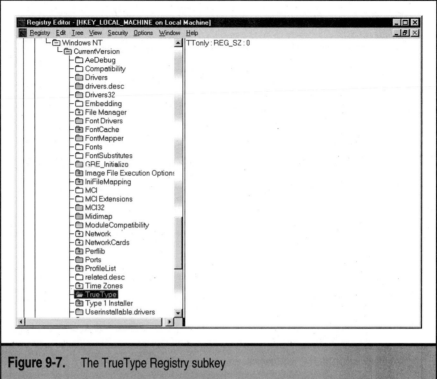

Figure 9-7. The TrueType Registry subkey

5. In the Value Name box, type **TTonly** and then select REG_SZ as the data type, as shown here:

6. Click OK. This will cause the SZ Editor dialog box to pop up.

7. In the Radix group, select Binary and then type **1** to allow Windows-based applications to use only TrueType fonts.

8. Click OK to add the new value.

Font Caching

The font cache is used to store many different fonts in memory. The size of the cache can greatly affect the amount of memory available in the system. Parameters, such as the minimum and maximum amount of memory that can be used for font caching, are located in the following Registry subkey: HKEY_LOCAL_MACHINE\ SOFTWARE\Microsoft\Windows NT\CurrentVersion\FontCache.

Be extremely cautious if you attempt to modify the default parameter values because they can negatively affect overall system performance if not set properly. In fact, it is recommended that you let Windows NT manage this subkey unless your system requires a large number of fonts (such as in a print shop) or you are using an international version of Windows NT. These are the only times when it may be beneficial to experiment with the FontCache subkey parameters.

The FontCache parameters and their respective values and descriptions are listed in Table 9-3.

FontCache Parameter	Data Value	Default Value	Description
MaxSize	REG_DWORD	0×80 (hexadecimal)	The maximum amount of memory address space reserved for font cache.
MinIncrSize	REG_DWORD	0×4	The minimum amount of memory (4Kb) used with each font cache size increment.

Table 9-3.   FontCache Parameters

FontCache Parameter	Data Value	Default Value	Description
MinInitSize	REG_DWORD	0×4	The minimum amount of memory (4Kb) initially committed per font cache.

Table 9-3.   FontCache Parameters (*continued*)

Print Logging

Every time a print job is serviced, NT logs the event in the Event Viewer's System log. You can imagine that it does not take long for the log to become cluttered with print informational messages. Depending on how the Event Viewer is configured to handle the log file when it grows to a certain size, it can quickly consume disk space or it may even halt logging of system events, which could have devastating results.

In addition to taking up disk space, print event logging also momentarily diverts NT's attention from other more important tasks. Although print logging effects on performance are not alarming, you still should minimize its impact on system performance. You can choose among error, warning, or informational event logging. It is recommended that you keep error or error and warning event logging turned on.

There are two ways to modify print event logging: through the Printers folder and through the Registry. The safest and easiest way is through the Printers folder, though both methods are described here.

To modify print event logging through the Printers folder, do the following:

1. Choose Start | Settings | Printers and open the Printers folder.

2. From the File menu, select Server Properties.

3. Select the Advanced tab.

4. Check the print event logging options that you want to use, as shown in Figure 9-8. Then click OK.

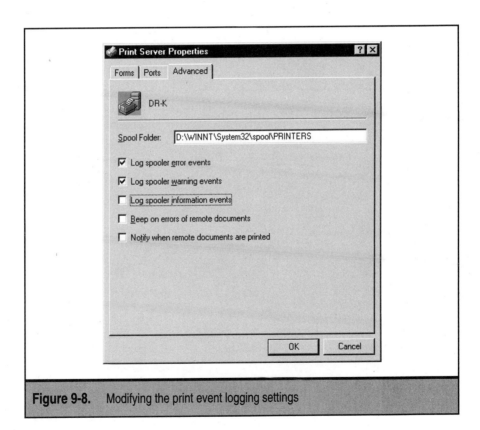

Figure 9-8. Modifying the print event logging settings

To modify print event logging through the Registry, do the following:

1. Start the Registry Editor by typing **REGEDT32** at the command prompt or in the Start | Run box.

2. Open the following subkey (as shown in Figure 9-9): HKEY_LOCAL_MACHINE\SYSTEM\CurrentControlSet\ Control\Print\Providers.

3. From the Edit menu, select Add Value to display the Add Value dialog box.

4. In the Value Name box, type **EventLog** and then select REG_DWORD as the data type.

5. Click OK. This will cause the DWORD Editor dialog box to pop up.

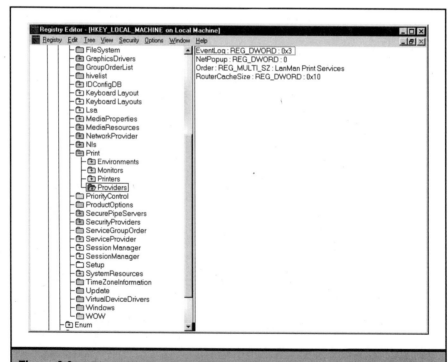

Figure 9-9. Disabling print event logging using the Registry

6. In the Radix grouping, select Decimal and then type **1** for error event logging only or **3** for error and warning event logging. Then click OK.

Tweaking the Spooler Service

The Windows NT spooler service is responsible for almost every aspect of printing. It is actually a collective arrangement of printing components that work together to process print requests. It consists of five separate components that act as a single entity and are responsible for receiving, processing, scheduling, and distributing print jobs. These five components are summarized in Table 9-4.

Spooler Component	Associated Files	Description
Router	Winspool.drv Spoolss.exe Spoolss.dll	The router is responsible for passing control of the print job to the appropriate print provider.
Local print provider	Localspl.dll	The local print provider handles many local printing tasks such as writing the print job to a spool file, keeping track of administrative information (user name, document name, data type), and polling installed print processors for recognition purposes.

Table 9-4. Print Spooler Components

Spooler Component	Associated Files	Description
Remote print providers	Win32sp.dll Nwprovau.dll	Remote print providers are used when the printing device is remote (such as a Windows NT print server). NT supplies two versions: one for Windows Network print servers (Win32sp.dll) and one for Novell NetWare (Nwprovau.dll).
Print processors	Windows: Winprint.dll Macintosh: Sfmpsprt.dll	Print processors work closely with the printer driver to despool print jobs and can alter the print job's data type, if necessary.
Print monitors	Localmon.dll Hpmon.dll Lprmon.dll Sfmmon.dll MARKVISION DECMON	There are two types of print monitors: language monitors and port monitors. Language monitors support bidirectional print devices, and port monitors control the I/O port to which the print device is connected.

Table 9-4.   Print Spooler Components (*continueWSS*

Even though the print spooler service is very important for printing, it does not have a higher priority than most other applications. In fact, it has the default priority, which is typically 7 for the Windows NT Workstation and 9 for the Windows NT Server, like every other noncritical system process.

To give the printing process a boost, you can modify the various priorities associated with the spooler service. These settings can be changed only through the Registry. The most notable performance boosts from these Registry modifications will be on print servers that service a large number of print jobs or a large number of printing devices. It is not advisable to change the default spooler settings on workstations or servers that are not very busy, primarily because the performance difference may not be noticeable enough to warrant messing with the Registry.

There are three spooler priorities that are worth experimenting with on busy print servers: PortThreadPriority, SpoolerPriority, and SchedulerThreadPriority. Their properties are listed in Table 9-5. These services are located in the following key: HKEY_LOCAL_MACHINE\SYSTEM\CurrentControlSet\Control\Print.

Parameter	Data Type	Data Value	Description and Recommendation
PortThread Priority	REG_DWORD	0 (indicates that the default value is used)	This parameter sets the priority level for each defined printing port's thread. Consider increasing this value to between 8 and 10 for servers.

Table 9-5. Maximizing Spooler Priority Levels

Parameter	Data Type	Data Value	Description and Recommendation
Spooler Priority	REG_DWORD	0×20 (NORMAL_ PRIORITY_ CLASS) Note: Not listed if default values are used	Sets the priority class for the print spooler. This parameter is a replacement for the PriorityClass parameter used with Windows NT version 3.51 and earlier. If the default setting is used, there will not be a visible entry for this parameter. Consider increasing this value to between 12 and 14 for servers.
Scheduler Thread Priority	REG_DWORD	0 (indicates that the default value is used)	Sets the priority of the scheduler thread, which is responsible for assigning print jobs to ports. Consider increasing this value to between 12 and 14 for servers.

Table 9-5. Maximizing Spooler Priority Levels (*continued*)

NOTE: Thread priority ranges between 1 (idle) and 31 (real time), where the higher number has higher priority. Threads relating to the printing process can have priorities ranging from 1 (idle) to 14 (high).

As Table 9-5 shows, SpoolerPriority does not appear in the Registry if the default setting is used. To change this priority, you must add the SpoolerPriority setting manually. To add the SpoolerPriority value, do the following:

1. Start the Registry Editor by typing **REGEDT32** at the command prompt or entering it in the Start | Run box. Go to HKEY_LOCAL_MACHINE\SYSTEM\CurrentControlSet\ Control\Print.

2. Select Add Value from the Edit menu to display the Add Value dialog box.

3. In the Value Name box, type **SpoolerPriority** and then select REG_DWORD as the data type.

4. Click OK. This will cause the DWORD Editor dialog box to pop up.

5. In the Radix grouping, select Hex and then type 8 to boost the priority to HIGH_PRIORITY_CLASS, as shown here:

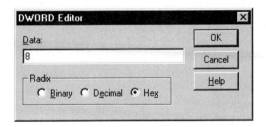

6. Click OK to add the new value.

Optimizing the Spooler File

As long as the print spooling option is enabled, Windows NT spools the print jobs to disk before actually sending them to the printer. The default location for the spool file (%SYSTEMROOT%\System32\

spool\printers) is on the same partition as the rest of the system files, and the increased load caused by read and write operations on the drive can severely hamper performance if the server has to support a large number of print requests.

One of the easiest ways to increase printing performance is to move the spooling file to a different location. More specifically, you should change the default location to a new directory on another physical drive. The spooler location change is especially critical to maintaining optimal performance if Windows NT is acting as a print server. As with most system changes, it can be accomplished through the Registry; however, there is also a simpler way to change the location of the print spool file. Use the following steps to modify the spool file's location:

NOTE: If you change the default spool file location through the user interface (as described here), this change will apply to all printers.

1. Create a new spool file directory, preferably on a separate physical drive. Putting the directory on a separate physical drive ensures that the spool file workload does not interfere with the workload associated with the normal operation of Windows NT. In other words, the disk subsystem will not be bombarded with both system requests and print spooler requests.

2. If the new spool file directory is located on an NTFS volume, set the proper permissions for this new directory. For example, give the Authenticated Users group Change permission.

NOTE: In Windows NT versions 3.51 and earlier, you must use the Registry to modify the spool file location.

3. Choose Start | Settings | Printers and open the Printers folder.

4. From the File menu, select Server Properties.

5. Select the Advanced tab.

6. To modify the spool file location, type the new path for the new spool folder that you created earlier.

You also have the option of modifying the print spool file location through the Registry. The parameter is located in the following Registry subkey: HKEY_LOCAL_MACHINE\SYSTEM\Current ControlSet\Control\Print.

You must then add (or modify) the following:

▼ Value name: DefaultSpoolDirectory

■ Data type: REG_SZ

■ Value: New path location of the spool file

▲ Default value: %SYSTEMROOT%\System32\spool\printers

The advantage of using the Registry to modify the print spool file location is that you can change the location for individual print devices. For instance, if a Windows NT print server is home to five different heavily used print devices, you can direct each print device to use a separate print spool file. To change the print spool file location for individual print devices, simply go to the print device's subkey (located under the subkey defined earlier) and modify the SpoolDirectory parameter so it points to another directory. Also, if you have enough physical disks, you can spread the workload of those print spooler files to separate physical disks, which will greatly improve the disk read and write times while spooling because each physical disk has its own heads to perform the spooling functions.

Whether you change the print spool file location through the Printers folder or the Registry, the modifications will not take effect until the system is restarted.

Network Printing

Network printing is a common approach in many environments because of its scalability and flexibility. Instead of configuring each workstation with its own print device, one or more printers can be shared over the network, and network-aware print devices can be conveniently located throughout the network instead of being confined to the location of the server or workstation. This section discusses opportunities for boosting printing performance and efficiency and for reducing the effects of printing on the rest of the environment.

Network Protocols

The most common protocols used to print over an NT network are TCP/IP and Data Link Control (DLC). The protocol that you choose will depend both on the configuration of your print server and on the protocols that are supported by your print device. For instance, if the Windows NT print server is already running TCP/IP, then it is better to use TCP/IP instead of adding another protocol stack to the server's configuration.

DLC is typically used to connect to mainframe environments, but it can also be used to connect to Hewlett-Packard print devices that are directly connected to the network. Other manufacturers rarely provide print device connectivity through DLC. Like TCP/IP, DLC only needs to be installed on the Windows NT print server. Clients can print to the DLC-enabled HP print device without having the DLC protocol stack installed. However, this protocol has many limitations. For instance, DLC is a nonroutable protocol so, depending on the network topology, it may encounter boundaries that it cannot cross. Also, Microsoft's implementation of DLC does not support communication between machines (other than print devices and mainframes) because it is not designed to work with the Redirector or Server services.

NOTE: The DLC Registry entries are located in the HKEY_LOCAL_ MACHINE\SYSTEM\CurrentControlSet\Services\DLC subkey.

TCP/IP, on the other hand, is widely supported by various print device manufacturers. This gives you a greater number of choices, which increases scalability and flexibility for printing.

Registry entries for TCP/IP network printing support are located in the following subkeys:

▼ HKEY_LOCAL_MACHINE\SOFTWARE\Microsoft\LPDSVC

■ HKEY_LOCAL_MACHINE\SOFTWARE\Microsoft\TcpPrint

▲ HKEY_LOCAL_MACHINE\SYSTEM\CCS\Services\ LPDSVC

For more information on optimizing network configurations and protocols, refer to Chapter 5.

Reducing Print Browsing Traffic

Any time a printer is shared from a Windows NT workstation or print server, its existence is announced to the rest of the network. A broadcast message is issued by the spooler service every 10 minutes, which adds to the traffic that already exists on the network and can affect network performance.

The good news is that you can choose among several options to reduce the amount of traffic generated by print device sharing on a network. All of these modifications are performed through the Registry in the following subkey: HKEY_LOCAL_MACHINE\ SYSTEM\CurrentControlSet\Control\Print\.

This subkey contains three parameters that you can use to manage the print browsing traffic: DisableServerThread, ServerThread Timeout, and NetPrinterDecayPeriod. These three parameters can dramatically affect network performance.

▼ **DisableServerThread** This parameter completely removes the spooler's ability to broadcast messages notifying other machines of shared print devices. The default value is 1, which means that notification is enabled. Changing this value to 0 disables notification. It is recommended that you keep this Registry parameter enabled. Otherwise, users will only be able to connect to the print device manually. For example, a user would have to know the UNC name for the printer (*SERVERNAME**PRINTERNAME*) to connect.

- **ServerThreadTimeout** This parameter specifies the length of time that passes between print browsing notifications. Modify this value instead of disabling notification altogether. The default value is 360,000 ms (6 minutes). Increasing this value can greatly reduce the amount of print browsing traffic on the network. It is recommended that you at least triple this value (1,080,000 ms, or 18 minutes) to reduce the frequency of announcements.

▲ **NetPrinterDecayPeriod** This value represents the amount of time that the machine sharing the print device caches the share print device lists. Depending on how much you increase the ServerThreadTimeout parameter, you should change this value to maintain the print browse list. For example, if you set ServerThreadTimeout to more than one hour, you should increase this parameter to one and a half hours, or at least 1.5 times the ServerThreadTimeout parameter value.

Greater Efficiency with Printer Pools

In an environment with more than one print device, sometimes a particular print device will be used more heavily, and other print devices may be underutilized. To combat this problem, Windows NT can tie printing resources together into a single entity called a *printer pool.*

A printer pool is a logical grouping of two or more identical print devices. Printer pools are viewed as a single print device, and all the printers that participate in the pool are shared under one share name. Any configuration changes made to the printer pool affect every print device in the pool. Therefore, all print devices in a pool must use the same print device driver, and for greater efficiency, the print devices should be identical. You can, however, mix different print connection types to include more print devices. For instance, you can include both network and local printers in a pool. Figure 9-10 shows mixed print connection types in a printer pool on Windows NT.

The use of printer pools allows Windows NT to more effectively and efficiently use printing resources. When a print job is sent to a printer pool, Windows NT hands the print job off to the first available print device. This way, no one print device is favored, and print jobs are less likely to experience delays.

Printer pools involve a few inconveniences. First, users do not know which print device will service a print request. However, if you physically group the print devices close together, users will be able to find their print jobs. You should also use separator files when implementing printer pools to help users differentiate one print job from another.

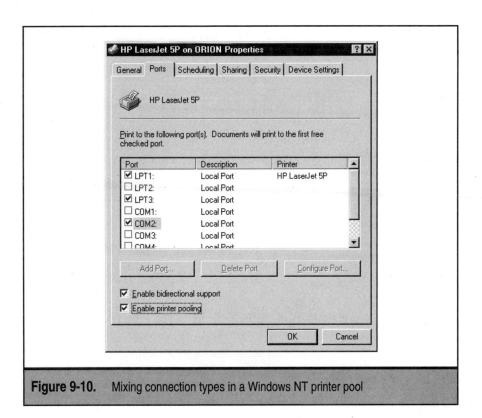

Figure 9-10. Mixing connection types in a Windows NT printer pool

Another inconvenience relates to the processing that occurs when one of the print devices experiences technical problems, such as a print jam or mechanical failure. In this case, any print job that is sent to that print device may never be printed because no built-in intelligence tells NT to redirect the print jobs to another, operational print device. However, the efficiency gained from printer pools far outweighs the few inconveniences they pose.

CREATING A PRINTER POOL   If you have the proper hardware (that is, several identical print devices or print devices that use a common print device driver), the process of creating a printer pool is extremely easy. To configure a printer pool on Windows NT, do the following:

NOTE: The following steps assume that the print devices have already been created. If any of the print devices has not been defined, refer to "Creating a Printer" earlier in this chapter.

1. Choose Start | Settings | Printers and open the Printers folder.

2. Select the print device by clicking the print device icon.

3. Go to the print device's Ports tab on the Properties page by right-clicking the print device icon, selecting Properties, and then clicking the Ports tab.

4. Select Enable Printer Pooling on the Ports tab to enable printer pooling, as shown in Figure 9-11.

5. Select all of the ports that the printer pool will use. For example, if the printer pool will contain three print devices, select the port location for each device.

6. Click the Sharing tab and enable sharing.

7. In the Share Name box, type the name for the printer pool that will be displayed in the browse list. Then click OK.

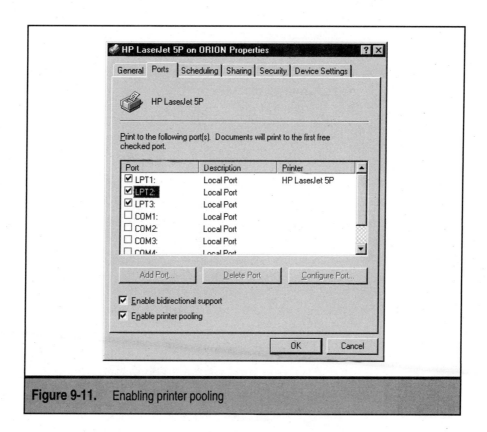

Figure 9-11. Enabling printer pooling

Scheduling

Scheduling is one of the most underutilized Windows NT printing configurations. Many users do not realize its true effectiveness, especially in environments where the printing workloads are vastly disparate in size. For example, your environment may typically print large and small print jobs throughout the day, but the large print jobs may not be needed immediately or even on that day. In other words, though the smaller print jobs may be needed at once, the large jobs could be printed after hours. If scheduling is not used, those large print jobs can tie up the print devices for considerable amounts of time and keep the smaller, more urgent jobs from printing in a timely fashion.

Printer scheduling is the best solution in this situation. It allows you to define and configure a printer with different names signifying different scheduling priorities. After a print device is defined, you can configure another instance for printing large print jobs after hours. Give the second instance of the print device a different name, such as AFTER HOURS PRINTING, and then change its scheduling properties accordingly. This will give clients another print device option to use to print large print jobs. Instead of printing large print jobs to their normal default printer, they can send them to the AFTER HOURS PRINTING print device. The print job will be queued on the Windows NT print server until the time you specified in the scheduling properties for that print device.

Here's how to configure another instance of a printer and change its scheduling properties on the Windows NT print server:

1. Choose Start | Settings | Printers and open the Printers folder.

2. Double-click the Add Printer icon to begin adding another print device definition for a given printer. Be sure to configure this instance of the print device exactly as the original.

3. When the Add Printer Wizard prompts you for the name of the printer, type a name that describes what the print device is used for, such as **AFTER HOURS PRINTING**.

4. After the print device instance has been created, right-click the print device icon and choose Properties.

5. In the print device's Properties dialog box, select the Scheduling tab as shown in Figure 9-12.

6. Change the Available property so that the print device is available only after hours (for example, from 5:00 P.M. to 6:00 A.M.).

As users print to this print device instance, the print jobs will be spooled and stored in the disk subsystem on the Windows NT print server until 5:00 P.M. Since the print jobs are stored on the print server's hard disk until the print device becomes available, you need to make sure there is ample disk space to hold them. It is also a good

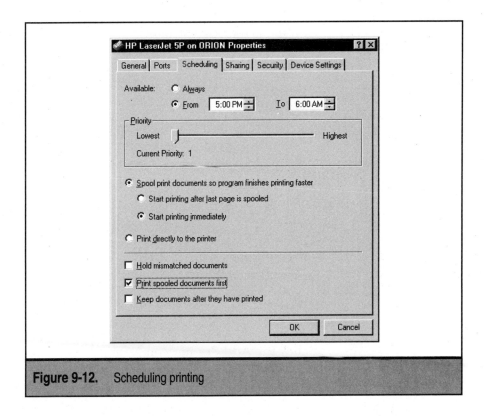

Figure 9-12.   Scheduling printing

idea to configure a separate spooler file, preferably on a separate hard disk drive, to ensure adequate read and write times as well as storage space.

CONCLUSION

Although printing is rarely regarded as a means of boosting performance, this chapter has shown otherwise. You can indeed improve printing performance and, as a direct result, increase overall system performance. This chapter discusses which print device hardware specifications affect printing performance the most and recommends ways to tweak Windows NT printing performance on workstations and servers.

CHAPTER 10

Tuning with the Registry

The Windows NT Registry is a repository containing a wealth of information pertaining to the system configuration. It is a database that uniquely describes a system's hardware configuration, security policy, installed system and application software, user-specific settings, file associations, and much more. Unfortunately, users rarely fully understand the Registry's capabilities and uses, in part because of its complexity and because many are intimidated by the potentially disastrous effects that a manual configuration change may have on the overall system. These concerns are justified; the Registry is not a Windows NT component that should be taken lightly. Windows NT relies heavily on the Registry to operate, and thus it is critical that you understand its approach to system configuration so you can fully grasp and make use of the Registry's capabilities.

Many of NT's default values provide moderate to good performance. However, the default system and environment variables may not meet the specific demands placed on the system by your organization, so to get the most out of the system, you will need to make some configuration changes. Throughout this book, many system configuration changes have been recommended to optimize specific system components or subsystems. Some of these can be accomplished through an application or system interface, but others require direct manipulation of the Windows NT Registry. Unfortunately, there is not always an application or system interface that you can use to make configuration changes to boost performance. To truly uncover the performance capabilities of Windows NT, you will often need to tweak settings particular to your system configuration by changing the Registry.

This chapter gives you the information and survival skills you need to manipulate the Registry so you can boost performance while maintaining system reliability. This chapter focuses on four key topics related to system performance and the Windows NT Registry:

▼ The Registry and its role in system performance. Many of the recommendations in this book require you to directly edit the Registry.

■ How to safely modify the Registry.

- ■ The importance of backing up the Registry to maintain system reliability and stability.

- ▲ How to keep the Registry operating efficiently so the database itself does not negatively affect system performance.

HOW THE WINDOWS NT REGISTRY CAN BOOST PERFORMANCE

How is familiarizing yourself with the Registry going to help you boost performance? For starters, Windows NT's default settings in many cases simply cannot give you the level of performance that you expect and need. In addition, there are a limited number of ways to optimize server performance through the UI, whereas all configuration parameters can be tweaked through the Registry. By familiarizing yourself with the Registry's organization, you will learn where to find those configuration parameters and what settings to use for each parameter. Figure 10-1 presents a simplified version of the Registry organization.

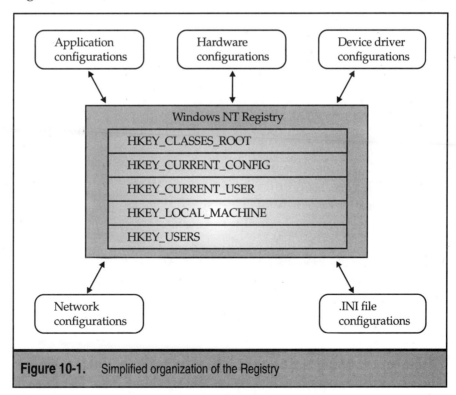

Figure 10-1.   Simplified organization of the Registry

As an IT professional responsible for the well-being of your Windows NT environment, it is essential that you know where various types of system configuration information are located in the Registry and how to change these settings to get the best performance from Windows NT. To effectively optimize Windows NT, you will need to be well informed about the Registry.

Beyond .INI Files

Earlier versions of Windows operating systems relied on .INI files for configuration parameters. However, .INI files offered only primitive organization, lacked security, did not provide user-specific settings, and suffered from other limitations as well.

For backward compatibility, Windows NT allows applications to use .INI files, and NT also keeps the following .INI files so that older programs can write to and reference these files:

▼ WIN.INI

■ SYSTEM.INI

■ CONTROL.INI

■ LANMAN.INI

▲ PROTOCOL.INI

The Registry consists of keys and subkeys, which may or may not contain value entries. The Registry keys are analogous to the bracketed headings in .INI files, and the Registry value entries correspond to the information located below the headings in the .INI files. This is the extent to which .INI file structure is similar to Registry organization. Unlike .INI files, the Registry permits multiple configuration levels with subkeys and allows multiple types of values.

All information pertaining to .INI files can be found in the following key: HKEY_LOCAL_MACHINE\SOFTWARE\Microsoft\ Windows NT\CurrentVersion\IniFileMapping. The subkeys under this location contain a string value, which essentially serves as a pointer to the Registry location containing the information located within the .INI file section. Each string either begins with SYS or USR, corresponding to HKEY_LOCAL_MACHINE\SOFTWARE or HKEY_CURRENT_USER, respectively. For example, the File Manager (WINFILE.INI) subkey contains the value entry Settings and has a string value of #USR:Software\Microsoft\File Manager \Settings, which translates to the following key: HKEY_CURRENT _USER\Software\Microsoft\File Manager\Settings. In this location you will find the configuration settings for the File Manager for the user currently logged in.

The symbol in front of the string value also is meaningful in .INI file mapping. These symbols appear in addition to the SYS and USR designation mentioned earlier. Table 10-1 describes all possible symbols in the IniFileMapping subkey.

Symbol	Meaning
!	All configuration modifications are made to both the Registry and the appropriate .INI file.
#	If Windows NT was installed on a machine that previously ran Windows 3.1, the Registry value will change to the value specified in the .INI file whenever a new user logs on.
@	Windows NT will not use the associated .INI file even if the requested data cannot be found in the Registry.

Table 10-1. IniFileMapping Symbols

WINDOWS NT REGISTRY ARCHITECTURE

The Registry is an organized conglomeration of hardware-, software-, and user-related information. It includes information regarding the devices present on the system, operating system and application configuration parameters, user profiles, and much more. The basic structure of the Registry, shown in Figure 10-2, looks much like a tree with its roots, branches, and leaves turned upside down. The Registry's structure is hierarchical, with multiple configuration levels specified by keys, subkeys, value entries, and values. A value entry is a parameter within the key or subkey, while a value is the specific value for the parameter.

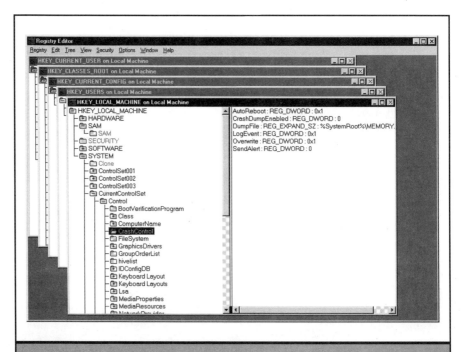

Figure 10-2.   Registry structure, with keys, subkeys, value entries, and values

Keys and Subkeys

A *key* is a top level of organization in the Registry. Each key can have subkeys branching off of it and can also contain value entries or values. Each subkey can, in turn, be considered the key for the information branching off of it.

There are five keys in the Registry that are called *root keys* or *hives*. These are permanent keys within the Registry, and they represent the highest level of organizational structure. Notice that in Figure 10-2, each window within the Registry represents a root key. The five root keys are described in Table 10-2.

In fact, the system actually perceives there to be six root keys in the Registry, but only five can be seen with REGEDT32. The missing root key is HKEY_DYN_DATA, and even though it does not appear to exist, it nonetheless serves a purpose. HKEY_DYN_DATA serves as a middleman between the Registry and a few other system components, such as device drivers and Win32-based applications.

Registry Root Key	Contents
HKEY_CLASSES_ROOT	File associations and OLE information.
HKEY_CURRENT_CONFIG	Hardware configuration information.
HKEY_CURRENT_USER	Information about the user currently logged on, such as desktop settings and network connections.
HKEY_LOCAL_MACHINE	System configuration information and parameters, such as hardware, software, and security settings.
HKEY_USERS	Local user account information. Information on each user is stored in a separate subkey.

Table 10-2.   Registry Root Keys (or Hives)

For example, Performance Monitor queries this root key when gathering performance statistics on a Windows NT machine.

The Registry information is divided into categories under the root keys. Root keys are hard-coded within the Windows NT operating system; you cannot delete them, nor can you add another root key to the Registry.

Interestingly, some of the root keys are subkeys of other root keys. The root keys that are also subkeys of other root keys are linked to one another. Table 10-3 lists the root keys and their respective links.

Where is the Registry information stored? By default, all Registry information is stored in the %SYSTEMROOT%\System32\Config directory. This includes SYSTEM.ALT and .LOG files, which serve as backup files. Table 10-4 lists the files you will find in the %SYSTEMROOT%\System32\Config directory and their Registry root keys and paths.

HKEY_LOCAL_MACHINE

The HKEY_LOCAL_MACHINE root key contains information pertaining to hardware devices and software installed on the system, including bus types, system memory, device drivers, and startup

Root Key	Corresponding Root Key and Link (Path)
HKEY_CLASSES_ROOT	HKEY_LOCAL_MACHINE\SOFTWARE\Classes
HKEY_CURRENT_CONFIG	HKEY_LOCAL_MACHINE\SYSTEM\CurrentControlSet\Hardware Profiles\Current
HKEY_CURRENT_USER	HKEY_USERS (current user logged on)

Table 10-3. Registry Root Key Links

Filename	Root Key and Path
SAM	HKEY_LOCAL_MACHINE\SAM
SECURITY	HKEY_LOCAL_MACHINE\SECURITY
SYSTEM	HKEY_LOCAL_MACHINE\SYSTEM
NTUSER	HKEY_CURRENT_USER
DEFAULT	HKEY_USERS\DEFAULT
SOFTWARE	HKEY_LOCAL_MACHINE\SOFTWARE

Table 10-4.   Filenames and Root Key Paths

parameters. The first level below HKEY_LOCAL_MACHINE has five subkeys—HARDWARE, SAM, SECURITY, SOFTWARE, and SYSTEM—as shown in Figure 10-3.

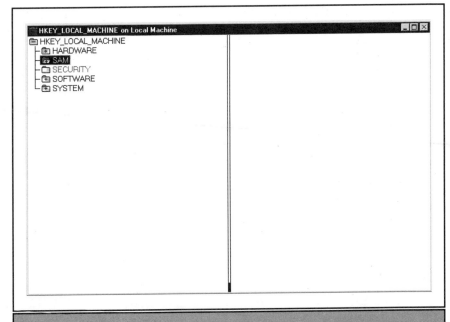

Figure 10-3.   Subkeys defined under HKEY_LOCAL_MACHINE

HKEY_LOCAL_MACHINE\HARDWARE   This subkey contains all the hardware information for the root key. It is a volatile subkey because its information is discarded when the system shuts down and rebuilt when the machine restarts. On Intel-based platforms, NTDETECT. COM is responsible for gathering hardware characteristics and passing this information to this subkey. NTDETECT.COM detects hardware components such as the following:

- ▼ Bus type
- ■ Adapter type
- ■ Communication ports (for example, whether the port is a COM or parallel port)
- ■ Keyboard
- ■ Mouse
- ■ Video
- ▲ Floppy disks

The information then is passed down to the subkeys under HKEY_LOCAL_MACHINE\HARDWARE, listed here:

- ▼ **HARDWARE\DESCRIPTION**   Receives hardware descriptions collected by NTDETECT.COM.
- ■ **HARDWARE\DEVICEMAP**   Contains the mappings of devices to device drivers.
- ■ **HARDWARE\OWNERMAP**   Similar to HARDWARE\ DEVICEMAP in that it maps drivers to devices, but this key relates to the system's bus types. For example, the PCI bus driver is mapped to the PCI bus.
- ▲ **HARDWARE\RESOURCEMAP**   Contains resource mappings that the devices use, such as physical memory ranges and interrupts.

HKEY_LOCAL_MACHINE\SAM   As shown in Figure 10-4, this subkey is dimmed; the information contained in this subkey is unreadable by

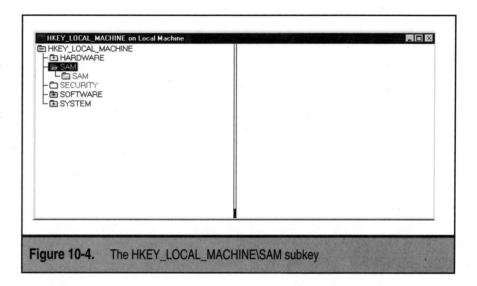

Figure 10-4.   The HKEY_LOCAL_MACHINE\SAM subkey

default. This subkey contains sensitive account information such as user passwords and domain associations. This subkey is directly linked to the HKEY_LOCAL_MACHINE\SECURITY subkey.

HKEY_LOCAL_MACHINE\SECURITY   As with the HKEY_LOCAL_MACHINE\SAM subkey, the information in this subkey cannot be accessed by default because of security concerns. This subkey defines user and group permissions and includes information regarding whether to install device drivers, add printers, install applications, and so on.

HKEY_LOCAL_MACHINE\SOFTWARE   This subkey stores application-specific information such as paths to executables and licensing information. The application settings in this subkey are applied globally because HKEY_LOCAL_MACHINE is the same for every user who logs onto the machine. This is unlike HKEY_CURRENT _USER\Software settings, because those settings are tailored for individual user accounts; for example, one user may execute completely different applications than another, so application settings are not applied systemwide.

You can also find information pertaining to the Windows NT operating system in this key. HKEY_LOCAL_MACHINE\ SOFTWARE\Microsoft\Windows NT\Current Version contains Windows NT operating system information such as the build number and the actual %SYSTEMROOT% directory path.

HKEY_LOCAL_MACHINE\SYSTEM   This subkey is of major importance to Windows NT because it contains detailed information on previous control sets, the current control set, Windows NT setup, and disks for the Disk Administrator. When the Disk Administrator prompts you to write disk signatures, the information, such as drive letters and RAID settings, is stored in the HKEY_LOCAL_MACHINE\ SYSTEM\DISK subkey.

The current control set is important to the operation of Windows NT; it defines the profile used by the system. Subkeys under CurrentControlSet provide detailed information on services running on the machine, the computer name, instructions for NT in case the system crashes (for example, whether to reboot, produce a crash dump, and so on), and directory paths to the Registry information files. The previous control sets are used for additional hardware profiles and the Last Known Good Configuration profile.

HKEY_CLASSES_ROOT

HKEY_CLASSES_ROOT is an alias for the HKEY_LOCAL_MACHINE\ SOFTWAE\Classes subkey, which houses information regarding file associations, shortcuts, OLE, and so on. Every registered filename extension has its own key with a REG_SZ value that essentially points to the application that will be launched to work with the specified filename extension. For example, when you double-click a filename with the .TXT extension from Windows NT Explorer, Notepad's association with this type of extension launches Notepad to read the file. Most systems have a large number of registered applications such as the ones shown in Figure 10-5.

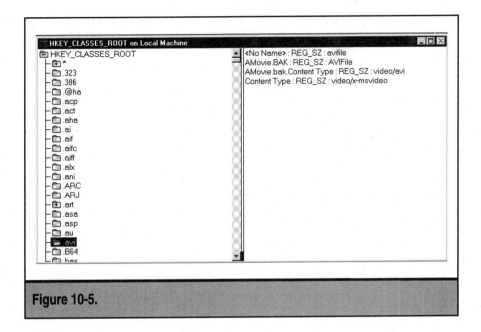

Figure 10-5.

HKEY_CURRENT_CONFIG

The HKEY_CURRENT_CONFIG root key was introduced in
Windows NT 4.0 for compatibility reasons for users running
applications on both the Windows 95/98 platform and Windows NT.
This key is actually an alias of the HKEY_LOCAL_MACHINE
\SYSTEM\CurrentControlSet\Hardware Profiles\Current subkey.
Figure 10-6 shows that these two keys are the same.

HKEY_CURRENT_USER

The HKEY_CURRENT_USER root key contains information
regarding the user currently logged on. It contains user preferences
such as desktop preferences, keyboard layout schemes, network
drive mappings, and software preferences. These preferences are
local in contrast to the global preferences contained in the HKEY
_LOCAL_MACHINE root key. HKEY_CURRENT_USER is a subset
of the HKEY_USERS*USERNAME* subkey, where *USERNAME* is the

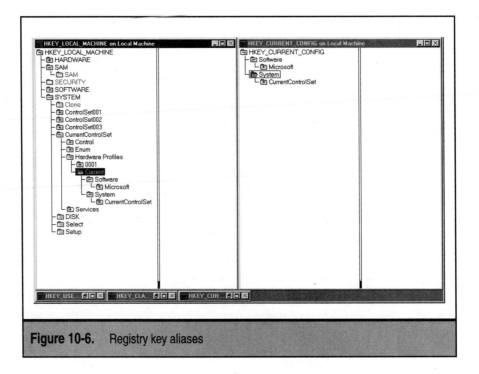

Figure 10-6. Registry key aliases

name of the user currently logged on. Common subkeys contained within the HKEY_CURRENT_USER root key are the following:

▼ AppEvents

■ Console

■ Control Panel

■ Environment

■ Keyboard Layout

■ Network

■ Printers

■ Software

■ UNICODE Program Groups

▲ Windows 3.1 Migration Status

NOTE: When a user is not logged on, the system uses the \DEFAULT key.

HKEY_USERS

HKEY_USERS contains a subkey for each user account. However, it may sometimes appear to contain only two subkeys—\DEFAULT and one identified by the security ID (SID). Typically, only two subkeys will be visible, like the ones shown in Figure 10-7. This key contains the profiles of all users logged onto the system. Note that profiles for user accounts accessing the system remotely are not loaded into this key but are loaded into the Registry of their local machines.

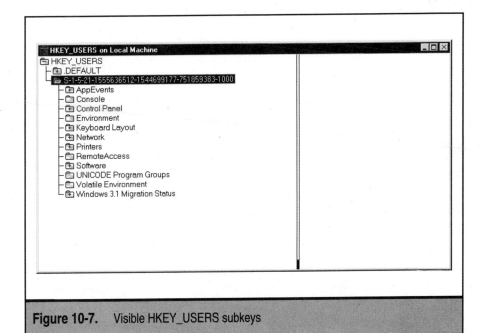

Figure 10-7.   Visible HKEY_USERS subkeys

Value Entries and Values

The information contained within the Registry is maintained by value entries. A value entry has three components: the value name, the value's data type (listed in Table 10-5), and the actual value. The most common data types are REG_BINARY, REG_DWORD, and REG_SZ. You will likely use these common data types to modify settings than any other data types.

Value Data Type	Description
REG_BINARY	Raw binary data that can also be displayed in hexadecimal (hex) format. Most of the system's hardware components use this data type, and their settings can be viewed in Windows NT Diagnostics.
REG_DWORD	A 32-bit number (4 bytes) that can be displayed in binary, hex, or decimal format. This value type is usually used for device drivers and services.
REG_DWORD_BIG_ENDIAN	A 32-bit number.
REG_EXPAND_SZ	An expandable data string that represents environment variables. The variables, such as %SYSTEMROOT% and %USERNAME%, are replaced by the actual values.
REG_LINK	A unicode symbolic link. This type typically links to another Registry key or subkey. For example, the HKEY_CURRENT_USER root key aliases a HKEY_USERS subkey.
REG_MULTI_SZ	An array of strings. Each string is separated by a NULL character.
REG_NONE	No value type.
REG_SZ	A string that usually represents a description. This description is readable (that is, not cryptic).

Table 10-5.   Registry Value Data Types

BUILT-IN REGISTRY EDITORS

Windows NT supplies two versions of the Registry Editor:
REGEDIT.EXE and REGEDT32.EXE. Both allow you to directly
modify the Registry on the local machine as well as on remote
machines. However, there are some subtle differences between them
that you should be aware of. These differences determine whether
you should use one or the other.

REGEDIT

REGEDIT, shown in Figure 10-8, is the 16-bit version of the Registry
Editor that is also included with Windows 95 and 98. On Windows NT
systems, REGEDIT is installed by default in the %SYSTEMROOT%
directory. Although you can use REGEDIT to view hives, keys,

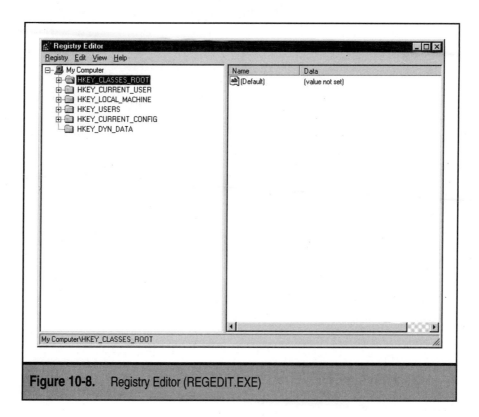

Figure 10-8.   Registry Editor (REGEDIT.EXE)

subkeys, and so on, it does not include all the functionality or data types that its counterpart, REGEDT32, does.

REGEDIT's functionality is somewhat limited because it does not let you set Registry key security or view or edit some value data types. The data types that you cannot modify are REG_EXPAND_SZ and REG_MULTI_SZ. For instance, if you try to view REG_EXPAND_SZ, the editor displays a binary data type rather than a string data type. Moreover, if you attempt to modify these data types, REGEDIT saves them as REG_SZ data types, which prevents the relevant parameter from performing its duties.

REGEDIT does have one advantage over its counterpart: its extensive search capabilities. You can use REGEDIT's Find dialog box, shown here, to search for keys, values, and data within the Registry structure. REGEDIT's search capabilities far exceed those of REGEDT32.EXE.

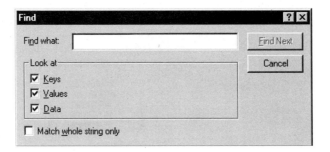

Because REGEDIT combines rather limited functionality with robust search capabilities, you should use it only to search for Registry information. This approach helps ensure that the Registry does not lose security-related information—or become corrupt.

Searching the Registry

To search for a key, a value, or data using REGEDIT, do the following:

1. Open REGEDIT either by selecting it from the Start | Run menu or typing REGEDIT at the command prompt.

2. In the left pane of REGEDIT, select My Computer. This allows the search algorithm to search the entire Registry.

3. From the File menu, choose Find to display the Find dialog box.

4. In the Find What box, type the key name, value name, or data value that you are searching for.

5. Click Find Next to start the search.

REGEDT32

REGEDT32, shown in Figure 10-9, is the Registry Editor commonly used for Windows NT and is located in the %SYSTEMROOT%\System32 directory. It does not have the clean, intuitive user interface of REGEDIT, but instead looks and feels like the File Manager. Despite its appearance, however, REGEDT32 is the Registry Editor of choice because it offers more functionality than REGEDIT, such as Registry

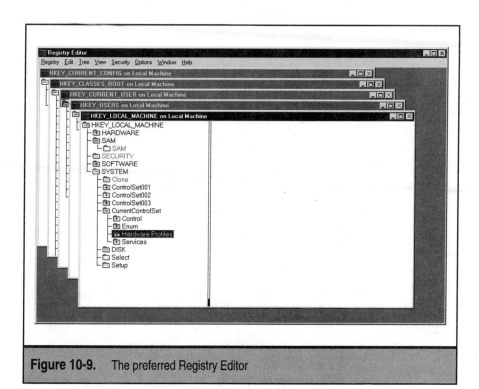

Figure 10-9.   The preferred Registry Editor

security management, the ability to modify any Registry parameter, and a special read-only mode.

Because REGEDT32 can perform more operations than REGEDIT, you have more flexibility with configuration settings. One important option that you should always use is Read-Only Mode. This option will not allow any changes to be saved to the Registry so you can safely peruse the Registry. It is recommended that you use this option until you are ready to make a specific configuration change.

Creating a Key

As you are preparing your server for blazingly fast performance, you are bound to come across a situation where you will need to add a key to the Registry. You may also sometimes need to install a driver or service that does not have its own installation program to guide you through setup procedures and make Registry changes on its own; this, too, may require adding a key to the Registry.

To create or add a Registry key, do the following:

1. Select the key or subkey under which you want the new key to appear.

2. Choose Add Key from the Edit menu to display the Add Key dialog box.

NOTE: The Add Key option will not appear if you are in read-only mode. To disable read-only mode, uncheck Read-Only Mode on the Options menu. You will also need appropriate access rights to add a key.

3. In the Key Name box, shown here, type the name of the key you want to add.

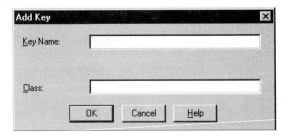

4. If you already know the class to which this key belongs, you can specify it in the Class box, or you can leave this box blank for now. It is recommended that you keep the Class box blank.

Adding a Value

Adding a value means adding a parameter to an existing key or to a key that you have just created. When you add a value, you must also assign it an appropriate data type.

To add a value to the Registry, do the following:

1. Select the key or subkey under which this value will exist.

2. Choose Add Value from the Edit menu to display the Add Value dialog box, shown here:

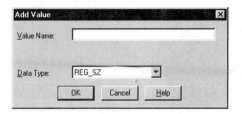

3. In the Value Name box, type the name of the value to be added.

4. In the Data Type pull-down menu, select the appropriate data type for the value to be added.

5. Click OK. A dialog box appropriate for the data value selected now appears. For example, if the data type is REG_SZ, the String Editor dialog box appears as shown here:

6. Type the value corresponding to the data type.

Viewing or Modifying Remote Registries

When you start REGEDT32, by default it opens the Registry of the local machine. However, you can also view or modify the Registry on a remote Windows NT machine, if you have the appropriate permissions. To view or modify the Registry on a remote Windows NT machine, choose Select Computer from the Registry menu. You can either browse a list of machines to choose from, or you can type the machine name in the Computer box. Once the remote Registry hives are loaded, you can work with it just as you would the local Registry.

Removing Registry Information

The ability to delete Registry keys or value entries is necessary to maintain the Registry, but it is also one of the most dangerous options you have. To delete a key or value entry, either select Delete from the Edit menu or press the DELETE key.

CAUTION: If you accidentally delete a key or value, there is little you can do to restore it.

Backing Up the Registry

It is important that you keep an up-to-data backup copy of the Registry for emergencies, such as the inadvertent deletion of a key or value. The most common way to back up the Registry is to use one the following methods:

▼ **Backup Program**   You can use either NT's built-in backup program (NTBACKUP.EXE) or a third-party backup program to back up the Registry to tape. Note that some third-party backup programs cannot back up the Registry.

■ **Repair Disk Utility (RDISK.EXE)**   On domain controllers used in small (1,000 users or less) domains or stand-alone servers, use the /S option.

▲ **REGEDT32** This Registry Editor can be used to manually save individual keys by using the Save Key or Save Subtree As option located under the Registry menu.

Backing up the Registry on a regular basis is crucial to the stability of the system. If the Registry becomes corrupted either by a system process or direct modification, the entire machine can be rendered useless unless you have properly prepared for such a disaster.

Importing and Exporting Registry Files

REGEDT32 offers an alternative option for backing up the Registry. You can also use this approach to view a remote machine's Registry. By using the Save Key option under the Registry menu, you can save copies of Registry keys and subkeys in data files. These files can later be used to restore or replace a key or even rebuild the entire Registry. There is one exception, however. You cannot use the Save Key option to save volatile keys. In other words, you cannot save keys that are created at startup and deleted when the system is shut down. Some volatile keys, such as HKEY_LOCAL_MACHINE\Hardware, have some nonvolatile subkeys that can be saved.

SAVING A KEY OR SUBKEY To save a key or subkey using REGEDT32, do the following:

1. Select the key or subkey that you want to save.

2. Select Save Key from the Registry menu to display the Save Key dialog box, shown here:

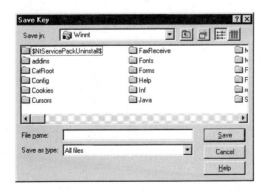

3. Type the name of the file. It is recommended that you use the name of the key as the name of the file.

RESTORING A PREVIOUSLY SAVED KEY OR SUBKEY   To restore a previously saved key using REGEDT32, follow these steps:

1. Click the key that you want to restore from a data file.

2. Select Restore from the Registry menu to display the Restore Key dialog box, shown here:

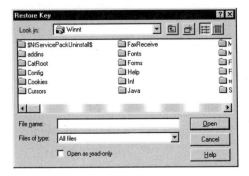

3. Browse for the location of the data file or type the full path and filename.

4. Click Open. You will be warned that you are about to overwrite the key and all of its subkeys.

5. Click Yes to continue.

TWEAKING THE REGISTRY FOR OPTIMAL PERFORMANCE

Clearly, Windows NT relies heavily on the Registry for system configuration information. Users often think of the Registry as the place to go to tune the system for optimal performance, especially if the UI—for instance, the Control Panel—does not have the instrumentation needed to perform such tweaks. Rarely, however, do users look at the Registry itself as a component to be optimized. How can you ensure that the Registry operates as effectively and efficiently as possible for Windows NT?

You have already seen that the Registry is an excellent place for fine-tuning system components since it contains hardware, software, and user configuration settings. You will now see that the Registry presents an opportunity to boost NT performance, not by adding or modifying a Registry configuration parameter, but by modifying the database itself.

A Lean, Mean, Configuration Machine

The Registry is a massive organizational structure containing almost everything you could ever want to know about a Windows NT system. For instance, when you add, modify, or remove hardware and software components, most, if not all, of the changes are reflected in the Registry. However, sometimes when hardware or software components are removed, they leave behind remnants of their existence. It is not uncommon to find Registry entries for a component that used to be a part of the system but was long ago deleted. Do not hastily assume that Windows NT is at fault for leaving defunct or invalid information in the Registry. Most often, it is the hardware component or application's uninstall program, or lack thereof, that does not completely remove its entries from the Registry. In fact, application entries are usually the ones left behind in the Registry, since the Registry's hardware inventory procedures are volatile, meaning that Windows NT always builds its hardware inventory at startup.

The Registry can quite easily accumulate fatty deposits left over from installing, uninstalling, and removing software components, but to get the best possible performance out of NT, the Registry must be kept lean and mean. All those fragments left behind from applications and system components need to be cleaned out from the Registry so that invalid data is not referenced or the Registry database does not grow large with unneeded information.

Cleaning the Registry

If you have ever tried to remove all references to an application by hand, you know how agonizing this process can be. Many of today's applications try to help by including an uninstall utility, which attempts to remove all of the application's code, data, and Registry entries. Uninstall utilities not only save you considerable time; they also reduce the risk that you will damage or corrupt the Registry with manual Registry edits.

Although many developers are building in uninstall utilities, there still are a large number of applications without one. Moreover, available uninstall utilities vary in how well they perform their duties. Consequently, Microsoft has developed its own utility, called RegClean (see "RegClean" just ahead for information on how to obtain this utility), to help reduce the clutter in the Registry. There are also a growing number of third-party utilities that are not application specific that are designed to remove invalid Registry entries.

ADD/REMOVE PROGRAMS   Windows NT provides its own means of removing applications and invalid Registry entries through the Add/Remove Programs applet available from the Control Panel (see Figure 10-10). Most applications can be installed through this applet, and most applications can be removed through it as well.

Although the Add/Remove Programs applet may appear to be the perfect solution for uninstalling applications and removing their associated entries from the Registry, in most cases, the applet simply kicks off an application's uninstall utility. If the application does not have an uninstall utility or if it has been deleted or corrupted, you are out of luck. Even if the system is able to start the application's uninstall utility, you still have to rely on the application to remove itself completely, including any Registry entries it may have added.

REGCLEAN   The RegClean utility searches the Registry for invalid entries and then removes them. RegClean 4.1a or higher is compatible with Windows NT 4.0 and later. The latest version of this utility can be located at Microsoft's FTP site (**ftp://ftp.microsoft.com/Softlib/mslfiles/regclean.exe**).

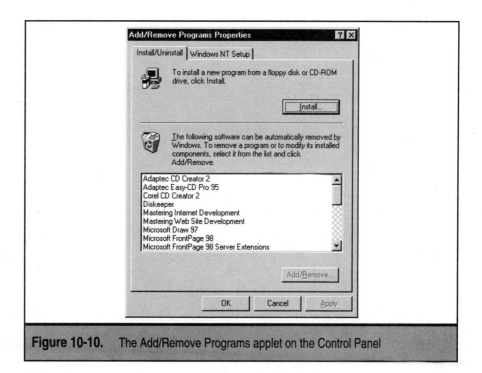

Figure 10-10. The Add/Remove Programs applet on the Control Panel

 CAUTION: As with any program or utility that can modify the Registry, it is critical that you back up the Registry before you execute RegClean.

When you run RegClean, as shown in Figure 10-11, it scans the Registry to find any erroneous values or invalid entries. If it finds any errors, it writes them to a file called UNDO.REG before removing them from the Registry. It is recommended that you review UNDO.REG with a text editor, such as Notepad, to see what changes have been made to the Registry. The UNDO.REG file is also created as a safeguard against the accidental removal of entries or values that are still needed. Figure 10-12 shows an example of the contents of the UNDO.REG file after running RegClean.

 NOTE: RegClean is not designed to fix a corrupted Registry.

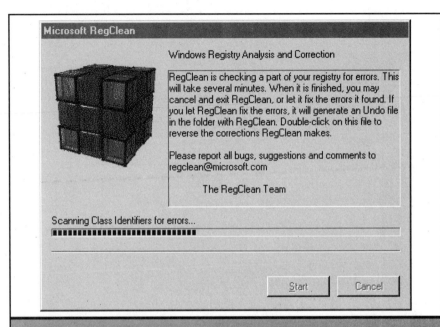

Figure 10-11. Cleaning the Registry with RegClean

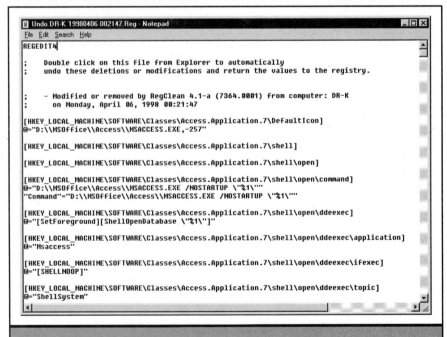

Figure 10-12.

To install RegClean, do the following:

1. Double-click the RegClean executable that you downloaded from Microsoft's FTP site to extract the files needed to run RegClean.

2. Go to the directory that you specified in step 1 and double-click the RegClean executable to start the program.

You can optionally create a shortcut to RegClean or add it to the Programs folder for easier accessibility.

NORTON UNINSTALL DELUXE   The Norton Uninstall Deluxe utility, shown in Figure 10-13, is designed to help clean a Windows NT system. It can be used to uninstall applications (more efficiently than the Add/Remove Programs applet in the Control Panel), move applications and their Registry pointers to another partition, remove invalid Registry entries, and much more. Additional

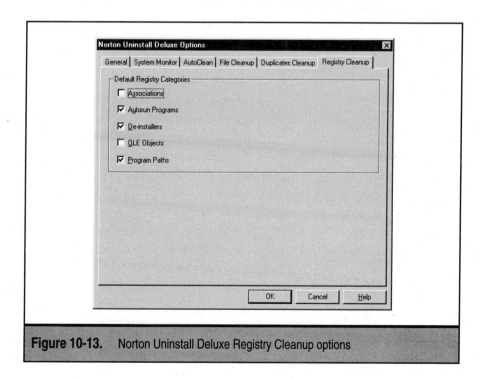

Figure 10-13.   Norton Uninstall Deluxe Registry Cleanup options

product information can be found at Symantec's web site
(**http://www.symantec.com/**).

For the best results from Norton Uninstall Deluxe's feature for
removing invalid Registry entries, install this utility immediately
after you install Windows NT; this way, the utility can maintain a
list of all changes to the system and use this information when
uninstalling an application. Even if you install Norton Uninstall
Deluxe on an existing system, however, it can still successfully
uninstall applications and remove invalid Registry entries. After
installation, it forces you to scan through files on all partitions and
review the Registry before it allows you to use the uninstall or
Registry entry removal features. The directory structure, file, and
Registry scan collects information that Norton Uninstall Deluxe
stores in its database to use to clean the system.

CONCLUSION

The Windows NT Registry is a critical component of the system. It is
also one of the most daunting and least understood components in
Windows NT. However, to effectively optimize the system, you need
to understand the organization of the Registry, how to make
configuration changes in the Registry, and the consequences of
changing the Registry.

Many of the configuration parameters you need to change to
increase system performance can be modified only through the
Registry; not every parameter setting can be easily accessed and
modified through the UI. In addition, the Registry itself must be
maintained and optimized so that Windows NT can work as
efficiently as possible.

This chapter described the Registry's organizational structure,
explained how to use the available tools to properly tune the system,
and directed you to the locations of important system keys. This
chapter also provided solid recommendations on how to maintain
and keep the Registry operating as efficiently as possible.

CHAPTER 11

Internet Information Server and the Proxy Server

The Internet's popularity has exploded in the past few years, providing companies and end users with more than just information, entertainment, and communication. While the possibilities of using the Internet seem endless, those responsible for supplying this wealth of information realize it does not come without a price.

Many companies are looking to host their own web sites in-house instead of through third-party Internet service providers (ISPs). This allows the company to have more control over the content and provides for easier administration and maintenance by the IT staff.

However, there are two important considerations with this arrangement. First, it is imperative that the web site maintains adequate response times for requests originating from the Internet or intranet. For instance, if a user attempts to connect to a company's web site to download their latest and greatest device drivers, but cannot due to an extremely busy server, the user might become frustrated and look elsewhere for the utilities. The more frequently this happens, the more the company appears unreliable—and the more damage done to their future reputation. Secondly, the company must provide adequate security to discourage, or ideally prevent, unauthorized access to the web server and to the company's intellectual property.

Successful implementation of an Internet/intranet web site is easily accomplished with Microsoft's Internet Information Server (IIS). IIS, bundled with Windows NT, can be complemented with the Proxy Server for increased security and performance, and is easily managed through a graphical interface. The goal of using IIS is to provide exceptional performance without diminishing security.

OPTIMIZING INTERNET INFORMATION SERVER

Many of the optimization recommendations, such as memory, the network subsystem, the disk subsystem, and others discussed in this book must be applied when configuring IIS for optimal performance. In addition to the recommendations provided throughout this book, tuning parameters specific to IIS configurations and optimizing the system components contribute to overall system performance. This portion of the chapter provides recommendations to specific IIS parameters.

While it is understood that many companies employ different versions of IIS, most of the recommendations presented here are not version-specific, unless otherwise noted.

Optimizing Hardware for IIS Performance

One of the most frequently asked questions when sizing a web server is "How many users can IIS support with a particular hardware configuration?" Unfortunately, there are no recipes or simple answers to this question. Identifying the hardware requirements for a web server is a complex, dynamic process. The number of users connecting simultaneously, as well as their usage patterns, will almost always vary significantly each time they request information from IIS services.

You cannot determine hardware requirements based on just a few parameters. In fact, even when you do define the variety of factors that affect IIS performance, they will constantly change. However, by using the capacity planning procedures described in Chapter 2, you can begin to determine the basic hardware requirements of the web server and scale accordingly. These procedures will also help you proactively identify system bottlenecks and changing hardware requirements.

Web server capacity planning is by far the most effective way to determine workloads placed on the system. You can begin sizing the web server by identifying parameters, such as whether or not the web pages are static or dynamic, what type of database is used, what type of server-scripting is used, and so on. This is assuming, of course, that Windows NT will be used only as a web server. If other functionality is built into the server, there will be additional hardware requirements.

The single most important hardware component for IIS is memory. Ensuring the overall efficiency and performance of the server consideration for all hardware components is important, but memory is key.

Memory

IIS and its related services (World Wide Web, FTP, and Gopher) must reside in memory. When determining how much memory is enough for the web server, take into account the additional resources needed for IIS and its services, the memory to be used by Windows NT and other services on the machine, and the memory requirements for generating dynamic content.

The more memory IIS has to use, the faster it can process user requests. To provide substantial performance the minimum amount of physical memory recommended for an IIS system is 64MB. This recommendation is for a web server primarily supplying static information. If dynamic information is used, the memory requirements may double or triple. For more information on memory, refer to Chapter 4.

INCREASING THE AMOUNT OF L2 CACHE A large amount of L2 cache on any system can significantly improve performance. This is especially true for IIS systems because their instruction paths involve many different components that take advantage of the L2 cache. It is recommended that you configure the IIS system with at least 1MB of L2 cache. For more information on L2 and other forms of cache, refer to Chapter 4.

Processor

Overall, the processing power required by basic IIS services is minimal. However, additional workloads placed on the server by dynamic content can significantly increase processing power requirements. Avoid configuring the web server with anything less than a Pentium 166MHz processor, even if you're only providing static HTML pages. If you anticipate supporting 1,000 or more simultaneous connections with static content a Pentium Pro class or higher is the recommended minimum processor. However, if the same scenario were to include dynamic content, it is highly recommended that you either incorporate a Pentium class or higher SMP machine or to architect the load balance on two or more machines.

Network Subsystem

Providing high-speed network access to client machines is critical to IIS performance. If clients are unable to obtain information from IIS in a timely manner, the results could be damaging to your business. Consider these factors when estimating the network hardware requirements for IIS:

▼ Simultaneous user support

■ Data transfers between the client and the IIS system

■ Connection types between IIS and the Internet

▲ Bandwidth usage limitations when configured with the Internet Service Manager (ISM)

There are many choices, such as the ones outlined in Table 11-1, for the connection type between IIS and the Internet. Of course, the higher the bandwidth, the more users you can adequately support. However, cost also has a major influence in determining the connection type.

Connection Type	Bandwidth	Recommended Maximum Number of Supported Clients
56K	56 Kbps	50
ISDN	64-128 Kbps	100
Frame Relay	56 Kbps-1. 544 Mbps	50-1,000
Dedicated 256K	256 Kbps	200
Fractional T1	128 Kbps-1.544 Mbps	100-1,000
T1	1.544 Mbps	1,000
T3	45 Mbps	1,000 or more

Table 11-1. Common External (WAN) Connection Types

Perform a rough calculation of the expected network traffic generated between IIS and the Internet before you make any hardware purchases. You can use a simple formula, such as

$$\text{Required bandwidth} = \text{number of users connecting per second} \\ \times \text{total number of bytes transferred} \\ \times 8 \text{ (for bps)}$$

to get a general idea of anticipated network requirements. For example, if 120 users connect each minute (2 users per second) and 10K of data is transferred to and from the client machine, then the connection type needs to support 20K per second (160Kbps). In this example, a 56Kbps connection would not satisfy those requirements.

The bandwidth of the NIC is also critical especially if a connection is made to a database on the internal network or IIS serves as an Intranet server. Typically, a 10-Mbps Ethernet adapter or a Token Ring adapter running at 16 Mbps is suitable for many environments. However, if IIS provides dynamic content, these connection types can quickly become saturated. Consequently, if a 100-Mbps or greater network segment is present, it is recommended that you use an adapter capable of supporting a minimum of 100 Mbps. Table 11-2

Connection Type	Bandwidth (in Mbps)
Token Ring	4
	16
Ethernet	10
Fast Ethernet	100
Gigabit Ethernet	1,000
ATM	622
FDDI	100

Table 11-2. Common Internal (LAN) Connection Types

provides a list of some of the connection types available to Windows NT on internal networks.

For more information on optimizing the network subsystem, refer to Chapter 5.

IIS Services

As mentioned earlier, IIS brings three powerful Internet-related services to Windows NT: WWW, FTP, and Gopher. They are all managed in a centralized location, either through the ISM (as shown in Figure 11-1) or through the Microsoft Management Console (MMC) with the IIS snap-in (as shown in Figure 11-2). Each location brings its own functionality to IIS and, as a result, each can affect how well the server performs. However, the MMC is specific only to IIS versions 4.0 and later.

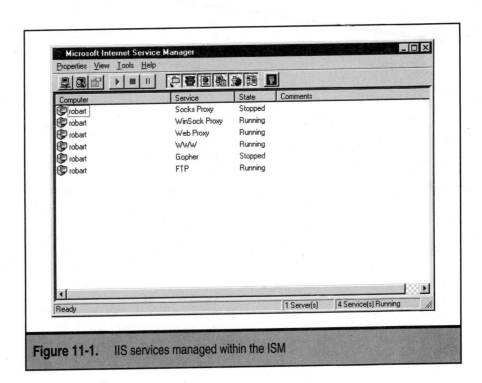

Figure 11-1.   IIS services managed within the ISM

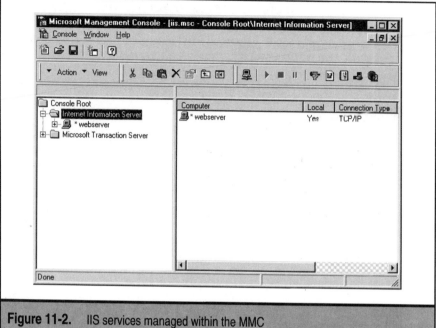

Figure 11-2. IIS services managed within the MMC

NOTE: The Gopher service is no longer supported in IIS versions 4.0 and later.

WWW (Web) Services

The WWW service, also known as the Web Service, is the most commonly used IIS service. As you can see in Figure 11-3, this service manages web browser-related traffic, virtual servers, web browsing authentication, and much more. This service also allows you to tweak some web-related network settings such as bandwidth throttling. Other performance tuning options for this service are discussed in the "Optimizing IIS Network Performance" section later in this chapter.

FTP Services

FTP is the File Transfer Protocol of the Internet and can affect how well the system performs. It provides file transfer services for users

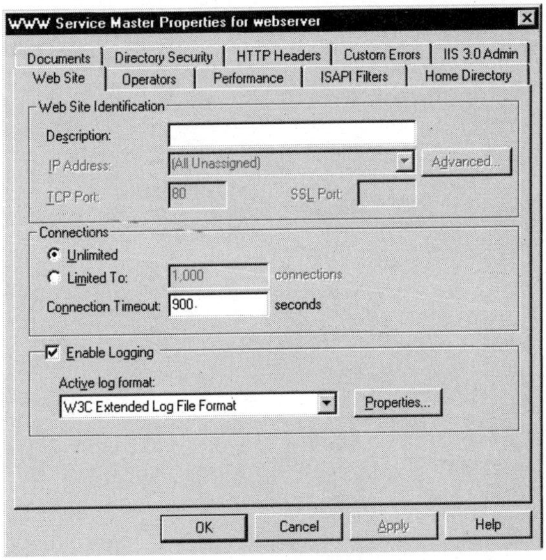

Figure 11-3.   Web service properties

connecting either through the web browser, the command prompt, or a third-party FTP utility.

LIMITING THE NUMBER OF FTP CONNECTIONS   There may be times when the number of users trying to access the FTP service on IIS can cause overall server performance to quickly and significantly decline. It is highly recommended that you place the FTP service on a separate server if you expect high numbers of simultaneous hits. This allows the web-servicing capabilities of the server not to be compromised by the large volume FTP requests and provides positive security measures.

On a single server, the default number of simultaneous FTP connections is 1,000. Limiting the number of simultaneous connections to the FTP service will help to prevent a decline in system performance and will allow you more control over the service. A customized message can be displayed to those users who have been temporarily denied access to the FTP service. To limit the number of FTP connections to the server, do the following:

1. Open REGEDT32 and go to the following key, as shown in Figure 11-4.

   HKEY_LOCAL_MACHINE\
     SYSTEM\
       CurrentControlSet\
         Services\
           MSFTPSVC\
             Parameters

2. Double-click the MaxConnections value entry to edit the value.

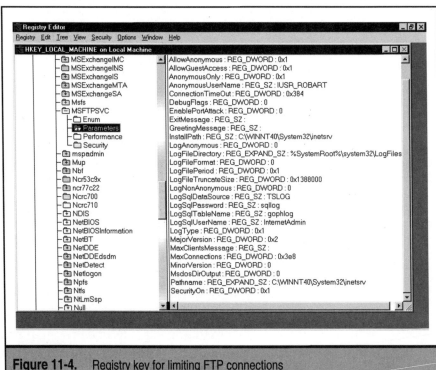

Figure 11-4.   Registry key for limiting FTP connections

3. In the DWORD editor, change the Radix value from Hex to Decimal.

4. Type in the number of simultaneous FTP connections allowed, and click OK.

5. Exit the Registry Editor.

6. Restart the FTP service from the ISM to implement the changes.

With IIS version 4.0 and later, the process of limiting connections is simplified, and does not require direct Registry manipulation. Limiting the number of FTP connections is done through the FTP Service Master Properties dialog box, as shown in Figure 11-5.

CONTROLLING FTP LOGGING   IIS gives you the option to enable logging, or tracking, of FTP-related information. Some of the information you may want to keep track of includes who is

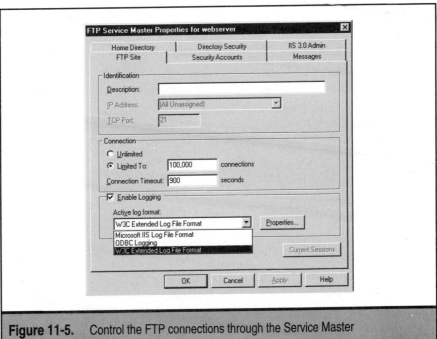

Figure 11-5.   Control the FTP connections through the Service Master Properties dialog box

accessing your FTP server and the types of transactions they are processing.

By default, IIS has always enabled logging of FTP-related information, though not all companies are required to or are interested in tracking FTP server activity. It is generally recommended that you keep logging for troubleshooting and informational purposes. These benefits outweigh any negative effects that logging might have on IIS performance. Performance fluctuations will vary from site to site depending on the amount of information being processed and written to disk. The more information being logged (i.e., the more connections, usage patterns, etc.), the greater the effect will be on performance.

You can log FTP-related information to a standard log file or to an ODBC data source such as a SQL Server database. Using the standard logging mechanism impacts performance significantly less than logging connection information to a SQL database. (For more information on SQL Server performance, refer to Chapter 12.) However, the benefits of logging to a SQL database include immediate and up-to-date information and the ability to create custom reports with tools such as Access and Crystal Reports.

When connection information is sent to a standard log file, it is stored in a 64K memory buffer. Only when the memory buffer reaches capacity does the FTP service write the connection information to the file. You can change the size of the memory buffer through the Registry to suit your FTP service needs. Increasing the size will slightly increase performance, but the connection information will be written to disk less frequently.

On the other hand, if you decrease the memory buffer size, performance will slightly decrease, but the log file will be more up-to-date. You must balance how current you want your information to be with the effects that a smaller buffer will have on performance.

To change the size of the memory buffer (and the frequency of writes to the disk), do the following:

1. Open REGEDT32 and go to this key:

   HKEY_LOCAL_MACHINE\
     SYSTEM\
      CurrentControlSet\
       Services\
        InetInfo\
         Parameters

2. Select Add Value from the Edit menu.

3. In the Value Name box located in the Add Value dialog box, type **LogFileBatchSize**.

4. Choose REG_DWORD as the data type from the drop down box provided, and click OK.

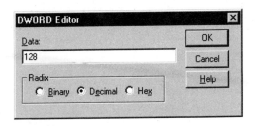

5. In the DWORD editor, select the Decimal radix and type in the memory buffer size. Click OK.

6. Close the Registry Editor and restart the FTP service.

Gopher Services

The Gopher service is a file and directory service where access to specified files and directories is given to users coming in from the Internet. It provides descriptions of those files and directories, along with a listing of other Gopher servers.

The use of Gopher services is declining due to the increasing popularity of graphical web sites and search engines. In fact, IIS versions 4.0 and later no longer support Gopher services. If your Windows NT environment does not require such a service, it is recommended that you permanently disable the service by using the Services applet within the Control Panel.

DISTRIBUTING THE LOAD

It is not uncommon to hear about certain web sites receiving
thousands or even hundreds of thousands of hits per day. How do
these web sites manage such high volumes of traffic? The workload
can actually be distributed across two or more identical web servers.
Clients connecting to a particular web site are oblivious to which
server is processing their request. Figure 11-6 illustrates a client
system connecting to a web site for a total of three times. Each time
the client connects, a different server seamlessly handles the request.

You can configure your web site to distribute the load among
multiple servers using two primary methods. The first uses a
Domain Name System (DNS) to associate multiple IP addresses
(i.e. multiple servers) with a single domain name entry, such as

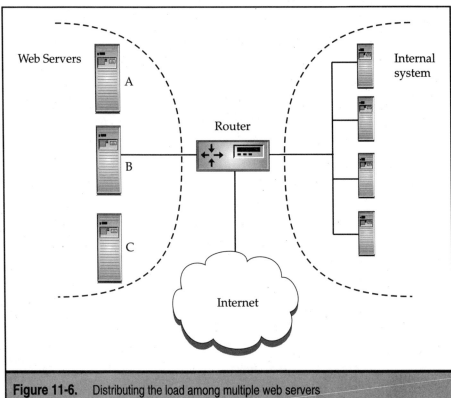

Figure 11-6.   Distributing the load among multiple web servers

www.microsoft.com. When the client machine requests information from **http://www.microsoft.com/**, the request may be handled by any of the IP addresses defined in DNS for that domain name. For a more detailed explanation of DNS and other network-related topics, refer to Chapter 5.

The second approach uses clustering technology, grouping together multiple servers that have the same functionality but appear as a single web server. Distributing workloads and providing an effective fault-tolerant solution, which results in increased availability and reliability, contribute to the growing popularity of clustering. Clustering solutions also provides a checks-and-balances system among all the servers participating in the cluster. For instance, if a change is made or a component is added to the web site, all the information is propagated throughout the cluster. Clustering technology is becoming the wave of the future to distribute workloads, provide high availability, and maintain reliability. Currently, Microsoft has incorporated a two-machine clustering solution in Windows NT Enterprise Edition, and support for more machines can be expected in the future. Table 11-3 provides a list of vendors who offer either hardware- or software-based clustering solutions for Windows NT.

USING THE PERFORMANCE MONITOR TO OPTIMIZE IIS

The Performance Monitor uses many of the objects and counters normally employed to gauge overall system health as well as specific IIS objects and counters. The objects specifically related to IIS are:

- ▼ Active Server Pages
- ■ FTP Service
- ■ Internet Information Services Global
- ▲ Web Service

Product	Company	Contact Information
Digital Clusters for Windows NT	Digital Equipment	1-800-354-9000 http://www.digital.com/
EnVista Availability Manager	Amdahl	1-408-746-6000 http://www.amdahl.com/
Isis Availability Manager	Isis Distributed Systems (wholly owned by Stratus)	1-800-563-9012 http://www.isis.com/
NCR LifeKeeper for Windows NT	NCR	1-800-225-5627 http://www.ncr.com/
Octopus SASO for NT	Octopus Technologies (The Qualix Group)	1-800-919-1009 http://www.octopustech.com/
RADIO Cluster	Stratus	1-888-723-4672 http://www.stratus.com/
StandbyServer for Windows NT	Vinca	1-800-934-9530 http://www.vinca.com/

Table 11-3.   Clustering Solutions for Windows NT

The following sections will examine how to use the Performance Monitor to gauge IIS system performance and will highlight the most important counters to watch.

Analyzing IIS Caching

File system cache is a critical component for optimizing IIS system performance. Since IIS is so memory-intensive, it relies heavily on the file system cache. Use the Performance Monitor to analyze the effectiveness of the cache, but do not attempt to change any cache configurations directly. Analyzing the cache will tell you if IIS is supplied with an ample amount of cache and physical memory. For a more detailed analysis of the file system cache and memory, refer to Chapter 4.

Cache Efficiency

Monitoring the percentage of cache hits is extremely important. The goal is to achieve a cache hit rate of 70 percent or more. High percentages translate into exceptional performance.

The most common type of cache read on an IIS system is the Memory Descriptor List (MDL) Read because it reflects how the server retrieves contiguous pages of information. This may vary, however, with each IIS configuration as well as with the content being provided. Use the Performance Monitor to verify that the MDL Read is the primary cache read on your server. You can do this by monitoring the Cache object every few hours during a 24-hour period. Various types of reads can occur on an IIS system including:

▼ **MDL read**   MDL reads retrieved pages containing data from the file system cache.

■ **Copy read**   When a process request is made to read a file, the file system copies the data from the cache into the application's buffer (within main memory).

■ **Fast read**   Fast reads retrieve data directly from the cache. Fast reads typically occur after the initial read request.

▲ **Pin read**   A pin read occurs when data is mapped into the cache so it can be modified and written back to the disk. Data is *pinned* in the cache, meaning that it stays in the same memory location and cannot be paged out to disk. This method reduces the number of page faults that may occur when requesting data.

Once you have identified the primary cache read method your system uses, the Performance Monitor can analyze the percent cache hits ratio for that particular cache read. For example, if you determine that the MDL Read is the most common type of cache read, examine the Cache: MDL Read Hits % counter to check its efficiency. The counter should have a value of at least 70 percent or higher for optimal performance.

What can you do if the cache read counter is less than 70 percent? When the value is less than 70 percent, it usually signifies that the system does not have enough physical memory. First, check the Memory: Cache Faults/sec, Memory: Page Faults/sec, and Memory: Pages/sec counters. These values should be very small if the system has an adequate amount of physical memory. In order to improve the cache hit ratio, add more physical memory to the system. Windows NT uses a portion of the additional physical memory to add to the file system cache and improve the cache hit ratio, as well as overall system performance. Therefore, the more memory the higher chance you have of a cache hit.

Cache Size

How much file system cache is enough to manage cache read requests? Keep the cache size as large as possible to maintain system performance and efficiency. Moreover, you cannot identify a specific cache size, because it will vary with every system configuration.

Monitor the counters listed in Table 11-4 to determine if the cache size is large enough to hold a sufficient amount of IIS-related data. Closely analyze the times when the cache size is at its smallest value to determine if the cache hits ratio is low (70 percent or lower). If the smallest cache size is coupled with a low cache hit ratio, check the available memory on the system. Typically, the available system

Object	Counter
Memory	Available Bytes
	Cache Bytes
	Cache Faults/sec
	Page Faults/sec
Cache	MDL Read Hits %

Table 11-4. Counters for Monitoring Cache Size and Efficiency

memory will be low as well. The combination of these factors will cause a decrease in performance and signify that the system needs more physical memory to accommodate IIS caching requirements.

OPTIMIZING IIS NETWORK PERFORMANCE

One apparent option for fine-tuning IIS network performance can be found under the Web Service Properties Performance tab shown in Figure 11-7. Other configuration settings require a scrutiny of performance statistics gathered from the Performance Monitor or other monitoring utilities. Whether you are supplying information to the Internet with a T3 network connection, or to an intranet, these

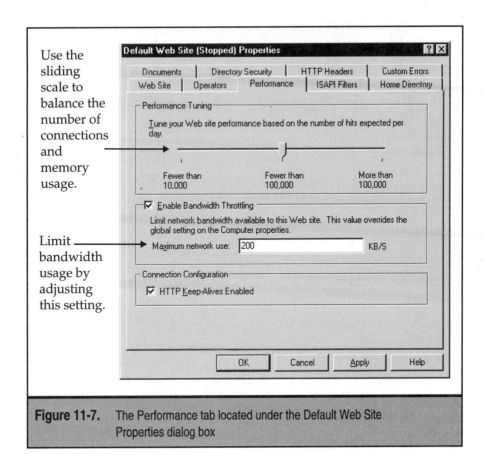

Figure 11-7.   The Performance tab located under the Default Web Site Properties dialog box

network performance recommendations are guaranteed to boost network performance and response times.

It is also important to understand how these settings may affect other system components, such as the amount of memory and processing power IIS will use.

Balancing Network Connections and Memory

IIS makes it easier to improve upon one aspect of performance without compromising another. The sliding scale, shown in Figure 11-7, allows you to tune the server's performance based upon the number of connections you anticipate per day. Adjusting the sliding scale helps IIS decide how much memory it can use for web services.

NOTE: This option can be applied either globally or to each web server on your network. Settings configured per server overwrite the Default Web Site Properties.

Microsoft recommends setting the sliding scale higher than your anticipated connections. A higher setting will increase the amount of memory the server uses and increase connection response times. However, there may be more connections than you realize. Web browsers connecting to the web server typically make more than one connection to help transfer information to the client machine. If the actual number of hits on the web server is 1,000 then there may be as many as 4,000 actual connections.

Controlling Network Resource Consumption

Increased performance often comes from the ability to control resources rather than just tweaking them. Network resource consumption strategies, such as limiting the network bandwidth available to the web site and limiting the number of connections, epitomizes good control of resources, and can significantly improve the web server's performance.

By selecting Enable Bandwidth Throttling within the Default Web Site Properties dialog box (see Figure 11-7), you can specify the exact amount of bandwidth each web site is able to use. Otherwise, you can enable this on a per site basis.

How much permitted network usage do you allow? The answer depends on the bandwidth of the Internet connection as well as how frequently the web site is being connected to. For example, if the web server has a dedicated 56K link to the Internet, limiting bandwidth usage may have adverse effects rather than improving IIS performance. Users trying to connect may experience unusually slow response times or may frequently receive Server Busy messages. In order to find the most suitable bandwidth limitation value and determine the web server's typical bandwidth requirements, analyze the web Service: Bytes Total/sec counter using the Performance Monitor. It is recommended not to limit network bandwidth usage below 50 percent of the link's capacity, because it can degrade response times.

Limiting the number of connections also provides more control over web server resources, and can improve IIS performance. Changing the default setting of Unlimited to a specific number ensures that accepted connections are processed in a more timely and efficient manner. To limit the number of connections to the web server, do the following:

1. Open the Microsoft Management Console (MMC) and locate the web site under the IIS component add-in.

2. Right-click the Default web Site and select Properties.

3. Within the Connections section under the web Site tab, click the Limited To: radio button, as shown in Figure 11-8.

4. In the connections box (now enabled), type in the maximum number of connections permitted at this web site.

5. Click OK to exit.

6. Close the MMC.

Before enabling this option, determine the ratio between server performance and the number of simultaneous connections it is supporting. For instance, if the web server's performance begins to decline while supporting 850 connections, then limit the number of

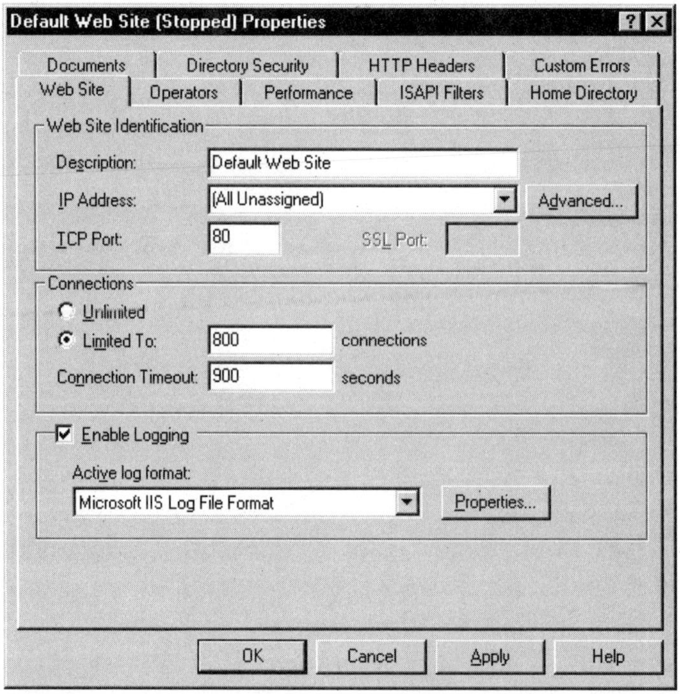

Figure 11-8. Limiting the number of permitted connections

simultaneous connections to a value below 850 (e.g., 800 connections). To determine an accurate ratio, monitor the counters listed in Table 11-5.

OPTIMIZING SERVER-BASED SCRIPTING

Information from the web has become a popular and efficient way of conducting business in a global marketplace. Many companies use the Web to dynamically present product, company, service, and other types of information to otherwise unreachable markets. Shopping at online stores, making airline reservations, and checking bank account information are just a few of the things you can do

Object	Counter	Recommended Value
Memory	Page Faults/sec	< 250
	Pages/sec	< 20
	Available Memory	> 4MB
Processor	% Processor Time	< 50
	Interrupts/sec	3,500 (for Pentium class or higher machines)
PhysicalDisk	% Disk Time	< 55
	Avg. Disk Queue Length	< 2
Web Service	Current Anonymous Users	The number of anonymous users connected simultaneously
	Current Non-Anonymous Users	The number of non-anonymous users connected simultaneously
	Maximum Connections	The maximum number of established connections associated with the Web service.

Table 11-5. Counters for determing the Ratio Between Server Performance and the Number of Simultaneous Connections

directly on the web, regardless of your physical location. Figure 11-9 illustrates how you can design your own computer system using Dell's online store.

Behind the scenes, server-based scripting on an IIS system allows companies to create and manage dynamic content on their web sites. Server-based scripting includes, but is not limited to, the Common Gateway Interface (CGI), the Internet Server API (ISAPI), Java, Active

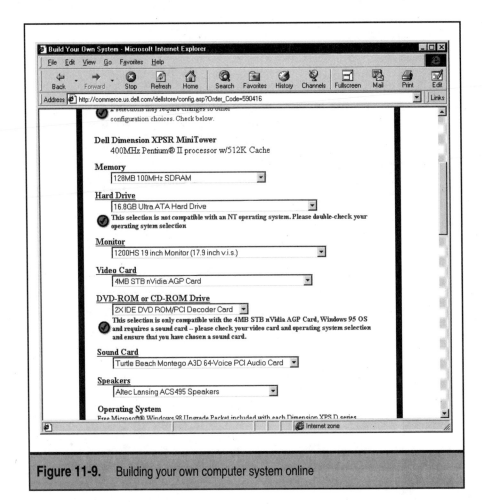

Figure 11-9. Building your own computer system online

Server Pages (ASP), audio, and video. The type of server-based scripting you choose to implement is important because each script can significantly impact the performance of IIS and, consequently, affect how your company does business over the Internet. This section will identify the server-based scripting types that have the most profound effect on resource requirements and IIS performance and provide ways of optimizing the scripts to minimize negative performance.

The Common Gateway Interface

CGI has been the most common method of communicating from a web site to an external data source. As the name implies, CGI acts as a gateway between a web server and other resources, such as a database or an e-mail program. Moreover, CGI is portable across many different operating system platforms including UNIX, Windows NT, and Windows 95, and can be written either as executables or as scripts to be read by an interpreter. The scripts, themselves, can be written in many different languages, including PERL (Practical Extraction and Reporting Language) and Sun Microsystems' Java.

Despite its popularity and portability among other operating systems, CGI requires more server resources (memory and processing power) than other server-based scripts, such as ISAPI or ASP. CGI usually has slower response times because applications or scripts run a separate process each time a client request is received. As the number of requests increase, the resource requirements to support those requests also increases. This can cause a severe slowdown in performance, and decreases client response times. On the other hand, ISAPI and ASP applications are loaded into memory only once, no matter how many times the application is used. CGI applications can take as much as five times the resources to run compared to ISAPI or ASP. As a result, it is recommended that you use ISAPI or ASP applications in place of CGI-based applications to prevent poor performance when providing dynamic content on an IIS system.

NOTE: FastCGI is a successor to CGI that incorporates improvements that enhance performance. Although it reduces some of the overhead associated with CGI, FastCGI scripts and executables still run in separate memory spaces thus requiring more resources than ISAPI or ASP.

Active Server Pages

ASP is at the forefront of dynamic content creation enabling you to run ActiveX Scripts and ActiveX Server Components on the client or the server. By executing the ActiveX Scripts and ActiveX Server Components on the server rather than the client, you achieve client-side operating system independence without compromising the dynamic content. Moreover, the time it takes for data to be transferred to and from client and server is drastically reduced because all the processing is done on the server. Only the resulting HTML code is transferred back to the client.

ASP supports both JScript and VBScript natively, and ActiveX scripting plug-ins are available for interpreters such as REXX, PERL, and other scripting interpreters. ActiveX Server Components can be created in Java, Visual Basic, Visual C++, and other languages. ASP also extends its compatibility by easily integrating with any ODBC-compliant database such as, Microsoft SQL Server, Oracle, and Sybase.

From a performance point of view, ASP is only loaded once, and runs as a multi-threaded service. Moreover, it is optimized to manage a large number of users-initiated requests, and can significantly reduce the amount of network traffic generally associated with dynamic content. As mentioned earlier, ASP only passes the resulting HTML code to the client, which is significantly less than the transfer of ActiveX components or executables.

Improving ASP Performance

Although you benefit immediately by using ASP, there are ways to improve its performance characteristics.

BUFFERING ASP APPLICATIONS   Typically, IIS transfers ASP requested data to the client as it is generated. However, this can result in diminished performance needed for transfers across the network or Internet connection. By buffering the ASP application's response to the client, you can deliver the content in its entirety and, consequently, improve the client response time. The additional memory needed is minimal, and the benefits of buffering far exceed the cost of supplying additional memory resources to the ASP application. To enable buffering for ASP applications, do the following:

1. Open the Microsoft Management Console (MMC) and locate the web site under the IIS component add-in, as shown in Figure 11-10.

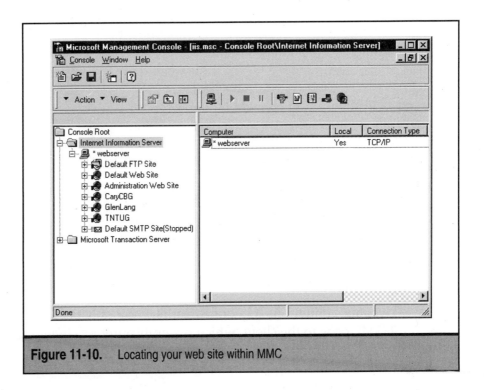

Figure 11-10.   Locating your web site within MMC

2. Right-click the site and select Properties to display the site properties.

3. Under the Home/Virtual Directory tab, click the Configuration button located in the Application Settings section.

4. Under the App Options tab shown in Figure 11-11, select the Enable Buffering option to buffer ASP applications, and click OK.

5. Click OK again to exit the Application Configuration dialog box.

6. Close MMC.

MINIMIZING RESOURCES USED BY ASP APPLICATIONS   Each time a client initiates a request to an ASP application, IIS is able to maintain a session state for each client. Maintaining session state information requires memory, processor, and other resources on the server. As

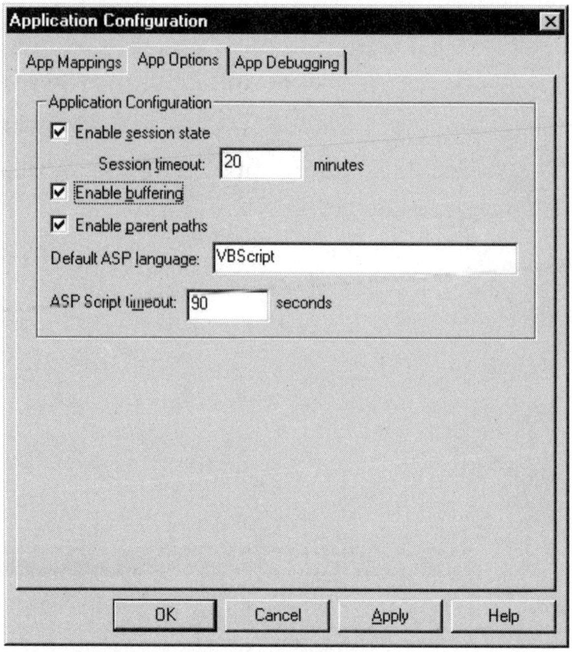

Figure 11-11.   Enabling ASP buffering

more users connect to the web site, the number of session states also increases. Session state information is kept by IIS unless the client disconnects or the session timeout value expires.

In previous versions of IIS, you could only disable session state information for the entire server, not on a per-application basis. In the current version of IIS, disabling session state information entirely could affect system functionality, and is not recommended. If you need to keep session information, minimize the duration of the session state in order to gain more control over system resources. Minimizing session state duration is especially beneficial for sites with large numbers of user connections. To minimize the session state timeout value, do the following:

1. Open the Microsoft Management Console (MMC) and locate the web site under the IIS component add-in.

2. Right-click the Default Web Site option and select Properties.

3. Under the Home Directory tab, click the Configuration button located in the Application Settings section.

4. Under the App Options tab, set the Session Timeout value to the minimum amount of time to maintain session state information, as shown in Figure 11-12, and click OK.

5. Click OK again to exit the Application Configuration dialog box.

6. Close the MMC.

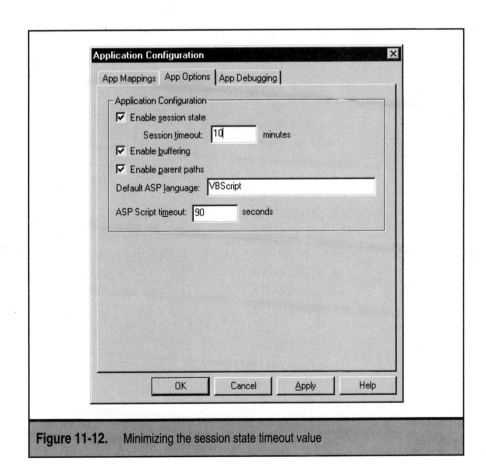

Figure 11-12. Minimizing the session state timeout value

OPTIMIZING THE PROXY SERVER

Available bandwidth to the Internet is a valuable resource for any company whether it is a dial-on-demand or a T3 connection. The amount of traffic flowing through this connection can easily consume much, if not all, of the bandwidth. In addition, traffic originating from the Internet can flood internal networks and pose serious security risks. These concerns are paramount for anyone connected to the Internet, especially considering its explosion in popularity.

Microsoft's Proxy Server is designed to minimize the security risks associated with direct connection to the Internet, and to enhance network performance by policing traffic originating from the Internet. The Proxy Server wastes no time in providing performance enhancements and security to an NT networked environment. Upon installation, the Proxy Server blocks all inbound traffic originating from the Internet that has not been initiated by a network client, as shown in Figure 11-13.

To take advantage of the Proxy Server's capabilities, it is imperative to optimize the server to accommodate inbound and outbound traffic without degrading system performance. This section illustrates how the Proxy Server has been designed to enhance performance, and pinpoints key tuning elements to help you increase the performance of the server itself.

NOTE: For large scale Internet server installations, you should also consider the alternative of employing a full-blown firewall product.

INTEGRATION WITH IIS

The Proxy Server acts as a firewall and content cache server that seamlessly integrates with IIS. Its combined security- and performance-related services are extremely beneficial to any environment, providing improved response times for clients and reducing network congestion all from a single point of administration. Microsoft claims overall network performance can be improved by an average of 50 percent when using content caching.

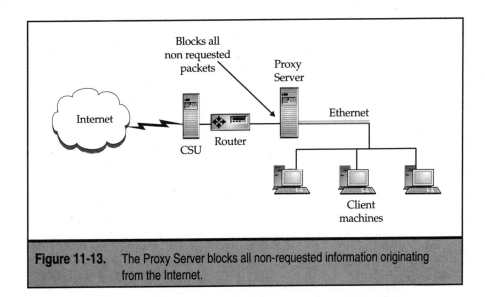

Figure 11-13. The Proxy Server blocks all non-requested information originating from the Internet.

The proxy services work alongside the WWW, FTP, and Gopher services provided by IIS, and are controlled with the ISM. Figure 11-14 illustrates how the proxy services can be easily managed through the ISM.

OPTIMIZING HARDWARE CONFIGURATIONS

As with IIS, it is difficult to knowprecisely how many users the Proxy Server can support. Trying to configure the Proxy Server to adequately manage anticipated workloads can easily become a daunting task.

Optimal hardware configuration is critical to prevent the Proxy Server from becoming a bottleneck, to optimize system performance, and to enhance security. While the most critical components are the amount of physical memory and the processor, you must not disregard the disk and network subsystems. Here are a few suggestions for optimizing the hardware configuration for the Proxy Server:

▼ Provide the Proxy Server with an ample amount of memory. Base memory configurations should be a minimum of 64MB.

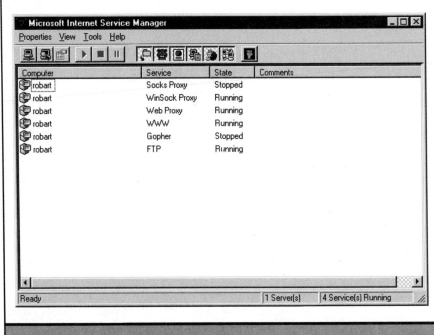

Figure 11-14. Centralized administration of IIS and Proxy Server services

- Use a high-end Pentium class or higher machine. For large sites, consider employing SMP machines or implementing proxy arrays to balance workloads.

- Use a RAID configuration, such as RAID 0 (disk striping) or RAID 1 (disk mirroring), whenever possible. For more information on configuring the disk subsystem, refer to Chapter 6.

- ▲ If a 100-Mbps or higher network segment is present, use a 100-Mbps NIC on the Proxy Server to link the server to the segment. This reduces contention at the server and allows the proxy to handle more requests simultaneously. For more information on network configurations and design issues, refer to Chapter 5.

Table 11-6 outlines the hardware recommendations based upon the anticipated number of users the Proxy Server will support. It is important to note that these are minimum hardware configurations which may vary due to usage patterns, network topology, Internet connectivity bandwidth, and so on.

SECURING YOUR ENVIRONMENT
WITHOUT DIMINISHING PERFORMANCE

Microsoft Proxy Server version 2.0 or higher exhibits firewall-class security that is comparable to traditional firewall technologies. In general, proxy servers have only been designed to enhance performance, but now IP-based security measures are incorporated in the Proxy Server, tightening security through the Web Proxy and WinSock services.

Traditionally, more concern has been placed on outside clients gaining access to internal networks, and less attention has been given to internal clients accessing non-business-related Internet sites. However, the popularity surge of the Internet has increased

Number of Client Machines	Recommended Server Configuration
0-300	Pentium 166 or higher 64MB RAM
300-1,000	Pentium Pro or higher 96MB RAM
1000-2,000	Dual Pentium 166 or higher 128MB RAM
2000-3,000	Dual Pentium Pro or higher 512MB RAM

Table 11-6.   Recommended Hardware Requirements

awareness for restricting access to some external, non-business-related sites, even at the risk of affecting performance and productivity. The Proxy Server can be configured to alleviate much of this concern through its built-in security measures such as packet, IP address, and domain filtering mechanisms, granting access only to administrator specified sites.

The Local Address Table

The local address table (LAT) defines what IP address ranges constitute your internal network. Any IP addresses not defined within the LAT are considered external to your network. You can let the Proxy Server construct the LAT from the Local Address Table Configuration dialog box, shown in Figure 11-15, but then it is recommended that you manually set the range of IP addresses in the internal network. Be sure to exclude the external NIC IP and any other external IP address in the LAT; otherwise, the Proxy Server will not be able to determine that you have an interface connecting to external networks.

NOTE: You can use RFC 1918-compliant private IP addresses listed in Table 11-7 for the internal network, because any traffic generated within the internal network will not pass through the Proxy Server into the Internet or other external networks.

The LAT is primarily a security measure for the Proxy Server. However, it can further enhance network performance by limiting

TCP/IP Subnet Class	Private IP Address Range
Class A	10.0.0.0-10.255.255.255
Class B	172.16.0.0-172.31.255.255
Class C	192.168.0.0-192.168.255.255

Table 11-7. RFC 1918 Private IP Address Ranges That Can Be Used for the Internal Network

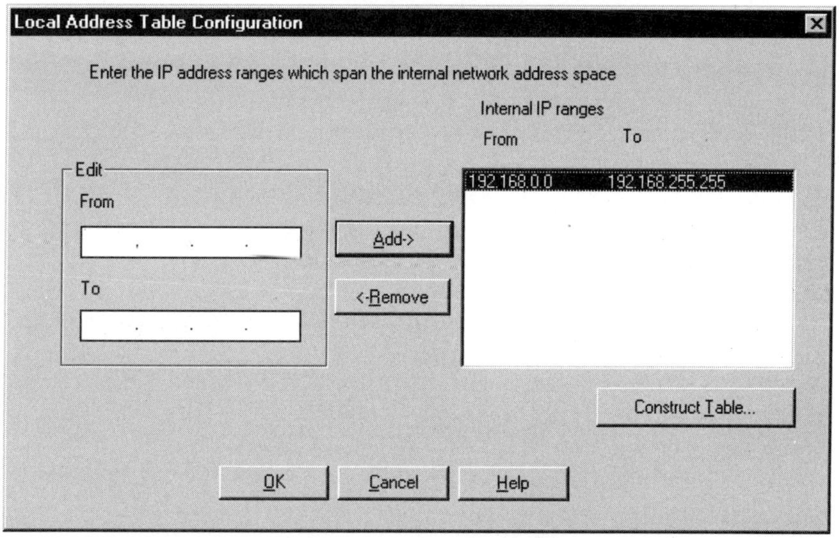

Figure 11-15. Manually configuring the LAT

external access to the internal network as well as defining which internal clients can use the Internet connection. If the Proxy Server is the only gateway to the Internet, it will block all internal client-initiated requests to the Internet. The client may still generate traffic on the internal network, the intranet, but its requests to access the Internet will be denied.

Minimizing the Number of LAT Updates

WinSock Proxy clients rely on the Proxy Server and the LAT for a variety of services such as identification and destination information, specifically making WinSock requests to TCP port 1745 for this information. The Proxy Server also will transfer the contents of the LAT to the client every time the server restarts or the Configuration Refresh Time of the LAT has expired.

Depending on the number of clients supported by the WinSock Proxy service, you may want to reduce the number of times the clients are updated with new LATs. If you have a large number of supported clients, reducing the refresh rates will greatly reduce the traffic generated on the internal network and improve network performance. It will also free the server resources spent to process the transfers. To reduce the number of LAT refreshes, do the following:

1. Open the MSPCLNT.INI file located in MSP\CLIENTS directory with a text editor, such as NOTEPAD. This is shown in Figure 11-16.

2. Scroll down through the file until you locate the [Common] bracket heading.

3. Change the following line

   ```
   Configuration Refresh Time (Hours)=6
   ```

   to

   ```
   Configuration Refresh Time (Hours)=1000000000
   ```

4. Save the file, and exit the text editor.

Caching

In addition to providing a secure network environment connected to the Internet, the Proxy Server can also enhance network performance by caching traffic data. The Proxy Server can be configured to cache frequently accessed content, as shown in Figure 11-17, which can significantly reduce the amount of traffic passing through the company's Internet connection into the LAN.

The Proxy Server's caching mechanisms are similar to memory caching detailed in Chapter 4. When a client requests connection to an external site, the Proxy Server checks to see if the content is in its cache. If the cache contains the data, the Proxy Server will directly satisfy the request, saving precious Internet connection bandwidth. Caching not only reduces bandwidth consumption, it also increases client response time. Plus, the data is received at LAN speeds, which are much faster than typical Internet connections.

There are two types of caching techniques supported by the Proxy Server, passive and active caching.

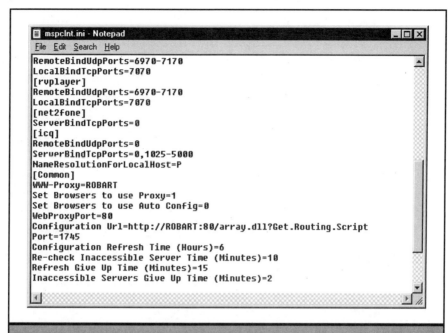

Figure 11-16. Contents of the MSPCLNT.INI file

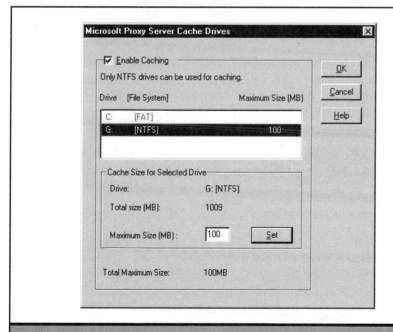

Figure 11-17. Enabling caching on the Proxy Server

Passive Caching

The Proxy Server's most basic form of caching is called *passive caching,* because the proxy's cache contains only the information requested by the client. This form of caching is analogous to caching techniques used with the client-based web browsers. When a client makes an HTTP request, the Proxy Server captures the request checking to see if the requested information is contained within the cache. If it is not in the cache or if the Time To Live (TTL) expiration value has expired, then the Proxy Server retrieves the information from the remote Internet site. Once it receives the information, the Proxy Server transmits it to the client and places it in the cache for future use. If the cache has reached its capacity, the older information is discarded, and the new information stored in the cache is given a TTL expiration value.

Active

Active caching goes beyond the capabilities of passive caching, is enabled by default, and significantly improves the rate at which data is retrieved from the web. Active caching supercedes passive caching by having the server update specific information located in the cache. This is in contrast to passive caching because the client is not the only entity requesting that the cache be updated. For example, the proxy can initiate requests for specific information during periods of low utilization, thus reducing the likelihood of outdated information.

Active caching can be disabled without disrupting passive caching as shown in Figure 11-18. Although this will reduce memory and processing requirements, the benefits of active caching far outweigh the resources that it uses.

The Proxy Server's active caching optimizes the cache using the following scenarios:

▼ Frequently retrieved information from a web site or other Internet-related site can receive a high priority refreshed rate in the cache.

▲ Periods of inactivity or low utilization of the Proxy Server will be used proficiently because the Proxy Server will generate requests to the Internet sites to update the cache.

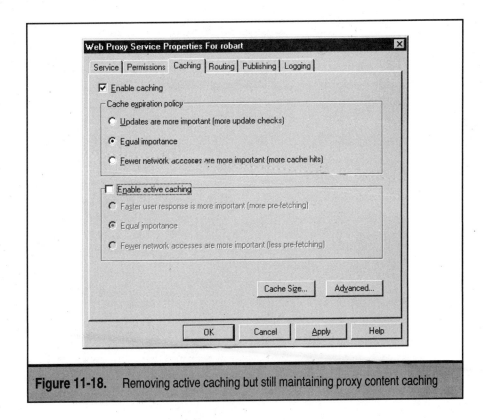

Figure 11-18. Removing active caching but still maintaining proxy content caching

It is highly recommended that you incorporate the Proxy Server's active caching techniques because of the significant performance benefits. These performance benefits include a reduction in network traffic during peak times of the day, more accurate data being passed to the client, increased client response times, and reduced bandwidth consumption on the Internet connection.

Server-Based Content Caching versus Client-Side Caching

Why worry about caching on the Proxy Server when web browsers use their own caching mechanisms? Server-based content caching significantly improves network performance because it is not specifically geared towards a single client. For instance, when one client makes a request for content on Microsoft's web site, the cache on the Proxy Server, as well as the client's web browser, is updated.

When another client requests information from Microsoft's web site, the client receives content provided by the Proxy Server's cache instead of directly from the web site. The content from the cache is received at a much faster rate (LAN speeds) and the Internet connection is less likely to be congested from traffic. If the Proxy Server is not configured to use some form of caching, then each additional client that does not have the web site in its cache would need to seek the information by going through the Internet connection.

Configuring the Cache Location and Size

During installation, the Proxy Server prompts you to specify whether or not to enable caching as well as the location and size of the cache. With the benefits of using content caching being apparent, the next important step is to properly configure the location and size of the cache.

NOTE: The content cache can only be used on an NTFS partition.

    These options can also be changed within the Web Proxy Service Properties dialog box at any time.

LOCATION   For optimal performance, the cache should be placed on a separate physical drive because of the frequent read and write requests made by clients or by the server itself. For instance, when a client makes a request using any of the web-based protocols, the Proxy Server reads the content cache to see whether or not the request can be satisfied. If you are unable to place the cache on its own physical drive, then you should place it on the hard disk drive with the least amount of activity.

SIZE   The size of the cache is as important, if not more important, than the physical location. Unfortunately, there is not a single correct answer to specifying an adequate amount of cache, because it all depends on a number of factors:

▼ The number of users the Proxy Server is configured to support.

■ The amount of client activity. Is the frequency of Internet usage high, moderate, or low?

■ The number of different sites (e.g., web or FTP sites) they are connecting to.

■ The sites refresh rate.

■ The content size of the sites.

▲ The bandwidth of the Internet connection.

Generally speaking, the larger the cache size, the better the chance that the Proxy Server will satisfy requests with its cache. Of course, size is also dependent on the amount of space available on the disk subsystem.

NOTE: The maximum amount of disk space that can be dedicated to the cache on a per disk basis is 10GB!

Table 11-8 presents some guidelines in determining the cache size to support an anticipated number of users. Again, it is important to remember that these recommendations may vary significantly as a result of the sheer number of factors involved in calculating the cache size.

Number of Users	Minimum Cache Size
0-300	500MB
301-1,000	1-2GB
1,001-2,000	2-4GB
2,001-3,000	4-6GB

Table 11-8. Minimum Cache Size Recommendations

DISABLING SERVICES

Any proxy service constantly running consumes system resources. Therefore, it is important that you disable any unneeded service to minimize the amount of resources the Proxy Server needs to operate. Some environments require certain services, such as WinSock, to allow FTP or Telnet access, while others may not. Although these services require a minimal amount of resources (e.g., approximately 400K memory for each service), these resources can be used for other, more important, server responsibilities.

The WinSock Proxy Service

The WinSock Proxy service is used to permit WinSock-compliant applications, such as Telnet and news-related services, to pass through the Proxy Server. It extends beyond the Web Proxy supported protocols (HTTP, FTP, Gopher, and SSL) with support for most non-web-based protocols, such as RealAudio, NetShow, IRC, and more.

Two requirements must be established before a client can use non-web-based services provided by the WinSock Proxy service. First, and most obvious, the WinSock Proxy service must be running. Second, the client must install the WinSock Proxy client software provided by the Proxy Server. No other configuration is necessary no matter how many WinSock applications are used by the client. The WinSock Proxy client software enables the client to communicate transparently with the Proxy Server without having to manually configure each WinSock application.

From a performance perspective, this singles out the client machines needing non-web-based access to the Internet or another external network. By limiting the WinSock services to clients with the required software you can reduce the amount of traffic generated by WinSock applications.

Many environments either do not allow non-web-based access outside the internal network or simply do not have a need for those types of services. If this is the case, it is highly recommended that you disable the WinSock service to decrease resource consumption.

Disabling the service through the ISM is a temporary solution because when the server is restarted, the WinSock Proxy service will be running. To permanently disable the service, do the following:

1. Double-click the Services applet within the Control Panel.

2. Scroll down the list of services until you find Microsoft WinSock Proxy Service.

3. Click the service to highlight it, and then click Stop to stop the service.

4. Once the service has stopped, either double-click the service, or select it and click Startup to display the service's startup parameters.

5. Within the Startup Type section of the Service properties dialog box, shown in Figure 11-19, select either Manual or Disabled.

6. Click OK, then click Close.

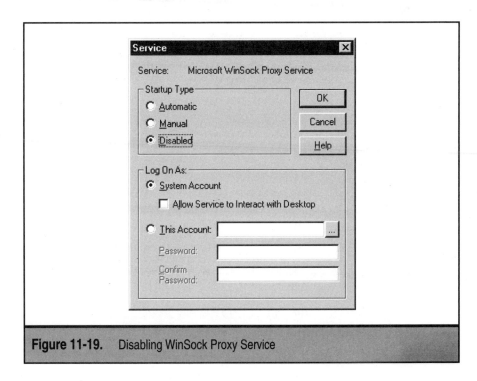

Figure 11-19.   Disabling WinSock Proxy Service

NOTE: If you select the Manual Startup option, you can then enable or disable the service manually from the ISM. Otherwise, you must go back into the Services applet and change the Startup Type from Disabled to Manual or Automatic before restarting the Microsoft WinSock Proxy Service.

The Socks Proxy Service

As noted earlier, clients that cannot reach Internet or external network-related services by using the WinSock Proxy to pass through the Proxy Server, use the Socks service instead. However, these client types, including Macintosh and UNIX, can use the Web Proxy for web browsing, provided the browser supports http proxying. If your Windows NT environment does not consist of these platforms, then the service is not needed, and can be disabled.

You can turn off this service through the IIS Internet Service Manager (ISM) or through the Registry. Using the ISM, however, is only a temporary solution to disabling the service. Anytime the Proxy Server is restarted the Socks service will also restart. To disable the Socks service permanently by modifying its Registry parameter, do the following:

1. Start REGEDT32 from a command prompt or the Start | Run menu by typing **REGEDT32.**

2. Locate the following subkey, as shown in Figure 11-20.

   HKEY_LOCAL_MACHINE\
    SYSTEM\
     CurrentControlSet\
     Services\
      W3Proxy\
       Parameters\
       Socks

3. Double-click the SocksServiceEnabled value entry to edit its value.

4. In the REG_DWORD dialog box, change the default value from 1 to 0.

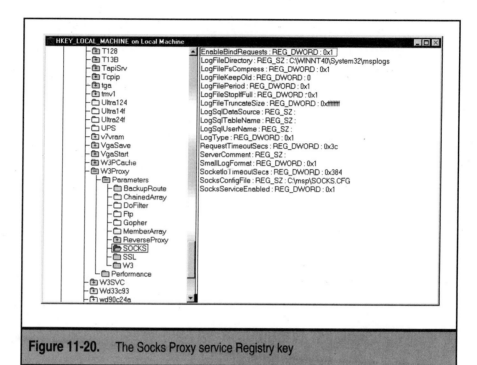

Figure 11-20. The Socks Proxy service Registry key

5. Click OK.

6. Exit the Registry Editor and restart the system for changes to take effect.

Completely disabling the Socks service saves valuable memory resources. If a Macintosh or UNIX client becomes a part of your environment or an existing client needs access through the Proxy Server, you must go through these steps again to change the setting back to the default value.

CONCLUSION

Internet Information Server has greatly impacted the way companies conduct business on the Internet as well as how they provide information through an intranet infrastructure. Without a successful IIS system, businesses can be severely hurt and reputations can be compromised. High-performance IIS systems are key to providing information to the world in a timely and efficient manner. Equally important is the combination of IIS and the Proxy Server, used to increase performance as well as to secure the company network. This chapter analyzed the factors influencing IIS performance, and provided solid recommendations aimed at boosting the performance of both IIS and the Proxy Server.

CHAPTER 12

Optimizing SQL Server

Tuning any BackOffice application is a complex task, and tuning SQL Server is no different. Many factors have a tremendous impact on how well your SQL Server database applications will perform and, to be honest, there is no possible way to discuss all of them here. This chapter is not intended to be an all-inclusive SQL Server tuning guide for someone who considers themselves to be *primarily* a full-time database professional. This chapter is for the serious NT infrastructure professional, facing situations such as these:

▼ Your boss says, "Here, you're in charge of making this database run fast since you know NT." Don't laugh; this happens more than you think.

■ You want to know how the database and associated applications affect server performance.

▲ You want to know enough about SQL Server tuning that you can participate in designing applications that you'll eventually help to maintain.

This chapter is for NT experts who need to learn more about SQL Server tuning and how it may affect overall system performance. It offers hands-on tips for tuning a SQL Server system while minimizing performance degradation on Windows NT. The recommendations here focus not on every possible tuning parameter, but rather on the issues that will produce the best performance gains.

NOTE: Portions of this chapter are adapted from the following *Windows NT Magazine* articles written by Brian Moran: "SQL Server 6.5 Introduces Insert Row Locking" (January, 1997), "Seven Tips for Speeding Large Data Loads with the Bulk Copy Program" (February, 1997), "Tuning Your Database with SQL Trace" (May, 1998). The chapter also incorporates information from Brian's monthly column. All of this material is used with permission.

PLANNING FOR OPTIMAL SYSTEM PERFORMANCE

As with other Windows NT systems, every component plays an important role in how well the server performs. For instance, a system with a powerful processor, ample amount of RAM, and a slow disk drive will more than likely fail to meet the needs of the environment simply because the disk subsystem is inadequate. However, depending on the functional configuration of the server, some system components are more important than others. The most influential hardware components on SQL Server performance are the processor, memory, and the disk subsystem. When designing a SQL Server, it is important that you make sure the hardware components complement one another so one inadequate component does not destroy the performance capabilities of an otherwise awesome server.

Processor

Choosing to use a single fast processor or multiple processors is the first major configuration issue you face when designing a SQL Server. The decision should be based upon the types of transactions the database will primarily be handling, even though SQL Server relies heavily on server processing power. There is no one correct answer, but a little knowledge of how SQL Server uses CPU resources will allow you to make a more informed choice.

SQL Server is implemented as a single process, multi-threaded application that can efficiently take advantage of multiple processors. However, SQL Server 6.5 does not know how to run individual queries in a parallel manner. It may be able to run three queries simultaneously across multiple processors, but it cannot break a single query into multiple threads running across those same three processors.

You need to understand the types of transactions (OLTP vs. OLAP) you plan to run on the server before you choose between faster processors or more processors. *OLTP* stands for *online transaction processing systems*, i.e., systems with many users and many quickly executed transactions. For example, airline reservation systems often use OLTP to offer customers quick and efficient reservations. On the other hand, *OLAP* stands for *online analytical systems*, and is commonly used to describe queries within a data warehouse. Compared to OLTP, OLAP systems tend to have fewer users and transactions, and each individual query consumes more resources.

Investing in an SMP-capable motherboard, even if you're just starting out with a single processor, is highly recommended.

Regardless of the types of transactions you run, you will then be able to scale the solution for future expansion without having to throw out your initial system purchase. It is anticipated that future versions of SQL Server will support parallelism within queries, meaning that transactions, such as OLAP queries, will take complete advantage of SMP architectures.

Using more processors provides better optimization for OLTP systems since SQL Server will be able to run simultaneous multiple queries. Performance of OLTP systems requires an emphasis on *user throughput,* which involves tracking the number of people using the system during a given period of time. On the other hand, SQL Server often handles OLAP systems more efficiently with faster processors than with multiple processors.

Memory

How much physical memory does your system need? To help you through this difficult decision during the initial configuration stage, use the principles of monitoring memory performance presented in Chapter 4.

Windows NT and SQL Server both tend to devour as much memory as you can feed them. This reason alone, and since memory is relatively inexpensive, should motivate you to configure the server with as much memory as possible. Although the minimum required amount of memory is 16MB, it is recommended that you initially configure the server with a minimum of 64MB for peak performance. Moreover, production servers can benefit immensely with initial configurations of 128MB or more. In fact, it is not uncommon to find large-scale SQL Server installations with up to a gigabyte of RAM.

L2 Cache

The amount of L2 cache available on the system is an important design consideration because SQL Server is a processor-intensive application, and the L2 cache size definitely contributes to increased processing performance. SQL Server running on SMP machines should always have at least 512K of L2 cache available, while 1MB or greater is optimal.

Disk Subsystem

You can take one giant tuning step forward if your initial configurations help to speed up your disk subsystem-related I/O, which is the slowest thing a computer knows how to do. Many performance problems stem from ill-configured disk subsystems, so it is important not to further exaggerate this bottleneck. Properly configuring the disk subsystem by using multiple disks and an intelligent, hardware-based RAID controller can boost many types of database operations. Where budgets allow, steer clear of software RAID solutions on your SQL Server machines. NT's software RAID solutions tend to use up a great deal of valuable processor time. Refer to Chapter 6 for more information on the disk subsystem and on related options such as hardware and software RAID.

You have won half the battle when you implement a hardware-based RAID solution, but to win the war you must choose the proper RAID level for SQL Server. RAID 10 is an ideal choice for your data devices, but its high cost may be impractical for many sites. On the other hand, RAID 5 (stripe sets with parity) provides reasonable read/write performance for data devices, but RAID 1 (straight mirroring) is for much faster write-intensive operations. RAID 1 ends up being a more efficient choice over RAID 5, because maintaining the transaction log is basically just a series of sequential writes.

Implement the following real-world solution to economically combine both performance and fault tolerance. Place your data on a RAID 5 array with at least three, and preferably four, physical disks. Now, place your log device on a separate RAID 1 array. If you can afford it, put your OS, SQL Server configuration, and page files on a separate RAID 1 array. Otherwise, place these items on the array that has the most free space.

Using SQL Server with Caching Disk Controllers

Hardware-based disk controllers that support write back offer great performance benefits. However, the potential to cause data corruption exists if they cannot guarantee to perform all log writes in all circumstances. Therefore, it is imperative that you consult the hardware vendor to ensure that their RAID controller is appropriate for write back use in a SQL Server database system. For example, the SMART-1 and SMART-2 caching disk controllers from Compaq (**http://www.compaq.com**) are proven, reliable controllers for use with SQL Server.

Don't Use Segments

SQL Server supports a concept called *segments,* which allows you to manually partition data across separate physical disks. It is recommended that you avoid using segments because it requires a lot of manual work and precise knowledge of the I/O usage patterns exhibited by your application. If you do manage to come up with an efficient solution, your applications I/O patterns may change over time, making your initial solution a potential bottleneck. RAID provides the same benefits without any of the downsides associated with segments. Apparently Microsoft agrees with this advice since segments will not be supported in future versions of SQL Server.

FAT versus NTFS

You can place your SQL Server devices on either a NTFS or FAT partition. The device creation, even with large database devices, happens almost immediately on NTFS partitions. However, creating large database devices on FAT partitions can take a long time.

There is actually not much difference between running SQL Server on FAT vs. NTFS once the devices have been created. Writing to a FAT partition may be a little faster (less than 5 percent) but the speed comes with some sacrifices. You cannot take advantage of NT-level security on your device files, and FAT does not offer dynamic marking of bad disk sectors like NTFS does.

Installation Tuning Tips

After the initial hardware configuration, you are faced with several installation options that can potentially affect the performance of SQL

Server. These installation options are important, but they will not necessarily make or break server performance. This section is intended to demystify some of the misconceptions surrounding SQL Server's installation options and how they can affect performance.

Choosing a Sort Order During SQL Server Installation

Many people choose the binary sort during installation because Microsoft claims it is 20 to 25 percent faster than other sort orders. Keep in mind that *sort speed* only affects sort, so you are not really improving server performance by 20 percent across the board. The inconvenience of developing systems using binary sort offsets any possible performance gain.

Network Protocol Performance

SQL Server Network Libraries (see Figure 12-1), commonly referred to as *NETLIBs* in SQL Server lingo, are not the same things as network protocols. NETLIBs are special communication layers that abstract the network so a SQL Server client application developer

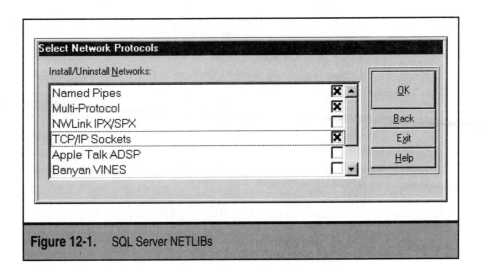

Figure 12-1.   SQL Server NETLIBs

does not have to write directly to the network. This is always a confusing issue since SQL Server supports the following NETLIBs:

▼ Named Pipes

■ Multi-Protocol

■ NWLink IPX/SPX

■ TCP/IP Sockets

■ AppleTalk ADSP

■ Banyan VINES

▲ DECNet Sockets

NETLIBs can run on any of NT's supported underlying protocols including Named Pipes and Multi-Protocol, which are network protocol independent. Microsoft testing has shown that the TCP/IP Sockets NETLIB is slightly faster than the other choices, but the difference is negligible and the network is rarely the bottleneck. Consequently, it is not necessary to make a decision concerning the NETLIB based on performance considerations.

One notable exception is Named Pipes over IPX/SPX (see "Troubleshooting Slow Client Performance" later in this chapter). Generally speaking, you will want to use the NETLIB that is the most compliant with your existing network protocols.

ENCRYPTION WITH MPN   The multi-protocol NETLIB (MPN) provides an optional ability to encrypt data as it travels over the wire. Microsoft claims that using the encryption capabilities of this NETLIB incurs a performance penalty of approximately 25 percent for network communication. Keep in mind that network communication is rarely the bottleneck in a typical database application and is unlikely to have much impact on overall system performance.

TUNING SQL SERVER FOR OPTIMAL PERFORMANCE

The many tuning options available to you make squeezing every drop of performance out of SQL Server a challenge. However, these options allow you to break away from the default settings and customize SQL Server to fit the needs of your environment, while still achieving the highest level of performance. Two additional components in your arsenal are the Bulk Copy Program (BCP) and Insert Row Locking (IRL) that, when properly implemented, can help you achieve greater levels of performance.

SQL Server Configuration Options

Sp_configure is one of the most important tools in your tuning arsenal. The settings discussed in this section are the ones that will have the most impact on system performance, but they are not inclusive of every setting available within sp_configure.

Affinity Mask

If the system is configured with more than one processor, the affinity mask can be used to prevent SQL Server from using certain processors. Through Windows NT, affinity mask allows you to limit the running of SQL Server threads to specific processors. This is similar to the /NUMPROC parameter placed in the BOOT.INI file limiting the number of processors Windows NT can use.

Why would you ever do this? Processor architectures typically assign certain low-level tasks to specific fixed processors. For example, SQL Server's Books Online (BOL) tells us that an eight-CPU Intel-based machine runs all I/O handling through the first processor (CPU = 0) and all delayed processor call interrupts for the first network interface are handled by the last processor (CPU = 7). In this case, SQL Server performance, on a busy server with heavy network and I/O loads, might improve by preventing SQL Server from using the first and last processors. Although using the affinity mask sounds promising for performance, do not change this value unless you have a solid understanding of the affinity mask and have a powerful system.

Backup Buffer Size

The backup buffer size controls how much memory is available for buffering data during the dump, restore, and Bulk Copy Program

(BCP) operations. The setting represents 32-page increments; the default setting of five gives us a buffer area of 160 pages, or 320K. The buffer is used as a bucket to temporarily store data as it moves in and out of SQL Server during the dump, restore, and BCP operations. Increasing this value may noticeably speed up these operations as long as your disk subsystem is fast enough to keep up.

Backup Threads

This parameter controls the number of threads SQL Server uses when performing the striped dump and load operations. SQL Server allows you to dump a database into multiple dump devices. You can increase dump/load throughput if you match this value to the number of devices that you are simultaneously dumping to or loading from. As a result, the faster data can be dumped or loaded, the better your overall database performance.

Hash Buckets

Hash buckets track a fixed number of memory-stored pages and informs SQL Server of which pages are available when a request is made. At any given point, a memory-based data cache cannot hold the large number of pages (2K) contained in a database. Before accessing a page, SQL Server must first determine whether the page is already loaded into memory or the disk I/O will be required.

Think of a hash bucket as the first page of a linked list or chain of pages that will be searched to find a cached page. SQL Server doesn't know if the page is cached, and it uses a hashing algorithm to scan the entire hash chain that contains this particular page. If the hash chains become too long, page access times can decline because more memory is needed to conduct the search. For servers configured with up to 192MB of memory, keep chain lengths to a maximum of four pages. However, when using the default settings, servers with as little as 92MB of memory may contain chains exceeding four pages in length.

To determine the length of your hash chains, run DBCC SQLPERF (HASHSTATS). Table 12-1 is an example of the information displayed from running this command. Look at the Longest and

Type	Items	Buckets	Chains	Longest	Average
TABLOCK	2	101	2	1	1.0
PAGLOCK	3	1,031	3	1	1.0
BUFHASH	35,214	16,001	16,001	5	2.20074
DESHASH	311	256	114	14	2.72807

Table 12-1.   Determining hash chain length

Average values for BUFHASH; ideally, both of these numbers should be less than four.

Running the command DBCC BUFCOUNT will provide you with a list of the ten longest chains.

```
**** THE 10 LONGEST BUFFER CHAINS ****
bucket number = 1786     chain size = 5
bucket number = 2381     chain size = 5
bucket number = 2427     chain size = 5
bucket number = 2429     chain size = 5
bucket number = 2510     chain size = 5
bucket number = 2556     chain size = 5
bucket number = 2668     chain size = 5
bucket number = 2683     chain size = 5
bucket number = 2810     chain size = 5
bucket number = 9549     chain size = 5
The Smallest Chain Size is: 1
The Average Chain Size is: 2.203925
```

In this example, the ten longest chains are all greater than four so you may want to increase the current setting for hash buckets. Tune the hash length by running DBCC SQLPERF (HASHSTATS) and increase the number of hash buckets until the command reports an average chain length for BUFHASH <=4. You will not need to tune this parameter unless your system has at least 128MB of RAM.

The "Locking Parameters"

Locking parameters work together to control how and when multiple page locks on a table are escalated to a single table lock. Each parameter has an effect on the escalation, so it is important to consider all of these as a single tuning unit. In most cases, SQL Server 6.5 does not allow row-level locking so page locks are the lowest level of lock granularity available. It is anticipated that future versions of SQL Server will support both page- and row-level locking, thus allowing the server to choose the most sensible method on a case by case basis.

Locks are acquired when you access data in a table. The exact type of lock and how long it is held depend on a number of factors. Typically, SQL Server starts acquiring locks at the page level (pages are 2K in size) and holds them for a certain amount of time. For instance, updating 1,000 rows, with 20 rows on each data page, means that you will need 50 individual page locks (1,000 rows / 20 rows per page = 50 pages). This is not a huge number, but locking individual pages with larger data sets can become very time-intensive.

Sometimes, SQL Server automatically escalates individual page locks to a single table lock to avoid holding a massive amount of single page locks. This escalation reduces the number of locks you'll need to complete an operation, but you end up getting an exclusive table lock which blocks everyone else from accessing the data during the duration of the transaction. As you can see, the decision of when to escalate from page to table lock is a trade-off between resource usage and multi-user access. Guessing the correct "escalation point" isn't always easy, but it will have a big impact on how well your system performs in a multi-user environment. The following three parameters control when SQL Server escalates from page to table locks.

LE THRESHOLD MAXIMUM   This setting represents the fixed number of single page locks SQL Server will acquire within a single statement before escalating to a table lock. By default, SQL Server escalates to a table lock if a single SQL command locks more than 200 pages. Imagine a big data warehouse with a 1G table that has 512,000 2K pages. These pages contain an average of 20 rows per page totaling slightly more than 10,000,000 rows. At the default value of 200 this table will escalate to an exclusive table lock by updating only 4,000 rows out of 10,000,000. This almost guarantees a serious blocking problem in a multi-user system. This example demonstrates the need to escalate based on what percentage of the table is locked rather than how many single pages are locked.

LE THRESHOLD PERCENT   This parameter escalates when a specified percentage of the table, usually starting at 20 percent, has been locked.

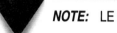

NOTE: LE threshold maximum always will override this setting.

From the 10,000,000-row table example, assume that LE threshold percent = 20 and threshold maximum = 200. The threshold percent will not take effect since escalation still occurs after reaching the fixed maximum number of 200 pages. Therefore it is important to properly configure the parameters for the desired effect.

There may be times where it is more beneficial to apply the LE threshold percent equal to the midsize table rather than the largest table. Otherwise, you run the risk of consuming too many resources before SQL Server escalates.

LE THRESHOLD MINIMUM   This setting is simple to understand, and rarely needs to be changed. Regardless of the values of our first two LE parameters, escalation to a table lock will not occur until the specified LE threshold minimum number of pages has been locked. Similar to the other LE parameters, LE threshold minimum refers to the number of locks that occur with each command rather than with each transaction.

Running the following SQL batch on the 10,000,000-row table example never causes SQL Server to escalate to a table lock.

```
DECLARE @KeyValue int
DECLARE @MaxRowsInTable int
SELECT @MaxRowsInTable = (select count(*) from Table)
SELECT @KeyValue = 1
BEGIN TRAN
While @KeyValue <= @MaxRowsInTable
```

```
Update TABLE set DataValue = "new value" Where PrimaryKey
                            = @KeyValue

COMMIT TRAN
```

However, adding the TABLOCK optimizer hint to the update command line would lock the entire table each time:

```
Update TABLE  (TABLOCK) set DataValue = "new value" Where
                            PrimaryKey = @KeyValue
```

Locks

You either have enough locks or you don't. Each configured lock takes up 28 bytes, so you don't want to arbitrarily set locks through the roof. However, queries will fail if you run out of locks during processing. The best thing to do in a new system is set the locks higher than necessary to avoid query failures. Over a period of time, use the Performance Monitor to monitor Locks: Total Locks usage over a reasonable period of time. Determine the maximum number of locks used, and then add 10-15 percent as a safety factor.

Max Async I/O

Heavily used by CHECKPOINT and BCP, max async I/O controls how many asynchronous I/O threads SQL Server releases to handle batch I/Os. Setting this value too high can seriously degrade performance so do not change it unless you plan on monitoring the effects. Monitor the PhysicalDisk: Avg. Disk Queue Length counter and increase the max async I/O until you see the disk queue length equal to or greater than four times the number of physical disks in your array. It is also recommended that you change this value only if the system is using hardware-based RAID.

Max Lazywrite I/O

Similar to max async I/O, max lazywrite I/O throttles the number of I/O threads used by the lazywriter. The lazywriter process is responsible for making sure the configured number of free buffers is available in the SQL Server data cache. If the actual number of free buffers drops below the configured value, the lazywriter begins flushing dirty pages. As you tweak this parameter, keep in mind the same concepts used for tuning max async I/O. In most cases, it is more beneficial to either set max lazywrite I/O to the same value as max async I/O or leave it at the default setting.

Max Worker Threads

This setting acts like a mini transaction processing (TP) monitor, measuring how physical NT-level threads manage SQL Server connections. SQL Server will ask Windows NT to assign a separate thread to every new connection until the number of user connections is greater than the max worker threads. After that point, SQL connections are managed in a round robin fashion among a pool of NT-level threads. You will need to experiment with this parameter for optimal performance, but keep in mind that every SQL user does not need to have their own NT thread. In fact, this value should be relatively low compared to the number of user connections.

Memory

Memory is, without question, the single most important, but often overlooked, sp_configure tuning parameter there is. In most cases, if you do not change the default value, it could have crippling effects on performance, since SQL Server will be limited to either 8MB or 16MB, depending on how much RAM is available during installation. This setting controls the maximum amount of memory that SQL Server will ever be allowed to use. Contrary to popular belief, though, it does not mean SQL will actually use all of this memory.

As mentioned earlier, SQL Server tends to devour memory. You should give SQL Server as much memory as you can without causing excessive paging. Increasing the memory dedicated to SQL Server beyond the paging point can severely hamper performance. There should be little or no paging in a dedicated SQL Server box once the system has reached a steady state. Table 12-2 is a guideline for setting initial memory configurations.

When configuring the memory parameter, it is critical to closely analyze its effects on memory performance. You can increase the memory allocation only if the system is not experiencing abnormal

System Memory (in MB)	SQL Server Memory Allocation (in MB)	SQL Server Memory Allocation (in 2K units)
16	4	2,048
24	8	4,096
32	16	8,192
64	40	20,480
128	100	51,210
256	216	110,592
512	464	237,568

Table 12-2. Initial Memory Configurations

amounts of paging. Refer to Chapter 4 for more information on tuning memory performance.

Open Objects

This parameter controls the number of database objects, including—but not limited to—tables, indexes, views, and procedures that can be open at any one time. The structure for each open object does not consume a lot of memory (about 70 bytes), but it can degrade performance if the configuration is too low.

Here's an undocumented technique for determining how high you can set this value. Use the undocumented Database Consistency Checker command DBCC DES to print information about the open objects that the server is currently using. The number of entries from the DBCC DES list will tell you how many objects are in use. The following code shows a simple technique for automating the process.

```
/* Technique for capturing DBCC output is explained in detail.
*/

/* create our wrapper procedure */
```

```
create proc ShowDes as
dbcc des
/* create a storage table for the procedure output */
create table DesOutput (DESInfo varchar(255))
/*
populate the storage table traceon(3604) command prints the DES
output back to the client rather than writing to the error log
*/
insert DesOutput
EXEC master..xp_cmdshell 'isql -Q" dbcc traceon(3604) dbcc
des" -E'
/*
```

Now count the number of objects. Each descriptor in the DES output takes up 9 lines, so we can divide the total number of lines in our table by 9. But first we need to throw out the 9 header rows generated by running the command. The final formula becomes

```
Open Objects = (Number of rows in DesOutput - 9) / 9
*/
declare @OpenObjects int
select @OpenObjects = (select count(*) -9 from DesOutput) / 9
select "Open Objects = ", @OpenObjects
```

Priority Boost

This setting forces SQL Server to run at a higher than normal base thread priority. Sounds like a good idea, but in practice it does not offer much performance improvement, and can very easily cause your system to become unstable.

Procedure Cache

This parameter controls how SQL Server's memory space is split between data and procedure usage. The memory parameter discussed earlier controls the maximum amount of memory SQL Server can use. In contrast, a variety of other system parameters affect how much memory the "base engine" needs at system start up. By default, this setting allocates 30 percent of remaining memory after system startup to the procedure cache. The remaining 70 percent is given to the data cache. This setting will almost always need to be changed especially if your server has a large amount of memory. In many cases, the data cache can make better use of the additional memory which may also reduce the amount of disk I/O needed. It is imperative that you strike a balance between the memory used for the procedure cache and the memory used for data.

Each instance of all stored procedures is managed with a procedure buffer. For example, if there are ten separate procedures in use, then there are ten different procedure buffers, each taking up 122 bytes of procedure cache. At system startup, a fixed number of buffers are allocated based upon the configured values for memory and procedure cache. If the SQL Server has 500 procedure buffers available, there can be no more than 500 procedures loaded into memory before 701 error messages appear. The system is prevented from loading any more procedures and errors are generated even if there is plenty of available space in the procedure cache.

Use the SQL Server-Procedure Cache object to measure allocation of both the cache and the buffers. Cache tracks actual space usage while the buffer counters are tracking the number of fixed procedure buffers available. Procedure Cache Used % and Procedure Buffers Used % are the two most important counters in this object to monitor. Reduce the procedure cache if both of these counters are very low over a sustained period of time.

SMP Concurrency

SMP concurrency controls the number of threads SQL Server releases to Windows NT for execution. This parameter limits the number of processors SQL Server can use at any given time. By default, SMP concurrency is set to 0 which tells SQL Server to auto-configure and use $N-1$ processors (where N is the number of processors in the computer). Table 12-3 illustrates various SMP concurrency settings. The value of -1 means N processors, while any positive value means that number of processors.

For most SQL Server configurations, modifying the SMP concurrency setting may cause the system to become unstable. For

Number of Processors	SMP Concurrency Setting	Number of Processors Used by SQL Server
4	0 (default)	3
4	–1	4
4	2	2
4	4	4

Table 12-3. Example SMP Concurrency Settings

example, two CPU-bound queries executed at the same time have the potential to utilize all available CPU time. This can starve other processes from processing time, cause the system to become sluggish, and prevent important tasks, such as I/O calls and network handlers, from being accomplished.

Nevertheless, in certain situations, you might get a noticeable performance boost by running SQL Server on all available processors. This is especially true if you're running on a dual SMP machine as opposed to a machine with four or more processors. Setting SMP concurrency equal to –1 is beneficial in some cases, but it all depends on your application's *transaction profile*, or the types of queries your application runs on a regular basis. For instance, in a dual-processor SMP machine, setting the value to 0 allows SQL Server to utilize one single processor for one user query. If you graphed Processor: % Processing Time, the utilization graph would look like a "sawtooth" pattern, indicating that one CPU is underutilized when SMP concurrency is left at the default value of 0. However, a setting of –1 enables two user queries to be performed simultaneously, which dramatically increases the amount of work to be accomplished. However, the downside to a –1 SMP concurrency setting is a processor bottleneck if the transaction profile is processor-intensive. Change the SMP concurrency setting to –1 only in relatively pure OLTP environments running simple queries with fast execution times.

Asynchronous Read-Ahead Operations

SQL Server 6.5 uses asynchronous *read-ahead (RA) threads* to address the limitations of standard table scanning. This allows SQL Server to use multiple threads for I/O operations even though only a single thread is processing the actual user query. The query threads and RA threads operate independently of one another, so the query doesn't even know that RA is operating. All the query thread knows is that it doesn't have to issue a "get page" request because data is always in the cache.

Without RA threads, SQL Server uses a single worker thread to query a get page request. This request reads a 2K page from disk if the referenced page is not already in cache, and it is unlikely that large tables will store that many pages in cache. As a result, the query will issue a large number of single get page requests. Parallel read-ahead allows SQL Server to use multiple background threads to perform disk I/O before the worker thread requests a particular page. This minimizes the amount of disk I/O because the worker threads are finding the requests in the cache rather than on disk. The process is extremely efficient because the RA thread performs its I/O in 16K extents rather than 2K pages, matching the block size used in most Intel-based disk controllers. Performance can be dramatically improved by reading pages into the cache even before the query requests them.

A SQL Server environment can benefit from RA threads without any additional modification. There is little, if any, reason to change the default settings in order to improve read-ahead performance.

TEMPDB in RAM (MB)

TEMPDB is used for a variety of important query functions. It is normally created on disk devices, and can be placed in memory just like a RAM disk. Data in a database will still end up in SQL Server's data cache before it can be used regardless of TEMPDB's placement into memory. For example, querying a 10MB temporary table while TEMPDB is in memory could actually consume 20MB of SQL Server's memory. It is possible to have the TEMPDB setting increase the performance of certain individual operations, but in most cases it is recommended that you place TEMPDB in memory.

Tuning the Bulk Copy Program

The Bulk Copy Program (BCP) is the most practical way to handle high-speed data loads in SQL Server. This command-line program moves data between an existing database table, or view, and an operating-system file stored in ASCII or machine format. BCP has many uses, but it's especially helpful for moving large data sets between SQL Server and other database systems, and for dealing with extracts from external data feeds or legacy systems.

BCP is a C-language client that communicates with the database using special BCP extensions in the DB-Library API (a SQL Server-specific programming interface). Importing or exporting data with an Open Database Connectivity (ODBC)-enabled application such as Microsoft Access is often easier because Microsoft doesn't provide a GUI interface for BCP, and the command-line syntax can be arcane and difficult to master. ODBC-enabled applications are OK for small data sets, but avoid ODBC applications when you're bulk loading a lot of data because ODBC applications load data using standard Insert statements, which is much slower than BCP.

Increasing BCP's Performance

BCP is the best solution for improving the speed of large bulk copies, and performance can vary significantly with different uses. While BCP is not the most user-friendly interface in the world, future versions may provide a more attractive, easier-to-use interface. The following sections are recommendations for improving BCP's performance.

ALWAYS USE FAST BCP You can load data in either fast or slow BCP mode. Obviously, fast BCP is quicker, but you pay a price. Fast BCP forces you to set a database option, *Select into/bulk copy* with sp_db option that lets non-logged operations occur. Do not leave this option on in production databases because it can prevent you from backing up your transaction log. Fast mode also requires that you drop any indexes on the target table—and BCP will revert to slow mode if you forget to remove even one index.

Transaction log activity accounts for the biggest speed difference between slow and fast BCP. Slow mode adds a log for each line of data added with an Insert statement. Fast BCP does not log individual rows, but logs new space allocations only when *extents* are linked into the table's page chain. Extents are 16K buffers in blocks of eight pages, used to manage data.

Data loads can run faster if you drop the indexes, run fast BCP, and then re-create the indexes. If your table has a clustered index, sort the data before running BCP and create an index using the sorted_data option, which tells SQL Server no to re-sort the data before creating the index.

RUN BCP FROM THE SERVER   Running BCP on the same machine as SQL Server is a great way to boost performance because it eliminates a great deal of network overhead. Consider the following scenario: Server A runs SQL Server and stores the data files. You invoke BCP from Workstation X and load data into Server A. BCP does not run as part of SQL Server, so the data is copied first to Workstation X, and is immediately sent back to Server A to be loaded. By running BCP directly from the server you can move a large data file around the network twice, once to the BCP client machine and once to the SQL Server, and eliminate any unnecessary network traffic. However, copying the remote data file to the server with NT's ordinary file copy command and then running BCP locally is still faster than the other scenario. Even if you do not run BCP from the server, avoid running BCP against a remote data file, because this process needlessly moves the file around the network.

USE LOCAL NAMED PIPES   When BCP runs on the same machine as SQL Server, it uses local named pipes, which greatly speeds up processing time. Local pipes comprise an interprocess communication (IPC) mechanism that completely bypasses the network to optimize processes running on the same machine. Local pipes act like a TCP/IP loopback so data never goes to the NT Redirector. By comparison, network named pipes send data through the Redirector, even if both processes run locally on the same machine. Local pipes can work up to 300 percent faster than network named pipes.

PLACE BCP AND SQL SERVER DATA ON SEPARATE DISKS   Running BCP through a local pipe reduces network overhead, but can introduce disk I/O-related bottlenecks. To avoid these bottlenecks, write BCP data files to a fast RAID array on a physical drive separate from your SQL Server devices. If maintaining separate drives is not practical, run benchmarks with your data and servers to determine which is worse, the network overhead involved with a remote BCP or the contention on the disk while BCP and SQL Server fight for the same disk I/O bandwidth.

INSTALL SQL SERVER SERVICE PACKS   Service Pack 1 (SP1) for SQL Server 6.5 included two useful enhancements that, according to Microsoft benchmarks, can improve BCP load times up to 700 percent and provide throughput rates of approximately 3.5 MBps. First, an engine optimization lets BCP write one extent at a time using n private buffers rather than writing one page at a time using a single public buffer area. Using SP_CONFIGURE 'BACKUP BUFFER SIZE,' experiment to find the best setting for n between 1 and 10. If your disk subsystem can handle the load, this action will greatly increase BCP speed.

NOTE: Always apply the latest available service pack for SQL Server.

Enabling the new *Table lock on bulk load* option in the sp_table option activates the second improvement in SP1. This option tells SQL Server to hold one exclusive table lock rather than grab individual locks as each new extent is linked into the page chain. Previously, BCP locked at the extent level, which could deplete the number of configured locks when a program is loading large data sets. Locking at the table level lets SQL Server acquire a single lock for the duration of the BCP load. Now, you can load larger data batches without exhausting the fixed supply of locks. Be sure the batch size equals the number of rows in the loaded table. These two enhancements speed data loading with BCP in the fast, non-logged mode, but they don't provide much change when using the slow, logged version of BCP.

USE NATIVE MODE   BCP can work with data in a native SQL Server format or in an ASCII representation. Native format uses slightly less disk space and runs a little faster because the data is not converted to ASCII format. Native mode does not provide the same performance boost as using a local named pipe, but every little bit helps.

Tuning Insert Row Locking

Arguments over row- versus page-level locking can take on near religious importance in some database circles. In SQL Server 6.5, Microsoft introduced Insert Row Locking (IRL), which is the first step towards a more robust lock model.

Why does a database need locks at all? The answer is simple: Locks provide consistent and concurrent access to data in a multi-user environment, while preventing simultaneous updates of the same data. With locks, you can be sure that while your airline agent is selling you that aisle seat, another agent is not promising the same seat to someone else. Lose the locks, and airline agents can sell the same seat to more than one person. Although they do that anyway, those mistakes are not the database's fault.

Tradition Rules

Previously, a page (2K in SQL Server) was the lowest level of lock granularity in SQL Server. One row, such as a customer record, is always less than 2K because a row must fit on one page. Even though a page contains many rows, only one record update can occur at a time. Row locks solve the problem by providing a finer level of granularity. With row locking, you can edit multiple records simultaneously because only individual rows are locked rather than the whole page. This allows for more simultaneous updates, thus increasing usability and boosting system performance.

IRL Tackles the Hot Page Problem

One of the most common concurrency issues SQL Server designers face is the *hot page* insert problem. A hot page occurs when multiple users try to insert data on the same page at the same time, creating a bottleneck with the potential to cripple high concurrency OLTP applications. Let us now closely examine how a hot page occurs and how IRL solves the problem.

A table is a linked list of 2K pages. Unless a clustered index exists, there is no explicit sort order. The last page in the chain is like a bucket, and all new rows go into it. SQL Server continues to add new pages to the end of the chain when the current bucket fills up. When no index exists on a table, data is inserted to the last page. Only one user at a time can grab the lock; all others must wait. The last page becomes a serious bottleneck as more users are added, and contention for the page becomes more severe.

You can add a clustered index to force a sort order upon the underlying table. SQL Server inserts data in its sorted location rather than on the last page in the data chain, eliminating the problem of everyone vying for access to one page. As good as it sounds, this solution does not solve the problem entirely. For example, a clustered index can be assigning key values using the Identity property and inserting data in *sorted order*. Unfortunately, the counter behavior of Identity means that sorted order is always on the last page, reintroducing the problem we were trying to solve in the first place.

NOTE: Primary keys create a unique index on the key. You can use Identity to auto-generate ascending key values similar to the counter data type found in Microsoft Access.

The solution is to put a clustered index on every table and never use it with an Identity column. This should eliminate contention in the data pages. But what happens when you add a non-clustered (NC) index to a column defined with an Identity property? This method introduces a hot page in the leaf level of the NC index because SQL Server inserts a row on the last page in the leaf level every time you add a new data row. No matter how you slice it, you introduce a hot page whenever you use an index with an Identity column. Sometimes contention occurs on the data pages, and other times it occurs on index pages. Either way it produces a limitation.

IRL eliminates this particular hot page problem by implementing row-level concurrency for insert operations. You do not get a hot spot because inserts do not block each other in either the data or index pages. IRL offers massive performance improvements of up to 40 percent for applications that are highly concurrent, but it provides little or no benefit to low-concurrency applications.

IRL Caveats

IRL solves important problems, but it also has a few caveats. Conduct extensive testing before enabling IRL in a production application because it may cause more problems than it solves. The following list summarizes IRL's caveats:

▼ IRL works only for inserts. Updates, deletes, and selects must be dealt with in the traditional manner.

■ If a clustered index exists, you must declare it unique. Otherwise, IRL will not be available for the table.

■ By default, IRL is disabled, and you must manually turn it on for specific tables.

■ IRL can introduce deadlock situations because it allows more sequential transactions to now occur concurrently. For example, suppose two users have locks on separate objects and each user wants a lock on the other's object. The deadlock occurs because each user is waiting for the other to release their lock; neither process can finish, therefore SQL Server kills one of the processes.

▲ Using IRL can potentially double the size of your transaction log during rollback operations.

MAINTAINING SQL SERVER PERFORMANCE

In order to keep SQL Server running at its best, you need to keep up with the changing requirements of your environment. This may include reconfiguring options for optimal performance, changing the primary transaction processing method used, rebuilding components, applying service packs, and much more. The important thing to remember is that you must routinely maintain the server if effective and efficient performance is to continue.

Managing Indexes

Rebuilding indexes in the proper order during maintenance operations is of the utmost importance due to the differences in clustered and NC indexes, most notably in the storage order. A clustered index stores the data pages in a table in sorted order based on the index key while an NC index imposes no sort order on the data pages at all. Always remember to rebuild the clustered index first, otherwise, SQL Server is forced to rebuild the NC indexes.

Applying the Latest Service Pack

Service packs provide a wealth of enhancements such as bug fixes, performance upgrades, security patches, and much more. It is imperative that you keep SQL Server up-to-date with the latest service pack in order to ensure optimal performance and to help guarantee reliability and stability.

Rebuilding the Registry

There may come a time when a disaster forces you to reinstall Windows NT entirely, or to rebuild the Registry from scratch on a machine that is also configured with SQL Server. A worse scenario would be to discover that, after reinstalling Windows NT or the Registry, all of the SQL Server Registry settings are lost while the data devices still exist.

The easiest way of returning the Registry back into a functional state is by using the undocumented RegistryRebuild option available within the SQL Server Setup program. RegistryRebuild is not supposed to be a secret, nonetheless, Microsoft left it out of the SQL Server 6.5 documentation. Using the command

```
setup /t RegistryRebuild = On
```

rebuilds the necessary SQL Server Registry entries and registers all the SQL Server-related services with the NT Service Control Manager.

CAUTION: Use the exact capitalization and spacing that you see here. If you do not, SQL Server will not recognize the setup switch, and may proceed with the full setup program, producing unexpected results.

RegistryRebuild uses the size and location of the master device to repopulate the Registry keys. Setup will also ask you for the size of the original master device (in megabytes) and for its fully qualified path. You can determine the size by looking at the original master device, which is created in \mssql\data\master.dat by default. While an accurate size is not important because size isn't stored in the Registry, the server definitely will not start without the correct location of the original master device.

Setup also will ask you what sort order and character set to install. Don't worry if you cannot remember which ones you picked the first time you installed SQL Server; Setup does not store your responses in the Registry. However, Setup *does* listen when you decide which network protocols you want SQL Server to support, so make sure to select all the protocols you need. Forgetting one protocol won't hurt your data, but it may keep certain applications from connecting correctly.

DESIGNING DATABASE APPLICATIONS FOR PERFORMANCE

SQL Server is the fastest relational database management system for Windows NT, according to Microsoft. Even though SQL Server cranks out high numbers on the Transaction Processing Council's C Benchmark (TPC-C), there is no guarantee your applications will run just as fast. This section offers sound recommendations to improve SQL Server and database application performance using SQL Trace.

Many factors, including hardware, the network, SQL Server configuration options, and application design, affect the performance of a database system. Most knowledgeable database professionals realize tuning their data-access application to interact with SQL Server is key to achieving the best performance.

SQL Trace

SQL Trace is a built-in utility that monitors and records database activity in SQL Server 6.5. The utility operates by capturing SQL statements or remote procedure calls (RPCs) sent to any SQL Server 6.5 system. This server activity can be displayed by creating filters that focus on the actions of particular users, applications, or work-station. You can save trace activity to disk in an ISQL/w-compatible script, replayable against a SQL Server, or set up an activity log file. Capturing the SQL command and performance information can help you analyze and fine-tune your system.

SQL Trace is the most powerful tool available to SQL Server. It lets you see the big picture of application-level interaction in SQL Server without having to know about the application or its source code. Modern data access mechanisms abstractions such as Open Database Connectivity (ODBC), Object Linking and Embedding Database (OLE DB), distributed component object model (DCOM), Remote Data Objects (RDO), ActiveX Data Object (ADO), and Data Access Object (DAO) are all great programming tools except they don't provide behind-the-scenes information.

The following code demonstrates how ODBC applications often do surprising things:

```
SELECT "dbo"."authors"."au_id" FROM "dbo"."authors"
Go
SELECT substring('NY',status/1024&1+1,1) from
master..sysdatabases where name=DB_NAME()
Go
```

```
CREATE proc #odbc#sa2ce584(@P1 varchar(11),@P2 varchar(11),@P3
varchar(11),@P4 varchar(11),@P5 varchar(11),@P6
varchar(11),@P7 varchar(11),@P8 varchar(11),@P9
varchar(11),@P10 varchar(11)) as SELECT
"au_id","au_lname","au_fname","phone","address","city","state",
"zip","contract" FROM "dbo"."authors" WHERE "au_id" = @P1 OR
"au_id" = @P2 OR "au_id" = @P3 OR "au_id" = @P4 OR "au_id" =
@P5 OR "au_id" = @P6 OR "au_id" = @P7 OR "au_id" = @P8 OR
"au_id" = @P9 OR "au_id" = @P10
go
#odbc#sa2ce584 "172-32-1176", "213-46-8915", "238-95-7766",
"267-41-2394", "274-80-9391", "341-22-1782", "409-56-7008",
"427-17-2319", "472-27-2349", "486-29-1786"
go
#odbc#sa2ce584 "527-72-3246", "648-92-1872", "672-71-3249",
"712-45-1867", "722-51-5454", "724-08-9931", "724-80-9391",
"756-30-7391", "807-91-6654", "846-92-7186"
go
#odbc#sa2ce584 "893-72-1158", "899-46-2035", "998-72-3567",
"998-72-3567", "998-72-3567", "998-72-3567", "998-72-3567",
"998-72-3567", "998-72-3567", "998-72-3567"
go
```

This simple SQL Trace output shows all the Transact-SQL (T-SQL) commands Microsoft Access issued when the attached link was opened to the pubs..authors table in Datasheet View. Read on to discover where all these statements came from.

First, Access runs a SELECT statement and returns all the values for the au_id primary key column. Then, it creates a stored procedure that accepts 10 parameters, and runs a SELECT statement similar to the following:

```
SELECT
"au_id","au_lname","au_fname","phone","address","city","state",
"zip","contract"
FROM "dbo"."authors" WHERE
"au_id" = @P1 OR "au_id" = @P2 OR "au_id" = @P3 OR "au_id" =
@P4 OR "au_id" = @P5 OR "au_id" = @P6 OR "au_id" = @P7 OR
"au_id" = @P8 OR "au_id" = @P9 OR "au_id" = @P10
```

Access must run the procedure three times to return all 24 rows; two calls for 10 rows each and one call for the final four rows.

This simple example demonstrates an important point: ODBC applications using data-access middleware rarely do exactly what you think they are doing. The final outcome may be the same with or without middleware, but ODBC may not always make the most efficient choice. Nonetheless, ODBC can be efficient and flexible—providing several ways to accomplish the same result, and allowing developers to better tune their systems. However, this flexibility is both a blessing and a curse. It is great to know your options, but miserable if the ODBC applications developer allows defaults that you don't want or need. SQL Trace lets you see ODBC's choices and determine whether they are appropriate for your environment.

Running SQL Trace

You can run SQL Trace, found under SQL Server's main menu, as a GUI utility, or through the xp_sqltrace stored procedure interface.

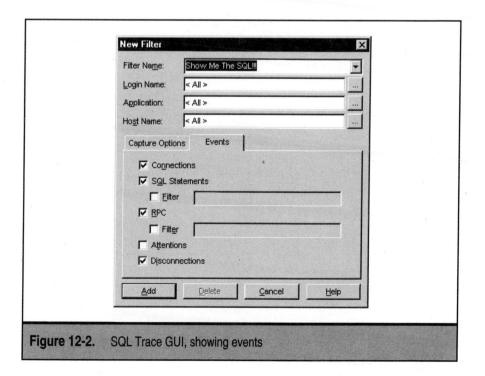

Figure 12-2.   SQL Trace GUI, showing events

The GUI version, a visual wrapper around xp_sqltrace, is easy to use and helpful for ad hoc troubleshooting. Figure 12-2 shows you the simple GUI version, and Figure 12-3 shows SQL Trace's stored procedure interface.

Figure 12-2 shows editing the filter properties of the trace "Show Me The SQL!!!" The appropriate options have been selected to display the trace onscreen, using a separate window for each connection. The trace will be logged to a .SQL file for replay and to a .LOG file for future analysis. The Filter dialog box on the Events tab, shown in Figure 12-3, permits filtering at the statement level so only T-SQL statements referencing the TopSecretTable object are shown.

The extended stored procedure version can be more useful than the GUI version when performing a full application profile. Xp_sqltrace offers more option control, and the audit mode can run long traces

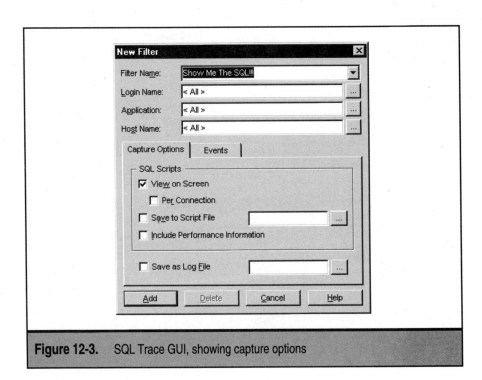

Figure 12-3.   SQL Trace GUI, showing capture options

without tying up a machine overnight. Also, a timed SQLExec task can be used to stop and start traces.

> **NOTE:** Set the xp_sqltrace command-line option @FullText to 1 if you want to capture the entire executed T-SQL batch.

Running xp_sqltrace is straightforward, but repeatedly typing all those option settings is quite tedious. One shortcut you might consider is to create stored procedure wrappers around xp_sqltrace and set the desired options. The following are two stored procedures you can use to get started:

```
CREATE PROC sp_StartSQL Trace
/* This procedure accepts a directory such as c:\SQL Trace\
and writes the trace file to that directory, appending time
and date information as part of the name. This addition lets
you keep multiple traces in the same directory and lets you
stop and start without worrying about naming conventions
*/
@TraceLogDirPath varchar(255)
as
DECLARE @CurrTime datetime
DECLARE @TraceLogFileName varchar(255)
SELECT @CurrTime = getdate()
SELECT @TraceLogFileName = convert(char(10), @CurrTime , 104)
+ "_" + datename(hh, @CurrTime) + "." + datename(mi,
@CurrTime) + "." + datename(ss, @CurrTime)
SELECT @TraceLogFileName = @TraceLogDirPath + "SQL TraceLog_"
+ @TraceLogFileName
SELECT "Auditing to --> ", @TraceLogFileName exec
master..xp_SQL Trace audit, @eventfilter = 31, @FullText = 1,
@FullFilePath = @TraceLogFileName
GO
CREATE PROC sp__StopSQL TraceAudit
/* If you run this procedure without parameters, you'll get
```

```
the name of the last SQL Trace audit file created. EventCode =
0 means that the trace is stopped. EventCode = 31 means that
it is running. Running the procedure with the fully qualified
name of the file SQL Trace is logging to will stop the
trace:*/
@AuditFilePath varchar(255) = NULL
as
IF (@AuditFilePath = NULL) exec master..xp_SQL Trace audit
ELSE
exec xp_SQL Trace audit, @FullFilePath = @AuditFilePath
GO
```

What effect does running SQL Trace have on security and performance? While SQL Trace is accessible on client machines, setting appropriate permission levels on xp_sqltrace within the master database can easily control security. By default, only the SA has permission to run xp_sqltrace.

When you monitor a database, keep the overhead low to avoid significantly skewing or misrepresenting results. Performance issues are negligible when xp_sqltrace information is logged to a text file on a server that is not completely I/O bound. If the server is I/O bound, write the log file to a remote network share, and hope that you don't encounter a bottleneck.

Loading SQL Trace Output for Analysis

SQL Trace output is almost useless in its raw form because it includes an overwhelming amount of information. To make life easier, first load the trace files back into a SQL Server table. Now, run queries against it to gain an understanding of what activity the server was performing and to quickly pinpoint inefficient parts of the application. The more clever the queries you write to analyze data, the more valuable SQL Trace will become.

Table 12-4 lists the information that a SQL Trace log file captures as a standard ASCII file with tab-delimited columns.

Component	Definition
Event	Specifies the event (e.g., START, PAUSE, ACTIVE, CONNECT, DISCONNECT, SQL, ATTENTION) as varchar(12) unless @IntegerEvents = 1.
UserName	Specifies the username of the person who generated the event.
ID	Specifies a unique, increasing identifier for connections.
SPID	Specifies the SQL Server process identification number.
StartTime	Specifies the start time of executed language statements or remote stored procedure calls. For connect and disconnect events, specifies the time that the user logged in.
EndTime	Specifies the ending time of executed language statements or remote stored procedure calls. For disconnect events, specifies the disconnect time.
Application	Specifies the application that generated the event.
Data	Specifies the language statement or remote stored procedure call as varchar(255) unless @FullText = 1.
Duration	Specifies the execution running time in milliseconds of the language statement or remote stored procedure call. For disconnect events, specifies the elapsed time in seconds since the user logged in.
CPU	Specifies the amount of CPU time used in milliseconds.
Reads	Specifies the number of disk reads.

Table 12-4. Information in a SQL Trace Log File

Component	Definition
Writes	Specifies the number of synchronous disk writes.
NT_Domain	Specifies the NT domain name of the user who generated the event.
NT_User	Specifies the NT username of the person who generated the event.
HostName	Specifies the name of the host that generated the event.
HostProcess	Specifies the host process ID number for the host that generated the event.

Table 12-4. Information in a SQL Trace Log File (continued)

It is easy to load your trace data into SQL Server for analysis using the bulk copy program (BCP). The log file is now tab-delimited, and the SQL Server table exactly matches the file layout.

```
CREATE TABLE SQL Trace
(
Event        char(12) NOT NULL,
UserName     char(30) NOT NULL,
ID           int NOT NULL,
SPID         int NOT NULL,
StartTime    datetime NULL,
EndTime      datetime NULL,
Application  char(30) NULL,
Data         varchar(255) NULL,
Duration     int NULL,
CPU          int NULL,
Reads        int NULL,
Writes       int NULL,
NT_Domain    varchar (30) NULL,
NT_User      varchar (30) NULL,
HostName     varchar (30) NULL,
HostProcess  decimal (10) NULL
)
```

To run BCP with SQL Trace, type the following:

```
bcp pubs..SQL Trace in c:\activity.log -Usa -Psecret -S -c
```

Keep in mind that you must also run xp_sqltrace with the @FullText option = 1 to capture the entire T-SQL batch. Unfortunately, SQL Server does not efficiently handle character strings longer than 255 bytes. To hold SQL commands longer than 255 bytes, you need to create a column with a text datatype having each text column consume at least one 2K database page. Feel free to create more than one table to handle large command trace files.

Table 12-5 illustrates keeping only the first 255 bytes of the SQL command. When working with large files, this approach saves a tremendous amount of space. The Data column is defined as varchar(255). If you want to load the entire SQL command, create a second identical table, with the Data column defined as text, and call it SQLTraceText. If you are working with a lot of space or have a small trace file, this definition allows you to load the entire SQL command. You can always open the trace log directly to grab the entire command, but make sure you have a good text editor because opening a 50MB file with Notepad takes time.

If you load SQL commands exceeding 255 bytes into your SQL Trace table, you will see BCP warning messages such as *DB-LIBRARY error: Attempt to bulk-copy an oversized row to the SQL Server*. You can ignore these messages, because they are only telling you that BCP is truncating the data field.

Analyzing SQL Trace Output

Now that you have loaded your trace log into a SQL Server table, you need to prioritize your tuning tasks. Do you spend more time tuning a query that takes two minutes to run and executes once, or tuning a query that takes one second to run but executes 100,000 times during the application? Choose the latter answer and start your trace analysis by looking for two types of queries: slow queries and frequently executed queries (even if each individual execution is very fast).

Start this process with the following query:

```
SELECT avg(duration) "Avg Duration",max(duration) "Max
Duration", sum(duration) "Sum Duration",count(*) "Tran
Count",substring(data, 1, 50) "Query"
FROM SQL Trace WHERE username = "BatchProcess
```

```
GROUP BY substring(data, 1, 50)
ORDER BY sum(duration)
```

This query gives the average, maximum, and total execution time of each query listed, beginning with those that are most time-consuming. At this stage, focus on what the application is doing as a whole, and don't get bogged down in low-level query tuning details. Table 12-5 shows output from a sample SQL Trace.

Query	Average Duration (in ms)	Maximum Duration (in ms)	Summary Duration (in ms)	Transaction Count
SELECT a,b,c FROM Table4	12,553	33,326	1,004,240	80
Exec BigStoredProc param1, param2	8	3,153	755,040	94,380
sp_cursoropen NULL, "SELECT * FROM BigTable where x=10 order by Name", 2, 8, NULL	47,190	47,190	47,190	1
sp_cursorfetch 201788208, 1, 0, 1	5	46	18,875	3,775
SELECT a,b,c FROM Table10	1	16	271	271
INSERT into Data1 VALUES (1, 2, 3)	9	63	324	36
SELECT a,b,c FROM Table5	139	156	278	2
SELECT x,y,z FROM Table9	23	33	184	8
SELECT x,y,z FROM Table2	2	16	16	8

Table 12-5. Result Set of a SQL Trace

The three most important rules of SQL Server tuning are:

▼ Make the slow queries run faster.

■ Spend the most time tuning queries that consume the most resources.

▲ Reduce the number of transactions SQL Server has to perform.

The first two rules are self-explanatory, but the third is less obvious. If you need to return 1,000 rows from a table called MyData, executing one query that returns 1,000 rows is much faster than executing 1,000 queries returning one row each. Surprisingly, many ODBC settings cause your applications to execute only one query at a time. With these rules in mind, examine the results of the sample trace.

Pay attention to the three rules, and don't worry about the specific SQL commands. Which queries take the most time to run? Which queries are run most frequently? Can you reduce the total number of queries executed? These questions are easy to answer using the summarized SQL Trace data, but are almost impossible to answer without the data.

What does the trace data tell you? The first query in the table consumes the most time, as shown in the Summary Duration column. At 12,553 milliseconds (ms) this query has one of the highest average execution times, but only executes 80 times. You can tune this slow query either by eliminating a join or by reindexing.

The second query in the table is the second largest time hog because it runs so frequently. As common sense tells you, you can solve that problem by not running the query as often. Eliminate the need to lock the application by rewriting the procedure to require fewer invocations. Sometimes rewriting the procedure is easy, and sometimes you need to change the entire application. In either case, the first step to solving the problem is understanding it.

The third and fourth queries go hand in hand. The third query opens a server-side ODBC cursor, and the fourth query fetches rows from it. In the fourth query,

```
sp_cursorfetch 201788208, 1, 0, 1
```

the last parameter (1) tells you how many rows are being returned with each invocation of the fetch. Remember the third rule: Reduce the number of transactions SQL Server must process. In this case, you are fetching 3,775 rows from the cursor opened in the third query, and using 3,775 SQL calls to do it. Using ODBC, set the fetch size to 100 (a reasonable size for client-side caching) and reduce the number of fourth query calls from 3,775 to 38. This adjustment provides a huge savings (50 percent to 100 percent) in total execution time.

Optimizing Stored Procedure Usage

Since stored procedures (SP) are compiled, they should execute faster than normal SQL statements. In reality, however, the issue is a little more complicated—and sometimes being precompiled adversely affects performance.

Stored procedures are reusable, but not re-entrant, which means that before the same SP can be run simultaneously, multiple copies of the SP must be cached. The following simple example shows how an SP can slow performance:

```
CREATE PROC ListCustomers
@TargetCustId int
as
SELECT * FROM Customers
WHERE CustId >= @TargetCustId
```

This example operates according to the following assumptions:

> 100,000 customers with CustId ranging from 1-100,000
> Unique NC index on Customers.CustId

Assume that there are no plans to use the SP in cache, and that User1 executes ListCustomers 100,000 to return a single customer. SQL Server will use the index to process this query and will leave the plan in cache after it is done. Now, User1 and User2 run the procedure at exactly the same time with the following commands:

```
User1 = ListCustomers 100,000
User2 = ListCustomers 1
```

Also assume that User2 gets the already cached plan first, which means that the query will use a plan stating "use the index." This makes sense for User1's request, but using an NC index to process User2's request is horribly inefficient because a table scan is cheaper.

Compiling does not always increase performance. Many SPs will have widely varying optimal plans based upon parameters passed into the procedure, and recompiling may make sense in this case.

When to Recompile

It is difficult to know exactly when to recompile an SP. However, here are two common ways to qualify SP recompiling:

▼ Using *Exec sp_MyProc with recompile* will force a new plan for only the current invocation of the procedure. This procedure makes sense when reusing cached plans and, in some rare circumstances, for creating new plans.

▲ Using *Create sp_MyProc with recompile* will force a new plan to be compiled every time the stored procedure is run. This makes sense if "recompiling" is the normal SP behavior you want.

There is a subtle difference to understand between these two techniques. The first option will compile a new plan for the SP invocation leaving the new plan and all other plans in cache when it is finished. If you use this option on an SP that runs frequently (i.e. 1,000 times), you will end up with 1,000 copies of the plan in cache. This would quickly consume the entire available procedure cache! The second option is actually the better choice when recompiling for normal usage. If the SP is created using WITH RECOMPILE, the old plans are not cached after they are used, and the available procedure cache is not consumed at such a high rate.

ODBC Call Syntax

SP calls to front-end applications can have a surprising impact on overall system performance. Applications can call a SQL Server procedure using T-SQL or RPC invocation methods, as shown in the following ODBC examples:

```
SQLExecDirect(hstmt, "EXECUTE sp_helpdb 'pubs' ", SQL_NTS);
SQLExecDirect(hstmt, "{ call sp_helpdb ('pubs') }", SQL_NTS);
```

The first ODBC call uses the T-SQL invocation method sending the SP call across the network as an ASCII string. Unfortunately, SQL Server does not know an SP has been called until the string has been parsed. The second example uses the RPC invocation method, packaging the SP call in an efficient manner immediately recognized by SQL Server. The string is not parsed since SQL Server already knows it is an SP. The T-SQL method handles parameters by sending input across the network as strings regardless of the underlying data type. However, the more efficient RPC method passes parameters as native SQL Server data types. For instance, an integer will remain an integer as it is passed across the network, and after the server parses the query. RPC call syntax can easily offer 20-25 percent performance gains over the T-SQL method.

You may not be an ODBC programmer, but it is very easy to see the call methods used. Run the SQL Trace described earlier, and review the EVENT column in the log output. SPs called as RPCs will have RPC categorized as their EVENT, while SPs called as T-SQL will show SQL as their EVENT.

TROUBLESHOOTING SLOW CLIENT PERFORMANCE

Windows 95 clients using SQL Server-based applications may experience abnormally slow performance if they are also using the Named Pipes and the IPX/SPX protocols. Removing the IPX/SPX protocol is a quick fix to change the applications from intolerably slow to lightning fast performance levels. This is only a temporary fix because it does not really pinpoint or remove the problem. What if the Windows 95 clients depended on the IPX/SPX protocol to communicate and collaborate with other machines on the network? This section not only describes the problem, it also presents a workaround for those clients that must keep the IPX/SPX protocol stack loaded.

The problem is a result of a networking enhancement called *direct hosting,* implemented by Microsoft to increase communication speeds. Direct hosting lets the client bypass the NetBIOS layer when communicating with the server over IPX. Unfortunately, the Windows 95 direct-hosting technology seriously slows processing when used over Named Pipes, the default—and most commonly used—SQL Server NetLib.

A simple solution is to avoid using direct hosting with IPX over Named Pipes. There are two ways of doing this. The first solution, though not a recommended one, is to disable direct hosting. Although this technique works, it requires direct manipulation of the Registry, and can slow the performance of other applications. The better solution involves changing the SQL Server IPX mechanism to something other than Named Pipes, such as IPX sockets or the Multi-Protocol NetLib. The SQL Client Configuration Utility provides a GUI for setting up all client-site networking information, making this task a breeze.

USING THE PERFORMANCE MONITOR TO OPTIMIZE PERFORMANCE

In addition to the counters mentioned earlier in this chapter, the following counters can have a tremendous impact on performance, and should be monitored to help gauge SQL Server performance:

▼ **Cache: Number of Free Buffers**   The number of cache buffers currently in the free buffer pool. Running out of free buffers is expensive, so this statistic should not be lower than the threshold specified by the parameter of sp_configure. Lazywriter will normally ensure that the number of free buffers does not fall below the threshold. If it does, you may need to either increase the max async I/O and max lazywrite I/O parameters, and/or increase the free buffer threshold. Lazywriter cannot keep up with the load if this parameter is consistently below the configured value of free buffers. You may need a faster disk subsystem, or you may be able to help the situation by increasing the configured value for max lazywrite IO.

■ **Cache Hit Ratio (CHR)**   The percentage of time required to find data in cache instead of being read from a disk. Because reading from the cache is much cheaper than reading from disk, you want this ratio to be high. You can use the memory parameter of sp_configure to increase the cache hit ratio by increasing the amount of data cache memory. However, some transactions can cause the cache hit ratio to be artificially high (80-90 percent). For example, certain transactions may request a page multiple time. In all likelihood, once the first request is satisfied, the data cache will satisfy all future requests.
In theory, Cache Hit Ratio is an important statistic, but it can also be misleading. RA can skew the number by reading necessary pages in from disk on a separate processor thread before a query actually needs them. This will cause the Cache Hit Ratio to be very high even if the data cache is constantly being flushed by the RA Manager. This can happen if the RA-Physical Reads/sec is high, or the I/O–Lazy Writes/sec is high. Providing aggregate value when SQL Server is started is another problem of CHR. Think about it; you begin to test a new application after a month of great CHR numbers. Unfortunately, the old CHR numbers may offset poor CHR numbers for the new application, and you will never be the wiser. Therefore, stop and restart your SQL services whenever possible before running this test.

■ **I/O-Batch Writes/sec**   The number of 2K pages written to disk per second using batch I/O. It is optimal for Batch Writes/sec to be high. The primary user of batch I/O is the checkpoint process. You will see this number jump up when the following operations occur:

Checkpoint
BCP
Dump

Sometimes checkpoint operations will degrade the system, especially if they take too long. Check this counter if you see transaction throughput rates drop off unexpectedly on a regular basis. If the counter is high during the transaction drop off you may need to tune the checkpoint process. However, you may be able to increase the Max Async I/O if your disks are fast enough, and you drop the recovery interval so each checkpoint has less work to do.

- **I/O-Lazy Writes/sec**   The lazywriter system process whose main task is to flush out batches of dirty, aged buffers and make them available to user processes by placing them in the free buffer pool. However, buffers containing changes must be written back to disk before they can be reused for a different page.

  The maximum number of batched asynchronous I/Os performed by the lazywriter can be tuned by adjusting the server's max lazywrite I/O parameter through SQL Enterprise Manager or sp_configure. Though specific to lazywriter, this parameter is comparable to max async I/O, which controls batch I/O such as BCP and checkpoints. Setting the parameter too low can hinder performance, while setting it too high can flood the disk subsystem with writes, thus slowing down disk reads.

- **I/O-Log Writes/sec**   This counter is a great indicator of several problems. As BOL says, it is bad news if this counter matches the max sequential I/O rate for the disk containing your log. You may need faster disks for the log, or you may simply need to redesign how transactions are handled by your application. For example, you have an ODBC application doing a large number of single row inserts. By default, each INSERT statement will require an immediate write to the transaction log. Limit the maximum insert rate you can support so that it equals the speed for writing log records. This speed could be 60-70 writes per second for a typical disk. You can dramatically increase throughput for your application by using manual transaction control with the BEGIN TRANSACTION and COMMIT TRANSACTION commands. Try batching a few hundred inserts together in a single transaction, and you will see throughput for your INSERT-based application increase dramatically.

- **I/O-Trans. per Log Record**   The number of transactions packed into a log record before a log record is written to disk. Because log records must be physically written to disk before a transaction is considered complete, system throughput is limited by the rate in which log writes are completed. If the log writes from many transactions are packed into a single physical write, throughput can be improved. It may be possible to increase the number of transactions per log record by adjusting the log write sleep parameter of sp_configure.

- **I/O-Transactions/sec**   The number of Transact-SQL command batches (not transaction batches) executed per second. This statistic is affected by all constraints, including I/O, number of users, cache size, complexity of requests, and others.

This counter is a great indicator of throughput on your system; high Transactions/sec means good throughput. Unfortunately, the name is very confusing because the counter does not really measure transactions; it is measuring the number of batches being executed. For example, one batch might include 100 commands and register one transaction in this counter.

This counter offers a great one-stop technique for making regular system health checks. You will know that something is wrong if you see this number beginning to drop off suddenly on a production system that is basically doing the same routine procedures.

Use this counter along with the I/O-Log Writes/sec to determine if your application is bound by the speed at which you can write to the log disk. Your application is almost definitely log bound if I/O-Transactions/sec and I/O-Log Writes/sec tend to mirror each other. This indicates that each transaction or batch being processed is requiring a physical log write due to inefficient transaction management.

▲ **RA-Physical Reads/sec**   Physical reads issued by the Read
Ahead Manager. Each read consists of eight 2K pages or 16K
reads. This counter provides a general idea of how busy
read-ahead is in terms of actual physical I/O.

CONCLUSION

This chapter was designed to highlight the most important and
influential factors affecting SQL Server performance. It examined
a variety of issues, such as hardware configurations, installation,
SQL Server configuration options, and database application design.
Although the recommendations here are not intended to be
all-inclusive, they are proven to help you achieve the best possible
performance boost, and to minimize any negative effects that SQL
Server might have on your overall system performance.

CHAPTER 13

Optimizing Exchange Server

erformance optimization and capacity analysis for a Microsoft Exchange environment should be performed separately from optimization and analysis for the main Windows NT design configuration. Although Exchange Server is a component of the Microsoft Backoffice suite of products, the demands of electronic communication add a new level of server and infrastructure capacity stress that should be modeled separately. Also, many organizations start with file and print access as their primary networking functions and only later add electronic messaging to the environment.

This chapter describes how Exchange should be configured and tuned to improve system performance. In many networking environments, it is not necessary to completely reconfigure the servers and organizational structure according to all of the recommendations in this chapter, but suggestions are made to help you understand how performance can be improved. This chapter provides strategies for determining the current performance of an existing Exchange environment and tips for tuning this environment and for projecting and modeling future demands to proactively manage the use of the messaging application.

MICROSOFT EXCHANGE FUNDAMENTALS

Microsoft Exchange Server is a client-server electronic messaging system that splits functions and tasks between an Exchange Server and an Exchange client. Core Exchange Server functions include routing messages between users and sending and receiving messages over the Internet. Core Exchange client functions include composing messages and sorting messages within a folder in Exchange. The performance in an Exchange environment thus depends on the optimization of the client, the communication link between the client and the Exchange Server, the Exchange Server's performance, and the communication link between the Exchange Server and any external data source such as the Internet or the WAN connection to another Exchange Server. Electronic message communication typically is *bursty*, or *asynchronous*, meaning that messages are created by a user or queued by the messaging server and then sent either on demand or after a specified delay to complete the electronic transaction.

Microsoft Exchange Server runs as a set of Windows NT services, and the demands of these services affect the server that is running Microsoft Exchange. Because of this, the Windows NT management tools described earlier in this book, such as the Event Viewer (to log the status of errors), the Performance Monitor (to review server performance), and the Task Manager (to review operating server drivers), all can be used to analyze the operations of an Exchange environment. As noted in previous chapters, a variety of built-in tools provided by Windows NT as well as third-party add-in tools are available to help analyze the NT environment, and these can also be used to analyze Exchange Server.

The databases used to store electronic messages in Exchange Server use the Microsoft Jet database technology. Jet is a highly efficient information storage system that does not require a separate database management system such as SQL Server to store and retrieve information. However, like any database, it needs to be configured and tuned properly to make it work as efficiently and effectively as possible.

The Exchange environment relies on Windows NT security to authenticate user access to electronic messages stored in a user's personal mailbox and to access information stored in public storage locations as well as the shared information of other users (such as calendars and shared message folders). Exchange's tight integration with Windows NT security means that user authentication is handled through Windows NT domain controllers, and this authentication process places demands on LAN and WAN infrastructure performance.

Microsoft Exchange Server uses the concept of public and private folders for the storage of user information. A private folder is a user's personal message storage mailbox; when a user receives an electronic message, the message is stored in the user's private folder. Messages by default are stored on the Exchange Server to enable centralized message storage management. However, a user can store messages in offline folders or separate data files to use mobile messaging, as detailed later in this chapter.

Public messages are stored in public folders for which security access is shared by multiple users. The creator or owner of the public folder controls security access. Dozens of options are available that give users specific permissions to public folders and the messages they contain. These permissions include reading, modifying, or deleting any message, and changing or deleting only those messages created by the user.

Many organizations use public folders to store, or post, a copy of a message for shared access by multiple users rather than sending the message to multiple users as e-mail. This use of Microsoft Exchange public folders reduces the number of messages sent, received, managed, and stored within Exchange, which reduces traffic on the network and thus improves system-wide performance.

In addition to handling electronic message storage, the Microsoft Exchange Server also manages external message communications, including communication with the Internet, other Exchange Servers, and other LAN or legacy message systems such as Microsoft Mail, IBM/Lotus cc:Mail, Lotus Notes, Profs, and SNADs. The connector service provides both inbound and outbound message communications with these other environments. These services, of course, place additional demands on the server and the LAN and WAN infrastructure.

Exchange also handles workgroup electronic communications functions such as faxing, voicemail, document imaging, and document management. Add-ins to Microsoft Exchange typically run as additional Windows NT services. These services can be configured and installed on the same Exchange Server that manages the user's private folders and the organizational public folders, or the services can be installed on completely separate NT servers. The procedures for distributing these functions to improve individual server performance are outlined later in this chapter, in the section "Creating Multiserver Configurations."

While Exchange Server security is tightly integrated with Windows NT security, the user directory, distribution lists, and address book are maintained separately in the current version of Exchange. This will not be the case in a Windows NT 5 environment with Active Directory, but for now, Exchange users and resources are managed and maintained separately from the rest of the system. The management utility, Exchange Administrator (ADMIN.EXE), can manage the resources of a single Exchange Server or of all Exchange Servers at a single site or in an organization's global system.

Key to Exchange Server optimization is knowing which components depend on Windows NT and which do not. This topic is discussed throughout this chapter. The core components of Exchange include the information stores (which hold both private and public information), directory store, message transfer agent (MTA), connectors, and logging service, as shown in Figure 13-1.

The Information Stores

The information stores in Microsoft Exchange are the databases where message information is stored. The information stores are also commonly known as the message databases. Each message has a unique message ID number assigned to it. This ID is used for tracking as a message is routed from user to user or from an internal user to an external user.

The message ID is also used to ensure that there is only one copy of each message stored on the Exchange Server. Even if a message is sent to multiple users, only one copy of the message is stored in the message database. Each user has a link between the private inbox

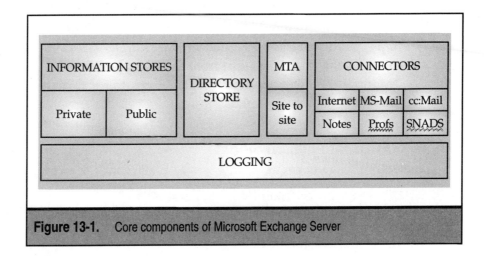

Figure 13-1. Core components of Microsoft Exchange Server

message list and the message itself. When the user accesses the message, the actual message from the information store is then opened and sent to the user. This one-message storage approach minimizes disk storage space. Only after every user who references a message no longer needs access to that message is the message finally deleted from the Exchange Server.

The information stores are large, single files that are created larger than the storage capacity needed for the existing messages. The purpose of preallocating disk space on the Exchange Server is to ensure that the server has enough storage space to manage incoming and outgoing messages. The information store databases are automatically created by the Exchange Server during installation and dynamically change in size to accommodate the storage demands of the server. Users do not have direct access to the message stores. Unlike file-based message systems, which allow users access to the server data directory that stores all messages, Exchange Server allows users access to messages only when using Exchange client software such as Outlook, POP3, or Web.

Exchange Server also automatically defragments and compresses the message stores to keep the message system running efficiently, as discussed later in this chapter.

Conceptually, this is how the information stores work: When users log on to review their electronic messages, they see only a table of contents of their messages that shows, for each message, who sent the message, when the message was sent, the subject of the message, and other information displayed in table format. When a user highlights a message and either presses ENTER or double-clicks the message, the message is sent from the Exchange database to the user. This approach reduces server-to-client data traffic to only the information requested by users.

Private Information Store

The private information store is where all of the users' mailboxes and messages for a site or organization are stored. Each message in the private information store is assigned a message ID number. An organization can have just one private information store, or it can distribute the storage of user mailboxes across multiple servers.

When multiple servers are used, it is most logical to distribute user mailboxes based on sites. This way, users in one city can access their mailboxes (the private information store) on the Exchange Server at their site, while others in another city can access their mailboxes (and the corresponding private information store) on the Exchange Server at their site. However, for organizations with hundreds of users, the users' mailboxes may be distributed across multiple Exchange Servers that reside in the same site. These two configurations are shown in Figure 13-2.

You need to consider several critical performance components when distributing users across multiple Exchange Servers. The advantage of having all users at a site on a single Exchange Server is that there is virtually no delay time when sending a message from one user to another since the server will have the only copy of the mail message, and the sender and recipient can reference this message ID number. However, if the users were on two different servers, the message would need to be routed from one Exchange Server to the other. This would cause traffic in physically routing a copy of the message from one server to the other, and it would also create additional storage demands since a copy of the message would need to reside on each server. In cases where messages are predominantly routed within a site and within a specific workgroup, it is usually best to keep all users in the workgroup on the same

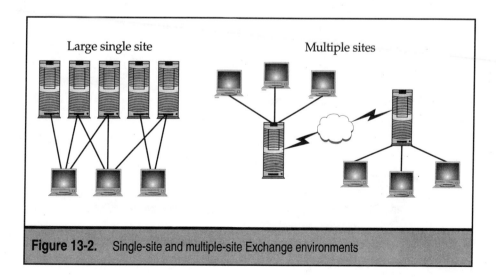

Figure 13-2.   Single-site and multiple-site Exchange environments

server to reduce server-to-server traffic or external traffic between servers.

The Microsoft Exchange Resource Kit (available for downloading from the Microsoft home page at **http://www.microsoft.com/ exchange/**) contains a utility that helps organizations move users from one Exchange Server to another. The Move User utility provides the services necessary to transfer a user's messages and address book from one server to another.

NOTE: The private information store file typically is stored on the Exchange Server in **\\server\share\exchsrvr\mdbdata\priv.edb**.

Public Information Store

The public information store is the message database for shared folders on the Exchange Server. Like the private store, the public information store contains mail messages. However, the public information store is accessible, by default, to all users at the Exchange Server site, not just to an individual. In addition, through folder-level security, administrators and network users can assign security rights to individual users, groups of users, or all users in the organization to allow access to a public folder or series of public folders.

Microsoft Exchange public folders can store information centrally within an organization to provide services similar to an intranet. Just as an intranet can store company templates, marketing documents, policy information, and the like, the Exchange public folders can store common information. This strategy of using Exchange to store common shared information can drastically reduce the number of messages that are sent to "all users" and so help alleviate message traffic, routing, and storage problems on the network. A sample public folder hierarchy is shown in Figure 13-3.

NOTE: The public information store file typically is stored on the Exchange Server in **\\server\share\exchsrvr\mdbdata\pub.edb**.

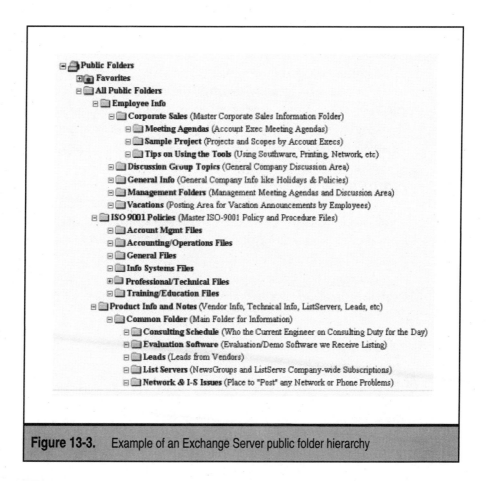

Figure 13-3.   Example of an Exchange Server public folder hierarchy

The Directory Store

In addition to the message database, one additional database is
crucial in the Microsoft Exchange environment. The directory store,
or directory database, contains all of the resource information
available to users in the Exchange organization such as a list of users,
distribution lists, and routes to external resources (such as the
Internet). Although some people complain that Windows NT does
not have a directory service, the Microsoft Exchange directory store
maintains a very structured directory system. The top level of the
Exchange environment is the *organization*, which can be split into *sites*

that are grouped by *distribution lists* made up of individual *users*. The master catalog of Exchange resources is called the *Global Address List*. This entire directory structure is shown in Figure 13-4.

Organizations that have multiple messaging systems commonly need to share directories or address books across the various messaging systems. This function requires the swapping of user and distribution lists from messaging system to messaging system and is called *directory synchronization*. Directory synchronization allows an organization to maintain a single directory of users across multiple messaging systems. With Microsoft Exchange Server 5.5 and the inclusion of LDAP version 3 directory capabilities, organizations now can choose between implementing a directory synchronization process or using an on-demand directory lookup process.

Although directory synchronization adds a service load on the synchronization server that varies from 1 to 5 percent of total

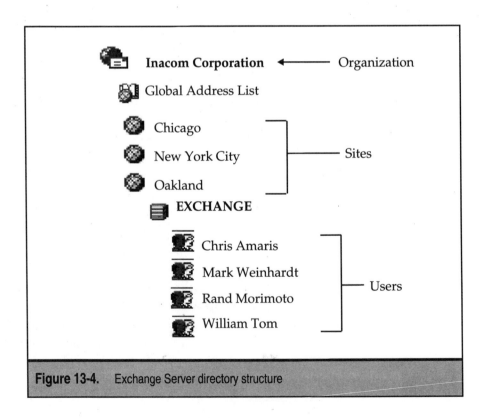

Figure 13-4.   Exchange Server directory structure

processor use, any user access to the directory is immediate and does not put additional load demands on the server. Through LDAP, a directory request is issued to the host system and displayed on demand. Even though this does not put a load on the Exchange Server, it does require the client to issue a request for a directory view to the remote system for each directory request.

NOTE: The directory store file typically is stored on the Exchange Server in \\server\share\exchsrvr\mdbdata\dir.edb.

The Message Transfer Agent (MTA)

The message transfer agent routes X.400 or RPC messages withina Microsoft Exchange environment. These messages are typically external to the current Exchange Server but are internal to the Exchange site or organization. If a user resides in a different city within the organization that has a separate Exchange Server, Microsoft Exchange uses the message transfer agent to route the message, via the Exchange site-to-site connection, to the remote user. It is through the MTA that the message is routed within the first server and then forwarded to the Exchange site connector, Internet mail connector, or other external gateway for routing to the second server.

To assess Exchange Server performance, you need to analyze the number of messages that are routed internally to a single server, routed to another server within the organization, or routed to individuals outside of the organization. The capacity planning and performance analysis tools discussed in the section "Capacity Planning for an Exchange Environment" later in this chapter can be used to help assess the demand that internal message routing places on servers. As a general rule, when analyzing the statistics of messages being processed by the MTA, the key factors to look at are the message sources and destinations. If your organization has multiple Exchange Servers at a single site where more than 40 percent of the MTA message volume is between internal servers at the site, you should consider moving the users or groups of users to the same server. The majority of MTA traffic should be site-to-site message communications, with only a small portion of the traffic being internal site communications.

Connectors

Connectors are Windows NT services running on an Exchange Server that manage inbound and outbound communication with the other messaging systems. Connectors perform directory synchronization with the other messaging system so that a single address contains Exchange Server users, distribution lists, and resource information as well as the external mail system information services.

There are three different methods for interconnecting multiple sites. For communication within an organization but to a different site, the Microsoft Exchange Site Connector provides the most comprehensive connection between servers. For communication with the Internet, an external connector called the Internet Mail Service is used. For communication with other messaging systems, Microsoft provides connectors to MS-Mail, cc:Mail, Lotus Notes, Profs, SNADs, and X.400.

Two critical factors in Exchange Server performance are the number of messages transmitted and the processor bandwidth of the Exchange Server, which manages inbound and outbound communication and the synchronization of user lists. Care needs to be taken when analyzing these processes to determine the quantity and scope of bandwidth demands on the environment in processing this information. There are three predefined performance monitoring utilities for analyzing the Exchange Server connectors:

▼ Microsoft Exchange Server IMS Statistics

■ Microsoft Exchange Server IMS Traffic

▲ Microsoft Exchange Server IMS Queues

These can be found in the Start | Programs | Microsoft Exchange folder. They monitor outgoing message volume, incoming message volume, and message queue length. The message volume for both incoming and outgoing messages should be less than 60 percent of the total message traffic of the organization. If the message volume exceeds 60 percent, you should assess the total byte count of connector message communications by comparing the total bytes sent and received with the total throughput capacity of the connector. If communication throughput exceeds 70 percent of the total message volume, connector performance is being degraded, and you should either increase the bandwidth capacity of the connector (for faster connection to the Internet or to the external messaging system) or move the connector to a different server. This will greatly improve Exchange Server performance by offloading the performance demands of the system connector.

Logging

Microsoft Exchange uses the same logging mechanism as Microsoft Windows NT, so every error in Microsoft Exchange, and potentially every message being sent or received in an Exchange environment, can be logged and tracked. The administrator of the Exchange environment can activate various message tracking and logging options. To activate message tracking and logging, do the following:

1. Choose Start | Programs | Microsoft Exchange Server | Microsoft Exchange Administrator to Start the Exchange Administrator program.

2. Choose Site | Server | Connectors and select the connect option you want to use.

3. On the Diagnostics Logging tab, turn on logging for each of the functions desired, as shown in Figure 13-5.

Microsoft Exchange uses the Microsoft Windows NT Event Viewer utility to store, look up, and manage logged events. This tracking monitors problems with Exchange services (such as errors in MTA message routing or in connecting to the Internet to send SMTP messages), internal message routing, logon and logoff by Exchange users, and automatic message store compaction notification.

Remember in logging that the more logging options activated, the more frequently the Exchange Server will write to the disk logs,

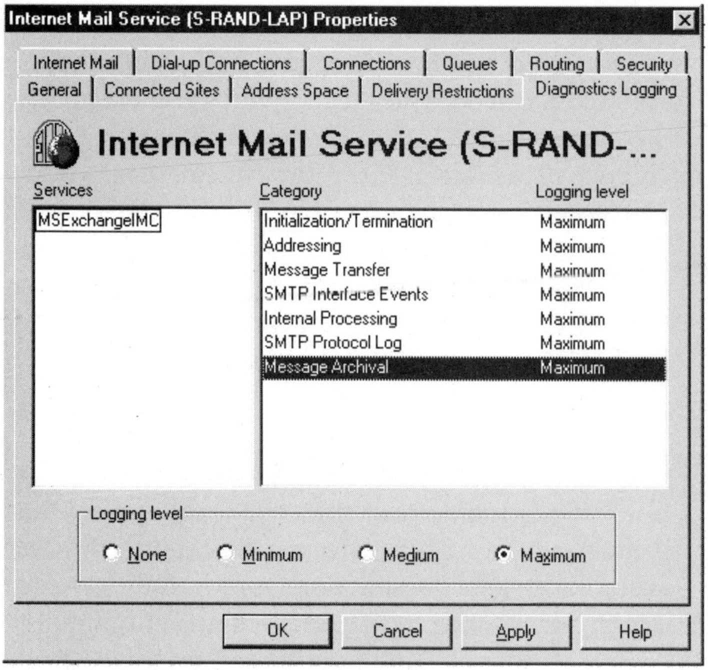

Figure 13-5. Enabling diagnostic logging in Exchange Server

requiring I/O storage space on the server and system processing time for managing the information storage. Since Exchange Server performs extensive logging to track message activity and back up message transactions to protect against corruption of the information store database, this additional logging doubles the read and write operations performed on the server.

However, logs do provide detailed information on the system status that can help a trained administrator understand Exchange Server processes.

CONFIGURING HARDWARE FOR OPTIMAL PERFORMANCE

Since Microsoft Exchange works under Windows NT, all of the factors that effect NT Server performance described throughout this book also affect the performance of Exchange Server, and the unique requirements of Exchange Server, such as its multiple message databases, services, and logging, add additional stress to the NT Server in a Microsoft Exchange environment.

The workload that Microsoft Exchange Server experiences ultimately depends on the number of users Exchange Server must support. How many users can Exchange Server support? This question cannot be answered with complete accuracy because so many factors must be considered, including hardware. A better way to phrase this question is, "What hardware configuration is needed to support a certain number of active users?"

This question raises two points. First, you should start the planning process by determining how many users the server must support and how they will be interacting with the server. For example, will users use the server only lightly, or will they be generating hundreds of messages per day? Second, you need to base your hardware configuration on the number of active users, not simply on the number of accounts or mailboxes on the server. For instance, a system may have more than 500 mailboxes, but only 200 users may be expected to use the messaging system concurrently.

This brings us to the question of what hardware configurations promote optimal performance with different numbers of active users. The following sections address this question and recommend hardware based on the number of users. The components that most affect Exchange Server performance are memory, the disk subsystem, and the processor.

RAM and CPU Configuration

Although every operating environment is unique and the optimal configuration differs from organization to organization, you can use some simple rules of thumb to determine the server size and amount of RAM needed for an Exchange Server. Many people think that Microsoft Exchange requires a "big" server compared to their existing e-mail server. Given the same number of messaging users on Microsoft Exchange, an organization can typically have the same server configuration as for a comparable e-mail messaging system.

However, if you add functionality or consolidate users under a single Exchange Server, a larger file server may be needed. It is the added groupware functionality, such as routing documentation, intranet document management, network faxing, group and personal scheduling, and remote dial-up access, that increases demands and requires a faster server processor and more memory in an Exchange Server.

The number of processors your system needs depends on the number of users you plan to support and their expected usage profiles. For medium- to large-scale environments, you are strongly advised to use a multiprocessor system or at least to invest in a system with multiprocessor capability to prevent the processor from becoming a bottleneck.

Since Microsoft Exchange is multithreaded, it can take advantage of multiprocessor systems. It is optimized to run on systems with up to four processors, and systems with more than four processors will see little improvement over a four-processor system. Moreover, it is more efficient to offload services to another Microsoft Exchange Server than to add more CPUs to a server with four processors, because then you won't place additional loads on other system components, such as memory and the disk subsystem.

NOTE: If the system is to be configured with more than one processor, it is imperative that you use as large an L2 cache as possible because each processor has equal access to the L2 cache, and the more processors you have, the less L2 cache space a processor will have for itself. You may need to purchase as much as a 2MB L2 cache for a multiprocessor system.

In a Windows NT environment, system memory plays as important a role as processor speed in determining the server's ability to manage network resources. The more memory a Windows NT Server has, the more file system cache space is available for the disk subsystem and the better the system performance. In a network environment in which hundreds of users access the same file server, a server with more system memory can service disk read and write requests from main memory rather than having to constantly access the hard disks in the server. As mentioned in Chapter 4, main memory is several orders of magnitude faster than the disk subsystem, so cached information access significantly improves performance.

Also, add-in applications such as search engines and document indexing and management utilities also increase the demands on memory.

Microsoft Exchange, like Windows NT, can handle as much memory as you can throw at it. However, Microsoft Exchange has its own special way of optimizing the system's memory configuration, using the Exchange Performance Optimizer. Microsoft Exchange allocates some of the system memory to the buffer cache, which consists of many 4Kb database buffers. Any change in the amount of memory on the system affects the size of the buffer cache.

NOTE: Any time the server's hardware configuration is changed, you should run the Performance Optimizer to allow Microsoft Exchange to reconfigure settings. For more information, refer to "Using the Performance Optimizer" later in this chapter.

When you run the Performance Optimizer, Exchange will see whether you have increased or decreased the amount of system memory, and it will then figure out how much memory should be used for the buffer cache. The buffer cache is similar to NT's own file system cache and SQL Server's memory allocation mechanism, though it is completely separate from either of these. Even more surprising, Microsoft Exchange does not rely on the NT file system cache for disk related I/O; instead, it relies on its buffer cache. In this sense, Microsoft Exchange is more independent of the operating system than other applications.

The benefits of Microsoft Exchange's ability to dedicate a portion of system memory for its own buffer cache are amazing, especially in terms of performance. One of the most notable advantages of Exchange Server's buffer cache is that it increases the number of cache hits. The higher the percentage of cache hits, the less reliant the application is on the disk subsystem. For more information on cache and memory, consult Chapter 4.

Another way in which Microsoft Exchange effectively uses memory resources is by automatically reconfiguring the Server service. After installation, Microsoft Exchange changes the NT Server service setting to Maximize Throughput for Network Applications. This sounds like a good idea, but what, if any, performance gain does this give you? The advantage is this: This setting increases the likelihood that Windows NT will page system cache memory before it pages memory used by network applications such as Microsoft Exchange. Because Exchange hardly ever relies on the system cache, paging will not have a significant effect on Exchange Server performance.

To reassure yourself that this configuration change has taken place, you can check the Server service settings by doing the following:

1. Click the Network applet on the Control Panel or right-click the Network Neighborhood icon and select Properties. This brings up the Network Properties screen.

2. On the Services tab, select the Server service and click the Properties button to bring up the Server Service Properties dialog box:

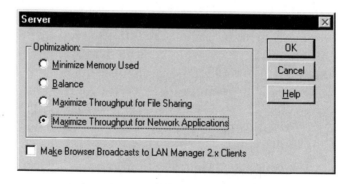

3. Make sure that the Server service is set to Maximize Throughput for Network Applications.

4. Click OK in the Server dialog box and then click Close in the Network dialog box.

5. When NT prompts you to restart the machine, select Yes.

Typically, a Microsoft Exchange Server in a highly optimized server configuration should have 32MB of base memory, plus 4MB of memory for each add-in application (such as a fax program or search engines), plus 8MB of RAM for each 1GB of disk storage space in the system. Thus, a server with 12GB of disk storage space that has Microsoft Exchange installed on top of Windows NT should have approximately 116 to 128MB of memory installed. For servers with less demand on server resources, such as archived data stores or small office servers with large disk space needs, the actual amount of memory for the server can be significantly lower.

Table 13-1 shows examples of the number of users and common baseline configurations for an Exchange Server. Although Table 13-1 suggests server configurations, it is advised that you run a capacity analysis utility (described in detail in the section "Capacity Planning for an Exchange Environment" later in this chapter) to determine the server performance capabilities needed for your organization.

For large and very large workgroups or organizations, you may want to split users or services across multiple servers (as described in the section "Creating Multiserver Configurations" later in this chapter) rather than continue to add more RAM or more processors. In general, one high-end machine should serve a maximum of 1,000 active users using only messaging (just e-mail) or 500 to 700 active users using GroupWare functionality in addition to messaging. However, to gauge the actual number of users the server can support, you must use a capacity analysis utility, such as LoadSim or Dynameasure.

Hard Drive Configuration

In Microsoft Exchange, the disk storage requirements of the server are directly related to the message storage requirements of the organization. Microsoft Exchange stores user name and folder information in the directory store, user mailbox information in the information store, and messages in the message database. The network administrator does not have to worry about how to manage these storage units. All the administrator needs to do is provide adequate disk storage space to meet the needs of the organization.

Users per File Server	Electronic Mail Only	E-mail/Scheduling/Document Management/Faxing
20	486 processor 1GB disk space 32MB RAM	Pentium processor 2GB disk space 32MB RAM
50	Pentium processor 2GB disk space 48MB RAM	Pentium processor 3GB disk space 64MB RAM
100	Pentium processor 3GB disk space 64MB RAM	Pentium processor 4GB disk space 96MB RAM
200	Dual-processor Pentium 6GB disk space 96MB RAM	Dual-processor Pentium 6GB disk space 128MB RAM
500	Dual-processor Pentium 8GB disk space 160MB RAM	Dual-processor Pentium 8GB disk space 196MB RAM
750	3-processor Pentium 12GB disk space 196MB RAM	3-processor Pentium 12GB disk space 256MB RAM
1,000	Dual-processor RISC 16GB disk space 256MB RAM	Dual-processor RISC 16GB disk space 256MB RAM
1,500	4-processor RISC 20GB disk space 384MB RAM	4-processor RISC 24GB disk space 512MB RAM

Table 13-1. Sample Server Configurations for Microsoft Exchange

The type of hard drive hardware (Fast/Wide SCSI, SCSI-2, PCI or EISA controller, etc.) can affect server access performance. See Chapter 6 for recommendations on disk subsystem hardware and hard drive configurations. Obviously, the faster the drive speed, the faster the disk transfer speed and the better the hardware performance. The key to configuring and managing the disk subsystem for Microsoft Exchange is to separate the transaction logs, message databases, and Exchange program files onto different physical drives.

Boot Drive

The boot drive is the default location of the %SYSTEMROOT% directory that contains NT executables, DLLs, and much more. It is also the default installation drive for many Exchange Server components. Having both the Windows NT files and the Microsoft Exchange program files on the boot drive of the server does not drastically affect server performance. It is common to have a 2 or 4GB boot drive to store all of this information.

The boot drive is also the default location for the Windows NT pagefile. You can move this paging file to a different drive location, but if the drive you put it on is not accessible at startup, the system will not boot. The paging file setup is important because if the system runs out of RAM, the system will write the overflow information to the system pagefile. As data is read from the server hard drive and then overflows back to the server drive, the drive read/write operation can become a server bottleneck. Further, when the initial pagefile size is exceeded, NT begins allocating additional disk space to the pagefile dynamically. When the pagefile is initially created, disk space is allocated contiguously on the server drive. However, when NT is forced to extend the size of the pagefile dynamically, it allocates additional disk space wherever space is available. This creates a fragmented pagefile on the server, which can drastically reduce overall system performance. The obvious solution is to have sufficient RAM in the server to prevent the swapping of information to disk in the first place.

Data Drive

The data drive typically is where the Exchange Server's message databases are stored: the private information store, public information store, and directory store. Microsoft Exchange versions 4.0, 5.0, and 5.5 Standard Edition have a limit of 16GB of storage space for each message store. However, Microsoft Exchange version

5.5 Enterprise Edition provides virtually unlimited storage capacity (a theoretical maximum of 16 terabytes).

By default, the message databases are stored on the same drive that contains the Exchange program files. For better performance, you should move these stores from the default location to a separate volume of their own. When you use the Performance Optimizer, it will likely configure the system in this way.

Log Drive

Microsoft Exchange automatically logs all message transactions in separate message logs to enable the recovery of lost messages in the event of a system failure. The log files are typically stored in the same directory as the main message databases. Because messages are stored both in the information store and in the log files on the server, extensive disk write sequences are performed. Therefore, it is best to place these files on separate drives.

Exchange Server Drive Configuration

For an optimal configuration, place the Windows NT system files and pagefile on a dedicated boot drive, the Exchange information store databases on a dedicated data drive, and the log files on a third hard drive subsystem. An Exchange Server runs more efficiently reading and writing information on multiple drive units than on a single drive subsystem that can become a bottleneck.

Disk Fault Tolerance

Disk fault tolerance is critical in minimizing the loss of information caused by system failure. You can implement disk fault tolerance through either the system hardware or software. Microsoft Windows NT provides software disk fault tolerance through disk mirroring and disk striping, whereas hardware disk fault tolerance would require the purchase of a disk controller that supports hardware fault tolerance.

When possible, though, you should use hardware fault tolerance. The advantages of hardware fault tolerance over software fault tolerance include the following:

▼ **Faster performance**   Because hardware fault tolerance is managed by a controller card or other hardware device, processing performance is not compromised. Software fault tolerance requires that a certain level of the operating system and system processor be available to manage the fault tolerance of the operating software.

▲ **Error trapping**   In a system that uses software fault tolerance, a hard drive subsystem failure may cause the server to halt network operating system functions. A system with hardware fault tolerance may be able to isolate the disk failure from the operating system functions and prevent the operating system from halting processing operations.

If your file server hardware vendor provides utilities to create fault-tolerant disk configurations for the server, you should use the hardware fault tolerance options for disk mirroring, duplexing, or data striping rather than the software options included in the Windows NT disk administrator.

In an optimized Exchange environment that has a separate boot drive, data drive, and log file drive, you should consider the following approaches to fault tolerance:

▼ **Boot drive**   Drive mirroring is a good way to protect system boot processes because a mirrored boot drive offers redundancy if bootup fails. NT cannot boot without a valid boot drive.

■ **Data drive**   The data drive in an Exchange environment is typically the largest volume on the server. The optional implementation of RAID level 5 provides an $N+1$ fault tolerance scheme, meaning that one backup drive is added to the entire array of data drives to provide the necessary fault tolerance capabilities.

▲ **Log drive**   Since the log drive stores only message logs, the log drive does not require a fault-tolerant configuration. By definition, the log drive is a backup of the primary data drive information, so it provides redundant services anyway.

Using the Performance Optimizer

During the Microsoft Exchange installation process, but after the Exchange Server software has been installed, the Performance Optimizer utility (PERFWIZ.EXE) is invoked. The Performance Optimizer reviews common server configuration settings on the Exchange Server and reconfigures database location, registry, and disk configuration settings and modifies the default parameters to improve the performance of the Exchange Server. By default, the Performance Optimizer tests a series of set parameters and tunes the Exchange Server automatically.

After the initial installation of the server, PERFWIZ.EXE can be run at any time to confirm the general optimization of the server. However, unless the server hardware has been modified, the Performance Optimizer will typically not find any objects to change since the utility is intended to compare server parameter settings with the hardware configuration of the system. It is highly recommended that you Run Performance Optimizer if you add memory to the server, update the hard drive configuration (such as by adding a new drive to a RAID set or a new physical drive to offload log files), or install a new network adapter.

The Performance Optimizer can also be run in manual mode to allow you to select specific options to review and tune. To invoke the Performance Optimizer in manual mode, simply run PERFWIZ.EXE –V to view a series of screens like the one shown in Figure 13-6. The –V switch tells Performance Optimizer to run in verbose mode. Verbose mode provides more detail about disk performance, buffer allocation, and other parameters. Parameter values can be set manually. Table 13-2 describes these parameters and their values.

NOTE: Although the Performance Optimizer provides more than four pages of user-modifiable parameters, the parameters listed in Table 13-2 are the only ones whose values change based on the size or optimization of the Exchange Server environment.

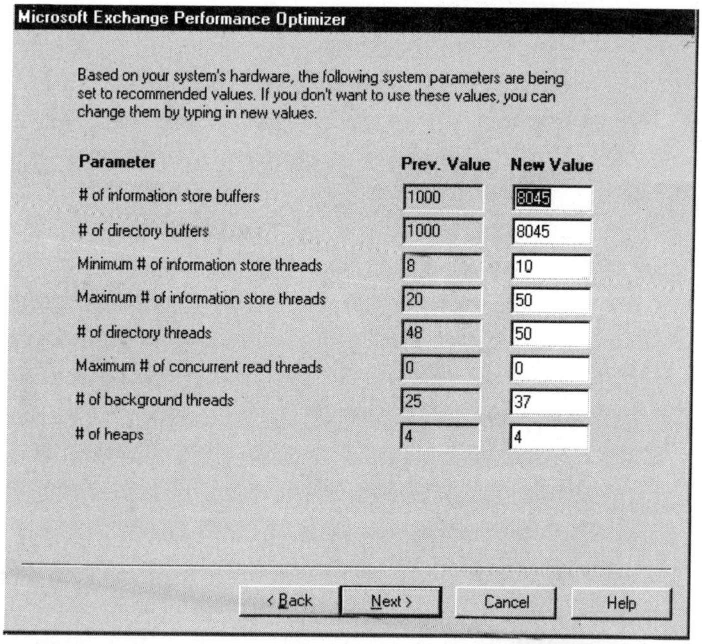

Figure 13-6.   Sample Performance Optimization manual configuration screen

Before the Performance Optimizer can make tuning modifications, the server must have the necessary hardware configuration. The Performance Optimizer only fine-tunes the server; it cannot make the actual hardware run any faster. For instance, if the server has only a single drive partition for the boot drive, data drive, and log files, the Performance Optimizer cannot reconfigure the hard drives to divide them into multiple physical sets. Thus, the key to improving server performance still is configuring the system with the proper hardware as described in the previous section. Given the proper hardware configuration, the Performance Optimizer will analyze the system and make any appropriate changes to improve Exchange Server performance.

Parameter	Description	Default	Reason to Modify
Number of Information Store Buffers	Number of buffers allocated to the information store. This is the cache buffer for information store transactions. This value can be increased to improve the performance on heavily accessed information message store servers. The size of each buffer is 4Kb.	1,000	Check the perfmon object for message queue length. If messages to the private information store are bottlenecking at the server, increase this parameter value. In general, allocate 50Kb per user. Thus, for a server with 500 users, allocate a total buffer space of 25,000Kb, or about 6,500 buffers.
Number of Directory Buffers	Number of buffers allocated to the directory. In networks with many users in the global address list, as the number of directory requests increases, a larger directory buffer can improve response time for directory resolution. The size of each buffer is 4Kb.	1,000	Check the perfmon object for the directory store request length. If the number of queued requests remains above 0 for an extended period of time, increase the number of directory buffers by 1,000.

Table 13-2. Performance Optimizer Parameter Settings

Parameter	Description	Default	Reason to Modify
Minimum Number of Information Store Threads	Minimum number of threads within a process that the information store can initiate.	8	Keep the minimum number of threads below the maximum to allow the Exchange Server to dynamically adjust the required thread allocation for the memory and processor as required. However, if the Exchange Information Store Thread object remains at the maximum for an extended period of time during the day, increase both the maximum and minimum numbers of threads to reduce the amount of dynamic allocation time necessary to adjust the server parameter.

Table 13-2. Performance Optimizer Parameter Settings (*continued*)

Parameter	Description	Default	Reason to Modify
Maximum Number of Information Store Threads	Maximum number of threads within a process that the information store can initiate.	20	The maximum number of information store threads must be greater than or equal to the minimum number of threads and should be set at a level that maintains the Exchange Information Store Thread perfmon object at or below this maximum. If the object exceeds this maximum, increase this value by 4 and restart the information store service.
Number of Directory Threads	Number of threads that the directory can initiate.	48	The number of directory store threads should be greater than or equal to the demands determined by the perfmon object Exchange Directory Store Thread. If the object exceeds this limit, increase this value by 4 and restart the directory store service.

Table 13-2.   Performance Optimizer Parameter Settings (*continued*)

Parameter	Description	Default	Reason to Modify
Number of Background Threads	Number of threads available for background tasks and gateway in and out processes and to the send and deliver thread pool.	25	Background threads should be increased when the perfmon object Background Threads reaches 80 percent of the maximum. Increase this value by 4 and restart the Exchange Server services.
Maximum Number of Concurrent Read Threads	Maximum number of threads available to service replication requests.	0	For networks with multiple sites and WAN-based connectors, increase the maximum number of concurrent read threads by 1 for each external site in direct first-level communication with the Exchange Server, up to a maximum of approximately 10.
Number of Private Information Store Send and Deliver Threads	Number of threads the private information store can use to send or deliver messages to mailboxes.	2	For networks with multiple private information store servers at a single site, increase this value by 1 for each additional private information store server at the site in direct first-level communication with the Exchange Server, up to a maximum of approximately 10.

Table 13-2.   Performance Optimizer Parameter Settings (*continued*)

Parameter	Description	Default	Reason to Modify
Number of Public Information Store Send and Deliver Threads	Number of threads the public information store can use to send or deliver messages to public folders.	2	For networks with multiple public information store servers at a single site, increase this value by 1 for each additional public information store server at the site in direct first-level communication with the Exchange Server, up to a maximum of approximately 10.
Number of Information Store Gateway In and Out Threads	Number of threads that a connector can initiate to or from the information store when receiving or sending messages. If an organization has heavy interserver or Internet traffic, increasing the number of threads will improve message throughput.	1	Increase this value only if the server has multiple processors to handle simultaneous thread processing. Increase this value by 2 for each processor added to the server.

Table 13-2. Performance Optimizer Parameter Settings (*continued*)

Parameter	Description	Default	Reason to Modify
Number of Information Store Users	Number of users currently configured as the maximum for the information store on the Exchange Server.	500	Increase this value to match the maximum number of users using this Exchange Server.
Number of Concurrent Connections to LAN-MTAs and RAS LAN-MTAs	Number of connections the Exchange Server can make to external services such as other Exchange sites or dynamic RAS sites.	40	Increase this value to match the number of simultaneous connections for LAN-based sites and RAS connections for users accessing this server.
Number of LAN-MTAs and X.400 Gateways	Number of connections to external X.400 sites.	20	Increase this value to match the number of simultaneous connections for X.400 sites on the network accessing this server.

Table 13-2. Performance Optimizer Parameter Settings (*continued*)

CREATING MULTISERVER CONFIGURATIONS

One way to increase the number of users in an organization without overloading a single server is to distribute users and message processing services across multiple servers. This approach also provides distributed functions, reducing the potential for failure at a central point in the environment. By distributing server functions, large organizations can distribute the management of large sets of users and functions to multiple individuals (via the Internet, fax routing, document management, e-mail, and the company intranet).

Multiserver Configurations

In organizations with hundreds of users and extensive demands for groupware functions, a single server cannot be upgraded with enough memory, processing speed, or disk or network I/O capacity to efficiently handle all of the communication demands. The solution is to distribute the Exchange Server functions across multiple servers. Load analysis tools (see "Capacity Planning for an Exchange Environment" later in this chapter) can be used to determine load demands on a server and whether an additional server is necessary to handle the functions.

Private and Public Store Servers

The private and public information databases can be stored on two separate servers. You can set up a server with the private information store as its only message database, thus dedicating a single server to mailbox management for individual users.

Private store servers let you distribute user mailboxes based on the performance capabilities of the Exchange Server in the environment. As the number of users in your organization increases, you can improve performance by distributing the load across multiple servers.

As with the private information store, you can place public information stores on a single dedicated server. Dedicated public store servers are common in organizations that use Exchange to meet their groupware and intranet needs. For example, a business might commonly use the public database to store template documents and publicly accessible messages.

Application Servers

Many third-party add-in services for Exchange provide fax, voicemail, document routing, or other electronic communication services. These services can be added to an existing Exchange Server as additional NT services, or, depending on the transaction volume or Exchange Server capacity, they can be set up on a dedicated application server.

Most organizations distribute add-in application server functions to a dedicated server only when more than about 100 people will be using the server for normal messaging and calendaring function. For a small organization, workgroup, or site, a single Exchange/add-in application server combination is adequate. However, in many cases, distributing server functions to an additional server is dictated by the add-in software itself. For example, the server may not have enough slots available to incorporate the extra adapters that the software requires.

Table 13-3 describes some of the add-in software configuration options for Exchange.

Third-Party Add-in Option	Performance Effects
Inbound and outbound faxing	Fax adapter boards are required to send and receive faxes. Boards vary in hardware type from ISA to PCI. Boards that offload processing to the fax adapter itself place less load on the server processor. Fax software can be installed on a dedicated server to distribute processing load from the Exchange Server to the fax server.
Document routing	Document routing places demands on the server processor and disk subsystem. As a document is routed from user to user, the Exchange Server has to determine the intended recipient, the location of the recipient, and the route for forwarding documents or providing notification. Routed files are stored on the server disk, creating disk read and write demands

Table 13-3.   Add-in Software for Exchange and Its Effects on Performance

Document management	Document management software enables users to check documents into and out of the server. Document management involves creating an index or card file for each document as it is accessed, tracking the document status, and storing the document, thus placing a load on the server and disk subsystem.
Pager gateway	Numeric and text pager links require that a modem be installed on the server to dial and send pager information. Because most modems use standard serial port communication processes that are interrupt driven, every time the modem is invoked to send a page, the processor is interrupted to communicate with the modem. If many pages are sent throughout the day, server performance may be degraded.
Voicemail integration	Voicemail integration allows the Exchange Server to act as voicemail server. This requires an adapter to link the Exchange Server to the phone switch or PBX to accept incoming phone calls. Messages are stored, and in addition, a data stream is created to ensure that the entire message is received. Voice messages can be very large, and file and disk storage management is important in ensuring the Exchange Server communications.

Table 13-4. Add-in Software for Exchange and Its Effects on Performance (*continued*)

Web, POP3, and IMAP messaging	Access to Exchange Server messages over the Internet requires that the Microsoft Internet Information Server (IIS) be activated. IIS could be installed on the Exchange Server or on a separate server, depending on the number of mailboxes being used for access and the security controls used for external access.

Table 13-5.   Add-in Software for Exchange and Its Effects on Performance (*continued*)

CAPACITY PLANNING FOR AN EXCHANGE ENVIRONMENT

Capacity planning for an Exchange environment has three phases during the life of the server. The first occurs prior to the purchase and installation of the Exchange Server software and is used to determine the size and capabilities needed for the new server. The second occurs after the server has been installed and used; this phase is used to confirm that the server configuration is adequate for the demands of the environment. The third phase occurs when the demands on the server change (for example, when the number of users increases, new add-in applications are used, or inbound and outbound message traffic increases); in this phase, incremental capacity analysis is needed to ensure that the server continues to meet the needs of the organization. Capacity planning was addressed in detail in Chapter 2. This section focuses on additional components specific to Exchange Server.

Sizing a New Server Configuration

Before you deploy Microsoft Exchange for your messaging environment, you should conduct tests to determine the server processor, amount of memory, and size of disk storage appropriate for your organization. For organizations already using electronic messaging, historical information on message traffic should be readily available. Organizations new to electronic messaging or that will be using some of the advanced groupware capabilities of Exchange will have to estimate server use and demands.

Several options are available for determining the size of Exchange Server you need. Integrated into Exchange is a free utility called Load Simulator, or LoadSim (LOADSIM.EXE), and third-party add-in utilities provide analysis components for estimating the requirements for an Exchange messaging system.

Using LoadSim

The LoadSim program simulates both user-initiated actions and background processes in an offline Exchange prototype server.

LoadSim simulates these user-initiated actions (based on user interaction):

▼ User actions for sending, receiving, replying to, saving, deleting, and forwarding electronic messages

■ User interaction with public folders

■ User interaction with Microsoft Scheduler for personal and group scheduling

▲ User interaction with electronic forms, views, and access

LoadSim simulates these background processes (based on server transactions):

▼ Transmission and receipt of external messages (Internet messages, MS-Mail messages, and site-to-site messages)

■ Replication of public folders among multiple sites

▲ Automatic database compaction and defragmentation

User-initiated actions directly affect the interaction between the client and server. Background processes affect server performance based on server-invoked transactions. When analyzing the impact of each of these types of processes on the Exchange Server, you will find that user-initiated actions typically increase in proportion to the number of users and the activity of the users within the environment, and the background processes of the server increase in proportion to the number of additional servers, sites, and external connections of the organization.

LoadSim is not a stand-alone modeling simulator, but rather an actual load generating utility. LoadSim creates actual messages and traffic on a network based on the specified load parameters so that actual network and server performance can be measured.

LoadSim categorizes the effects of load on the server into four levels of input and output: Very Light, Light, Medium, and Heavy. Table 13-4 shows the basic differences among these categories.

DETERMINING USER TRAFFIC PATTERNS   To effectively use the results of LoadSim, you need to determine whether users are very light, light, medium, or heavy users of messaging. Most messaging administrators do not know their users' message traffic patterns. However, organizations already using Exchange Server or the Windows Messaging and Outlook client can use the STORSTAT.EXE utility to analyze historical user traffic. This utility is contained in the Microsoft Backoffice Resource Kit or can be downloaded from the Microsoft web site.

The Storstat utility analyzes a user's mailbox and creates a one-page report showing the average number of messages sent, messages received, and messages with attachments; the average size

Parameter	Very Light	Light	Medium	Heavy
# of Nondefault Folders	0	20	40	60
# of Messages per Folder	0	5	5	5
# of Messages in User's Inbox	0	1	4	9
# of Messages in Deleted Items	0	1	1	1
Usage (Hrs/Day)	12	8	8	8
# of Messages Sent per Day	4	5	15	30
# of Messages Received per Day	10	23	66	120

Table 13-6.   LoadSim Standard Parameters

of messages; and other statistics. All a user needs to do is execute the STORSTAT.EXE utility from any Windows 95 or Windows NT workstation, and the utility automatically generates a report for the user's message box. The report generated is similar to the following:

```
*********************************************************
Service Provider: Microsoft Exchange Server
Message Store: Mailbox - Rand Morimoto
*********************************************************
Total msgs in entire store: 2500
Average messages sent per day is 27.33
Largest number of msgs sent a day is 49
Average number of recipients on a message is 3
Average number of replies per day is 6
Average number of forwards per day is 2
Average number of msgs received per day is 27.33
Maximum number of msgs received in a day is 83
Largest # of messages in any folder is 987
Average folder size is 1847.53K
Number of Inbox rules is 3
```

GRAPHING USE   After analyzing average user messaging traffic with the Storstat utility, you can better calculate messaging use with LoadSim. Rather than creating a report based solely on averages, LoadSim works on the basis of ninety-fifth percentile statistics. This means that when the LoadSim utility is expected to process a mail message in less than 2 seconds, it counts as successful only transactions that take 2 seconds or less to complete—if one transaction takes 3 seconds and a second transaction that takes 1 second, the first transaction is not counted, even though the two transactions together take an average of 2 seconds. This approach provides a more accurate picture of events.

The graphs LoadSim generates show the number of users per server based on the relative score of acceptable performance. This score is based on a series of predetermined acceptable response times based on the responses meeting the set criteria ninety-five percent of the time in typical user demand requests to an Exchange Server. The predetermined ninety-fifth percentile for acceptable responses to users for read transactions is 301 ms. Other ninety-fifth percentile ratings for responses are as follows: Send = 1,212 ms, Reply = 701 ms, Reply All = 822 ms, Forward = 962 ms, Move = 401 ms, and Delete = 411 ms.

LoadSim then uses a predetermined weighting factor, based on the number of times the function is performed during an average day, as a multiplier for these response times. The result is the score that is then used to determine the maximum number of users that a specific Exchange Server configuration can support. The greater the processing capacity of the server, the greater the tolerance of the score and the more users that can be added to the server.

LoadSim provides a good relative comparison of server configurations based on predetermined transaction numbers. By using the STORSTAT.EXE utility to calculate real user messaging transactions and fitting this information into one of the LoadSim models, a messaging administrator can estimate the number of users that can share a server. For a free utility with fixed values, LoadSim provides a good analysis of the demands on Exchange Server performance.

NOTE: The LOADSIM.EXE program is on the Exchange CD in the SUPPORT\LOADSIM directory and is accompanied by a LOADSIM.DOC installation and use document.

Bluecurve Dynameasure

A number of third-party utilities are available to analyze capacity and performance for a Windows NT environment. However, the program that currently provides the best analysis for Exchange Server is Dynameasure, from Bluecurve Software (**http://www.bluecurve.com**) Dynameasure provides graphs, charts, and reports similar to those LoadSim provides, but measurements are based on user-defined message sizes and other criteria, which provides significant flexibility for simulating actual user activities for a given server configuration.

LoadSim provides only four levels of input criteria comparison, measured for a fixed length of time using an offline Exchange prototype server. Dynameasure, on the other hand, allows user-defined input criteria based on dozens of variable options, as shown in Figure 13-7, that are measured for the time and duration defined by the user.

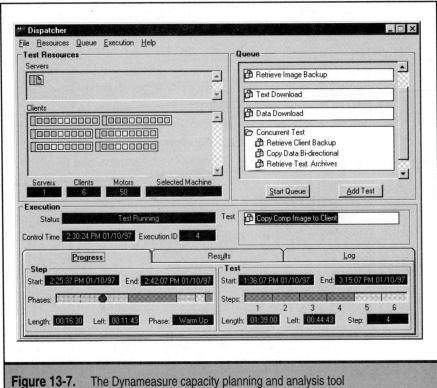

Figure 13-7.   The Dynameasure capacity planning and analysis tool

Dynameasure can be invoked on an existing Exchange Server in production use.

These advantages enable you to determine the characteristics of the organization's users and check these characteristics against the actual Exchange Server in the organization. Tests should be conducted in a controlled state, so you can put as much or as little load on the Exchange Server as you like. The tests should also be conducted in a nonproduction environment so the organization's day-to-day use of Exchange Server is not affected; however, performing tests on an existing server provides exact analysis of capacity and capabilities. Also, by performing tests at various times and for various durations, you can determine Exchange Server performance at different times of the day. Many utilities test a server over an extended period of time and average the results throughout time. However, in real life, system demands vary from morning to midday to afternoon, and

Dynameasure lets you analyze test results from these time periods to determine server impact.

During any server capacity analysis, the component being tested (in this case, Microsoft Exchange) should not be the only environment tested. Just as other processes (such as mainframe access, file and print access, and data warehouse interactions) can affect Exchange performance, the implementation and use of Exchange can affect other applications. Testing should include other demands on the network to ensure that the new messaging system does not negatively affect the performance of the rest of the environment.

Dynameasure analyzes and measures file and print access as well as SQL/database access on the network. This analysis can be conducted independently, or it can be conducted as part of the entire Exchange Server testing process. Figure 13-8 shows a graph that provides comparative information on an Exchange Server's CPU use, disk use, and network I/O.

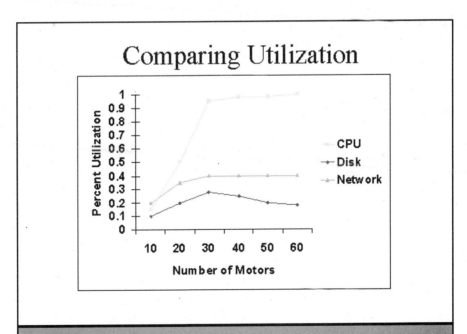

Figure 13-8.   A server performance graph based on Dynameasure analysis

Using the Performance Monitor for Capacity Planning

As an organization extends the services provided by the Exchange environment or adds users, you need to be able to determine whether an existing server is being overloaded or is running efficiently. You will need to answer such questions as why is the network running so slowly, why do messages take so long to be sent and received, and why do users complain that messages never get through to the recipient. You will need to determine whether there is a bottleneck in the network, and if there is, where does it reside. Obvious bottlenecks include the server processor, memory, disk capacity, and network adapter, but Internet connections, mail relay servers, WAN connections, third-party add-in applications, and so on can also be bottlenecks.

As described in Chapter 8, the Performance Monitor utility (PERFMON.EXE) is built into Windows NT. In addition to the performance tests outlined throughout this book, the Performance Monitor provides testing counters specific to Exchange Server:

▼ **MSExchangeDB: Log Byte Writes per Second** This counter indicates the rate that data is written to the log files on the server, or the linear information processing capabilities of the Exchange environment. If the number of log bytes increases during the day, this indicates that more information is being processed by the server. This statistic is used to identify the peak communication times for the Exchange Server, and this information can then be used in reviewing the Log Sessions Waiting object to determine if a bottleneck exists during peak transaction periods.

■ **MSExchangeDB: Log Sessions Waiting** This counter indicates the number of sessions waiting for log commit so a transaction can be completed. Whereas the Log Byte Writes per Second value reflects the log writing capability of the Exchange Server, Log Sessions Waiting reflects the server capacity. The Log Sessions Waiting counter should be 0 for a server that has plenty of bandwidth to handle transaction requests; however, in busy server environments, this number will be greater than 0. When log sessions are waiting, the server does not have enough capacity to manage the transactions being requested. If the Log Sessions Waiting value is greater than 2 for more than 50 percent of the active operations of the server, server performance is not adequate. If this occurs often, a faster server processor, hard disk subsystem, or LAN or WAN I/O is needed. By reviewing the individual Performance Monitor statistics for server processor, disk I/O, LAN or WAN I/O, and RAM use, you can determine which of these individual components may be the bottleneck on the server.

■ **MSExchangeMTA: MTA Queue Is Backlogged**   Since the MTA manages messages to other Exchange Servers and external message sources such as the Internet, if the MTA queue is backlogged, external communication processing is overloaded. As with the Log Sessions Waiting object, the MTA queue is optimized at 0, where no transactions are queued and waiting to be processed. You should be concerned if the value of this object exceeds 0 for more than just a few minutes and never clears to 0 over an extended period. By assessing the status of other queues such as those for the Internet Mail Server, MS-Mail Connector, and cc:Mail Connector, you can track performance bottlenecks for external communications to a specific connector or series of connectors in the organization.

▲ **MSExchangeIS: Private Information Store or Public Information Store Are Backlogged**   When the private or public information stores are backlogged, message delivery processing for individual user mailboxes or shared public folders is overloaded. This state can be caused by several factors: For the private information store object, a large number of users may be accessing the Exchange private information store, the messages being read or written by users may be large, or many messages may be being distributed between users. For the public store object, the organization may be using document management or document routing software, or it is using an Exchange Server as an intranet where large datasets are being managed and manipulated. Again, both of these numbers should ideally be 0, and they definitely should not remain above 0 for an extended period of time. If they remain greater than 0 throughout a day, hardware I/O components such as the processor, disk capacity, RAM use, and network I/O should be evaluated to determine what needs to be upgraded to keep these values at 0.

When reviewing and analyzing Performance Monitor statistics for Exchange, don't expect them to tell you exactly where the problem resides. The statistics gathered from the Performance Monitor objects will tell you only that a problem exists. You must then use these Performance Monitor components to identify the object that is the root of the problem. In most cases, problems occur because of improperly configured or tuned hardware components (such as improperly configured drives, caching, and LAN adapters) that affect performance in the Exchange Server environment. When properly used, the Performance Monitor can alert you to impending problems in Exchange or other related server components.

Planning for Additional Load on an Existing Server

You also need to analyze what an increase in the number of users or a change in server function demands will do to the performance of the environment. The goal is to determine the current performance of the server and the expected growth of the organization and then model this growth to determine whether the server will be sufficient or additional servers will be needed

Collecting Baseline Data

You need baseline data to perform comparative analysis of the environment. In an Exchange Server environment, you should collect baseline statistics on server processor use, server RAM use, network LAN and WAN bandwidth use, number of messages sent and received by users at the site, and gateway and connector traffic.

Start by creating a baseline standard for the working environment at different times of the day since loads may vary from morning to midday to evening. Then assess server performance for various levels of system capacity during these different time periods and at different times of the day, week, and month. Then if a problem occurs in the network, you can run a performance analysis on the system and compare the current performance with the baseline.

You should not simply collect baseline information once and then file it away for any future system comparison. Instead, you should periodically collect new baseline statistics to ensure that the data includes any changes and updates and reflects the current status of the network. For example, if users are added to the network, the baseline needs to be changed. Similarly, adding new applications or services to the network, such as Internet connectivity, software, network faxing, remote network access, or enhanced WAN connectivity capabilities, affects network performance, and new baseline statistics should be collected.

Modeling Performance Requirements

With up-to-date baseline information in place, you can model and project with relative accuracy the affects of any future changes in the environment. For example, suppose that an organization has added 20 new users to the network twice before, and that each time performance measurements have been taken to establish a new baseline. In the future, when the organization wants to add 20 more users to the network, the historical data from the previous additions can be analyzed. If the addition of 20 users has decreased network performance by 3 percent each time, you can estimate that another addition of 20 users will also decrease network performance by approximately 3 percent, assuming that other factors remain constant.

However, you should not rely solely on this estimation if you want to maintain Microsoft Exchange Server performance. You also need to actually model performance. First, be sure you have baseline data on current system performance. Next, determine the expected increase in demand or growth on the network. Finally, set up a performance modeling utility such as LoadSim or Bluecurve's Dynameasure to model the additional load. The utility will be better able to determine the effects of the new load on the capacity and capabilities of the environment.

USING REPLICATION TO MINIMIZE COMMUNICATION TRAFFIC

In many Exchange environment configurations, you may not need to constantly upgrade servers, LAN connections, and WAN router links to maintain the performance capability of the environment. Instead of tuning and upgrading servers to handle message workloads, you can use strategies that extend the existing infrastructure to handle the increased demands. These strategies include implementing replication services from server to server and using public folders for centralized message storage.

Fundamentals of Replication Services

As organizations begin to deploy public folder shares, share schedules, and electronically route information throughout the organization, the need to communicate outside of a single Microsoft Exchange Server to other Exchange Servers in different business units becomes extremely critical. Microsoft Exchange provides a mechanism for replicating selected information from one server to another.

The replication information can be anything from a single folder to the entire public folder structure of the entire organization. What you replicate depends on whether users at other Exchange Servers or different sites need to access the shared information. For example, if an organization stores only corporate policies, marketing documents, and global client information in public folders, the entire public folder structure can be shared; this type of information is valuable to all members of the organization and should be readily available to everyone, regardless of where various employees are located.

However, if an organization divides its public information storage into global information and regional information, it may have some folders that can be replicated throughout the organization and other folders that have local business information that should not be replicated. In this case, the organization should designate for replication only those folders that have global corporate information and leave the rest of the folders locally accessible without replicating them to other sites.

Site-to-Site Replication

After you determine what information to store and what information to replicate to other sites, you need to configure your Microsoft Exchange Servers to replicate the required information, set up a security system to prevent users from accidentally or purposely deleting or modifying information, and manage the information that is replicated throughout the organization.

The Microsoft Exchange Server lets the Exchange administrator identify which folders should be replicated on other Exchange Servers and how often the information should be replicated. During the replication process, the Exchange Servers communicate with each other and compare the information to be replicated. The servers then determine which information is not identical and needs to be copied. Information may differ because something was added or deleted in the folder being replicated or the content of a message or object within the folder was modified. The Exchange Servers then determine what information needs to be sent and what information needs to be received between the two servers and begin the process of updating files, objects, and stored information.

The replication process can be configured to run continuously throughout the day whenever information changes and requires updating, or it can be performed at a specific time (or times) during the day. You will need to consider the trade-off between information that is always up-to-date and the impact of continuous updating on server performance. To keep information identical between sites, you need to implement continuous replication, but this replication may use 10 to 15 percent of the server's available processing bandwidth. Many organizations instead choose to replicate information between sites periodically throughout the day based on the organization's need for current information. You should run baseline comparisons with and without replication activated to determine the effects of replication on your server's capacity.

In determining the frequency of replication, you will need to weigh the bandwidth capability available to the Exchange Servers against the importance of having updated information on both servers. If an organization requires up-to-date information all the time, but the Exchange Server updates information only once a night, users may be using information that is an entire day old and of little value. Such an organization may want to update information hourly, for example. However, if the Exchange Servers are connected by an old and very slow 19.2K data line, a full replication process may tie up the entire bandwidth of the line, leaving no available bandwidth for other business purposes.

Maintaining Replicated Information

Once information has been replicated, you need to determine how it should be maintained. If the information is relatively static, like company policies or procedures, it may need to be reviewed once a quarter or once a year. However, if the information needs to be updated weekly or monthly, like company marketing or product information, then the old information will need to be deleted so it is not accidentally used or accessed (or unnecessarily taking up disk storage space). The information can then be updated on the server.

OPTIMIZING SERVER PERFORMANCE THROUGH ONGOING MAINTENANCE

You know that defragmenting hard drives and compressing files improves information access on a workstation or in a general database environment. These same steps can be used to improve the performance of Microsoft Exchange since the Exchange Server is nothing more than a database of messages. Exchange Server automatically compacts and defragments its databases. However, there are different levels of tuning that you should know about. In the following discussions, note that IS maintenance and compaction are automated server maintenance operations, and defragmentation is a manual server maintenance process.

IS Maintenance

Information systems maintenance is the automatic tuning of the Exchange Server's information store. This tuning takes place between 1:00 A.M. and 6:00 A.M.

IS maintenance includes the following operations:

▼ **Tombstone compression**   When a message is deleted by all users on the Exchange Server and no longer needs to be stored, the message is automatically eliminated from the Exchange Server. However, a hole still exists where the message used to reside. Tombstone compression fills in the hole with other active messages, leaving the end of the Exchange message store as free storage space for new messages.

■ **Index aging**   Index aging maintains the indexes created by users when they have different views of the information in a message store. There is always a default view that users see when they access a folder. However, different views of the information stored in a folder can be created on users' screens. An index is created for each view created by users and then stored on the Exchange Server. The indexes are maintained on the server as long as users access the different views, but if the indexes are not used, they are deleted from the system to free up disk space on the server.

▲ **Message expiration management**   The message database is cleaned up automatically based on the expiration dates. By default, the message database is cleaned up on a nightly basis.

Compaction

Compaction is the online defragmentation and reclamation of unused disk storage space. As shown in Figure 13-9, Exchange directory compaction is managed by the Garbage Collection Interval setting on

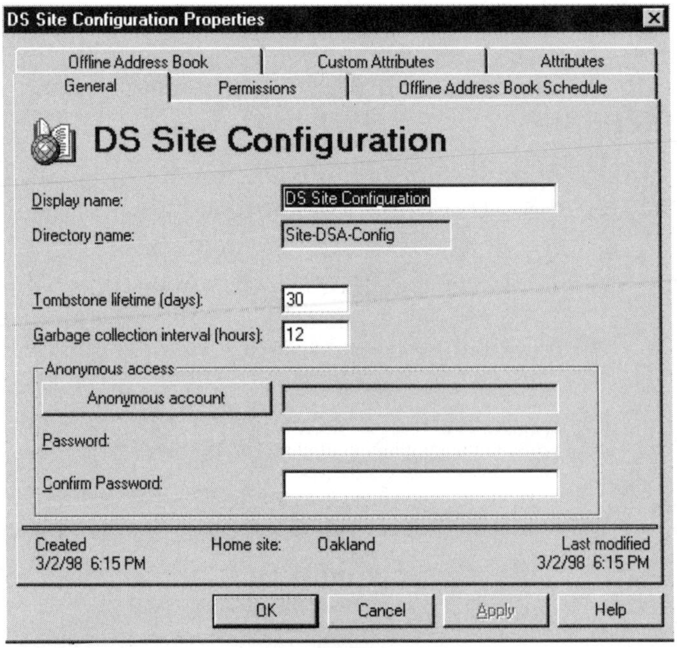

Figure 13-9. Exchange Administrator's Garbage Collection Interval setting for compaction

the General tab of the DS Site Configuration Properties page of the Exchange Administrator utility. The garbage collection interval is the interval after which expired tombstones are permanently deleted. After this deletion, the directory is defragmented, with open spaces in the message databases filled in with other messages. However, the size of the Exchange Server message database is not changed, and any unused space is marked as available for use. The only way to compact, defragment, and compress the message store database is through an offline compression operation called *defragmentation*.

Defragmentation

Defragmentation in Exchange refers to offline defragmentation of the Exchange message information stores. Offline defragmentation is more efficient than online defragmentation since the process has full access and full server bandwidth for managing the information store. During offline defragmentation, the Exchange services need to be stopped and the utilities run from a DOS or command prompt. In Exchange versions 4.0 and 5.0, the utility is called EDBUTIL.EXE, and in Exchange version 5.5, it is called ESEUTIL.EXE. During offline defragmentation, all expired tombstones are deleted, open spaces within the database are filled with messages compressed within the message store, and excess message database storage space is released, thus decreasing the size of the information store databases.

OPTIMIZING THE EXCHANGE CLIENT

We have reviewed the optimization capabilities of the server component of the Microsoft Exchange Server configuration. Now we will look at the client component in this client-server environment. In Microsoft Exchange, the client component is just as important as the server component. Whereas the server manages the messages and their transfer from server to server and from the server to the Internet or some other external destination, the client manages electronic forms, the filtering of message views, and the rich text viewing and display of Exchange messages.

Latest Release of the Client

Over the life of the Exchange Server product, there have been significant improvements in the client software used to access the Exchange Server software. The two main clients are the Exchange client and the Outlook client.

The Exchange client was the first-generation client software for Exchange. It supports DOS, 16-bit Windows, 32-bit Windows, and the Macintosh. The Exchange client is the client commonly found in Windows 95 (and also known as the Windows Messaging client). The Exchange client has separate programs for scheduling and an address book.

In mid-1997, Microsoft announced that new-generation systems would use the Outlook client. The Outlook client integrates messaging, calendaring, an address book, notes, journaling, and intranet capabilities in a single application. With the Outlook client, one program manages all electronic messaging and groupware functionality, facilitating cross-platform support by providing a single interface for multiple functions across multiple operating environments. Today, the Outlook client supports 16-bit Windows, 32-bit Windows, Macintosh, and web formats.

It is important to maintain the latest release of the Exchange or Outlook client to ensure the best performance of the client software. Since the client software provides 50 percent of the client-server functionality of Exchange, client performance is crucial to the overall user access to the system. The latest releases of the clients for Exchange are listed at the Microsoft Exchange Web site (**http://www.microsoft.com/exchange**) and frequently are downloadable (although some of the client updates require that an existing version reside on the hard drive of the system being upgraded).

Client Hardware Configuration

The client hardware is important in the client interaction with Exchange. Although the basic functions of Exchange can be run on low-performance web-based terminals, the full groupware capabilities of Exchange typically require a Windows 32-bit workstation or Apple Macintosh computer with 16MB or more of memory and at least 50MB of free disk space. The increased performance of the client system is needed since functions such as message sorting, filtering, and message management occur on the client system, not on the Exchange Server.

Using NetBIOS Names

Frequently overlooked in performance analyses of the Exchange environment is the effect of using Windows NetBIOS names to resolve client and server names. The Exchange client uses NetBIOS names to find the Exchange Server. Thus, if an organization uses TCP/IP as its sole communications protocol, the NetBIOS name needs to be resolved using a TCP/IP-compatible lookup process so the Exchange client can find the Exchange Server. Today, this process is handled by the Windows Internet Naming Server (WINS), Domain Name Service (DNS), or a static file on the client called the LMHOST file.

On a congested network, if a client needs to resolve a name with a LAN- or WAN-based WINS or DNS server, the client may take a long time to find and connect to the Exchange Server. If it takes a long time for a client to authenticate and access the Exchange Server, you should perform a test to determine how long the client is taking to resolve the NetBIOS name over the network. This can be accomplished through the use of built-in Windows tools such as PING.EXE, TRACERT.EXE, and NBTUTIL.EXE.

Using PST Instead of the Information Store

Many organizations that want to reduce network traffic use local personal store files (or PST files) to manage messages with minimal impact on the Exchange Server itself. A PST file is a separate file typically stored on a user's local hard drive; messages are copied from the Exchange Server to the PST when the user accesses the Exchange Server. The advantage of a PST file is that all messages are transferred once from the Exchange Server to the PST file, and then any time the user wants to access the file, the request is managed locally (no demands are placed on the LAN, WAN, or Exchange Server).

While the PST method offloads demands external to the client, it also eliminates all administrative benefits that Exchange Server provides. With a non-PST-configured Exchange client, the administrator can put limits on the age and storage demands of the Exchange client, forcing Exchange users to perform periodic maintenance of their mailboxes. Exchange also does not normally depend on users to back up their own PST files on a regular basis, but in a PST-based environment, it is up to each user to maintain a backup process for messages—obviously not a desirable procedure in organizations that place backup and network maintenance responsibilities in the hands of IS personnel. The PST method also does not enable users to roam from station to station or from operating system to operating system. Messages reside only in the PST file at a user's workstation; if the user decides to work remotely or from another workstation, the PST file does not follow the user.

The PST file method offloads a significant amount of bandwidth and storage demands from the Exchange Server and infrastructure. However, it is commonly thought to place too many responsibilities on users and drastically limits an organization's ability to leverage the centralized management and mobile access functions of the Exchange Server product.

Remote Access Exchange

For organizations that have remote and mobile users, Microsoft Exchange provides functionality that improves system performance and user efficiency and makes the mobile functions of Exchange highly desirable. Microsoft Exchange for remote users is handled by the exact same client software used by LAN-based users; thus, no retraining of users is needed, and no special software needs to be purchased. Only one additional step is required to activate an Exchange user for remote access: the creation of a file called the *Offline Store* (or the OST file) that is a replica of the user's message information stored on the Exchange Server.

When a user dials into Microsoft Exchange, the user can choose to work offline, creating messages that are queued in the OST file. When the user synchronizes offline and online messages, any messages stored in the offline queue are sent to the Exchange Server, and any messages waiting for the user on the Exchange Server are copied to the user's offline store file. The Exchange Server is automatically updated with any modifications or changes the user makes to the offline store file. Thus, if messages are deleted, moved, or edited, the changes are reflected on the Exchange Server after synchronization. If the user logs onto the network on the LAN, because all messages were synchronized offline from the remote system, the LAN-connected user sees the state of all messages just as if the user were working online. Changes are forwarded, updated, modified, and replicated across all platforms.

A common use of Microsoft Exchange's remote access function, beyond its use by traveling users, is to improve performance at remote sites that have limited WAN bandwidth to a centralized Exchange Server. Rather than installing an Exchange Server at every single site or connecting users full time over a slow 19.2K line, an organization can implement offline stores so users' messages are created and queued on their local hard drives. Users can then synchronize their message boxes, and outbound messages are sent to the Exchange Server, and inbound messages are retrieved to the client. This approach allows the use of Exchange in environments with limited bandwidth.

CONCLUSION

Optimizing a Microsoft Exchange Server environment is not much different from optimizing performance in a standard Microsoft Windows NT environment. The tools used to tune and optimize the two environments are similar. In addition, subcomponents of the tools and utilities provide analyses, baselining, tuning, and management functions specific to the electronic messaging components within Exchange.

It is crucial that you analyze capacity and project performance demands when implementing Microsoft Exchange. Few products place as many demands on the entire Windows NT infrastructure as electronic messaging. Exchange provides the messaging services many businesses now consider critical, from simple electronic mail messages to group calendar management. The new groupware capabilities that Exchange and third-party Exchange add-ins provide, such as voicemail integration, document routing, document imaging, and Internet connectivity, require client-server communications, transfer and storage of large files, and mobile computing—all of which stress the NT infrastructure more than ever before.

CHAPTER 14

Getting the Most Out of Systems Management Server

Systems Management Server (SMS) is an extremely complex and powerful management utility that can be used for tracking hardware and software inventory, troubleshooting, system diagnostics, software distribution, and much more. SMS is so complex that it requires careful planning and maintenance for successful implementation in any environment, large or small. For instance, even small SMS environments require a hierarchical structure to support the various servers in the SMS infrastructure.

Equally important, SMS must be tuned to suit the needs and functional requirements for each environment. If any SMS performance issue is ignored, it can not only affect the SMS servers' performance but can also drastically affect network and client performance.

This chapter is dedicated to providing sound recommendations in the areas that will have the largest impact on SMS and overall environment performance. These issues include, but are not limited to, planning and initial configuration, hardware considerations, and tuning-specific functionality.

PLANNING AND OPTIMIZING SITE STRUCTURE

The sheer complexity of SMS warrants considerable planning and testing before it is implemented in a production environment. Careful planning of the SMS structure and responsibilities will reduce the risks of degrading both your environment's efficiency and the quality of service. Before you attempt to determine hardware resource requirements, you must be completely familiar with the following:

▼ The functional role of SMS in the environment (inventory, software distribution, remote diagnostics, or any combination of these services)

■ The anticipated number and location of servers comprising the SMS hierarchy

■ The number of supported clients

▲ The existing Windows NT infrastructure

Figure 14-1 illustrates a sample site structure that will help you understand the SMS organization. The servers that comprise an SMS site and their functional roles in the environment are listed in Table 14-1.

SMS capacity planning should be a primary concern. Take advantage of the capacity planning procedures examined and

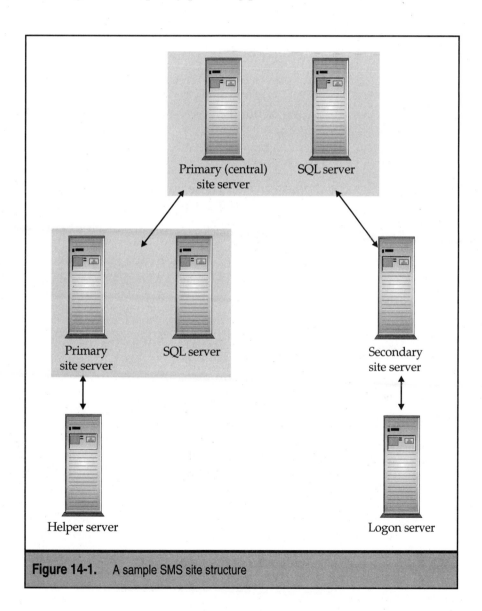

Figure 14-1. A sample SMS site structure

Server Type	Functional Role in an SMS Site
Primary site server	Manages the SMS site and any existing subsites; must have a SQL Server database to store system, job, inventory, and status information; serves as primary logon server.
Secondary site server	Same functionality as the Primary site server except for two cases: 1. It passes information to the Primary site server above it in the hierarchy because it does not have its own SQL Server database. 2. It has limited ability to manage the site (i.e., it relies on the Primary site server for management).
SQL Server	Contains the SMS data device, database, log device, and data log.
Helper server	As the name implies, the helper server is used to reduce the workload of a site server by taking on some of the SMS services. These include the Despooler, Inventory Data Loader, Inventory Processing, and the Scheduler.
Logon server	Authenticates users; provides logon scripts; temporarily stores client inventory files until the site server can request them and later process the files; minimizes communication between client machines and site servers.

Table 14-1. SMS Server Types and Their Respective Functional Roles in the Environment

outlined in Chapter 2 because they can be immensely beneficial during the SMS planning stages. By using the important decision-making techniques from Chapter 2, proper planning and optimizing of site configurations can help you tame SMS and manage the environment more efficiently.

Considerations for SQL Server Planning and Optimization

SMS relies heavily on SQL Server for maintaining management information such as inventory, jobs, and other operations. SQL Server must be installed and configured for SMS before you can even begin installing SMS. As part of your SMS planning, refer to Chapter 12 for ways to boost SQL Server performance.

In addition to the SQL Server tuning recommendations made in Chapter 12, there are several other SQL Server and SMS tuning options available. These include configuring a dedicated SQL Server, device and database size, and using SQL Server scripts.

Segment SQL Server and SMS

Both SMS and SQL Server are resource-intensive servers, requiring considerable amounts of memory, processing power, and disk space for optimal performance. Ideally, SQL Server should have its own machine, dedicated to SMS functionality, to minimize resource contention and improve performance. This is especially true in large environments of several thousand or more clients. Moreover, a SQL Server may already exist in the environment, and if so you will want to adapt it for SMS.

If you must use a single machine for both SMS and SQL Server, it is imperative that you configure the machine with the proper amount of hardware. For example, a minimum recommended hardware configuration running both SMS and SQL Server is the following:

▼ 96MB of RAM (32MB for each: Windows NT, SQL Server, and SMS)

■ 2GB of disk space

▲ Dual Pentium processor

It is important to note those are the minimum recommendations. Depending upon the number of client machines to be supported, these minimums may not be adequate for optimal performance.

Device and Database Sizing

An SMS database requires a corresponding transaction log on the SQL Server device. This transaction log is primarily used by SMS for logging queries and executions against the SMS database. Proper sizing of the SMS database and transaction log is key to achieving and maintaining optimal performance. If these components reach capacity, unpredictable results could occur and cause SMS to become unstable.

Proven planning methods can help you more accurately set the database size. To begin with, you must have a good approximation of the number of client machines to be supported by SMS, because these numbers influence the database size. More specifically, the SMS database contains information updated by a Management Information File (MIF) for each client machine, which is loaded, when the client logs on for the first time.

Starting with a minimum of 20MB, size the initial capacity of the SMS device and database. Then add the expected number of client machines to be supported by SMS. The client machine information updated by a MIF will each take approximately 35KB of space. Therefore, an SMS database that will support 100 client machines (20MB + (35KB × 100 client machines)) will need to be at least 24MB.

NOTE: The above calculation does not factor in the number of packages (jobs) or other information that may be stored in the database. Consequently, it is recommended that you supply the device and database with at least an extra 10 percent capacity.

Using the size of the SMS device and database as a baseline, calculate the initial size of the transaction log file and device. Typically, the size of the transaction log file and device is 15 percent of the SMS database. For example, if the size of the SMS database is 60MB, then set the initial size of the transaction log file and device to 9MB.

TEMPDB is the last device and database configuration to affect SMS and SQL Server performance. As mentioned in Chapter 12, TEMPDB is used to temporarily store the results of queries. Allocate

25 percent of the SMS database for the TEMPDB database device and 20 percent for the TEMPDB log device.

> **NOTE:**   Placing TEMPDB in RAM will not provide a noticeable performance improvement. In fact, it may cause SQL Server to consume more memory and slow performance. Refer to Chapter 12 for more information regarding TEMPDB in RAM.

Adjusting the Server Load

In addition to keeping SMS and SQL Server on separate machines, consider distributing the functions of each SMS system. The primary site server has the most responsibility within the SMS site structure, and should run only those services needed by SMS. In other words, place services, such as file and print sharing, printing, and so on with other servers.

Enlist Help

You can further enhance a site's performance by offloading some of a site server's responsibility to a helper server. A helper server is designed to do exactly what the name implies; help out the SMS site servers by taking on several specific tasks or services.

However, the helper server is limited to the number of services it can accept, including the Despooler, Inventory Data Loader, Inventory Processing, and the Scheduler as shown in Figure 14-2. By adjusting the workload of an SMS site server, you minimize the resource requirements of the site server and improve overall efficiency of the site structure. The SMS site server will no longer have the responsibility of running senders, processing MIF files, or accessing SQL Server for inventory purposes.

Network Considerations

Whether SMS is communicating with other servers in the SMS site structure, performing logon processes, or being used for remote diagnostics, it depends on the network to gather and push

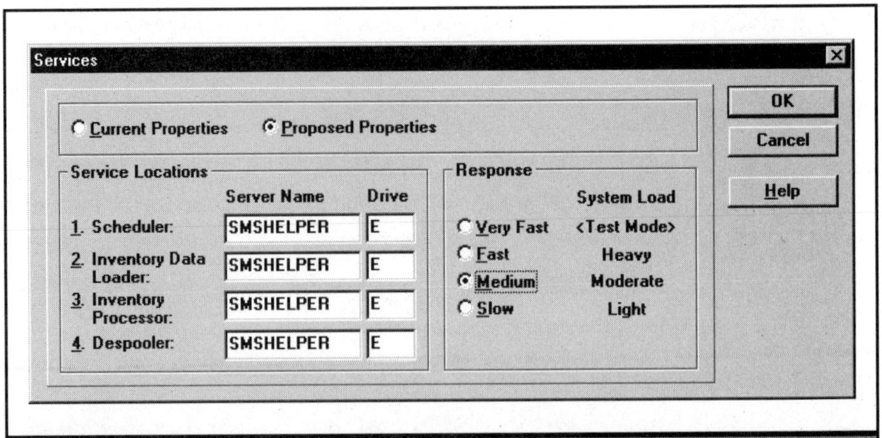

Figure 14-2. Offloading specific services from a site server to a helper server

information to or from the client machines. Exactly how much of the network SMS uses depends primarily on the network topology, the number of SMS clients, and the frequency of performing SMS-related functions such as inventory and software distribution.

SMS has a utility called Network Monitor, shown in Figure 14-3, used for monitoring the effects SMS has on the network. This utility is a more full-featured version than the one bundled with Windows NT Server. Among other things, it is not confined to only monitoring traffic on the host machine. Instead, the SMS version of Network Monitor can be used to monitor the entire network segment.

Some networks may be close to reaching a saturation point with the amount of traffic being generated while others are running optimally, servicing the Windows NT environment in the fastest, most efficient way possible. In either case, an improperly planned SMS installation can wreak havoc on the network infrastructure with the sheer amount of network-related traffic it can easily generate. This section shows you a variety of ways to reduce the impact SMS has on your network. You may want to refer to Chapter 5 for more information regarding network performance.

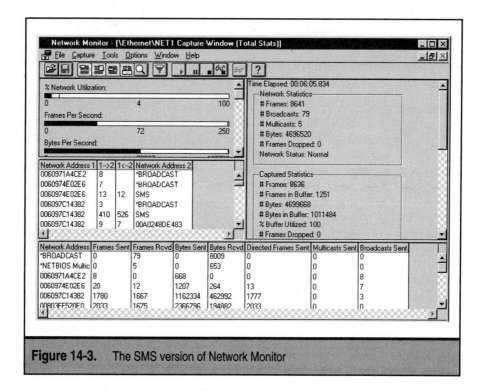

Figure 14-3.   The SMS version of Network Monitor

Minimize Available Bandwidth

Once a job has been defined and scheduled, the job, depending on the SMS site structure, must transfer the information to other sites in the hierarchy. An uncontrolled job traversing the network can potentially impact network performance depending on:

▼ The package size

■ The frequency of defining jobs

■ The number of sites receiving the job

▲ Network segment bandwidth

To minimize the impact a job or jobs have on network segments, you must control the amount of available bandwidth the sender uses.

Use the Sender Manager to control the amount of available bandwidth at specified times of the day, reduce the number of concurrent connections, and lower the total number of retries to be performed. For instance, during normal business hours you can allow the sender only 40 percent available bandwidth for jobs and specify only three concurrent connections to three sites. You may specify higher available bandwidth and more concurrent connections during after-hours, because network utilization is much lower.

Segment the Network

Rarely will you find an NT environment where the administrators simultaneously plan a network infrastructure while planning an SMS site installation. Instead, it is more common to find companies planning to integrate an SMS site with the existing network structure. If you do not carefully plan the SMS site integration, you could potentially slow performance rather than reap the benefits promised by SMS.

The importance of segmenting the network was originally examined in Chapter 5, and the same holds true for an SMS site structure. Adding SMS generated traffic to already existing network traffic can potentially cause network-related bottlenecks. You can help to reduce the overhead of SMS generated network traffic by physically segmenting the network with routers and subnets.

SMS and RAS

While users may primarily connect to a network via a LAN, many Windows NT environments are not limited to this configuration. Users can also connect to the network through Remote Access Service (RAS) when they are out on the road or dialing in from home. The connection speed is slow at best (14.4-, 28.8-, 33.6-, or 56-bps), especially when compared to LAN speeds. As a result, it is important to note any effects that the link speed may have on SMS-related functions, such as hardware and software inventory, software distribution, and remote diagnostics.

When SMS clients log on to the network, they process a logon script containing an SMS batch file (SMSLS.BAT) to request inventory or other related SMS functions. Unfortunately, for those logging on remotely through RAS this presents some serious complications. For instance, the connection's bandwidth is easily saturated due to the amount of communication occurring between the client and server. This, in turn, can cause the client to wait tremendously long periods of time before beginning any specific tasks, such as checking e-mail.

The most obvious solution for clients using RAS is to bypass the script entirely and avoid any SMS logon processing. The key to this solution is to detect the RAS client before attempting to disable the SMS logon processes. You can use a BackOffice Resource Kit utility called RAS Connection Checker (CHECKRAS.EXE) to determine whether or not the client is connecting to the network through RAS.

Within the logon script execute the CHECKRAS before any SMS configurations to indicate whether or not to run the SMS logon process. When client machines log on, CHECKRAS is executed and returns one of the following codes:

▼ 0 No RAS connections

▲ 1 One or more RAS connections

If CHECKRAS returns a 0, some or all of the SMS logon processes can be skipped, allowing immediate access to the network. Otherwise, the client is not connecting through RAS and can communicate directly with SMS. For example, the following code can be inserted into the logon script to detect a RAS connection and disable SMS logon processes:

```
:CHECKRAS
CHECKRAS > nul
 if errorlevel 1 goto END
REM Run SMS Logon Processes
NET USE S: /DEL /Y
NET USE S:\\SMS_SERVER\SMS_SHR
```

```
CALL S:\RUNSMS.BAT
NET USE S: /DEL /Y
    .
    .
    .
: END
```

Another option for detecting clients connecting through RAS is to create a batch file, which will automatically search for an SMS connection. The batch file will place another file on the machine before dialing in and then remove the file after disconnecting. This solution can be implemented with or without user intervention. The following is a sample logon script eliminating user intervention to run the batch file:

```
@ECHO OFF
ECHO.
ECHO.
ECHO Company Name, Inc.
ECHO.
ECHO.
REM Check for Remote Connection
IF EXIST C:\REMOTE.TXT GOTO : END

REM Run SMS Logon Processes
NET USE S: /DEL /Y
NET USE S: \\SMS_SERVER\SMS_SHR
CALL S:\RUNSMS.BAT
NET USE S: /DEL /Y
: END

EXIT
```

Rolling Out SMS

Another effective way of planning and optimizing an SMS site configuration is to build a mock site and vigorously test it against your Windows NT environment. Microsoft recommends this lab testing approach and supplies a planning whitepaper, which includes detailed procedures for configuring a test environment. You can find it at **http://www.microsoft.com/smsmgmt/**.

If configuring an entirely separate SMS test environment is an affordable option, the benefits you gain will be tremendous. You can save enormous amounts of time and money in the long run by testing a variety of configuration and performance scenarios so that you avoid a frustrating SMS implementation.

If a separate test environment is not an option, try a pilot program approach where you start small and gradually add to the SMS site structure until most of the kinks are ironed out. You can then add to the site by department, by building, or by gradually converting a small number of client machines to SMS machines until the entire environment is part of the SMS site structure.

OPTIMIZING HARDWARE CONFIGURATIONS

An SMS environment may be limited to the following server configurations: a primary site, a secondary site, and the helper servers. Depending on the size of the network and the respective machines' raw power, you may have anywhere from one to several different SMS servers supporting the SMS site structure and client base. Optimizing the hardware configurations will not be difficult if you carefully plan and optimize site configuration and roughly estimate the number of clients SMS will be supporting.

Each major system component (memory, processor, disk subsystem, and network subsystem) plays a critical role in determining SMS' efficiency and ability to adequately support the site structure. Consequently, when you are configuring SMS servers it is extremely important to invest in the highest quality hardware you can afford for optimal performance.

Memory

On almost all Windows NT Servers, the amount and type of memory is vital to performance. Adding SMS to the configuration places even more importance on memory requirements because it, too, tends to devour memory. SMS server types influence the memory requirements because there are different active services for each configuration. The minimum memory requirement is 24MB (although 32MB minimum is recommended) in addition to the Windows NT memory requirements. Table 14-2 lists the memory requirements needed by each server type to adequately run SMS services.

NOTE: The memory requirements in Table 14-2 are for SMS services only. They do not include other services running on the server nor do they account for other SMS functionality, such as running the SMS Administrator.

Optimal memory configuration begins with 64MB, but minimum memory requirements can quickly multiply as the size of the SMS site increases. Keep in mind, these minimum memory requirements do not apply if SMS and SQL Server are on the same machine.

Processor

Microsoft's minimum processor requirement for an SMS system is a 486 DX2/66. SMS will indeed run on this processor, but be prepared for lengthy waits when using SMS. As a general rule of thumb, even small to medium sized sites should operate with a Pentium class or higher processor.

Server Type	Memory Required by SMS Services (in MB)
Primary site server	19
Secondary site server	16
Logon server	8

Table 14-2.   Memory Requirements for SMS Services on Different Server Configurations

Disk Subsystem

The disk subsystem requires balance between the fastest possible configuration and an adequate, fault-tolerant solution. Minimizing disaster is just as important if not more important than data transfer speeds. For example, if a fault-tolerant disk subsystem solution is not implemented and the primary site server crashes, it will be extremely difficult and time-consuming to rebuild SMS.

The disk subsystem is one of the slowest system components. In this regard, it easily fits the definition of a bottleneck, and can adversely affect all other main system components if not configured properly. To prevent the disk subsystem from slowing the server down any more than necessary, invest in a hardware-based RAID solution. This will ease the processor's burden of servicing I/O requests as well as give you more flexibility with configuration and fault tolerance. Although you have the option of using a software-based RAID solution, hardware RAID gives you the better end result of faster performance.

The type of RAID solution you choose can have a significant effect on SMS performance. If you choose to use RAID 0 (striping without parity) for its simplicity and extremely fast transfer rates, make sure you implement a solid backup scheme, because there is no inherent fault tolerance. The recommended alternative to RAID 0 is RAID 5 (striping with parity) because it offers exceptional performance and fault tolerance. Refer to Chapter 6 for more information on the disk subsystem and related topics.

Network Subsystem

As mentioned earlier in the Network Considerations section, the network subsystem performance directly impacts how fast SMS servers communicate with each other and how fast clients can be serviced. This performance impact is most important when the site is first established and when clients log on for the first time. Typically, one to four megabytes of data are transferred between SMS and client machines logging on for the first time.

To prevent SMS generated traffic from overwhelming or consuming the network bandwidth, place the SMS servers on a 100

Mbps or greater network segment. Though this may not be feasible for some environments because of the cost factors involved. Review other recommendations in the "Network Considerations" section, and in Chapter 5, to prevent network overload due to client/server generated traffic.

TUNING SMS CONFIGURATION PARAMETERS

The size and complexity of SMS warrants a large number of configuration parameters. However, the default values for SMS are not always the best settings to optimally run your specific environment.

Although there are many tuning configuration parameters, the ones examined in this section can offer the most significant improvements in performance.

Tuning the SMS Administrator

The SMS Administrator utility, shown in Figure 14-4, is one of the most important and most frequently used tools in the SMS arsenal. It allows you to perform various management duties including remote diagnostics and site configuration. On the other hand, the SMS Administrator is an extremely demanding resource, using approximately 4MB of RAM and almost 40MB of disk space all by itself. As if that were not enough, SMS Administrator requires more memory to operate as more client machines, each consuming 726 bytes, are added to the site. For instance, running SMS Administrator with a site that has 1000 SMS client machines would require ((4 + 1000 (726 bytes)) which roughly translates to 5MB just to run the application.

Remember, the above calculation is useful simply for determining the base amount of memory needed by SMS Administrator to run the client machines, not necessarily for performing any operations. Depending on the number of client machines and the operation being performed, the SMS Administrator can potentially consume a

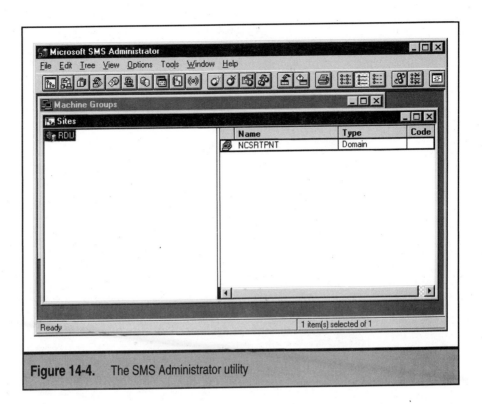

Figure 14-4.   The SMS Administrator utility

substantial amount of RAM. As a result, you should avoid running the SMS Administrator on site servers, especially those servers already burdened with heavy workloads. One option would be to install the SMS Administrator on a separate Windows NT machine to offload some of the responsibility of the SMS site servers.

Optimizing Site Properties

The Site Properties dialog box, shown in Figure 14-5, may be the last place you would look to fine-tune SMS, but it can influence site performance with regards to the service response intervals. The settings available for your site's response interval are very simple: Slow, Fast, and Very Fast. At first glance, you may suspect the Very Fast setting would automatically make the site scream with speed.

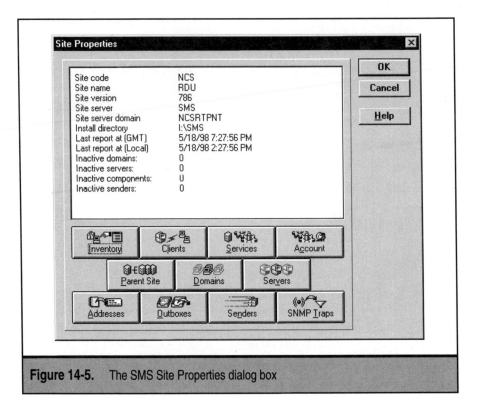

Figure 14-5.   The SMS Site Properties dialog box

Unfortunately, the frequency setting for polling SMS services does not necessarily translate into faster performance. In fact, the higher the frequency, the more stress is put on SMS to process the polling. On the other hand, setting the service response interval to Slow will reduce server workload, but may not service the site as promptly as you would like.

There is no right or wrong answer to setting the service response intervals, because it will depend on the size of your SMS site, the server's current workload, and the server's processing power. The key here is to strike a balance between the frequency of polling and the capacity of the server.

Optimizing Logging

Logging is a very useful mechanism for troubleshooting SMS processes. However, it can also significantly slow overall system performance due to the processing overhead and space requirements, which need to be closely monitored.

When you initially install the SMS site in a test environment, and then finally in a production environment, keep logging enabled to help determine the cause of any problems that may arise. Depending on the site configuration and your comfort level, the longer you keep logging enabled the easier it will be to iron out problems and to analyze log files for troubleshooting purposes.

NOTE: Place the SMS log file on its own physical disk drive (not a logical partition) to minimize disk-related I/O.

You can also use the SMS Service Manager, shown in Figure 14-6, to enable or disable the tracing of each SMS service activity. Some of these SMS services are listed here:

▼ SMS_EXECUTIVE

■ SMS_HIERARCHY_MANAGER

■ SMS_INVENTORY_AGENT_NT

■ SMS_INVENTORY_DATA_LOADER

■ SMS_INVENTORY_PROCESSOR

■ SMS_LAN_SENDER

■ SMS_MAINTENANCE_MANAGER

▲ SMS_SCHEDULER

The tracing of each SMS service is enabled each time the service, or the server itself, is started and disabling through SMS Service

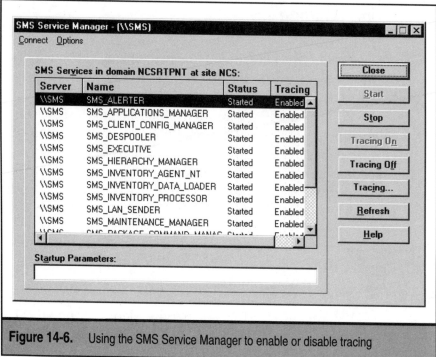

Figure 14-6. Using the SMS Service Manager to enable or disable tracing

Manager is only a temporary solution. To permanently disable tracing for individual services, do the following:

1. Open REGEDT32 either by typing **REGEDT32** at the command prompt or selecting it from the Start | Run menu.

2. Open the following key, as shown in Figure 14-7:

   HKEY_LOCAL_MACHINE\
     Software\
       Microsoft\
       SMS\
         Tracing\

3. Underneath the key specified above you will notice a subkey referencing each SMS service running on the server. Change the Enable parameter from 1 to 0 within the defining subkey to disable tracing of a particular service.

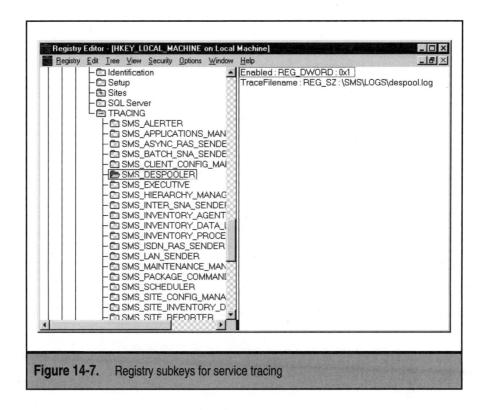

Figure 14-7.   Registry subkeys for service tracing

4. Close REGEDT32 and restart the SMS service using the Services applet within the Control Panel.

OPTIMIZING SMS MANAGEMENT FUNCTIONS

As mentioned earlier, SMS is an enterprise management solution often used for inventory, software distribution, and remote diagnostics. Fine-tuning the following support services will help SMS to operate more efficiently and better serve your environment.

Scheduling

Scheduling is the backbone for many SMS services, including inventory collections, software distributions, and more. This section will focus on Scheduler, which is the component responsible for monitoring and controlling SMS schedules, and how it may affect SMS performance and the overall Windows NT environment, and provide recommendations to optimize scheduling.

Scheduling Jobs

An essential part of distributing applications to client machines is scheduling job delivery. In an environment with less than 30 client machines scheduling may not impact performance as much as it would in medium to large environments. Nonetheless, no matter how large the site, knowing how many client machines to send the job and when to schedule the job are equally important.

Obviously, there are numerous factors to consider in deciding when and how to schedule jobs. These include the following:

▼ Number of client machines

■ Package size

■ Network bandwidth

▲ SMS site structure

Unfortunately, there is no clear answer as to when to schedule a job. Keep in mind that it is better to continuously send jobs to a small number of client machines over a sustained period of time. For example, for a site with 100 clients, schedule four jobs at different times of the day, each sending jobs to 25 clients. This is particularly important when you are simultaneously sending mandatory jobs to several SMS client machines, because the client does not have the option not to install the application.

CAUTION: Although scheduling jobs after normal business hours is an exceptional idea, do not rely on this technique entirely. You must also schedule jobs at different times, even during non-business hours, to avoid server and network congestion and contention.

The benefits to this approach are that SMS does not have as much information to process, which relieves stress on the processor, and the network's bandwidth is not overloaded. This improves the server's performance and minimizes the risk of traffic congestion on the network.

Scheduling Hardware and Software Inventories

Inventory collection is one of the most commonly used SMS functions. As each client logs on, this function gathers hardware and software client configuration information, such as whether or not the client has a package as well as other file and driver configurations. First-time client logons can potentially bottleneck SMS servers, the site's SQL Server, SMS client machines, and the network segment, because as much as 4MB of data is pushed to the client before hardware or software inventories are even started. Automatic execution of inventories for each new client machine is not part of the initial SMS configuration. However, if you do configure inventory to run immediately for any new client machine, it will place a larger burden on the network segment.

Client machines already integrated into the SMS site with hardware or software inventories will only propagate changes to their respective MIF files. It is still very important to control the number of inventories given to the client machines to reduce processing and bandwidth requirements.

When deciding the appropriate intervals to run hardware and software inventories, you should consider the following:

▼ The frequency of hardware or software changes on client machines

■ The space needed to store this information

▲ The frequency of updating the information

Generally speaking, the amount of hardware configuration changes a client machine may experience is minimal. Therefore, you should consider scheduling hardware inventories less frequently than software inventories.

NOTE: The default inventory frequency is once a week (every 7 days).

Scheduling hardware inventories every two weeks or once a month is usually suitable for most environments. While hardware inventories are not necessary every time the client logs on, or even every week, software inventories are usually needed more frequently. Changes to the client machine's software configuration could be as frequent as weekly or as infrequent as twice in one year. Of course, the frequency of changes depends entirely on your environment's policy and the user. The point of scheduling out the frequency of the software inventories is to minimize the impact on SMS.

AN ALTERNATIVE TO SOFTWARE INVENTORY   If you want a more comprehensive look at the actual software loaded on a client machine, use SMS' software audit feature. While the inventory agent runs software inventory, a software audit is performed from the client machine. Either AUDIT16.EXE or AUDIT32.EXE runs on the client with instructions coming from a rule file called AUDIT.RUL. Software auditing can be used to check application versions running on the client as well as locating defective driver versions.

Optimizing File Collection

As an administrative tool, SMS has the ability to collect specified files from client machines, such as file version information. If you plan to use file collection, you should devise a mechanism to delete the collected files once they are no longer needed. Information about the collected files is stored in the SMS database, but the actual file resides on the site server. Deleting the file from the site server will also purge the information from the SMS database.

CONTROLLING USER GROUP COLLECTION   SMS automatically collects the associated MIF file for all global user groups in every SMS domain and all trusted domains. As you can see, there is potential for accumulating a large number of user group MIF files. Some of these MIF files may also be duplicates, as in one for each site in the SMS domain.

Especially important for large sites, it is recommended that you reduce the MIF file collection frequency to reduce the distribution between sites and to minimize the workload for each SMS system responsible for distribution. To reduce or completely disable user group MIF file collection, use the Set Global User Groups (SETGUG.EXE).

Prevent Inventory Resynchronizations

A resynchronization is required when new inventory information does not coincide with current information existing in the database. To initiate a resynchronization, the Inventory Data Loader is responsible for creating an inventory command file called RESYNC.CFG (located in SITE.SRV\MAINCFG.BOX\ INVDOPSM.BOX\DOMAIN_X.000) from the resync command, and replicates it to all SMS logon servers in the SMS site. When the client logs on, it searches the RESYNC.CFG file for its SMS ID. If the SMS ID is found, the client sends a complete inventory, and the file is marked as a resync file. Both the client and the logon server keep track of the update so that another resynchronization is not performed.

As you can see, this generates more work for both the SMS systems and the client machine, not to mention increasing network traffic. A relatively few number of resynchronizations in an SMS site will have little or no impact on overall performance. For medium to large sites, however, numerous resynchronizations can significantly slow performance and may even bring the SMS site to its knees.

Unfortunately, SMS does not have any built-in mechanisms to automatically minimize or prevent resynchronizations. Therefore, it is up to you to periodically check the number of duplicate machines using the SMS Database Manager, shown in Figure 14-8. If duplicate names exist, you should delete the older ones.

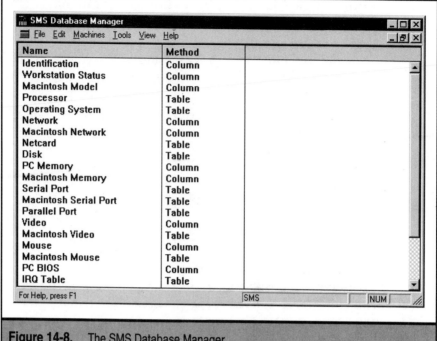

Figure 14-8. The SMS Database Manager

CAUTION: Deleting all duplicate machine entries may cause an increase in resynchronizations rather than minimizing or preventing them.

An easier, more efficient way of minimizing or preventing resynchronizations is with a BackOffice Resource Kit utility called Resync-File Cleaner (DUMPSYNC.EXE). DUMPSYNC will clean the RESYNC.CFG file of duplicate names on all SMS logon servers in the SMS site.

DUMPSYNC must be run from SMS\SITE.SRV\INVDOM.BOX\ DOMAIN.000 for each SMS site to be cleaned. Depending on the size of your environment, run DUMPSYNC anywhere from once a week to once a month to ensure those resynchronizations are minimized or entirely prevented.

The syntax for DUMPSYNC is as follows:

DUMPSYNC [*DAYS*] [/DUMP]

where

▼ *DAYS* is the number before a resynchronization request is removed from RESYNC.CFG. In addition to removing resynchronization requests from RESYNC.CFG, the associated SMSID.CFG files are deleted from SITE.SRV\MAINCFG.BOX\ INVDOM.BOX\DOMAIN.000\INVENCFG.BOX.

▲ /DUMP displays the complete contents of RESYNC.CFG.

MAINTAINING AN OPTIMAL SMS CONFIGURATION

SMS can be one of the most high maintenance BackOffice applications because of its complexity and reliance on system components. SMS is one server application that you must periodically maintain to keep in optimal running condition.

Installing the Latest Service Pack

As with Windows NT Server and all other Microsoft BackOffice applications, it is important to keep up-to-date with the latest service pack (SP). Service packs provide a wealth of enhancements such as bug fixes, performance upgrades, security patches, and much more. Applying the latest service pack helps to ensure optimum system performance and helps to guarantee reliability and stability. It is also important to note that service packs are cumulative and that subsequent SPs contain enhancements not found in previous service packs.

SMS SP3 and above provide faster client logon times due to an important performance enhancement to client processing. Many of the files previously executed from the logon server, such as inventory processing, are now installed locally on the client machine. Only the initial client logon will take longer and subsequent logons will run faster because of local client processing and minimized network traffic. Logon times will also increase for clients logging on through slow communication links. Table 14-3 compares the drive space requirements for two client types before and after SP3.

The end result is that the amount of information transferred between client and server after installation is significantly reduced

Client Operating System	Drive Space Requirements Before SP3 (MB)	Drive Space Requirements After SP3 (MB)
Windows 95	2.7	3.8
Windows NT	2.9	3.2

Table 14-3.   Comparing Drive Space Requirements Before and After SP3.

resulting in faster logon times. According to Microsoft, network traffic is reduced approximately 50 to 75 percent depending on the client operating system.

Another notable performance enhancement with SP3 involves SMS' remote control capabilities. Surprisingly enough, the current version of Windows NT remote control does not perform as well as previous versions. This was because earlier versions of Windows NT could use an SMS accelerated video driver to improve screen transfers. Now, SP3 contains an accelerated video driver to match the video enhancements in Windows NT version 4.0 and later. (Refer to Chapter 7 for more information on video performance.) As a result, this problem no longer exists, and video performance while running remote control has improved considerably.

Routinely Checking SMS System Directories

Old or unused files on SMS site server wastes disk space and may even significantly slow server performance. Some SMS processes continually retry jobs or scan all files in their associated directory, which increases the amount of processing the server must do. Consequently, it is imperative to check the SMS system directories to ensure that files are correctly processed and disk space is used efficiently. Moreover, routinely checking these directories can help you troubleshoot problems with SMS. Table 14-4 lists the most important system directories to monitor and sheds light on what to look for.

NOTE: Before you begin maintenance on the directories listed in Table 14-4, you must stop the corresponding SMS service to avoid any complications.

Monitoring SMS Data Device and Database Size

The data device and database size will naturally grow as the number of client machines and packages increase. It is not uncommon for the data device and database to reach near capacity over a short period of time. However, when such an occasion does arise, it can have disastrous effects on performance for both SMS and SQL Server. The SMS database has a finite limit, and when it reaches capacity, insert or update operations will generate errors and fail. As a result, it is imperative to monitor the growth of the SMS data device and database to prevent possible corruption and stability problems.

The procedure for monitoring the size of the SMS database is not readily apparent because it is not as simple as running the Performance Monitor to watch a specific counter. You can use SQL Enterprise Manager's Manage Databases feature to determine the size of the SMS database, but you must work with the limitation of manually and periodically checking the size. Of course, it would be much easier to somehow trigger an alert that would notify you before the database reached capacity. SQL Enterprise Manager's Alerts can trigger alerts, but it is severely limited since it will only alert you when the database has reached capacity.

The best solution to this problem is not the easiest, but it is highly recommended that you invest the time and effort to create the solution. You can create a user-defined counter within SQL Server by using a script and the sp_spaceused procedure. For more information on creating a user-defined script to monitor database size, consult Microsoft's Knowledge Base located at **http://support.microsoft.com/** and search for article Q163036.

SMS System Directory	What to Monitor
LOGS	Logging is useful for troubleshooting the SMS services and components. However, they can easily take up large amounts of disk space and can degrade system performance. By default, each log uses up to 128KB. Delete old or unused logs.
SITE.SRV\ INVENTRY.BOX	The Inventory Processor monitors this directory and deletes files when the inventory data is written to the SITE.SRV\DATALOAD.BOX\ DELTAMIF.COL directory. A backlog may indicate that the Inventory Processor is not running or is too busy to process the files.
SITE.SRV\ INVENTRY.BOX\ HISTORY	The history files located in this directory are updated with each inventory record update. However, if the inventory record is deleted, the corresponding history file is not deleted. Unchecked, this directory can grow to consume vast amounts of disk space. It is recommended that you delete all history files more than two months old.
SITE.SRV\ INVENTRY.BOX\ BADMIFS	The Inventory Processor places unprocessed MIF files in this directory. Ideally, this directory should always be empty.
SITE.SRV\ INVENTRY.BOX\ BADRAWS	The Inventory Processor places unprocessed inventory files in this directory. Ideally, this directory should always be empty.
SITE.SRV\ DATALOAD.BOX\ DELTAMIF.COL	This directory stores MIF files that are ready to be processed by the Data Loader. A backlog of files in this directory may indicate that the SQL Server database is unavailable or that the Data Loader is overloaded.

Table 14-4.   SMS System Directories to Routinely Monitor

SMS System Directory	What to Monitor
SITE.SRV\ DATALOAD.BOX\ DELTAMIF.COL\ PROCESS	The Data Loader uses this directory to store ready-to-process MIF files. The files are either processed and moved to the SITEREP.BOX directory, or not processed and moved to the BADMIFS directory. A backlog may indicate that the SQL Server database is unavailable or that the Data Loader is overloaded.
SITE.SRV\ DATALOAD.BOX\ DELTAMIF.COL\ BADMIFS	Ideally, this directory should always be empty. Any MIF files in this directory may indicate a problem with the Data Loader.
SITE.SRV\ SITEREP.BOX	The Data Loader uses this directory to store MIF files ready to be sent to a parent site. When Site Reporter detects a queue of MIF files, it creates a system job to send these files to the parent site. A backlog may indicate that the Site Reporter is not running or is overloaded, or that there is a problem with the connection to the primary site.
SITE.SRV\ MAINCFG.BOX\ PCMDOM.BOX	This directory contains the package instruction files for each client machine. However, when a client machine is deleted, the corresponding package instruction file is not automatically deleted. Delete any package instruction file older than the last simple maintenance job.
LOGON.SRV\ PCMINS.BOX	Perform the same procedure as in the SITE.SRV\MAINCFG.BOX\PCMDOM.BOX section above to ensure that the old package instruction files are not replicated.

Table 14-4. SMS System Directories to Routinely Monitor (*continued*)

SMS System Directory	What to Monitor
SITE.SRV\ SCHEDULE.BOX	SMS components use this directory to store system job instructions for the Scheduler. The Scheduler uses the instructions to start specified system jobs. A backlog may indicate that the Scheduler is not running or is overloaded.
SITE.SRV\SENDER. BOX\ REQUESTS	The Scheduler places send request files for the sender to this directory. The appropriate sender monitors its directory (below this one) and processes the requests. A backlog may indicate that the sender is overloaded, is not running, or cannot connect to the target site.
SITE.SRV\SENDER. BOX\ TOSEND	The Scheduler places compressed jobs and Despooler instruction files in this directory. A backlog may indicate that the sender is overloaded, is not running, or cannot connect to the target site.
SITE.SRV\ DESPOOLR.BOX\ RECEIVE	The Despooler monitors and processes the compressed Despooler instruction files in this directory. Once the Despooler processes the files and verification is received, files are moved to the STORE directory. A backlog may indicate that the Despooler is overloaded.

Table 14-4.   SMS System Directories to Routinely Monitor (*continued*)

Use the Performance Monitor both to monitor your defined counter and to ensure that the SMS data device and database are not approaching capacity. As a general rule of thumb, any database utilization should not exceed 70 percent of capacity. You can minimize the time you spend watching this counter by configuring automatic alerts should the counter exceed the recommended value. If utilization increases above 70 percent, be sure to increase the counter value. At this point, it is also recommended that you manually remove files, or use SQL's DBCLEAN utility or the BackOffice Resource Kit scripts described below to clear unwanted information, such as old history files, duplicate records, and old client machine entries.

OPTIMIZING SMS WITH THE PERFORMANCE MONITOR

SMS does not have a defined object to be monitored with the Performance Monitor. This does not mean, however, that you cannot use the Performance Monitor to gauge SMS performance. Use the Performance Monitor's Process object to monitor important SMS processes including, but not limited to, the following:

- ▼ PREINST
- ■ SITEINS
- ■ SMS
- ▲ SMSEXEC

In addition to these processes, it is strongly recommended that you monitor the following system components:

- ▼ Disk Subsystem (refer to Chapter 6)
- ■ Network Subsystem (refer to Chapter 5)
- ■ Memory (refer to Chapter 4)
- ▲ Processor

CONCLUSION

SMS is an extremely powerful, complex, and resource-intensive enterprise management solution. This chapter delved into various planning considerations and highlighted important areas for optimization. With the combination of careful planning and optimization, SMS can be implemented successfully in your Windows NT environment, and you can reap the benefits of its management capabilities.

WINDOWS
NT
Professional
Library

APPENDIX A

Windows NT Performance Monitor Objects and Counters

Throughout this book, there have been many references to Performance Monitor objects and counters that can be used to gauge performance of specific system components. This appendix provides a complete listing of objects and counters available to Windows NT. (Note that this information can also be found with the Performance Monitor itself, and in the Microsoft Windows NT Resource Kit.) You can monitor the objects and counters listed here with the Performance Monitor or with a third-party utility to gather system statistics, troubleshoot performance problems, monitor system activity, locate and minimize bottlenecks, and much more.

Object	Counter	Description	Default Scale
Active Server Pages	Debugging Requests	The number of debugging document requests.	1
	Errors during Script Runtime	The number of requests that failed due to runtime errors.	1
	Errors from ASP Preprocessor	The number of requests that failed due to preprocessor errors.	1
	Errors from Script Compilers	The number of requests that failed due to script compilation errors.	1
	Errors/Sec	The number of errors per second.	1
	Memory Allocated	The total amount of memory, in bytes, currently allocated by active server pages.	0.0001
	Request Bytes In Total	The total size, in bytes, of all requests.	0.0001
	Request Bytes Out Total	The total size, in bytes, of responses sent to clients. This does not include standard HTTP response headers.	0.0001
	Request Execution Time	The number of milliseconds that it took to execute the most recent request.	0.001
	Request Wait Time	The number of milliseconds that the most recent request was waiting in the queue.	0.001
	Requests Disconnected	The number of requests that were disconnected due to communication failure.	1
	Requests Executing	The number of requests currently executing.	1

Object	Counter	Description	Default Scale
	Requests Failed Total	The total number of requests that failed due to errors, authorization failure, and rejections.	1
	Requests Not Authorized	The number of requests that failed due to insufficient access rights.	1
	Requests Not Found	The number of requests for files that were not found.	1
	Requests Queued	The number of requests waiting for service from the queue.	1
	Requests Rejected	The total number of requests not executed because there were insufficient resources to process them.	1
	Requests Succeeded	The number of requests that executed successfully.	0.1
	Requests Timed Out	The number of requests that timed out.	1
	Requests Total	The total number of requests since the service was started.	0.1
	Requests/Sec	The number of requests executed per second.	1
	Script Engines Cached	The number of script engines in the cache.	1
	Session Duration	The number of milliseconds that the most recent session persisted.	1,000
	Sessions Current	The current number of sessions being serviced.	0.1
	Sessions Timed Out	The number of sessions that timed out.	0.1
	Sessions Total	The total number of sessions since the service was started.	0.1
	Template Cache Hit Rate	The percent of requests found in the template cache.	1
	Template Notifications	The number of templates invalidated in the cache due to change notification.	1
	Templates Cached	The number of templates currently cached.	1
	Transactions Aborted	The number of transactions aborted.	1
	Transactions Committed	The number of transactions committed.	1

Object	Counter	Description	Default Scale
	Transactions Pending	The number of transactions in progress.	1
	Transactions Total	The total number of transactions since the service was started.	1
	Transactions/Sec	The number of transactions started per second.	1
AppleTalk Object	AARP Packets/Sec	The number of AARP packets per second received by AppleTalk on this port.	0.1
	ATP ALO Response/Sec	The number of ATP At-Least-Once transaction responses per second on this port.	1
	ATP Packets/Sec	The number of ATP packets per second received by AppleTalk on this port.	0.1
	ATP Recvd Release/Sec	The number of ATP transaction release packets per second received on this port.	0.1
	ATP Response Timeouts	The number of ATP release timers that have expired on this port.	1
	ATP Retries Local	The number of ATP requests retransmitted on this port.	0.1
	ATP Retries Remote	The number of ATP requests retransmitted to this port.	0.1
	ATP XO Response/Sec	The number of ATP Exactly-Once transaction responses per second on this port.	0.1
	Average Time/AARP Packet	The average time, in milliseconds, taken to process an AARP packet on this port.	1
	Average Time/ATP Packet	The average time, in milliseconds, taken to process an ATP packet on this port.	1
	Average Time/DDP Packet	The average time, in milliseconds, taken to process a DDP packet on this port.	1
	Average Time/NBP Packet	The average time, in milliseconds, taken to process an NBP packet on this port.	1
	Average Time/RTMP Packet	The average time, in milliseconds, taken to process an RTMP packet on this port.	1
	Average Time/ZIP Packet	The average time, in milliseconds, taken to process a ZIP packet on this port.	1

Object	Counter	Description	Default Scale
	Bytes In/Sec	The number of bytes received per second by AppleTalk on this port.	0.0001
	Bytes Out/Sec	The number of bytes sent per second by AppleTalk on this port.	0.0001
	Current NonPaged Pool	The current amount of nonpaged memory resources used by AppleTalk.	0.0001
	DDP Packets/Sec	The number of DDP packets per second received by AppleTalk on this port.	0.1
	NBP Packets/Sec	The number of NBP packets per second received by AppleTalk on this port.	0.1
	Packets Dropped	The number of packets dropped due to resource limitations on this port.	1
	Packets In/Sec	The number of packets received per second by AppleTalk on this port.	0.1
	Packets Out/Sec	The number of packets sent per second by AppleTalk on this port.	0.1
	Packets Routed In/Sec	The number of packets routed in on this port.	1
	Packets Routed Out/Sec	The number of packets routed out on this port.	1
	RTMP Packets/Sec	The number of RTMP packets per second received by AppleTalk on this port.	0.1
	ZIP Packets/Sec	The number of ZIP packets per second received by AppleTalk on this port.	0.1
Browser Object	Announcements Domain/Sec	The rate at which a domain has announced itself to the network.	1
	Announcements Server/Sec	The rate at which the servers in this domain have announced themselves to this server.	1
	Announcements Total/Sec	The sum of Announcements Server/Sec and Announcements Domain/Sec.	1
	Duplicate Master Announcements	The number of times that the master browser has detected another master browser on the same domain.	1
	Election Packets/Sec	The rate at which browser election packets have been received by this workstation.	1
	Enumerations Domain/Sec	The rate at which domain browse requests have been processed by this workstation.	1

Object	Counter	Description	Default Scale
	Enumerations Other/Sec	The rate at which browse requests processed by this workstation were not domain or server browse requests.	1
	Enumerations Server/Sec	The rate at which server browse requests have been processed by this workstation.	1
	Enumerations Total/Sec	The rate at which browse requests have been processed by this workstation. This is the sum of Enumerations Server, Enumerations Domain, and Enumerations Other.	1
	Illegal Datagrams/Sec	The rate at which incorrectly formatted datagrams have been received by the workstation.	1
	Mailslot Allocations Failed	The number of times the datagram receiver has failed to allocate a buffer to hold a user mailslot write.	1
	Mailslot Opens Failed/Sec	The rate at which mailslot messages received by this workstation were to be delivered to mailslots that are not present on this workstation.	1
	Mailslot Receives Failed	The number of mailslot messages that couldn't be received due to transport failures.	1
	Mailslot Writes Failed	The total number of mailslot messages that have been successfully received, but that were unable to be written to the mailslot.	1
	Mailslot Writes/Sec	The rate at which mailslot messages have been successfully received.	1
	Missed Mailslot Datagrams	The number of mailslot datagrams that have been discarded due to configuration or allocation limits.	1
	Missed Server Announcements	The number of server announcements that have been missed due to configuration or allocation limits.	1
	Missed Server List Requests	The number of requests to retrieve a list of browser servers that were received by this workstation but could not be processed.	1
	Server Announce Allocations Failed/Sec	The rate at which server (or domain) announcements failed due to lack of memory.	1

Object	Counter	Description	Default Scale
	Server List Requests/Sec	The rate at which requests to retrieve a list of browser servers were processed by this workstation.	1
Cache Object	Async Copy Reads/Sec	The frequency of reads from pages of the file system cache that involve a memory copy of the data from the cache to the application's buffer. The application regains control immediately, even if the disk must be accessed to retrieve the page.	1
	Async Data Maps/Sec	The frequency with which an application using a file system, such as NTFS, maps a page of a file into the file system cache to read the page and does not wait for the page to be retrieved if it is not in main memory.	1
	Async Fast Reads/Sec	The frequency of reads from the file system cache that bypass the installed file system and retrieve the data directly from the cache. Normally, file I/O requests invoke the appropriate file system to retrieve data from a file, but this path permits data to be retrieved from the cache directly (without file system involvement) if the data is in the cache. Even if the data is not in the cache, one invocation of the file system is avoided. If the data is not in the cache, the request (application program call) will not wait until the data has been retrieved from disk, but will get control immediately.	0.1
	Async MDL Reads/Sec	The frequency of reads from the file system cache that use a memory descriptor list (MDL) to access the pages. The MDL contains the physical address of each page in the transfer, thus permitting direct memory access (DMA) of the pages. If the accessed pages are not in main memory, the calling application program will not wait for the pages to fault in from disk.	1

Object	Counter	Description	Default Scale
	Async Pin Reads/Sec	The frequency with which data is read into the file system cache preparatory to writing the data back to disk. Pages read in this fashion are pinned in memory at the completion of the read. The file system regains control immediately, even if the disk must be accessed to retrieve the page. While pinned, a page's physical address will not be altered.	1
	Copy Read Hits %	The percentage of cache copy read requests that hit the cache—e.g., when a disk read was not needed to provide access to the page in the cache. A copy read is a file read operation that is satisfied by a memory copy from a page in the cache to the application's buffer. The LAN redirector uses this method for retrieving information from the cache, as does the LAN server for small transfers. This method is used by the disk file systems as well.	1
	Copy Reads/Sec	The frequency of reads from pages of the file system cache that involve a memory copy of the data from the cache to the application's buffer. The LAN redirector uses this method for retrieving information from the file system cache, as does the LAN server for small transfers. This method is used by the disk file systems as well.	1
	Data Flush Pages/Sec	The number of pages the file system cache has flushed to disk as a result of a request to flush or to satisfy a write-through file write request. More than one page can be transferred on each flush operation.	1
	Data Flushes/Sec	The rate at which the file system cache has flushed its contents to disk as a result of a request to flush or to satisfy a write-through file write request. More than one page can be transferred on each flush operation.	1

Object	Counter	Description	Default Scale
	Data Map Hits %	The percentage of data maps in the file system cache that were resolved without having to retrieve a page from the disk because the page was already in physical memory.	1
	Data Map Pins/Sec	The frequency with which data maps in the file system cache resulted in the pinning of a page in main memory, an action usually preparatory to writing to the file on disk. While pinned, a page's physical address in main memory and virtual address in the file system cache will not be altered.	1
	Data Maps/Sec	The frequency with which a file system, such as NTFS, maps a page of a file to the file system cache to read the page.	1
	Fast Read Not Possibles/Sec	The frequency with which an application program interface (API) function call attempts to bypass the file system to get to data in the file system cache that could not be retrieved without invoking the file system.	1
	Fast Read Resource Misses/Sec	The frequency of cache misses necessitated by the lack of available resources to satisfy the request.	1
	Fast Reads/Sec	The frequency of reads from the file system cache that bypass the installed file system and retrieve the data directly from the cache. Normally, file I/O requests invoke the appropriate file system to retrieve data from a file, but this path permits direct retrieval of data from the cache without file system involvement if the data is in the cache. Even if the data is not in the cache, one invocation of the file system is avoided.	0.1

Object	Counter	Description	Default Scale
	Lazy Write Flushes/Sec	The rate at which the lazy writer thread wrote to disk. Lazy writing is the process of updating the disk after the page has been changed in memory, so that the application that changed the file does not have to wait for the disk write to be complete before proceeding. More than one page can be transferred by each write operation.	1
	Lazy Write Pages/Sec	The rate at which the lazy writer thread wrote to disk. Lazy writing is the process of updating the disk after the page has been changed in memory, so that the application that changed the file does not have to wait for the disk write to be complete before proceeding. More than one page can be transferred on a single disk write operation.	1
	MDL Read Hits %	The percentage of memory descriptor list (MDL) read requests to the file system cache that hit the cache—e.g., requests that did not require disk accesses to provide memory access to the pages in the cache.	1
	MDL Reads/Sec	The frequency of reads from the file system cache that use a memory descriptor list (MDL) to access the data. The MDL contains the physical address of each page involved in the transfer and thus can employ a hardware direct memory access (DMA) device to effect the copy. The LAN server uses this method for large transfers out of the server.	1
	Pin Read Hits %	The percentage of pin read requests that hit the file system cache—e.g., requests that did not require a disk read to provide access to the page in the file system cache. While pinned, a page's physical address in the file system cache will not be altered. The LAN redirector uses this method for retrieving data from the cache, as does the LAN server for small transfers. This is usually the method used by the disk file systems as well.	1

Object	Counter	Description	Default Scale
	Pin Reads/Sec	The frequency with which data is read into the file system cache preparatory to writing the data back to disk. Pages read in this fashion are pinned in memory at the completion of the read. While pinned, a page's physical address in the file system cache will not be altered.	1
	Read Aheads/Sec	The frequency of reads from the file system cache in which the cache detects sequential access to a file. The read aheads permit the data to be transferred in larger blocks than those being requested by the application, reducing the overhead per access.	1
	Sync Copy Reads/Sec	The frequency of reads from pages of the file system cache that involve a memory copy of the data from the cache to the application's buffer. The file system will not regain control until the copy operation is complete, even if the disk must be accessed to retrieve the page.	1
	Sync Data Maps/Sec	The frequency with which a file system, such as NTFS, maps a page of a file to the file system cache to read the page and waits for the page to be retrieved if it is not in main memory.	1
	Sync Fast Reads/Sec	The frequency of reads from the file system cache that bypass the installed file system and retrieve the data directly from the cache. Normally, file I/O requests invoke the appropriate file system to retrieve data from a file, but this path permits direct retrieval of data from the cache without file system involvement if the data is in the cache. Even if the data is not in the cache, one invocation of the file system is avoided. If the data is not in the cache, the request (application program call) will wait until the data has been retrieved from disk.	0.1

Object	Counter	Description	Default Scale
	Sync MDL Reads/Sec	The frequency of reads from the file system cache that use a memory descriptor list (MDL) to access the pages. The MDL contains the physical address of each page in the transfer, thus permitting direct memory access (DMA) of the pages. If the accessed page(s) are not in main memory, the caller will wait for the pages to fault in from the disk.	1
	Sync Pin Reads/Sec	The frequency with which data is read into the file system cache preparatory to writing the data back to disk. Pages read in this fashion are pinned in memory at the completion of the read. The file system will not regain control until the page is pinned in the file system cache if the disk must be accessed to retrieve the page. While pinned, a page's physical address in the file system cache will not be altered.	1
Client Service for NetWare Object	Bytes Received/Sec	The rate at which bytes come in to the redirector from the network. This includes all application data as well as network protocol information (such as packet headers).	0.0001
	Bytes Total/Sec	The rate at which the redirector is processing data bytes. This includes all application and file data in addition to protocol information such as packet headers.	0.0001
	Bytes Transmitted/Sec	The rate at which bytes are leaving the redirector to go to the network. This includes all application data as well as network protocol information (such as packet headers).	0.0001
	Connect NetWare 2.x	Counts connections to NetWare 2.x servers.	1
	Connect NetWare 3.x	Counts connections to NetWare 3.x servers.	1
	Connect NetWare 4.x	Counts connections to NetWare 4.x servers.	1

Object	Counter	Description	Default Scale
	File Data Operations/Sec	The rate at which the redirector is processing data operations. One operation includes (hopefully) many bytes (we say "hopefully" here because each operation has overhead). To determine the efficiency of this path, divide Bytes/Sec by this counter to find the average number of bytes transferred per operation.	1
	File Read Operations/Sec	The rate at which applications are asking the redirector for data. Each call to a file system, or each similar application program interface (API) call, counts as one operation.	1
	File Write Operations/Sec	The rate at which applications are sending data to the redirector. Each call to a file system, or each similar application program interface (API) call, counts as one operation.	1
	Packet Burst IO/Sec	The sum of Packet Burst Read NCPs/Sec and Packet Burst Write NCPs/Sec.	1
	Packet Burst Read NCP Count/Sec	The rate of NetWare Core Protocol requests for Packet Burst reads. Packet Burst is a windowing protocol that improves performance.	1
	Packet Burst Read Timeouts/Sec	The rate at which the NetWare service needs to retransmit a Burst Read request because the NetWare server took too long to respond.	1
	Packet Burst Write NCP Count/Sec	The rate of NetWare Core Protocol requests for Packet Burst writes. Packet Burst is a windowing protocol that improves performance.	1
	Packet Burst Write Timeouts/Sec	The rate at which the NetWare service needs to retransmit a Burst Write request because the NetWare server took too long to respond.	1

Object	Counter	Description	Default Scale
	Packets Received/Sec	The rate at which the redirector is receiving packets (also called SMBs, or server message blocks). Network transmissions are divided into packets. The average number of bytes received in a packet can be obtained by dividing Bytes Received/Sec by this counter. Some packets received may not contain incoming data; for example, an acknowledgment to a write made by the redirector would count as an incoming packet.	0.1
	Packets Transmitted/Sec	The rate at which the redirector is sending packets (also called SMBs, or server message blocks). Network transmissions are divided into packets. The average number of bytes transmitted in a packet can be obtained by dividing Bytes Transmitted/Sec by this counter.	0.1
	Packets/Sec	The rate the redirector is processing data packets. One packet includes many bytes due to protocol overhead. To determine the efficiency of this path, divide Bytes/Sec by this counter to find the average number of bytes transferred per packet. You can also divide this counter by Operations/Sec to determine the average number of packets per operation, another measure of efficiency.	0.1
	Read Operations Random/Sec	The rate at which, on a file-by-file basis, reads occur that are not sequential. If a read occurs using a particular file handle and then is followed by another read that is not the next contiguous byte, this counter is incremented by one.	0.1
	Read Packets/Sec	The rate at which read packets are being placed on the network. Each time a single packet is sent with a request to read data remotely, this counter is incremented by one.	0.1
	Server Disconnects	The number of times a server has disconnected your redirector.	1

Object	Counter	Description	Default Scale
	Server Reconnects	The number of times your redirector has had to reconnect to a server to complete a new active request. You can be disconnected by the server if you remain inactive for too long. Locally, even if all your remote files are closed, the redirector will keep your connections intact for (nominally) ten minutes. Such inactive connections are called dormant connections. Reconnecting is expensive in time.	1
	Server Sessions	The total number of security objects the redirector has managed. For example, a logon to a server followed by a network access to the same server will establish one connection, but two sessions.	1
	Write Operations Random/Sec	The rate at which, on a file-by-file basis, writes occur that are not sequential. If a write occurs using a particular file handle and then is followed by another write that is not the next contiguous byte, this counter is incremented by one.	0.1
	Write Packets/Sec	The rate at which writes are being sent to the network. Each time a single packet is sent with a request to write remote data, this counter is incremented by one.	0.1
FTP Service	Bytes Received/Sec	The rate that data bytes are received by the FTP service.	0.0001
	Bytes Sent/Sec	The rate that data bytes are sent by the FTP service.	0.0001
	Bytes Total/Sec	The sum of Bytes Sent/Sec and Bytes Received/Sec. This is the total rate of bytes transferred by the FTP service.	0.0001
	Current Anonymous Users	The number of users who currently have anonymous connections using the FTP service.	1
	Current Connections	The current number of connections established with the FTP service.	1
	Current NonAnonymous Users	The number of users who currently have non-anonymous connections using the FTP service.	1

Object	Counter	Description	Default Scale
	Maximum Anonymous Users	The maximum number of users who have established concurrent anonymous connections using the FTP service (since service startup).	1
	Maximum Connections	The maximum number of simultaneous connections established with the FTP service.	1
	Maximum NonAnonymous Users	The maximum number of users who have established concurrent non-anonymous connections using the FTP service (since service startup).	1
	Total Anonymous Users	The total number of users who have established anonymous connections with the FTP service (since service startup).	1
	Total Connection Attempts	The number of connections that have been attempted using the FTP service (since service startup). This counter is for all instances listed.	1
	Total Files Received	The total number of files received by the FTP service.	1
	Total Files Sent	The total number of files sent by the FTP service since service startup.	1
	Total Files Transferred	The sum of Files Sent and Files Received. This value is the total number of files transferred by the FTP service since service startup.	1
	Total Logon Attempts	The number of logons that have been attempted using the FTP service (since service startup).	1
	Total NonAnonymous Users	The total number of users who have established non-anonymous connections with the FTP service (since service startup).	1

Object	Counter	Description	Default Scale
ICMP Object	Messages Outbound Errors	The number of ICMP messages that this entity did not send due to problems discovered within ICMP, such as lack of buffers. This value does not include errors discovered outside the ICMP layer, such as the failure of IP to route the resultant datagram. In some implementations, none of the error types are included in the value of this counter.	1
	Messages Received Errors	The number of ICMP messages that the entity received but determined to contain errors (bad ICMP checksums, bad length, etc.).	1
	Messages Received/Sec	The rate at which ICMP messages are received by the entity. The rate includes those messages received in error.	0.1
	Messages Sent/Sec	The rate at which the entity attempted to send ICMP messages. The rate includes those messages sent in error.	0.1
	Messages/Sec	The total rate at which ICMP messages are sent and received by the entity. The rate includes those messages received or sent in error.	0.1
	Received Address Mask	The number of ICMP Address Mask Request messages received.	1
	Received Address Mask Reply	The number of ICMP Address Mask Reply messages received.	1
	Received Dest Unreachable	The number of ICMP Destination Unreachable messages received.	1
	Received Echo Reply/Sec	The rate of ICMP Echo Reply messages received.	0.1
	Received Echo/Sec	The rate of ICMP Echo messages received.	0.1
	Received Parameter Problem	The number of ICMP Parameter Problem messages received.	1
	Received Redirect/Sec	The rate of ICMP Redirect messages received.	0.1
	Received Source Quench	The number of ICMP Source Quench messages received.	1

Object	Counter	Description	Default Scale
	Received Time Exceeded	The number of ICMP Time Exceeded messages received.	1
	Received Timestamp Reply/Sec	The rate of ICMP Timestamp Reply messages received.	0.1
	Received Timestamp/Sec	The rate of ICMP Timestamp (request) messages received.	0.1
	Sent Address Mask	The number of ICMP Address Mask Request messages sent.	1
	Sent Address Mask Reply	The number of ICMP Address Mask Reply messages sent.	1
	Sent Destination Unreachable	The number of ICMP Destination Unreachable messages sent.	1
	Sent Echo Reply/Sec	The rate of ICMP Echo Reply messages sent.	0.1
	Sent Echo/Sec	The rate of ICMP Echo messages sent.	0.1
	Sent Parameter Problem	The number of ICMP Parameter Problem messages sent.	1
	Sent Redirect/Sec	The rate of ICMP Redirect messages sent.	0.1
	Sent Source Quench	The number of ICMP Source Quench messages sent.	1
	Sent Time Exceeded	The number of ICMP Time Exceeded messages sent.	1
	Sent Timestamp Reply/Sec	The rate of ICMP Timestamp Reply messages sent.	0.1
	Sent Timestamp/Sec	The rate of ICMP Timestamp (request) messages sent.	0.1
Image Object	Exec Read Only	Image space is the virtual address space in use by the selected image with this protection. Execute/ read-only memory is memory that can be executed as well as read.	1
	Exec Read/Write	Image space is the virtual address space in use by the selected image with this protection. Execute/read/write memory is memory that can be executed by programs as well as read and written to.	1

Object	Counter	Description	Default Scale
	Exec Write Copy	Image space is the virtual address space in use by the selected image with this protection. Execute/write/copy memory is memory that can be executed by programs as well as read and written to. This type of protection is used when memory needs to be shared between processes. If the sharing processes only read the memory, then they will all use the same memory. If a sharing process wants write access, then a copy of this memory will be made for that process.	1
	Executable	Image space is the virtual address space in use by the selected image with this protection. Executable memory is memory that can be executed by programs but cannot be read or written to. This type of protection is not supported by all processor types.	1
	No Access	Image space is the virtual address space in use by the selected image with this protection. No Access protection prevents a process from writing to or reading these pages and will generate an access violation if either is attempted.	1
	Read Only	Image space is the virtual address space in use by the selected image with this protection. Read Only protection prevents the contents of these pages from being modified. Any attempts to write or modify these pages will generate an access violation.	1
	Read/Write	Image space is the virtual address space in use by the selected image with this protection. Read/Write protection allows a process to read, modify, and write to these pages.	1

Object	Counter	Description	Default Scale
	Write Copy	Image space is the virtual address space in use by the selected image with this protection. Write Copy protection is used when memory is shared for reading but not for writing. When processes are reading this memory, they can share the same memory; however, when a sharing process wants to have read/write access to this shared memory, a copy of that memory is made for writing to.	1
Internet Information Services Global	Cache Flushes	The number of times a portion of the memory cache has expired due to file or directory changes in an Internet Information Services directory tree.	1
	Cache Hits	The total number of times a file open, directory listing, or service-specific object request was found in the cache.	0.001
	Cache Hits %	The ratio of cache hits to all cache requests.	1
	Cache Misses	The total number of times a file open, directory listing, or service-specific object request was not found in the cache.	0.1
	Cached File Handles	The number of open file handles cached by all of the Internet Information Services.	0.1
	Current Blocked Async I/O Requests	The number of current requests temporarily blocked due to bandwidth throttling settings.	0.1
	Directory Listings	The number of cached directory listings cached by all of the Internet Information Services.	0.1
	Measured Async I/O Bandwidth Usage	The measured bandwidth of asynchronous I/O averaged over a minute.	0.1
	Objects	The number of cached objects cached by all of the Internet Information Services. The objects include file handle tracking objects, directory listing objects, and service-specific objects.	0.1
	Total Allowed Async I/O Requests	The total number of requests allowed by bandwidth throttling settings (counted since service startup).	0.1

Object	Counter	Description	Default Scale
	Total Blocked Async I/O Requests	The total number of requests temporarily blocked due to bandwidth throttling settings (counted since service startup).	0.1
	Total Rejected Async I/O Requests	The total number of requests rejected due to bandwidth throttling settings (counted since service startup).	0.1
IP Object	Datagrams/Sec	The rate at which IP datagrams, including those in error, are received from or sent to the interfaces. Any forwarded datagrams are not included in this rate.	0.1
	Datagrams Received/Sec	The rate at which IP datagrams, including those in error, are received from the interfaces.	1
	Datagrams Received Header Errors	The number of input datagrams discarded due to errors in their IP headers, including bad checksums, version number mismatch, other format errors, time-to-live exceeded, and errors discovered in processing their IP options.	1
	Datagrams Received Address Errors	The number of input datagrams discarded because the IP address in their IP header's destination field was not a valid address that could be received at this entity. This count includes invalid addresses (such as 0.0. 0.0) and addresses of unsupported classes (such as Class E). For entities that are not IP gateways and therefore do not forward datagrams, this counter includes datagrams discarded because the destination address was not a local address.	1
	Datagrams Forwarded/Sec	The rate of input datagrams for which this entity was not the final IP destination, as a result of which an attempt was made to find a route to forward the datagrams to that final destination. In entities that do not act as IP gateways, this rate includes only those packets that were source-routed via this entity and for which Source-Route option processing was successful.	1

Object	Counter	Description	Default Scale
	Datagrams Received Unknown Protocol	The number of locally-addressed datagrams received successfully but discarded because of an unknown or unsupported protocol.	1
	Datagrams Received Discarded	The number of input IP datagrams for which no problems were encountered to prevent their continued processing, but which were discarded (for example, for lack of buffer space). This counter does not include any datagrams discarded while awaiting reassembly.	1
	Datagrams Received Delivered/Sec	The rate at which input datagrams are successfully delivered to IP user-protocols (including ICMP).	0.1
	Datagrams Sent/Sec	The rate at which IP datagrams are supplied to IP for transmission by local IP user protocols (including ICMP). This counter does not include any datagrams counted in Datagrams Forwarded.	0.1
	Datagrams Outbound Discarded	The number of output IP datagrams for which no problems were encountered to prevent their transmission to their destination, but which were discarded (for example, for lack of buffer space). This counter includes datagrams counted in Datagrams Forwarded if any such packets met this (discretionary) discard criterion.	1
	Datagrams Outbound No Route	The number of IP datagrams discarded because no route could be found to transmit them to their destinations. This counter includes any packets counted in Datagrams Forwarded that meet this "no route" criterion.	1
	Fragments Received/Sec	The rate at which IP fragments that need to be reassembled at this entity are received.	0.1
	Fragments Reassembled/Sec	The rate at which IP fragments are successfully reassembled.	0.1

Object	Counter	Description	Default Scale
	Fragment Reassembly Failures	The number of failures detected by the IP reassembly algorithm (for whatever reason—time-outs, errors, etc.). This is not necessarily a count of discarded IP fragments since some algorithms (notably RFC 815) can lose track of the number of fragments by combining them as they are received.	1
	Fragmented Datagrams/Sec	The rate at which datagrams are successfully fragmented at this entity.	0.1
	Fragmentation Failures	The number of IP datagrams that have been discarded because they needed to be fragmented at this entity but could not be (for example, because their Don't Fragment flag was set).	1
	Fragments Created/Sec	The rate at which IP datagram fragments were generated as a result of fragmentation at this entity.	0.1
Logical Disk Object	% Disk Read Time	The percentage of elapsed time that the selected disk drive is busy servicing read requests.	1
	% Disk Time	The percentage of elapsed time that the selected disk drive is busy servicing read or write requests.	1
	% Disk Write Time	The average number of read requests that were queued for the selected disk during the sample interval.	1
	% Free Space	The ratio of the free space available on the logical disk unit to the total usable space provided by the selected logical disk drive	1
	Avg. Disk Bytes/Read	The average number of bytes transferred from the disk during read operations.	0.01
	Avg. Disk Bytes/Transfer	The average number of bytes transferred to or from the disk during write or read operations.	0.01
	Avg. Disk Bytes/Write	The average number of bytes transferred to the disk during write operations.	0.01

Object	Counter	Description	Default Scale
	Avg. Disk Queue Length	The average number of both read and write requests that were queued for the selected disk during the sample interval.	100
	Avg. Disk Read Queue Length	The average number of read requests that were queued for the selected disk during the sample interval.	100
	Avg. Disk Sec/Read	The average time, in seconds, of a data read from the disk.	1,000
	Avg. Disk Sec/Transfer	The average time, in seconds, of a disk transfer.	1,000
	Avg. Disk Sec/Write	The average time, in seconds, of a data write to the disk.	1,000
	Avg. Disk Write Queue Length	The average number of write requests that were queued for the selected disk during the sample interval.	100
	Current Disk Queue Length	The number of requests outstanding on the disk at the time the performance data is collected. This includes requests in service at the time of the snapshot. This is an instantaneous length, not an average over the time interval. Multi-spindle disk devices can have multiple requests active at one time, but other concurrent requests are awaiting service. This counter may reflect a transitory high or low queue length, but if there is a sustained load on the disk drive, it is likely that this value will consistently be high. Requests experience delays proportional to the length of this queue minus the number of spindles on the disks. This difference should average less than 2 for good performance.	10
	Disk Bytes/Sec	The rate at which bytes are transferred to or from the disk during write or read operations.	0.0001
	Disk Read Bytes/Sec	The rate at which bytes are transferred from the disk during read operations.	0.0001

Object	Counter	Description	Default Scale
	Disk Reads/Sec	The rate of read operations on the disk.	1
	Disk Transfers/Sec	The rate of read and write operations on the disk.	1
	Disk Write Bytes/Sec	The rate at which bytes are transferred to the disk during write operations.	0.0001
	Disk Writes/Sec	The rate of write operations on the disk.	1
	Free Megabytes	The amount of unallocated space on the disk drive, in megabytes (1 megabyte = 1,048,576 bytes).	1
Memory Object	% Committed Bytes in Use	The ratio of Memory: Committed Bytes to Memory: Commit Limit. (Committed memory is physical memory in use for which space has been reserved in the paging file should it need to be written to disk. The commit limit is determined by the size of the paging file. If the paging file is enlarged, the commit limit increases, and the ratio is reduced.)	1
	Available Bytes	The amount of physical memory available to processes running on the computer, in bytes. It is calculated by summing space on the Zeroed, Free, and Standby memory lists. Free memory is ready for use; Zeroed memory is pages of memory filled with zeros to prevent later processes from seeing data used by a previous process. Standby memory is memory removed from a process's working set (its physical memory) on route to disk, but which is still available to be recalled.	0.00001
	Cache Bytes	The number of bytes currently being used by the file system cache. The file system cache is an area of physical memory that stores recently used pages of data for applications. Windows NT continually adjusts the size of the cache, making it as large as it can while still preserving the minimum required number of available bytes for processes.	0.00001

Object	Counter	Description	Default Scale
	Cache Bytes Peak	The maximum number of bytes used by the file system cache since the system was last restarted. This value may be larger than the current size of the cache. The file system cache is an area of physical memory that stores recently used pages of data for applications. Windows NT continually adjusts the size of the cache, making it as large as it can while still preserving the minimum required number of available bytes for processes.	0.00001
	Cache Faults/Sec	The number of faults that occur when a page sought in the file system cache is not found there and must be retrieved from elsewhere in memory (a soft fault) or from disk (a hard fault). The file system cache is an area of physical memory that stores recently used pages of data for applications. Cache activity is a reliable indicator of most application I/O operations. This counter counts the number of faults, without regard for the number of pages faulted in each operation.	0.1
	Commit Limit	The amount of virtual memory that can be committed without having to extend the paging file(s). It is measured in bytes. (Committed memory is physical memory for which space has been reserved in the disk paging files. There can be one paging file on each physical drive.) If the paging file(s) are expanded, this limit increases accordingly.	0.000001
	Committed Bytes	The amount of committed virtual memory, in bytes. (Committed memory is physical memory for which space has been reserved in the disk paging file in case it needs to be written back to disk.)	0.000001

Object	Counter	Description	Default Scale
	Demand Zero Faults/Sec	The number of page faults that require a zeroed page to satisfy the fault. Zeroed pages, pages emptied of previously stored data and filled with zeros, are a security feature of Windows NT. They prevent processes from seeing data stored by earlier processes that used the memory space. Windows NT maintains a list of zeroed pages to accelerate this process. This counter counts the number of faults, without regard to the number of pages retrieved in response to the fault.	0.1
	Free System Page Table Entries	The number of page table entries not currently in use by the system.	0.01
	Page Faults/Sec	The average number of pages faulted per second. This is measured in numbers of pages faulted, but because only one page is faulted in each fault operation, this value is also equal to the number of page fault operations. A page fault occurs when a process references a page in virtual memory that is not in its working set (its space in physical memory). This counter includes both hard faults (those that require disk access) and soft faults (where the faulted page is found elsewhere in physical memory). Most processors can handle large numbers of soft faults without significant consequences. However, hard faults, which require disk access, can cause delays.	1

Object	Counter	Description	Default Scale
	Page Reads/Sec	The average number of times the disk was read to resolve hard page faults in each second. This counts the number of read operations, without regard to the number of pages retrieved in each operation. (Hard page faults occur when a process references a page in virtual memory that is not in its working set or elsewhere in physical memory and so must be retrieved from disk.) This counter was designed as a primary indicator of the kinds of faults that cause systemwide delays. It includes reads in response to faults in the file system cache (usually requested by applications) and in noncached mapped memory files. Compare the value of Page Reads/Sec to the value of Pages Input/Sec to find the average number of pages read during each read operation.	1
	Page Writes/Sec	The average number of times pages were written to disk to free up space in physical memory. Pages are written to disk only if they are changed while in physical memory, so they are likely to hold data, not code. This counter counts write operations, without regard to the number of pages written in each operation.	1
	Pages Input/Sec	The average number of pages read from disk to resolve hard page faults. (Hard page faults occur when a process refers to a page in virtual memory that is not in its working set or elsewhere in physical memory and so must be retrieved from disk.) When a page is faulted, the system tries to read multiple contiguous pages into memory to maximize the benefit of the costly read operation. Compare Pages Input/Sec to Page Reads/Sec to find the average number of pages read into memory in each read operation.	1

Object	Counter	Description	Default Scale
	Pages Output/Sec	The average number of pages written to disk to free up space in physical memory. Pages are written back to disk only if they are changed in physical memory, so they are likely to hold data, not code. A high rate of pages output may indicate a memory shortage. Windows NT writes more pages back to disk to free up space when physical memory is in short supply. This counter counts the number of pages and can be compared to other counts of pages without conversion.	1
	Pages/Sec	The number of pages read from or written to disk to resolve hard page faults. (Hard page faults occur when a process requires code or data that is not in its working set or elsewhere in physical memory and so must be retrieved from disk.) This counter was designed as a primary indicator of the kinds of faults that cause systemwide delays. It is the sum of Memory: Pages Input/Sec and Memory: Pages Output/Sec. It is counted in numbers of pages, so it can be compared to other counts of pages, such as Memory: Page Faults/Sec, without conversion. It includes pages retrieved in response to faults in the file system cache (usually requested by applications) and noncached mapped memory files.	1
	Pool Nonpaged Allocs	The number of calls to allocate space in the nonpaged pool. The nonpaged pool is an area of system memory for objects that cannot be written to disk and so must remain in physical memory as long as they are allocated. It is measured in numbers of calls to allocate space, regardless of the amount of space allocated in each call.	0.01

Object	Counter	Description	Default Scale
	Pool Nonpaged Bytes	The number of bytes in the nonpaged pool, an area of system memory (physical memory used by the operating system) for objects that cannot be written to disk but which must remain in physical memory as long as they are allocated. Memory: Pool Nonpaged Bytes is calculated differently than Process: Pool Nonpaged Bytes, so this value may not equal Process: Pool Nonpaged Bytes: _Total.	0.00001
	Pool Paged Allocs	The number of calls to allocate space in the paged pool. The paged pool is an area of system memory (physical memory used by the operating system) for objects that can be written to disk when they are not being used. It is measured in number of calls to allocate space, regardless of the amount of space allocated in each call.	0.01
	Pool Paged Bytes	The number of bytes in the paged pool, an area of system memory (physical memory used by the operating system) for objects that can be written to disk when they are not being used. Memory: Pool Paged Bytes is calculated differently than Process: Pool Paged Bytes, so this value may not equal Process: Pool Paged Bytes: _Total.	0.00001
	Pool Paged Resident Bytes	The current size of the paged pool, in bytes. The paged pool is an area of system memory (physical memory used by the operating system) for objects that can be written to disk when they are not being used. Space used by the paged and nonpaged pools are taken from physical memory, so a pool that is too large denies memory space to processes.	0.00001
	System Cache Resident Bytes	The number of bytes of pageable operating system code in the file system cache. This value is a component of Memory: System Code Resident Bytes, which represents all pageable operating system code that is currently in physical memory.	0.00001

Object	Counter	Description	Default Scale
	System Code Resident Bytes	The number of bytes of operating system code currently in physical memory that can be written to disk when not in use. This value is a component of System Code Total Bytes, which also includes operating system code on disk. System Code Resident Bytes (and System Code Total Bytes) does not include code that must remain in physical memory and cannot be written to disk.	0.00001
	System Code Total Bytes	The number of bytes of pageable operating system code currently in virtual memory. It is a measure of the amount of physical memory being used by the operating system that can be written to disk when not in use. This value is calculated by summing the bytes in NTOSKRNL.EXE, HAL.DLL, the boot drivers, and file systems loaded by NTLDR/OSLOADER. This counter does not include code that must remain in physical memory and cannot be written to disk.	0.00001
	System Driver Resident Bytes	The number of bytes of pageable physical memory being used by device drivers. It is the working set (physical memory area) of the drivers. This value is a component of Memory: System Driver Total Bytes, which also includes driver memory that has been written to disk. Neither System Driver Resident Bytes nor System Driver Total Bytes includes memory that cannot be written to disk.	0.00001
	System Driver Total Bytes	The number of bytes of pageable virtual memory currently being used by device drivers. (Pageable memory can be written to disk when it is not being used.) It includes physical memory (Memory: System Driver Resident Bytes) and code and data written to disk. It is a component of Memory: System Code Total Bytes.	0.00001

Object	Counter	Description	Default Scale
	Transition Faults/Sec	The number of page faults resolved by recovering pages that were being used by another process sharing the page, or were on the modified page list or the standby list, or were being written to disk at the time of the page fault. The pages were recovered without additional disk activity. Transition faults are counted according to the number of faults, but because only one page is faulted in each operation, this value is equal to the number of pages faulted.	0.1
	Write Copies/Sec	The number of page faults caused by attempts to write that have been satisfied by copying the page from elsewhere in physical memory. This is an economical way of sharing data since a page is copied only when it is written to; otherwise, the page is shared. This counter counts the number of copies, without regard for the number of pages copied in each operation.	1
NBT Connection Object	Bytes Received/Sec	The rate at which bytes are received by the local computer over an NBT connection to some remote computer. All the bytes received by the local computer over the particular NBT connection are counted.	0.0001
	Bytes Sent/Sec	The rate at which bytes are sent by the local computer over an NBT connection to some remote computer. All the bytes sent by the local computer over the particular NBT connection are counted.	0.0001
	Bytes Total/Sec	The rate at which bytes are sent or received by the local computer over an NBT connection to some remote computer. All the bytes sent or received by the local computer over the particular NBT connection are counted.	0.0001
NetBEUI Object	Bytes Total/Sec	The sum of Frame Bytes/Sec and Datagram Bytes/Sec. This is the total rate of bytes sent to or received from the network by the protocol, but it counts only the bytes in frames (packets) that carry data.	0.0001

Object	Counter	Description	Default Scale
	Connection Session Timeouts	The number of connections that were dropped due to a session timeout. This number is an accumulator and shows a running total.	1
	Connections Canceled	The number of connections that were canceled. This number is an accumulator and shows a running total.	1
	Connections No Retries	The total count of connections that were successfully made on the first try. This number is an accumulator and shows a running total.	1
	Connections Open	The number of connections currently open for this protocol. This counter shows the current count only and does not accumulate over time.	1
	Connections with Retries	The total count of connections that were made after retrying the attempt. A retry occurs when the first connection attempt failed. This number is an accumulator and shows a running total.	1
	Datagram Bytes Received/Sec	The rate at which datagram bytes are received by the computer. A datagram is a connectionless packet whose delivery to a remote computer is not guaranteed.	0.0001
	Datagram Bytes Sent/Sec	The rate at which datagram bytes are sent from the computer. A datagram is a connectionless packet whose delivery to a remote computer is not guaranteed.	0.0001
	Datagram Bytes/Sec	The rate at which datagram bytes are processed by the computer. This counter is the sum of datagram bytes that are sent as well as received. A datagram is a connectionless packet whose delivery to a remote computer is not guaranteed.	0.0001
	Datagrams Received/Sec	The rate at which datagrams are received by the computer. A datagram is a connectionless packet whose delivery to a remote computer is not guaranteed.	0.1
	Datagrams Sent/Sec	The rate at which datagrams are sent from the computer. A datagram is a connectionless packet whose delivery to a remote computer is not guaranteed.	0.1

Object	Counter	Description	Default Scale
	Datagrams/ Sec	The rate at which datagrams are processed by the computer. This counter displays the sum of datagrams sent and datagrams received. A datagram is a connectionless packet whose delivery to a remote computer is not guaranteed.	0.1
	Disconnects Local	The number of session disconnections that were initiated by the local computer. This number is an accumulator and shows a running total.	1
	Disconnects Remote	The number of session disconnections that were initiated by the remote computer. This number is an accumulator and shows a running total.	1
	Expirations Ack	The count of T2 timer expirations.	1
	Expirations Response	The count of T1 timer expirations.	1
	Failures Adapter	The number of connections that were dropped due to an adapter failure. This number is an accumulator and shows a running total.	1
	Failures Link	The number of connections that were dropped due to a link failure. This number is accumulator and shows a running total.	1
	Failures No Listen	The number of connections that were rejected because the remote computer was not listening for connection requests.	1
	Failures Not Found	The number of connection attempts that failed because the remote computer could not be found. This number is an accumulator and shows a running total.	1
	Failures Resource Local	The number of connections that failed because of resource problems or shortages on the local computer. This number is an accumulator and shows a running total.	1
	Failures Resource Remote	The number of connections that failed because of resource problems or shortages on the remote computer. This number is an accumulator and shows a running total.	1

Object	Counter	Description	Default Scale
	Frame Bytes Received/Sec	The rate at which data bytes are received by the computer. This counter counts only the frames (packets) that carry data.	0.0001
	Frame Bytes Rejected/Sec	The rate at which data bytes are rejected. This counter counts only the bytes in data frames (packets) that carry data.	0.0001
	Frame Bytes Re-Sent/Sec	The rate at which data bytes are resent by the computer. This counter counts only the bytes in frames that carry data.	0.0001
	Frame Bytes Sent/Sec	The rate at which data bytes are sent by the computer. This counter counts only the bytes in frames (packets) that carry data.	0.0001
	Frame Bytes/Sec	The rate at which data bytes are processed by the computer. This counter is the sum of data frame bytes sent and received. This counter counts only the bytes in frames (packets) that carry data.	0.0001
	Frames Received/Sec	The rate at which data frames are received by the computer. This counter counts only the frames (packets) that carry data.	0.1
	Frames Rejected/Sec	The rate at which data frames are rejected. This counter counts only the frames (packets) that carry data.	0.1
	Frames Re-Sent/Sec	The rate at which data frames (packets) are resent by the computer. This counter counts only the frames (packets) that carry data.	0.1
	Frames Sent/Sec	The rate at which data frames are sent by the computer. This counter counts only the frames (packets) that carry data.	0.1
	Frames/Sec	The rate at which data frames (or packets) are processed by the computer. This counter is the sum of data frames sent and data frames received. This counter counts only those frames (packets) that carry data.	0.1
	Packets Received/Sec	The rate at which packets are received by the computer. This counter counts all packets processed, including control as well as data packets.	0.1

Object	Counter	Description	Default Scale
	Packets Sent/Sec	The rate at which packets are sent by the computer. This counter counts all packets sent by the computer, including control as well as data packets.	0.1
	Packets/Sec	The rate at which packets are processed by the computer. This count is the sum of Packets Sent and Packets Received per second. This counter includes all packets processed, including control as well as data packets.	0.1
	Piggyback Ack Queued/Sec	The rate at which piggybacked acknowledgments are queued. Piggyback acknowledgments are acknowledgments to received packets that are to be included in the next outgoing packet to the remote computer.	0.1
	Piggyback Ack Timeouts	The number of times that a piggyback acknowledgment could not be sent because there was no outgoing packet to the remote system on which to piggyback. A piggyback ack is an acknowledgment to a received packet that is sent along in an outgoing data packet to the remote computer. If no outgoing packet is sent within the timeout period, then an ack packet is sent, and this counter is incremented.	0.1
	Window Send Average	The running average number of data bytes that were sent before waiting for an acknowledgment from the remote computer.	1
	Window Send Maximum	The maximum number of bytes of data that will be sent before waiting for an acknowledgment from the remote computer.	1
NetBEUI Resource Object	Times Exhausted	The number of times all the resources (buffers) were in use. The number in parentheses following the resource name is used to identify the resource in Event Log messages.	1

Object	Counter	Description	Default Scale
	Used Average	The current number of resources (buffers) in use at this time. The number in parentheses following the resource name is used to identify the resource in Event Log messages.	1
	Used Maximum	The maximum number of NetBEUI resources (buffers) in use at any point in time. This value is useful in sizing the maximum resources provided. The number in parentheses following the resource name is used to identify the resource in Event Log messages.	1
Network Interface Object	Bytes Received/Sec	The rate at which bytes are received at the interface, including framing characters.	0.0001
	Bytes Sent/Sec	The rate at which bytes are sent from the interface, including framing characters.	0.0001
	Bytes Total/Sec	The rate at which bytes are sent and received at the interface, including framing characters.	0.0001
	Current Bandwidth	An estimate of the interface's current bandwidth in bits per second (bps). For interfaces that do not vary in bandwidth or for those where no accurate estimation can be made, this value is the nominal bandwidth.	0.000001
	Output Queue Length	The length of the output packet queue (in packets). If this value is more than 2, delays are being experienced, and the bottleneck should be found and eliminated if possible. Since the requests are queued by NDIS in this implementation, this value will always be 0.	1
	Packets Outbound Discarded	The number of outbound packets that were chosen to be discarded, even though no errors had been detected to prevent their being transmitted. One possible reason for discarding such a packet could be to free up buffer space.	1
	Packets Outbound Errors	The number of outbound packets that could not be transmitted because of errors.	1

Object	Counter	Description	Default Scale
	Packets Received Discarded	The number of inbound packets that were chosen to be discarded, even though no errors had been detected to prevent their being deliverable to a higher-layer protocol. One possible reason for discarding such a packet could be to free up buffer space.	1
	Packets Received Errors	The number of inbound packets that contained errors preventing them from being deliverable to a higher-layer protocol.	1
	Packets Received Non-Unicast/ Sec	The rate at which non-unicast (e.g., subnet broadcast or subnet multicast) packets are delivered to a higher-layer protocol.	0.1
	Packets Received Unicast/Sec	The rate at which (subnet) unicast packets are delivered to a higher-layer protocol.	0.1
	Packets Received Unknown	The number of packets received via the interface that were discarded because of an unknown or unsupported protocol.	1
	Packets Received/Sec	The rate at which packets are received at the network interface.	0.1
	Packets Sent Non-Unicast/ Sec	The rate at which packets are requested to be transmitted to non-unicast (e.g., subnet broadcast or subnet multicast) addresses by higher-level protocols. The rate includes the packets that were discarded or not sent.	0.1
	Packets Sent Unicast/Sec	The rate at which packets are requested to be transmitted to subnet-unicast addresses by higher-level protocols. The rate includes the packets that were discarded or not sent.	0.1
	Packets Sent/Sec	The rate at which packets are sent on the network interface.	0.1
	Packets/Sec	The rate at which packets are sent and received on the network interface.	0.1
Network Segment Object	% Broadcast Frames	The percentage of network bandwidth that is made up of broadcast traffic on this network segment.	1

Object	Counter	Description	Default Scale
	% Multicast Frames	The percentage of network bandwidth that is made up of multicast traffic on this network segment.	1
	% Network Utilization	The percentage of network bandwidth in use on this network segment.	1
	Broadcast Frames Received/ Second	The number of broadcast frames received per second on this network segment.	0.1
	Multicast Frames Received/ Second	The number of multicast frames received per second on this network segment.	0.1
	Total Bytes Received/ Second	The number of bytes received per second on this network segment.	0.0001
	Total Frames Received/ Second	The total number of frames received per second on this network segment.	0.0001
NWLink IPX Object	Bytes Total/Sec	The sum of Frame Bytes/Sec and Datagram Bytes/Sec. This is the total rate of bytes sent to or received from the network by the protocol, but it counts only the bytes in frames (packets) that carry data.	0.0001
	Connection Session Timeouts	The number of connections that were dropped due to a session timeout. This number is an accumulator and shows a running total.	1
	Connections Canceled	The number of connections that were canceled. This number is an accumulator and shows a running total.	1
	Connections No Retries	The total count of connections that were successfully made on the first try. This number is an accumulator and shows a running total.	1
	Connections Open	The number of connections currently open for this protocol. This counter shows the current count only and does not accumulate over time.	1

Object	Counter	Description	Default Scale
	Connections with Retries	The total count of connections that were made after retrying the attempt. A retry occurs if the first connection attempt fails. This number is an accumulator and shows a running total.	1
	Datagram Bytes Received/Sec	The rate at which datagram bytes are received by the computer. A datagram is a connectionless packet whose delivery to a remote computer is not guaranteed.	0.0001
	Datagram Bytes Sent/Sec	The rate at which datagram bytes are sent from the computer. A datagram is a connectionless packet whose delivery to a remote computer is not guaranteed.	0.0001
	Datagram Bytes/Sec	The rate at which datagram bytes are processed by the computer. This counter is the sum of datagram bytes that are sent as well as received. A datagram is a connectionless packet whose delivery to a remote computer is not guaranteed.	0.0001
	Datagrams Received/Sec	The rate at which datagrams are received by the computer. A datagram is a connectionless packet whose delivery to a remote computer is not guaranteed.	0.1
	Datagrams Sent/Sec	The rate at which datagrams are sent from the computer. A datagram is a connectionless packet whose delivery to a remote computer is not guaranteed.	0.1
	Datagrams/Sec	The rate at which datagrams are processed by the computer. This counter displays the sum of datagrams sent and datagrams received. A datagram is a connectionless packet whose delivery to a remote computer is not guaranteed.	0.1
	Disconnects Local	The number of session disconnections that were initiated by the local computer. This number is an accumulator and shows a running total.	1
	Disconnects Remote	The number of session disconnections that were initiated by the remote computer. This number is an accumulator and shows a running total.	1
	Expirations Ack	The count of T2 timer expirations.	1

Object	Counter	Description	Default Scale
	Expirations Response	The count of T1 timer expirations.	1
	Failures Adapter	The number of connections that were dropped due to an adapter failure. This number is an accumulator and shows a running total.	1
	Failures Link	The number of connections that were dropped due to a link failure. This number is an accumulator and shows a running total.	1
	Failures No Listen	The number of connections that were rejected because the remote computer was not listening for connection requests.	1
	Failures Not Found	The number of connection attempts that failed because the remote computer could not be found. This number is an accumulator and shows a running total.	1
	Failures Resource Local	The number of connections that failed because of resource problems or shortages on the local computer. This number is an accumulator and shows a running total.	1
	Failures Resource Remote	The number of connections that failed because of resource problems or shortages on the remote computer. This number is an accumulator and shows a running total.	1
	Frame Bytes Received/Sec	The rate at which data bytes are received by the computer. This counter counts only the frames (packets) that carry data.	0.0001
	Frame Bytes Rejected/Sec	The rate at which data bytes are rejected. This counter counts only the bytes in data frames (packets) that carry data.	0.0001
	Frame Bytes Re-Sent/Sec	The rate at which data bytes are resent by the computer. This counter counts only the bytes in frames (packets) that carry data.	0.0001
	Frame Bytes Sent/Sec	The rate at which data bytes are sent by the computer. This counter counts only the bytes in frames (packets) that carry data.	0.0001

Object	Counter	Description	Default Scale
	Frame Bytes/Sec	The rate at which data bytes are processed by the computer. This counter is the sum of data frame bytes sent and received. This counter counts only the byte in frames (packets) that carry data.	0.0001
	Frames Received/Sec	The rate at which data frames are received by the computer. This counter counts only the frames (packets) that carry data.	0.1
	Frames Rejected/Sec	The rate at which data frames are rejected. This counter counts only the frames (packets) that carry data.	0.1
	Frames Re-Sent/Sec	The rate at which data frames (packets) are resent by the computer. This counter counts only the frames (packets) that carry data.	0.1
	Frames Sent/Sec	The rate at which data frames are sent by the computer. This counter counts only the frames (packets) that carry data.	0.1
	Frames/Sec	The rate at which data frames (packets) are processed by the computer. This counter is the sum of data frames sent and data frames received. This counter counts only those frames (packets) that carry data.	0.1
	Packets Received/Sec	The rate at which packets are received by the computer. This counter counts all packets processed, including control as well as data packets.	0.1
	Packets Sent/Sec	The rate at which packets are sent by the computer. This counter counts all packets sent by the computer, including control as well as data packets.	0.1
	Packets/Sec	The rate at which packets are processed by the computer. This count is the sum of Packets Sent and Packets Received per second. This counter includes all packets processed, including control as well as data packets.	0.1

Object	Counter	Description	Default Scale
	Piggyback Ack Queued/Sec	The rate at which piggybacked acknowledgments are queued. Piggyback acknowledgments are acknowledgments to received packets that are to be included in the next outgoing packet to the remote computer.	0.1
	Piggyback Ack Timeouts	The number of times that a piggyback acknowledgment could not be sent because there was no outgoing packet to the remote system on which to piggyback. A piggyback ack is an acknowledgment to a received packet that is sent along in an outgoing data packet to the remote computer. If no outgoing packet is sent within the timeout period, then an ack packet is sent, and this counter is incremented.	0.1
	Window Send Average	The running average number of data bytes that were sent before waiting for an acknowledgment from the remote computer.	1
	Window Send Maximum	The maximum number of bytes of data that will be sent before waiting for an acknowledgment from the remote computer.	1
NWLink NetBIOS Object	Bytes Total/Sec	The sum of Frame Bytes/Sec and Datagram Bytes/Sec. This is the total rate for bytes sent to or received from the network by the protocol, but it counts only the bytes in frames (packets) that carry data.	0.0001
	Connection Session Timeouts	The number of connections that were dropped due to a session timeout. This number is an accumulator and shows a running total.	1
	Connections Canceled	The number of connections that were canceled. This number is an accumulator and shows a running total.	1
	Connections No Retries	The total count of connections that succeeded on the first try. This number is an accumulator and shows a running total.	1

Object	Counter	Description	Default Scale
	Connections Open	The number of connections currently open for this protocol. This counter shows the current count only and does not accumulate over time.	1
	Connections with Retries	The total count of connections that were made after retrying the attempt. A retry occurs if the first connection attempt fails. This number is an accumulator and shows a running total.	1
	Datagram Bytes Received/Sec	The rate at which datagram bytes are received by the computer. A datagram is a connectionless packet whose delivery to a remote computer is not guaranteed.	0.0001
	Datagram Bytes Sent/Sec	The rate at which datagram bytes are sent from the computer. A datagram is a connectionless packet whose delivery to a remote computer is not guaranteed.	0.0001
	Datagram Bytes/Sec	The rate at which datagram bytes are processed by the computer. This counter is the sum of datagram bytes that are sent as well as received. A datagram is a connectionless packet whose delivery to a remote computer is not guaranteed.	0.0001
	Datagrams Received/Sec	The rate at which datagrams are received by the computer. A datagram is a connectionless packet whose delivery to a remote computer is not guaranteed.	0.1
	Datagrams Sent/Sec	The rate at which datagrams are sent from the computer. A datagram is a connectionless packet whose delivery to a remote computer is not guaranteed.	0.1
	Datagrams/Sec	The rate at which datagrams are processed by the computer. This counter displays the sum of datagrams sent and datagrams received. A datagram is a connectionless packet whose delivery to a remote computer is not guaranteed.	0.1
	Disconnects Local	The number of session disconnections that were initiated by the local computer. This number is an accumulator and shows a running total.	1

Object	Counter	Description	Default Scale
	Disconnects Remote	The number of session disconnections that were initiated by the remote computer. This number is an accumulator and shows a running total.	1
	Expirations Ack	The count of T2 timer expirations.	1
	Expirations Response	The count of T1 timer expirations.	1
	Failures Adapter	The number of connections that were dropped due to an adapter failure. This number is an accumulator and shows a running total.	1
	Failures Link	The number of connections that were dropped due to a link failure. This number is an accumulator and shows a running total.	1
	Failures No Listen	The number of connections that were rejected because the remote computer was not listening for connection requests.	1
	Failures Not Found	The number of connection attempts that failed because the remote computer could not be found. This number is an accumulator and shows a running total.	1
	Failures Resource Local	The number of connections that failed because of resource problems or shortages on the local computer. This number is an accumulator and shows a running total.	1
	Failures Resource Remote	The number of connections that failed because of resource problems or shortages on the remote computer. This number is an accumulator and shows a running total.	1
	Frame Bytes Received/Sec	The rate at which data bytes are received by the computer. This counter counts only the frames (packets) that carry data.	0.0001
	Frame Bytes Rejected/Sec	The rate at which data bytes are rejected. This counter counts only the bytes in data frames (packets) that carry data.	0.0001
	Frame Bytes Re-Sent/Sec	The rate at which data bytes are resent by the computer. This counter counts only the bytes in frames that carry data.	0.0001

Object	Counter	Description	Default Scale
	Frame Bytes Sent/Sec	The rate at which data bytes are sent by the computer. This counter counts only the bytes in frames (packets) that carry data.	0.0001
	Frame Bytes/Sec	The rate at which data bytes are processed by the computer. This counter is the sum of data frame bytes sent and received. This counter counts only the bytes in frames (packets) that carry data.	0.0001
	Frames Received/Sec	The rate at which data frames are received by the computer. This counter counts only the frames (packets) that carry data.	0.1
	Frames Rejected/Sec	The rate at which data frames are rejected. This counter counts only the frames (packets) thatcarry data.	0.1
	Frames Re-Sent/Sec	The rate at which data frames (packets) are resent by the computer. This counter counts only the frames or packets that carry data.	0.1
	Frames Sent/Sec	The rate at which data frames are sent by the computer. This counter counts only the frames (packets) that carry data.	0.1
	Frames/Sec	The rate at which data frames (packets) are processed by the computer. This counter is the sum of data frames sent and data frames received. This counter counts only those frames (packets) that carry data.	0.1
	Packets Received/Sec	The rate at which packets are received by the computer. This counter counts all packets processed, including control as well as data packets.	0.1
	Packets Sent/Sec	The rate at which packets are sent by the computer. This counter counts all packets sent by the computer, including control as well as data packets.	0.1
	Packets/Sec	The rate at which packets are processed by the computer. This count is the sum of Packets Sent and Packets Received per second. This counter includes all packets processed, including control as well as data packets.	0.1

Object	Counter	Description	Default Scale
	Piggyback Ack Queued/Sec	The rate at which piggybacked acknowledgments are queued. Piggyback acknowledgments are acknowledgments to received packets that are to be included in the next outgoing packet to the remote computer.	0.1
	Piggyback Ack Timeouts	The number of times that a piggyback acknowledgment could not be sent because there was no outgoing packet to the remote system on which to piggyback. A piggyback ack is an acknowledgment to a received packet that is sent along in an outgoing data packet to the remote computer. If no outgoing packet is sent within the timeout period, then an ack packet is sent, and this counter is incremented.	0.1
	Window Send Average	The running average number of data bytes that were sent before waiting for an acknowledgment from the remote computer.	1
	Window Send Maximum	The maximum number of bytes of data that will be sent before waiting for an acknowledgment from the remote computer.	1
NWLink SPX Object	Bytes Total/Sec	The sum of Frame Bytes/Sec and Datagram Bytes/Sec. This is the total rate of bytes sent to or received from the network by the protocol, but it counts only the bytes in frames (packets) that carry data.	0.0001
	Connection Session Timeouts	The number of connections that were dropped due to a session timeout. This number is an accumulator and shows a running total.	1
	Connections Canceled	The number of connections that were canceled. This number is an accumulator and shows a running total.	1
	Connections No Retries	the total count of connections that succeeded on the first try. This number is an accumulator and shows a running total.	1

Object	Counter	Description	Default Scale
	Connections Open	The number of connections currently open for this protocol. This counter shows the current count only and does not accumulate over time.	1
	Connections with Retries	The total count of connections that were made after retrying the attempt. A retry occurs if the first connection attempt fails. This number is an accumulator and shows a running total.	1
	Datagram Bytes Received/Sec	The rate at which datagram bytes are received by the computer. A datagram is a connectionless packet whose delivery to a remote computer is not guaranteed.	0.0001
	Datagram Bytes Sent/Sec	The rate at which datagram bytes are sent from the computer. A datagram is a connectionless packet whose delivery to a remote computer is not guaranteed.	0.0001
	Datagram Bytes/Sec	The rate at which datagram bytes are processed by the computer. This counter is the sum of datagram bytes that are sent as well as received. A datagram is a connectionless packet whose delivery to a remote computer is not guaranteed.	0.0001
	Datagrams Received/Sec	The rate at which datagrams are received by the computer. A datagram is a connectionless packet whose delivery to a remote computer is not guaranteed.	0.1
	Datagrams Sent/Sec	The rate at which datagrams are sent from the computer. A datagram is a connectionless packet whose delivery to a remote computer is not guaranteed.	0.1
	Datagrams/Sec	The rate at which datagrams are processed by the computer. This counter displays the sum of datagrams sent and datagrams received. A datagram is a connectionless packet whose delivery to a remote computer is not guaranteed.	0.1
	Disconnects Local	The number of session disconnections that were initiated by the local computer. This number is an accumulator and shows a running total.	1

Object	Counter	Description	Default Scale
	Disconnects Remote	The number of session disconnections that were initiated by the remote computer. This number is an accumulator and shows a running total.	1
	Expirations Ack	The count of T2 timer expirations.	1
	Expirations Response	The count of T1 timer expirations.	1
	Failures Adapter	The number of connections that were dropped due to an adapter failure. This number is an accumulator and shows a running total.	1
	Failures Link	The number of connections that were dropped due to a link failure. This number is an accumulator and shows a running total.	1
	Failures No Listen	The number of connections that were rejected because the remote computer was not listening for connection requests.	1
	Failures Not Found	The number of connection attempts that failed because the remote computer could not be found. This number is an accumulator and shows a running total.	1
	Failures Resource Local	The number of connections that failed because of resource problems or shortages on the local computer. This number is an accumulator and shows a running total.	1
	Failures Resource Remote	The number of connections that failed because of resource problems or shortages on the remote computer. This number is an accumulator and shows a running total.	1
	Frame Bytes Received/Sec	The rate at which data bytes are received by the computer. This counter counts only the frames (packets) that carry data.	0.0001
	Frame Bytes Rejected/Sec	The rate at which data bytes are rejected. This counter counts only the bytes in data frames (packets) that carry data.	0.0001
	Frame Bytes Re-Sent/Sec	The rate at which data bytes are resent by the computer. This counter counts only the bytes in frames that carry data.	0.0001

Object	Counter	Description	Default Scale
	Frame Bytes Sent/Sec	The rate at which data bytes are sent by the computer. This counter counts only the bytes in frames (packets) that carry data.	0.0001
	Frame Bytes/Sec	The rate at which data bytes are processed by the computer. This counter is the sum of data frame bytes sent and received. This counter counts only the bytes in frames (packets) that carry data.	0.0001
	Frames Received/Sec	The rate at which data frames are received by the computer. This counter counts only the frames (packets) that carry data.	0.1
	Frames Rejected/Sec	The rate at which data frames are rejected. This counter counts only the frames (packets) that carry data.	0.1
	Frames Re-Sent/Sec	The rate at which data frames (packets) are resent by the computer. This counter counts only the frames or packets that carry data.	0.1
	Frames Sent/Sec	The rate at which data frames are sent by the computer. This counter counts only the frames (packets) that carry data.	0.1
	Frames/Sec	The rate at which data frames (packets) are processed by the computer. This counter is the sum of data frames sent and data frames received. This counter counts only those frames (packets) that carry data.	0.1
	Packets Received/Sec	The rate at which packets are received by the computer. This counter counts all packets processed, including control as well as data packets.	0.1
	Packets Sent/Sec	The rate at which packets are sent by the computer. This counter counts all packets sent by the computer, including control as well as data packets.	0.1
	Packets/Sec	The rate at which packets are processed by the computer. This count is the sum of Packets Sent/Sec and Packets Received/Sec. This counter includes all packets processed, including control as well as data packets.	0.1

Object	Counter	Description	Default Scale
	Piggyback Ack Queued/Sec	The rate at which piggybacked acknowledgments are queued. Piggyback acknowledgments are acknowledgments to received packets that are to be included in the next outgoing packet to the remote computer.	0.1
	Piggyback Ack Timeouts	The number of times that a piggyback acknowledgment could not be sent because there was no outgoing packet to the remote system on which to piggyback. A piggyback ack is an acknowledgment to a received packet that is sent along in an outgoing data packet to the remote computer. If no outgoing packet is sent within the timeout period, then an ack packet is sent, and this counter is incremented.	0.1
	Window Send Average	The running average number of data bytes that were sent before waiting for an acknowledgment from the remote computer.	1
	Window Send Maximum	The maximum number of bytes of data that will be sent before waiting for an acknowledgment from the remote computer.	1
Objects Object	Events	The number of events in the computer at the time of data collection. This is an instantaneous count, not an average over the time interval. An event is used when two or more threads want to synchronize execution.	0.1
	Mutexes	The number of mutexes in the computer at the time of data collection. This is an instantaneous count, not an average over the time interval. Mutexes are used by threads to ensure that only one thread is executing some section of code.	1
	Processes	The number of processes in the computer at the time of data collection. This is an instantaneous count, not an average over the time interval. Each process represents the running of a program.	1

Object	Counter	Description	Default Scale
	Sections	The number of sections in the computer at the time of data collection. This is an instantaneous count, not an average over the time interval. A section is a portion of virtual memory created by a process to store data. A process may share sections with other processes.	0.1
	Semaphores	The number of semaphores in the computer at the time of data collection. This is an instantaneous count, not an average over the time interval. Threads use semaphores to obtain exclusive access to data structures that they share with other threads.	0.1
	Threads	The number of threads in the computer at the time of data collection. This is an instantaneous count, not an average over the time interval. A thread is the basic executable entity that can execute instructions in a processor.	0.1
Paging File Object	% Usage Peak	The peak usage of the page file instance, in percent. See also the Process: Page File Bytes Peak counter.	1
	Usage	The percentage of the page file instance in use. See also the Process: Page File Bytes counter.	1
Physical Disk Object	% Disk Read Time	The percentage of elapsed time that the selected disk drive is busy servicing read requests.	1
	% Disk Time	The percentage of elapsed time that the selected disk drive is busy servicing read or write requests.	1
	% Disk Write Time	The percentage of elapsed time that the selected disk drive is busy servicing write requests.	1
	Avg. Disk Bytes/Read	The average number of bytes transferred from the disk during read operations.	0.01
	Avg. Disk Bytes/Transfer	The average number of bytes transferred to or from the disk during write or read operations.	0.01

Object	Counter	Description	Default Scale
	Avg. Disk Bytes/Write	The average number of bytes transferred to the disk during write operations.	0.01
	Avg. Disk Queue Length	The average number of both read and write requests that were queued for the selected disk during the sample interval.	100
	Avg. Disk Read Queue Length	The average number of read requests that were queued for the selected disk during the sample interval.	100
	Avg. Disk Sec/Read	The average time, in seconds, of a data read from the disk.	1,000
	Avg. Disk Sec/Transfer	The average time, in seconds, of a disk transfer.	1,000
	Avg. Disk Sec/Write	The average time, in seconds, of a data write to the disk.	1,000
	Avg. Disk Write Queue Length	The average number of write requests that were queued for the selected disk during the sample interval.	100
	Current Disk Queue Length	The number of requests outstanding on the disk at the time the performance data is collected. This includes requests in service at the time of the snapshot. This is an instantaneous length, not an average over the time interval. Multi-spindle disk devices can have multiple requests active at one time, but other concurrent requests are awaiting service. This counter may reflect a transitory high or low queue length, but if there is a sustained load on the disk drive, this value will likely be consistently high. Requests experience delays proportional to the length of this queue minus the number of spindles on the disks. This difference should average less than 2.	10
	Disk Bytes/Sec	The rate at which bytes are transferred to or from the disk during write or read operations.	0.0001
	Disk Read Bytes/Sec	The rate at which bytes are transferred from the disk during read operations.	0.0001

Object	Counter	Description	Default Scale
	Disk Reads/Sec	The rate of read operations on the disk.	1
	Disk Transfers/Sec	The rate of read and write operations on the disk.	1
	Disk Write Bytes/Sec	The rate at which bytes are transferred to the disk during write operations.	0.0001
	Disk Writes/Sec	The rate of write operations on the disk.	1
Process Object	% Privileged Time	The percentage of elapsed time that the threads of the process have spent executing code in privileged mode. When a Windows NT system service is called, the service will often run in privileged mode to gain access to system-private data. Such data is protected from access by threads executing in user mode. Calls to the system can be explicit or implicit, such as page faults or interrupts. Unlike some early operating systems, Windows NT uses process boundaries for subsystem protection in addition to the traditional protection of user and privileged modes. These subsystem processes provide additional protection. Therefore, some work done by Windows NT on behalf of your application may appear in other subsystem processes in addition to the privileged time in your process.	1
	% Processor Time	The percentage of elapsed time that all of the threads of this process used the processor to execute instructions. An instruction is the basic unit of execution in a computer, a thread is the object that executes instructions, and a process is the object created when a program is run. Code executed to handle some hardware interrupts and trap conditions are included in this count.	1

Object	Counter	Description	Default Scale
	% User Time	The percentage of elapsed time that this process' threads have spent executing code in user mode. Applications, environment subsystems, and integral subsystems execute in user mode. Code executing in user mode cannot damage the integrity of the Windows NT Executive, kernel, and device drivers. Unlike some early operating systems, Windows NT uses process boundaries for subsystem protection in addition to the traditional protection of user and privileged modes. These subsystem processes provide additional protection. Therefore, some work done by Windows NT on behalf of your application may appear in other subsystem processes in addition to the privileged time in your process.	1
	Elapsed Time	The total elapsed time (in seconds) this process has been running.	0.0001
	Handle Count	The total number of handles currently open by this process. This number is the sum of the handles currently open by each thread in this process.	1
	ID Process	The unique identifier of this process. ID process numbers are reused, so they identify a process only for the lifetime of that process.	0.1
	Page Faults/Sec	The rate of page faults by the threads executing in this process. A page fault occurs when a thread refers to a virtual memory page that is not in its working set in main memory. This will cause the page not to be fetched from disk if it is on the standby list and hence already in main memory or if it is in use by another process with which the page is shared.	0.1

Object	Counter	Description	Default Scale
	Page File Bytes	The current number of bytes this process has used in the paging file(s). Paging files are used to store pages of memory used by the process that are not contained in other files. Paging files are shared by all processes, and lack of space in paging files can prevent other processes from allocating memory.	0.000001
	Page File Bytes Peak	The maximum number of bytes this process has used in the paging file(s). Paging files are used to store pages of memory used by the process that are not contained in other files. Paging files are shared by all processes, and lack of space in paging files can prevent other processes from allocating memory.	0.000001
	Pool Nonpaged Bytes	The number of bytes in the nonpaged pool, a system memory area where space is acquired by operating system components as they accomplish their appointed tasks. Nonpaged pool pages cannot be paged out to the paging file, but instead remain in main memory as long as they are allocated.	0.00001
	Pool Paged Bytes	The number of bytes in the paged pool, a system memory area where space is acquired by operating system components as they accomplish their appointed tasks. Paged pool pages can be paged out to the paging file when they are not accessed by the system for sustained periods of time.	0.00001
	Priority Base	The current base priority of this process. Threads within a process can raise and lower their own base priorities relative to the process' base priority.	1
	Private Bytes	The current number of bytes this process has allocated that cannot be shared with other processes.	0.00001
	Thread Count	The number of threads currently active in this process. An instruction is the basic unit of execution in a processor, and a thread is the object that executes instructions. Every running process has at least one thread.	1

Object	Counter	Description	Default Scale
	Virtual Bytes	The current size, in bytes, of the virtual address space the process is using. Use of virtual address space does not necessarily imply corresponding use of either disk or main memory pages. Virtual space is finite, and by using too much, the process can limit its ability to load libraries.	0.000001
	Virtual Bytes Peak	The maximum number of bytes of virtual address space the process has used at any one time. Use of virtual address space does not necessarily imply corresponding use of either disk or main memory pages. Virtual space is, however, finite, and by using too much, the process may limit its ability to load libraries.	0.000001
	Working Set	The current number of bytes in the working set of this process. The working set is the set of memory pages touched recently by the threads in the process. If free memory in the computer exceeds a threshold, pages are left in the working set of a process even if they are not in use. If free memory falls below a threshold, pages are trimmed from working sets. If they are needed, they will then be soft-faulted back into the working set before they leave main memory.	0.00001
	Working Set Peak	The maximum number of bytes in the working set of this process at any point in time. The working set is the set of memory pages touched recently by the threads in the process. If free memory in the computer exceeds a threshold, pages are left in the working set of a process even if they are not in use. If free memory falls below a threshold, pages are trimmed from working sets. If they are needed, they will be soft-faulted back into the working set before they leave main memory.	0.00001
Process Address Space Object	Bytes Free	The total unused virtual address space of this process.	0.0001

Object	Counter	Description	Default Scale
	Bytes Image Free	The amount of virtual address space that is not in use or reserved by images within this process.	0.0001
	Bytes Image Reserved	The sum of all virtual memory reserved by images running within this process.	0.0001
	Bytes Reserved	The total amount of virtual memory reserved for future use by this process.	0.0001
	ID Process	The unique identifier of this process. ID process numbers are reused, so they identify a process only for the lifetime of that process.	1
	Image Space Exec Read Only	The virtual address space in use by the images being executed by the process. This is the sum of all the address space with this protection allocated by images run by the selected process. Execute/ read-only memory is memory that can be executed as well as read.	0.00001
	Image Space Exec Read/Write	Image space is the virtual address space in use by the images being executed by the process. This is the sum of all the address space with this protection allocated by images run by the selected process. Execute/read/write memory is memory that can be executed by programs as well as read and written to and modified.	0.00001
	Image Space Exec Write Copy	Image space is the virtual address space in use by the images being executed by the process. This is the sum of all the address space with this protection allocated by images run by the selected process. Execute/write/copy memory is memory that can be executed by programs as well as read and written to. This type of protection is used when memory needs to be shared between processes. If the sharing processes only read the memory, then they will all use the same memory. If a sharing process needs write access, then a copy of this memory will be made for that process.	0.00001

Object	Counter	Description	Default Scale
	Image Space Executable	Image space is the virtual address space in use by the images being executed by the process. This is the sum of all the address space with this protection allocated by images run by the selected process. Executable memory is memory that can be executed by programs but cannot be read or written to. This type of protection is not supported by all processor types.	0.00001
	Image Space No Access	Image space is the virtual address space in use by the images being executed by the process. This is the sum of all the address space with this protection allocated by images run by the selected process. No Access protection prevents a process from writing to or reading from these pages and will generate an access violation if either is attempted.	0.00001
	Image Space Read Only	Image space is the virtual address space in use by the images being executed by the process. This is the sum of all the address space with this protection allocated by images run by the selected process. Read Only protection prevents the contents of these pages from being modified. Any attempts to write or modify these pages will generate an access violation.	0.00001
	Image Space Read/Write	Image space is the virtual address space in use by the images being executed by the process. This is the sum of all the address space with this protection allocated by images run by the selected process. Read/Write protection allows a process to read, modify, and write to these pages.	0.00001

Object	Counter	Description	Default Scale
	Image Space Write Copy	Image space is the virtual address space in use by the images being executed by the process. This is the sum of all the address space with this protection allocated by images run by the selected process. Write Copy protection is used when memory is shared for reading but not for writing. When processes are reading this memory, they can share the same memory; however, when a sharing process wants read/write access to this shared memory, a copy of that memory is made for writing to.	0.00001
	Mapped Space Exec Read Only	Mapped space is virtual memory that has been mapped to a specific virtual address (or range of virtual addresses) in the process' virtual address space. Execute/read-only memory is memory that can be executed as well as read.	0.00001
	Mapped Space Exec Read/Write	Mapped space is virtual memory that has been mapped to a specific virtual address (or range of virtual addresses) in the process' virtual address space. Execute/read/write memory is memory that can be executed by programs as well as read and modified.	0.00001
	Mapped Space Exec Write Copy	Mapped space is virtual memory that has been mapped to a specific virtual address (or range of virtual addresses) in the process' virtual address space. Execute/write/copy memory is memory that can be executed by programs as well as read and written to. This type of protection is used when memory needs to be shared between processes. If the sharing processes only read the memory, then they will all use the same memory. If a sharing process needs write access, then a copy of this memory will be made for that process.	0.00001

Object	Counter	Description	Default Scale
	Mapped Space Executable	Mapped space is virtual memory that has been mapped to a specific virtual address (or range of virtual addresses) in the process' virtual address space. Executable memory is memory that can be executed by programs but cannot be read or written to. This type of protection is not supported by all processor types.	0.00001
	Mapped Space No Access	Mapped space is virtual memory that has been mapped to a specific virtual address (or range of virtual addresses) in the process' virtual address space. No Access protection prevents a process from writing to or reading from these pages and will generate an access violation if either is attempted.	0.00001
	Mapped Space Read Only	Mapped space is virtual memory that has been mapped to a specific virtual address (or range of virtual addresses) in the process's virtual address space. Read Only protection prevents the contents of these pages from being modified. Any attempts to write to or modify these pages will generate an access violation.	0.00001
	Mapped Space Read/Write	Mapped space is virtual memory that has been mapped to a specific virtual address (or range of virtual addresses) in the process's virtual address space. Read/Write protection allows a process to read, modify, and write to these pages.	0.00001
	Mapped Space Write Copy	Mapped space is virtual memory that has been mapped to a specific virtual address (or range of virtual addresses) in the process's virtual address space. Write Copy protection is used when memory is shared for reading but not for writing. When processes are reading this memory, they can share the same memory; however, when a sharing process wants to have write access to this shared memory, a copy of that memory is made.	0.00001
	Reserved Space Exec Read Only	Reserved space is virtual memory that has been reserved for future use by a process but has not been mapped or committed. Execute/read-only memory is memory that can be executed as well as read.	0.00001

Object	Counter	Description	Default Scale
	Reserved Space Exec Read/Write	Reserved space is virtual memory that has been reserved for future use by a process but has not been mapped or committed. Execute/read/write memory is memory that can be executed by programs as well as read and modified.	0.00001
	Reserved Space Exec Write Copy	Reserved space is virtual memory that has been reserved for future use by a process but has not been mapped or committed. Execute/write/copy memory is memory that can be executed by programs as well as read and written to. This type of protection is used when memory needs to be shared between processes. If the sharing processes only read the memory, then they will all use the same memory. If a sharing process needs write access, then a copy of this memory will be made for that process.	0.00001
	Reserved Space Executable	Reserved space is virtual memory that has been reserved for future use by a process but has not been mapped or committed. Executable memory is memory that can be executed by programs but cannot be read or written. This type of protection is not supported by all processor types.	0.00001
	Reserved Space No Access	Reserved space is virtual memory that has been reserved for future use by a process but has not been mapped or committed. No Access protection prevents a process from writing to or reading from these pages and will generate an access violation if either is attempted.	0.00001
	Reserved Space Read Only	Reserved space is virtual memory that has been reserved for future use by a process but has not been mapped or committed. Read Only protection prevents the contents of these pages from being modified. Any attempts to write to or modify these pages will generate an access violation.	0.00001

Object	Counter	Description	Default Scale
	Reserved Space Read/Write	Reserved space is virtual memory that has been reserved for future use by a process but has not been mapped or committed. Read/Write protection allows a process to read, modify, and write to these pages.	0.00001
	Reserved Space Write Copy	Reserved space is virtual memory that has been reserved for future use by a process but has not been mapped or committed. Write Copy protection is used when memory is shared for reading but not for writing. When processes are reading this memory, they can share the same memory; however, when a sharing process wants read/write access to this shared memory, a copy of that memory is made.	0.00001
	Unassigned Space Exec Read Only	Unassigned space is mapped and committed virtual memory in use by the process that is not attributable to any particular image being executed by that process. Execute/read-only memory is memory that can be executed as well as read.	0.00001
	Unassigned Space Exec Read/Write	Unassigned space is mapped and committed virtual memory in use by the process that is not attributable to any particular image being executed by that process. Execute/read/write memory is memory that can be executed by programs as well as read and written to.	0.00001
	Unassigned Space Exec Write Copy	Unassigned space is mapped and committed virtual memory in use by the process that is not attributable to any particular image being executed by that process. Execute/write/copy memory is memory that can be executed by programs as well as read and written to. This type of protection is used when memory needs to be shared between processes. If the sharing processes only read the memory, then they will all use the same memory. If a sharing process needs write access, then a copy of this memory will be made for that process.	0.00001

Object	Counter	Description	Default Scale
	Unassigned Space Executable	Unassigned space is mapped and committed virtual memory in use by the process that is not attributable to any particular image being executed by that process. Executable memory is memory that can be executed by programs, but cannot be read or written to. This type of protection is not supported by all processor types.	0.00001
	Unassigned Space No Access	Unassigned space is mapped and committed virtual memory in use by the process that is not attributable to any particular image being executed by that process. No Access protection prevents a process from writing to or reading from these pages and will generate an access violation if either is attempted.	0.00001
	Unassigned Space Read Only	Unassigned space is mapped and committed virtual memory in use by the process that is not attributable to any particular image being executed by that process. Read Only protection prevents the contents of these pages from being modified. Any attempts to write to or modify these pages will generate an access violation.	0.00001
	Unassigned Space Read/Write	Unassigned space is mapped and committed virtual memory in use by the process that is not attributable to any particular image being executed by that process. Read/Write protection allows a process to read, modify, and write to these pages.	0.00001
	Unassigned Space Write Copy	Unassigned space is mapped and committed virtual memory in use by the process that is not attributable to any particular image being executed by that process. Write Copy protection is used when memory is shared for reading but not for writing. When processes are reading this memory, they can share the same memory; however, when a sharing process wants read/write access to this shared memory, a copy of that memory is made for writing to.	0.00001

Object	Counter	Description	Default Scale
Processor Object	% DPC Time	The percentage of time that the processor spent receiving and servicing deferred procedure calls (DPCs) during the sample interval. (DPCs are interrupts that run at a lower priority than standard interrupts.) % DPC Time is a component of % Privileged Time because DPCs are executed in privileged mode. They are counted separately and are not a component of the interrupt counters.	1
	% Interrupt Time	The percentage of time the processor spent receiving and servicing hardware interrupts during the sample interval. This value is an indirect indicator of the activity of devices that generate interrupts, such as the system clock, the mouse, disk drivers, data communication lines, network interface cards, and other peripheral devices. These devices normally interrupt the processor when they have completed a task or require attention. Normal thread execution is suspended during interrupts. Most system clocks interrupt the processor every 10 milliseconds, creating a background of interrupt activity.	1
	% Privileged Time	The percentage of non-idle processor time spent in privileged mode. (Privileged mode is a processing mode designed for operating system components and hardware-manipulating drivers. It allows direct access to hardware and all memory. The alternative, user mode, is a restricted processing mode designed for applications, environment subsystems, and integral subsystems. The operating system switches application threads to privileged mode to obtain operating system services.) % Privileged Time includes time servicing interrupts and DPCs. A high rate of privileged time may be attributable to a large number of interrupts generated by a failing device.	1

Object	Counter	Description	Default Scale
	% Processor Time	The percentage of time that the processor is executing application or operating system processes (not idle). This counter was designed as a primary indicator of processor activity. It is calculated by measuring the time that the processor spends executing the thread of the idle process in each sample interval and then subtracting that value from 100 percent. (Each processor has an idle thread that consumes cycles when no other threads are ready to run.)	1
	% User Time	The percentage of non-idle processor time spent in user mode. (User mode is a restricted processing mode designed for applications, environment subsystems, and integral subsystems. The alternative, privileged mode, is designed for operating system components and allows direct access to hardware and all memory. The operating system switches application threads to privileged mode to obtain operating system services.)	1
	APC Bypasses/Sec	The rate at which kernel APC interrupts were avoided. APC Bypasses/Sec is the rate at which kernel APC interrupts were avoided.	1
	DPC Bypasses/Sec	The rate at which deferred procedure calls (DPCs) on all processors were avoided. (DPCs are interrupts that run at a lower priority than standard interrupts.)	1
	DPC Rate	The rate at which deferred procedure calls (DPCs) are added to the processor's DPC queue between the timer tics of the processor clock. DPC objects are queued to this processor's DPC queue per clock tick. (DPCs are interrupts that run at a lower priority than standard interrupts. Each processor has its own DPC queue.) This counter measures the rate at which DPCs are added to the queue, not the number of DPCs in the queue.	1

Object	Counter	Description	Default Scale
	DPCs Queued/Sec	The overall rate at which deferred procedure calls (DPCs) are added to the processor's DPC queue. (DPCs are interrupts that run at a lower priority than standard interrupts. Each processor has its own DPC queue.) This counter measures the rate at which DPCs are added to the queue, not the number of DPCs in the queue.	1
	Interrupts/Sec	The average number of hardware interrupts the processor is receiving and servicing in each second. It does not include DPCs, which are counted separately. This value is an indirect indicator of the activity of devices that generate interrupts, such as the system clock, the mouse, disk drivers, data communication lines, network interface cards, and other peripheral devices. These devices normally interrupt the processor when they have completed a task or require attention. Normal thread execution is suspended during interrupts. Most system clocks interrupt the processor every 10 milliseconds, creating a background of interrupt activity.	0.01
RAS Port Object	Alignment Errors	The total number of alignment errors for this connection. Alignment errors occur when a byte received is different from the byte expected.	1
	Buffer Overrun Errors	The total number of buffer overrun errors for this connection. Buffer overrun errors occur when the software cannot handle the rate at which data is received.	1
	Bytes Received	The total number of bytes received for this connection.	1
	Bytes Received/Sec	The number of bytes received per second.	1
	Bytes Transmitted	The total number of bytes transmitted for this connection.	1
	Bytes Transmitted/Sec	The number of bytes transmitted per second.	1

Object	Counter	Description	Default Scale
	CRC Errors	The total number of CRC errors for this connection. CRC errors occur when the frame received contains erroneous data.	1
	Frames Received	The total number of data frames received for this connection.	1
	Frames Received/Sec	The number of frames received per second.	1
	Frames Transmitted	The total number of data frames transmitted for this connection.	1
	Frames Transmitted/Sec	The number of frames transmitted per second.	1
	Percent Compression In	The compression ratio for bytes being received.	1
	Percent Compression Out	The compression ratio for bytes being transmitted.	1
	Serial Overrun Errors	The total number of serial overrun errors for this connection. Serial overrun errors occur when the hardware cannot handle the rate at which data is received.	1
	Timeout Errors	The total number of timeout errors for this connection. Timeout errors occur when an expected byte is not received in time.	1
	Total Errors	The total number of CRC, timeout, serial overrun, alignment, and buffer overrun errors for this connection.	1
	Total Errors/Sec	The total number of CRC, timeout, serial overrun, alignment, and buffer overrun errors per second.	1
RAS Total Object	Alignment Errors	The total number of alignment errors for this connection. Alignment errors occur when a byte received is different from the byte expected.	1
	Buffer Overrun Errors	The total number of buffer overrun errors for this connection. Buffer overrun errors occur when the software cannot handle the rate at which data is received.	1
	Bytes Received	The total number of bytes received for this connection.	1
	Bytes Received/Sec	The number of bytes received per second.	1

Object	Counter	Description	Default Scale
	Bytes Transmitted	The total number of bytes transmitted for this connection.	1
	Bytes Transmitted/Sec	The number of bytes transmitted per second.	1
	CRC Errors	The total number of CRC errors for this connection. CRC errors occur when the frame received contains erroneous data.	1
	Frames Received	The total number of data frames received for this connection.	1
	Frames Received/Sec	The number of frames received per second.	1
	Frames Transmitted	The total number of data frames transmitted for this connection.	1
	Frames Transmitted/Sec	The number of frames transmitted per second.	1
	Percent Compression In	The compression ratio for bytes being received.	1
	Percent Compression Out	The compression ratio for bytes being transmitted.	1
	Serial Overrun Errors	The total number of serial overrun errors for this connection. Serial overrun errors occur when the hardware cannot handle the rate at which data is received.	1
	Timeout Errors	The total number of timeout errors for this connection. Timeout errors occur when an expected byte is not received in time.	1
	Total Connections	The total number of remote access connections.	1
	Total Errors	The total number of CRC, timeout, serial overrun, alignment, and buffer overrun errors for this connection.	1
	Total Errors/Sec	The total number of CRC, timeout, serial overrun, alignment, and buffer overrun errors per second.	1
Redirector Object	Bytes Received/Sec	The rate of bytes coming in to the redirector from the network. It includes all application data as well as network protocol information (such as packet headers).	0.0001

Object	Counter	Description	Default Scale
	Bytes Total/Sec	The rate the redirector is processing data bytes. This includes all application and file data in addition to protocol information (such as packet headers).	0.0001
	Bytes Transmitted/Sec	The rate at which bytes are leaving the redirector to go to the network. It includes all application data as well as network protocol information (such as packet headers).	0.0001
	Connects Core	The number of connections to servers running the original MS-Net SMB protocol, including MS-Net itself and Xenix and VAXs.	1
	Connects LAN Manager 2.0	Counts connections to LAN Manager 2.0 servers, including LMX servers.	1
	Connects LAN Manager 2.1	Counts connections to LAN Manager 2.1 servers, including LMX servers.	1
	Connects Windows NT	Counts connections to Windows NT computers.	1
	Current Commands	The number of requests to the redirector that are currently queued for service. If this number is much larger than the number of network adapter cards installed in the computer, then the network(s) and/or the server(s) being accessed are seriously bottlenecked.	1
	File Data Operations/Sec	The rate the redirector is processing data operations. One operation includes (hopefully) many bytes (we say "hopefully" here because each operation has overhead). To determine the efficiency of this path, divide Bytes/Sec by this counter to find the average number of bytes transferred per operation.	1
	File Read Operations/Sec	The rate at which applications are asking the redirector for data. Each call to a file system, or each similar application program interface (API) call, counts as one operation.	1

Object	Counter	Description	Default Scale
	File Write Operations/Sec	The rate at which applications are sending data to the redirector. Each call to a file system, or to a similar application program interface (API) call, counts as one operation.	1
	Network Errors/Sec	Counts serious unexpected errors that generally indicate that the redirector and one or more servers are having serious communication difficulties. For example, an SMB (server message block) protocol error will generate a network error. This results in an entry in the system event log, so look there for details.	1
	Packets Received/Sec	The rate at which the redirector is receiving packets (also called SMBs, or server message blocks). Network transmissions are divided into packets. The average number of bytes received in a packet can be obtained by dividing Bytes Received/Sec by this counter. Some packets received may not contain incoming data; for example, an acknowledgment to a write operation by the redirector would count as an incoming packet.	0.1
	Packets Transmitted/Sec	The rate at which the redirector is sending packets (also called SMBs, or server message blocks). Network transmissions are divided into packets. The average number of bytes transmitted in a packet can be obtained by dividing Bytes Transmitted/Sec by this counter.	0.1
	Packets/Sec	The rate the redirector is processing data packets. One packet includes (hopefully) many bytes (we say "hopefully" here because each packet has protocol overhead). To determine the efficiency of this path, divide Bytes/Sec by this counter to find the average number of bytes transferred per packet. You can also divide this counter by Operations/Sec to determine the average number of packets per operation, another measure of efficiency.	0.1

Object	Counter	Description	Default Scale
	Read Bytes Cache/Sec	The rate at which applications are accessing the file system cache by using the redirector. Some of these data requests are satisfied by retrieving the data from the cache. Requests that miss the cache cause a page fault.	0.0001
	Read Bytes Network/Sec	The rate at which applications are reading data across the network. This occurs when data sought in the file system cache is not found there and must be retrieved from the network. Dividing this value by Bytes Received/Sec indicates the proportion of application data traveling across the network.	0.0001
	Read Bytes Non-Paging/Sec	Counts those bytes read by the redirector in response to normal file requests by an application when they are redirected to come from another computer. In addition to file requests, this counter includes other methods of reading across the network, such as named pipes and transactions. This counter does not count network protocol information, just application data.	0.0001
	Read Bytes Paging/Sec	The rate at which the redirector is attempting to read bytes in response to page faults. Page faults are caused by the loading of modules (such as programs and libraries), by a miss in the file system cache, or by files directly mapped to the address space of applications (a high-performance feature of Windows NT).	0.0001
	Read Operations Random/Sec	The rate at which, on a file-by-file basis, reads occur that are not sequential. If a read occurs using a particular file handle and then is followed by another read that is not the next contiguous byte, this counter is incremented by one.	0.1

Object	Counter	Description	Default Scale
	Read Packets Small/Sec	The rate at which reads less than one-fourth of the server's negotiated buffer size are performed by applications. Too many of these could indicate a waste of buffers on the server. This counter is incremented once for each read. It does not count packets.	0.1
	Read Packets/Sec	The rate at which read packets are being placed on the network. Each time a single packet is sent with a request to read data remotely, this counter is incremented by one.	0.1
	Reads Denied/Sec	The rate at which the server is unable to accommodate requests for raw reads. When a read is much larger than the server's negotiated buffer size, the redirector requests a raw read which, if granted, permits the transfer of the data without lots of protocol overhead on each packet. To accomplish this, the server must lock out other requests, so the request is denied if the server is really busy.	1
	Reads Large/Sec	The rate at which reads more than two times the server's negotiated buffer size are made by applications. Too many of these could place a strain on server resources. This counter is incremented once for each read. It does not count packets.	1
	Server Disconnects	The number of times a server has disconnected the redirector.	1
	Server Reconnects	The number of times the redirector has had to reconnect to a server to complete a new active request. You can be disconnected by the server if you remain inactive for too long. Locally, even if all your remote files are closed, the redirector will keep your connections intact for (nominally) ten minutes. Such inactive connections are called dormant connections. Reconnecting is expensive in time.	1

Object	Counter	Description	Default Scale
	Server Sessions	The total number of security objects the redirector has managed. For example, a logon to a server followed by a network access to the same server will establish one connection, but two sessions.	1
	Server Sessions Hung	The number of active sessions that are timed out and unable to proceed due to a lack of response from the remote server.	1
	Write Bytes Cache/Sec	The rate at which applications on your computer are writing to the file system cache using the redirector. The data may not leave your computer immediately; it can be retained in the cache for further modification before being written to the network. This reduces network traffic. Each write of a byte into the cache is counted here.	0.0001
	Write Bytes Network/Sec	Write Bytes Network/sec is the rate that your applications are writing data across the network. Either the system Cache was bypassed, as for Named Pipes or Transactions, or else the Cache wrote the bytes to make room for other data. Dividing this counter by Bytes Transmitted/Sec will indicate the "efficiency" of data written to the network, since all of these bytes are real application data (see Transmitted Bytes/Sec).	0.0001
	Write Bytes Non-Paging/Sec	The rate at which bytes are written by the redirector in response to normal file outputs by an application when they are redirected to another computer. In addition to file requests, this counter includes other methods of writing across the network, such as named pipes and transactions. This counter does not count network protocol information, just application data.	0.0001

Object	Counter	Description	Default Scale
	Write Bytes Paging/Sec	The rate at which the redirector is attempting to write bytes changed in the pages being used by applications. The program data changed by modules (such as programs and libraries) that were loaded over the network are paged out when no longer needed. Other output pages come from the cache.	0.0001
	Write Operations Random/Sec	The rate at which, on a file-by-file basis, writes occur that are not sequential. If a write occurs using a particular file handle and then is followed by another write that is not the next contiguous byte, this counter is incremented by one.	0.1
	Write Packets Small/Sec	The rate at which writes are performed by applications that are less than one-fourth of the server's negotiated buffer size. Too many of these could indicate a waste of buffers on the server. This counter is incremented once for each write; it counts writes, not packets.	0.1
	Write Packets/Sec	The rate at which writes are being sent to the network. Each time a single packet is sent with a request to write remote data, this counter is incremented by one.	0.1
	Writes Denied/Sec	The rate at which the server is unable to accommodate requests for raw writes. When a write is much larger than the server's negotiated buffer size, the redirector requests a raw write, which, if granted, permits the transfer of the data without lots of protocol overhead on each packet. To accomplish this, the server must lock out other requests, so the request is denied if the server is really busy.	1
	Writes Large/Sec	The rate at which writes are performed by applications that are more than two times the server's negotiated buffer size. Too many of these can place a strain on server resources. This counter is incremented once for each write; it counts writes, not packets.	1

Object	Counter	Description	Default Scale
Server Object	Blocking Requests Rejected	The number of times the server has rejected blocking SMBs due to an insufficient number of free work items. This value indicates whether the MaxWorkItem or MinFreeWorkItems server parameters may need tuning.	1
	Bytes Received/Sec	The number of bytes the server has received from the network. This value indicates how busy the server is.	0.0001
	Bytes Total/Sec	The number of bytes the server has sent to and received from the network. This value provides an overall indication of how busy the server is.	0.0001
	Bytes Transmitted/Sec	The number of bytes the server has sent on the network. This value indicates how busy the server is.	0.0001
	Context Blocks Queued/Sec	The rate at which work context blocks had to be placed on the server's FSP queue to await server action.	0.1
	Errors Access Permissions	The number of times opens on behalf of clients have failed with STATUS_ACCESS _DENIED. This value can indicate whether somebody is randomly attempting to access files in the hope of getting at something that was not properly protected.	1
	Errors Granted Access	The number of times accesses to files opened successfully were denied. This value can indicate attempts to access files without proper access authorization.	1
	Errors Logon	The number of failed logon attempts to the server. The value can indicate whether password-guessing programs are being used to crack the security on the server.	1
	Errors System	The number of times an internal server error was detected. Unexpected errors usually indicate a problem with the server.	1
	File Directory Searches	The number of searches for files currently active in the server. This value indicates current server activity.	1

Object	Counter	Description	Default Scale
	Files Open	The number of files currently opened in the server. This value indicates current server activity.	1
	Files Opened Total	The number of successful open attempts performed by the server on behalf of clients. This value is useful in determining the amount of file I/O, the overhead for path-based operations, and the effectiveness of open locks.	0.001
	Logon Total	The total number of interactive logons, network logons, service logons, successful logons, and failed logons since the machine was last rebooted.	10
	Logon/Sec	The rate of all interactive logons, network logons, service logons, successful logons, and failed logons.	10
	Pool Nonpaged Bytes	The number of bytes of nonpageable computer memory that the server is currently using. This value is useful for determining the values of the value entry MaxNonpagedMemoryUsage in the Windows NT Registry. For more information, see REGENTRY.HLP on the Windows NT Resource Kit CD.	0.0001
	Pool Nonpaged Failures	The number of times allocations from the nonpaged pool have failed. This value indicates that the computer's physical memory is too small.	1
	Pool Nonpaged Peak	The maximum number of bytes of nonpaged pool the server has had in use at any one point. This value indicates how much physical memory the computer should have.	0.0001
	Pool Paged Bytes	The number of bytes of pageable computer memory the server is currently using. This value can help in determining good values for the MaxPagedMemoryUsage parameter.	0.0001
	Pool Paged Failures	The number of times allocations from the paged pool have failed. This value indicates that the computer's physical memory or page file is too small.	1

Object	Counter	Description	Default Scale
	Pool Paged Peak	The maximum number of bytes of paged pool the server has had allocated. This value indicates the proper sizes of the page file(s) and physical memory.	0.0001
	Server Sessions	The number of sessions currently active in the server. This value indicates current server activity.	1
	Sessions Errored Out	The number of sessions that have been closed due to unexpected error conditions. This value indicates how frequently network problems are causing dropped sessions on the server.	1
	Sessions Forced Off	The number of sessions that have been forced to log off. This value can indicate how many sessions were forced to log off due to logon time constraints.	1
	Sessions Logged Off	The number of sessions that have terminated normally. This value is useful in interpreting the Sessions Timed Out and Sessions Errored Out statistics; it allows percentage calculations.	1
	Sessions Timed Out	The number of sessions that have been closed because their idle time exceeded the AutoDisconnect parameter for the server. This value indicates whether the AutoDisconnect setting is helping to conserve resources.	1
	Work Item Shortages	The number of times STATUS_DATA_ NOT _ACCEPTED was returned at receive indication time. This occurs when no work item is available or can be allocated to service the incoming request. This value indicates whether the InitWorkItems or MaxWorkItems parameter may need to be adjusted.	1
Server Work Queues Object	Active Threads	The number of threads currently working on a request from the server client for this CPU. The system keeps this number as low as possible to minimize unnecessary context switching. This is an instantaneous count for the CPU, not an average over time.	1

Object	Counter	Description	Default Scale
	Available Threads	The number of server threads on this processor not currently working on requests from a client. The server dynamically adjusts the number of threads to maximize server performance.	1
	Available Work Items	Every request from a client is represented in the server as a work item, and the server maintains a pool of available work items per CPU to speed up processing. This is the instantaneous number of available work items for this CPU. A sustained near-zero value indicates the need to increase the MinFreeWorkItems Registry value for the server service. This value will always be 0 in the blocking queue instance.	1
	Borrowed Work Items	Every request from a client is represented in the server as a work item, and the server maintains a pool of available work items per CPU to speed up processing. When a CPU runs out of work items, it borrows a free work item from another CPU. An increasing value of this running counter may indicate the need to increase the MaxWorkItems or MinFreeWorkItems Registry value for the server service. This value will always be 0 in the blocking queue instance.	1
	Bytes Received/Sec	The rate at which the server is receiving bytes from the network clients on this CPU. This value is a measure of how busy the server is.	0.0001
	Bytes Sent/Sec	The rate at which the server is sending bytes to the network clients on this CPU. This value is a measure of how busy the server is.	0.0001
	Bytes Transferred/Sec	The rate at which the server is sending and receiving bytes with the network clients on this CPU. This value is a measure of how busy the server is.	0.0001
	Context Blocks Queued/Sec	The rate at which work context blocks had to be placed on the server's FSP queue to await server action.	1

Object	Counter	Description	Default Scale
	Current Clients	The instantaneous count of the clients being serviced by this CPU. The server actively balances the client load across all of the CPUs in the system. This value will always be 0 in the blocking queue instance.	1
	Queue Length	The current length of the server work queue for this CPU. A sustained queue length of greater than four may indicate processor congestion. This is an instantaneous count, not an average over time.	1
	Read Bytes/Sec	The rate the server is reading data from files for the clients on this CPU. This value is a measure of how busy the server is.	0.0001
	Read Operations/Sec	The rate the server is performing file read operations for the clients on this CPU. This value is a measure of how busy the server is. This value will always be 0 in the blocking queue instance.	1
	Total Bytes/Sec	The rate the server is reading and writing data to and from the files for the clients on this CPU. This value is a measure of how busy the server is.	0.0001
	Total Operations/Sec	The rate the server is performing file read and file write operations for the clients on this CPU. This value is a measure of how busy the server is. This value will always be 0 in the blocking queue instance.	1
	Work Item Shortages	Every request from a client is represented in the server as a work item, and the server maintains a pool of available work items per CPU to speed up processing. A sustained value greater than zero indicates the need to increase the MaxWorkItems Registry value for the server service. This value will always be 0 in the blocking queue instance.	1
	Write Bytes/Sec	The rate the server is writing data to files for the clients on this CPU. This value is a measure of how busy the server is.	0.0001

Object	Counter	Description	Default Scale
	Write Operations/Sec	The rate the server is performing file write operations for the clients on this CPU. This value is a measure of how busy the server is. This value will always be 0 in the blocking queue instance.	1
System Object	% Registry Quota in Use	The percentage of Total Registry Quota Allowed that is currently being used by the system.	1
	% Total DPC Time	The average percentage of time that all processors spent receiving and servicing deferred procedure calls (DPCs). (DPCs are interrupts that run at a lower priority than the standard interrupts.) It is the sum of Processor: % DPC Time for all processors on the computer divided by the number of processors. System: % Total DPC Time is a component of System: % Total Privileged Time because DPCs are executed in privileged mode. DPCs are counted separately and are not a component of the interrupt count.	1
	% Total Interrupt Time	The average percentage of time that all processors spent servicing interrupts. It is the sum of Processor: % Interrupt Time for all processors on the computer divided by the number of processors. DPCs are counted separately and are not a component of the interrupt count. This value is an indirect indicator of the activity of devices that generate interrupts, such as the system timer, the mouse, disk drivers, data communication lines, network interface cards, and other peripheral devices.	1

Object	Counter	Description	Default Scale
	% Total Privileged Time	The average percentage of non-idle time all processors spent in privileged (kernel) mode. It is the sum of Processor: % Privileged Time for all processors on the computer divided by the number of processors. System: % Total User Time and System: % Total Privileged Time sum to % Total Processor Time, but not always to 100%. (Privileged mode is a processing mode designed for operating system components and which allows direct access to hardware and all memory. The operating system switches application threads to privileged mode to obtain operating system services. The alternative, user mode, is a restricted processing mode designed for applications and environment subsystems.)	1
	% Total Processor Time	The average percentage of time that all processors on the computer are executing non-idle threads. This counter was designed as the primary indicator of processor activity on multiprocessor computers. It is equal to the sum of Process: % Processor Time for all processors divided by the number of processors. It is calculated by summing the time that all processors spend executing the thread of the idle process in each sample interval, subtracting that value from 100%, and dividing the difference by the number of processors on the computer. (Each processor has an idle thread, which consumes cycles when no other threads are ready to run.) For example, on a multiprocessor computer, a value of 50% means that all processors are busy for half of the sample interval, or that half of the processors are busy for all of the sample interval.	1

Object	Counter	Description	Default Scale
	% Total User Time	The average percentage of non-idle time all processors spent in user mode. It is the sum of Processor: % User Time for all processors on the computer divided by the number of processors. System: % Total User Time and System: % Total Privileged Time sum to % Total Processor Time, but not always to 100%. (User mode is a restricted processing mode designed for applications, environment subsystems, and integral subsystems. The alternative, privileged mode, is designed for operating system components and allows direct access to hardware and all memory. The operating system switches application threads to privileged mode to obtain operating system services.)	1
	Alignment Fixups/Sec	The rate at which alignment faults are fixed by the system.	1
	Context Switches/Sec	The combined rate at which all processors on the computer are switched from one thread to another. Context switches occur when a running thread voluntarily relinquishes the processor, is preempted by a higher-priority ready thread, or switches between user mode and privileged (kernel) mode to use an Executive or subsystem service. It is the sum of Thread: Context Switches/Sec for all threads running on all processors in the computer and is measured in number of switches. There are context switch counters on the System and Thread objects.	0.01
	Exception Dispatches/Sec	The rate of exceptions dispatched by the system.	1
	File Control Bytes/Sec	The overall rate at which bytes are transferred for all file system operations that are neither reads nor writes, including file system control requests and requests for information about device characteristics or status. It is measured in number of bytes.	0.001

Object	Counter	Description	Default Scale
	File Control Operations/Sec	The combined rate of file system operations that are neither reads nor writes, such as file system control requests and requests for information about device characteristics or status. This is the inverse of System: File Data Operations/Sec and is measured in number of operations.	1
	File Data Operations/Sec	The combined rate of read and write operations on all logical disks on the computer. This is the inverse of System: File Control Operations/Sec.	1
	File Read Bytes/Sec	The overall rate at which bytes are read to satisfy file system read requests for all devices on the computer, including reads from the file system cache. It is measured in number of bytes.	0.0001
	File Read Operations/Sec	The combined rate of file system read requests for all devices on the computer, including requests to read from the file system cache. It is measured in number of reads.	1
	File Write Bytes/Sec	The overall rate at which bytes are written to satisfy file system write requests for all devices on the computer, including writes to the file system cache. It is measured in number of bytes.	0.0001
	File Write Operations/Sec	The combined rate of file system write requests for all devices on the computer, including requests to write to data in the file system cache. It is measured in number of writes.	1
	Floating Emulations/Sec	The rate of floating emulations performed by the system.	1
	Processor Queue Length	The number of threads in the processor queue. There is a single queue for processor time even on computers with multiple processors. Unlike the disk counters, this counter counts ready threads only, not threads that are running. A sustained processor queue value of greater than two threads generally indicates processor congestion.	10

Object	Counter	Description	Default Scale
	System Calls/Sec	The combined rate of calls to Windows NT system service routines by all processes running on the computer. These routines perform all of the basic scheduling and synchronization of activities on the computer and provide access to nongraphic devices, memory management, and name space management.	0.1
	System Up Time	Total time (in seconds) that the computer has been operational since it was last started.	0.00001
	Total APC Bypasses/Sec	The combined rate at which kernel asynchronous procedure call (APC) interrupts on all processors were avoided. This value is the sum of Processor: APC Bypasses/Sec for all processors divided by the number of processors.	1
	Total DPC Bypasses/Sec	The combined rate at which deferred procedure calls (DPCs) on all processors were avoided. (DPCs are interrupts that run at a lower priority than standard interrupts.) This value is the sum of Processor: DPC Bypasses/Sec for all processors divided by the number of processors.	1
	Total DPC Rate	The combined rate at which deferred procedure calls (DPCs) are added to the DPC queues of all processors between timer tics of each processor's system clock. (DPCs are interrupts that run at a lower priority than standard interrupts.) Each processor has its own DPC queue. This counter measures the rate at which DPCs are added to the queue, not the number of DPCs in the queue. It is the sum of Processor: DPC Rate for all processors on the computer divided by the number of processors.	1

Object	Counter	Description	Default Scale
	Total DPCs Queued/Sec	The combined rate at which deferred procedure calls (DPCs) are added to the DPC queue of all processors on the computer. (DPCs are interrupts that run at a lower priority than standard interrupts.) Each processor has its own DPC queue. This counter measures the rates at which DPCs are added to the queue, not the number of DPCs in the queue. It is the sum of Processor: DPCs Queued/Sec for all processors on the computer divided by the number of processors.	1
	Total Interrupts/Sec	The combined rate of hardware interrupts received and serviced by all processors on the computer. It is the sum of Processor: Interrupts/Sec for all processors divided by the number of processors, and it is measured in number of interrupts. It does not include DPCs, which are counted separately. This value is an indirect indicator of the activity of devices that generate interrupts, such as the system timer, the mouse, disk drivers, data communication lines, network interface cards, and other peripheral devices. These devices normally interrupt the processor when they have completed a task or require attention. Normal thread execution is suspended during interrupts. Most system clocks interrupt the processor every 10 milliseconds, creating a background of interrupt activity.	0.01
TCP Object	Connection Failures	The number of times TCP connections have made a direct transition to the CLOSED state from the SYN-SENT state or the SYN-RCVD state, plus the number of times TCP connections have made a direct transition to the LISTEN state from the SYN-RCVD state.	1

Object	Counter	Description	Default Scale
	Connections Active	The number of times TCP connections have made a direct transition to the SYN-SENT state from the CLOSED state.	1
	Connections Established	The number of TCP connections for which the current state is either ESTABLISHED or CLOSE-WAIT.	1
	Connections Passive	The number of times TCP connections have made a direct transition to the SYN-RCVD state from the LISTEN state.	1
	Connections Reset	The number of times TCP connections have made a direct transition to the CLOSED state from either the ESTABLISHED state or the CLOSE-WAIT state.	1
	Segments Received/Sec	The rate at which segments are received, including those received in error. This count includes segments received on currently established connections.	0.1
	Segments Retransmitted/Sec	The rate at which segments are retransmitted—e.g., the number of segments transmitted containing one or more previously transmitted bytes.	0.1
	Segments Sent/Sec	The rate at which segments are sent, including those on current connections, but excluding those containing only retransmitted bytes.	0.1
	Segments/Sec	The rate at which TCP segments are sent or received using the TCP protocol.	0.1
Telephony	Active Lines	The number of telephone lines serviced by this computer that are currently active.	1
	Active Telephones	The number of telephone devices that are currently being monitored.	1
	Client Apps	The number of applications that are currently using telephony services.	1
	Current Incoming Calls	The number of current incoming calls being serviced by this computer.	1
	Current Outgoing Calls	The number of current outgoing calls being serviced by this computer.	1

Object	Counter	Description	Default Scale
	Incoming Calls/Sec	The rate of incoming calls answered by this computer.	1
	Lines	The number of telephone lines serviced by this computer.	1
	Outgoing Calls/Sec	The rate of outgoing calls made by this computer.	1
	Telephone Devices	The number of telephone devices serviced by this computer.	1
Thread Object	% Privileged Time	The percentage of elapsed time that this thread has spent executing code in privileged mode. When a Windows NT system service is called, the service will often run in privileged mode to gain access to system-private data. Such data is protected from access by threads executing in user mode. Calls to the system can be explicit or implicit, such as page faults or interrupts. Unlike some early operating systems, Windows NT uses process boundaries for subsystem protection in addition to the traditional protection of user and privileged modes. These subsystem processes provide additional protection. Therefore, some work done by Windows NT on behalf of your application may appear in other subsystem processes in addition to the privileged time in your process.	1
	% Processor Time	The percentage of elapsed time that this thread used the processor to execute instructions. An instruction is the basic unit of execution in a processor, and a thread is the object that executes instructions. Code executed to handle some hardware interrupts and trap conditions is included in this count.	1

Object	Counter	Description	Default Scale
	% User Time	The percentage of elapsed time that this thread has spent executing code in user mode. Applications, environment subsystems, and integral subsystems execute in user mode. Code executing in user mode cannot damage the integrity of the Windows NT Executive, kernel, and device drivers. Unlike some early operating systems, Windows NT uses process boundaries for subsystem protection in addition to the traditional protection of user and privileged modes. These subsystem processes provide additional protection. Therefore, some work done by Windows NT on behalf of your application may appear in other subsystem processes in addition to the privileged time in your process.	1
	Context Switches/Sec	The rate of switches from one thread to another. Thread switches can occur either inside of a single process or across processes. A thread switch can be caused either by one thread asking another for information, or by a thread being preempted by another, higher-priority thread's becoming ready to run. Unlike some early operating systems, Windows NT uses process boundaries for subsystem protection in addition to the traditional protection of user and privileged modes. These subsystem processes provide additional protection. Therefore, some work done by Windows NT on behalf of an application may appear in other subsystem processes in addition to the privileged time in the application. Switching to the subsystem process causes one context switch in the application thread. Switching back causes another context switch in the subsystem thread.	0.01
	Elapsed Time	The total elapsed time (in seconds) this thread has been running.	0.0001

Object	Counter	Description	Default Scale
	ID Process	The unique identifier of this process. ID process numbers are reused, so they identify a process only for the lifetime of that process.	1
	ID Thread	The unique identifier of this thread. ID thread numbers are reused, so they identify a thread only for the lifetime of that thread.	1
	Priority Base	The current base priority of this thread. The system can raise the thread's dynamic priority above the base priority if the thread is handling user input, or lower it toward the base priority if the thread becomes compute bound.	1
	Priority Current	The current dynamic priority of this thread. The system can raise the thread's dynamic priority above the base priority if the thread is handling user input, or lower it toward the base priority if the thread becomes compute bound.	1
	Start Address	Starting virtual address for this thread. The thread state is the current state of the thread. Valid values are: 0 Initialized 1 Ready 2 Running 3 Standby 4 Terminated 5 Waiting 6 Transition 7 Unknown	1

Object	Counter	Description	Default Scale
	Thread Wait Reason	Applicable only when the thread is in the wait state. Valid values are: 0 Waiting for a component of the Windows NT Executive 1 Waiting for a page to be freed 2 Waiting for a page to be mapped or copied 3 Waiting for space to be allocated in the paged or nonpaged pool 4 Waiting for an execution delay to be resolved 5 Suspended 6 Waiting for a user request 7 Waiting for a component of the Windows NT Executive 8 Waiting for a page to be freed 9 Waiting for a page to be mapped or copied 10 Waiting for space to be allocated in the paged or nonpaged pool 11 Waiting for an execution delay to be resolved 12 Suspended 13 Waiting for a user request 14 Waiting for an event pair high 15 Waiting for an event pair low 16 Waiting for an LPC receive notice 17 Waiting for an LPC reply notice 18 Waiting for virtual memory to be allocated 19 Waiting for a page to be written to disk 20+ (Reserved for future use)	1
Thread Details Object	User PC	The current user program counter for this thread.	
UDP Object	Datagrams No Port/Sec	The rate of received UDP datagrams for which there was no application at the destination port.	0.1
	Datagrams Received Errors	The number of received UDP datagrams that could not be delivered for reasons other than the lack of an application at the destination port.	1

Object	Counter	Description	Default Scale
	Datagrams Received/Sec	The rate at which UDP datagrams are delivered to UDP users.	0.1
	Datagrams Sent/Sec	The rate at which UDP datagrams are sent from the entity.	0.1
	Datagrams/Sec	The rate at which UDP datagrams are sent or received by the entity.	0.1
Web Service	Anonymous Users/Sec	The rate at which users are making anonymous connections using the Web service.	1
	Bytes Received/Sec	The rate at which data bytes are received by the Web service.	0.0001
	Bytes Sent/Sec	The rate at which data bytes are sent by the Web service.	0.0001
	Bytes Total/Sec	The sum of Bytes Sent/Sec and Bytes Received/Sec. This is the total rate of bytes transferred by the Web service.	0.0001
	CGI Requests/Sec	The rate at which CGI requests are simultaneously being processed by the Web service.	1
	Connection Attempts/Sec	The rate at which connections using the Web service are being attempted.	1
	Current Anonymous Users/Sec	The number of users who currently have anonymous connections using the Web service.	1
	Current Blocked Async I/O Requests	The number of current requests temporarily blocked due to bandwidth throttling settings.	1
	Current CGI Requests	The current number of CGI requests that are simultaneously being processed by the Web service.	1
	Current Connections	The current number of connections established with the Web service.	1
	Current ISAPI Extension Requests	The current number of ISAPI Extension requests that are simultaneously being processed by the Web service.	1
	Current NonAnonymous Users	The number of users who currently have non-anonymous connections using the Web service.	1

Object	Counter	Description	Default Scale
	Delete Requests/Sec	The rate at which HTTP requests using the DELETE method are made. Delete requests are generally used for file removals.	1
	Files Received/Sec	The rate at which files are received by the Web service.	1
	Files Sent/Sec	The rate at which files are sent by the Web service.	1
	Files/Sec	The rate at which files are transferred— e.g., the rate that files are sent and received by the Web service.	1
	Get Requests/Sec	The rate at which HTTP requests using the GET method are made. Get requests are generally used for basic file retrievals or image maps, though they can be used with forms.	1
	Head Requests/Sec	The rate at which HTTP requests using the HEAD method are made. Head requests generally indicate that a client is querying the state of a document that the client already has to see if it needs to be refreshed.	1
	ISAPI Extension Requests/Sec	The rate at which ISAPI Extension requests are simultaneously being processed by the Web service.	1
	Logon Attempts/Sec	The rate at which logons using the Web service are being attempted.	1
	Maximum Anonymous Users	The maximum number of users who established concurrent anonymous connections using the Web service (counted since service startup).	1
	Maximum CGI Requests	The maximum number of CGI requests simultaneously processed by the Web service.	1
	Maximum Connections	The maximum number of simultaneous connections established with the Web service.	1
	Maximum ISAPI Extension Requests	The maximum number of ISAPI Extension requests simultaneously processed by the Web service.	1

Object	Counter	Description	Default Scale
	Maximum NonAnonymous Users	The maximum number of users who established concurrent non-anonymous connections using the Web service (counted since service startup).	1
	Measured Async I/O Bandwidth Usage	The measured bandwidth of asynchronous I/O averaged over a minute.	1
	NonAnony- mous Users/Sec	The rate at which users are making non-anonymous connections using the Web service.	1
	Not Found Errors/Sec	The rate of errors due to requests that couldn't be satisfied by the server because the requested document could not be found. These are generally reported as an HTTP 404 error code to the client.	1
	Other Request Methods/Sec	The rate at which HTTP requests are made that do not use the GET, POST, PUT, DELETE, TRACE, or HEAD method. These may include LINK or other methods supported by gateway applications.	1
	Post Requests/Sec	The rate at which HTTP requests using the POST method are made. Post requests are generally used for forms or gateway requests.	1
	Put Requests/Sec	The rate at which HTTP requests using the PUT method are made.	1
	System Code Resident Bytes	The number of system code resident bytes.	1
	Total Allowed Async I/O Requests	The total number of requests allowed by bandwidth throttling settings (counted since service startup).	1
	Total Anonymous Users	The total number of users who established an anonymous connection with the Web service (counted since service startup).	1
	Total Blocked Async I/O Requests	The total number of requests temporarily blocked due to bandwidth throttling settings (counted since service startup).	1

Object	Counter	Description	Default Scale
	Total CGI Requests	Total Common Gateway Interface (CGI) requests are custom gateway executables (.EXE files) that the administrator can install to add forms processing or other dynamic data sources. CGI requests spawn a process on the server, which can be a large drain on server resources. The count is the total since service startup.	1
	Total Connection Attempts	The number of connections that have been attempted using the Web service (counted since service startup).	1
	Total Delete Requests	The number of HTTP requests using the DELETE method (counted since service startup). Delete requests are generally used for file removals.	1
	Total Files Received	The total number of files received by the Web service (counted since service startup).	1
	Total Files Sent	The total number of files sent by the Web service (counted since service startup).	1
	Total Files Transferred	The sum of Files Sent and Files Received. This is the total number of files transferred by the Web service (counted since service startup).	1
	Total Get Requests	The number of HTTP requests using the GET method (counted since service startup). Get requests are generally used for basic file retrievals or image maps, though they can be used with forms.	1
	Total Head Requests	The number of HTTP requests using the HEAD method (counted since service startup). Head requests generally indicate that a client is querying the state of a document that the client already has to see if it needs to be refreshed.	1

Object	Counter	Description	Default Scale
	Total ISAPI Extension Requests	Total ISAPI Extension Requests are custom gateway dynamic link libraries (.DLL files) that the administrator can install to add forms processing or other dynamic data sources. Unlike CGI requests, ISAPI requests are simple calls to a DLL library routine; thus they are better suited to high-performance gateway applications. The count is the total since service startup.	1
	Total Logon Attempts	The number of logons that have been attempted using the Web service (counted since service startup).	1
	Total Method Requests	The number of HTTP GET, POST, PUT, DELETE, TRACE, HEAD, and other method requests (counted since service startup).	1
	Total Method Requests/Sec	The rate at which HTTP requests using the GET, POST, PUT, DELETE, TRACE, or HEAD method are made.	1
	Total NonAnony-mous Users	The total number of users who established a non-anonymous connection with the Web service (counted since service startup).	1
	Total Not Found Errors	The number of requests that couldn't be satisfied by the server because the requested document could not be found. These are generally reported as an HTTP 404 error code to the client. The count is the total since service startup.	1
	Total Other Request Methods	The number of HTTP requests that are not GET, POST, PUT, DELETE, TRACE, or HEAD methods (counted since service startup). These may include LINK or other methods supported by gateway applications.	1
	Total Post Requests	The number of HTTP requests using the POST method (counted since service startup). Post requests are generally used for forms or gateway requests.	1

Object	Counter	Description	Default Scale
	Total Put Requests	The number of HTTP requests using the PUT method (counted since service startup).	1
	Total Rejected Async I/O Requests	The total number of requests rejected due to bandwidth throttling settings (counted since service startup).	1
	Total Trace Requests	The number of HTTP requests using the TRACE method (counted since service startup). Trace requests allow the client to see what is being received at the end of the request chain and to use the information for diagnostic purposes.	1

INDEX

N